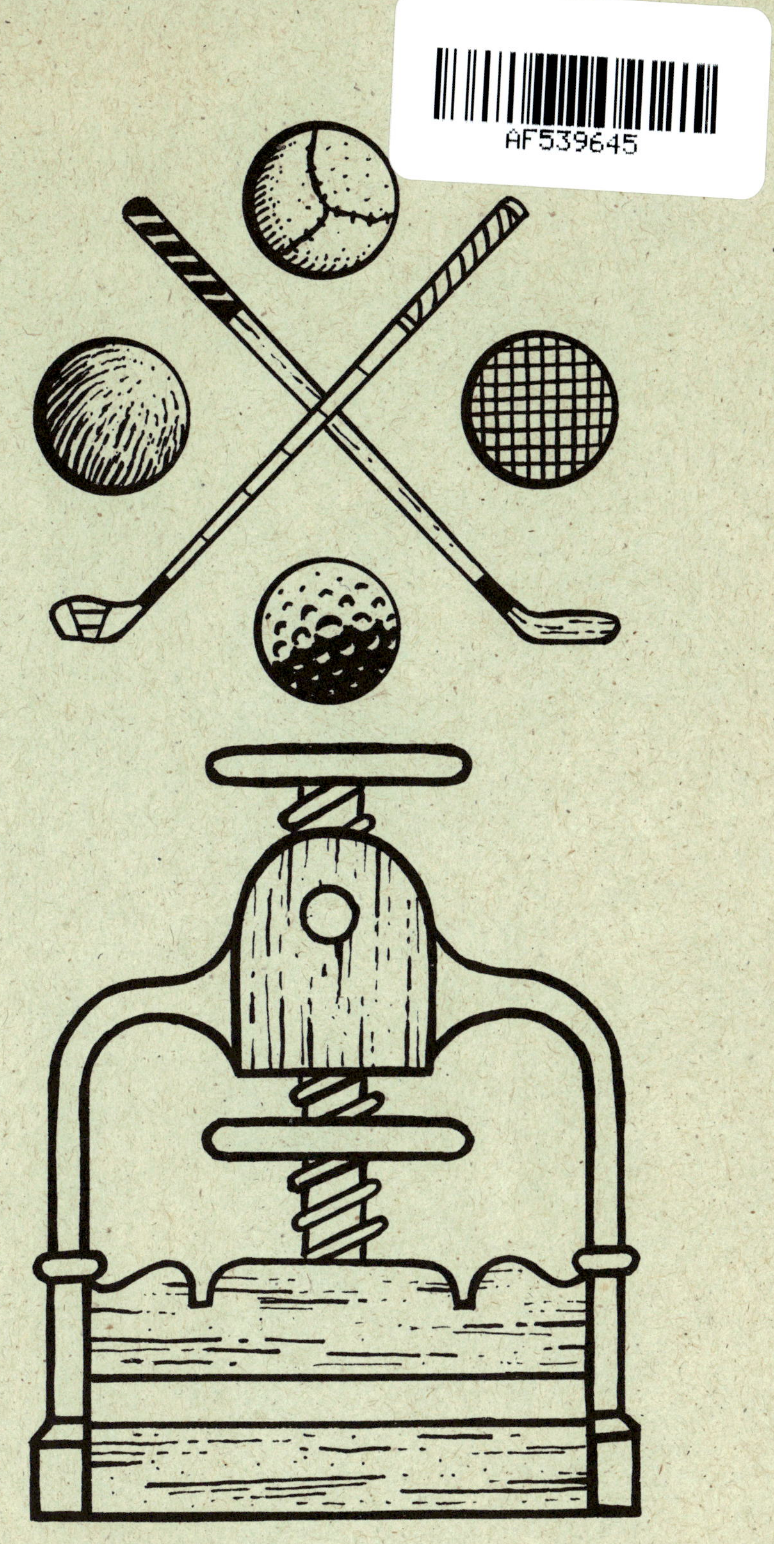

The Game of Golf
and
The Printed Word
1566-1985

The Game of Golf and The Printed Word 1566-1985

A Bibliography of Golf Literature in the English Language by

Richard E. Donovan
and
Joseph S. F. Murdoch

With an introductory essay by
Herbert Warren Wind

Castalio Press
Endicott, New York
1987

Library of Congress Catalog Card Number: 87-071494

International Standard Book Number: 0-943895-00-6 trade edition
International Standard Book Number: 0-943895-01-4 limited edition

Manufactured in the United States of America

Printed by:
Haddon Craftsmen, Inc.
Scranton, Pennsylvania

Published and Distributed by:

Castalio Press
PO Box 7070
Endicott, New York 13760

To my wife, Angie for her love and patience. To my children; Kathy, Pat, Terri, and Michelle for their love and understanding, who grew up amidst all the books.

Dick Donovan

To my wife, Betty who with appreciation, started me on my way to a much beloved library of golf books.

Joe Murdoch

ACKNOWLEDGEMENTS

A great many people have provided assistance in the preparation of this book. I wish to thank Janet Seagle, USGA Museum and Library, Far Hills, New Jersey; Jean Bryant, Ralph Miller Library, Industry Hills, California; The Honourable Company of Edinburgh Golfers, Muirfield, Scotland; Bobby Burnet, Royal and Ancient Golf Club of St. Andrews; to that wonderful group of private collectors around the world who allowed me entree to their collections: Alastair Johnston, Cleveland, Ohio; Ralph & Karen Elder, Annandale, Virginia; George & Susan Lewis, Mamaroneck, New York; Jerry Davis, Encino, California; Rusty Mott, Sheffield, Massachusetts; Pat Kennedy, Burlington, Vermont; Tony Hawkins, Chislehurst, England; David White, Brighton, England; Sara Baddiel, London, England; Tim Smartt [Order of the Bathtub] Lewes, England; Archie Baird [CX], Aberlady, Scotland; George Colville, Musselburgh, Scotland; David Hamilton, Glasgow, Scotland; Peter Crabtree, Keighley, England; Philip Truett, London, England and to four individuals who wish to remain anonymous [two in the US, one each in Canada and England]. I especially want to thank my son Patrick without whose computer expertise and overall preparation this book would not be. To my daughter, Terri, who in her breaks from the University of Vermont, travelled with me and assisted in the research; to my daughters Kathy and Michelle, for assistance in the detailed preparation of entries; to my wife Angie, for her many suggestions on the formatting and design; to Herbert Warren Wind, for his introductory essay; to Aksel Paddersen, for the cover design and photographs; to Gary Schoonover for his technical support and expertise and lastly to David Earl, Managing Editor, Golf Illustrated Magazine, for overall editorial direction and photographic and dust jacket text preparation.

TABLE OF CONTENTS

INTRODUCTION

It comes as very good news that, at this time when interest in golf books, ancient and modern, is growing spectacularly, a new, extensive bibliography, "The Game of Golf and The Printed Word, 1566-1985," is arriving on the scene. Subtitled "A Bibliography of Golf Literature in the English Language," it is the joint work of Richard E. Donovan and Joseph S. F. Murdoch, the latter for many years the good shepherd of the Golf Collectors' Society. It is a considerably expanded successor to Murdoch's "The Library of Golf," a bibliography that was published in 1968. Whereas that guide introduced the reader to about nine hundred golf books, both well-known and recondite, the new bibliography is a far more ambitious and inclusive work. Donovan, a bookseller whose hobby is collecting golf books, has ranged far and wide searching out books on golf, golf club histories, golf club handbooks, golf pamphlets, and verse and songs about the game. The result of his industry is evident in the new bibliography, which includes some four thousand and seven hundred entries. (I would add, however, that the four different historical eras into which Donovan divides the game are distinctly personal, as are his remarks on the golf balls introduced in the last score or so of years.)

Such a detailed golf bibliography is a boon indeed, for no other game has a literature that compares with golf's. While the first books about golf and its charms did not appear until the middle of the eighteenth century, the game had been played a long time before that. Sir Guy Campbell, a sound golf historian as well as an able golf-course architect, came to the conclusion that a rudimentary form of golf had probably been played on the east coast of Scotland as far back as the twelfth century. However, for quite some time golf was a point-to-point game. The players started at some natural or man-made feature and tried to reach a similar feature in the fewest number of strokes. It was only when the game developed into a series of individual holes that formed a course—usually of eight, twelve, or eighteen holes—that golf came into its own as a prepossessing game and not just a nice change for young men bowed down by archery practice.

If golf is the game with the finest literature, I would guess that this derives naturally from the fact that people love to talk golf. A man "on hold" waiting for a moment to describe his round of 87 blow by blow to his companions, each of whom fortunately has a glass in hand, finds himself entertained by the odd way some of his chums are carrying on about their rounds, the condition of fairways, the churlishness of certain caddies, or a new course they have just played for the first time. A game that is pleasant to talk about is conducive to writing about and reading about. I do not think that many people would disagree that at the core of golf's appeal is the happy fact that each course has its own personality as does each hole of that course. At the turn of the century—indeed, until the middle of this century—I would imagine that the course that was best known not only to British golfers but to golfers around the world was the Old Course at St. Andrews. If a golfer referred to the eleventh hole on the Old Course, into the mind of his listeners popped a clear picture of that difficult par 3, its downsloping green guarded by those deep pits, Strath Bunker and Hill Bunker. Or if a fellow in another group happened to mention the seventeenth at St. Andrews, his listeners' eyes would light up with a clear picture of the 450-yard Road Hole, its fairway breaking from left-to-right to a raised green complete with its Scylla and Charybdis—the deep, high-banked Road Bunker on the left, and on the right, behind the green, the town road itself.

I would presume that today the course that is best known to golfers around the world might be Augusta National, inasmuch as the Masters tournament is held on that course annually and is widely telecast. I would imagine that golfers from Dornoch to Melbourne are now well acquainted, for example, with the thirteenth at Augusta National, that 465-yard par 5, and they know just when a golfer should try to carry the creek before the green with his second and when he shouldn't. They undoubtedly appreciate such niceties as how very hard the short sixteenth plays when the pin is set on the narrow shelf at the back-right corner of this green, with that gaping bunker close behind it.

Certainly one of the great attractions of golf is how difficult a game it is to play well. With the sole exception of croquet, it is the only outdoor game in which the player hits a stationary ball from a stationary stance. It looks easy, but one soon understands that a golf swing is not a natural swing at all, although it may appear to be when you watch a champion. One must understand the intricate technique that lay behind the lazy timing and the lyrical grace of Bobby Jones or the measured movements that set up Nicklaus' explosive deliverance at impact of the immense power he has generated. A very small percentage of the world's golfers are capable of standing up to the pressure in a competition more rigorous than the Saturday-afternoon tournament at their club, but, on the other hand, golf is one of the rare lifetime sports in which a stripling of nine and a graybeard of eighty-one play with equal earnestness.

But I ramble. I should not be chattering on about how wonderful a game golf is—that is fairly apparent—and I should be concerning myself with the literature of golf. We know that quite a few spirited if hard-to-read golf books came out before 1880. That decade saw the publication of three watershed books on golf: "Golf: A Royal and Ancient Game," by Robert Clark; "The Art of Golf," by Sir Walter Simpson; and "Hints on the Game of Golf," by Horace G. Hutchinson. From the 1880s on, many diverting and enlightening books of golf have been written. The first gripping books that a golfer meets depend on when he was born and where he was raised. As a fellow who grew up in a small but intensely golf-conscious town near Boston in the 1920s and 1930s, I was fortunate in that two very good books on golf were part of the family library. The first was "The Duffer's Handbook of Golf," by Grantland Rice and Clare Briggs. The contributions to golf by Rice cannot be overstated. As one of our country's first syndicated sports columnists and as the editor of *"The American Golfer,"* a superb monthly magazine published by Conde Nast, he saw no reasons why Americans should not know as much about Bobby Jones and Walter Hagen as they did about Ty Cobb and Babe Ruth. Clare Briggs was a cartoonist who may be best remembered by most people for his daily and Sunday comic strip called "Mr. and Mrs.," but no artist since Briggs has captured the essence of the game and the inescapable excesses of its devotees as clearly and crisply as he did. The second book was "Down the Fairway," by Robert T. Jones, Jr., and O. B. Keeler. This is one of the game's classics. In 1926, at the age of twenty-four, Bobby, who had been regarded since 1916 as the greatest golf talent in our country, won the British Open for the first time that spring and then went on to win the United States Open for the second time that summer. His relief and pleasure at finally having lived up to expectations no doubt had something to do with his wish to set down what the game of golf—competitive golf—is like for someone who happens to become an outstanding golfer at an early age and then is supposed to perform wonders.

This early reading gave me a good background, and when I was later introduced to Bernard Darwin's books, I realized just how remarkable a writer he was. Golf was only one of Darwin's enthusiasms, and we are fortunate that he chose to write as frequently as he did about the game. There has been no one I know of who has been as thoroughly saturated with golf as Darwin. His essays on the game are in a class by themselves.

A further word about Richard E. Donovan, the moving force behind

"The Game of Golf and The Printed Word," is called for. Now in his early fifties, Donovan runs his bookselling business in Endicott, New York. (That is the city where the annual PGA Tour event, the B. C. Open, is played at the En-Joie Golf Club.) Donovan made connections with game at the age of twelve, when he started to caddie at the nearby Binghamton Country Club. He was in his late teens when he saw "Follow the Sun," the movie about Ben Hogan's career. It had a terrific impact on him: he decided to become a professional golfer. When he discovered that he did not have the requisite talent to be a successful touring pro, Donovan went to work a an administrator in the Aerospace Division of the General Electric Company. This called for many trips back and forth across the country, and in 1970 he had his fill of travel. That year he became a bookseller in Endicott, and he slowly but surely built up a fine clientele.

In September 1976, when Donovan was playing a few holes at his home course at the end of a working day, a curious realization suddenly hit him when he birdied the fifteenth, a 433-yard par 4, by playing an almost perfect 5-iron approach two feet from the hole. "It was such a deeply satisfying shot and, in addition to that, it was such a beautiful evening out there on the course I found myself saying inwardly, 'I have an antiquarian book business. Why don't I specialize in antiquarian golf books?'" From that moment on, Donovan has done so.

In 1979, when Donovan was in Philadelphia on a book-buying trip, he got together with Joe Murdoch and they spent the first of many evenings talking about golf books over a few drinks in the golf library in Murdoch's home in Lafayette Hill. Many visits later, Donovan suggested that it was probably time for Murdoch to bring his bibliography of golf books up to date, and he wondered if Murdoch would consider collaborating with him on that project. With characteristic graciousness, Murdoch replied that he didn't have the energy needed for the amount of work a new addition would require. He encouraged Donovan to undertake a new bibliography, and he volunteered to be of whatever assistance he could. In 1986 and 1987, Donovan, in order to make certain that he had not overlooked any books that belonged in the bibliography, spent several months in Great Britain scouring every nook and cranny. There are different concepts of the material a golf bibliography should include—in their separate prefaces, Murdoch and Donovan present their individual points of view—but there is no disputing the completeness of "The Game of Golf and The Printed Word." It is sure to be a boon for the ever-increasing battalions of collectors.

Herbert Warren Wind

PREFACE

The game of golf and the printed word are two pure art forms, each esthetically pleasing and delightfully rewarding. It was, as history proved, predestined that both would evolve in the mid-fifteenth century.

A major role-player of the day was King James II of Scotland, whom we can thank for our first reference to the game, as he decreed in 1457 that citizens should desist from playing golf. About ten years earlier in Mainz, Germany, Johann Gutenberg was perfecting the movable type printing press, thus enabling the history of golf to be passed down in a permanent form.

War, insidious as it is, also makes a significant contribution, as the bowmakers and Smities, who forged the weapons of the day, were to become the future clubmakers. We can also thank the Scottish balladeers for transferring their praise of battles to the wondrous deeds of the golfer of yore, oral history, which would eventually transpose to poetry in golf's earliest literature.

Some five hundred plus years and over four thousand pieces of printed literature later, in 1976 to be exact, the idea for this bibliography was born. Combining my love of the game as a bookseller, and my love of the printed word, I felt that I was in a unique position to accomplish the task. But what a task! First, building my personal library, then tracking down any printed references I could lay my eyes on. Each new find would be cherished and recorded.

After about three years, armed with a little arrogance and hundreds of unrecorded titles, I finally made contact with Joe Murdoch, who dispels the adage, "nothing new in golf." For in 1968, Joe made one of the most significant contributions to the printed word with his bibliography, "The Library of Golf." It was and is a legacy of a man's admiration of the game of golf and the printed word. Over the years Joe and I have spent many enjoyable afternoons at his clubhouse for luncheons and later in his library discussing the literature and historical aspects of the game. In 1981 Joe blessed my efforts to attempt to produce as complete a golf bibliography as possible, and has been, much to his chagrin, my mentor ever since.

In arranging the style of this bibliography, I considered many approaches: standard author title with details, by subject, chronological and so on. What I was looking for was something unique to tie the game and the literature together. When one contemplates golf history, one dominant feature has literally forged changes in the game. That is the magnificent loved/hated sphere, the golf ball. Our early historical references indicate that the featherie golf ball was in use up until about 1860. About 1848 a revolutionary discovery, the gutta percha ball, bounced into the golf world and brought about a change in a club design and, because of its cheaper price, many new players were introduced to the game. In 1898, the rubber cored ball was introduced and once again new adherents were converted to the game. Architects were rethinking their philosophy of course design and clubmakers, in an effort to meet increased demands, introduced the technology of mass production. The introduction of the hard core golf ball in 1962 enabled longer distance...farther and farther.

Literature likewise evolved as a result of the golf ball. ..."And yee, my clubs, you must no more prepare to make your bals flee whistling in the aire," is one of the earliest references in verse form. The gutta percha brought forth our first instruction book; the rubber-core era gives us our first look at architecture and biographies; and finally, the hard core era curiously gives rise to the scholarly researched historical material.

I have arranged the bibliography into four eras:

The Featherie	1620 to 1850
The Gutta Percha	1851 to 1900
The Rubber Core	1901 to 1960
The Hard Core	1961 to 1985

An introductory essay precedes each era, providing a perspective on the significance of the literature and the authors of the that era. Entries are arranged by author and title and listed in alphabetical sequence, location where published, publisher, year, edition, pagination, binding, illustrator, size, and an assigned reference number. Additionally there is a "Short Title Index" and a "Author Index" and as an afterthought an index of "Golf Club Histories." This was decided on the basis of they being one of my enigmas during the research phase. It was one of the most difficult areas to locate material on, as so many are privately produced and in general are in a limited printing. It was evident to me that future historians will come to rely on this information for historical research data as, in a great many cases, it will be the only record of the early development of the game and a look at the sociological impact it had on a geographical area.

A few words are in order as to what is and what is not contained in the bibliography. First, only works published in the English language, however there are a few bilingual (and in one case, in braille] works listed. I have excluded material on "turfgrass" as this is quite well covered in James Beard's, Turfgrass Bibliography from 1672-1972." And I am sure I will take a little flak for including those multitudinous productions of what are known in the UK as "Golf Club Handbooks." These little gems have been produced since about the early 1900's up to the present day. Once again, like club histories, these contribute significantly to the history of the game as many clubs and courses were disbanded due to war or for economic reasons. In fact, one of the primary producers of these handbooks was bombed during World War II and as such we have no complete record of what has been published and what are listed herein are the results of what I have physically seen. I am sure there are literally hundreds more to be included, so I call upon the club managers, secretaries and historians to communicate to me any information on omissions regarding handbooks and also club histories, and help to contribute to a later revised edition.

A. J. Balfour in 1890 wrote, "A tolerable day, a tolerable green, a tolerable opponent supply, or ought to supply, all that any reasonably constituted human being should require in the way of entertainment. With a fine sea view, and a clear course in front of him, the golfer should find no difficulty in dismissing all worries from his mind, and regarding golf, even it may be very indifferent golf, as the true and adequate end of man's existence." I would like to think today that Mr. Balfour would add "and waiting at home would be a golf library."

In closing, I must say that the body of golf literature, so vast that no other sport or game has produced as much, surely is indicative of man's fascination with and love of the game, and, as such has provided me one of the most rewarding experiences that I have been involved with: the knowledge gained and passed on, the personal interchanges with the most interesting and personable collectors, and last, but not least, the most enjoyable sessions with Joe Murdoch, who I dragged out of retirement to contribute his vast knowledge, as his writings in the essays demonstrate. The result proves a blend of Irish Mist and Scottish Dew.

Richard E. Donovan
Endicott, New York

PREFACE

Some years ago, in 1968 to be exact, Gale Research Company, Detroit, Michigan, was kind enough to publish my "The Library of Golf, 1743-1966; A Bibliography of Golf Books, Indexed Alphabetically, Chronologically and by Subject Matter." I never met, nor do I know to this day, the designer of the book, Mr. Richard Kinney, but whatever virtue the book possessed was considerably enhanced by Mr. Kinney's design. I delight in feeling that is a book of considerable charm because of its distinguished appearance. I make no such claim as to is content.

It must have tested the considerable patience of the publisher, Mr. Samuel Ruffner, when the book entered the market place for it is a matter of record that long lines did not form seeking it in book shops. It is testimony to Mr. Ruffner's patience, however, that the book finally went out of print some fifteen years later. I know nothing about publishing but I suspect that I would have nothing to do with a book that took fifteen years to sell.

It is of some satisfaction to me, as a golf-book collector, that the hobby—that of collecting golf books—has grown tremendously and there are now known collectors around the world. If we have grown in numbers, I am not sure that we have grown in stature. The more prestigious book dealers in London, New York, Los Angeles and other book-collecting capitals still look somewhat askance at the sight of an ill-shod, corduroy-coated individual who may invade his shop to ask, always somewhat plaintively, "Do you have any golf books?"

On the other hand, it is selfish pleasure to know that major auction houses, such as Phillips', Sotheby's and Christie's, now conduct sales of golf books (and other golfing artifacts) which attract a goodly number of bidders and, by my standards, an inordinate amount of money.

This bit of history is just preface to the point that Richard E. Donovan, book-dealer in Endicott, New York, suggested that a new edition of "The Library of Golf" might be in order and that he and I, in concert, might collaborate on the effort in an attempt to correct the mistakes of the past and add those books which had been published in the intervening years. He further suggested that I might have missed a few in my bibliography. I found it difficult to reconcile myself with that fact but became convinced that I should join the team when he began to mention some golf-book titles that were unknown to me.

The result of our partnership is presented here.

The attendant bibliography presents, as I suppose is inevitable in any collaboration, some compromises. My idea of just what constitutes a book does not always agree with Dick's. (Try to find a truly satisfactory definition of a book!) His concept of golf literature is not always mine.

I would confess that Dick's concept is larger than mine and, to his credit, there are titles listed herein which I may not have entertained but which add to our knowledge of the game.

Perhaps just one more point should be emphasized. As in my now rapidly-aging book, this book is concerned only with golf literature. It does not attempt to establish just who invented the game or where it started. If Donovan or Murdoch have opinions on the subject, they will not be mentioned here.

We offer this book to golf-book collectors who are twice blessed. They love the grandest game of all. . . and they love books. Of the latter sin, the famed Dr. Rosenbach once offered the opinion that this sport was the second-most enjoyable experience a man could enjoy.

Because I have devoted myself in my retirement from what was once described as a "laughingly business career," to a life of leisure and an occasional martini, I am not quite sure that I appreciate Dick Donovan shaking me loose from my favorite table on the veranda of the Clubhouse. Inspired, however, by his industry and indefatigable research, I like to think we offer you a book of some merit and, hopefully, of great interest. Of just how much merit it offers or of how much interest it holds, you might write to Donovan—not me.

Plaudits should be directed to him. Jeers and comments of derision, we would remind you, are unacceptable when one plays the game of golf.

Joseph S.F. Murdoch
Lafayette Hill, Pennsylvania

Part I

The Featherie Era

1620-1850

THE FEATHERIE ERA 1620-1850

It is obvious, as will be seen later, that golf was played in Scotland before 1620, but for our purposes, we define the era as beginning in 1618 when a monopoly was given to James Melvill for the making of feather balls. Studiously avoiding our earlier assertion that we would enter into the arena of historical facts, we commend you to read Chapter 22 of Robert Browning's "A History of Golf" for any conjecture as to the form and make of earlier balls.

The literature of the game of golf, regrettably, does not follow the development of the game in those early years. It may be appropriate to note that Raymond Chandler, perhaps more noted for whodunit in a garret, rather than whodidit on a golf course, once observed, "When a book—any sort of book—reaches a certain intensity of artistic performance, it becomes literature." The earliest references to golf in this era can hardly be described as "intense." However, these early references are of great interest to the collector.

Printing, as we recognize it today, came to Scotland early in the sixteenth century. The earliest references to the game were not printed. They were the work of scribes and thus, the now famous Acts of Parliament written in 1457 (with later additions) constitute the first mention of the game. The first printing came a full century later, in 1566 and this printing, and some of the subsequent printings of The Acts, is a prize that many golf collectors would like to win. Some of the later printings, which are very desirable, are the 1618 edition and the 1682 edition.

If the game was in full flower in this early era, the few devotees of the game obviously did not feel any great compulsion to commit their love of the game to paper. Nothing appeared.

I had cited, in my "Library of Golf," that the earliest English printed reference (as opposed to the Scottish) was "Instructions to a Son," written by the Marques of Argyle and published in England in 1689. Some years later we discovered an earlier edition, printed in 1616 and we had the great pleasure of seeing one of these earlier editions on display when we toured the home of the Argyles, Inverrary Castle. We remember it especially because we had the greatest urge to practice the ancient British sport of "smash and run." It was only the presence of guards, who appeared to be in much better condition and much faster of foot, that prevented us from the deed. In all truth, the reference is fleeting and not too important; but to a collector, it would be a prize.

Other early references, if they cannot be defined as "literature," would include "The Muses Threnodie" (1638), "Westminster Drollery" (1671), and the discovery by Dr. Henry W. Meikle, in 1938, of an early diary maintained by an Edinburgh medical student, Thomas Kincaid, in 1687/88.

As the number of printed books proliferated—none of which was designed to acquaint the world with the mystery of golf—it should be mentioned that the third edition of "Encyclopedia Britannica" (1797) was the first of that increasingly popular type of publication to mention the game. In those late years of the 18th and early 19th centuries, various books on sports, such as Hoyle, Strutt and Stonehenge, appeared and each of them mentioned golf, usually, as a game peculiar to the Scots.

The Reverend T. F. Dibdin, one of the early collectors of books, wrote his famous "Bibliographical & Antiquarian and Picturesque Tour of the Northern Counties of England and in Scotland" in 1838, which includes a delightful account of an evening spent with the golfers of St. Andrews.

That same year, "A Series of Original Portraits and Caricature Etchings with Biographical Sketches and Illustrative Anecdotes" by John Kay, Edinburgh, appeared. It is a book of some fascination for anyone interested in Scotland and of great appeal to golf collectors because it included the (now) famous portrait of Alexander McKeller, "Cock o' the Green" and certainly one of the first great golf fanatics.

It was not until some years later that I learned of another portrait in the book is of some golfing interest. John Osbourne, York Place, Edinburgh, is another subject of Kay's observation. He is one of the early Captains of the Honourable Company of Edinburgh Golfers, and his house was to become the abode of a succession of veterinarians, each named Baird. One of the notable golf collectors of today, Archie Baird, and a retired veterinarian, still lived in that ancient home when I first visited him in 1970.

Toward the end of this featherie era, a couple of histories appeared which are of some appeal to collectors. They are: "A History of St. Andrews" by Rev. C. J. Lyon and "A History of St. Andrews" by another Reverend, Charles Roger. Both of these have references to golf.

I was bold enough in my earlier bibliography to write that "the first important contribution to the literature of golf appeared in 1721 with the publication of a small volume of poetry entitled 'Glotta,' written by James Arbuckle, a student at Glasgow University and printed by William Duncan of that city."

I am amazed now at my boldness, for I now freely confess that I "copped" the line from Hopkinson (Cecil Hopkinson: "Collecting Golf Books," 1938) and I have not, to this day, seen a copy of it. I will admit to some comfort when a copy was sold at one of the British auctions in later years for a price which the British would admit was "a pretty sum."

Some twenty years later, "The Goff" appeared, first published in 1743 (later editions, 1763 and 1793). It is considered, generally, in any of its three editions, to be the grand prize for any collector.

As a collector, not as a savant, I must mention that the third edition includes the first reference in print to a golf collector. He was, sadly enough to a book collector, a club collector. Depending upon one's definition of "scarce" or "rare," it is not easily found today, and it is somewhat interesting to me to learn that the United States Golf Association began their current "rare book" program in 1980 with a reprint, in one volume, of all three editions. Not too many years later, with the growth of interest in collecting golf books, the reprint is now becoming a collectors' item.

Some eighty years later, the first book to attempt some sort of history of the game appeared with the publication of "The Rules of the Thistle Club" in 1824. Written by James Cundell, secretary of the club, it is of some interest to learn that he sent the manuscript to a fellow club member, Sir Walter Scott, asking Scott to critique his article. Scott returned it with a note that he could do nothing to add to its excellence. I add the note, as I did in my revision (1978) of my bibliography, that I did not originally list the title for the very simple reason that I did not know what it was. The title would indicate, I like to think most would agree, a simple sheet of rules. We know now that it is a very important contribution to the literature of golf and perhaps of more importance than the earlier poetry. Robert Clark, recognizing its importance, reprinted it in his great book in 1875.

A decade later (than "Thistle Club"), "Golfiana" by George Fullerton Carnegie was published; another long poem and—from stories passed down to us—printed privately for distribution among his many friends. The second edition, printed the same year, is said to be distinguished by the price (10/6) printed on the cover. A third edition, with some poems added, was published in 1842.

A note of bibliographic mystery is introduced at this point. Harry B. Wood's bibliography, contained in "Golfing Curios and the Like" (1910), mentions a fourth edition of this book (1862). Cecil Hopkinson disputes the possibility, pointing out that no known copies of such an edition have been found. Just recently (1986), reports have circulated that there is such an edition hidden away in a library in Europe. Your humble compilers of this epic have now established the validity of the book.

For those who are intrigued with the spread of golf throughout the world, it is interesting to note that the second edition of Thomas Mathison's "The Goff" was dedicated to "All the Lovers of Goff in Europe, Asia, Africa, and America." Of the actual playing of the game in those faraway places, there is fragmentary evidence. It has been established as the Scots emigrated from their native land, they carried their "sticks." Just recently (late 1986) , a research project regarding the emigration of Scots turned up evidence that as early as 1743, clubs and balls were shipped from Scotland to Charleston, South Carolina, in America. Some fifty years later, in Charleston and Savannah, Georgia, newspapers, advertisements appeared announcing "golf balls" (which presumes dancing and, perhaps, the consumption of spirits). It is a matter of record that in 1779 a newspaper in New York City carried an advertisement offering "excellent clubs and the veritable Caledonian Balls." It has been presumed that his notice was inserted to attract the eyes of the Scottish troops who were then stationed in that city.

There is also a small but significant pamphlet, written by Dr. Benjamin Rush of Philadelphia and printed by the famed colonial printer, James Dunlop, in 1772. It is entitled "Sermons to Gentlemen upon Temperance and Exercise" which we must confess does not appeal to us. It does however give us the first appearance in North America, of information on the game—"Golf is an exercife which is much ufed by the Gentlemen in Scotland. A large common in which there are feveral little holes is chofen for the purpofe. It is played with little leather balls fluffed with feathers; and flicks made fomewhat in the form of a handy-wicket. He who puts a ball into a given number of holes, with the feweft flokes, gets the game. The late Dr. M'Kenzie, Author of the effay on Health and Long Life, ufed to fay, that a man would live ten years the longer for ufing this exercife once or twice a week." One can assume that Dr. Rush picked up this information while attending the University of Edinburgh for his medical studies.

Thus endeth the first era of golf.

A Member

100. *St. Andrews to the Play, Dedicated to the Royal and Ancient Golfing Club*. Bangor, Wales: Privately Printed, 1st ed. 1854, 8p, wrappers, 18.5cm.

Actis and Constititionis

120. *The Actis and Constitutions of the Realme of Scotland maid in Parliamentis haldin be the rycht excellent, hie and mychtie Princeis King's James the first, Second, Third, Feird, Fyfth, and in tyme of Marie now Queen of Scottis*. Edinburgh: Robert Lekpreuik, 1st ed. 1566 [engraved title page] vellum, 26.5cm. later printings.

Adamson, H[enry]

140. *The Muses Threnodie: or Mirthful Mournings on the death of Mr. Gall. Containing variety of Poetical Descriptions, Moral Instructions, Historical Narritives and Devine Observation, with the most remarkable Antiquities of Scotland, especially of Perth*. Perth, Scotland: James Cant & Robert Morrison, 2d ed. 1774, 261p, appendix 200p, folding map, leather, 18cm. note: first edition not located.

Arbuckle, James

160. *Glotta, A Poem Humbly Inscribed to the Right Honourable The Marquees of Carnarron*. Glasgow: William Duncan, 1st ed. 1721, 22p, wrappers, 18cm.

Carnegie, George Fullerton

180. *Golfiana, or, Niceties Connected with the Game of Golf*. Leith, Scotland: Privately Printed, 1st ed. 1833, 8p, wrappers, 15cm.

185. 2d ed. Edinburgh: Wm. Blackwood and Alexander Hill, 1833, 16p, wrappers, 15cm.

190. 3d ed. Edinburgh: William Blackwood, 1842, 26p, wrappers, 15.5cm.

195. 4th ed. Edinburgh: William Blackwood, 1863, 24p, boards, 13.5cm.

[Cundell, James]

210. *Rules of the Thistle Club: with some historical notices relative to the progress of the game of golf in Scotland*. Edinburgh: Privately Printed, 1st ed. 1824, 50p, illustrated wrappers, 21cm.

220. limited ed. facsimile [1900 copies] slipcased. Far Hills, New Jersey: USGA, 1983, 50p, 1/4 cloth, boards, 20.5cm, introduction by Joseph C. Dey Jr.

Depping, George Bernhard

240. *Evenings Entertainments; or, Delineations of the manners and customs of various nations, interspersed with geographical notices, historical and biographical anecdotes, and descriptions in natural history. 2 Volumes.* London: Henry Colburn, 1st ed. 1811, unknown pagination, leather, note: this entry from the British Museum records.

250. *Depping's Evening Entertainments: comprising delineations of the manners and customs of various nations.* Philadelphia: David Hogan, 1st American ed. 1812, 424p, illustrated by Atherton, leather, 18cm, later printings.

Grierson, James

270. *Delineations of St. Andrews.* Edinburgh: Peter Hill, 1st ed. 1807, 244p, illustrated, leather, 19cm.

280. 2d ed. 1823, 224p, illustrated, leather, 19cm.

290. 3d ed. 1838, St. Andrews: Joseph Cook, 264p, illustrated, cloth, 19cm. later printings.

[Honourable Company of Edinburgh Golfers]

310. *Laws to be Observed by the Members of the Golfing Company in Playing Golf.* [Edinburgh] Privately Printed, 1st ed. 1775, 4p, wrappers, 27cm.

[Hoyle, Edmond]

330. *Hoyle's Games Improved.* London: J.F.&C.Rivington/T. Payne, UK ed. 1790, 290p, illustrated, leather, 15.5cm. note: first edition in which the game of golf appeared.

340. American ed. Boston: Edward Cotton, 1814, 296p, illustrated, leather, 12.5cm. note: first American edition in which the game of golf appeared.

Mathison, Thomas

360. *The Goff; A Heroi-Comical Poem in Three Cantos.* Edinburgh: Privately Printed, 1st ed. 1743, 22p, wrappers, 19.5cm.

370. 2d ed. Edinburgh: James Reid, 1763, 22p, wrappers 22cm.

380. 3d ed. Edinburgh: Peter Hill, 1793, 32p, wrappers, 23.5cm, note: imprint is identified as second edition but is actually the third edition.

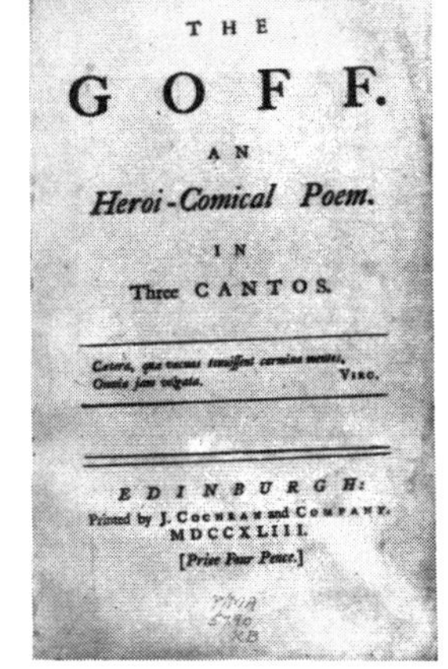
THE
GOFF.
AN
Heroi-Comical Poem.
IN
Three CANTOS.
Cetera, quae vacuas tenuissent carmine mentes,
Omnia jam vulgata. VIRG.
EDINBURGH:
Printed by J. COCHRAN and COMPANY.
MDCCXLIII.
[*Price Four Pence.*]

390. limited ed. facsimile of all 3 editions [1400 copies] slipcased, Far Hills, New Jersey: USGA, 1981, unpaginated, 1/4 cloth, boards, 25.5cm, preface by Harry W. Easterly.

400. special presentation ed. [500 copies] slipcased, Far Hills, New Jersey: USGA, 1981, unpaginated, 1/4 cloth, boards, 25.5cm, preface by Harry W. Easterly.

Musselburgh Golf Club

420. *Laws of the Musselburgh Golf Club. [Established A.D. 1774] with some notices Respecting The Game.* Musselburgh, Scotland: Privately Printed, 1st ed. 1829, 20p, wrappers, 21.5cm.

[Rush, Benjamin]

440. *Sermons to Gentlemen upon Temperance and Exercise.* Philadelphia: John Dunlap, 1st ed. 1772, 44p, wrappers, 19cm.

450. *Sermons To the Rich and Famous, On Temperance and Exercise.* London: Edward & Charles Dilly, 1st UK ed. 1772, 80p, wrappers, 15.5cm.

Strutt, Joseph

470. *The Sports and Pastimes of the People of England: Rural and Domestic Recreations, May-Games, Mummeries, Pageants, Processions and Pompous Spectacles, from the earliest period to the present time.* London: J. White, limited ed. large paper, 1801, 301p, illustrated, leather, raised bands, 29.5cm, subsequent editions.

Part II

The Gutta Percha Era

1851-1900

THE GUTTA PERCHA ERA 1851-1900

If the years are not precise, it suits our purpose to delineate the era of the gutta percha ball as this half-century. Historians—and the various books on golf history—will satisfy any curiosity you may have as to the exact years which witnessed the tremendous growth of golf from small corners in Scotland to the four corners of the world (if, indeed, a round globe can be said to have four corners).

The literature of golf enjoyed an increase in quantity as the five decades passed a corresponding growth and by the end of the era, the turn of the present century, it may be said that the penmen of the day were enthusiastically foisting upon the not-too-unwilling shoulders of golfers more and more books. It remains to the individual to decide whether this deluge of books should be described as literature.

It should be added that it was in this era that we become more aware of the growing interest in collecting golf artifacts. Smith's book (1866), with the advertisement on the back cover, makes us accept this growing interest.

"The Golfer's Manual, being an Historical and Descriptive Account of the National Game of Scotland" by "A Keen hand," published in 1857, is the first of the important book to be published in this era. "A Keen Hand" was H. B. Farnie, then a young St. Andrews University student, who was to later become a journalist, the author of several guide (tourist) books; later the editor of a Fife newspaper and, still later, a music critic of some distinction. The book was to go into a second and third edition with the text unchanged with fresh title pages bound into the first edition folios. In 1947, some 90 years later, a reprint was published, distinguished by an introduction by Bernard Darwin. Any one of the three original editions are uncommon and the 1947 reprint is becoming a prize. This book was really the first book on golf and the first book to offer instruction. It might be damned for the later distinction; it is honored for the earlier distinction.

With some exceptions, and again as in the first era, poetry made up most of the entries in the first decades of this era. We can only theorize, as we did in our earlier book, that these poems (lays) were composed by enthusiastic followers of the game and, stimulated, perhaps, with a glass or two, they would rise at their meetings to extol the virtues of the game. Reaching some favor with fellow-Club-members, the authors would publish them in attractive form to distribute among friends. They were never published in great numbers and most of them today are in that category of scarce. Some, perhaps, rare.

"Songs of the Innerleven Club," "Poems on Golf," "Golfiana" (Brown), and "Blackheath Golfing Lays" are some of these; it is the fortunate collector who finds one today.

Some serious writers—or, some writers writing seriously—began to write of the game and to gather (or collect) stories and accounts of the game as played in earlier days. Robert Chambers, son of one of the brother-founders of the famous Edinburgh printers and, later, publishers, was one of the first of these. He was also one of the better players of his day.

His first book (perhaps, more a pamphlet!) was "A Few Rambling Remarks on Golf," even today a most charming title, and following closely upon the heels (or spine) of Farnie's book, also a book of instruction. It was subsequently published four years later under the title "Gymnastics, Golf and Curling," and some twenty years later, under his son's name, as "Golfing."

Some other books, equally important in contributing to our knowledge of the game are: George Robb's "Historical Gossip about Golf and Golfers" (1863) which might be described as the first anthology. "The Golfer's Year Book of 1866," edited by Robert Howie Smith which is one of the first books to immortalize the names of members of the Clubs than known and "The Golfer's Handbook," some years later (1881), by Robert Forgan, Jr., son of the famous clubmaker, was a lively compilation of instruction and historical information. This latter book was to go into six editions, the final edition with the title changed to "The Golfer's Manual."

Generally recognized as "the masterpiece of golf literature" in this—or any other—era is the anthology, "Golf: A Royal and Ancient Game" which was compiled and edited by Robert Clark, an Edinburgh printer. An enthusiastic golfer, even if not described as one of the better players of his time, Clark become interested in collecting as much as could be found of the early writings of golf. He mounted his collection of these writings in a book of handsome production and, even today, the paper, the binding and, not incidentally, the contents, excite the interest of the knowledgeable collector.

Clark was the first—ever a canny Scot—of many who would follow who would complicate the lives of collectors by issuing the same book in a limited number of 50 copies. He published, from the same printed forms, an edition of 50 copies, numbered, which was to become even more of a collector's item than the same (very desirable) first edition. He did not even stop there. Further enhancing the desirability of the book to collectors (then, and now!) he had bound up some "Presentation" copies. Of these, it is difficult to number them. Hopkinson mentions "a few"; the learned Royal and Ancient Golf Club Librarian, Mr. Burnet, has stated in his catalogue of that marvelous library that were "twelve."

I am not sure about Donovan but I can tell you that Murdoch is not about to cast a ballot. Having been "burned" a few times in making positive statements about the limitations of certain books, Murdoch is not about to make a guess. Let me say; if you have one of the "First," you have a prize; if you have one of the "Presentation," you do not have to worry about educating your children.

Clark's great book went into a second and third edition (1893 and 1899), both published by Macmillan, and either of these is, too, very desirable.

It is said, I believe by Horace Hutchinson, that "in 1885 golf was an eccentricity affected by a few; by 1890 it had become a general fashion." He was referring to the spread of golf from Scotland to England.

Certainly no account of the literature of this era would be complete without acknowledging the contributions made by Hutchinson. His first book was 1886; a small, thin book of instruction which he sent to William Blackwood, the Edinburgh publisher, for consideration. Blackwood, according to Hutchinson, agreed to publish it, "for I am sure there must be something in that book. Ever since I read it, I have been trying to play according to its advice and the result is that I've entirely lost any little idea of the game I ever had."

The book was published (by Blackwood) and went into fourteen editions.

Despite any confusion he may have caused—even as Toski and Ballard and Haney do today—Hutchinson contributed greatly to the literature in this (and the next) era which we are examining. He wrote a succession of fine books, "British Golf Links," "Bert Edward, the Golf Caddie," "Aspects of Golf" and his great triumph, "Golf," from the Badminton Library of Sports, which first appeared in 1890. This latter book is still today one of the most entertaining and informative books on the game that one can read. It went into many later editions and any one of them can be read today with as much pleasure and enjoyment as the day it was published.

To quote myself, which is not always the most reliable source, "in the ten-year era from 1890, 48 books would be written on the game, including the first biography of a golfer (F. G. Tait); the first book describing the more renowned courses (or links) (Hutchinson); the first golfing novel (Stobart); the first American book (Lee); the first book written by a woman (Kennard); and the first book by a working professional (Park)."

In the last ten years of the half-century the game spread around the world and, happily, writers were there to make a record of it. The books of this era are most interesting to read and most instructive for anyone who may be interested in the history of the game. I am not sure that they all met the standard which we define as literature; but then, how many of us play to par?

Thus endeth the second era of golf.

A Member [Dr. Stone]

500. *The Duffers' Golf Club Papers, to which is added: a day on the ladies links.* Montrose, Scotland: Privately Printed, 1st ed. 1891, 71p, leather, 18.5cm.

Aikman, George

520. *A Round of the Links: Views of the Golf Greens of Scotland, from water colour drawings by John Smart.* [Edinburgh, Scotland] Privately Printed, limited, signed ed. [no limitation cited] 1893 [20p] illustrated, decorative cloth, 42cm.

530. limited ed. facsimile [500 copies] slipcased, Towie Barclay Castle, Scotland: Heritage Press, 1980 [20p] illustrated, 1/4 leather, gilt stamped cloth, 43cm.

540. *Pen and Pencil Sketches on the Game of Golf.* [Edinburgh, Scotland] Privately Printed, 1st ed. 1893 [40p] illustrated, cloth, 42cm, after drawings by John Smart.

Andre, Richard

560. *Colonel Bogey's Sketch Book: comprising an eccentric collection of scribbles and scratches found in disused lockers and swept up in the pavilion together with Sunday after-dinner sayings of the Colonel.* London: Longmans Green, 1st ed. 1897, 44p, illustrated, 1/4 cloth, illustrated boards, 21.5cm.

Balfour, J. Stuart

580. *Spalding's Athletic Library: Golf, containing list of implements and their uses, glossary of technical terms and latest revised rules of the game.* New York: American Sports Publishing, 1st ed. 1893, 24p, illustrated, wrappers, 17.5cm. note: this is the first of the Spalding's publications on golf. Title changed in 1895, for later editions see entry "Spalding's Official Golf Guide."

Balfour, James

600. *Reminiscences of Golf on St. Andrews Links.* Edinburgh: David Douglas, 1st ed. 1887, 68p, wrappers, 16.5cm.

610. limited ed. facsimile [300 copies] Carlinville, Illinois: Chas. A. Bud Dufner, 1982, 68p, illustrated wrappers, 16.5cm.

Barrie, James

630. *Historical Sketch of the Hawick Golf Club, with complete list of members, constitution and rules, etc, and appended.* Hawick, Scotland: James Edgar, 1st ed. 1898, 183p, illustrated, cloth, 18.5cm.

Baxter, Peter

650. *Golf in Perth and Perthshire: Traditional, Historical and Modern.* Perth, Scotland: Thomas Hunter, 1st ed, 1899, 183p, cloth, 20cm.

Beckwith, J.P.

670. *The Golf Links Located in Florida and Nassau.* [St. Augustine, Florida] Privately Printed, 1st ed. 1900 [42p] illustrated, illustrated wrappers, 15cm.

[Bennett, Andrew]

690. *The Book of St. Andrews Links: containing plan of golf course, description of the greens, rules of the game, bye-laws of the links, regulations for starting, golfing rhymes, etc.* St. Andrews & Edinburgh: J.&G. Innes & J.Menzies, limited ed. [1000 copies] 1898, 80p, illustrated, wrappers, 18.5cm.

700. limited ed. [200 copies] facsimile, slipcased, London: Ellesborough Press, 1984, 80p, illustrated, leather, aeg, raised bands, 18.5cm.

[Brooks Brothers]

720. *The Links Book.* New York: Brooks Brothers, 1st ed. 1900, 112p, illustrated by Will Bradley, wrappers, 10cm.

[Brown, Thomas]

740. *Golfiana or A Day At Gullane.* NP: Privately Printed, 1st ed. 1869, 15p, wrappers, 22.5cm.

Caesar, William

760. *Carnoustie Golf Links Bazaar 1892.* Carnoustie, Scotland: Privately Printed, 1st ed. 1892, 65p, decorative boards and cloth, 21cm.

Camp, Walter and Lillian Brooks

780. *Drives and Puts: A book of golf stories.* Boston: L.C. Page, 1st ed. 1899, 243p, illustrated, decorative cloth, 17.5cm.

Carruth, Hayden

800. *A Hand-Book of Golf for Bears*. New York: R.H.Russell, 1st ed. 1900 [56p] illustrated by Frank Ver Beck, 1/4 cloth, illustrated boards, 23.5cm.

[Chambers, Charles E.S.]

820. *Golfing: A Handbook to the Royal and Ancient Game, with a list of clubs, rules etc., also golfing sketches and poems.* Edinburgh: W.&R. Chambers, 1st ed. 1887, 134p, illustrated, decorative cloth, 18cm.

Chambers, Robert

840. *A Few Rambling Remarks on Golf, with the rules as laid down by the Royal and Ancient Club of St. Andrews.* Edinburgh: W.&R. Chambers, 1st ed. 1862, 31p, illustrated, illustrated wrappers, 15cm.

850. limited ed. facsimile [1900 copies] slipcased, Far Hills, New Jersey: USGA, 1983, 31p, illustrated, 1/4 cloth, illustrated boards, 15cm, introductory essay by Joseph C. Dey.

[Chambers, Robert]

860. *Gymnastics, Golf and Curling*. London and Edinburgh: W.&R. Chambers, [ca1866] 1st ed, 94p, illustrated, illustrated wrappers, 14cm. later printing.

[Clark, Robert]

880. *Golf: A Royal and Ancient Game*. Edinburgh: R.&R. Clark, limited ed. large paper, signed [50 copies] 1875, 284p, illustrated, decorative cloth, 24cm, additional illustrations.

890. limited ed. presentation copy, 1875, 284p, illustrated, decorative cloth, 28.5cm. note: an unknown limited number of copies of the large paper edition prepared for Robert Clark. Copies are somewhat different with a photograph of Robert Clark and signed by him.

900. 1st trade ed. Edinburgh: R.&R. Clark, 1875, 284p, illustrated, decorative cloth, 24cm.

910. 2d ed. rev. London: Macmillan, 1893, 304p, illustrated, decorative cloth, 20.5cm.

920. 3d ed. rev. London: Macmillan, 1899, 304p, illustrated, decorative cloth, 21cm.

930. reprint of 2d ed. East Ardsley, England: EP Publishing, 1975, 304p, illustrated, cloth, 21.5cm.

940. abridged reprint ed. Newtongrange, Scotland: Lang Syne, 1984, 100p, illustrated, illustrated wrappers, 21cm.

950. *Poems on Golf.* Edinburgh: Privately Printed, special presentation ed. 1867, 78p, pebble grain cloth, 22.5cm. note: list of subscribers not contained in this small limited number of presentation copies.

960. 1st ed. [subscribers ed.] Edinburgh: Privately Printed, 1867, 78p, cloth, 22.5cm.

Compton, C.H.

980. *The Antiquity of Golf, A paper read at the Congress of the British Archaelological Association.* London: Privately Printed, 1st ed. [1881] 13p, wrappers, 23cm.

Cunningham, Andrew S.

1000. *Inverkeithing, North Queens Ferry, Limekilns, Charlestown, The Ferryhills: Their Antiquities & Recreation Resources-History of Dunfermline Golf Club and Plan of Course.* Dunfermline, Scotland: W. Clark, 1st ed. [1899] 181p, illustrated, cloth, 18.5cm.

Currente, Calamo [James McHardy]

1020. *Half Hours with an Old Golfer.* London: George Bell, 1st ed. 1895, 178p, illustrated by G.A. Laundry, decorative cloth, 18.5cm.

[Dalrymple, W.]

1040. *Handbook of Golf: with diagrams and positions and instructions from amateur and professional champions.* Edinburgh: W.H. White, 1st ed. 1895, 116p, illustrated, wrappers, 15.5cm.

1050. *The Golfer's Referee.* by the editor of 'The Golfer'. Edinburgh/ London: W.H.White/Simpkin, Marshall, Hamilton and Kent, 1st ed. [1897] 99p, decorative cloth, 16cm.

deAula, W. [pseud for Hall Maxwell]

1070. *St. Andrews: Ancient and Modern.* Edinburgh: Privately Printed, 1st ed. 1870, 71p, illustrated, wrappers, 16.5cm.

Dwight, James

1090. *Golf: A Handbook For Beginners.* Boston: Overman Wheel Co. 1st ed. [ca1895] 82p, illustrated, illustrated wrappers, 17cm.

Everard, Harry Stirling Crawford

1110. *Golf In Theory and Practice: Some Hints to Beginners.* London: George Bell, 1st ed. 1896, 194p, illustrated, decorative cloth, 18.5cm. later printing. note: In 1897 an imprint states first published January 1897. Apparently a printing error.

Fairbanks, Walter

1130. *Some Hints on Learning Golf.* Denver, Colorado: Privately Printed, 1st. ed. [ca1900] 15p, wrappers, 17.5cm.

Farnie, Henry Brougham] by A Keen Hand

1140. *The Golfer's Manual, being an historical and descriptive account of the national game of Scotland.* Cupar, Scotland: Whitehead and Orr, 1st ed. 1857, 96p, illustrated, decorative cloth, 16cm.

1141. 2d ed. Cupar, Scotland: John C. Orr, 1862, 96p, cloth, illustrated, 14.5cm.

1142. 3d ed. St. Andrews: J. Cook, 1870, illustrated, wrappers, 14.5cm.

1143. limited ed. facsimile [750 copies] slipcased, London: Dropmore Press, 1947, 84p, illustrated, 1/4 cloth, illustrated boards, 20cm.

1144. reprint ed. New York: Vantage Press, 1965, 89p, illustrated, 20.5cm.

Fitzpatrick, Hugh Louis

1150. *Golf Don'ts: Admonitions that will help the novice to play well and scratch men to play better.* New York: Doubleday Page, 1st ed. 1900, 114p, decorative cloth, 16cm.

Fleming, David Hay

1170. *Historical Notes & Extracts Concerning The Links of St. Andrews 1552-1893.* St. Andrews: Citizens Office, 1st ed. 1893, 112p, wrappers, 16.5cm.

Flint, Violet [pseud for J.E. Thompson]

1190. *A Golfing Idyll or The Skipper's Round with the Deil on the Links of St. Andrews.* [St. Andrews] Privately Printed, 1st ed. 1892, 30p, wrappers, 19cm.

1200. 2d ed. St Andrews: W.C. Henderson, 1893, 36p, illustrated wrappers, 18.5cm.

1210. 3d ed. St Andrews: W.C. Henderson, 1897, 35p, illustrated by A. Islay, decorative cloth and illustrated wrappers, 23cm.

1220. limited ed. facsimile of 3d ed. [250 copies] Droitwich, England: Grant Books, 1978, 35p, illustrated by A. Islay, 1/4 cloth, illustrated boards, 24.5cm, preface by H.R. Grant.

Forgan, Robert

1230. *The Golfer's Handbook, including History of the Game, Hints to Beginners, the Feat of Champion Golfers, Lists of Leading Clubs and Their Office-Bearers, etc.* Cupar, Scotland: John Innes, 1st ed. 1881, 83p, illustrated, illustrated boards, 18cm.

1235. 2d ed. Cupar, Scotland/London: John Innes/Marcus Ward, 1883, 72p, illustrated, boards, 18cm.

1240. 3d ed. Edinburgh: John Menzies, [ca1884] 70p, illustrated, illustrated boards, 19.5cm.

1245. 4th ed. London: Simpkin, Marshall, Hamilton, Kent, 1890, 80p, illustrated, decorative cloth, 18.5cm.

1250. Forgan's Special Edition, London: Simpkin, Marshall, Hamilton, Kent [ca1891] 80p, illustrated, decorative cloth, 18.5cm. later printings. note: this edition identical to the fourth edition.

1255. 5th ed. not located.

1260. *The Golfer's Manual, including History of the Game; Special Uses of the Different Clubs; Hints to Beginners; History of Golf Balls; The Feats of Champion Golfers; Golfiana; Glossary of Technical Terms, New Rules of the Game.* London: Simpkin, Marshall, Hamilton, Kent, 6th ed. rev. [1897] 84p, illustrated, decorative cloth, 18.5cm. note: previously titled "The Golfer's Handbook."

1265. 7th ed. rev. [ca1907] 100p, illustrated, cloth, 18.5cm.

1270. 8th ed. not located.

Game of Golf

1280. *The Game of Golf: including short course of instruction, list of clubs and accessories; rules of golf revised to date, etiquette of golf and pictures of celebrated professional golfers.* Chicago: Hibbard, Spencer, Bartlett, 1st ed. 1900, 103p, illustrated, wrappers, 17cm, introduction by John D. Dunn.

Glynes, Webster

1300. *The Maiden: A Golfing Epic.* [England] Privately Printed, 1st ed. [ca1893] 19p, cloth, 20.5cm.

Golf in California

1340. *Golf in California.* Chicago: Santa Fe Railroad, 1st ed. 1900, 47p, illustrated, illustrated wrappers, 15cm.

Golf Links on the Grand Rapids & Indiana Railway

1360. *Golf Links on the Grand Rapids & Indiana Railway.* Grand Rapids, Michigan: Grand Rapids & Indiana Railway, 1st ed. [ca1900] [24p] illustrated, illustrated wrappers, 19.5cm.

Golfer [George Robb]

1380. *Historical Gossip About Golf and Golfers.* Edinburgh: Privately Printed, 1st ed. 1863, 58p, wrappers, 16.5cm.

Golfer's Guide to the Game and Greens of Scotland

1400. *Golfer's Guide to the Game and Greens of Scotland.* Edinburgh: W.H. White, 1st ed. 1894, 208p, decorative cloth, 18.5cm. edited by W. Dalrymple. note: title change in 1895 edition. "Golfer's Guide for the United Kingdom."

Golfer's Guide for the United Kingdom

1420. *Golfer's Guide for the United Kingdom 1895.* Edinburgh: W.H. White, 2d ed. 1895, 304p, illustrated, decorative cloth, 18.5cm. edited by W. Dalrymple. note: See "Golfer's Guide to the Game and Greens of Scotland."

1430. 3d ed. Edinburgh: W.H. White, 1896, 334p, illustrated, decorative cloth, 18.5cm.

1440. 4th ed. not located.

1450. 5th ed. not located.

Golfer's Guide Annual

1470. *Golfer's Guide Annual 1899.* Edinburgh: W.H. White, 6th ed. 1899, 476p, illustrated, decorative cloth, 18.5cm. note: title change. See "Golfer's Guide for the United Kingdom."

Golfer's Handbook

1490. *Golfer's Handbook.* Edinburgh: The Golf Agency, 1899, 1st ed. not located.

1500. 2d ed. 1900, 189p, cloth, 13cm.

1510. 3d ed. 1901. not located.

1520. 4th ed. 1902. 297p, illustrated, cloth, 13cm.

1530. 5th ed. 1903. not located.

1540. 6th ed. 1904. not located.
1550. 7th ed. 1905. 538p, illustrated, cloth, 13.5cm.
1560. 8th ed. 1906, 833p, illustrated, cloth, 13.5cm.
1570. 9th ed. 1907. 796p, illustrated, cloth, 13.5cm.
1580. 10th ed. 1908, 987p, illustrated, cloth, 13.5cm.
1590. 11th ed. Edinburgh: Scottish Newspaper, 1909, 1035p, illustrated, cloth, 13.5cm.
1600. 12th ed. 1910. not located.
1610. 13th ed. 1911, 1119p, illustrated, cloth, 13.5cm.
1620. 14th ed. 1912. 1071p, illustrated, cloth, 13.5cm.
1630. 15th ed. 1913, 947p, illustrated, decorative cloth, 13.5cm.
1640. 16th ed. 1914, 1062p, illustrated, cloth, 13.5cm.
1650. 17th ed. 1915. not located.
1660. 18th ed. 1916. not located.
1670. 19th ed. 1917. not located.
1680. 20th ed. 1918. not located.
1690. 21st ed. 1919. 722p, illustrated, cloth, 13.5cm.
1700. 22d ed. 1920. 947p, illustrated, cloth, 13.5cm.
1710. 23d ed. 1921, Edinburgh: Golfer's Handbook, 1005p, illustrated, cloth, 13cm.
1720. 24th ed. 1922, 1051p, illustrated, cloth, 13.5cm.
1730. 25th ed. 1923, 1131p, illustrated, decorative cloth, 13.5cm.
1740. 26th ed. 1924, 1207p, illustrated, cloth, 13cm.
1750. 27th ed. 1925, 1283p, illustrated, cloth, 13cm.
1760. 28th ed. 1926, 1335p, illustrated, cloth, 13cm.
1770. 29th ed. 1927, 891p, illustrated, cloth, 19cm.
1780. 30th ed. 1928, 859p, illustrated, cloth, 19cm.
1790. 31st ed. 1929, 875p, illustrated, cloth, 19cm.
1800. 32d ed. 1930, 883p, illustrated, cloth, 19cm.
1810. 33d ed. 1931, 887p, illustrated, cloth, 19cm.
1820. 34th ed. 1932, 869p, illustrated, cloth, 19cm.
1830. 35th ed. 1933, 875p, illustrated, cloth, 19cm.
1840. 36th ed. 1934, 919p, illustrated, cloth, 18.5cm.
1850. 37th ed. 1935, 947p, illustrated, cloth, 19cm.
1860. 38th ed. 1936, 951p, illustrated, cloth, 19cm.
1870. 39th ed. 1937, 959p, illustrated, cloth, 19cm.
1880. 40th ed. 1938, 979p, illustrated, cloth, 19cm.
1890. 41st ed. 1939, 955p, illustrated, cloth, 18.5cm.
1900. 42d ed. 1940, 915p, illustrated, cloth, 18.5cm.
1910. 43d ed. 1941, 915p, illustrated, cloth, 18.5cm.

1920. 44th ed. 1947, 779p, illustrated, cloth, 18.5cm.
1930. 45th ed. 1948, 767p, illustrated, cloth, 18.5cm.
1940. 46th ed. 1949, 847p, illustrated, cloth, 18.5cm.
1950. 47th ed. 1950, 911p, illustrated, cloth, 18.5cm.
1960. 48th ed. 1951, 931p, illustrated, cloth, 18.5cm.
1970. 49th ed. 1952, 919p, illustrated, cloth, 18.5cm.
1980. 50th ed. 1953, 950p, illustrated, cloth, 18.5cm.
1990. 51st ed. 1954, 966p, illustrated, cloth, 18.5cm.
2000. 52d ed. 1955, 991p, illustrated, cloth, 18.5cm.
2010. 53d ed. 1956, 1031p, illustrated, cloth, 18.5cm.
2020. 54th ed. 1957, 1015p, illustrated, cloth, 18.5cm.
2030. 55th ed. 1958, 1059p, illustrated, cloth, 18.5cm.
2040. 56th ed. 1959, 1059p, illustrated, cloth, 18.5cm.
2050. 57th ed. 1960, 1059p, illustrated, cloth, 18.5cm.
2060. 58th ed. 1961, 1059p, illustrated, cloth, 18.5cm.
2070. 59th ed. 1962, Glasgow: The Golfer's Handbook, 1055p, illustrated, cloth, 18.5cm.
2080. 60th ed. 1963, 1055p, illustrated, cloth, 18.5cm.
2090. 61st ed. 1964, 1055p, illustrated, cloth, 18.5cm.
2100. 62d ed. 1965, 1073p, illustrated, cloth, 18.5cm.
2110. 63d ed. 1966, 1080p, illustrated, cloth, 18.5cm.
2120. 64th ed. 1967, 1075p, illustrated, cloth, 18.5cm.
2130. 65th ed. 1968, 1045p, illustrated, cloth, 18.5cm.
2140. 66th ed. 1969, 1015p, illustrated, cloth, 18.5cm.
2150. 67th ed. 1970, 1018p, illustrated, cloth, 18.5cm.
2160. 68th ed. 1971, 1034p, illustrated, cloth, 18.5cm.
2170. 69th ed. 1972, 1022p, illustrated, cloth, 18.5cm.
2180. 70th ed. 1973, 1031p, illustrated, cloth, 18.5cm.
2190. 71st ed. 1974, 1059p, illustrated, cloth, 18.5cm.
2200. 72d ed. 1975, 1037p, illustrated, cloth, 18.5cm.
2210. 73d ed. 1976, 1037p, illustrated, cloth, 18.5cm.
2220. 74th ed. 1977, 683p, illustrated, cloth, 21cm.
2230. 75th ed. 1978, 694p, illustrated, cloth, 21cm.
2240. 76th ed. 1979, 704p, illustrated, cloth, 21cm.
2250. 77th ed. 1980, 696p, illustrated, cloth, 21cm.
2260. 78th ed. 1981, 680p, illustrated, cloth, 21cm.
2270. 79th ed. 1982, 680p, illustrated, cloth, 21cm.
2280. 80th ed. 1983, 744p, illustrated, cloth, 21cm.
2290. 81st ed. 1984, London: Macmillan/Golf Monthly, 770p, illustrated, cloth, 21cm.

2300. 82d ed. 1985, London: Macmillan, 822p, illustrated, cloth and wrappers, 21cm.

Golfing Annual

2600. *Golfing Annual 1887-1888.* London: Horace Cox, 1st ed. 1888, 226p, illustrated, decorative cloth, 18cm. edited by C. Robertson Bauchope.

2610. 2d ed. 1888-1889. 1889, 305p, illustrated, decorative cloth, 18cm. edited by John Bauchope.

2620. 3d ed. 1889-1890. 1890, 270p, illustrated, decorative cloth, 18cm. edited by David Scott Duncan.

2630. 4th ed. 1890-1891. 1891, 344p, illustrated, decorative cloth, 18cm. edited by David Scott Duncan.

2640. 5th ed. 1891-1892. 1892, 326p, illustrated, decorative cloth, 18cm. edited by David Scott Duncan.

2650. 6th ed. 1892-1893. 1893, 368p, illustrated, decorative cloth, 18cm. edited by David Scott Duncan.

2660. 7th ed. 1893-1894. 1894, 452p, illustrated, decorative cloth, 18cm. edited by David Scott Duncan.

2670. 8th ed. 1894-1895. 1895, 530p, illustrated, decorative cloth, 18cm. edited by David Scott Duncan.

2680. 9th ed. 1895-1896. 1896, 576p, illustrated, decorative cloth, 18cm. edited by David Scott Duncan.

2690. 10th ed. 1896-1897. 1897, 606p, illustrated, decorative cloth, 18cm. edited by David Scott Duncan.

2700. 11th ed. 1897-1898. 1898, 588p, illustrated, decorative cloth, 18cm. edited by David Scott Duncan.

2710. 12th ed. 1898-1899. 1899, 592p, illustrated, decorative cloth, 18cm. edited by David Scott Duncan.

2720. 13th ed. 1899-1900. 1900, 590p, illustrated, decorative cloth, 18cm. edited by David Scott Duncan.

2730. 14th ed. 1900-1901. 1901, 602p, illustrated, decorative cloth, 18cm. edited by David Scott Duncan.

2740. 15th ed. 1901-1902. 1902, 619p, illustrated, decorative cloth, 18cm. edited by David Scott Duncan.

2750. 16th ed. 1902-1903. 1903, 609p, illustrated, decorative cloth, 18cm. edited by David Scott Duncan.

2760. 17th ed. 1903-1904. 1904, 660p, illustrated, decorative cloth, 18cm. edited by David Scott Duncan.

2770. 18th ed. 1904-1905. 1905, 694p, illustrated, decorative cloth, 18cm. edited by David Scott Duncan.

2780. 19th ed. 1905-1906. 1906, 752p, illustrated, decorative cloth, 18cm, edited by David Scott Duncan.

2790. 20th ed. 1906-1907. 1907, 644p, illustrated, decorative cloth, 18cm. edited by David Scott Duncan.

2800. 21st ed. 1907-1908. 1908, 684p, illustrated, decorative cloth, 18cm. edited by David Scott Duncan.

2810. 22d ed. 1908-1909. 1909, 734p, illustrated, decorative cloth, 18cm. edited by David Scott Duncan.

2820. 23d ed. 1909-1910. 1910, 760p, illustrated, decorative cloth, 18cm. edited by David Scott Duncan.

Hassall, John

2840. *The Seven Ages of Golf.* London: Fine Arts Society, 1st.ed. 1899 [18p] illustrated, pictorial portfolio, 42cm, introduction by Horace Hutchinson.

2850. limited ed. signed [260 copies] 1899 [18p] Illustrated, pictorial portfolio, 42cm, introduction by Horace Hutchinson.

Hillinthorn, Gerald

2870. *Your First Game of Golf.* London: Day, 1st ed. [ca1891] 27p, illustrated, illustrated wrappers, 18.5cm.

Hughes, W.E.

2890. *Chronicles of the Blackheath Golfers, with illustrations and portraits.* London: Chapman and Hall, 1st ed. 1897, 245p, illustrated decorative cloth, 25cm.

Hutchinson, Horace Gordon

2910. *A Golfing Pilgrim on Many Links.* London: Methuen, 1st ed. 1898, 287p, decorative cloth, 19.5cm. later printings.

2920. 1st American ed. New York: Scribner's, 1898, 287p, decorative cloth, 19cm.

2930. *Aspects of Golf.* Bristol, England: J.W. Arrowsmith, 1st ed. 1900, 150p, illustrated wrappers, 16cm.

2940. *British Golf Links; A Short Account of the Leading Golf Links of the United Kingdom.* London: J.S. Virtue, limited ed. large paper [250 copies] 1897, 331p, illustrated, wrappers, 39.5cm. note: issued in wrappers for individual custom binding as ordered, in protective box.

2950. 1st trade ed. 1897, 331p, illustrated, decorative cloth, 32cm.

2960. *Famous Golf Links.* edited by, with Andrew Lang, H.S.C. Everard, T. Rutherford Clark. London: Longmans, Green, 1st ed. 1891, 199p, illustrated, decorative cloth, 19cm.

2970. *Golf: The Badminton Library.* London: Longmans, Green, limited ed. large paper [250 copies] 1890, 495p, illustrated, 1/2 leather/decorative cloth, 24.5cm.

2980. small deluxe ed. 1890, 463p, illustrated,1/2 leather, decorative cloth, 19cm.

2990. 1st ed. 1890, 463p, illustrated, decorative cloth, 18.5cm.

3000. 2d ed. 1890, 463p, illustrated, decorative cloth, 18.5cm.

3010. 3d ed. rev. 1892, 469p, illustrated, decorative cloth, 18.5cm.

3020. 4th ed. rev. 1893, 480p, illustrated, decorative cloth, 18.5cm.

3030. 5th ed. rev. 1895, 480p, illustrated, decorative cloth, 18.5cm.

3040. 6th ed. 1898, 483p, illustrated, decorative cloth, 18.5cm.

3050. 7th ed. rev. 1901, 481p, illustrated, decorative cloth, 18.5cm.

3060. 8th ed. rev. 1902, 481p, illustrated, decorative cloth, 18.5cm.

3070. 9th ed. 1911, 481p, illustrated, decorative cloth, 18.5cm.

3080. *Golfing: The Oval Series of Games*. London: George Routledge, 1st ed. 1893, 120p, illustrated, 1/4 cloth/illustrated boards, 18.5cm. later printings.

3090. *Golf: A Complete History of the Game, together with directions for selection of implements, the rules, and a glossary of golf terms*. Philadelphia: Penn, 1st American ed. 1900, 179p, decorative cloth, 14.5cm. US title of "Golfing, The Oval Series of Games." later printings.

3100. *Hints on the Game of Golf*. Edinburgh: William Blackwood, 1st ed. 1886, 69p, illustrated, illustrated linen cloth, 17cm. later printings.

3110. *The Book of Golf and Golfers*. London: Longmans, Green, 1st ed. 1899, 316p, illustrated, cloth, 22cm. later printings.

Irwin, J.F.

3130. *Golf Sketches*. London: Simpkin, Marshall, Hamilton, Kent, 1st ed. [ca1892] [17p] illustrated, illustrated wrappers, 24cm.

J.A.C.K. [J. McCullough]

3150. *Golf in the Year 2000; or, What Are We Coming To*. London: T. Fisher Unwin, 1st ed. 1892, 159p, wrappers, 18.5cm.

3160. facsimile ed. Cincinnati, Ohio: Old Golf Shop, 1984, 159p, cloth 18.5m.

Jackson, David

3180. *Golf Songs and Recitations*. Cupar, Scotland: Privately Printed, 1st ed. 1886, 32p, illustrated, illustrated wrappers, 16.5cm.

Kennard, Edward [Mrs]

3200. *The Sorrows of A Golfer's Wife*. London: F.V. White, 1st ed. 1896, 312p, decorative cloth, 18cm.

Kerr, John

3220. *The Golf Book of East Lothian.* Edinburgh: Privately Printed, limited ed. signed, large paper [250 copies] 1896, 516p/34p appendix, illustrated, 1/2 leather, gilt stamped boards, 28.5cm.

3230. limited ed. signed, small paper [500 copies] Edinburgh: Privately Printed, 1896, 516p/34p appendix, illustrated, decorative cloth, 24.5cm.

Kip, Charles A.

3250. *The Amateur Championship Golf Competition at the Morris County Golf Club.* New York: Privately Printed, limited ed. [100 copies] 1898 [58p] illustrated, cloth, 36cm. preface by Van Tassel Sutphen.

[Knight, William Angus] by A Novice

3270. *On the Links; Being Golfing Stories by Various Hands, with Shakespeare on Golf, by a Novice; also Two Rhymes on Golf by Andrew Lang.* Edinburgh: David Douglas, 1st ed. 1889, 63p, illustrated, illustrated boards, 17cm.

3280. *Shakespeare on Golf: with special reference to St. Andrews Links.* Edinburgh: David Douglas, 1st ed. 1885, 24p, wrappers, 11.5cm.

Knight, William Angus and T.T. Oliphant

3300. *Stories of Golf: with Rhymes on Golf, also Shakespeare on Golf.* London: Heinemann, 2d ed. rev. 1894, 146p, decorative cloth, 17.5cm. Previous title "On the Links."

Lang, Andrew and others

3320. *A Batch of Golfing Papers.* London: Simpkin, Marshall, Hamilton, Kent, 1st ed. 1892, 123p, cloth, 15.5cm.

3325. pbk. ed. 1892, 123p, wrappers, 15cm.

3330. 1st American ed. New York: M.F. Mansfield, 1897, 120p, decorative cloth, 16.5cm.

Lee, James P.

3350. *Golf in America.* New York: Dodd, Mead, 1st ed. 1895, 194p, decorative cloth, illustrated, 17cm.

3360. *Golf and Golfing: A practical manual.* New York: Dodd, Mead, 2d ed. 1895, 194p, cloth, 15.5cm. photographs eliminated from this edition.

Life Magazine

3380. *Fore! Life's Book for Golfers.* New York: Life Publishing, 1st ed. 1900 [60p] 1/4 cloth, illustrated boards, illustrated, 28.5cm.

Linskill, W.T.

3400. *Golf.* London: George Bell, 1st ed. 1889, 54p, illustrated, decorative cloth, 17cm.

3410. 2d ed. rev. 1892, 58p, illustrated, decorative cloth, 17cm, later printings.

Lockyer, Joseph Norman and W. Rutherford

3430. *The Rules of golf: being the St. Andrews rules for the game, codified and annotated.* London: Macmillan, 1st ed. 1896, 114p, cloth, 12cm.

3440. 1st American ed. New York: Macmillan, 1896, 114p, cloth, 13cm.

3445. pbk ed. 1896, 114p, wrappers, 13cm.

Low, John Laing

3460. *F.G. Tait: A Record, Being His Life, Letters and Golfing Diary.* London: J. Nisbet, 1st ed. 1900, 304p, decorative cloth and decorative vellum, 21cm, introduction by Andrew Lang.

MacArthur, Charles

3480. *The Golfer's Annual for 1869-1870.* Ayr, Scotland: Henry & Grant, 1st ed. 1870, 143p, boards, 16cm.

Mackern, Louie [Mrs] and M. Boys

3500. *Our Lady of the Green [a book of ladies golf]*. London: Laurence and Bullen, 1st ed. 1899, 233p, decorative cloth, 18.5cm.

Marsh, Thomas

3520. *Blackheath Golfing Lays*. [London] Privately Printed, 1st ed. 1873, 143p, boards, 17cm.

McBain, J. and W. Fernie

3540. *Golf: Dean's Champion Handbooks*. London: Dean & Son, 1st ed. [ca1899] 63p, illustrated, illustrated linen wrappers, 18cm.

McCullough, J.

3560. *Golf: Containing practical hints with rules of the game*. London: Ward, Locke, 1st ed. 1899, 62p, wrappers, 18.5cm.

McPherson, J. Gordon

3580. *Golf and Golfers, Past and Present*. Edinburgh: William Blackwood, 1st ed, 1891, 100p, illustrated, decorative cloth, 17.5cm, introduction by A.J. Balfour.

Monifieth Golf Links

3600. *Monifieth Golf Links Bazaar Book*. Dundee, Scotland: John Leng, 1st ed. 1899, illustrated, illustrated wrappers, 24.5cm.

Most Convenient Setting Forth

3620. *A Most Convenient Setting Forth of Much Interesting Information Regarding Golf... also the new rules as adopted by the Royal and Ancient Golf Club of St. Andrews, and the rulings thereon of the United States Golf Amateur Association*. New York: Rogers, Peet, 1st ed. 1900, 4p, tartan cloth, 10cm.

Newman, Joseph

3650 *The Official Golf Guide of America for 1900*. Garden City, New York: Privately Printed, 2d ed. 1900, 384p, illustrated, wrappers, 26.5cm.

Newman, Josiah

3660. *The Official Golf Guide of the United Stated and Canada 1899*. New York: Privately Printed, 1st ed. 1899, 374p, illustrated, wrappers, 27.5cm.

Old Golfer [L. Everage]

3670. *Golf on a New Principle: Iron Clubs Superseded.* Bournemouth, England: F.J. Brighth, 1st ed. 1897, 169p, illustrated, illustrated boards, 18cm.

Park, Jr., William

3690. *The Game of Golf.* London: Longmans, Green, 1st ed. 1896, 277p, illustrated, decorative cloth, 19cm. later printings.

Peck, Samuel Minturn

3710. *The Golf Girl*. New York: Frederick A. Stokes, 1st ed. 1899, 15p, illustrated by Maud Humphrey, illustrated boards, 27cm.

Peter, H. Thomas

3730. *Reminiscences of Golf and Golfers*. Edinburgh: James Thin, 1st ed. [ca1890] 55p, decorative linen boards, 13.5cm.

3740. limited ed. facsimile [250copies] Clinton, Illinois: Chas A. Bud Dufner, 1985, 55p, decorative cloth, 14cm.

Potter, E.C.

3760. *Midlothian Melodies, Mnemonic Maunderings of the Merry Muse*. Chicago: Privately Printed, 1st ed. 1900, 52p, cloth, 17.5cm.

Ralston, William

3780. *North Again, Golfing This Time.* London: Simpkin, Marshall, Hamilton, Kent, 1st ed. [ca1894] 25p, illustrated, illustrated wrappers, 20.5cm.

S., R.A.

3800. *The Links: An Auld Kirk Allegory.* Edinburgh: J. Gardner Hitt, 1st ed. [ca1895] 14p, wrappers, 21cm.

Scriba

3820. *Tour Round Scottish Golf Links.* Newcastle, England: Privately Printed, offprint [ca1888] 14p, wrappers, 16cm. note: from the Newcastle Daily Journal Sept.1 & 17, 1888.

Senat, Prosper L.

3840. *Through the Greens and Golfer's Year Book, Philadelphia Section; containing the field maps and official data of the prominent golf clubs and association for 1898, with supplementary map of the Morris County Links.* Philadelphia: Golfer's Year Book, 1st ed. 1898, 80p, illustrated, wrappers, 26.5cm.

Simpson, Walter Grindley

3860. *The Art of Golf.* Edinburgh: David Douglas, 1st ed. 1887, 186p, illustrated, 1/4 leather, illustrated boards, 22cm.

3870. 2d ed. rev. 1892, 186p, illustrated, 1/4 leather, illustrated boards, 21.5cm.

3880. 1st American ed. of 2d UK ed. New York: G.P. Putnam's, 1892, 186p, illustrated, 1/4 leather, illustrated boards, 22cm.

3890. limited ed. facsimile [1400 copies] slipcased, Far Hills, New Jersey: USGA, 1982, 186p, illustrated, decorative cloth, 21.5cm, preface by Harry Easterly, Jr.; an appreciation of The Art of Golf by Ben Crenshaw.

3900. special presentation ed. [500 copies] slipcased, Far Hills, New Jersey: USGA, 1982, 186p, illustrated, decorative cloth, 21.5cm, preface by Harry Easterly, Jr.; an appreciation of The Art of Golf by Ben Crenshaw.

Smith, Garden C.

3920. *Golf.* London: Lawrence & Bullen, 1st ed. 1897, 104p, illustrated, cloth, 18.5cm, with a contribution by Mrs. Mackern.

3925. pbk. ed. 1897, 104p, illustrated, 18cm.
3930. 1st American ed. New York: Frederick A. Stokes, [ca1897] 96p, illustrated, decorative cloth, 18cm.

3940. *The World of Golf: The Isthmian Library.* London: A.D. Innes, 1st ed. 1898, 330p, decorative cloth, illustrated, 19cm.

Smith, James Greig

3960. *Woodspring.* Bristol, England: Privately Printed, 1st ed. 1898, 157p, illustrated, leather, raised bands, teg, 22.5cm.

Smith, Robert Howie

3980. *The Golfer's Yearbook for 1866.* Ayr, Scotland: Smith & Grant, 1st ed. 1867, 88p, illustrated wrappers, 16cm.

Somerville, John

4000. *A Foursome at Rye.* Rye, England: J.I. Deacon, 1st ed. 1898, 61p, illustrated wrappers, 19cm.

Spalding's Official Golf Guide

4020. *Spalding's Official Golf Guide 1895.* New York: American Sports Publishing, 2d ed. 1895, 43p, illustrated, illustrated wrappers, 17cm, revised by L.B. Stoddard. note: For first edition see J. Stuart Balfour.
4030. 3d ed. 1897, 133p, illustrated, illustrated wrappers, 17cm, edited by C.S. Cox.
4040. 4th ed. 1898, 169p, illustrated, illustrated wrappers, 16.5cm, edited by C.S. Cox.
4050. 5th ed. 1900, 191p, illustrated, illustrated wrappers, 16.5cm, edited by C.S. Cox.
4060. 6th ed. 1901, 220p, illustrated, illustrated wrappers, 17cm, edited by C.S. Cox.
4070. 7th ed. 1902, 182p, illustrated, illustrated wrappers, 17cm, edited by C.S. Cox.
4080. 8th ed. 1903, 174p, illustrated, illustrated wrappers, 17cm, edited by C.S. Cox.
4090. 9th ed. 1904, 136p, illustrated, illustrated wrappers, 17cm, edited by C.S. Cox.
4100. 10th ed. 1905, 180p, illustrated, illustrated wrappers, 17cm, edited by C.S. Cox.
4110. 11th ed. 1906, not located.
4120. 12th ed. 1907, 179p, illustrated, illustrated wrappers, 17cm,

edited by Chas. Kirchner and Thos. Bendelow.

4130. 13th ed. 1908, 182p, illustrated, illustrated wrappers, 17cm, edited by Thos. Bendelow and Chas. Kirchner.

4140. 14th ed. 1909, 245p, illustrated, illustrated wrappers, 17cm, edited by Thos. Bendelow.

4150. 15th ed. 1910, 237p, illustrated, illustrated wrappers, 17cm, edited by Thos. Bendelow.

4160. 16th ed. 1911, 238p, illustrated, illustrated wrappers, 17cm, edited by Thos. Bendelow.

4170. 17th ed. 1912, 227p, illustrated, illustrated wrappers, 17cm, edited by Thos. Bendelow.

4180. 18th ed. 1913, 264p, illustrated, illustrated wrappers, 17cm, edited by Thos. Bendelow.

4190. 19th ed. 1914, 289p, illustrated, illustrated wrappers, 17cm, edited by Thos. Bendelow.

4200. 20th ed. 1915, 251p, illustrated, illustrated wrappers, 17cm, edited by Thos. Bendelow.

4210. 21st ed. 1916, 223p, illustrated, illustrated wrappers, 17cm, edited by Thos. Bendelow.

4220. 22d ed. 1917, 275p, illustrated, illustrated wrappers, 17cm, edited by Grantland Rice.

4230. 23d ed. 1918, 209p, illustrated, illustrated wrappers, 17cm, edited by Grantland Rice.

4240. 24th ed. 1919, 218p, illustrated, illustrated wrappers, 17cm, edited by Grantland Rice.

4250. 25th ed. 1920, 135p, illustrated, illustrated wrappers, 17cm, edited by Grantland Rice.

4260. 26th ed. 1921, 183p, illustrated, illustrated wrappers, 17cm, edited by Grantland Rice.

4270. 27th ed. 1922, 180p, illustrated, illustrated wrappers, 17cm, edited by Grantland Rice.

4280. 28th ed. 1923, 240p, illustrated, illustrated wrappers, 17cm, edited by Grantland Rice.

4290. 29th ed. 1924, 227p, illustrated, illustrated wrappers, 17cm, edited by Grantland Rice.

4300. 30th ed. 1925, 147p, illustrated, illustrated wrappers, 17cm, edited by Grantland Rice.

4310. 31st ed. 1926, 141p, illustrated, illustrated wrappers, 17cm, edited by Grantland Rice.

4320. 32d ed. 1927, 151p, illustrated, illustrated wrappers, 17cm, edited by Grantland Rice.

4330. 33d ed. 1928, 173p, illustrated, illustrated wrappers, 17cm, edited by Grantland Rice.

4340. 34th ed. 1929, 177p, illustrated, illustrated wrappers, 17cm, edited by Grantland Rice.

4350. 35th ed. 1930, 194p, illustrated, illustrated wrappers, 17cm, edited by Grantland Rice.

4360. 36th ed. 1931, 224p, illustrated, illustrated wrappers, 17cm, edited by Grantland Rice.

Stewart, James Lindsey

4380. *Golfiana Miscellanea: Being a Collection of Interesting Monographs on the Royal and Ancient Game of Golf.* edited by. London: Hamilton, Adams, 1st ed. 1887, 300p, cloth, 21cm.

[Stewart, T. Ross]

4400. *Lays of the Links: A Score of Parodies.* Edinburgh: David Douglas, 1st ed. 1895, 68p, cloth, 16cm.

Stobart, M.A.

4420. *Won at the Last Hole: A Golfing Romance.* London: Cassell, 1st ed. 1893, 99p, illustrated by Major Hopkins, wrappers, 18cm.

Sutphen, William G. Van Tassel

4450. *The Golfer's Alphabet.* New York: Harper's, 1st ed. 1898 [112p] illustrated by A.B. Frost, 1/4 cloth, illustrated boards, 23cm.

4460. facsimile ed. Rutland, Vermont: Charles E. Tuttle, 1967 [58p] illustrated by A.B. Frost, 1/4 cloth illustrated boards, 21cm.

4470. *The Golficide and other Tales of the Fair Green.* New York: Harper's, 1st ed. 1898, 227p, illustrated, 1/2 cloth boards, 17cm.

4480. 1st UK ed. London: Harper's, 1898, 227p, illustrated, decorative cloth, 17cm.

Sweney, H.R.

4500. *Keep Your Eye on the Ball and Your Right Knee Stiff... A short and concise treatise on golf.* Albany, New York: Privately Printed, 1st ed. 1898, 78p, illustrated, illustrated boards, 15cm.

Thomson, John

4520. *Golfing and other Poems and Songs*. Glasgow: William Hodge, 1st ed. 1893, 84p, illustrated, cloth, 20cm.

Twaddler

4540. *Golf Twaddle, containing a few hints to duffers*. Edinburgh: John Menzies, 1st ed. [ca1897] 32p, wrappers, 18cm.

Victim [D.W.C. Falls]

4560. *An A.B.C. of Golf*. New York: Blanchard Press, 1st ed. 1898 [28p] illustrated, illustrated burlap cloth, 26cm. later printings.

W., G. B.

4580. *The Phraseology of Golf: Illustrated by Outlines and Adapted by G.B.W.* London: Simpkin, 1st ed. 1893 [56p] illustrated, boards, 10cm.

Whigham, H[enry] J[ames]

4600. *How to Play Golf*. Chicago: Herbert S. Stone, 1st ed. 1897, 313p, illustrated, decorative cloth, 19.5cm. later printings.

4605. 2d ed. 1898, 335p, illustrated, decorative cloth, 19.5cm.

4610. 3d ed. not located.

4615. 4th ed. not located.

4620. 5th ed. 1900, 339p, illustrated, decorative cloth, 19.5cm.

4625. 6th ed. 1903, 277p, illustrated, decorative cloth, 19.5cm.

W[oodhead], E[rnest]

4640. *The Yorkshire Union of Golf Clubs, First County Championship*. Huddersfield, England: Privately Printed, 1st ed 1894, 22p, illustrated, illustrated wrappers, 21cm.

Woodward, E.J.

4660. *Golf Greens of England, Ireland and Wales.* [London] The Field, 1st ed. 1897 [166p] illustrated wrappers, 18cm.

4670. 2d ed. rev. 1900 [144p] illustrated, illustrated wrappers, 17.5cm.

Wright & Ditson

4690. *Wright & Ditson Golf Guide.* Boston: Wright & Ditson, 1st ed. 1900, 60p, illustrated, wrappers, 15.5cm. later printings.

Part III

The Rubber Core Era

1901-1960

THE RUBBER CORE ERA 1901-1960

Historians, who are noted for their precision, would more accurately peg this era from 1898, when Mr. Haskell produced his home-made rubber-wound, to 1959, when one of the great unknown figures in golf history, Jim Bartsch, embarked on his search for a one-piece ball. But then, what is a couple of years when you are contemplating five hundred years of history?

If the previous (Gutta Percha) era produced a plethora of golf books, especially in the last decade of that era, this new era of golf produced books in awesome quantities. Regrettably, quantity does always bespeak quality. In the earlier part of the era golf literally exploded in popularity everywhere and, seemingly, all at once. In America, this popularity gained a new impetus with the winning of the United States Open in 1913 by the young amateur, Francis Ouimet.

If many of those who took up the game were more accustomed to holding baseball bats or hoes, it became obvious to a number of writers that an aching void had to be filled, that of telling these novices how to play the game. Eager to supply the neophytes with the nuances, (they never mentioned the nuisances!) of the game, printing presses spewed forth a barrage of advice, instruction and explanation. These books seldom made sense but they were snapped up by the new devotees of the game. Most of them could hardly be described as literature.

It is in this era that the term—some may say epithet—"golf writer" was first used; the man in the sports department of a newspaper who had some knowledge of the game and who could submit prose which didn't often make sense to the sports editor but was understood by the increasing number of readers who had taken up the game. This era, thus, becomes a time when it is probably more appropriate to emphasize the names of the writers rather than the titles of books.

Leading the way into this era and one who gained a special reputation through is coverage of the game is Bernard R. M. Darwin, grandson of Charles Darwin, the evolutionist, and happily, for a lot of golfbook collectors as yet unborn, an absolute fanatic about golf. Many posies have been tossed to the feet of Darwin, but to this day, no tribute is more graceful nor more winning than that written by Herbert Warren Wind: to quote in part, "Thanks to Bernard, golf has acquired the sturdiest literature of any game. The best is Darwin's—about two dozen books in all—and the rest is as good as it is largely because he showed the writers who came after him how golf could and should be written."

Darwin, as Wind hinted, brought a new style to golf reporting, extending his coverage beyond the prosaic "who won." This almost-lyrical form of golf writing led to a succession of fine writers—and foremost among them, Herb Wind—who produced a truly fine literature of the game. Darwin, without question, led the way to that high standard, and his books which followed his first reporting are even today very much worth reading, which may be, when one thinks about it, one of the criteria upon which literature is judged.

Contemporaries of Darwin were Frank Moran, perhaps the earliest of the Scottish golf writers and Robert Browning—not he of Elizabeth—who edited *Golfing* magazine for forty-five years. Both were fine writers, and if they did not win the fame that Darwin enjoyed, their writings on the game are just as enjoyable.

In this era, too, came Henry Longhurst, he of the velvet pen and the soft voice, who startled the world of television when it became popular by remaining quiet. Henry felt, uniquely, that if the viewers were watching the picture, he did not have to tell them what was going on. How much more enjoyable would be golf on TV if more "commentators" would take his position. His many books on golf are, each of them, treasures.

In the previous era, the first club history was published (Blackheath), quickly followed by the little-known history of the Hawick Golf Club; but this era now in focus saw a proliferation of such histories (Crail, Royal Burgess, Garden City and St. Andrews in America) but one of the finest is one of the first to be published after 1900; Everard's great history of The Royal and Ancient Golf Club of St. Andrews, the first golf book to contain beautiful color illustrations.

As mentioned before, this, too, was the era when a great spate of books on instruction was foisted upon the unresisting shoulders of new golfers, led by those great soldiers of the links, Vardon, Taylor and Braid. They were to lead the parade of professionals who more often in the words of a ghost writer bequeathed unto us their advice as to how to play like they did. Sadly, and no matter how hard we tried, the lessons were not too well learned. A succession of champions tried, heaven knows; George Duncan, Travis, Travers, Wethered and Tolley . . . Sarazen, Armour, Alliss (the elder) - and much later, Alliss (the younger) . . . Snead, Nelson and Hogan . . . Palmer, Player, Casper and Nicklaus. Each of them tried. And still we foozle.

We have hinted at the presence of "ghosts." It would be unfair to imply that these great champions could not write; we know that to be wrong because without exception all of them could write their name. We would suspect, however, that Herb Graffis, Roger Ganem, Oscar Fraley, Ken Bowden and many writers who will never be known hit more keys of the typewriter than those whose name appeared on the title page ever hit golf balls.

The history of golf literature would not be as concise as it should be if special notice was not given to "The Haunted Major," first published in 1902 and still in print; truly a record of longevity which is remarkable. Other long-living books, from a publishing standpoint, include those delightful stories by P. G. Wodehouse which have appeared under a number of different titles; A. J. Morrison's "A New Way to Better Golf;" Percy Boomer's "On Learning Golf," and, more recently, Ben Hogan's "Five Lessons."

The annual publications which offer so much information about the championships and other statistical data were born in the previous (Gutty) era, but this current era saw the proliferation of such books, starting with the granddaddy of them all, "The Golfer's Handbook," first published in 1899 and still going strong today (1987). Others to follow would include "Nisbet's Annual Golf Yearbook," edited by John Low; "The American Golf Guide and Year Book," published (as the title would indicate) in the United States; and the annual "Spalding Guides," which were published from 1893 to 1931. Because of their transitory content, many of these books have disappeared, but all are fascinating to the true golf buff who has an interest in the past achievements of old champions and the preservation of the records of the past.

It is, perhaps, unfair to attempt to select a few book titles from the many which occupy this era. In writing of it, one's imagination is led in many directions.

One, for example, is the field of course architecture. It was during this era that the difficult art achieved a degree of professionalism. Books by Colt, Thomas, Hunter, Wethered & Simpson and Mackenzie were published and began to educate the uneducated player as to the subtlety of the game and how the planning of a course was just a bit more than moving around a lot of earth . . . a lesson which some of the more modern architects never seemed to learn.

In the field of humor, one must mention P. G. Wodehouse and G. C. Nash, with his delightful letters to "The Secretary," and certainly George Houghton, who stumbled across the best-selling idea of creating a "golf addict," which represents most golfers, and duly capitalized upon this simple invention to produce books which occupy an entire shelf in any serious collector's library.

It was also in this era that the game grew, somewhat insidiously, into other countries and, inevitably, the literature —or a reasonable facsimile—grew. D. G. Soutar, emigrant from Carnoustie, went to Australia and proceeded to corrupt a large part of the populace into playing golf. He wrote the first book to be published in that part of the world, "The Australian Golfer," in 1906; the book is today a rare prize for any collector. In South Africa, a transplanted Yorkshireman, R. G. Fall, who by his own confession was not very good at the game, loved it and was later to start publication of the magazine *South African Golf.* As early as 1918 he was sensible enough to make record of the early history of the game in that country with his "History of Golf at the Cape." It may be thin, but it is brave and, more valuably, a record of the game as it was introduced and played at that end of the world.

Within the context of the assignment given me, this is a very difficult era to cover. It was a era, as intimated earlier, that the game literally exploded in its popularity and those vultures of the press, the golf writers, were not slow to recognize its increasing fascination and the need for books on the subject. They, the writers, were more than pleased to provide the books. It is rather ironic that very few, if any, of them became rich; nor produced literature.

Thus endeth the third era of golf.

A.G. Spalding

4800. *Golf Reporters Almanac 1958*. Chicopee, Massachusetts: A.G. Spalding, 1st ed. 1958, 159p, illustrated, illustrated wrappers, 17.5cm. later printings.

4810. *Kro-Flite Kronicles or Grey Matters for Golfers*. London: A.G. Spalding, 1st ed. [ca1935] [20p] illustrated by Frederic Parker, illustrated wrappers, 20cm.

Acree, Edward C.

4830. *Golf Simplified*. with Jock Hutchinson and Bill Hutchinson. Chicago: Ziff Davis, 1st ed. [1946] 118p, illustrated, cloth, 23.5cm.

Adams, Frederick Upham

4850. *John Henry Smith: A Humorous Romance of Outdoor Life*. New York: Doubleday, Page, 1st ed. 1905, 346p, illustrated by A.B. Frost, decorative cloth, 19.5cm.

4860. *John Henry Smith, A Golfing Romance*. London: Hutchinson, 1st UK ed. 1905, 346p, illustrated by A.B. Frost, decorative cloth, 19.5cm.

4870. *John Henry Smith: A Humorous Romance of Outdoor Life*. New York: Fenno, reprint [ca1905] 346p, illustrated by A.B.Frost, decorative cloth, 19cm.

4880. pbk. ed. reprint. New York: Fenno [ca1905] 346p, illustrated by A.B. Frost, illustrated wrappers, 19cm.

Adams, Herbert

4900. *Death Off the Fairway*. London: The Crime Club, 1st ed. 1936, 283p, cloth, 18.5cm. later printing.

4910. *Death on the First Tee*. London: Macdonald, 1st ed. 1957, 192p, cloth, 18.5cm.

4920. *John Brand's Will*. London: Methuen, 1st ed. 1933, 267p cloth, 19cm. later printings.

4930. *The Golf House Murder*. Philadelphia: Lippincott, 1st American ed. [1933] 316p, cloth, 19cm. American title of "John Brand's Will."

4940. *One To Play*. London: Macdonald, 1st ed. 1949, 224p, cloth, 18.5cm.

4950. *The 19th Hole Mystery.* London: The Crime Club, 1st ed. 1939, 252p, cloth, 18.5cm.

4960. *The Body in the Bunker.* London: The Crime Club, 1st ed. 1935, 283p, cloth, 18.5cm.

4970. 1st ed. American ed. Philadelphia: Lippincott [1935] 309p, cloth, 19cm.

4980. *The Perfect Round: Tales of the Links.* London: Methuen, 1st ed. 1927, 214p, illustrated, cloth, 19cm. later printing.

4990. *The Secret of Bogey House.* London: Methuen, 1st ed. 1924, 252p, cloth, 18.5cm.

Adams, Robert Winthrop

5010. *Timing Your Golf Swing.* New York: Citadel Press, 1st ed. [1957] 62p, illustrated, cloth, 26.5cm, foreword by Francis Ouimet. A 45rpm phonograph record included.

5020. *What Club Fits You?* New York: Citadel Press, offprint [1957] [6p] illustrated, illustrated wrappers, 20cm, offprint from Golfing Magazine.

Aitchison, Thomas S. and George Lorimer.

5040. *Reminiscences of the Old Bruntsfield Links Golf Club 1866-1874.* Edinburgh: Privately Printed, 1st ed. 1902, 126p, illustrated, decorative cloth, 24.5cm.

Akerman, E.J.B.

5060. *The Leatherjackets Golfing Society 1928-1949.* [Bristol, England] Privately Printed, 1st ed. 1949, 69p, cloth, 27cm.

Alderley Edge Golf Club

5080. *Alderley Edge Golf Club [Handbook].* Hants & London: Temple Publicity Services [ca1960] 12p, illustrated, illustrated wrappers, 18.5cm.

All Weather Golf Practices

5100. *All Weather Golf Practices.* London: All Weather Golf Practice, 1st ed. [ca1927] 36p, illustrated, illustrated wrappers, 12cm.

Allen, Leslie

5120. *Murder in the Rough.* New York: Five Star Mysteries, 1st ed. [1946] 157p, illustrated wrappers, 18cm.

Allerton, Mark [pseud for William Ernest Cameron]

5140. *Golf Faults Remedied, containing also rules worth remembering.* London: World of Golf, 1st ed. [ca1911] 26p, wrappers, 19.5cm

5150. *The Girl on the Green.* London: Methuen, 1st ed. 1914, 295p, cloth, 19cm.

Allerton, Mark and Robert Browning.

5170. *Golf Made Easy: A book for the man who plays but wants to play better.* London: Cassell, 1st ed. 1910, 134p, illustrated wrappers, 19cm.

Allison, Benjamin R.

5190. *The Rockaway Hunting Club.* Cedarhurst, New York: Privately Printed, 1st ed. slipcased, 1952, 236p, illustrated, decorative cloth, 25.5cm.

Allison, Willie

5210. *The First Golf Review.* edited by. London: Bonar, 1st ed. 1950, 92p, illustrated, cloth, 24.5cm.

Alliss, Percy

5230. *Better Golf.* London: A&C Black, 1st ed. 1926, 189p, illustrated, cloth, 20cm, introduction by George W. Greenwood.

5240. 2d ed. rev. 1933, 152p, illustrated, cloth, 19cm.

5250. *Making Golf Easier.* Edinburgh: Stoddart & Malcolm, 1st ed. 1933, 51p, illustrated, illustrated wrappers, 18.5cm.

Alliss, Peter

5270. *Drive and Bunker Shot [Flicker Book].* London: Flick-A-Book, 1st ed.[ca1955] [100p] illustrated, wrappers, 7.5cm.

Ambrose, Charles

5290. *The West Sussex Golf Club and Course [Handbook].* Pulborough, England: Privately Printed [ca1938] 24p, illustrated, wrappers, 18.5cm.

American Annual Golf Guide and Year Book

5310. *American Annual Golf Guide and Year Book 1916*. New York: Angus, 1st ed. 1916, 321p, illustrated, cloth, 19cm, edited by P.C. Pulver.

5320. 2d ed. 1917, 412p, illustrated, cloth, 19cm, edited by P.C. Pulver.

5330. 3d ed. 1918, 385p, illustrated, cloth, 19cm, edited by W.H. Follett.

5340. 4th ed. 1920, 436p, illustrated, cloth, 19cm, edited by W.H. Follett.

5350. 5th ed. 1921, 440p, illustrated, cloth, 19cm, edited by W.H. Follett.

5360. 6th ed. 1922, 456p, illustrated, cloth, 19cm, edited by W.H. Follett.

5370. 7th ed. 1923, 554p, illustrated, cloth, 19cm, edited by John G. Anderson.

5380. 8th ed. 1924, 550p, illustrated, cloth, 19cm, edited by John G. Anderson.

5390. 9th ed. 1925, 511p, illustrated, cloth, 19cm, edited by J. Lewis Brown.

5400. 10th ed. 1926, 602p, illustrated, cloth, 19cm, edited by J.Lewis Brown.

5410. 11th ed. 1927, 609p, illustrated, cloth, 19cm, edited by J.Lewis Brown.

5420. 12th ed. 1928, 626p, illustrated, cloth, 19cm.

5430. 13th ed. 1929, 625p, illustrated, cloth, 19cm.

5440. 14th ed. 1931, 528p, illustrated, cloth, 19cm.

American Golf Foundation

5460. *A Golf Club As A Business*. Chicago: American Golf Foundation, 1st ed. [ca1944] 16p, illustrated, illustrated wrappers, 28cm.

5470. *Example Golf Club By-Laws as Compiled from A Survey Made with the Cooperation of More than 1000 Golf Clubs*. Chicago: American Golf Foundation, 1st ed. [ca1947] 12p, illustrated wrappers, 28cm.

5480. *How To Secure More Members*. Chicago: American Golf Foundation, 1st ed. [ca1946] 15p, illustrated, illustrated wrappers, 28cm.

5490. *Suggestions for Golf Club By-Laws*. Chicago: American Golf Foundation, 1st ed. [ca1948] [6p] illustrated wrappers, 28cm.

5500. *What Is The American Golf Foundation*. Chicago: American Golf Foundation, 1st ed. [ca1945] 12p, illustrated, illustrated wrappers, 28cm.

American Golfer Magazine

5520. *Twelve Golf Lessons: the best advice from many of the game's most famous instructors*. New York: American Golfer Magazine, 1st ed. [1929] 32p, illustrated, illustrated wrappers, 23cm.

Andre, Richard

5540. *Golf Plays and Recitations*. London: R.A. Everett, 1st ed. 1904, 127p, decorative cloth, 18cm.

Andreason, Dale

5560. *Simplified Golf*. Palm Springs, California: Southwest, 1st ed. [1960] 64p, illustrated, illustrated wrappers, 21.5cm. later printing.

Andrews, Julia Lincoln

5580. *Golf: A Play in Two Acts*. New York: Samuel French, 1st ed. [1902] 39p, wrappers, 19cm.

Anstruther Golf Club

5600. *Anstruther Golf Club [Handbook]*. Derby & Cheltenham, England: New Centurion, 1953, 32p, illustrated, wrappers, 18.5cm.

Arbroath Golf Club

5620. *Arbroath Golf Club [Handbook]*. London: Vickery, Kyrle [ca1920] 21p, illustrated, illustrated wrappers, 18cm.

Armour, Richard

5640. *Golf Bawls*. New York: Beechhurst Press, 1st ed. [1946] 77p, illustrated by Herb Middlecamp, decorative cloth, 23cm.

Armour, Tommy

5660. *A Round of Golf with Tommy Armour.* New York: Simon & Schuster, 1st ed. 1959, 143p, illustrated by Merritt D. Cutler, cloth, 23cm.

5670. 1st UK ed. London: Hodder & Stoughton, 1960, 142p, cloth, 22.5cm.

5680. *How to Play Your Best Golf All the Time.* New York: Simon & Schuster, 1st ed. 1953, 151p, illustrated by Lealand Gustavson, cloth, 22.5cm, introduction by Grantland Rice. later printings.

5690. 1st UK ed. London: Hodder & Stoughton, 1954, 159p, illustrated by Lealand Gustavson, cloth, 22cm. later printings.

5700. pbk. ed. London: Hodder & Stoughton, 1954, 159p, illustrated by Lealand Gustavson, illustrated wrappers, 17.5cm, later printings.

5710. 2d ed. rev. Greenwich, Connecticut: Fawcett [1961] 160p, illustrated by Lealand Gustavson, illustrated wrappers, 17.5cm. later printings.

5720. facsimile ed. Stamford, Connecticut: Classics of Golf [1984] 151p, illustrated, decorative cloth, 22.5cm, introduction by Herbert Warren Wind, afterword by Herb Graffis.

5730. *Tommy Armour Speaks.* Cincinnati, Ohio: Macgregor, 1st ed. [ca1960] 20p, illustrated, illustrated wrappers, 21.5cm.

5740. *Tommy Armour Tells You How to Play Your Best Golf.* New York: Good Reading Service, abridged ed. [1956] 15p, illustrated, illustrated wrappers, 19.5cm, abridged from "How To Play Your Best Golf All the Time."

Arnold, A.E.

5760. *Putting and Spared Shots.* London: Methuen, 1st ed. 1939, 75p, illustrated, cloth, 16.5cm, foreword by Abe Mitchell.

Astle, M.J.

5780. *The Principles of Golf.* London & Edinburgh: W & R Chambers, 1st ed. [1923] 108p, illustrated by Marjorie Bates, decorative cloth, 18cm.

5790. 2d ed. rev. 1925, 109p, illustrated by Marjorie Bates, cloth, 18cm.

Atten, Howie

5810. *Chatten with Atten on Golf, Instructions Simplified.* [Chicago] Privately Printed, 1st ed. [1959] 37p, illustrated, spiral bound illustrated wrappers, 21.5cm.

Augusta National Golf Club

5830. *Augusta National Yearbook, published in connection with 2nd Annual Invitation Tournament April 4-5-6-7, 1935.* Augusta, Georgia: Augusta National Golf Club, 1st ed. [1935] 40p, illustrated, illustrated wrappers, 28cm.

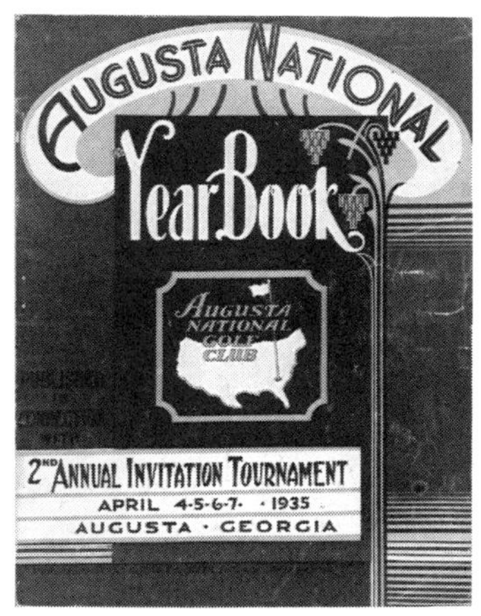

Ayton, L.B.

5850. *How to Play Worthing Golf Course [Handbook].* Bristol & London: Temple Publicity Services [ca1951] 20p, illustrated, illustrated wrappers, 18.5cm.

Ayton, Laurie and others.

5870. *Golf As Champions Play It.* Chicago: Associated Editors, 1st ed. [1928] 40p, illustrated, illustrated wrappers, 17cm.

B., A.

5890. *Told at the 19th Hole, Humorous St. Andrews Golfing Stories.* Cupar, Scotland: J. & G. Innes, 3d ed. [ca1928] 28p, illustrated, illustrated wrappers, 18cm. later printings. note: no copies of the first or second edition has been located.

B., C.J. [C.J. Billson] and P.S.W.

5910. *Horace on the Links: with notes from Horace Hutchinson's writings.* London: Swan, Sonnenschein, 1st ed. 1903, 100p, cloth, 17.5cm, foreword by Horace Hutchinson. later printing.

B., E.M. and G.R.T.

5930. *Humors and Emotions of Golf.* London: Blades, East & Blades, 1st ed. [ca1905] 93p, wrappers, 20.5cm.

Baert, Raymond

5950. *Adventures of Monsieur DuPont, Golf Champion.* London: Lawrence & Jellicoe, 1st English language ed [ca1913] [40p] illustrated, illustrated boards, 21cm.

Baffy

5970. *Golf Problems.* Bristol, England: Sports Times, 1st ed. [ca1928] 11p, wrappers, 14cm.

Bailey, Charles William

5990. *The Brain and Golf: Some Hints for Golfers from Modern Mental Science.* with a chapter on theory and practice by Bernard Darwin. London: Mills & Boon, 1st ed. 1923, 96p, illustrated, cloth, 19cm, foreword by Sir Charles S. Sherrington. later printing.

6000. 1st American ed. Boston: Small, Maynard [1924] 93p, illustrated, cloth, 19cm.

6010. *The Professor on the Golf Links: Some Sidelights on Golf from Modern Science.* London: Silas Birch, 1st ed. [1925] 91p, 1/4 cloth, boards, 18.5cm.

Bald Peak Country Club

6030. *The Bald Peak Country Club.* Melvin Village, New Hampshire: Privately Printed, 1st ed. [ca1920] 63p, illustrated, illustrated wrappers, 18.5cm.

Ballantine, R.E.

6050. *How to Play Ganton Golf Course.* London & Bristol: Temple Publicity Services [ca1952] 36p, illustrated, wrappers, 19cm.

Banes, Ford

6070. *Right Down Your Fairway.* New York: A.S. Barnes, 1st ed. [1947] [94p] illustrated, cloth, 22.5cm.

Bantock, Miles

6090. *On Many Greens: A Book of Golf and Golfers.* New York: Grosset & Dunlap, 1st ed. 1901, 167p, illustrated, decorative cloth, 17.5cm, introduction by Findlay Douglas.

Barker, Reg

6110. *Eighteen for Ever.* [Pretoria, South Africa] Privately Printed, 1st ed. [1959] 67p, illustrated by H.A. Niezen, wrappers, 18cm.

Barlow, Raymond G.

6130. *Golf for the Beginner and the Confused.* Philadelphia: Dorrance, 1st ed. [1954] 129p, illustrated by Bob Grams, cloth, 18.5cm.

Barnes, James M.

6150. *A Guide to Good Golf.* New York: Dodd Mead, 1st ed. 1925, 137p, illustrated, pictorial cloth, 20cm, foreword by Grantland Rice. later printings.

6160. 1st UK ed. London: John Lane, 1925, 137p, illustrated, cloth, 21cm, foreword by Grantland Rice. later printings.

6170. *Picture Analysis of Golf Strokes.* Philadelphia: Lippincott, 1st ed. 1919, 252p, illustrated, pictorial cloth, 28cm. later printings.

Barnett, Frank H.

6190. *A Brief History of Claremont Country Club.* Oakland, California: Privately Printed, 1st ed. 1960, 36p, wrappers, 19.5cm.

Barrington, John

6210. *The U.S. Golfer's Annual Handbook.* edited by. New York:. Crowell, 1st ed. [1958] 248p, cloth, 20cm, foreword by Joseph C. Dey, Jr.

Barton, Pam

6230. *A Stroke A Hole.* London: Blackie & Son, 1st ed. 1937, 88p, illustrated, cloth, 18cm. later printing.

6240. 1st American ed. New York: M.S. Mills, 1938, 88p, illustrated, cloth, 18cm.

Batchelor, Gerald

6260. *Golf Stories.* London: A & C Black, 1st ed. 1914, 131p, illustrated by E.W. Mitchell, decorative cloth, 18.5cm.

Bateman, Henry Mayo

6280. *Adventures At Golf.* London: Methuen, 1st ed. 1923, 50p, illustrated, illustrated boards, 27.5cm.

6290. 1st American ed. New York: Henry Holt, 1923, 50p, illustrated, decorative cloth, 28cm.

6300. reprint ed. *H M Bateman on Golf.* Weybridge, England: Whittet, 1977, 78p, illustrated, illustrated boards, 12.5cm. previously titled "Adventures At Golf."

Bauer, Aleck

6320. *Hazards:Those essential elements in a golf course without which the game would be tame and uninteresting.* Chicago: Toby Rubovits, 1st ed. 1913, 61p, illustrated, 1/4 cloth, boards, 20.5cm .

Bauer, Dave

6340. *Golf Techniques of the Bauer Sisters.* with Otis Dypwick.New York: Prentice-Hall, 1st ed. [1951] 89p, illustrated, cloth, 20.5cm.

Baughman, Ernest A.

6360. *How to Caddie.* Chicago: Privately Printed, 1st ed. [1914] 27p, wrappers, 15cm.

Baxter, John E.

6380. *Locker Room Ballads.* New York: Appleton, 1st ed. 1923, 76p, illustrated by James Montgomery Flagg, decorative cloth, 18.5cm.

Beaman, S.G. Hulme

6400. *The Adventures of Larry the Lamb.* London: George Lapworth, 1st ed. [ca1935] [16p] illustrated by Ernest Noble, illustrated wrappers, 21.5cm.

Beasley, Chauncey Haven

6420. *Golf in Latin.* Newport, Rhode Island: Privately Printed, 2d ed. [1954] 6p, illustrated wrappers, 23cm. note: first edition not located.

Beattie, James

6440. *The Club Toter.* Chicago: Allied Golf, 1st ed. [ca1929] 16p, illustrated, illustrated wrappers, 17.5cm.

Beck, Alfred

6460. *Hints on Golf for Everyone.* Filey, England: Privately Printed, 1st ed. [ca1925] 16p, wrappers, 16cm.

Beck, Fred

6480. *To H*!! with Golf.* New York: Hill & Wang, 1st ed. 1956, 223p, illustrated by Emax, cloth, 20cm.

Beck, Fred and O.K. Barnes

6500. *73 Years in a Sand Trap.* New York: A.A. Wynn, 1st ed. 1949, 159p, illustrated by Emax, cloth, 20cm.

Becker, Harland Aldrich

6520. *The Knack of Golf.* Santa Barbara, California: Pacific Coast Publications, limited ed. [250 copies] 1952, 208p, illustrated, cloth, 23cm, introduction by Jim Ferrier.

Bedford and County Golf Club

6540. *The Bedford and County Golf Club [Handbook].* Cheltenham, England: Ed. J. Burrow, 1938, 32p, illustrated, illustrated wrappers, 16cm.

Begbie, Harold

6560. *J. H. Taylor, or, The Inside of a Week.* London: Mills & Boon, 1st ed. 1925, 107p, illustrated, cloth, 18.5cm.

6570. pbk. ed. 1925, 107p, illustrated, illustrated wrappers, 18.5cm.

Behr, Max J.

6590. *What Is Amateurism? An inquiry to determine how it should be governed, addressed to the Executive Committee of the USGA.* [New York] Privately Printed, 1st ed. 1917, 10p, wrappers, 23cm.

Beldam, George W.

6610. *Golfing Illustrated: Gowan's Practical Picture Book, No. 2.* London: Gowan's & Gray, 1st ed. 1908, 70p, illustrated, illustrated wrappers, 14.5cm.

6620. *Great Golfers: Their Methods at a Glance.* London: Macmillan, 1st ed. 1904, 480p, illustrated, decorative cloth, 22cm, with contributions by Harold H. Hilton, J.H. Taylor, James Braid, Alex Herd, Harry Vardon.

6630. *The World's Champion Golfers: Their Art Disclosed by the Ultra-Rapid Camera. [11 Volumes].* London: Photocrom , 1st ed. [1924] various pages, illustrated, wrappers, 20.5cm. 10 volumes of instructions with a 1 volume key to interpretation of photos.

Beldam, George W. and J.H. Taylor.

6650. *Golf Faults Illustrated.* London: George Newnes, 1st ed. [ca1905] 140p, illustrated, pictorial cloth, 21.5cm.

6660. 2d ed. rev. [1905] 175p, illustrated, cloth, 21cm.

Belfore, Joe

6680. *Golfing Aids.* Detroit, Michigan: Privately Printed, 1st ed. [ca1940] 12p, illustrated, wrappers, 19cm.

Bendelow, Tom

6700. *Golf Courses by the American Park Builders.* Chicago: American Park Builders, 1st ed. [1926] 36p, illustrated, illustrated wrappers, 16cm.

Bennett, Andrew

6720. *St. Andrews Golf Club Centenary 1843-1943: Being the hundred years record of an historic Fife golf club.* St. Andrews: W.C. Henderson, 1st ed. 1943, 75p, illustrated, illustrated wrappers, 22cm.

Benson, Edward Frederic and E.H. Miles

6740. *A Book of Golf.* edited by. by J. Braid, J.A.T. Bramston, H.G. Hutchinson. London: Hurst & Blackett, 1st ed. 1903, 308p, illustrated, decorative cloth, 18.5cm.

6750. 1st American ed. New York: Dutton, 1903, 308p, illustrated, decorative cloth, 18.5cm.

Beres, Frank

6770. *Building 18 Holes Miniature Golf.* Woodbridge, New Jersey: Privately Printed, 1st ed. [1948] [7p] illustrated, illustrated wrappers, 27.5cm.

6780. *How to Build and the Forty Secrets of A Golf Driving Range.* Woodbridge, New Jersey: Privately Printed, 1st ed. [ca1948] 28p, illustrated, illustrated wrappers, 27.5cm.

Berg, Patty and Mark Cox.

6800. *Golf Illustrated.* New York: A.S. Barnes, 1st ed. [1950] 72p, illustrated, cloth, 23cm.

6810. 1st UK ed. *Golf for Women: Illustrated.* London: Cassell, 1951, 72p, illustrated, cloth, 21cm, foreword by L.B. Icely. UK title of "Golf Illustrated." later printing.

Berg, Patty and Otis Dypwick

6830. *Golf.* New York: A.S. Barnes, 1st ed. [1941] 81p, illustrated, cloth, 23cm, foreword by O.B. Keeler. later printings.

Berkeley, Earl of

6850. *Sound Golf By Applying Principles of Practice.* London: Seeley Service, 1st ed. [1936] 205p, cloth, 19.5cm.

Berrien, Edith Heal

6870. *Fiftieth Anniversary Women's Metropolitan Golf Association.* [New York] Privately Printed, 1st ed. [1950] 98p, illustrated, decorative cloth, 27.5cm.

Bertholy, Paul

6890. *The Bertholy Bombshell.* Southern Pines, North Carolina: Golf World, 1st ed. [ca1955] [12p] illustrated, illustrated wrappers, 22cm.

Bertie, C.H.

6910. *History of the Manly Golf Club.* Sydney, Australia: Privately Printed, 1st ed. 1946, 63p, illustrated, cloth, 24cm.

Betinis, James

6930. *Hit the Nail on the Head:The six fundamentals of golf.* Oaklawn, Illinois: West End Press, 1st ed. 1960, 67p, illustrated, wrappers, 18cm.

Birdie Book

6950. *Birdie Book: Pointers on Par.* Skokie, Illinois: Knollwood, 1st ed. [1958] 25p, illustrated, illustrated wrappers, 7.5cm.

Birkdale Golf Club

6970. *Birkdale Golf Club Golden Jubilee 1889-1939.* Southport, England: Privately Printed, 1st ed. 1939 [4p] illustrated, wrappers, 21cm.

6980. *The Birkdale Golf Club [Handbook].* Derby & Cheltenham, England: New Centurion [1952] 56p, illustrated, wrappers, 18cm.

Blatch, William Desmond

7000. *The Law Relating to Golf Clubs: being a guide to the various rates and taxes payable by a golf club and the methods of rating; with an outline of the law of selling intoxicants in a golf club and the liabilities of members and of legislation to planning.* London: Waterloo and Sons, 1st ed. 1943, 36p, cloth, 21.5cm.

7010. 2d ed. rev. 1946, 81p, decorative cloth, 21.5cm.

Blos

7030. *Fore! Forty Drawings by Mahood.* London: Hammond, Hammond, 1st ed. [1959] [40p] illustrated by Mahood, illustrated boards, 11cm, introduction by Dai Rees.

Board, John Arthur

7050. *The Right Way to Become A Golfer.* London: Right Way, 1st ed. [1948] 124p, illustrated, cloth, 18.5cm, foreword by Bernard Darwin. later printing.

Bond, G.L.

7070. *The Dunstable Book. [History of Dunstable Downs Golf Club].* Dunstable, England: Privately Printed, limited ed. [no limitation cited] 1931, 47p, illustrated by B.W.R. Batchelor, decorative cloth, 25cm.

Boomer, Percy

7090. *On Learning Golf.* London: John Lane, limited ed. signed and numbered [500 copies] 1942, 215p, illustrated, cloth, 20.5cm, foreword by Duke of Windsor.

7100. 1st trade ed. London: John Lane, 1942, 215p, illustrated, cloth, 20.5cm. later printings.

7110. 1st American ed. New York: Knopf, 1946, 258p, illustrated, cloth, 18cm. later printings.

Boros, Julius

7130. *How to Play Par Golf.* New York: Prentice-Hall, 1st ed. [1953] 191p, illustrated, cloth, 20.5cm , foreword by Fred J. Bowman.

7140. *The 3 Tenets for Better Golf.* Chicago: George S. May, 1st ed. [ca1956] [4p] illustrated, illustrated wrappers, 28cm.

Bottome, George McDonald

7160. *Golf for the Middle-Aged and Others.* London: Faber & Faber, 1st ed. 1946, 66p, illustrated, cloth, 20.5cm.

7170. *Modern Golf.* with J. Heron. London: Faber & Faber, 1st ed. 1949, 104p, illustrated, cloth, 20cm.

Bounds, Roger J.

7190. *Municipal Golf Courses: A Report Compiled by the Chamber of Commerce of the United States*. Washington, DC: Chamber of Commerce of the United States, 1st ed. 1930, 32p, wrappers, 27.5cm.

Bovis, John L.

7210. *The It of Golf: Simplified golf demonstrated as applied mechanics*. Cincinnati, Ohio: It-of-Golf, 1st ed. [1927] 59p, cloth, 17.5cm.

Boynton, Henry Walcott

7230. *The Golfer's Rubaiyat*. Chicago: Stone, 1st ed. 1901 [79p] illustrated, illustrated boards, 17cm.

7240. 1st UK ed. London: Grant & Richards, 1903, 70p, illustrated, boards, 17cm.

Braid, James

7260. *Advanced Golf, or, Hints and Instruction for Progressive Players*. London: Methuen, 1st ed. 1908, 322p, illustrated, cloth, 22cm. later printings.

7270. 1st American ed. Philadelphia: George Jacobs [ca1908] 322p, illustrated, cloth, 22cm. later printings.

7280. *Golf Guide and How To Play Golf*. London: British Sports Publishing, 1st ed. 1906, 144p, illustrated, cloth and illustrated wrappers, 17cm. later printings.

7290. *Ladies' Field Golf Book*. London: George Newnes, 1st ed. 1908, 85p, illustrated, cloth, 17.5cm.

Braid, James and Harry Vardon.

7310. *How To Play Golf*. New York: American Sports Publishing, 1st American ed. 1907, 123p, illustrated, cloth, 16cm. US title of James Braid's, "Golf Guide and How to Play Golf." later printings.

7315. pbk. ed. 1907, 123p, illustrated, illustrated wrappers, 16cm. later printings.

Bramshaw Golf Club

7330. *Bramshaw Golf Club [Handbook]*. Southhampton, England: Russell [ca1946] 24p, illustrated, wrappers, 18.5cm.

Brand Hall Golf Club

7350. *Brand Hall Golf Club [Handbook].* Birmingham & Worcester, England: Littleburg [ca1938] 16p, wrappers, 16.5cm.

Bray Golf Club

7370. *Bray Golf Club [Handbook].* London: Golf Clubs Association [ca1952] 23p, illustrated, wrappers,18.5cm.

Breeden, Marshall

7390. *Us Golfers and Our California Links: facts about all the golf links in California and fiction about the game o' gawf.* Los Angeles: Western Book, 1st ed. 1923, 46p, cloth, 22.5cm.

Brews, Sid

7410. *Golf in A Nutshell.* Capetown, South Africa: Vacuum Oil Co. 1st ed. [ca1937] [16p] illustrated, illustrated wrappers, 18.5cm.

Briggs, Clare

7430. *Golf: The Book of a Thousand Chuckles.* Chicago: P.F. Volland, 1st ed. [1916] [200p] illustrated by Clare Briggs, illustrated boards. 22.5cm.

Brinton, Alan

7450. *Mr. and Mrs. Golfer... cut their handicaps.* London: News Chronicle, 1st ed. [ca1954] 30p, illustrated, spiral bound illustrated wrappers, 25.5cm, with instructions by Percy and Peter Alliss.

Broadbent, W.F.

7470. *Golf: Fundamental Instructions.* London: Universal Publications, 1st ed. [1938] 90p, illustrated, wrappers, 16.5cm.

Brookuure, James H.

7490. *Notes on Golf Pertaining to the Art of Putting and the Short Approach Shots.* NP: Privately Printed, limited ed. signed [100 copies] 1935, 23p, illustrated, illustrated wrappers, 21.5cm.

Broughty Golf Club

7510. *Broughty Golf Club [Handbook].* Derby & Cheltenham, England: New Centurion [ca1953] 24p, illustrated, wrappers, 16cm.

Brown, George S.

7530. *First Steps to Golf.* London: Mills & Boon, 1st ed. 1913, 91p, illustrated, cloth, 19cm.

7540. 2d ed. rev. not located.

7550. 1st American ed. New York: James Pott, 1913, 91p, illustrated cloth, 19.5cm.

7560. 2d American ed. rev. Boston: Small, Maynard, 1924, 105p, illustrated, cloth, 19cm, with two added chapters by H.H. Hilton.

Brown, Horace

7580. *Murder in the Rough.* London: T.V. Boardman, 1st ed. 1948, 160p, illustrated wrappers, 18cm.

Brown, Innis

7600. *Getting Out of Trouble.* South Weymouth, Massachusetts: M.N. Arnold Shoe, 1st ed. [1934] [18p] illustrated, illustrated wrappers, 17cm.

7610. *How To Play Golf.* edited by. New York: American Sports Publishing, 1st ed. [1930] 128p, illustrated, illustrated wrappers, 17cm. later printings.

7620. *How To Putt Better.* South Weymouth, Massachusetts: M.N. Arnold Shoe Co. 1st ed. [1933] 20p, illustrated, illustrated wrappers, 17cm.

Brown, J. Lewis

7640. *Golf At Glens Falls Country Club.* Glens Falls, New York: Privately Printed, 1st ed. [1923] 63p, illustrated, pictorial boards, 21cm.

Brown, James

7660. *Songs of Golf.* St. Andrews, Scotland: W.C. Henderson, 1st ed. 1902, 58p, illustrated, wrappers, 16.5cm.

Brown, Kenneth

7680. *Putter Perkins.* Boston: Houghton Mifflin, 1st ed. 1923, 126p, illustrated by E.W. Kemble, decorative cloth, 19cm.

Brown, William Garrott

7700. *Golf.* Boston: Houghton Mifflin, 1st ed. 1902, 64p, 1/4 cloth, boards, 17.5cm.

Browning, Robert H.K.

7720. *A History of Golf: The Royal and Ancient Game.* London: J.M. Dent, 1st ed. 1955, 236p, illustrated, cloth, 22cm.

7730. 1st American ed. New York: Dutton [1955] 236p, illustrated, cloth, 22cm.

7740. facsimile ed. New York: Classics of Golf [1985] 236p, illustrated, cloth, 23cm, introduction by Herbert Warren Wind, afterword by S.L.McKinlay.

7750. *Aberdare Golf Club [Handbook].* London: Golf Clubs Association [ca1946] 15p, illustrated, wrappers, 18cm.

7760. *Aberdovey Golf Club [Handbook].* London: Golf Clubs Association [ca1947] 19p, illustrated, wrappers, 18cm.

7770. *Addington Golf Club [Handbook].* London: Golf Clubs Association [ca1946] 31p, illustrated, wrappers, 18cm.

7780. *Axe Cliff Golf Club [Handbook].* London: Golf Clubs Association, 1939, 23p, illustrated, wrappers, 18cm.

7790. *Ballater Golf Club [Handbook].* London: Golf Clubs Association [ca1947] 18p, illustrated, wrappers, 18.5cm.

7800. *Banchory Golf Club [Handbook].* London: Golf Clubs Association, 1938, 19p, illustrated, wrappers, 18cm.

7810. *Banstead Downs Golf Club [Handbook].* London: Golf Clubs Association [ca1951] 19p, illustrated, wrappers, 18cm.

7820. *Bath Golf Club [Handbook].* London: Golf Clubs Association, 1931, 24p, illustrated, wrappers, 18.5cm.

7830. *Bedfordshire Golf Club [Handbook].* London: Golf Clubs Association [ca1947] 27p, illustrated, wrappers, 18cm.

7840. *Beeston Fields Golf Club [Handbook].* London: Golf Clubs Association [ca1947] 15p, illustrated, wrappers, 18cm.

7850. *Bexhill Golf & Sports Club [Handbook].* London: Golf Clubs Association, 1938, 39p, illustrated, wrappers, 18cm.

7860. *Bexley Heath Golf Club [Handbook].* London: Golf Clubs Association [ca1947] 23p, illustrated, wrappers, 18cm.

7870. *Bin Down [Looe] Golf Club [Handbook].* London: Golf Clubs Association, 1939, 29p, illustrated, wrappers, 18cm.

7880. *Bolton Golf Club [Handbook].* London: Golf Clubs Association [ca1947] 23p, illustrated, wrappers, 18cm.

7890. *Brampton Golf Club [Handbook].* London: Golf Clubs Association [ca1952] 23p, illustrated, wrappers, 18cm.

7900. *Branford Golf Club [Handbook].* London: Golf Clubs Association, 1938, 31p, illustrated, wrappers, 18cm.

7910. *Bude and North Cornwall Golf Club. [Handbook].* London: Golf Clubs Association, 1932, 39p, illustrated, wrappers, 18cm.

7920. *Burhill Club [Handbook].* London: Golf Clubs Association [ca1949] 25p, illustrated, wrappers, 18.5cm.

7930. *Burton-On-Trent Golf Club [Handbook].* London: Golf Clubs Association [ca1953] 23p, illustrated, wrappers, 18cm.

7940. *Caernarvonshire Golf Club [Handbook].* London: Golf Clubs Association [ca1947] 18p, illustrated, wrappers, 18cm.

7950. *Callander Golf Club [Handbook].* London: Golf Clubs Association, 1939, 15p, illustrated, wrappers, 18cm.

7960. *Carmarthen Golf Club [Handbook].* London: Golf Clubs Association, 1939, 21p, illustrated, wrappers, 18.5cm.

7970. *Chigwell Golf Club [Handbook].* London: Golf Clubs Association [ca1951] 25p, illustrated, wrappers, 18cm.

7980. *Churston Golf Club [Handbook]*. London: Golf Clubs Association, 1939, 19p, illustrated, wrappers, 18.5cm.

7990. *Clevedon Golf Club [Handbook]*. London: Golf Clubs Association [ca1947] 25p, illustrated, wrappers, 18.5cm.

8000. *Coventry Golf Club [Handbook]*. London: Golf Clubs Association [ca1947] 27p, illustrated, wrappers, 18.5cm.

8010. *Crews Hill Golf Club [Handbook]*. London: Golf Clubs Association [ca1948] 24p, illustrated, wrappers, 18.5cm.

8020. *Crichel Park Golf Club [Handbook]*. London: Golf Clubs Association, 1938, 19p, illustrated, wrappers, 18cm.

8030. *Crieff Golf Club [Handbook]*. London: Golf Clubs Association, 1938, 19p, illustrated, wrappers, 18cm.

8040. *Cuddington Golf Club [Handbook]*. London: Golf Clubs Association, 1934, 23p, illustrated, wrappers, 18cm.

8050. *Dalmahoy Golf Club [Handbook]*. London: Golf Clubs Association, 1938, 27p, illustrated, wrappers, 18.5cm.

8060. *Dartford Golf Club [Handbook]*. London: Golf Clubs Association [ca1948] 17p, illustrated, wrappers, 18.5cm.

8070. *Duddington Golf Club [Handbook]*. London: Golf Clubs Association [ca1948] 25p, illustrated, wrappers, 18.5cm.

8080. *Dumfries and County Golf Club [Handbook]*. London: Golf Clubs Association, 1938, 19p, illustrated, wrappers, 18.5cm.

8090. *Ealing Golf Club [Handbook]*. London: Golf Clubs Association [ca1950] 15p, illustrated, wrappers, 18cm.

8100. *East Berks Golf Club [Handbook]*. London: Golf Clubs Association [ca1947] 20p, illustrated, wrappers, 18.5cm.

8110. *East Brighton Golf Club [Handbook]*. London: Golf Clubs Association [ca1947] 21p, illustrated, wrappers, 18cm.

8120. *East Herts Golf Club [Handbook]*. London: Golf Clubs Association [ca1947] 15p, illustrated, wrappers, 18.5cm.

8130. *East Renfrewshire Golf Club [Handbook]*. London: Golf Clubs Association, 1939, 17p, illustrated, wrappers, 18cm.

8140. *Edgbaston Golf Club [Handbook]*. London: Golf Clubs Association, 1939, 24p, illustrated, wrappers, 18cm.

8150. *Effingham Golf Club [Handbook]*. London: Golf Clubs Association [ca1947] 35p, illustrated, wrappers, 18cm.

8160. *Enfield Golf Club [Handbook]*. London: Golf Clubs Association [ca1948] 25p, illustrated, wrappers, 18.5cm.

8170. *Epsom Golf Club [Handbook]*. London: Golf Clubs Association [ca1947] 29p, illustrated, wrappers, 18.5cm.

8180. *Fulford Heath Golf Club [Handbook]*. London: Golf Clubs Association [ca1951] 19p, illustrated, wrappers, 18.5cm.

8190. *Fulneck Golf Club [Handbook]*. London: Golf Clubs Association [ca1948] 19p, illustrated, wrappers, 18.5cm.

8200. *Fulwell Golf Club [Handbook]*. London: Golf Clubs Association [ca1948] 26p, illustrated, wrappers, 18.5cm.

8210. *Ganton Golf Club [Handbook]*. London: Golf Clubs Association, 1939, 31p, illustrated, wrappers, 18.5cm.

8220. *Golf in Cornwall*. London: Golf Clubs Association [ca1952] 87p, illustrated, illustrated wrappers, 18.5cm.

8230. *Golf in Devon*. London: Golf Clubs Association [ca1952] 95p, illustrated, illustrated wrappers, 18.5cm.

8240. *Golf in Essex*. London: Golf Clubs Association [ca1952] 83p, illustrated, illustrated wrappers, 18.5cm.

8250. *Golf in Gloustershire*. London: Golf Clubs Association [ca1954] 53p, illustrated, illustrated wrappers, 18.5cm.

8260. *Golf in Hants & Dorset.* London: Golf Clubs Association [ca1955] 163p, illustrated, illustrated wrappers, 18.5cm.

8270. *Golf in Kent.* London: Golf Clubs Association [ca1952] 123p, illustrated, illustrated wrappers, 18.5cm.

8280. *Golf in Somerset.* London: Golf Clubs Association [ca1952] 59p, illustrated, illustrated wrappers, 18.5cm.

8290. *Golf in Surrey.* London: Golf Clubs Association [ca1957] 191p, illustrated, illustrated wrappers, 18.5cm.

8300. *Golf in Sussex.* London: Golf Clubs Association [ca1959] 103p, illustrated, illustrated wrappers, 18.5cm.

8310. *Golf in the Channel Islands.* London: Golf Clubs Association [ca1953] 35p, illustrated, illustrated wrappers, 18.5cm.

8320. *Golf in the Isle of Man.* London: Golf Clubs Association [ca1955] 39p, illustrated, illustrated wrappers, 18.5cm.

8330. *Golf on the Lancs Coast.* London: Golf Clubs Association [ca1957] 56p, illustrated, illustrated wrappers, 18.5cm.

8340. *Golf with Seven Clubs.* London: W. & G. Foyle, 1st ed. 1950, 93p, illustrated, illustrated wrappers, 18cm.

8350. *Goodwood Golf Club [Handbook].* London: Golf Clubs Association, 1939, 23p, illustrated, wrappers, 18.5cm.

8360. *Gosforth Golf Club [Handbook].* London: Golf Clubs Association [ca1947] 19p, illustrated, wrappers, 18cm.

8370. *Halifax Bradley Hall Golf Club [Handbook].* London: Golf Clubs Association [ca1948] 18p, illustrated, wrappers, 18.5cm.

8380. *Hallamshire Golf Club [Handbook].* London: Golf Clubs Association [ca1947] 16p, illustrated, wrappers, 18.5cm.

8390. *Harpenden Golf Club [Handbook]*. London: Golf Clubs Association [ca1946] 25p, illustrated, wrappers, 18.5cm.

8400. *Headingley Golf Club [Handbook]*. London: Golf Clubs Association [ca1947] 16p, illustrated, wrappers, 18.5cm.

8410. *Helensburgh Golf Club [Handbook]*. London: Golf Clubs Association, 1938, 23p, illustrated, wrappers, 18.5cm.

8420. *Henley Golf Club [Handbook]*. London: Golf Clubs Association, 1938, 19p, illustrated, wrappers, 18.5cm.

8430. *Highgate Golf Club [Handbook]*. London: Golf Clubs Association, 1936, 23p, illustrated, wrappers, 18.5cm.

8440. *Hockley Golf Club [Handbook]*. London: Golf Clubs Association [ca1949] 14p, illustrated, wrappers, 18.5cm.

8450. *Holyhead Golf Club [Handbook]*. London: Golf Clubs Association [ca1947] 10p, illustrated, wrappers, 18.5cm.

8460. *Hornsea Golf Club [Handbook]*. London: Golf Clubs Association [ca1947] 15p, illustrated, wrappers, 18.5cm.

8470. *Hunstanton Golf Club [Handbook]*. London: Golf Clubs Association [ca1950] 29p, illustrated, wrappers, 18.5cm.

8480. *Ilford Golf Club [Handbook]*. London: Golf Clubs Association [ca1952] 23p, illustrated, wrappers, 18.5cm.

8490. *Kingsthorpe Golf Club [Handbook]*. London: Golf Clubs Association [ca1946] 23p, illustrated, wrappers, 18.5cm.

8500. *Kingswood Golf Club [Handbook]*. London: Golf Clubs Association, 1938, 19p, illustrated, wrappers, 18.5cm.

8510. *Kirby Muxloe Golf Club [Handbook]*. London: Golf Clubs Association [ca1949] 19p, illustrated, wrappers, 18.5cm.

8520. *Knole Park Golf Club [Handbook]*. London: Golf Clubs Association [ca1951] 23p, illustrated, wrappers, 18.5cm.

8530. *Langland Bay Golf Club [Handbook]*. London: Golf Clubs Association [ca1955] 31p, illustrated, wrappers, 18.5cm.

8540. *Lansdown Golf Club [Handbook]*. London: Golf Clubs Association, 1932, 27p, illustrated, wrappers, 18.5cm.

8550. *Lee-On-The-Solent Golf Club [Handbook]*. London: Golf Clubs Association, 1931, 23p, illustrated, wrappers, 18.5cm.

8560. *Leek Golf Club Handbook]*. London: Golf Clubs Association [ca1947] 23p, illustrated, wrappers, 18.5cm.

8570. *Long Ashton Golf Club [Handbook]*. London: Golf Clubs Association [ca1948] 19p, illustrated, wrappers, 18.5cm.

8580. *Lothianburn Golf Club [Handbook]*. London: Golf Clubs Association [ca1948] 18p, illustrated, wrappers, 18cm.

8590. *Maidenhead Golf Club [Handbook]*. London: Golf Clubs Association, 1937, 14p, illustrated, wrappers, 18.5cm.

8600. *Mere Golf and Country Club [Handbook]*. London: Golf Clubs Association, 1938, 23p, illustrated, wrappers, 18.5cm.

8610. *Mersea Island Golf Club [Handbook]*. London: Golf Clubs Association, 1938, 23p, illustrated, wrappers, 18.5cm.

8620. *Minehead and West Somerset Golf Club [Handbook]*. London: Golf Clubs Association [ca1946] 27p, illustrated, wrappers, 18.5cm.

8630. *Moments with Golfing Masters*. London: Methuen, 1st ed. 1932 [100p] illustrated by Daniel Browning, cloth, 17cm.

8640. *Murcar Golf Club [Handbook]*. London: Golf Clubs Association, 1938, 25p, illustrated, wrappers, 18.5cm.

8650. *Nevin & District Golf Club [Handbook]*. London: Golf Clubs Association [ca1947] 19p, illustrated, wrappers, 18.5cm.

8660. *Newbury District Golf Club [Handbook]*. London: Golf Clubs Association, 1933, 24p, illustrated, wrappers, 18.5cm.

8670. *Newport Golf Club [Handbook]*. London: Golf Clubs Association [ca1953] 35p, illustrated, wrappers, 18.5cm.

8680. *North Cliff Golf Club [Handbook]*. London: Golf Clubs Association [ca1948] 24p, illustrated, wrappers, 18.5cm.

8690. *Olton Golf Club [Handbook]*. London: Golf Clubs Association [ca1948] 23p, illustrated, wrappers, 18.5cm.

8700. *Ormskirk Golf Club [Handbook]*. London: Golf Clubs Association, 1938, 21p, illustrated, wrappers, 18.5cm.

8710. *Oxley Park Golf Club [Handbook]*. London: Golf Clubs Association, 1947, 29p, illustrated, wrappers, 18.5cm.

8720. *Ponteland Golf Club [Handbook]*. London: Golf Clubs Association, 1939, 23p, illustrated, wrappers, 18.5cm.

8730. *Prestonfield Golf Club [Handbook]*. London: Golf Clubs Association [ca1948] 26p, illustrated, wrappers, 18cm.

8740. *Prestwick St. Nicholas Golf Club [Handbook]*. London: Golf Clubs Association, 1939, 24p, illustrated, wrappers, 18.5cm.

8750. *Purley Downs Golf Club [Handbook]*. London: Golf Clubs Association [ca1948] 23p, illustrated, wrappers, 18.5cm.

8760. *Robin Hood Golf Club [Handbook]*. London: Golf Clubs Association, 1938, 19p, illustrated, wrappers, 18.5cm.

8770. *Rothley Park Golf Club [Handbook]*. London: Golf Clubs Association [ca1949] 23p, illustrated, wrappers, 18.5cm.

8780. *Rowlands Castle Golf Club [Handbook]*. London: Golf Clubs Association [ca1948] 20p, illustrated, wrappers, 18.5cm.

8790. *Royal Winchester Golf Club [Handbook]*. London: Golf Clubs Association, 1934, 16p, illustrated, wrappers, 18.5cm.

8800. *Sandiway Golf Club [Handbook]*. London: Golf Clubs Association, 1939, 23p, illustrated, wrappers, 18.5cm.

8810. *Shaw Hill Golf Club [Handbook]*. London: Golf Clubs Association [ca1948] 20p, illustrated, wrappers, 18.5cm.

8820. *Shifnal Golf Club [Handbook]*. London: Golf Clubs Association [ca1948] 21p, illustrated, wrappers, 18cm.

8830. *Shipley Golf Club [Handbook]*. London: Golf Clubs Association [ca1948] 16p, illustrated, wrappers, 18.5cm.

8840. *Shrewsbury Golf Club [Handbook]*. London: Golf Clubs Association, 1939, 22p, illustrated, wrappers, 18.5cm.

8850. *Sickleholme Golf Club [Handbook]*. London: Golf Clubs Association, 1938, 14p, illustrated, wrappers, 18.5cm.

8860. *Sitwell Park Golf Club [Handbook]*. London: Golf Clubs Association [ca1948] 19p, illustrated, wrappers, 18.5cm.

8870. *St. Enodoc Golf Club [Handbook]*. London: Golf Clubs Association, 1934, 23p, illustrated, wrappers, 18.5cm.

8880. *St. George's Hill Golf Club [Handbook]*. London: Golf Clubs Association [ca1955] 39p, illustrated, wrappers, 18.5cm.

8890. *St. Leonard's Golf Club. [Handbook]*. London: Golf Clubs Association, 1938, 23p, illustrated, wrappers, 18.5cm.

8900. *Super Golf*. London: Simpkin, Marshall, Hamilton, Kent, 1st ed. 1919, 143p, illustrated, cloth, 16.5cm.

8910. *Sutton Coldfield Golf Club [Handbook]*. London: Golf Clubs Association [ca1948] 29p, illustrated, wrappers, 18.5cm.

8920. *The Aberystwyth Golf Club [Handbook]*. London: Golf Clubs Association, 1934, 27p, illustrated, wrappers, 18cm.

8930. *The Alloa Golf Club [Handbook]*. London: Golf Clubs Association [ca1948] 15p, illustrated, wrappers, 18cm.

8940. *The Alnmouth Golf Club [Handbook]*. London: Golf Clubs Association [ca1948] 27p, illustrated, wrappers, 18cm.

8950. *The Appleby Golf Club [Handbook]*. London: Golf Clubs Association [ca1946] 22p, illustrated, wrappers, 18cm.

8960. *The Ardeer Golf Club [Handbook]*. London: Golf Clubs Association [ca1948] 15p, illustrated, wrappers, 18cm.

8970. *The Arkley Golf Club [Handbook]*. London: Golf Clubs Association [ca1955] 15p, illustrated, wrappers, 18cm.

8980. *The Ashford Manor Golf Club [Handbook]*. London: Golf Clubs Association [ca1947] 15p, illustrated, wrappers, 18cm.

8990. *The Aspley Guise & Woburn Sands Golf Club [Handbook]*. London: Golf Clubs Association [ca1947] 17p, illustrated, wrappers, 18cm.

9000. *The Ayr Corporation Golf Courses [Handbook]*. London: Golf Clubs Association, 1933, 28p, illustrated, wrappers, 18cm.

9010. *The Barrow Golf Club [Handbook]*. London: Golf Clubs Association [ca1948] 19p, illustrated, wrappers, 17.5cm.

9020. *The Betchworth Park Golf Club [Handbook]*. London: Golf Clubs Association [ca1947] 17p, illustrated, wrappers, 18cm.

9030. *The Birkdale Golf Club [Handbook]*. London: Golf Clubs Association, 1934, 27p, illustrated, wrappers, 18cm.

9040. *The Birstall Golf Club [Handbook]*. London: Golf Clubs Association [ca1947] 24p, illustrated, wrappers, 18cm.

9050. *The Bishop Auckland Golf Club [Handbook]*. London: Golf Clubs Association [ca1947] 24p, illustrated, wrappers, 18cm.

9060. *The Blackburn Golf Club [Handbook]*. London: Golf Clubs Association [ca1947] 18p, illustrated, wrappers, 18.5cm.

9070. *The Blackmoor Golf Club [Handbook]*. London: Golf Clubs Association [ca1947] 24p, illustrated, wrappers, 18.5cm.

9080. *The Blackpool Golf Club [Handbook]*. London: Golf Clubs Association, 1939, 23p, illustrated, wrappers, 18cm.

9090. *The Blackpool North Shore Golf Club [Handbook]*. London: Golf Clubs Association [ca1947] 37p, illustrated, wrappers, 18.5cm.

9100. *The Borth & Ynyslas Golf Club [Handbook]*. London: Golf Clubs Association, 1934, 23p, illustrated, wrappers, 18cm.

9110. *The Bramley Golf Club [Handbook]*. London: Golf Clubs Association [ca1950] 20p, illustrated, wrappers, 18cm.

9120. *The Bramshaw Golf Club [Handbook]*. London: Golf Clubs Association [ca1947] 19p, illustrated, wrappers, 18cm.

9130. *The Brighton & Hove Golf Club [Handbook]*. London: Golf Clubs Association [ca1947] 27p, illustrated, wrappers, 18cm.

9140. *The Bristol & Clifton Golf Club [Handbook]*. London: Golf Clubs Association [ca1948] 27p, illustrated, wrappers, 18cm.

9150. *The Brocton Hall Golf Club [Handbook]*. London: Golf Clubs Association [ca1948] 11p, illustrated, wrappers, 18.5cm.

9160. *The Brokenhurst Manor Golf Club [Handbook]*. London: Golf Clubs Association, 1939, 25p, illustrated, wrappers, 18cm.

9170. *The Brookmans Park Golf Club [Handbook]*. London: Golf Clubs Association, 1938, 23p, illustrated, wrappers, 18cm.

9180. *The Burnham Beeches Golf Club [Handbook]*. London: Golf Clubs Association, 1938, 23p, illustrated, wrappers, 18cm.

9190. *The Bury Golf Club [Handbook]*. London: Golf Clubs Association [ca1947] 23p, illustrated, wrappers, 18.5cm.

9200. *The Bush Hill Park Golf Club [Handbook]*. London: Golf Clubs Association [ca1951] 15p, illustrated, wrappers, 18.5cm.

9210. *The Bushey Hall Golf Club [Handbook]*. London: Golf Clubs Association [ca1951] 15p, illustrated, wrappers, 17.5cm.

9220. *The Calcot Golf Club [Handbook]*. London: Golf Clubs Association [ca1952] 26p, illustrated, wrappers, 18cm.

9230. *The Calthorpe Golf Club [Handbook]*. London: Golf Clubs Association [ca1947] 21p, illustrated, wrappers, 18.5cm.

9240. *The Camberley Heath Golf Club [Handbook]*. London: Golf Clubs Association [ca1947] 19p, illustrated, wrappers, 18.5cm.

9250. *The Carlisle City Golf Club [Handbook]*. London: Golf Clubs Association [ca1947] 23p, illustrated, wrappers, 18cm.

9260. *The Castletown Golf Club [Handbook]*. London: Golf Clubs Association [ca1947] 19p, illustrated, wrappers, 18cm.

9270. *The Cathcart Castle Golf Club [Handbook]*. London: Golf Clubs Association, 1939, 20p, illustrated, wrappers, 18cm.

9280. *The Cavendish Golf Club [Handbook]*. London: Golf Clubs Association, 1938, 23p, illustrated, wrappers, 18.5cm.

9290. *The Chester [Curzon Port] Golf Club [Handbook]*. London: Golf Clubs Association [ca1947] 19p, illustrated, wrappers, 18cm.

9300. *The Chesterfield [Whitstable] Golf Club [Handbook]*. London: Golf Clubs Association [ca1947] 19p, illustrated, wrappers, 18cm.

9310. *The Childwall Golf Club [Handbook]*. London: Golf Clubs Association [ca1950] 19p, illustrated, wrappers, 18cm.

9320. *The Chipstead Golf Club [Handbook]*. London: Golf Clubs Association, 1938, 15p, illustrated, wrappers, 18.5cm.

9330. *The Cirencester Golf Club [Handbook]*. London: Golf Clubs Association [ca1949] 26p, illustrated, wrappers, 18cm.

9340. *The City of Newcastle Golf Club [Handbook]*. London: Golf Clubs Association [ca1952] 29p, illustrated, wrappers, 18cm.

9350. *The Clacton-On-Sea Golf Club [Handbook]*. London: Golf Clubs Association, 1939, 27p, illustrated, wrappers, 18.5cm.

9360. *The Cleveleys Hydro Golf Club [Handbook]*. London: Golf Clubs Association [ca1947] 22p, illustrated, wrappers, 18cm.

9370. *The Colchester Golf Club [Handbook]*. London: Golf Clubs Association [ca1948] 15p, illustrated, wrappers, 18cm.

9380. *The Cooden Beach Golf Club [Handbook]*. London: Golf Clubs Association [ca1950] 29p, illustrated, wrappers, 18.5cm.

9390. *The Croham Hurst Golf Club [Handbook]*. London: Golf Clubs Association [ca1955] 19p, illustrated, wrappers, 18cm.

9400. *The Deepdale [Scarborough] Golf Club [Handbook]*. London: Golf Clubs Association [ca1947] 25p, illustrated, wrappers, 18.5cm.

9410. *The Deeside Golf Club [Handbook]*. London: Golf Clubs Association, 1938, 19p, illustrated, wrappers, 18.5cm.

9420. *The Dewsbury District Golf Club [Handbook]*. London: Golf Clubs Association [ca1948] 23p, illustrated, wrappers, 18cm.

9430. *The Didsbury Golf Club [Handbook]*. London: Golf Clubs Association [ca1948] 16p, illustrated, wrappers, 18cm.

9440. *The Dinas Powis Golf Club [Handbook]*. London: Golf Clubs Association [ca1947] 19p, illustrated, wrappers, 18cm.

9450. *The Disley Golf Club [Handbook]*. London: Golf Clubs Association [ca1948] 20p, illustrated, wrappers, 18cm.

9460. *The Doncaster Golf Club [Handbook]*. London: Golf Clubs Association [ca1950] 19p, illustrated, wrappers, 18.5cm.

9470. *The Dulwich and Sydenham Hill Golf Club [Handbook]*. London: Golf Clubs Association [ca1952] 23p, illustrated, wrappers, 18.5cm.

9480. *The Dunscar Golf Club [Handbook]*. London: Golf Clubs Association [1948] 19p, illustrated, wrappers, 18cm.

9490. *The Dunstable Downs Golf Club [Handbook]*. London: Golf Clubs Association [ca1948] 31p, illustrated, wrappers, 18cm.

9500. *The Eaglescliffe & District Golf Club [Handbook]*. London: Golf Clubs Association [ca1938] 19p, illustrated, wrappers, 18cm.

9510. *The Eastbourne Downs Club [Handbook]*. London: Golf Clubs Association [ca1949] 20p, illustrated, wrappers, 18.5cm.

9520. *The Elgin Golf Club [Handbook]*. London: Golf Clubs Association [ca1947] 25p, illustrated, wrappers, 18cm.

9530. *The Exmouth Golf Club [Handbook]*. London: Golf Clubs Association, 1931, 28p, illustrated, wrappers, 18cm.

9540. *The Fairhaven Golf Club [Handbook]*. London: Golf Clubs Association, 1939, 27p, illustrated, wrappers, 18.5cm.

9550. *The Farnham Golf Club [Handbook]*. London: Golf Clubs Association [ca1955] 19p, illustrated, wrappers, 18cm.

9560. *The Filey Golf Club [Handbook]*. London: Golf Clubs Association, 1934, 30p, illustrated, wrappers, 18.5cm.

9570. *The Finchley Golf Club [Handbook]*. London: Golf Clubs Association, 1938, 19p, illustrated, wrappers, 18cm.

9580. *The Firbeck Hall Golf Club [Handbook]*. London: Golf Clubs Association, 1938, 25p, illustrated, wrappers, 18.5cm.

9590. *The Flackwell Heath Golf Club [Handbook]*. London: Golf Clubs Association [ca1952] 15p, illustrated, wrappers, 18cm.

9600. *The Fleetwood Club [Handbook]*. London: Golf Clubs Association, 1938, 19p, illustrated, wrappers, 18.5cm.

9610. *The Folkstone Golf Club [Handbook]*. London: Golf Clubs Association, 1932, 24p, illustrated, wrappers, 18.5cm.

9620. *The Formby Ladies Golf Club [Handbook]*. London: Golf Clubs Association [ca1953] 15p, illustrated, wrappers, 18.5cm.

9630. *The Freshwater Bay [I.O.W.] Golf Club [Handbook]*. London: Golf Clubs Association [ca1948] 30p, illustrated, wrappers, 18.5cm.

9640. *The Frinton Golf Club [Handbook]*. London: Golf Clubs Association, 1938, 31p, illustrated, wrappers, 18.5cm.

9650. *The Fulford [York] Golf Club [Handbook]*. London: Golf Clubs Association [ca1948] 19p, illustrated, wrappers, 18cm.

9660. *The Gerrards Cross Golf Club [Handbook]*. London: Golf Clubs Association [ca1947] 21p, illustrated, wrappers, 18.5cm.

9670. *The Glamorganshire Golf Club [Handbook]*. London: Golf Clubs Association [ca1955] 27p, illustrated, wrappers, 18.5cm.

9680. *The Glen Gorse Golf Club [Handbook]*. London: Golf Clubs Association [ca1953] 12p, illustrated, wrappers, 18cm.

9690. *The Golfer's Catechism:A vade mecum to the rules of golf.* London: H.O. Quinn, 1st ed. [ca1935] 88p, cloth, 15cm.

9700. *The Gosport and Stokes Bay Golf Club [Handbook]*. London: Golf Clubs Association [ca1948] 24p, illustrated, wrappers, 18.5cm.

9710. *The Grand Marine Hotel and Barton-on-Sea Golf Club [Handbook]*. New Milton, England: Privately Printed [ca1950] 15p, illustrated, illustrated wrappers, 18.5cm.

9720. *The Grange Park Golf Club [Handbook]*. London: Golf Clubs Association [ca1948] 16p, illustrated, wrappers, 18.5cm.

9730. *The Greenway Hall Golf Club [Handbook]*. London: Golf Clubs Association [ca1948] 19p, illustrated, wrappers, 18.5cm.

9740. *The Guildford Golf Club [Handbook]*. London: Golf Clubs Association [ca1948] 27p, illustrated, wrappers, 18.5cm.

9750. *The Hadley Wood Golf Club [Handbook]*. London: Golf Clubs Association [ca1948] 27p, illustrated, wrappers, 18.5cm.

9760. *The Harrogate Golf Club [Handbook]*. London: Golf Clubs Association [ca1947] 22p, illustrated, wrappers, 18.5cm.

9770. *The Hastings Golf Club [Handbook]*. London: Golf Clubs Association, 1934, 27p, illustrated, wrappers, 18.5cm.

9780. *The Hawick Golf Club [Handbook]*. London: Golf Clubs Association [ca1947] 18p, illustrated, wrappers, 18.5cm.

9790. *The Hayling Golf Club [Handbook]*. London: Golf Clubs Association, 1931, 24p, illustrated, wrappers, 18.5cm.

9800. *The Haywards Heath Golf Club [Handbook]*. London: Golf Clubs Association [ca1955] 19p, illustrated, wrappers, 18.5cm.

9810. *The Hendon Golf Club [Handbook]*. London: Golf Clubs Association [ca1950] 20p, illustrated, wrappers, 18.5cm.

9820. *The Herne Bay Golf Club [Handbook].* London: Golf Clubs Association [ca1948] 19p, illustrated, wrappers, 18.5cm.

9830. *The Hesketh Golf Club [Handbook].* London: Golf Clubs Association [ca1947] 19p, illustrated, wrappers, 18.5cm.

9840. *The Hessle Golf Club [Handbook].* London: Golf Clubs Association [ca1948] 11p, illustrated, wrappers, 18.5cm.

9850. *The Highwoods Bexhill-on-Sea Golf Club [Handbook].* London: Golf Clubs Association [ca1949] 25p, illustrated, wrappers, 18.5cm.

9860. *The Hillsborough Golf Club [Handbook].* London: Golf Clubs Association [ca1952] 15p, illustrated, wrappers, 18.5cm.

9870. *The Hindhead Golf Club [Handbook].* London: Golf Clubs Association, 1938, 23p, illustrated, wrappers, 18.5cm.

9880. *The Honiton Golf Club [Handbook].* London: Golf Clubs Association, 1939, 19p, illustrated, wrappers, 18.5cm.

9890. *The Huddersfield Golf Club [Handbook].* London: Golf Clubs Association [ca1947] 31p, illustrated, wrappers, 18.5cm.

9900. *The Hull Golf Club [Handbook].* London: Golf Clubs Association [ca1947] 17p, illustrated, wrappers, 18.5cm.

9910. *The Huntercombe Golf Club [Handbook].* London: Golf Clubs Association [1952] 27p, illustrated, wrappers, 18.5cm.

9920. *The Ilkley Golf Club [Handbook].* London: Golf Clubs Association, 1939, 23p, illustrated, wrappers, 18.5cm.

9930. *The Inverness Golf Club [Handbook].* London: Golf Clubs Association [ca1947] 29p, illustrated, wrappers, 18.5cm.

9940. *The Irvine Golf Club [Handbook].* London: Golf Clubs Association [ca1947] 25p, illustrated, wrappers, 18.5cm.

9950. *The Keighley Golf Club [Handbook]*. London: Golf Clubs Association [ca1946] 25p, illustrated, wrappers, 18.5cm.

9960. *The Kettering Golf Club [Handbook]*. London: Golf Clubs Association [ca1948] 27p, illustrated, wrappers, 18.5cm.

9970. *The King's Lynn Golf Club [Handbook]*. London: Golf Clubs Association [ca1949] 20p, illustrated, wrappers, 18.5cm.

9980. *The Kington Golf Club [Handbook]*. London: Golf Clubs Association [ca1950] 15p, illustrated, wrappers, 18.5cm.

9990. *The Knott End & Fleetwood Golf Club [Handbook]*. London: Golf Clubs Association [ca1949] 13p, illustrated, wrappers, 17.5cm.

10000. *The Leatherhead Golf Club [Handbook]*. London: Golf Clubs Association, 1938, 21p, illustrated, wrappers, 18.5cm.

10010. *The Leighton Buzzard Golf Club [Handbook]*. London: Golf Clubs Association [ca1948] 35p, illustrated, wrappers, 18.5cm.

10020. *The Lewes Golf Club [Handbook]*. London: Golf Clubs Association [ca1948] 25p, illustrated, wrappers, 18.5cm.

10030. *The Lindrick Golf Club [Handbook]*. London: Golf Clubs Association [ca1955] 23p, illustrated, wrappers, 18.5cm.

10040. *The Littlehampton Golf Club [Handbook]*. London: Golf Clubs Association, 1938, 27p, illustrated, wrappers, 18.5cm.

10050. *The Llandrindod Wells Golf Club [Handbook]*. London: Golf Clubs Association [ca1951] 29p, illustrated, wrappers, 18.5cm.

10060. *The Llandudno Golf Club [Handbook]*. London: Golf Clubs Association, 1937, 19p, illustrated, wrappers, 18.5cm.

10070. *The Ludlow Golf Club [Handbook]*. London: Golf Clubs Association [ca1947] 20p, illustrated, wrappers, 18.5cm.

10080. *The Lundin Golf Club [Handbook]*. London: Golf Clubs Association [ca1947] 20p, illustrated, wrappers, 18.5cm.

10090. *The Lytham [Green Drive] Golf Club [Handbook]*. London: Golf Clubs Association [ca1948] 23p, illustrated, wrappers, 18cm.

10100. *The Manchester Golf Club [Handbook]*. London: Golf Clubs Association [ca1953] 19p, illustrated, wrappers, 18.5cm.

10110. *The Mannings Heath Golf Club [Handbook]*. London: Golf Clubs Association, 1938, 25p, illustrated, wrappers, 18.5cm.

10120. *The Moray Golf Club [Handbook]*. London: Golf Clubs Association [ca1947] 23p, illustrated, wrappers, 18.5cm.

10130. *The Morecambe Golf Club [Handbook]*. London: Golf Clubs Association, 1934, 23p, illustrated, wrappers, 18.5cm.

10140. *The Morpeth Golf Club [Handbook]*. London: Golf Clubs Association [ca1948] 20p, illustrated, wrappers, 18.5cm.

10150. *The Mortonhall Golf Club [Handbook]*. London: Golf Clubs Association [ca1952] 19p, illustrated, wrappers, 18cm.

10160. *The Mullion Golf Club [Handbook]*. London: Golf Clubs Association [ca1949] 45p, illustrated, wrappers, 18.5cm.

10170. *The Muswell Hill Golf Club [Handbook]*. London: Golf Clubs Association [ca1951] 23p, illustrated, wrappers, 18.5cm.

10180. *The Naze Golf Club [Handbook]*. London: Golf Clubs Association, 1939, 27p, illustrated, wrappers, 18.5cm.

10190. *The New Golf Club, St. Andrews [Handbook]*. London: Golf Clubs Association [ca1946] 27p, illustrated, wrappers, 18.5cm.

10200. *The New Highwood Golf Club [Handbook]*. London: Golf Clubs Association [ca1947] 41p, illustrated, wrappers, 18.5cm.

10210. *The Newbattle Golf Club [Handbook]*. London: Golf Clubs Association [ca1947] 21p, illustrated, wrappers, 18.5cm.

10220. *The Newbury and Crookham Golf Club [Handbook]*. London: Golf Clubs Association [ca1952] 39p, illustrated, wrappers, 18cm.

10230. *The Newton Abbot Golf Club [Handbook]*. London: Golf Clubs Association, 1932, 35p, illustrated, wrappers, 18.5cm.

10240. *The North Manchester Golf Club [Handbook]*. London: Golf Clubs Association [ca1953] 23p, illustrated, wrappers, 18.5cm.

10250. *The North Shore Golf Club [Handbook]*. London: Golf Clubs Association, 1938, 39p, illustrated, wrappers, 18.5cm.

10260. *The Oakdale Golf Club [Handbook]*. London: Golf Clubs Association [ca1947] 19p, illustrated, wrappers, 18cm.

10270. *The Old Colwyn Golf Club [Handbook]*. London: Golf Clubs Association [ca1952] 11p, illustrated, wrappers, 18cm.

10280. *The Old Links [Bolton] Golf Club [Handbook]*. London: Golf Clubs Association [ca1948] 16p, illustrated, wrappers, 18.5cm.

10290. *The Panmure Golf Club [Handbook]*. London: Golf Clubs Association [ca1950] 14p, illustrated, wrappers, 18cm.

10300. *The Pannal Golf Club [Handbook]*. London: Golf Clubs Association [ca1946] 19p, illustrated, wrappers, 18.5cm.

10310. *The Parkstone Golf Club [Handbook]*. London: Golf Clubs Association, 1928, 40p, illustrated, wrappers, 18.5cm.

10320. *The Peebles Municipal Golf Course [Handbook]*. London: Golf Clubs Association [ca1947] 21p, illustrated, wrappers, 18.5cm.

10330. *The Penmaenmawr Golf Club [Handbook].* London: Golf Clubs Association [ca1955] 15p, illustrated, wrappers, 18cm.

10340. *The Penwortham Golf Club [Handbook].* London: Golf Clubs Association [ca 1949] 17p, illustrated, wrappers, 18.5cm.

10350. *The Perranporth Golf Club [Handbook].* London: Golf Clubs Association, 1938, 23p, illustrated, wrappers, 18.5cm.

10360. *The Piltdown Golf Club [Handbook].* London: Golf Clubs Association [ca1947] 21p, illustrated, wrappers, 18.5cm.

10370. *The Prenton [Cheshire] Golf Club [Handbook].* London: Golf Clubs Association [ca1949] 15p, illustrated, wrappers, 18.5cm.

10380. *The Preston Golf Club [Handbook].* London: Golf Clubs Association [ca1947] 18p, illustrated, wrappers, 18.5cm.

10390. *The Pwllheli Golf Club [Handbook].* London: Golf Clubs Association [ca1947] 31p, illustrated, wrappers, 18.5cm.

10400. *The Queen's Park Golf Club [Handbook].* London: Golf Clubs Association [ca1949] 31p, illustrated, wrappers, 18.5cm.

10410. *The Ramsey Golf Club [Handbook].* London: Golf Clubs Association [ca1948] 16p, illustrated, wrappers, 18.5cm.

10420. *The Reading Golf Club [Handbook].* London: Golf Clubs Association [ca1953] 27p, illustrated, wrappers, 18.5cm.

10430. *The Rhondda Golf Club [Handbook].* London: Golf Clubs Association [ca1948] 20p, illustrated, wrappers, 18.5cm.

10440. *The Rhyl Golf Club [Handbook].* London: Golf Clubs Association, 1940, 19p, illustrated, wrappers, 18.5cm.

10450. *The Ringway Golf Club [Handbook].* London: Golf Clubs Association [ca1949] 13p, illustrated, wrappers, 18.5cm.

10460. *The Rochdale Golf Club [Handbook]*. London: Golf Clubs Association [ca1948] 15p, illustrated, wrappers, 18.5cm.

10470. *The Roehampton Club [Handbook]*. London: Golf Clubs Association [ca1955] 27p, illustrated, wrappers, 18.5cm.

10480. *The Romford Golf Club [Handbook]*. London: Golf Clubs Association [ca1947] 19p, illustrated, wrappers, 18.5cm.

10490. *The Royal Aberdeen Golf Club [Handbook]*. London: Golf Clubs Association, 1940, 24p, illustrated, wrappers, 18cm.

10500. *The Royal Ashdown Forest Golf Club [Handbook]*. London: Golf Clubs Association [ca1948] 26p, illustrated, wrappers, 18cm.

10510. *The Royal County Down Golf Club [Handbook]*. London: Golf Clubs Association [ca1951] 28p, illustrated, wrappers, 18cm.

10520. *The Royal Cromer Golf Club [Handbook]*. London: Golf Clubs Association, 1938, 35p, illustrated, wrappers, 18cm.

10530. *The Royal Isle of Wight Golf Club [Handbook]*. London: Golf Clubs Association [ca1947] 20p, illustrated, wrappers, 18cm.

10540. *The Royal Jersey Golf Club [Handbook]*. London: Golf Clubs Association, 1939, 31p, illustrated, wrappers, 18.5cm.

10550. *The Royal Norwich Golf Club [Handbook]*. London: Golf Clubs Association [ca1949] 23p, illustrated, wrappers, 19cm.

10560. *The Royal Porthcawl Golf Club [Handbook]*. London: Golf Clubs Association [ca1951] 23p, illustrated, wrappers, 18.5cm.

10570. *The Royal Portrush Golf Club [Handbook]*. London: Golf Clubs Association [ca1949] 49p, illustrated, wrappers, 18.5cm.

10580. *The Rushcliffe Golf Club [Handbook]*. London: Golf Clubs Association [ca1953] 23p, illustrated, wrappers, 18.5cm.

10590. *The Rushmere Golf Club [Handbook]*. London: Golf Clubs Association [ca1948] 24p, illustrated, wrappers, 18.5cm.

10600. *The Ryde Golf Club [Handbook]*. London: Golf Clubs Association [ca1949] 15p, illustrated, wrappers, 18.5cm.

10610. *The Salisbury and South Wilts Golf Club [Handbook]*. London: Golf Clubs Association, 1928, 23p, illustrated, wrappers, 18.5cm.

10620. *The Sand Moor Golf Club [Handbook]*. London: Golf Clubs Association [ca1948] 21p, illustrated, wrappers, 18.5cm.

10630. *The Scarborough South Cliff Golf Club [Handbook]*. London: Golf Clubs Association, 1939, 31p, illustrated, wrappers, 18.5cm.

10640. *The Seacroft Golf Club [Handbook]*. London: Golf Clubs Association, 1939, 29p, illustrated, wrappers, 18.5cm.

10650. *The Seaford Golf Club [Handbook]*. London: Golf Clubs Association, 1938, 27p, illustrated, wrappers, 18.5cm.

10660. *The Sheringham Golf Club [Handbook]*. London: Golf Clubs Association, 1938, 21p, illustrated, wrappers, 18.5cm.

10670. *The Sherwood Forest Golf Club [Handbook]*. London: Golf Clubs Association [ca1948] 32p, illustrated, wrappers, 18.5cm.

10680. *The Sidmouth Golf Club [Handbook]*. London: Golf Clubs Association [ca1947] 29p, illustrated, wrappers, 18.5cm.

10690. *The Sonning Golf Club [Handbook]*. London: Golf Clubs Association, 1938, 23p, illustrated, wrappers, 18.5cm.

10700. *The South Herts Golf Club [Handbook]*. London: Golf Clubs Association, 1932, 28p, illustrated, wrappers, 18.5cm.

10710. *The South Shields Golf Club [Handbook]*. London: Golf Clubs Association [ca1948] 19p, illustrated, wrappers, 18.5cm.

10720. *The Southport & Ainsdale Golf Club [Handbook]*. London: Golf Clubs Association [ca1946] 29p, illustrated, wrappers, 18.5cm.

10730. *The Spalding Golf Club [Handbook]*. London: Golf Clubs Association [ca1951] 19p, illustrated, wrappers, 18.5cm.

10740. *The St. Annes Old Links Golf Club [Handbook]*. London: Golf Clubs Association [ca1946] 27p, illustrated, wrappers, 18.5cm.

10750. *The St. Ives Golf Club [Handbook]*. London: Golf Clubs Association [ca1949] 11p, illustrated, wrappers, 17.5cm.

10760. *The Stanley Park [Municipal] Golf Course [Handbook]*. London: Golf Clubs Association [ca1949] 26p, illustrated, wrappers, 18cm.

10770. *The Stanmore Golf Club [Handbook]*. London: Golf Clubs Association [ca1955] 19p, illustrated, wrappers, 18.5cm.

10780. *The Stinchcombe Hill Golf Club [Handbook]*. London: Golf Clubs Association [ca1948] 23p, illustrated, wrappers, 18.5cm.

10790. *The Stoneham Golf Club [Handbook]*. London: Golf Clubs Association [1947] 25p, illustrated, wrappers, 18cm.

10800. *The Strathpeffer Spa Golf Club [Handbook]*. London: Golf Clubs Association [ca1947] 19p, illustrated, wrappers, 18.5cm.

10810. *The Strawberry Hill Golf Club [Handbook]*. London: Golf Clubs Association [ca1951] 19p, illustrated, wrappers, 18cm.

10820. *The Stymie: A miscellany of golfing humor and wit*. Glasgow: Fraser, Asher, 1st ed. 1910, 104p, illustrated, illustrated wrappers, 20cm.

10830. *The Sunningdale Golf Club [Handbook]*. London: Golf Clubs Association [ca1950] 23p, illustrated, wrappers, 18.5cm.

10840. *The Swanage & Studland Golf Club [Handbook]*. London: Golf Clubs Association, 1939, 19p, illustrated, wrappers, 18.5cm.

10850. *The Swansea Bay Golf Club [Handbook]*. London: Golf Clubs Association [ca1948] 18p, illustrated, wrappers, 18.5cm.

10860. *The Swindon Golf Club [Handbook]*. London: Golf Clubs Association, 1934, 23p, illustrated, wrappers, 18.5cm.

10870. *The Tavistock Golf Club [Handbook]*. London: Golf Clubs Association, 1938, 17p, illustrated, wrappers, 18.5cm.

10880. *The Teignmouth Golf Club [Handbook]*. London: Golf Clubs Association [ca1948] 25p, illustrated, wrappers, 18.5cm.

10890. *The Tenby Golf Club [Handbook]*. London: Golf Clubs Association, 1938, 31p, illustrated, wrappers, 18.5cm.

10900. *The Thrope Hall Golf Club [Handbook]*. London: Golf Clubs Association [ca1949] 39p, illustrated, wrappers, 18.5cm.

10910. *The Tiverton Golf Club [Handbook]*. London: Golf Clubs Association [ca1947] 25p, illustrated, wrappers, 18.5cm.

10920. *The Trentham Golf Club [Handbook]*. London: Golf Clubs Association, 1938, 19p, illustrated, wrappers, 18.5cm.

10930. *The Truro Golf Club [Handbook]*. London: Golf Clubs Association [ca1947] 21p, illustrated, wrappers, 18.5cm.

10940. *The Ulverston Golf Club [Handbook]*. London: Golf Clubs Association, 1939, 23p, illustrated, wrappers, 18.5cm.

10950. *The Vale of Leven Golf Club [Handbook]*. London: Golf Clubs Association [ca1947] 25p, illustrated, wrappers, 18.5cm.

10960. *The Wakefield Golf Club [Handbook]*. London: Golf Clubs Association [ca1949] 23p, illustrated, wrappers, 18cm.

10970. *The Wanstead Golf Club [Handbook]*. London: Golf Clubs Association [ca1947] 31p, illustrated, wrappers, 18.5cm.

10980. *The Warren Golf Club [Handbook]*. London: Golf Clubs Association [ca1947] 35p, illustrated, wrappers, 18cm.

10990. *The Waterlooville Golf Club [Handbook]*. London: Golf Clubs Association [ca1948] 16p, illustrated, wrappers, 18cm.

11000. *The Wentworth Golf Club [Handbook]*. London: Golf Clubs Association [ca1953] 41p, illustrated, wrappers, 18.5cm.

11010. *The West Byfleet Golf Club [Handbook]*. London: Golf Clubs Association [ca1950] 21p, illustrated, wrappers, 18cm.

11020. *The West Herts Golf Club [Handbook]*. London: Golf Clubs Association [ca1952] 19p, illustrated, wrappers, 18.5cm.

11030. *The West Kent Golf Club [Handbook]*. London: Golf Clubs Association, 1939, 19p, illustrated, wrappers, 18.5cm.

11040. *The Westgate-on-Sea and Birchington Golf Club [Handbook]*. London: Golf Clubs Association, 1929, 24p, illustrated, wrappers, 18.5cm.

11050. *The Weston-super-Mare Golf Club [Handbook]*. London: Golf Clubs Association [ca1949] 29p, illustrated, wrappers, 18cm.

11060. *The Whitley Bay Golf Club [Handbook]*. London: Golf Clubs Association, 1939, 21p, illustrated, wrappers, 18.5cm.

11070. *The Whitsand Bay Golf Club [Handbook]*. London: Golf Clubs Association [ca1948] 23p, illustrated, wrappers, 18.5cm.

11080. *The Windwhistle Golf Club [Handbook]*. London: Golf Clubs Association [ca1948] 19p, illustrated, wrappers, 18.5cm.

11090. *The Winterfield Golf Club [Handbook]*. London: Golf Clubs Association, 1938, 19p, illustrated, wrappers, 18.5cm.

11100. *The Withington Golf Club [Handbook]*. London: Golf Clubs Association [ca1948] 25p, illustrated, wrappers, 18.5cm.

11110. *The Woodcote Park Golf Club [Handbook]*. London: Golf Clubs Association [ca1952] 25p, illustrated, wrappers, 18.5cm.

11120. *The Woolton Golf Club [Handbook]*. London: Golf Clubs Association [ca1948] 15p, illustrated, wrappers, 18.5cm.

11130. *The Worcestershire Golf Club [Handbook]*. London: Golf Clubs Association, 1939, 29p, illustrated, wrappers, 18cm.

11140. *The Workington Golf Club [Handbook]*. London: Golf Clubs Association [ca1949] 10p, illustrated, wrappers, 18cm.

11150. *The Worlebury Golf Club [Handbook]*. London: Golf Clubs Association, 1938, 19p, illustrated, wrappers, 18.5cm.

11160. *The Worthing Golf Club [Handbook]*. London: Golf Clubs Association, 1938, 47p, illustrated, wrappers, 18.5cm.

11170. *The Wrekin Golf Club [Handbook]*. London: Golf Clubs Association, 1938, 19p, illustrated, wrappers, 18cm.

11180. *The Yelverton Golf Club [Handbook]*. London: Golf Clubs Association [ca1951] 16p, illustrated, wrappers, 18cm.

11190. *Thorndon Park Golf Club [Handbook]*. London: Golf Clubs Association [ca1948] 19p, illustrated, wrappers, 18cm.

11200. *Thurlestone Golf Club [Handbook]*. London: Golf Clubs Association, 1939, 31p, illustrated, wrappers, 18.5cm.

11210. *Torbay Country Club [Handbook]*. London: Golf Clubs Association [ca1947] 33p, illustrated, wrappers, 18cm.

11220. *Trevose Golf Club [Handbook].* London: Golf Clubs Association, 1934, 37p, illustrated, wrappers, 18.5cm.

11230. *Troon Golf Club [Handbook].* London: Golf Clubs Association [ca1951] 23p, illustrated, wrappers, 18.5cm.

11240. *Tyneside Golf Club [Handbook].* London: Golf Clubs Association [ca1948] 19p, illustrated, wrappers, 18cm.

11250. *Tyrrells Wood Golf Club [Handbook].* London: Golf Clubs Association, 1939, 20p, illustrated, wrappers, 18.5cm.

11260. *Walsall Golf Club [Handbook].* London: Golf Clubs Association [ca1956] 35p, illustrated, wrappers, 18cm.

11270. *West Hove Golf Club [Handbook].* London: Golf Clubs Association, 1939, 16p, illustrated, wrappers, 18.5cm.

11280. *When You Are Off Your Game.* London: Liverpool & London & Globe Insurance, 1st ed. [ca1929] 48p, illustrated, wrappers, 10.5cm.

11290. *Woodbridge Golf Club [Handbook].* London: Golf Clubs Association [ca1948] 15p, illustrated, wrappers, 18.5cm.

11300. *York Golf Club [Handbook].* London: Golf Clubs Association [ca1951] 19p, illustrated, wrappers, 18.5cm.

Bryan, Dorothy and Marguerite.

11320. *Michael and Patsy on the Golf Links.* Garden City, New York: Doubleday, Doran, 1st ed. 1933 [30p] illustrated, illustrated boards, 20.5cm.

Bulger [pseud for William Wilson]

11340. *Echoes from the Links.* Edinburgh: J &J Gray, 1st ed. [1924] 92p, illustrated wrappers, 18cm.

Burke Golf Company

11360. *Golf As She Ought To Be Played.* Newark, Ohio: Burke Golf, 1st ed. [1929] 18p, illustrated, wrappers, 13cm.

11370. *Making the Clubhead Work.* Newark, Ohio: Burke Golf, 1st ed. [1931] 16p, illustrated, illustrated wrappers, 16cm.

Burke, Jack

11390. *Ten Lessons in Golf.* St. Paul, Minnesota: Brown & Bigelow, 1st ed. [ca1923] 32p, illustrated, illustrated wrappers, 15.5cm.

11400. *The Natural Way to Better Golf.* Garden City, New York: Hanover House, 1st ed. [1954] 151p, illustrated by Norman Todhunter, cloth, 23.5cm.

11410. 1st UK ed. London: Constable, 1955, 151p, cloth, 21.5cm.

11420. pbk. ed. New York: Bantam, 1955, 119p, illustrated wrappers, 18cm.

Burke, James Francis

11440. *Guard the Game of Golf Against the Danger of Becoming a Humdrum, Haphazard, Meaningless Pastime.* Chicago: Western Golf Association, 1st ed. 1925, 15p, wrappers, 20.5cm.

Burnham Ladies Golf Club

11460. *Burnham Ladies Golf Club [Handbook].* Gloucester & London: British Publishing [ca1947] 16p, illustrated, illustrated wrappers, 16.5cm.

Burns, Ralph F.

11480. *Historical Review of LaGrange Country Club 1899-1949.* La Grange, Illinois: Privately Printed, 1st ed. 1949, 32p, illustrated, illustrated wrappers, 28cm.

Burton, Miles

11500. *Tragedy At the Thirteenth Hole.* London: The Crime Club, 1st ed. [1933] 252p, cloth, 18.5cm.

11510. pbk. ed. London: The Crime Club [ca1934] 128p, illustrated wrappers, 22cm.

Burton, Percy

11530. *To Sweden & Denmark & Back: Being a brief diary of the tour of an English golf team.* [London] Privately Printed, 1st ed. 1947 [4p] illustrated, illustrated wrappers, 21cm.

Burton, Richard

11550. *Length with Discretion.* London: Hutchinson, 1st ed. [ca1940] 190p, illustrated, cloth, 18.5cm.

Business Man's Golf Course.

11570. *Business Man's Golf Course. Elements of Golf; Wooden Clubs; Iron Clubs; Approaching and Putting; Faults and Their Remedies; Co-Ordinating Your Game. Six Volumes.* Springfield, Massachusetts: Business Man's Golf Course [1924] 1st ed. 28p to 32p each, illustrated wrappers, 16.5cm.

Butler, William Meredith

11590. *The Golfer's Manual.* London: T. Werner Laurie, 1st ed. [ca1907] 171p, illustrated, decorative cloth, 19cm, introduction by Dr. Macnamara.

11600. *The Golfer's Guide.* Philadelphia: Lippincott, 1st American ed. [ca1907] 171p, illustrated, decorative cloth, 19cm, introduction by Dr. Macnamara. American title of "The Golfer's Manual."

Butte Country Club

11620. *Observing 30 Years with the Present Butte Country Club House.* Butte, Montana: Privately Printed, 1st ed. 1945 [10p] illustrated, illustrated wrappers, 28cm.

11630. *Observing 50 Years with the Butte Country Club 1899-1949.* Butte, Montana: Privately Printed, 1st ed. 1949 [18p] illustrated, illustrated wrappers, 27cm.

Buttress, Howard P. [Mrs]

11650. *A History of Women's Golf in Southern California.* edited by. [Los Angeles] Privately Printed, 1st ed. [ca1959] 59p, illustrated, wrappers, 20.5cm, compiled by Mrs. Edwin C. Berg, Mrs. George Midgley, Mrs. E.A. Winstanberg and Mrs. Glen Dudley.

Buxton & High Peak Golf Club

11670. *The Buxton & High Peak Golf Club [Handbook].* London: Golf Clubs Association [ca1948] 16p, illustrated, wrappers, 18cm.

C., W.K.

11690. *History of the Warrender Golf Club.* Edinburgh: Privately Printed, 1st ed. 1906, 31p, illustrated, wrappers, 16.5cm.

Caddie Manual

11710. *Caddie Manual.* St. Louis, Missouri: Burgess-Mason, 1st ed. [ca1920] 36p, illustrated, wrappers, 15.5cm.

Caddy Coloring Book

11730. *Caddy Coloring Book.* New York: Saalfield, 1st ed. 1950 [16p] illustrated, shaped illustrated wrappers, 27.5cm.

Caernarvonshire Golf Club

11750. *Caernarvonshire Golf Club [Handbook].* Derby & Cheltenham, England: New Centurion, 1937, 20p, illustrated, wrappers, 18.5cm.

Cain, Sylvia Potter

11770. *Instructions for Elementary Golfers.* [Palo Alto, California] Stanford University, 1st ed. [1939] 14p, wrappers, 21.5cm.

Calkins, Leighton

11790. *A System for Club Handicapping.* New York: Arthur Pottow, 1st ed. 1905 [8p] wrappers, 20.5cm.

Callaway, Lionel F.

11810. *New and Improved System of Simplified Handicapping for Golfers.* Ft. Lauderdale, Florida: Privately Printed, 1st ed. [1952] [25p] wrappers, 14cm.

Came Down Golf Club

11830. *The Came Down Golf Club [Handbook].* London: Golf Clubs Association, 1933, 22p, illustrated, wrappers, 18.5cm.

Camerer, Dave

11850. *Golf with the Masters: The secret to better golf.* New York: A.S. Barnes, 1st ed. [1955] 159p, illustrated, cloth, 24.5cm.

11860. *Improve Your Golf.* edited by. New York: Random House, 1st ed. [1958] 128p, illustrated, cloth, 23.5cm.

11870. pbk. ed. New York: Maco [1958] 128p, illustrated, illustrated wrappers, 23.5cm. later printing.

Campbell, Guy Colin

11890. *Golf At Prince's and Deal.* Sandwich, England: Privately Printed, 1st ed. [ca1950] 39p, illustrated, decorative boards, 24cm, foreword by Bernard Darwin.

11900. *Golf for Beginners.* London: C. Arthur Pearson, 1st ed. 1922, 124p, illustrated, decorative cloth, 18.5cm, forewords by J.L. Low and Cecil K. Hutchinson.

11910. 1st American ed. New York: F.A. Stokes, 1922, 124p, illustrated, decorative cloth, 18.5cm. later printings.

Campbell, Patrick

11930. *Round Ireland with a Golf Bag.* Dublin, Ireland: Irish Times, 1st ed. [ca1937] 31p, illustrated, illustrated wrappers, 24.5cm.

Canausa, F.C.

11950. *How To Win At Golf.* New York: Vantage Press, 1st ed. [1956] 91p, illustrated, cloth, 20cm, introduction by Floyd L. Parks.

Cannington Park Golf Club

11970. *Cannington Park Golf Club [Handbook].* London: Vickery Kyrle [ca1935] 11p, illustrated, illustrated wrappers, 18cm.

Carl, Henry M.

11990. *Analytic Physical Culture Golf: home exercises for automatic correct form and greater golf.* Chickasha, Oklahoma: Privately Printed, 1st ed. [ca1928] 88p, illustrated, wrappers, 20cm.

Carnoustie Golf Courses

12010. *Carnoustie Golf Course.* Carnoustie, Scotland: Carnoustie Golf Course Committee, 1st ed. 1931, 40p, illustrated, wrappers, 27cm. note: cover title " Carnoustie, The New Championship Golf Course."

12020. *Carnoustie Golf Course.* Carnoustie, Scotland: Three Private Citizens of Carnoustie, 1st ed. 1933, 44p, illustrated, wrappers, 26.5cm, forewords by James Wright, R.R. Webster Braille, J.W.A. Simpson.

12030. *Carnoustie and Its Golf Courses*. Carnoustie, Scotland: Privately Printed, 1st ed. 1937, 52p, illustrated, wrappers, 26.5cm, foreword by James Wright. note: cover title "Carnoustie Commentary."

12040. *Carnoustie Commentary, Championship Supplement*. Carnoustie, Scotland: Carnoustie Golf Course Committee, 1937, 16p, illustrated, wrappers, 26.5cm.

Cavalcade of Golf

12060. *Cavalcade of Golf: from King James to King [Bobby] Jones*. [London] Silver King, 1st ed. [ca1935] 9p, illustrated, illustrated wrappers, 14cm.

12070. *Cavalcade of Golf: from King James to Silver King*. London: Silvertown, 1st ed. [ca1938] [16p] illustrated, illustrated wrappers, 20.5cm.

Cavanagh, Walter

12090. *The Art of Golf*. Greenfield, Massachusetts: Privately Printed, 1st ed. [1927] 76p, illustrated, wrappers, 19.5cm.

Caw, William,

12110. *King James VI Golf Club, Record and Records*. Edinburgh: R.&R. Clark, 1st ed. 1912, 68p, illustrated, decorative cloth, 18.5cm.

Chadwick, H.H.

12130. *Golf in Vermont, A Directory of Courses*. Montpelier, Vermont: Vermont Development Commission, 1st ed. 1946, 13p, illustrated wrappers, 17.5cm.

Chambers, Charles E.S.

12150. *Early Golf At Bruntsfield and Leith*. [Edinburgh] Privately Printed, offprint, 1932, 10p, wrappers, 24.5cm, extracted from the 18th volume of the Book of the Old Edinburgh Club, April 1932.

Channon, Eric

12170. *Lewes Golf Club [Handbook]*. Bristol & London: Temple Publicity Services [ca1952] 20p, illustrated, wrappers, 18.5cm.

Chapman, Hay

12190. *Law of the Links: Rules, Principles and Etiquette of Golf.* San Francisco: Privately Printed, 1st ed. 1922, 61p, cloth, 17cm. later printing.

Chapman, Richard and Ledyard Sands

12210. *Golf As I Play It.* New York: Carlyle House, 1st ed. 1940, 158p, illustrated, cloth, 22.5cm, foreword by Grantland Rice.

Charles River Country Club

12230. *Life At the Charles River Country Club 1921-1946.* Newton Centre, Massachusetts: Privately Printed, 1st ed. 1946, 51p, illustrated, 1/4 cloth, illustrated boards, 30cm.

Chattell, C.C.

12250. *The Golfers' Guide 1908: A complete handbook of useful information for golf clubs and their members.* Chicago: Privately Printed, 1st ed. 1908, 289p, illustrated, decorative cloth, 22cm.

12260. 2d ed. 1909, 239p, illustrated, decorative cloth, 22cm.

Cheney, Edward

12280. *An Eightsome of "Golfing Badgers."* [New York] Privately Printed, 1st ed. [ca1945] [8p] illustrated, wrappers, 17cm.

Chislehurst Golf Club

12300. *Chislehurst Golf Club [Handbook].* Cheltenham & London: Ed J. Burrow [ca1928] 32p, illustrated, illustrated wrappers, 16.5cm.

Christie, Agatha

12320. *The Murder on the Links.* London: John Lane, 1923, 298p, cloth, 18.5cm. later printings.

12340. 1st American ed. New York: Dodd, Mead, 1923, 298p, cloth, 18.5cm. later printings.

Chronicles, Joe [pseud for Joe Chapman]

12370. *Uncle Jed, Caddie Master.* Philadelphia: Privately Printed, 1st ed. 1934, 229p, illustrated, cloth, 20cm.

Clapcott, C.B.

12390. *The History of Handicapping*. NP: Privately Printed, 1st ed. [ca1924] 10p, wrappers, 21.5cm.

12400. *The Rules of the Ten Oldest Golf Clubs from 1754-1848: together with the rules of the Royal Ancient Golf Club of St. Andrews for the years 1858, 1877, 1888*. Edinburgh: Golf Monthly, limited ed. [500 copies] 1935, 127p, cloth, 21.5cm.

Clark, Charles E.

12420. *The New Haven Country Club, The First Fifty Years 1898-1948*. New Haven, Connecticut: Privately Printed, 1st ed. 1949, 66p, illustrated, wrappers, 20.5cm.

Clarke, A.B. [Mrs]

12440. *History of Elie Golf House Club Jubilee 1925*. Elie, Scotland: Privately Printed, 1st ed. 1925, 15p, illustrated, illustrated wrappers, 25cm.

Clarke, Charles and Mottram Gilbert

12460. *Commonsense Golf*. London: Simpkin, Marshall, Hamilton & Kent, 1st ed. 1914, 132p, illustrated, cloth, 18cm.

12470. 1st American ed. New York: McBride, Nast, 1914, 132p, illustrated, cloth, 18cm.

Clarke, Jr., Fred C.

12490. *The Woodstock Country Club 1895-1959*. Woodstock, Vermont: Privately Printed, 1st ed. 1959, 61p, illustrated, illustrated wrappers, 28cm.

Cleveland, Charles Blair

12510. *Approaching and Putting: The key to a lower golf score*. New York: Crowell, 1st ed. 1953 150p, illustrated, cloth, 20cm, introduction by Walter Hagen.

Cliffer, Harold J.

12530. *Planning the Golf Club House*. Chicago: National Golf Foundation, 1st ed. 1956, 96p, illustrated, cloth, 27.5cm. later printing.

Clougher, T.R.

12550. *Golf Clubs of the Empire: The Golfing Annual 1926*. London: Clougher, 1st ed. not located.

12560. *Golf Clubs of the Empire: The Golfing Annual 1927*. London: Clougher, 2d ed. 1927, 352p, illustrated, decorative cloth, 22cm.

12570. *Golf Clubs of the Empire: The Golfing Annual 1928*. London: Clougher, 3d ed. 1928, 468p, illustrated, decorative cloth, 22cm.

12580. *Golf Clubs of the Empire: The Golfing Annual 1929*. London: Clougher, 4th ed. 1929, 512p, illustrated, decorative cloth, 22cm.

12590. *Golf Clubs of the Empire: The Golfing Annual 1930*. London: Clougher, 5th ed. 1930, 546p, illustrated, decorative cloth, 22cm.

12600. *Golf Clubs of the Empire: The Golfing Annual 1931*. London: Clougher, 6th ed. 1931, 528p, illustrated, decorative cloth, 22cm.

12610. *Golf Clubs of the Empire: The Golfing Annual 1932*. London: Clougher, 7th ed. 1932, 516p, illustrated, decorative cloth, 22cm.

Clow, Jr., William Ellsworth

12630. *Good Golf*. Lake Forest, Illinois: Privately Printed, 1st ed. 1942, 40p, illustrated, illustrated wrappers, 23cm.

Coffey, Martin E.

12650. *Golfing in Ireland*. Dublin: Harpers, 2d ed, 1953, 195p, illustrated, cloth, 21cm. note: for first edition see J.P. Murray, "Golfing in Ireland."

Colchester Golf Club

12670. *Colchester Golf Club [Handbook]*. Cheltenham & London: Ed. J. Burrow [ca1938] 16p, illustrated, wrappers, 16.5cm.

Coll, Ben,

12690. *I Love Golf*. Johnstown, Pennsylvania: Privately Printed, 1st ed. [1950] 64p, illustrated by John I. Coleman, illustrated wrappers, 19.5cm.

Collett, Glenna

12710. *Golf for Young Players*. Boston: Little Brown, 1st ed. 1926, 115p, illustrated, decorative cloth, 19cm, foreword by Elenora Randolph Sears.

12720. facsimile ed. Cincinnati, Ohio: Old Golf Shop, 1984, 115p, illustrated, cloth, 18.5cm, also a few of a limited edition bound in leather-for Curtis Cup participants, introduction by Glenna Collett Vare.

12730. *Ladies in the Rough*. New York: Knopf, 1st ed. 1928, 228p, illustrated, cloth, 20.5cm, with James M. Neville, foreword by Bobby Jones. later printing.

12740. 1st UK ed. London: Knopf, 1929, 208p, illustrated, cloth, 19cm, introduction by Bobby Jones.

Collier, Basil

12760. *Local Thunder*. London: William Heinemann, 1st ed. 1936, 284p, cloth, 19cm.

Colonel

12780. *Golfing By Numbers: One action for playing all strokes [except putting]*. London: Alexander-Ousley, 1st ed. 1927, 31p, illustrated by L.M. Duffy, cloth, 18.5cm.

Colt, Harry S. and C.H. Alison

12800. *Some Essays on Golf Course Architecture*. London: Country Life & George Newnes, 1st ed. 1920, 69p, illustrated, 1/4 cloth, boards, 18.5cm, with contributions by Dr. A. Mackenzie, Horace G. Hutchinson, John L. Low.

Colville, James

12820. *The Glasgow Golf Club 1787-1907*. Glasgow: John Smith, 1st ed. 1907, 172p, illustrated, cloth, 18.5cm.

Colwyn Bay Golf Club

12840. *Colwyn Bay Golf Club [Handbook]*. London: Golf Clubs Association, 1934, 19p, illustrated, wrappers, 18.5cm.

Compston, Archie and Stanley Anderson

12880. *Love on the Fairway: A Romance of the Open Championship*. London: T. Werner Laurie, 1st ed. 1936, 123p, illustrated by fforne, decorative cloth, 18.5cm, foreword by Henry Cotton.

Compston, Archie and Henry Longhurst

12900. *Go Golfing*. London: Duckworth, 1st ed. 1937, 105p, illustrated, cloth, 18cm.

Connolly, Robert

12920. *How to Become A Golfer and Have No One to Blame but Yourself*. Johannesburgh, South Africa: Little Man, 1st ed. [ca1955] illustrated, illustrated wrappers, 18.5cm.

Conroy, William

12940. *Fifty Years of Apawamis*. Rye, New York: Privately Printed, limited ed. [500 copies] 1940, 245p, illustrated, decorative cloth, 25.5cm.

Converse, A.D.

12960. *Toy Town Golf Course*. Winchenden, Massachusetts: Privately Printed, 1st ed. [ca1926] [26p] illustrated, illustrated boards, 20.5cm.

Cooper, David

12980. *Golfing Resorts on the Glasgow and South-Western Railway*. Glasgow: Glasgow and South-Western Railway, 1st ed. 1901, 48p, illustrated, illustrated wrappers, 14cm, later printings.

Cooper, Samuel W.

13000. *The Nineteenth Hole and Other Lyrics of the Links*. Philadelphia: Driver & Iron, 1st ed. [1921] 16p, illustrated, wrappers, 23.5cm.

Cortissoz, Royal

13020. *Nine Holes of Golf*. New York: Scribner, 1st ed. 1922, 97p, illustrated, decorative boards, 19cm.

13030. *The Ekwanok Country Club*. Manchester, Vermont: Privately Printed, 1st ed. 1937, 22p, illustrated, 1/4 cloth, boards, 30.5cm.

Cotton, Henry

13050. *Golf: Being a short treatise for the use of young people who aspire to proficiency in the Royal and Ancient game*. London: Eyre & Spottiswoode, 1st ed. 1931, 147p, illustrated, cloth, 18.5cm, foreword by Bernard Darwin. later printings.

13060. 1st American ed. New York: Coward-McCann, 1931, 147p, illustrated, cloth, 18.5cm, foreword by Bernard Darwin.

13070. *Hints on Play with Steel Shafts.* Liverpool, England: British Steel Golf Shafts, 1st ed. [ca1933] 40p, illustrated wrappers, 22cm.

13080. *My Golfing Album.* London: Country Life, 1st ed. 1959, 248p, illustrated, cloth, 25.5cm, later printing.

13090. *My Swing.* London: Country Life, 1st ed. 1952, 144p, illustrated, cloth, 21.5cm.

13100. *Some Golfing Ifs.* London: British Steel Golf Shafts, 1st ed. [ca1948] 40p, illustrated, illustrated wrappers and leather, 21.5cm.

13110. *This Game of Golf.* London: Country Life, 1st ed. 1948, 248p, illustrated, cloth, 25.5cm, foreword by Bernard Darwin. later printings.

13120. 1st American ed. New York: Scribner's, 1948, 248p, illustrated, cloth, 25.5cm, foreword by Bernard Darwin. later printings.

Country Club of York

13140. *Country Club of York Yearbook in which the History of the Club is Reviewed.* York, Pennsylvania: Privately Printed, 1st ed. 1929, 77p, illustrated, 1/4 cloth, boards, 22cm.

Cousins, Geoffrey

13160. *Golfers At Law: The rules of golf, how they were evolved by pioneers, developed by events and the habits of golfers, influenced by national and international forces, and modified by official decisions.* London: Stanley Paul, 1st ed. 1958, 144p, illustrated, cloth, 19.5cm.

13170. 1st American ed. New York: Knopf, 1959, 201p, illustrated, cloth, 18.5cm, foreword by Joseph Dey, Jr.

Coventry Hearsall Golf Club

13190. *Coventry Hearsall Golf Club [Handbook].* Derby & Cheltenham, England: New Centurion, 1937, 24p, illustrated, wrappers, 18.5cm.

Cox, Wiffy

13210. *How to Cut Strokes Off Your Golf Score.* New York: Employee Relations, 1st ed. [1960] 14p, illustrated by Robert J. Lee, illustrated wrappers, 18cm, as told to Joe Gambatese.

Cox, William J.

13230. *Can I Help You? The Guide to Better Golf.* London: Ernest Benn, 1st ed. 1954, 95p, illustrated, cloth, 24.5cm, foreword by Tom Scott.

13240. *Play Better Golf.* London: Frederick Muller, 1st ed. 1952, 96p, illustrated, cloth, 18cm, introduction by Tom Scott.

13250. *W. J. Cox and Golf.* London: Niblick Publishing, 1st ed. [ca1936] 32p, illustrated, illustrated wrappers, 19cm.

Crane, Charles E.

13270. *Brattleboro Country Club.* Brattleboro, Vermont: Vermont Peoples National Bank, 1st ed. 1926, 32p, illustrated, illustrated wrappers, 15.5cm.

Crane, Leo

13290. *California Golf Directory.* Fresno, California: Privately Printed, 1st ed. [1953] 58p, illustrated wrappers, 21cm.

Craven, Frank

13310. *The 19th Hole, A Comedy in Three Acts.* New York: Samuel French, 1st ed. [1928] 104p, illustrated, illustrated wrappers, 19cm.

Crawford, Macgregor & Canby

13330. *Golf: The Game of Games.* Dayton, Ohio: Crawford, Macgregor & Canby, 1st ed. [ca1922] 24p, illustrated, illustrated wrappers, 17.5cm, later printings.

13340. *How Boys Can Enjoy Golf.* Dayton, Ohio: Crawford, McGregor & Canby, 2d ed [1920] [8p] illustrated, illustrated wrappers, 15cm. note: first edition not located.

13350. *Stepping Stones To A Golf Course.* [Dayton, Ohio] Crawford, McGregor & Canby, 1st ed. [1921] 24p, illustrated, illustrated wrappers, 18cm.

Crawley, Leonard

13370. *Playfair Golf Annual 1950*. London: Playfair Books, 1st ed. 1950, 208p, illustrated, illustrated wrappers, 18cm, foreword by Bernard Darwin, 18cm.

13380. *Playfair Golf Annual 1951*. London: Playfair Books, 2d ed. 1951, 210p, illustrated, illustrated wrappers, 18cm.

13390. *Playfair Golf Annual 1952*. London: Playfair Books, 3d ed. 1952, 176p, illustrated, illustrated wrappers, 18cm.

13400. *Playfair Golf Annual 1953*. London: Playfair Books, 4th ed. 1953, 240p, illustrated, illustrated wrappers, 18cm.

13410. *The Golfing Year 1954*. London: Playfair, 5th ed. 1954, 208p, illustrated, cloth, 21.5cm. note: previously titled "Playfair Golf Annual."

Cremin, Eric

13430. *Par Golf*. edited by John Fennell. Sydney & London: Angus & Robertson, 1st ed. 1952, 127p, illustrated, cloth, 20cm, foreword by Norman Von Nida.

Crews, D.D. and J.G Germuga

13450. *Caddie Handbook*. Rochester, New York: Privately Printed, 1st ed. [1946] 14p, illustrated wrappers, 15cm.

Crogen, Corrine

13470. *Golf Fundamentals for Students and Teachers*. Palo Alto, California: N-P, 1st ed. [1960] 79p, illustrated, wrappers, 28cm.

13480. *Golf Fundamentals*. Palo Alto, California: N-P, 2d ed. rev. 1964, 83p, illustrated, illustrated wrappers, 28cm.

13490. 3d ed. rev. Long Beach, California: Privately Printed, 1973, 105p, illustrated, illustrated wrappers, 28cm.

Crombie, Charles

13510. *The Rules of Golf Illustrated*. London: Golf Illustrated, 1st ed. [ca1905] [50p] illustrated, illustrated boards, 29cm.

13520. *Some of the Rules of Golf*. London: Ariel Press, reprint ed. [1966] [26p] illustrated,boards, 30.5cm, introduction by Alan Jenkins.

13530. 1st American ed. reprint, New York: Taplinger, 1966 [26p] illustrated, 1/2 cloth, illustrated boards, 30.5cm, introduction by Alan Jenkins.

Cromie, Robert A.

13550. *New Angles on Putting and Chipping: Based on the principle originated and perfected by the late Mark G. Harris.* Chicago: Reilly & Lee, 1st ed. 1960, 48p, illustrated by William O'Brien, illustrated wrappers, 34cm, foreword by Lloyd Mangrum.

Croome, A.C.M.

13570. *The Camberley Heath Golf Club.* Camberley, England: Privately Printed, 1st ed. 1913, 22p, illustrated, cloth, 14cm.

Cummings, George Lewis

13590. *It Goes Where You Hit It: A treatise on golf.* [Toronto] Privately Printed, 1st ed. [1948] 56p, illustrated, decorative cloth, 24.5cm, later printing.

Cunningham, Andrew S.

13610. *Lundin Links, Upper & Lower Largo and Leven.* Portobello, Scotland: Thomas Adams, 1st ed. 1913, 132p, wrappers, 21.5cm. later printing.

13620. *The Golf Clubs Round Largo Bay: Inner Leven, Leven, Leven Thistle, Lundin, Wemyss, Methil, Leven Ladies and Lundin Ladies.* Leven, Scotland: Purves & Cunningham, 1st ed. 1909, 146p, illustrated, cloth, 17.5cm.

Cunningham, Carl

13640. *Down the Middle.* NP: Privately Printed, 1st ed. [1952] [30p] illustrated, wrappers, 17cm.

Curtiss, Frederic H. and John Heard

13660. *The Country Club 1882-1932.* Brookline, Massachusetts: Privately Printed, 1st ed. 1932, 212p, illustrated, decorative cloth, 26cm.

13670. special presentation ed. [5 copies] 1932, 213p, illustrated, full leather, raised bands, teg, 26cm.

Dalbeattie Golf Club

13690. *The Book of Dalbeattie Golf Club.* Dalbeattie, Scotland: Privately Printed, 1st ed. [1912] 51p, illustrated, illustrated wrappers, 24.5cm.

Daly, Fred

13710. *Golf As I See It*. London: Sporting Handbooks, 1st ed. [1951] 126p, illustrated, cloth, 18.5cm.

Dann, Marshall

13730. *Golfdom's Greatest Tournaments*. Detroit, Michigan: Packard Sports Library, 1st ed. [1952] 14p, illustrated, illustrated wrappers, 18cm.

Dante, James [Jim] and Leo Diegel

13750. *The Nine Bad Shots of Golf and What to Do About Them*. New York: Whittlesey House, 1st ed. [1947] 189p, illustrated, cloth, 20cm, in collaboration with Len Elliot. later printings.

13760. 1st UK ed. London: Herbert Jenkins, 1948, 158p, illustrated, cloth, 19cm, later printings.

13770. 1st Canadian ed. Toronto: McGraw-Hill [1948] 189p, illustrated, cloth, 20.5cm.

13780. pbk. ed. New York: Cornerstone Library, 1961, 186p, illustrated, illustrated wrappers, 20cm, later printings.

Dante, Joseph [Joe] and Len Elliott

13800. *Stop that Slice*. New York: Thomas Y. Crowell, 1st ed. [1953] 60p, illustrated by Bill Crawford, cloth, 25cm.

13810. pbk. ed. New York: McGraw-Hill [1953] 59p, illustrated by Bill Crawford, illustrated wrappers, 25cm.

13820. 1st UK ed. London: Herbert Jenkins, 1954, 112p, illustrated by Bill Crawford, cloth, 19.5cm.

Darsie, Darsie L.

13840. *My Greatest Day in Golf*. New York: A.S. Barnes, 1st ed. [1950] 210p, illustrated, cloth, 21.5cm.

13850. 1st UK ed. London: Alvin Redman, 1952, 254p, illustrated, cloth, 21.5cm, with Arthur J. Lacey.

Darwin, Bernard

13870. *A Day's Golf At Leeds Castle, May 15th, 1934*. London: Privately Printed, 1st ed. 1934, 8p, illustrated, cloth, 29cm.

13880. *A Friendly Round*. London: Mills & Boon, 1st ed. 1922, 142p, cloth, 19cm.

13890. *A Golfer's Gallery by Old Masters*. London: Country Life, 1st ed. [ca1920] 19p text, 18 mounted plates, illustrated, boards, 40.5cm.

13900. limited ed. signed [500 copies] [ca1920] 19p text, 19plates, illustrated, cloth, 43.5cm. note: one additional plate.

13910. *A Round of Golf on the L[ondon] & N[orth] E[astern] R[ailway]*. [London] London & Northeastern Railway, 1st ed. [ca1925] 127p, illustrated, cloth, 20cm.

13920. *A Round of Golf on the London & North Eastern Railway*. [London] London & Northeastern Railway, 2d ed. [ca1927] 153p, illustrated, wrappers, 18cm.

13930. 3d ed. 1937, 126p, illustrated, illustrated wrappers, 21.5cm.

13940. *About These New Rules, Bernard Darwin Explains....* London: Twiss & Brownings & Hallows, 1st ed. [ca1954] [6p] illustrated, illustrated wrappers, 20cm.

13950. *Aldeburgh Golf Club [Handbook]*. London: Golf Clubs Association, 1939, 27p, illustrated, wrappers, 18cm.

13960. *Ashridge Golf Club [Handbook]*. London: Golf Clubs Association, 1938, 29p, illustrated, wrappers, 18cm.

13970. *Berkhamsted Golf Club [Handbook]*. London: Golf Clubs Association [ca1946] 19p, illustrated, wrappers, 18 cm.

13980. *British Golf*. London: Collins, 1st ed. 1946, 47p, illustrated, decorative boards, 22 cm.

13990. *Burhill Club [Handbook]*. London: Golf Clubs Association, 1939, 23p, illustrated, illustrated wrappers, 18.5cm.

14000. *Come to Britain for Golf: Golf in Great Britain and Northern Ireland*. London: Travel Association of Great Britain & Northern Ireland, 1st ed. [ca1946] [8p] illustrated, illustrated wrappers [folder] 23cm.

14010. *Every Idle Dream*. London: Collins, 1st ed. 1948, 254p, illustrated by Elinor Darwin, cloth, 21.5cm.

14020. *Golf Between Two Wars.* London: Chatto & Windus, 1st ed. 1944, 227p, illustrated, cloth, 20.5 cm. later printing.

14030. facsimile ed. New York: Classics of Golf [1985] 227p, illustrated, cloth, 22.5cm, introduction by Herbert Warren Wind, afterword by Ben Crenshaw.

14040. *Golf From the Times: a reprint, revised and re-arranged of some articles on Golf by The Times Special Contributor.* London: The Times, 1st ed. [ca1912] 141p, cloth, 21cm.

14050. *Golf In Great Britain and Ireland.* London: Travel Association of Great Britain & Ireland, 1st ed. [ca1930] 39p, illustrated, wrappers, 13cm.

14060. *Golf: Pleasures of Life Series.* London: Burke, 1st ed. 1954, 222p, illustrated, cloth, 21.5 cm.

14070. *Golf: Some Hints and Suggestions.* London: Country Life, 1st ed. 1920, 32p, illustrated wrappers, 18.5cm.

14080. *Golfing By Paths.* London: Country Life, 1st ed. 1946, 203p, illustrated, cloth, 21 cm.

14090. *Green Memories.* London: Hodder & Stoughton, 1st ed. [ca1928] 332p, illustrated, cloth, 22cm.

14100. *Harewood Downs Golf Club [Handbook].* London: Golf Clubs Association, [ca1948] 25p, illustrated, wrappers, 18.5cm.

14110. *Hints on Golf, with supplement on Golfing Kit.* London: Burberry's, 1st ed. [1912] 55p, illustrated, 1/4 cloth, boards and wrappers, 21.5cm.

14120. *Hunstanton Golf Club [Handbook]*. London: Golf Clubs Association, 1928, 28p, illustrated, wrappers, 18.5cm.

14130. *James Braid*. London: Hodder & Stoughton, 1st ed. 1952, 196p, illustrated, cloth, 20cm.

14140. facsimile ed. limited. [200 copies] Cincinnati, Ohio: Old Golf Shop, 1981, 196p, illustrated, leather, 20cm.

14150. *Knole Park Golf Club [Handbook]*. London: Golf Clubs Association, 1926, 28p, illustrated, wrappers, 18.5cm.

14160. *Life Is Sweet Brother*. London: Collins, 1st ed. 1940, 285p, illustrated, cloth, 21.5 cm.

14170. *North Foreland Golf Club [Handbook]*. London: Golf Clubs Association, 1939, 29p, illustrated, wrappers, 18.5cm.

14180. *North Hants Golf Club [Handbook]*. London: Golf Clubs Association [ca1949] 15p, illustrated, wrappers, 18cm.

14190. *Out of the Rough*. London: Chapman & Hall, 1st ed. [ca1932] 336p, decorative cloth, 18.5cm.

14200. *Pack Clouds Away*. London: Collins, 1st ed. 1941, 288p, cloth, 21.5 cm.

14210. *Playing the Like*. London: Chapman & Hall, 1st ed. 1934, 246p, decorative cloth, 18.5 cm.

14220. *Prince's Golf Club [Handbook]*. London: Golf Clubs Association, 1938, 27p, illustrated, wrappers, 18.5cm.

14230. *Rubs of the Green*. London: Chapman & Hall, 1st ed. 1936, 260p, decorative cloth, 18.5 cm.

14240. *Second Shots: Casual Talks about Golf*. London: George Newnes, 1st ed. 1930, 178p, illustrated, cloth, 15.5cm.

14250. *Six Golfing Shots By Six Famous Players*. London: Dormeuil Freres, 1st ed. [1927] 46p, illustrated, wrappers, 23cm.

14260. *St. Enodoc Golf Club [Handbook]*. London: Golf Clubs Association [ca1947] 41p, illustrated, wrappers, 18.5cm.

14270. *Tee Shots and Others*. London: Kegan Paul, Trench, Trubner, 1st ed. 1911, 271p, illustrated by E.W. Mitchell, decorative cloth, 18.5 cm.

14280. 1st American ed. Philadelphia: David McKay [ca1911] 271p, illustrated by E.W. Mitchell, decorative cloth, 18.5cm.

14290. limited ed. facsimile, numbered, slipcased [1500 copies] Far Hills: New Jersey, USGA, 1984, 271p, decorative cloth, 19.5cm, introductory essay by Lady Joyce Heathcoat Amory.

14300. *The Beaconsfield Golf Club [Handbook]*. London: Golf Clubs Association [ca1947] 23p, illustrated, wrappers, 18cm.

14310. *The Bogner Golf Club [Handbook]*. London: Golf Clubs Association, 1938, 29p, illustrated, wrappers, 18cm.

14320. *The Burnham & Berrow Golf Club [Handbook]*. London: Golf Clubs Association, 1938, 31p, illustrated, wrappers, 18cm.

14330. *The Carlisle & Silloth Golf Club [Handbook]*. London: Golf Clubs Association [ca1946] 23p, illustrated, wrappers, 18cm.

14340. *The Crowborough Beacon Golf Club [Handbook]*. London: Golf Clubs Association, 1934, 27p, illustrated, wrappers, 18.5cm.

14350. *The Dorset Golf Club [Handbook]*. London: Golf Clubs Association, 1932, 32p, illustrated, wrappers, 18cm.

14360. *The Downe Golf Club [Handbook]*. London: Golf Clubs Association [ca1947] 39p, illustrated, wrappers, 18cm.

14370. *The East Devon Golf Club [Handbook]*. London: Golf Clubs Association [ca1947] 27p, illustrated, wrappers, 18.5cm.

14380. *The Farnham Golf Club [Handbook]*. London: Golf Clubs Association, 1938, 21p, illustrated, wrappers, 18cm.

14390. *The Formby Golf Club [Handbook].* London: Golf Clubs Association, 1934, 27p, illustrated, wrappers, 18.5cm.

14400. *The Frilford Heath Golf Club [Handbook].* London: Golf Clubs Association, 1938, 23p, illustrated, wrappers, 18.5cm.

14410. *The Golf Courses of the British Isles.* London: Duckworth, 1st ed. 1910, 253p, illustrated by Harry Roundtree, decorative cloth, 22 cm.

14420. 1st American ed. New York: Appleton, 1911, 253p, illustrated by Harry Roundtree, cloth, 22cm.

14430. *The Golf Courses of Great Britain.* London: Jonathan Cape, 2d ed. 1925, 287p, illustrated, cloth, 23cm. note: eliminated from this the second edition of "The Golf Courses of the British Isles" are the courses of Ireland.

14440. *The Hayling Golf Club [Handbook].* London: Golf Clubs Association [ca1947] 23p, illustrated, wrappers, 18.5cm.

14450. *The Ifield Golf and Country Club [Handbook].* London: Golf Clubs Association [ca1947] 24p, illustrated, wrappers, 18.5cm.

14460. *The Ilkley Golf Club [Handbook].* London: Golf Clubs Association, 1931, 24p, illustrated, wrappers, 18.5cm.

14470. *The Liphook Golf Club [Handbook].* London: Golf Clubs Association [ca1947] 19p, illustrated, wrappers, 18.5cm.

14480. *The Lucifer Golfing Society.* London: Privately Printed, 1st ed. 1942, 24p, illustrated, illustrated wrappers, 18.5cm, with Carlton Levick.

14490. *The New Golf Club St. Andrews [Handbook].* London: Golf Clubs Association, 1923, 24p, illustrated, wrappers, 18.5cm.

14500. *The Rochester and Cobham Park Golf Club [Handbook].* London: Golf Clubs Association, 1938, 15p, illustrated, wrappers, 18.5cm.

14510. *The Royal Ashdown Forest Golf Club [Handbook].* London: Golf Clubs Association, 1938, 23p, illustrated, wrappers, 18cm.

14520. *The Royal Blackheath Golf Club [Handbook].* London: Golf Clubs Association, 1938, 31p, illustrated, illustrated wrappers, 18cm.

14530. *The Royal Cinque Ports Golf Club [Handbook].* London: Golf Clubs Association, 1935, 31p, illustrated, wrappers, 18cm.

14540. *The Royal Liverpool Golf Club [Handbook].* London: Golf Clubs Association, 1922, 28p, illustrated, wrappers, 18.5cm.

14550. *The Royal North Devon Golf Club [Handbook].* London: Golf Clubs Association, 1921, 24p, illustrated, wrappers, 18cm.

14560. *The Royal West Norfolk Golf Club [Handbook].* London: Golf Clubs Association, 1923, 28p, illustrated, wrappers, 18.5cm.

14570. *The Royal Wimbledon Golf Club [Handbook].* London: Golf Clubs Association, 1922, 24p, illustrated, wrappers, 18.5cm.

14580. *The Rye Golf Club [Handbook].* London: Golf Clubs Association, 1939, 25p, wrappers,18cm.

14590. *The Saunton Golf Club [Handbook].* London: Golf Clubs Association, 1926, 20p, illustrated, wrappers, 18cm.

14600. *The Sundridge Park Golf Club [Handbook].* London: Golf Clubs Association [ca1946] 23p, illustrated, wrappers, 18.5cm.

14610. *The Tandridge Golf Club [Handbook].* London: Golf Clubs Association, 1925, 35p, illustrated, wrappers, 18cm.

14620. *The Teignmouth Golf Club [Handbook]*. London: Golf Clubs Association, 1925, 40p, illustrated, wrappers, 18cm.

14630. *The Walton Heath Golf Club [Handbook]*. London: Golf Clubs Association, 1937, 31p, illustrated, wrappers, 18.5cm.

14640. *The West Lancashire Golf Club [Handbook]*. London: Golf Clubs Association, 1934, 28p, illustrated, wrappers, 18.5cm.

14650. *The West Surrey Golf Club [Handbook]*. London: Golf Clubs Association, 1938, 21p, illustrated, wrappers, 18.5cm.

14660. *The West Sussex Golf Club [Handbook]*. London: Golf Clubs Association, 1935, 31p, illustrated, wrappers, 18.5cm.

14670. *The Working Golf Club [Handbook]*. London: Golf Clubs Association [ca1949] 22p, illustrated, wrappers, 18.5cm.

14680. *The World That Fred Made: An Autobiography*. London: Chatto & Windus, 1st ed. 1955, 256p, illustrated, cloth, 21 cm.

14690. *West Hill Golf Club [Handbook]*. London: Golf Clubs Association [ca1946] 20p, illustrated, wrappers, 18.5cm.

14700. *West Kent Golf Club [Handbook]*. London: Golf Clubs Association [ca1951] 19p, illustrated, wrappers, 18.5cm.

14710. *Willingdon Golf Club [Handbook]*. London: Golf Clubs Association [ca1947] 25p, illustrated, wrappers, 18cm.

14720. *Worplesdon Golf Club [Handbook]*. London: Golf Clubs Association [ca1946] 23p, illustrated, wrappers, 18.5cm.

Darwin, Bernard and others

14740. *A History of Golf in Britain*. and H. Gardiner-Hill, Guy Campbell, Henry Cotton, Henry Longhurst, Leonard Crawley, Enid Wilson, Lord Brabazon. London: Cassell, 1st ed. 1952, 312p, illustrated, cloth, 27.5 cm.

Davis, Joe

14760. *Blue Book of Chicago Golfers*. edited by. Chicago: W.S. Chambers, 1st ed. [1925] 300p, illustrated, leatherette, 24.5cm.

Davis, Joe G.

14780. *Major Golf Trophies*. Chicago: G.A. Soden, 1st ed. 1928 [60p] illustrated, illustrated wrappers, 23cm.

Davis, Robert H. [Bob]

14800. *Do You Know How A Golf Ball Is Made*. Buffalo, New York: U.S. Rubber, 1st ed. [ca1928] [38p] illustrated, wrappers, 16cm, introduction by Irvin S. Cobb.

14810. *The Way of A Caddie with A Man*. New York: United States Rubber, 1st ed. [1926] [12p] wrappers, 16cm.

De C.B., R.

14830. *Golfballistics*. Port-Louis, Mauritius: Privately Printed, limited ed. [no limitation cited] 1941, 51p, illustrated, wrappers, 19cm, presumed pseudonym of Roger Bacon, introduction by Henry Cotton.

Debenham, Betty

14850. *The Carlisle and Silloth Golf Club [Handbook]*. London: Golf Clubs Association [ca1950] 15p, illustrated, wrappers, 19cm.

14860. *The Luffenham Heath Golf Club [Handbook]*. London: Golf Clubs Association [ca1950] 19p, illustrated, wrappers, 18.5cm.

14870. *The Peterborough Milton Golf Club [Handbook]*. London: Golf Clubs Association [ca1950] 15p, illustrated, wrappers, 18.5cm.

Debenham, Robert

14890. *Metropolitan Golf Club 1908-1929*. Melbourne: Australia, Privately Printed, 1st ed. 1929 [36p] illustrated, tied wrappers, 21.5cm.

Deeside Golf Club

14910. *History of Deeside Golf Club 1903-1953*. Aberdeen, Scotland: Privately Printed, 1st ed. 1953, 28p, illustrated, decorative cloth, 21.5cm.

deGarmo, Louis

14930. *Play Golf and Enjoy It.* New York: Greenberg, 1st ed. [1954] 95p, illustrated, cloth, 20cm, introduction by Grantland Rice.

Delaware and Hudson Railroad

14950. *Golf: A Directory of Courses in the Summer Paradise on the Delaware and Hudson Line.* Albany, New York: Delaware and Hudson Railroad, 1st ed. [ca1916] [28p] illustrated, illustrated wrappers, 9cm.

Demaret, James [Jimmy]

14970. *My Partner, Ben Hogan.* New York: McGraw-Hill, 1st ed. [1954] 214p, illustrated by Murray Olderman, cloth, 20 cm.

14980. 1st UK ed. London: Peter Davies [1954] 214p, illustrated, cloth, 20cm.

14990. pbk. ed. London: Panther, 1957, 187p, illustrated, illustrated wrappers, 17.5cm.

Detroit Golf Club

15010. *Detroit Golf Club: A Chronicle of Forty Years of Substantial Achievement, 1899-1939.* Detroit, Michigan: Privately Printed, limited ed. [1000 copies] 1939, 68p, illustrated, pictorial cloth, 30.5cm.

DeWitt, William O.

15030. *DeWitt's Golf Year Book.* Miami: DeWitt's Golf Year Book, 1st ed. [1953] 316p, illustrated, illustrated wrappers, 23cm.

15040. 2d ed. 1958, 552p, illustrated wrappers, 23cm.

15050. 3d ed. 1960, 520p, illustrated wrappers, 23cm.

Dickinson, Patric

15070. *A Round of Golf Courses: A Selection of the Best Eighteen.* London: Evans Brothers, 1st ed. 1951, 159p, illustrated, cloth, 22cm, foreword by Bernard Darwin.

Diehl, Robert W. and Tom Vardon

15090. *The Diehl-Vardon Manual.* St. Paul, Minnesota: Western Golf Publishing, 1st ed. [1927] 87p, illustrated, decorative cloth, 24.5cm.

15100. 2d ed. rev. [1929] 119p, illustrated, illustrated wrappers, 25.5cm.

Direlton Castle Golf Club

15120. *Direlton Castle Golf Club, 1854-1954 First Centenary.* Gullane, Scotland: Privately Printed, 1st ed. 1954, 24p, illustrated, illustrated wrappers, 18.5cm.

Divotee

15140. *Its Moral Beauty.* London: Mills & Boon, 1st ed. 1923, 120p, cloth, 19cm.

Dix, Harold

15160. *A Handbook on the Rules of Golf.* Girard, Kansas: Haldeman Julius, 1st ed. [1927] 32p, wrappers, 15cm.

Dixon, H. Macneile

15180. *Golf-and How!* London: Printing Consultants, 1st ed. [ca1949] 87p, illustrated, cloth, 18.5 cm, foreword by James Braid.

Dods, Marcus

15200. *The Bunker At the Fifth.* Edinburgh: William Hodge, 1st ed. [ca1927] 186p, cloth, 18.5cm.

Dow, James Gordon

15220. *The Crail Golfing Society 1786-1936; Being the History of an Eighteenth Century Golf Club in the East Neuk of Fife.* Edinburgh: Golf Monthly, limited ed. [250 copies] 1936, 99p, illustrated, cloth, 22 cm.

Drury, Tom

15240. *Blackwell Golf Club, Worcestershire, A History.* Worcestershire, England: Privately Printed, 1st ed. [ca1953] 40p, illustrated, wrappers, 22cm.

Dubb, Abel [pseud for John B. Sanborn]

15260. *Why Golf.* Chicago: Privately Printed, 1st ed. 1921, 29p, illustrated by John Sanborn, wrappers, 16 cm.

Duffer, Joe

15280. *The Power Swing.* New York: Waverlynn, 1st ed. [1949] [20p] illustrated, felt wrappers, 15.5cm.

Duke, Will

15300. *Fair Prey.* London: T.V. Beardman, 1st ed. 1958, 187p, cloth, 18.5cm.

Dunbar Golf Club

15320. *Dunbar Golf Club [Handbook].* Derby & Cheltenham, England: New Centurion [ca1955] 36p, illustrated, wrappers, 13.5cm.

Duncan, George

15340. *Golf At the Gallop.* London: Sporting Handbooks, 1st ed. 1951, 192p, illustrated, cloth, 21.5cm, edited by Edgar Turner.

15350. *Golf for Women.* London: T. Werner Laurie, 1st ed. [ca1912] 185p, illustrated, decorative cloth, 18cm.
15360. 1st American ed. New York: J. Pott [ca1913] 185p, illustrated, decorative cloth, 18.5 cm.

15370. *Present Day Golf.* London: Hodder & Stoughton, 2d ed. rev. [1922] 111p, illustrated, cloth, 21.5cm. note: see #15390, Bernard Darwin's chapters eliminated from this edition.

Duncan, George and Bernard Darwin

15390. *Present Day Golf.* London: Hodder & Stoughton, 1st ed. [ca1921] 309p, illustrated, cloth, 21.5cm.
15400. 1st American ed. New York: George H. Doran [1921] 309p, illustrated, cloth, 22cm.

Dunlop Caddie

15420. *Leaves from My Diary.* Birmingham, England: Dunlop Rubber, 1st ed. [ca1919] 40p, illustrated by Ernest Noble, illustrated boards, 25cm.

Dunlop Rubber

15440. *The Making of a 'Maxfli'.* London: Dunlop Rubber, 1st ed. [ca1924] 31p, illustrated, boards, 18cm.

Dunlop-Hill, Noel

15460. *History of the Scottish Ladies Golfing Association 1903-1928.* London: Mortons, 1st ed. 1929, 62p, illustrated, decorative cloth, 23 cm.

Dunn, J.

15480. *Golf From Rabbit to Tiger.* London: Thorsons, 1st ed. 1955, 134p, illustrated, cloth, 21.5cm, foreword by Max Faulkner.

Dunn, John Duncan

15500. *Elements of the Golf Swing.* NP: General Cigar, 1st ed. [1930] 24p, illustrated, illustrated wrappers, 17cm.

15510. *Golf.* Los Angeles: Privately Printed, 1st ed. [1941] 40p, illustrated, illustrated wrappers, 16cm.

15520. *How to Drive-How to Approach-How to Putt. 3 Volumes.* Chicago: Thos. E. Wilson, 1st ed. slipcased, 1922, 58p, 49p, 47p, illustrated, wrappers, 19.5cm.

15530. *Intimate Golf Talks.* New York: G.P. Putnam's, 1st ed. [1920] 240p, illustrated, pictorial cloth, 19cm. with Elon Jessup.

15540. *Natural Golf: A book of fundamental instruction which shows the golfer how to develop his own natural style.* New York: G.P. Putnam's, 1st ed. boxed, 1931, 199p, illustrated, cloth, 27.5 cm, foreword by A.C. Gregson.

15550. *The A. B. C. of Golf.* New York: Harper & Bros, 1st ed. [1916] 120p, illustrated, cloth, 16.5cm.

Dunn, Seymour

15570. *Golf Fundamentals: Orthodoxy of Style.* Lake Placid, New York: Privately Printed, 1st ed. 1922, 283p, illustrated, cloth, 31 cm. later printings.

15580. *Golf Fundamentals.* reprint ed. Norwalk, Connecticut: Golf Digest, 1977, 283p, illustrated, leather, 22cm.

15590. *Standardized Golf Instructions.* New York: Privately Printed, 1st ed. [1934] 153p, illustrated, cloth, 15 cm. later printings.

15600. pbk. ed. [5 Volumes]. New York: Privately Printed [1934] illustrated, illustrated wrappers, 15.5cm.

15610. *The Complete Golf Joke Book.* New York: Stravon, 1st ed. 1953, 128p, illustrated by Al Ross, cloth, 21cm.

15620. pbk. ed. New York: Rainbow [1953] illustrated, illustrated wrappers, 20cm.

Dunning, Bob

15640. *Green Construction.* Tulsa, Oklahoma: Privately Printed, 1st ed. [ca1960] 11p, illustrated wrappers, 21.5cm.

Duties of A Caddie

15660. *The Duties of A Caddie.* London: Silverstone 1st ed. [ca1932] 16p, illustrated, illustrated wrappers, 15.5cm.

Dutra, Olin

15680. *All You Need to Know to Start Golf: with Groove Your Swing.* Louisville, Kentucky: Hillerich & Bradsby, 1st ed. [1941] 31p, illustrated, illustrated wrappers, 21.5cm.

15690. *Golf Doctor.* [Los Angeles] Camday, 1st ed. [1948] 205p, illustrated, illustrated wrappers, 11.5cm, foreword by Grantland Rice.

Dutra, Olin and others

15710. *Your Guide To Golf in Southern California, Where and How To Play.* and Bill Hickey, Chas Lacey, Bill McHie and Joe Novak. Los Angeles: Privately Printed, 1st ed. [1940] 80p, illustrated, wrappers, 18.5cm.

East, J. Victor

15730. *Better Golf in 5 Minutes.* Englewood Cliffs, New Jersey: Prentice- Hall, 1st ed. [1956] 202p, illustrated, cloth, 22.5cm, introduction by Irving R. Allen. later printing.

Eaton Golf Club

15750. *Eaton Golf Club [Handbook].* London: Golf Clubs Association [ca1948] 32p, illustrated, wrappers, 18cm.

Edgar, J. Douglas

15770. *The Gate To Golf.* Washington, DC: Privately Printed, 1st ed. 1920, 61p, illustrated, cloth, 21.5 cm. accompanied by "The Gate."

15780. 1st UK ed. St. Albans, England: Edgar & Co. [1920] 61p, illustrated, cloth, 21.5cm.

15790. limited ed. facsimile, slipcased [100 copies] London: Ellesborough Press, 1983, 61p, illustrated, leather, raised bands, aeg, 21cm.

Edinburgh Burgess Golfing Society

15810. *History of the Edinburgh Burgess Golfing Society.* Edinburgh: Privately Printed, [1906] 1st ed, 54p, illustrated, illustrated wrappers, 12cm.

15820. reprint ed. Broxburn, Scotland: Alna Press [ca 1984] 46p, illustrated, illustrated wrappers, 12cm.

Edmonstone, C.G.

15840. *A Study of Golf from Its Mechanical Aspect.* Kent, England: Edall Press, 1st ed. [ca1910] 36p, illustrated, wrappers, 17.5cm.

Edwards, Leslie

15860. *Golf on Merseyside and District.* Liverpool, England: Littlebury, 3d ed. [ca1954] 48p, illustrated, illustrated wrappers, 18.5cm. note: have not located the first or second edition.

15870. *Wallasey Golf Club [Handbook].* London: Temple Publicity Services [ca1960] 12p, illustrated, illustrated wrappers, 18.5cm, with W. H. Davies.

Edwards, R. Stafford

15890. *Wee Burn Country Club: History, Reorganization, By-Laws, Regulations.* Darien, Connecticut: Privately Printed, 1st ed. 1949, 34p, wrappers, 17.5cm.

Edwards, Russ

15910. *The Golpher: His Origin and His Finish.* Washington, DC: Fireside Golphers, 1st ed. [1929] 40p, illustrated, illustrated boards, 15.5cm.

Elliss, A.D.

15930. *History of the Royal Melbourne Golf Club, Vol I, 1891 to 1941.* Melbourne, Australia: Robertson & Mullems, 1st ed. 1941, 128p, illustrated, decorative cloth, 21.5cm.

Erskine Park Golf Club

15950. *Erskine Park Golf Club Silver Anniversary 1925-1950.* South Bend, Indiana: Privately Printed, 1st ed. 1950 [60p] illustrated wrappers, 21.5cm.

Evans, Jr., Charles [Chick]

15970. *Caddy Manual.* Chicago: Norbert Hackett, 1st ed. [1928] 32p, illustrated, illustrated wrappers, 16cm.

15980. *Chick Evans Guide to Better Golf.* St. Paul, Minnesota: Brown & Bigelow, 1st ed. [ca1924] 47p, illustrated, illustrated wrappers, 15.5cm.

15990. *Chick Evans' Golf Book: The Story of the Sporting Battles of the Greatest of all Amateur Golfers.* Chicago: Thos. E. Wilson, limited ed. signed [999 copies] [1921] 343p, illustrated, decorative leather, 23cm.

16000. 1st trade ed. [1921] 343p, illustrated, cloth, 19cm.

16010. limited ed. facsimile [30 copies] Cincinnati, Ohio: Old Golf Shop 1978, 343p, illustrated, gilt leather, 21.5cm, issued for the Chick Evans Invitational, Forest Hills Country Club.

16020. limited ed. facsimile [425 copies] Muirfield, Ohio: Privately Printed, 1985, 343p, illustrated, gilt stamped leather, raised bands, 19cm, published for The Memorial Tournament of 1985.

16030. *Golf for Boys and Girls.* Chicago: Windsor Press, 1st ed. [1954] 112p, illustrated by Frank C. Murphy, decorative cloth, 28cm.

Evans, Jr., Charles [Chick] and Barrie Payne

16050. *Ida Broke: The Humor and Philosophy of Golf.* New York: Dutton, 1st ed. [1929] 302p, illustrated by McDuffer, cloth, 20.5cm, introduction by Grantland Rice.

Evans, Webster and Tom Scott

16070. *In Praise of Golf: An Anthology for all Lovers of the Game.* London: Frederick Muller, 1st ed. 1950, 63p, illustrated, decorative boards, 13.5cm.

Everard, Harry Stirling Crawford

16090. *A History of the Royal and Ancient Golf Club, St. Andrews from 1754-1900.* Edinburgh: William Blackwood, 1st ed. 1907, 306p, illustrated, decorative cloth, 25cm.

Exmoor Country Club

16110. *Exmoor Country Club Semi-Centennial Year 1896-1946.* Highland Park, Illinois: Privately Printed, 1st ed. 1946 [48p] illustrated, cloth, 28cm.

Fable of the Lost Golf Ball

16130. *The Fable of the Lost Golf Ball.* Chicago: J.L. Sugden Advertising, 1st ed. [ca1940] 10p, illustrated, illustrated boards, 17.5cm.

Facts About the Course at Garden City, L.I.

16150. *Facts About the Course at Garden City, L.I. where the National Amateur Championship will be played September 1st to 6th, 1913.* Brooklyn, New York: Brooklyn Daily Eagle, 1st ed. 1913 [200p] illustrated, wrappers, 12.5cm.

Facts About the Links of the Detroit Country Club

16170. *Facts About the Links of the Detroit Country Club where the U.S. Amateur Championship will be played August 28-September 4.* Brooklyn, New York: Brooklyn Daily Eagle, 1st ed. 1915 [24p] illustrated, wrappers, 12.5cm.

Facts About the Merion Course

16190. *Facts About the Merion Course at Ardmore, Pa. where the National Amateur Golf Championship will be played September 4th to 9th 1916.* Brooklyn, New York: Brooklyn Daily Eagle, 1st ed. 1916 [14p] illustrated, wrappers, 20cm.

Fairlie, Walter Edwin

16210. *The Old Course of St. Andrews: Plans with names of holes and bunkers.* St. Andrews: W.C. Henderson, 1st ed. [1908] [20p] illustrated, linen wrappers, 17.5cm.

Fairview Country Club

16230. *Fairview Country Club Twenty-Fifth Anniversary 1904-1929.* Elmsford, New York: Privately Printed, 1st ed. 1929, 95p, illustrated, 1/4 cloth, boards, 21.5cm.

Fall, Robert Geoffrey

16250. *A Short History of the Mowbray Golf Club.* Cape Town, South Africa: Privately Printed, 1st ed. 1939, 23p, illustrated, illustrated wrappers, 21.5cm.

16260. *Golfing in Southern Africa, Edition 1958.* Cape Town, South Africa: South African Golf, 1st ed. 1958, 324p, illustrated, decorative cloth, 23.5cm.

16270. *Southern Africa Golf Annual 1967-68.* Cape Town, South Africa: South African Crafts & Hobbies, 2d ed. 1968, 224p, illustrated, illustrated wrappers, 28cm. note: previously titled "Golfing in Southern Africa."

16280. *History of Golf at the Cape: In which is also treated the origin of the Game of Golf, Golf Stories and a Register of S.A. clubs.* Cape Town, South Africa: Argus, 1st ed. 1918, 48p, wrappers, 21cm.

Farmington Country Club

16300. *Farmington Country Club, Historical Sketch and Chain of Title*. Charlottesville, Virginia: Privately Printed, 1st ed. [ca1932] [5p] illustrated wrappers, 15.5cm.

Farrar, Guy B.

16320. *The Royal Liverpool Golf Club, A History 1869-1932*. Birkenhead, England: Willmer, 1st ed. 1933, 309p, illustrated, decorative cloth, 24cm.

16330. *The Royal Liverpool Golf Club [Handbook]*. London: Golf Clubs Association [ca1947] 19p, illustrated, wrappers, 18.5cm.

Farrell, J. [Major]

16350. *Golf*. London: William Jackson, 1st ed. [ca1930] 30p, cloth, 17cm.

Farrell, Johnny

16370. *How to Play Your Golf Course*. Chicago: Wilson-Western Sporting Goods, 1st ed. 1929, 19p, illustrated, illustrated wrappers, 21cm.

16380. *If I Were in Your Golf Shoes*. New York: Henry Holt, 1st ed. [1951] 87p, illustrated, cloth, 19cm, introduction by Robert T. Jones, Jr.

16390. *The Weekend Golfer*. London: Herbert Jenkins, 1st UK ed. 1952, 96p, illustrated, cloth, 19.5cm, foreword by Robert T. Jones, Jr. UK title of "If I Were in Your Golf Shoes."

16400. *Johnny Farrell on Golf Sportsmanship, Rules of the Game Which are Commonly Broken*. Chicago: Wilson-Western Sporting Goods, 1st ed. 1929, 19p, illustrated, illustrated wrappers, 20cm.

16410. *Putting to Win*. Springfield, Massachusetts: A.R. Metcalfe, 1st ed. [ca1929] [10p] illustrated, wrappers, 14cm.

Fascination of Golf

16430. *The Fascination of Golf*. London: W.T. Henley's, 1st ed. [ca1918] [44p] illustrated, illustrated wrappers, 24cm.

Faulkner, Max and Louis T. Stanley

16450. *The Faulkner Method.* London: Hutchinson, 1st ed. 1952, 62p, illustrated, cloth, 21cm.

Faust, W.H. [Commander]

16470. *This Hectic Game of Golf.* Ann Arbor, Michigan: Privately Printed, 1st ed. [ca1930] 20p, illustrated wrappers, 21cm.

Faxon, Dike

16490. *History of Echo Lake Country Club 1899-1956.* Westfield, New Jersey: Privately Printed, 1st ed. 1956, 100p, illustrated, wrappers, 20.5cm.

Fenn, H.B.

16510. *A Box of Matches: Containing Forty Ways to Play Golf; or, The Handicapper's Hoyle.* New York: Brooks Brothers, 1st ed. 1922, 48p, illustrated, leather and illustrated wrappers, 11.5cm.

Fereday, Len

16530. *The Burbage Common [Hinckley] Golf Club [Handbook].* Bristol & London: Temple Publicity Service [ca1951] 12p, illustrated, wrappers, 18cm.

Ferndown Golf Club

16550. *Ferndown Golf Club [Handbook].* London: Golf Clubs Association, 1939, 37p, illustrated, wrappers, 18cm.

Ferrier, James [Jim]

16570. *Golf Shots.* Sydney, Australia: Bulletin, 1st ed. [1940] 32p, illustrated, illustrated wrappers, 30cm.

16580. *Low Score Golf.* Chicago: Little Sports Library. Ziff-Davis, 1st ed. [1948] 127p, illustrated, illustrated boards, 17cm.

16590. pbk. ed. [1948] 127p, illustrated, illustrated wrappers, 20cm.

Fifty Miles of Golf Round London

16610. *Fifty Miles of Golf Round London.* London: Whitefriars Press, 1st ed. 1937, 272p, 1/4 cloth, illustrated boards, 18cm.

16620. 2d ed. rev. London: Week End, 1938, 258p, 1/4 cloth, illustrated boards, 18cm.

Fine, Benjamin and Howard

16640. *The Fine Method of Golf.* Skokie, Illinois: Fine Method of Golf, 1st ed. [1958] 60p, illustrated, illustrated wrappers, 20cm.

Fishbein, Morris [Dr]

16660. *To Golf or Not to Golf: the morale and hygienic significance of golf in war.* [Chicago] Golfdom Magazine [ca1943] [4p] wrappers, 23cm, offprint from Golfdom Magazine.

Fitch, George

16680. *Golf for the Beginner.* New York: Colliers, 1st ed. 1908, 15p, illustrated, illustrated wrappers, 16.5cm.

16690. 2d ed. rev. [1909] [28p] illustrated, decorative boards, 16cm.

Five Secrets of Winning Golf

16710. *Five Secrets of Winning Golf.* La Grange, Illinois: Sylvan Co. 1st ed. 1945, 26p, illustrated, illustrated wrappers, 19.5cm.

Fleager, H.A.

16730. *History of the Seattle Golf Club.* Seattle, Washington: Privately Printed, 1st ed. 1959 [14p] illustrated, suede leather, 22.5cm.

Fleishman, Alvin

16750. *Compend of Golf Supplemented by Atomic Golf Aids.* Baltimore, Maryland: Fleishman Co. 1st ed. [1946] 24p, wrappers, 18cm, with 10 'flash card' Atomic cards.

Fletcher, Charles

16770. *How to Play Bad Golf.* Los Angeles: Privately Printed, 1st ed. [1935] 24p, illustrated by Jud Wright, illustrated wrappers, 17.5cm.

Flippin, Harrison F. [Mrs]

16790. *Golf Is Fun.* Wynewood, Pennsylvania: Privately Printed, 1st ed. 1956 [18p] illustrated, illustrated wrappers, 21.5cm.

Floyd, Channing

16810. *The Little Golf Teacher.* New York: Privately Printed, 1st ed. [1925] 23p, illustrated, leatherette, 11.5cm.

Floyd, Frank Harris

16830. *The Mechanics of the Golf Swing and the Techniques of the Contestants at Oakmont, Pittsburgh, Open Tournament, 1927.* Detroit, Michigan: Privately Printed, 1st ed. 1927, 54p, illustrated wrappers, 19.5cm.

Follow Through [J. Sawyer Shaw]

16850. *The Essence of Golf.* Oswestry/London: Hughes/ Simpkin Marshall, 1st ed. [ca1954] 70p, illustrated, decorative cloth, 17cm, introduction by George Duncan.

Forbes, John D.

16870. *The Mt. Anthony Country Club.* Bennington, Vermont: Privately Printed, 1st ed. 1944, 23p, illustrated, wrappers, 23cm.

Ford, Doug

16890. *How I Play Inside Golf.* Englewood Cliffs, New Jersey: Prentice-Hall, 1st ed. [1960] 146p, illustrated by Lealand Gustavson, decorative cloth, 23cm, preface by Lawrence Robinson.

16900. *The Brainy Way to Better Golf.* London: Stanley Paul, 1st UK ed. 1961, 146p, illustrated by Lealand Gustavson, cloth, 21cm, preface by Lawrence Robinson. UK title of "How I Play Inside Golf." later printings.

16910. *Start Golf Young.* New York: Sterling, 1st ed. [1955] 124p, illustrated by Howard Morris, decorative cloth, 19.5cm.

16920. *Golf.* New York: Sterling, 2d ed. 1960, 124p, illustrated by Howard Morris, illustrated wrappers, 19.5cm, originally published in cloth under title "Start Golf Young."

16930. *Getting Started in Golf.* New York: Sterling, 1st ed. [1964] 124p, illustrated by Howard Morris, illustrated boards, 19cm, revised from "Start Golf Young."

16940. pbk. ed. New York: Cornerstone Library, 1964, 124p, illustrated by Howard Morris, illustrated wrappers, 20.5cm.

Forfar Golf Club

16960. *Forfar Golf Club [Handbook].* Cheltenham, England: Ed. J. Burrow [ca1923] 28p, illustrated, illustrated wrappers, 16.5cm.

Forrest, James

16980. *A Natural Golfer: Hand Action in Games.* London: Thomas Murby, 1st ed. 1938, 97p, illustrated, cloth, 24.5cm.

16990. 1st American ed. New York: Dutton, 1938, 97p, illustrated, cloth, 24.5cm.

17000. *Golf Made Easy.* London: Thomas Murby, 1st ed. 1933, 68p, illustrated, cloth, 24.5cm.

17010. 1st American ed. New York: Dutton, 1934, 68p, illustrated, cloth, 24.5cm, preface by W.G. Van Tassel Sutphen.

17020. *The Basis of the Golf Swing.* London: Thomas Murby, 1st ed. 1925, 60p, illustrated, cloth, 21.5cm.

17030. *The Golf Stroke.* London: Thomas Murby, 1st ed. 1930, 110p, illustrated, cloth, 24.5cm.

Fortrose and Rosemarkie Golf Club

17050. *The Fortrose and Rosemarkie Golf Club [Handbook].* London: Golf Clubs Association [ca1948] 21p, illustrated, wrappers, 18.5cm.

Foster, Cy

17070. *Golf Is Easy.* Columbus, Ohio: Privately Printed, 1st ed. 1950, 48p, illustrated, illustrated wrappers, 23cm.

Foster, N.R.

17090. *History of the Royal Wimbledon Golf Club-1865 to 1929.* [Wimbledon, England] Privately Printed, 1st ed. 1929, 27p, wrappers, 15cm.

Fowlie, Peter

17110. *The Science of Golf: A Study in Movement.* London: Methuen, 1st ed. 1922, 128p, illustrated, cloth, 18.5cm.

17120. 1st American ed. New York: Robert M. McBride, 1922, 128p, illustrated, cloth, 18.5 cm.

17130. *The Technique of the Golf Swing.* London: Methuen, 1st ed. 1934, 117p, illustrated, cloth, 18.5cm.

Fox, G.D.

17150. *The Golfer's Pocket Tip Book.* London: Mills & Boon, 1st ed. 1911, 126p, illustrated, leather, 14.5cm.

17160. 1st American ed. New York: James Pott [ca1915] 126p, illustrated, cloth, 14.5cm.

Fox, Jr., W.F.

17180. *Golf's Guardian Angels.* Detroit, Michigan: Packard Motors, 1st ed. 1954 [8p] illustrated, illustrated wrappers, 23.5cm.

Fraley, Oscar

17200. *Golf in Action.* New York: A.A. Wynn, 1st ed. [1952] 121p, illustrated, cloth, 27cm.

17210. pbk. ed. [1952] 120p, illustrated, illustrated wrappers, 27.5cm.

Francis, Joseph

17230. *Dutch Open Champion, 1959:"Papwa" Sewsunker Sewgoolum.* Durham, South Africa: Privately Printed, 1st ed. [1959] [48p] illustrated, illustrated wrappers, 18cm.

Francis, Richard Standish

17250. *Golf: Its Rules and Decisions.* New York: Macmillan, 1st ed. 1937, 411p, illustrated, cloth, 21.5cm, introduction by John C. Jackson.

17260. 2d ed. rev. 1939, 413p, illustrated, cloth, 21.5cm.

17270. *Rules of Golf with Interpretations.* [Boston, Massachusetts] Wright & Ditson, offprint [ca1937] 40p, leatherette, 17cm, offprint from "Golf: Its Rules and Decisions."

Frankenberg, H. Xavier Montanza

17290. *Golf Made Easy.* Chicago: Frankenberg Golf Foundation, 1st ed. [1948] 40p, illustrated, illustrated wrappers, 28cm.

Fraser's Golf Directory and Year Book

17310. *Fraser's Golf Directory and Year Book 1923.* Montreal: Fraser, 1st ed. 1923, 208p, illustrated, wrappers, 25.5cm, edited by Robert Ness Balsillie. note: title changed to "Fraser's International Golf Year Book."

17320. *Fraser's International Golf Year Book 1924*. Montreal: Fraser, 2d ed. 1924, 336p, illustrated, cloth, 25.5cm.

17330. *Fraser's International Golf Year Book 1925-1926*. Montreal/New York: Fraser, 3d ed. 1925, 432p, illustrated, cloth and wrappers, 25.5cm.

17340. *Fraser's International Golf Year Book 1926-1927*. Montreal/New York: Fraser, 4th ed. 1926, 436p, illustrated, wrappers, 25cm.

17350. *Fraser's International Golf Year Book 1927*. Montreal/ New York: Fraser, 5th ed. 1927, 466p, illustrated, wrappers, 25cm.

17360. *Fraser's International Golf Year Book 1928*. Montreal/ New York: Fraser, 6th ed. 1928, 480p, illustrated, wrappers, 25cm.

17370. *Fraser's International Golf Year Book 1929*. Montreal/ New York: Fraser, 7th ed. 1929, 438p, illustrated, wrappers, 24cm.

17380. *Fraser's International Golf Year Book 1930*. Montreal/ New York: Fraser, 8th ed. 1930, 440p, illustrated, wrappers, 25cm.

17390. *Fraser's International Golf Year Book 1931*. Montreal/ New York: Fraser, 9th ed. 1931, 456p, illustrated, wrappers, 25cm.

17400. *Fraser's International Golf Year Book 1932*. Montreal/ New York: Fraser, 10th ed. 1932, 388p, wrappers, 25.5cm.

17410. *Fraser's International Golf Year Book 1933*. Montreal/ New York: Fraser, 11th ed. 1933, 304p, wrappers, 25.5cm.

17420. *Fraser's International Golf Year Book 1934*. Montreal/ New York: Fraser, 12th ed. 1934, 312p, wrappers, 25.5cm.

17430. *Fraser's International Golf Year Book 1935*. Montreal/ New York: Fraser, 13th ed. 1935, 316p, wrappers, 25.5cm.

17440. *Fraser's International Golf Year Book 1936*. Montreal/ New York: Fraser, 14th ed. 1936, 336p, wrappers, 25.5cm.

17450. *Fraser's International Golf Year Book 1937*. Montreal/ New York: Fraser, 15th ed. 1937, 232p, wrappers, 25.5cm.

Fraser, Chick

17470. *Pictorial Golf: Chick Fraser Playing Driver, Midiron, Mashie Pitch, Putter. 4 Volumes [Flip Book]*. Los Angeles: Pictorial Golf, 1st ed. [1922] various pagination, illustrated, wrappers, 8.5cm.

Fraserburgh Golf Club

17490. *The Fraserburgh Golf Club [Handbook]*. London: Golf Clubs Association [ca1947] 27p, illustrated, wrappers, 18cm.

Freeborn, James Livingston

17510. *The Edgewood Club 1884-1937.* Tivoli, New York: Privately Printed, 1st ed. 1937, 40p, illustrated, cloth, 17.5cm.

Frome, David [pseud for Mrs. Zenith Brown]

17530. *The Strange Death of Martin Green.* Garden City, New York: The Crime Club-Doubleday, 1st ed. [1931] 309p, cloth, 19cm.

17540. *The Murder on the Sixth Hole.* London: Methuen, 1st UK ed. 1931, 309 p, cloth, 19cm, UK title of "Strange Death of Martin Green."

Fulford, Harry

17560. *Golf's Little Ironies.* London: Simpkin, Marshall, Hamilton, Kent, 1st ed. 1919, 141p, illustrated, cloth, 16.5cm.

17570. *Potted Golf.* Glasgow: Dalross, 1st ed. 1910, 147p, illustrated, cloth, 18cm, preface by J.H. Taylor.

Fullarton, J.R.

17590. *Instructions for Caddies.* Melbourne, Australia: Victoria Golf Association [ca1938] 24p, illustrated, illustrated wrappers, 18cm.

Fuller, Timothy

17610. *Reunion with Murder.* Boston: Little, Brown, 1st ed. 1941, 258p, cloth, 19cm.

17620. 1st UK ed. London: Heinemann, 1947, 153p, cloth, 18.5cm.

Gaal, Charlie and Nate Collier

17640. *Your Golf.* Rutherford, New Jersey: Gilio Publications, 1st ed. [1948] 93p, illustrated, spiral bound illustrated wrappers, 23cm.

Galbraith, William

17660. *Prestwick St. Nicholas Golf Club.* Prestwick, Scotland: Privately Printed, 1st ed. 1950, 180p, illustrated, cloth, 22cm.

Gallico, Paul

17680. *Golf Is A Friendly Game.* New York: Knopf, 1st ed. 1942, 274p, illustrated, cloth, 19.5cm.

Galvano, Phil

17700. *Seagram's Guide to Strategic Golf.* New York: Gemi Studio, 1st ed. [ca1960] 32p, illustrated, illustrated wrappers, 21cm.

17710. *Secrets of Accurate Putting and Chipping.* Englewood Cliffs, New Jersey: Prentice-Hall, 1st ed. [1957] 100p, illustrated, decorative cloth, 21cm, later printings.

17720. pbk. ed. [1960] 100p, illustrated, illustrated wrappers, 21cm, later printings.

17730. *The Gentle Arts of Putting and Chipping.* London: Stanley Paul, 1st UK ed. 1959, 100p, illustrated, cloth, 21cm, UK title "Secrets of Accurate Chipping & Putting."

Gardner, Don

17750. *Don Gardner's Golf Book: Three Point Method.* Springfield, Missouri: Cain Printing, 1st ed. [1947] 44p, illustrated by Steve Miller, illustrated wrappers, 21.5cm, later printings.

Gaskill, Bud [Willard]

17770. *Golf At A Glance.* New York: Arco, 1st ed. [1958] 128p, illustrated, cloth, 19.5cm.

17780. pbk. ed. New York: Arco [1958] 128p, illustrated, illustrated wrappers, 19.5cm, later printing.

Gaudin, J.W.

17800. *Method in Golf.* Leeds, England: Yorkshire Evening Post, 1st ed. [ca1929] 32p, illustrated, illustrated wrappers, 16cm.

General [Ernest Heywood]

17820. *Golf and How to Play It: being a treatise with hints; from the 'Putting Green' to the 'Tee' instead of the reverse.* Holborn, England: A.W. Gamage, 2d ed. [ca1912] 60p, illustrated, illustrated boards, 17cm. note: first edition not located.

Gerrits, Paul H.

17840. *The Golfer's Guide.* Appleton, Wisconsin: Privately Printed, 1st ed. [1947] 32p, illustrated, illustrated wrappers, 14.5cm.

Gibson, Nevin H.

17860. *The Encyclopedia of Golf: with the Official All-Time records.* New York: A.S. Barnes, 1st ed. [1958] 256p, illustrated, cloth, 24.5cm.

17870. 2d ed. rev. [1964] 310p, illustrated, cloth, 24.5cm.
17880. pbk. ed. 2d ed. rev. [1964] 310p, illustrated, wrappers, 20.5cm.

Gilbert, James

17900. *Boyce Hill Golf Club [Handbook]*. Cheltenham & London: Ed. J. Burrow [ca1938] 16p, illustrated, illustrated wrappers, 16.5cm.

Gill, Howard

17920. *Fun in the Rough from Golf Digest*. Englewood Cliffs, New Jersey: Prentice-Hall, 1st ed. [1957] 118p, illustrated, decorative cloth, 24.5cm.

Gillespie, Percy J.

17940. *Putting: A Revolution in the Art or Hoisting the Red Flag on the Putting Green*. Dublin, Ireland: Irish Goodwill Novelties, 1st ed. [ca1957] 44p, illustrated, illustrated wrappers, 12.5cm, introduction by J.B. Carr.

Gillon, Stair A.

17960. *The Honourable Company of Edinburgh Golfers At Muirfield, 1891-1914*. Edinburgh: Privately Printed, 1st ed. 1946, 58p, illustrated wrappers, 25cm.

Gilruth, J.D.

17980. *Arbroath Golf Course*. Arbroath, Scotland: T. Buncle, 1st ed. 1909, 159p, illustrated, illustrated wrappers, 18.5cm.

Gilson, C.J.L.

18000. *Golf: Warnes Recreation Books*. London: Frederick Warne, 1st ed. [ca1928] 64p, illustrated, illustrated wrappers, 18cm.

Glamorganshire Golf Club

18020. *Short History of the Glamorganshire Golf Club 1890-1950*. Penarth, Wales: Privately Printed, 1st ed. 1950 [24p] illustrated, illustrated wrappers, 21.5cm.

Gloucester Golf Club

18040. *Gloucester Golf Club [Handbook]*. Cheltenham & London: Ed. J. Burrow [ca1938] 28p, illustrated, illustrated wrappers, 16.5cm.

Glover, Thomas

18060. *Ladies Open Golf Championship May, 1902*. Edinburgh: Privately Printed, 1st ed. 1902, 15p, illustrated, decorative cloth, 27cm.

Goetz, Austin

18080. *The Golf Champ: A Farce Comedy In Three Acts*. Minneapolis, Minnesota: Northwestern Press, 1st ed. [1934] 92p, illustrated, wrappers, 19cm.

Golf and Other Sports At Del Monte

18120. *Golf and Other Sports At Del Monte*. Del Monte, California: Privately Printed, 1st ed. [ca1913] [32p] illustrated, illustrated wrappers, 23cm.

Golf and Ping Pong

18140. *Golf and Ping Pong*. Portsmouth, Virginia: Seaboard Air Line, 1st ed. [ca1903] 23p, illustrated, illustrated wrappers, 15.5cm, with Practical Golf Points by Walter J. Travis.

Golf At Del Monte California

18160. *Golf At Del Monte California*. Del Monte, California: Privately Printed, 1st ed. [ca1903] [32p] illustrated, illustrated wrappers, 17.5cm.

Golf Clubs of Devon

18180. *The Golf Clubs of Devon*. Dundee, Scotland: Simmath Press, 1st ed. [ca1935] 72p, illustrated, decorative cloth, 17.5cm.

Golf Clubs of Fife

18200. *The Golf Clubs of Fife*. Dundee, Scotland: Simmath Press, 1st ed. [ca1933] 44p, illustrated, decorative cloth, 17cm.

Golf Courses in Switzerland

18220. *Golf Courses in Switzerland*. Berne, Switzerland: Swiss Federal Railways, 1st ed. 1928, 8p, illustrated, illustrated wrappers, 18.5cm.

Golf Courses of New Hampshire

18240. *Golf Courses of New Hampshire*. Concord, New Hampshire: State Board of Publicity, 1929 [60p] illustrated, wrappers, 18.5cm. later printings.

Golf Courses on the G.W.R.

18260. *Golf Courses on the G.W.R.* London: Great Western Railway [ca1923] 72p, illustrated, illustrated wrappers, 18.5cm.

Golf Courses Served by the G.W.R.

18280. *Golf Courses Served by the G.W.R. and Where to Stay.* London: Great Western Railway, 1934, 55p, illustrated, illustrated wrappers, 22.5cm, foreword by Peter Lawless.

18290. *Golf Courses Served by the G.W.R. and Where to Stay.* London: Great Western Railway, 1937, 55p, illustrated, illustrated wrappers, 23cm, foreword by Harry S. Colt.

18300. *Golf Courses Served by the G.W.R. and Where to Stay.* London: Great Western Railway, 1939, 65p, illustrated by Margaret Bradley, illustrated wrappers, 23cm, foreword by J.S.F. Morrison.

Golf Illustrated Magazine

18320. *Fore! Golf Illustrated Annual.* London: Golf Illustrated Magazine, 1st ed. [ca1912] 96p, illustrated by Tom Wilkinson, illustrated wrappers, 24.5cm.

Golf in Bermuda

18340. *Golf in Bermuda.* Hamilton, Bermuda: Bermuda Golf Association, 1957 [8p] illustrated, illustrated wrappers, 20.5cm.

Golf in Britain

18360. *Golf in Britain.* London: British Travel Association, 1st ed. 1959, 35p, illustrated, illustrated wrappers, 23cm.

Golf in Germany

18380. *Golf in Germany.* Berlin: German Railroads, 1st ed. [ca1926] 4p, illustrated, illustrated wrappers, 22.5cm.

Golf in Italy

18400. *Golf in Italy.* Milan, Italy: Ferrovie Dello Stato [ca1935] 25p, illustrated, illustrated wrappers, 20cm.

Golf in Japan

18420. *Golf in Japan.* [Japan] Japanese Government Railways, 1934, 68p, illustrated, illustrated wrappers, 22cm.

Golf in Maine

18440. *Golf In Maine Annual Guide.* Bath, Maine: Harry C. Webber, 1st ed. 1930, 71p, illustrated, illustrated wrappers, 16cm, later printings.

Golf in Schools

18460. *Golf in Schools.* Chicago: Golf PROmotions, 1st ed. [ca1939] 15p, illustrated, illustrated wrappers, 29.5cm.

Golf in Scotland

18480. *Golf in Scotland.* Aberdeen, Scotland: Premier Advertising [ca1939] 119p, illustrated, illustrated wrappers, 24.5cm.

Golf in Town and County [Angus and Kincardine]

18500. *Golf in Town and County: The Golf Courses in Angus and Kincardine.* Aberdeen, Scotland: James Brown, 1st ed. [ca1932] 40p, wrappers, 21cm.

Golf in Yorkshire

18520. *Golf in Yorkshire.* Yorkshire, England: Yorkshire Evening Post [ca1934] 68p, illustrated, illustrated wrappers, 18cm.

Golf Know How

18540. *Golf Know How, An Amazing Encyclopedia of Golf Tips.* New York: Golf Know How, 1st ed. [1957] 48p, illustrated, illustrated wrappers, 21.5cm.

Golf Links of France

18560. *The Golf Links of France.* [France] Railways of France, 1st ed. [ca1930] 31p, illustrated, illustrated wrappers, 21cm, foreword by Wilbur Forrest.

Golf Made Easy thru Scotch Secrets

18580. *Golf Made Easy thru Scotch Secrets.* Pittsburgh: Scotch Golf System, 1st ed. [1936] 66p, wrappers, 20.5cm.

Golf Match Club

18600. *Golf Match Club: Record of Matches, 1897-1908.* [London] Privately Printed, 1st ed. 1909, 113p, cloth, 13.5cm, compiled by Walter Bovill.

18610. *Golf Match Club: Record of Matches, 1897-1928.* [London] Privately Printed, 2d ed. note: this edition not located.

18620. *Golf Match Club: Record of Matches 1897-1938.* [London] Privately Printed, 3d ed. 1939, 339p, cloth, 13.5cm, compiled by John C. Craigie.

Golf Mind vs. Business Mind

18640. *Golf Mind vs. Business Mind: The neutro-mental system for Golfer.* Chicago: Superior Service Press, 1st ed. [ca1924] 38p, wrappers, 18.5cm.

Golf Professional's Handbook of Business

18660. *Golf Professional's Handbook of Business: The best of pro business practices as contributed by professionals.* Providence, Rhode Island: United States Rubber Co. 3d ed. [1932] 95p, illustrated, cloth, 25cm, note: see also Herb Graffis "The Golf Club Organizers' Handbook."

Golf Service Book

18680. *Golf Service Book For Caddies and Members.* Philadelphia: Lippincott, 1st ed. [1922] 31p, illustrated, illustrated wrappers, 18cm.

18690. 2d ed. rev. [1938] 36p, illustrated, illustrated wrappers, 21cm.

Golf Technique and Guide of Southern California

18710. *Golf Technique and Guide of Southern California.* Los Angeles: McHie & McHie 1st ed. [1940] 112p, illustrated, illustrated wrappers, 15.5cm.

Golfers Guide and Official Handbook for Scotland

18730. *The Golfers Guide and Official Handbook for Scotland.* Glasgow: John McMurtrie, 1st ed. 1901, 416p, illustrated, decorative cloth, 12cm.

Golfers Guide To Happy Holidays

18750. *Golfers Guide To Happy Holidays.* London: Webster, 1st ed. [ca1924] 55p, illustrated wrappers, 18.5cm.

Golfers Magazine

18770. *The Grip in Golf.* [Chicago] Golfers Magazine, 1st ed. [1923] 131p, illustrated, cloth, 19.5cm.

Golfers Yearbook

18790. *Golfers Yearbook 1938*. New York: National Golf Review, 1st ed. 1938, 320p, illustrated, cloth, 30.5cm.

18800. *Golfers Yearbook 1939*. New York: National Golf Review, 2d ed. 1939, 112p, illustrated, wrappers, 29cm.

Golfers' Guide and Hand-Book

18820. *The Golfers' Guide and Hand-Book*. Melbourne, Australia: Page & Bird, 1st ed. 1931, 64p, illustrated, illustrated wrappers, 22cm.

Golfers' Record, 1903

18840. *The Golfers' Record, 1903*. Philadelphia: Golfers' Record, 1st ed. 1903, 208p, illustrated, decorative cloth, 15cm.

Golfing in Scotland At 100 Holiday Resorts.

18860. *Golfing in Scotland At 100 Holiday Resorts*. London: Ed. J. Burrow, 1st ed. [ca1936] 124p, illustrated, cloth, 18.5cm, introduction by Archie Compston.

Golfing in Southern England

18880. *Golfing in Southern England and On the Continent [including the Channel Islands]*. London: Southern Railway, 11th ed. 1931, 168p, illustrated, illustrated wrappers, 21cm, introduction by Robert Browning. note: earlier editions not located.

Golfing on Long Island

18900. *Golfing on Long Island*. New York: Long Island Railroad, 1st ed. 1902 [22p] illustrated, illustrated wrappers, 15cm.

Golfmasters

18920. *Golfmasters: A Sure Way to Play Better Golf*. Brooklyn, New York: Golfmasters, 1st ed. [1940] [64p] illustrated, illustrated wrappers, 32cm, by Jimmy Thompson, Sam Snead, Dick Metz, Harry Cooper, Byron Nelson, Denny Shute, Craig Wood, Henry Picard, Vic Ghezzi, Jimmy Hines, Ralph Guldahl, Paul Runyan, Johnny Revolta, Horton Smith. foreword by Grantland Rice. later printing.

Gordon, Charles A.

18940. *The Gordon Caddie Guide*. Detroit, Michigan: Privately Printed, 1st ed. [1921] 112p, cloth, 14.5cm.

Gordon, Hugh H.

18960. *Repair Your Own Golf Clubs.* NP: Dietz Press, 1st ed. [1959] 40p, illustrated by Milton Hull, illustrated wrappers, 18cm.

Gordon, Jack

18980. *Ten Commandments of the Golf Stroke.* Buffalo, New York: Privately Printed, 1st ed. [ca1929] 21p, illustrated by Urquhart Wilcox, wrappers, 19cm.

18990. reprint ed. Buffalo, New York: Broed [1969] 23p, illustrated by Urquhart Wilcox, wrappers, 19cm.

19000. *Understandable Golf.* Williamsville, New York: Privately Printed, 1st ed. [ca1926] 144p, illustrated, leatherette, 20.5cm.

19010. 2d ed. rev. [1926] 160p, illustrated, leatherette, 20.5cm.

Gorham Golf Book

19030. *The Gorham Golf Book.* New York: Gorham, 1st ed. 1903, 148p, illustrated by John Hassall, decorative leather, 10cm.

Goring & Streatley Golf Club

19050. *Goring & Streatley Golf Club [Handbook].* Cheltenham & London: Ed. J. Burrow [ca1938] 20p, illustrated, illustrated wrappers, 16.5cm.

Gottlieb, Bea

19070. *What Is This Thing Called Swing?* New York: Privately Printed, 1st ed. [1945] 16p, illustrated, wrappers, 18.5cm, later printings.

Gottlieb, Harry

19090. *Golf for Southpaws.* New York: A.A. Wynn, 1st ed. [1953] 120p, illustrated, cloth, 27.5cm, foreword by Leo Fraser.

19100. reprint ed. New York: Hill & Wang [1953] 120p, illustrated, cloth, 27.5cm.

Graffis, Herb

19120. *A Treasury of Golf Tips.* Chicago: Golfing, 1st ed. [ca1940] 31p, illustrated, illustrated wrappers, 18cm.

19130. *Golfing's Treasury of Golf Tips.* Chicago: Golfing Publications, 2d ed. 1963, 18p, illustrated, illustrated wrappers, 18.5cm. note: second edition of "A Treasury of Golf Tips."

19140. *Easy Cures for Your Ailing Golf.* Chicago: Bee Bindery, 1st ed. [ca1959] 26p, illustrated, illustrated wrappers, 15cm.

19150. *Fun and Larceny.* Louisville, Kentucky: Hillerich & Bradsby, 1st ed. [1936] [12p] illustrated, illustrated wrappers, 18cm.

19160. *Golf Facilities: Organization, Construction, Management, Maintenance.* Chicago: National Golf Foundation, 1st ed. 1949, 77p, illustrated, illustrated wrappers, 28cm, note: previously titled "The Golf Club Organizers Handbook."

19170. *Golfing's Dictionary of Golf Information.* edited by. Chicago: Golfing Publications, 1st ed. [1960] 22p, illustrated, illustrated wrappers, 19.5cm.

19180. *Golfing's Digest of Golf Lessons.* Chicago: Golfing Publications, 1st ed. [1955] 32p, illustrated, illustrated wrappers, 17.5cm.

19190. *Golfing's Picture Story of Good Golf.* edited by. Chicago: Golfing, 1st ed. [1954] 24p, illustrated, illustrated wrappers, 28cm.

19200. *More Golf Business for You.* Chicago: National Golf Foundation, 1st ed. [ca1954] [10p] wrappers, 21.5cm.

19210. *Planning the Professional's Shop.* Chicago: National Golf Foundation, 1st ed. 1951, 50p, illustrated, illustrated wrappers, 28cm, later printings.

19220. *Simply Golf.* edited by. Chicago: Golfing Publications 1st ed. [1959] 23p, illustrated, illustrated wrappers, 17.5cm.

19230. *Six Champions Tell You How.* edited by. Chicago: Golfing Magazine, 1st ed. [ca1953] 48p, illustrated wrappers, 18cm.

19240. *The Golf Club Organizers Hand-Book.* Chicago: Golfdom Magazine, 1st ed. 1931, 56p, illustrated, illustrated wrappers, 30.5cm. note: see also "Golf Facilities: Organization, Construction, Management, Maintenance.

19250. *The Primer of Good Golf.* edited by. Chicago: Golfing Publications, 1st ed. [1957] 31p, illustrated, illustrated wrappers, 18cm.

Grange-Over-Sands New Golf Club

19270. *Grange-Over-Sands New Golf Club [Handbook].* Bristol & London: Temple Publicity Services [ca1951] 28p, illustrated, illustrated wrappers, 18.5cm.

Grant, Arthur

19290. *Golf: The Pocket Professional.* London: Methuen, 1st ed. 1930, 60p, illustrated by Abel Petit, leatherette, 13.5cm.

Graves, Charles and Henry Longhurst

19310. *Candid Caddies.* London: Duckworth, 1st ed. 1935, 120p, illustrated by Bert Thomas, illustrated boards, 21cm, introduction by Bernard Darwin.

19320. 2d ed. rev. London: Citadel Press, 1947, 126p, 1/4 cloth, illustrated boards, 18.5cm.

Gray, Maxwell [pseud Mary Gleed Tuttiett]

19340. *The Great Refusal.* London: John Long, 1st ed. 1906, 381p, cloth, 21.5cm.

19350. reprint ed. London: Collins [1907] 446p, cloth, 21cm.

Green, Sandy

19370. *Don'ts for Golfers.* London: Gay & Hancock, 1st ed. 1925, 70p, decorative cloth, 11cm.

Greene, Kell

19390. *The Golf Swing of Bobby Jones: An Analysis of His Drive.* Chicago: Dixon Press, 1st ed. 1931, 76p, illustrated, boards, 17cm.

Greenways

19410. *Fifty Golf Hints for Beginners.* Sidcup, England: Kentish Times, 1st ed. [ca1928] 47p, wrappers, 12.5cm.

Greenwood, George W.

19430. *Golf Really Explained.* London: W. Foulsham, 1st ed. [ca1926] 86p, illustrated, illustrated wrappers, 16cm, later printings.

19440. 2d ed. rev. [ca 1946] 91p, illustrated, wrappers, 16cm, introduction by Henry Cotton.

Gregory's Guide for Golfers

19460. *Gregory's Guide for Golfers: A Complete Handbook containing High-Class maps showing the locations and giving Details of Golf Courses around Sydney.* Sydney: Gregory's, 1st ed. [ca1939] 112p, illustrated wrappers, 21.5cm.

19470. 2d ed. rev. 1947, 148p, illustrated wrappers, 21.5cm.

Greig, Ian

19490. *The King's Club Murder.* London: Ernest Benn, 1st ed. 1930, 288p, cloth, 21.5cm.

19500. *The Silver King Mystery.* New York: Henry Holt, 1st American ed. [1930] 279p, cloth, 19cm, American title of "The King's Club Murder."

Gribbin, T.M.

19520. *The Wilmslow Golf Club [Handbook].* London: Temple Publicity Services [ca1950] 32p, illustrated, illustrated wrappers, 18cm.

Gribbin, Thomas

19540. *Correct Caddy Conduct: What to Know and Do and Why.* Philadelphia: Privately Printed, 1st ed. [1920] 32p, illustrated, wrappers, 13.5cm.

Grierson, Francis

19560. *Boomerang Murder.* London: Hutchinson, 1st ed. 1951, 248p, illustrated, cloth, 18.5cm.

Griffin, Marcus

19580. *A History of the Concord Golf Club 1899-1939.* Sydney, Australia: Privately Printed, 1st ed. 1939, 44p, wrappers, 24.5cm.

Griffiths, E.M.

19600. *With Club and Caddie: Verses and Parodies.* with a few by M.G., B.G. and L.C.H.G. London: Gibbings, 1st ed. 1909, 117p, cloth, 17cm.

Griggs, Bruce E.

19620. *Golfgraphs.* Washington, DC: Privately Printed, limited ed. [no limitation cited] 1933 [112p] illustrated, gilt stamped leather, 23cm.

Grimsdell, R.

19640. *Golf In South Africa.* Johannesburg, South Africa: South African Railways & Harbours Administration, 1st ed. 1928, 95p, illustrated, illustrated wrappers, 21.5cm.

19650. 2d ed. rev. Pretoria, South Africa: South African Railways, 1936, 39p, illustrated, illustrated wrappers, 25cm.

Gross, Milton

19670. *Eighteen Holes in My Head.* New York: McGraw-Hill, 1st ed. [1959] 148p, illustrated by John Pierotti, cloth, 20.5cm, foreword by Jimmy Demaret.

Guide to Golf Clubs in and Around London

19690. *A Guide to Golf Clubs in and Around London.* London: Simpson Piccadilly [ca1955] [46p] illustrated wrappers, 18.5cm.

Guldahl, Ralph

19710. *Groove Your Golf [Flipbook].* Indianapolis, Indiana: International Sports, 1st ed. [1939] 221p, illustrated, leatherette, 9.5cm, foreword by Bobby Jones.

Gullik, Geoffrey M.

19730. *History of Lindrick Golf Club 1891-1951.* Lindrick, England: Privately Printed, 1st ed. 1951, 52p, illustrated, decorative cloth, 21.5cm.

Gundelfinger, Jr., Philip [Phil]

19750. *Golf's Who's Who: Records of the Pros, 1958.* Pittsburgh, Pennsylvania: Golf's Who Who, 1st ed. 1958, 128p, illustrated, illustrated wrappers, 21.5cm.

Gustavson, Lealand

19770. *Enjoy Your Golf.* New York: Harcourt, Brace, 1st ed. [1954] 157p, illustrated by Lealand Gustavson, decorative cloth, 19.5cm.

H., T.

19790. *A Barton Ballad.* Edinburgh: Privately Printed, 1st ed. 1918, 15p, wrappers, 21cm. note: presumed to be Tom Hunter.

Haas, Harry J.

19810. *Handbook for Caddies and Members: Teaching the Caddies by Illustrations: telling the members what they really know but frequently disregard.* Philadelphia: Lippincott, 31p, 1st ed. [1922] 31p, illustrated wrappers, 17.5cm.

19820. *Golf Service Book for Caddies and Members.* Philadelphia: Lippincott, 2d ed. rev. 1938, 36p, illustrated, illustrated wrappers, 21cm. note: previously titled "Handbook for Caddies and Members."

Hackbarth, John C.

19840. *The Key to Better Golf: A Mental Plan.* Madison, Wisconsin: Privately Printed, 1st ed. 1929, 183p, illustrated, leatherette, 23cm.

Haddington Municipal Golf Course

19860. *Haddington Municipal Golf Course [Handbook].* Derby & Cheltenham, England: New Centurion, 1953, 36p, illustrated, wrappers, 18cm.

Hagen, Walter

19880. *Golf Clubs and How To Use Them.* Detroit, Michigan: W.J. Brueckman, 1st ed. 1929 [22p] illustrated, illustrated wrappers, 17 cm.

19890. *The How and Why of Golf.* Grand Rapids, Michigan: L.A. Young, 1st ed. [ca1932] 31p, illustrated, illustrated wrappers, 15cm.

19900. *The Walter Hagen Story.* New York: Simon & Schuster, 1st ed. 1956, 341p, illustrated, cloth, 23cm, with Margaret Seaton Heck, introduction by H.G. Salinger.

19910. 1st UK ed. London: Heinemann, 1957, 299p, illustrated, cloth, 22cm.

19920. limited ed. reprint [250 copies] Muirfield Ohio: Memorial Tournament, 1977, 299p, illustrated, embossed leather, 25cm.

Hahn, Paul

19940. *Links Logic*. Ormond Beach, Florida: Privately Printed, 1st ed. [1951] 39p, illustrated, illustrated wrappers, 19.5cm.

Hall, Holworthy

19960. *Dormie One, and other Golf Stories*. New York: Century, 1st ed. 1917, 349p, illustrated, decorative cloth, 19cm.

19970. *Dormie One*. New York: Privately Printed, limited ed. [250 copies] 1944, 37p, wrappers, 19cm, offprint from "Dormie One and Other Golf Stories."

Hall, Ray

19990. *A Golf Plan for Schools*. Chicago: National Golf Foundation, 1st ed. [ca1952] [8p] illustrated, illustrated wrappers, 23cm.

Hallem, A.E.

20010. *Straight Road to Golf: How to Become an Accomplished Player*. Manchester, England: Allied Newspapers, 1st ed. [ca1928] 47p, illustrated, illustrated wrappers, 18.5cm.

Hamilton, B. C.

20030. *Golf: A Treatise on the Royal and Ancient Game, A Glossary of Golfing Terms*. NP: Vetric, 1st ed. 1947 [34p] illustrated, illustrated wrappers, 8cm.

Hamilton, Eddie

20050. *Golfing Gimmicks*. [Scotland] Scottish Sunday Press, 1st ed. 1958 [32p] illustrated, illustrated wrappers, 14cm.

Hamilton, Edward A. and Charles Preston

20070. *Golfing America*. Garden City, New York: Doubleday, 1st ed. [1958] 128p, illustrated, illustrated boards, 31cm, text by Al Laney.

Hammerton, J.A.

20090. *The Rubaiyat of a Golfer*. London: Country Life, 1st ed. 1946 [72p] illustrated by D.L. Ghilchik, cloth, 17.5cm.

Hammond, Daryn

20110. *The Golf Swing: The Ernest Jones Method.* London: Chatto & Windus, 1st ed. 1920, 159p, illustrated, cloth, 22cm, later printings.

20120. 1st American ed. New York: Brentano's, 1920, 159p, illustrated, cloth, 22cm, later printings.

Handy, Ike S.

20140. *It's the Damned Ball.* Houston, Texas: Anson Jones Press, 1st ed. 1951, 174p, illustrated by Sid Van Ulm, decorative leatherette, 23.5cm.

20150. reprint ed. 1953, 174p, decorative cloth, illustrated by Sid Van Ulm, 23cm.

20160. 2d ed. Chicago: Twentieth Century Press, 1961, 150p, illustrated by Mel Keefer, cloth, 23cm.

Harburn Golf Club

20180. *Harburn Golf Club [Handbook].* Cheltenham, England: Ed. J. Burrow [ca1939] 16p, illustrated, illustrated wrappers, 16.5cm.

Harcke, Byron

20200. *Fore: Golf Fundamentals.* Chicago: Chicago Park District, 1st ed. [ca1960] [12p] illustrated, illustrated wrappers, 13cm.

Hare, Burnham

20220. *The Golfing Swing Simplified and Its Mechanism Correctly Explained.* London: Methuen, 1st ed. 1913, 62p, illustrated, pictorial cloth, 17cm, later printings.

20230. 4th ed. rev. 1915, 56p, illustrated, pictorial cloth, 17cm.

20240. 5th ed. rev. 1920, 62p, illustrated, pictorial cloth, 17cm.

Harlow, Bob

20260. *Golf State, North Carolina.* edited by. Raleigh, North Carolina: Dept. of Conservation & Development [ca1953] 32p, illustrated, illustrated wrappers, 20cm.

20270. *True Golf Facts.* Pinehurst, North Carolina: Pinehurst Outlook, 1st ed. [ca1940] 57p, wrappers, 18.5cm.

Harpenden Golf Club

20290. *Harpenden Golf Club, 1894-1954, Diamond Jubilee Souvenir Handbook.* Harpenden, England: Golf Clubs Association, 1st ed. 1954, 40p, illustrated, wrappers, 18.5cm.

Harris, Mark G.

20310. *New Angles on Putting and Chip Shots.* Chicago: Reilly & Lee, 1st ed. [1940] 80p, illustrated, illustrated wrappers, 35cm.

Harris, Robert

20330. *Proposed New Rules of Golf, A Threat To The Game As a Sport.* [England] Privately Printed, 1st ed. [ca1949] [8p] wrappers, 20.5cm.

20350. *Sixty Years of Golf.* London: Batchworth Press, 1st ed. 1953, 131p, illustrated, cloth, 23cm.

Hattstrom, H.A.

20370. *Golf After Forty.* [Ridgefield, Connecticut] Hall, 1st ed. [1946] 160p, illustrated, decorative cloth, 21.5cm.

20380. pbk. ed. Chicago: Popular Mechanics Press [ca1954] 128p, illustrated, illustrated wrappers, 21cm.

20390. *On and Off the Green.* Evanston, Illinois: Shoreline Press, 1st ed. [ca1955] [24p] illustrated, illustrated wrappers, 21.5cm.

20400. *The In-Line Method of Putting and Approaching.* Evanston, Illinois: Hattstrom Specialties, 1st ed. [ca1959] 28p, illustrated, illustrated wrappers, 21cm. note: second edition of "On & Off the Green."

Haultain, Theodore Arnold

20420. *The Mystery of Golf: A briefe Account of Games in generall; their origine; Antiqutie; & Rampancie:and of the game ycleped Golf in particular:its Uniqueness; its Curiosness; and its Difficultie; its anatomical, philsophicall, and moral properties; together with diverse Concepts on other Matters to it, appertaining.* Boston: Houghton Mifflin, limited ed. [440 copies] slipcased, 1908, 151p, 1/4 cloth, boards, 19.5cm. note: special leather edition, full grain pigskin, blindtooled, inlays of green and purple, inner covers of pigskin, silk linings.

20430. 2d ed. rev. New York: Macmillan, 1910, 249p, illustrated, decorative cloth, 19cm.

20440. 1st UK ed. of 2d American ed. rev. London: Macmillan, 1910, 249p, illustrated, decorative cloth, 18.5cm, later printings.

20450. facsimile ed. slipcased, New York: Serendipity Press, 1965, 151p, 1/4 cloth, illustrated boards, 18cm, foreword by Herbert Warren Wind.

Haywood, Abel

20470. *The Manchester Golf Club: Being A Record of Its Early Days.* Manchester, England: Privately Printed, 1st ed. 1909 [10p] illustrated, wrappers, 18.5cm.

Haywood, John C.

20490. *The Silver Cleek.* New York: Mitchell Kennerley, 1st ed. [1908] 286p, illustrated by Gordon Grant, pictorial cloth, 18cm.

Hecker, Genevieve [Mrs Charles T. Stout]

20510. *Golf For Women.* New York: Baker & Taylor, 1st ed. [1904] 217p, illustrated, decorative cloth, 21cm, with a chapter by Rhona K. Adair.

Helme, Eleanor E.

20530. *After the Ball: Merry Memoirs of A Golfer, being the Story of Forty-Six Championships and other Golfing Occasions pursued with Club, Notebook and Pencil.* London: Hurst & Blackett, 1st ed. [ca1931] 320p, illustrated by Charles Ambrose, decorative cloth, 18.5cm.

20540. *Family Golf.* London: J.M. Dent, 1st ed. 1938, 272p, illustrated by Barbara Turner, cloth, 19.5cm, foreword by Joyce Wethered.

20550. *The Best of Golf, By Some Best of Golfers.* edited by. London: Mills & Boon, 1st ed. 1925, 64p, illustrated, cloth, 19cm.

20560. *The Lady Golfer's Tip Book.* London: Mills & Boon, 1st ed. 1923, 95p, illustrated, cloth, 18.5cm.

Helmer, Myra Bradwell and Inez Lenore Klumph

20580. *Father Gander Golf Book.* Chicago: Chicago Legal News, 1st ed. 1909 [42p] illustrated by Clarence G. Vollmer, decorative cloth, 23cm.

Henderson's Photographic Golf Instructor

20600. *Henderson's Photographic Golf Instructor.* Colombo, Ceylon [Sri Lanka] Privately Printed, 1st ed. [1923] 120p, illustrated, cloth, 21.5cm.

Henderson, J. Lindsay

20620. *The Records of the Panmure Golf Club.* Dundee, Scotland: Privately Printed, 1st ed. 1926, 52p, cloth, 18.5cm.

Henderson, L.J.

20640. *Golf By the Masters.* edited by. Sydney, Australia: Crescent Publishing Service, 1st ed. [ca1950] 48p, illustrated, illustrated wrappers, 28cm.

20650. *The P.G.A. Golfer's Guide.* Sydney, Australia: Crescent, 1st ed. 1949, 104p, illustrated wrappers, 13cm.

Henderson, Robert W.

20670. *Line of Flight, A Manual of Golf.* Bismarck, North Dakota: Privately Printed, 1st ed. [1939] 39p, illustrated, illustrated wrappers, 18.5cm.

Henley Golf Club

20690. *Henley Golf Club [Handbook].* Cheltenham, England: Ed. J. Burrow [ca1916] 36p, illustrated, illustrated wrappers, 16.5cm.

Hensley, Bill F.

20710. *North Carolina-Golf State U.S.A.* edited by. Raleigh, North Carolina: Dept. of Conservation & Development [ca1953] 16p, illustrated, illustrated wrappers, 24.5cm, text by Arnold Kirk.

Herd, Alexander [Sandy]

20730. *My Golfing Life.* London: Chapman & Hall, 1st ed. 1923, 246p, illustrated, cloth, 22cm, as told to Clyde Foster, foreword by Field Marshal Earl Haig.

20740. 1st American ed. New York: Dutton, 1923, 246p, illustrated, cloth, 22cm.

Herndon, Charles

20760. *Golf Made Easier.* Los Angeles: Parker Stone & Baird, 1st ed. [1930] 220p, illustrated, cloth, 20cm.

Herold, Donald [Don]

20780. *Love That Golf: It can be better than you think.* New York: A.S. Barnes, 1st ed. [1952] 137p, illustrated, cloth, 19cm.

20790. 1st UK ed. Kingswood, England: World's Work, 1953, 126p, illustrated, cloth, 19cm.

20800. pbk. ed. Kingswood, England: World's Work, 1955, 126p, illustrated, illustrated wrappers, 18.5cm.

Hetzel, Frederick W.

20820. *You Can Improve Your Golf with A Sling-Master.* East Orange, New Jersey: Privately Printed, 1st ed. [1956] 42p, illustrated, illustrated wrappers, 23cm.

Heywood, John

20840. *John Heywood's Guide To Lancashire, Cheshire, Derbyshire, Yorkshire and North Wales Golf.* Manchester, England: John Heywood, 1st ed. 1920, 162p, illustrated linen wrappers, 18cm.

20850. 2d ed. [1921] 182p, illustrated linen wrappers, 18cm.

Hezlet, May [Mrs M.E.L. Ross]

20870. *Ladies Golf.* London: Hutchinson, 1st ed. 1904, 336p, illustrated, decorative cloth, 20cm. later printings.

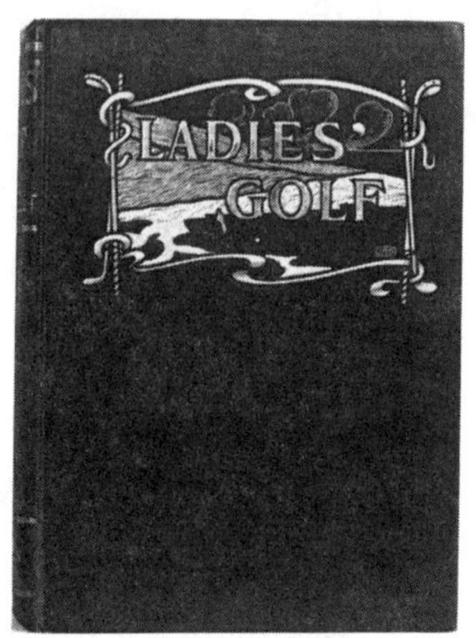

Hicks, Elizabeth Mary [Betty]

20890. *Fundamentals of Golf.* Chicago: J.A. Ducker, 1st ed. [1948] 20p, illustrated, illustrated wrappers, 18cm.

Hicks, Elizabeth Mary [Betty] and Ellen J. Griffin

20910. *Golf Manual for Teachers.* St. Louis, Missouri: C.V. Mosby, 1st ed. 1949, 312p, illustrated, decorative cloth, 21.5cm. later printing.

Highland Country Club

20930. *Highland Country Club 50th Anniversary 1901-1951.* Attleboro, Massachusetts: Privately Printed, 1st ed. 1951, 33p, illustrated, illustrated wrappers, 23cm.

Highman, Walter J.

20950. *A Heavenly Meeting, A Sequel.* Chicago: American Medical Association, offprint [1925] 7p, wrappers, 25.5cm, offprint from Archives of Dermatology & Syphilology.

Hill, J.C.H.

20970. *The Lyre On the Links and Other Verses.* London: John Bale, 1st ed. 1935, 60p, wrappers, 18.5cm.

Hillerich & Bradsby

20990. *Grand Slam Golf Classics.* Louisville, Kentucky: Hillerich & Bradsby, 1st ed. [ca1931] 62p, illustrated wrappers, 20cm, consultant-Innis Brown.

Hills, A.J.

21010. *Golf At Jasper Park.* Montreal: Canadian National Railways, 1st ed. [ca1927] [35p] illustrated, illustrated wrappers, 31.5cm.

Hillsborough Golf Club

21030. *The Hillsborough Golf Club [Handbook].* Derby & Cheltenham, England: New Centurion [ca1948] 20p, illustrated, wrappers, 16.5cm.

Hilton, Harold H.

21050. *Modern Golf.* New York: Outing, 1st ed. 1913, 140p, illustrated, decorative cloth, 17.5cm.

21060. *My Golfing Reminiscences.* London: James Nisbet, 1st ed. 1907, 247p, cloth, 19cm.

Hilton, Harold H. and Garden C. Smith

21080. *The Royal and Ancient Game of Golf.* London: Golf Illustrated, limited deluxe ed. [100 copies] 1912, 275p, illustrated, hand tooled decorative vellum, aeg, 30.5cm.

21090. limited ed. [900 copies] London: London & Countries Press, 1912, 275p, illustrated, gilt leather, aeg, 31cm.

Hime, Maurice

21110. *The Unlucky Golfer: His Handbook.* London: Simpkin, Marshall, Hamilton, Kent, 1st ed. 1904, 31p, illustrated by John R. Monsell, illustrated wrappers, 17cm.

Hindle, Darce

21130. *Links of Love, A Story of the Riviera.* London: John Long, 1st ed. 1904, 324p, decorative cloth, 19cm.

Hobson, William G.

21150. *It Ain't Necessarily So: Letters from Willie Appleseed to His Friend Frank.* New York: Privately Printed, 1st ed. [1959] 26p, illustrated, illustrated wrappers, 28cm.

Hodson, Bert

21170. *Your Best Way to Play The Chigwell Golf Course.* London: Broadway Plaistow [ca1952] 48p, illustrated, illustrated wrappers, 18cm.

Hogan, Ben

21190. *Five Lessons, The Modern Fundamentals of Golf.* New York: A.S. Barnes, deluxe ed. slipcased [1957] 127p, illustrated by Anthony Ravielli, cloth, 25cm, with Herbert Warren Wind, foreword by L. James.

21200. 1st trade ed.[1957] 127p, illustrated by Anthony Ravielli, cloth, 25.5cm.

21210. pbk. ed. New York: Cornerstone Library, 1962, 127p, illustrated, illustrated wrappers 20.5cm, later printings.

21220. reprint ed. Norwalk, Connecticut: Golf Digest, 1985, 127p, illustrated, cloth, 23cm, foreword by Nick Seitz.

21230. *The Modern Fundamentals of Golf.* London: Kaye & Ward, 1st UK ed. 1957, 127p, illustrated, cloth, 24.5cm. UK title of "Five Lessons, The Modern Fundamental of Golf."

21240. pbk. ed. London: Corgi, 1965, 127p, illustrated, illustrated wrappers, 18cm.

21250. *Here's Your Free Golf Lesson [Flipbook].* Baltimore, Maryland: Bromo-Seltzer, 1st ed. [ca1940] [56p] illustrated, illustrated wrappers, 5cm.

21260. *Power Golf.* New York: A.S. Barnes, 1st ed. [1948] 166p, illustrated, cloth, 22.5cm, foreword by Ed Dudley. later printings.

21270. 1st UK ed. London: Kaye & Ward, 1949, 190p, illustrated, cloth, 21.5cm. later printings.

21280. pbk. ed. New York: Pocket Books, 1953, 187p, illustrated, illustrated wrappers, 16cm, foreword by Ed Dudley.

21290. abridged ed. Louisville, Kentucky: Fawcett-Hayes [1960] 112p, illustrated, illustrated wrappers, 23.5cm.

21300. 2d abridged ed. rev. Greenwich, Connecticut: Fawcett [1960] 144p, illustrated, illustrated wrappers, 23.5cm.

Hogan, Ben and others

21320. *The Complete Guide to Golf.* and Cary Middlecoff, Sam Snead, Tommy Armour, Indianapolis: Bobbs-Merrill, 1st ed. [1955] 144p, illustrated, cloth, 24cm, foreword by Gene Littler.

21330. pbk. ed. New York: Maco Magazine [1955] 144p, illustrated, illustrated wrappers, 24cm.

Hon, Billy

21350. *Prominent Golfers in Caricature.* [Los Angeles] Privately Printed, 1st ed. 1930 [102p] illustrated, decorative leatherette, 29cm.

Hooper, Richard W.

21370. *The Game of Golf in East Africa.* edited by. Nairobi, Kenya: W. Boyd, 1st ed. 1953, 288p, illustrated, decorative cloth, 21.5cm.

Hopkins, Frank

21390. *Golf Holes They Talk About.* New York: Privately Printed, limited ed. signed [880 copies] 1927 [64p] illustrated, decorative cloth, 21cm.

Hopkinson, Cecil

21410. *Collecting Golf Books, 1743-1938.* London: Constable, 1st ed. 1938, 56p, cloth, 19cm.

21415. special presentation ed. [4 copies] 1938, 56p, leather, 19cm.

21420. pbk. ed. 1938, 56p, wrappers, 19cm.

21430. *Collecting Golf Books 1743-1938, to which has been added Bibliotheca Golfiana together with some notes and commentary by Joseph S.F. Murdoch.* Droitwich, England: Grant Books, limited ed. facsimile [250 copies} 1980, 90p, illustrated, cloth, 24cm, compiled and arranged by H.R. Grant.

Horne, W.B.J.

21450. *History of the Royal Wimbledon Golf Club 1865-1949.* London: Privately Printed, 1st ed. 1949, 28p, wrappers, 15cm.

Horton, Chester

21470. *Better Golf.* Chicago: John F. Dille, 1st ed. [1930] 58p, illustrated, illustrated wrappers, 23cm.

21480. *Chester Horton's Golf Lesson.* Albany, New York: Times-Union, 1st ed. [ca1925] 32p, illustrated, illustrated wrappers, 29cm, introduction by Chick Evans. note: imprint will vary as many newspapers in the US issued copies.

Hosmer, Howard C.

21500. *Through Half a Century: Commemorating the Fiftieth Anniversary of the Founding of the Country Club of Rochester.* Rochester, New York: Privately Printed, limited ed. [500 copies] 1945, 46p, illustrated, cloth, 22.5cm.

Hotchkiss, Horace L.

21520. *Origin and Organization of the Senior's Tournament.* [New York] Privately Printed, 1st ed. 1922, 32p, illustrated, wrappers, 22.5cm.

Houghton, George

21540. *An Addict's Guide to British Golf: A County by County Pictorial Directory.* London: Stanley Paul, 1st ed. 1959, 320p, illustrated, cloth, 21cm.

21550. *Confessions of A Golf Addict.* London: Museum Press, 1st ed. 1952, 84p, illustrated, wrappers, 21.5cm. later printings.

21560. *Confessions of A Golf Addict: An Anthology of carefree notes and drawings.* New York: Simon & Schuster, 1st ed. 1959, 182p, illustrated, cloth, 20.5cm, introduction by Ted Ray.

21570. *Golf Addict Visits the U.S.A.* London: Museum Press, 1st ed. 1955, 85p, illustrated, wrappers, 21cm. later printing.

21580. *Golf Addicts on Parade.* London: Country Life, 1st ed. 1959 [96p] illustrated, decorative cloth, 21.5cm, foreword by Cyril Tolley.

21590. *Golf Addicts Through the Ages.* London: Museum Press, 1st ed. 1956, 85p, illustrated, wrappers, 21cm.

21600. *Golf On My Pillow: Midnight Letters to A Son in Foreign Parts.* London: Stanley Paul, 1st ed. 1958, 144p, illustrated, decorative cloth, 21cm.
21610. pbk. ed. [1958] 142p, illustrated, illustrated wrappers, 18cm. later printings.

21620. *Golfer's ABC: A Golphabet for Addicts.* London: Museum Press, 1st ed. 1953 [52p] illustrated, wrappers, 25cm, verses by Hubert Simons.

21630. *More Confessions of A Golf Addict.* London: Museum Press, 1st ed. 1954, 86p, illustrated, wrappers, 21cm, later printing.

21640. *Portrait of A Golf Addict: A monograph in words and pictures.* London: Country Life, 1st ed. 1960, 102p, illustrated, decorative cloth, 21.5cm.
21650. 1st American ed. New York: Hart [1966] 151p, illustrated, illustrated wrappers, 17.5cm.

21660. *The Truth About Golf Addicts: An Anthology of carefree notes and drawings.* London: Museum Press, 1st ed. 1957, 194p, illustrated, cloth, 21cm, introduction by Ted Ray.

Hovanesian, Archie
21680. *Golf Is Mental.* New Britain, Connecticut: HB & HC, 1st ed. 1960, 98p, wrappers, 18.5cm.

How To Be A Good Caddie
21700. *How To Be A Good Caddie.* New York: Caxton Press, 1st ed. [1952] [16p] illustrated, illustrated wrappers, 13.5cm.

How To Improve Your Golf
21720. *How To Improve Your Golf: Lessons by British Masters.* London: Hutchinson, 1st ed. [ca1925] 88p, illustrated, cloth, 18.5cm.

How To Play the Old Course, St. Andrews
21740. *How to Play the Old Course, St. Andrews.* St. Andrews: J.&G. Innes, 1st ed. [ca1932] 44p, illustrated, illustrated wrappers, 17cm.

Howard, Robert Endersby

21760. *Lessons from Great Golfers.* London: Methuen, 1st ed. 1924, 175p, illustrated, cloth, 19cm.

Hughes, Henry

21780. *Golf for the Late Beginner.* London: John Long, 1st ed. 1911, 93p, illustrated, illustrated boards, 16.5cm, later printings.

21790. 1st American ed. New York: McBride Nast, 1913, 93p, illustrated, decorative cloth, 16.5cm, later printings.

21800. *Golf Practice for Players of Limited Leisure.* London: Thomas Murby, 1st ed. 1913, 93p, illustrated, illustrated boards, 18.5cm.

21810. 2d ed. rev. 1922, 96p, illustrated, decorative cloth, 18.5cm.

Hulse, Ronald W.

21830. *Dinsdale Spa Golf Club [Handbook].* London: Temple Publicity Services [ca1960] 16p, illustrated, illustrated wrappers, 18.5cm.

21840. *Hexham Golf Club [Handbook].* London: Temple Publicity Services [ca1960] 12p, illustrated, wrappers, 18.5cm.

Humorist On Golf

21860. *The Humorist on Golf.* London: Humorist, 1st ed. 1930, 80p, illustrated, illustrated wrappers, 24.5cm.

Hunter, David Smith

21880. *Golf Simplified: Cause and Effect.* Garden City, New York: Doubleday Page, 1st ed. 1921, 43p, illustrated, pictorial boards, 17cm, later printings.

21890. 1st UK ed. London: Hodder & Stoughton [1921] 64p, illustrated, cloth, 16.5cm.

Hunter, N.C.

21910. *The Losing Hazard.* London: Robert Hale, 1st ed. [1951] 252p, cloth, 21.5cm, later printing.

Hunter, Robert

21930. *The Links*. New York: Scribners', 1st ed. 1926, 163p, illustrated, decorative cloth, 22.5cm. note: In 1935 Golfdom Magazine purchased from Scribners' a few hundred unbound copies and bound them in a plain green cloth.

Hunter, Wille

21950. *The Easyway to Winning Golf: Methods of the Masters Authoritatively Explained*. Los Angeles: Easyway, 1st ed. [ca1935] 30p, illustrated wrappers, 16.5cm.

Hutchinson, Horace Gordon

21970. *Bert Edward, the Golf Caddie*. London: John Murray, 1st ed. 1903, 257p, cloth, 18.5cm, later printing.

21980. *Fifty Years of Golf*. London: Country Life, 1st ed. 1919, 229p, illustrated, cloth, 21.5cm.

21990. limited ed. facsimile [1500 copies] slipcased, Far Hills, New Jersey: USGA, 1985, 229p, illustrated, decorative cloth, 22.5cm, introduction by Peter Ryde.

22000. *Golf Greens and Greenkeeping*. edited by. London: Country Life, 1st ed. 1906, 219p, illustrated, cloth, 23cm.

22010. *The Lost Golfer*. London: John Murray, 1st ed. 1930, 335p, cloth, 18.5cm.

22020. *The New Book of Golf*. edited by. London: Longmans, Green, 1st ed. 1912, 361p, illustrated, decorative cloth, 19.5cm, contributors; May Hezlet, Bernard Darwin, James Sherlock, A.C.M. Croombe, C.K. Hutchinson. later printings.

Hutchinson, Jock

22040. *Better Golf*. Chicago: Chicago Tribune, 1st ed. [1928] 30p, illustrated, illustrated wrappers, 23cm.

Hyde, E. J.

22060. *The Story of the Pennant Hills Golf Club 1922-1959*. Sydney, Australia: Privately Printed, 1st ed. 1959, 55p, illustrated, cloth, 21.5cm.

Hyslop, Theodore B.

22080. *Mental Handicaps in Golf.* London: Bailliere, Tindall & Cox, 1st ed. 1927, 111p, decorative cloth, 16cm, forewords by Rolf Creasy & John Henry Taylor.

22090. 1st American ed. Baltimore, Maryland: Williams & Wilkins, 1927, 111p, decorative cloth, 16cm.

Ignotus

22110. *Golf in A Nutshell.* London: Country Life, 1st ed. 1919, 61p, boards, 16.5cm.

Igoe, Jr., James [Jim]

22130. *Hooks and Slices: A Parody on Golf.* Chicago: B.E. Callahan, 1st ed. [1950] [88p] illustrated by John Faulkner, cloth, 22.5cm.

Interesting Facts for Every Golfer

22150. *Interesting Facts for Every Golfer.* NP: Privately Printed, 1st ed. [ca1932] 23p, wrappers, 17.5cm.

Isles of Scilly Golf Club

22170. *Isles of Scilly Golf Club [Handbook].* Bristol & London: Temple Publicity Services [ca1950] 16p, illustrated, illustrated wrappers, 18cm.

Ito, Cho

22190. *Golfer's Treasures: Being an Alphabetical Arrangement of Theories and Hints from Great Golfers.* London: St. Catherine Press, 1st ed. 1925, 311p, illustrated, 1/4 cloth, boards, 18.5cm, foreword by Bernard Darwin.

James River Country Club

22210. *James River Country Club Twenty-Fifth Anniversary.* Newport News, Virginia: Privately Printed, 1st ed. 1957, 24p, illustrated, illustrated wrappers, 28cm.

James, Francis

22230. *Brancepeth Castle Golf Club [Handbook].* Bristol & London: Temple Publicity Services [ca1949] 16p, illustrated, illustrated wrappers, 18cm.

22240. *Llandudno Golf Club [Handbook]*. London: Temple Publicity Services [ca1960] 28p, illustrated, wrappers, 18.5cm.

22250. *The Hesketh Golf Club [Handbook]*. Bristol & London: Temple Publicity Services [ca1951] 23p, illustrated, illustrated wrappers, 18cm.

22260. *The Okehampton Golf Club [Handbook]*. Bristol & London: Temple Publicity Services [ca1951 16p, illustrated, illustrated wrappers, 18.5cm.

22270. *Warren Golf Club [Handbook]*. London: Temple Publicity Services [ca1960] 16p, illustrated, illustrated wrappers, 18.5cm.

James, Joseph [Joe]

22290. *Kill It Before It Moves: How Not to Play Golf in Several Humorous Lessons*. New York: A.S. Barnes, 1st ed. [1961] 54p, illustrated, cloth, 20.5cm.

James, Sid

22310. *From Tee To Cup*. Chicago: Wilson, 1st ed. [ca1955] 67p, illustrated, spiral bound wrappers, 18cm.

Jerome, Owen Fox

22330. *The Golf Club Murder*. New York: Edward J. Clode, 1st ed. [1929] 319p, cloth, 18.5cm.

22340. reprint ed. New York: Grosset & Dunlap [1929] 319p, cloth, 18.5cm.

Jessop, J.C.

22360. *Teach Yourself Golf*. London: English Universities Press, 1st ed. 1950, 201p, illustrated, cloth, 17.5cm.

22370. 2d ed. rev. 1960, 204p, illustrated, cloth, 17.5cm, later printings.

Johnson, J. W.

22390. *A Wonderful Golf Score*. NP: Privately Printed, 1st ed. [ca1920] 38p, illustrated wrappers, 19cm.

Johnson, Owen

22410. *Even Threes*. NP: NP, offprint [ca1930] 27p, wrappers, 20.5cm, offprint from the Golden Book, June 1930.

Jones, Ernest

22430. *Swing the Clubhead.* New York: Dodd, Mead, 1st ed. [1952] 126p, illustrated, cloth, 20cm, as told to David Eisenberg. later printings.

22440. 1st UK ed. London: Herbert Jenkins, 1953, 116p, illustrated, cloth, 19cm, with David Eisenberg, commentary by Bernard Darwin. later printings.

22450. reprint ed. Norwalk, Connecticut: Arno Press/Golf Digest, 1977, 126p, illustrated, decorative cloth, 21.5cm, later printings.

22460. *Swing's the Thing in Golf.* NP: Reader Mail, 1st ed. [1940] 31p, illustrated, illustrated wrappers, 18cm.

Jones, Ernest and Innis Brown

22480. *Swinging into Golf.* New York: Whittlesey House, 1st ed. 1937, 150p, illustrated, decorative cloth, 20.5cm, later printings.

22490. 1st UK ed. London: Nicholson & Watson, 1937, 150p, illustrated, cloth, 18.5cm. later printings.

22500. reprint ed. New York: Blue Ribbon, 1941, 150p, illustrated, cloth, 20.5cm.

Jones, Molly Sibbering

22520. *Golden Jubilee, The Story of the Southerndown Ladies Golf Club, 1905-1955.* Glamorgan, Wales: Privately Printed, 1st ed. 1958, 117p, illustrated, cloth, 21.5cm.

Jones, Robert Trent

22540. *Golf Course Architecture.* New York: Thompson & Jones, 1st ed. [ca1938] 39p, illustrated, wrappers, 19.5cm.

Jones, Jr., Robert Tyre

22560. *Bobby Jones On Golf.* New York: New Metropolitan Fiction, 1st ed. [1930] 112p, illustrated, illustrated wrappers, 30.5cm, introduction by Grantland Rice.

22570. 2d ed. rev. New York: One Time [1931] 112p, illustrated, illustrated wrappers, 30.5cm.

22580. *Golf Bobby Jones-Out of the Rough and Putt.* London: Flicker Productions, 1st ed. [1930] [100p] illustrated, wrappers, 7.5cm.

22590. *Golf Is My Game.* Garden City, New York: Doubleday, 1st ed. 1960, 255p, illustrated, cloth, 23cm.

22600. 1st UK ed. London: Chatto & Windus, 1961, 270p, illustrated, cloth, 23cm, foreword by Bernard Darwin.

22610. *Golf ShotsBy Bobby Jones-Driver and Mashie Shots.* London: Flicker Productions, 1st ed. [ca1930] [100p] illustrated, wrappers, 7.5cm.

22620. *How A College Or School Should Publicize The Showing of A Motion Picture on Golf.* New York: American Golf Institute, 1st ed. [ca1936] [4p] illustrated wrappers, 22.5cm.

22630. *How to Organize Golfers In A Municipality.* New York: American Golf Institute, 1st ed. [ca1936] 13p, illustrated, illustrated wrappers, 23cm.

22640. *How to Play Golf.* [New York] Bell Syndicate, 1st ed. [1929] 32p, illustrated, illustrated wrappers, 17 cm.

22650. 2d ed rev. [1930] 32p, illustrated, illustrated wrappers, 18.5cm.

22660. *How to Run A Golf Tournament.* New York: American Golf Institute, 1st ed. [ca1936] 32p, wrappers, 23cm.

22670. *My Twelve Most Difficult Shots.* St. Paul, Minnesota: B&B, 1st ed. [ca1929] 63p, illustrated, gilt stamped leather, 10cm, introduction by Grantland Rice.

22680. *Rights and Wrongs of Golf.* New York: A.G. Spalding, 1st ed. [1935] 45p, illustrated, illustrated wrappers, 17cm.

22690. 2d ed. rev. 1936, 53p, illustrated, leatherette, 17cm.

22700. *Some Tips from Bobby Jones.* [New York] A.G. Spalding, 1st ed. [ca1935] [22p] illustrated, illustrated wrappers, 15.5cm.

22710. *Suggestions How To See The Masters Tournament.* Augusta, Georgia: Augusta National Golf Club, 1st ed. [ca1949] [11p] wrappers, 15cm, later printings.

Jones, Jr., Robert Tyre and O.B. Keeler

22730. *Down the Fairway: The Golf Life and Play of Robert T. Jones, Jr.* New York: Minton, Balch, limited ed. signed, slip-cased [300 copies] 1927, 239p, illustrated, decorative cloth, 24cm, foreword by Grantland Rice.

22740. 1st trade ed. 1927, 239p, illustrated, decorative cloth, 21.5cm. later printings.

22750. 1st UK ed. London: George Allen & Unwin, 1927, 239p, illustrated, cloth, 21.5cm.

22760. reprint ed. New York: Blue Ribbon, 1927, 239p, illustrated, decorative cloth, 20.5cm. later printings.

22770. facsimile ed. Stamford, Connecticut: Classics of Golf, 1983, 239p, illustrated, cloth, 21.5cm, introduction by Herbert Warren Wind, afterword by Francis M. Bird.

Jones, Jr., Robert Tyre and Harold Lowe

22790. *Group Instructions in Golf: A Handbook for Schools and Colleges.* New York: American Sports Publications, 1st ed. 1939, 63p, illustrated, illustrated wrappers, 17cm.

Jones, Jr., Robert Tyre and others

22810. *Short Cuts to Par Golf.* and Gene Sarazen, Tommy Armour, Chick Evans, Harry Cooper, Walter Hagen, Horton Smith, Johnny Farrell, Bobby Cruickshank, Francis Ouimet. Louisville, Kentucky: Fawcett, 1st ed. 1931, 65p, illustrated, illustrated wrappers, 28cm.

Jones, Jr., Robert Tyre and Clifford Roberts

22830. *The Masters Tournament.* Augusta, Georgia: Privately Printed, 1st ed. [ca1952] [32p] illustrated, gilt stamped leather, aeg, 25cm.

Jordan, Harry Hall

22850. *Ye Golf Booke.* Brisbane, Australia: William Brooke, 1st ed. 1928, 43p, illustrated, illustrated wrappers, 18.5cm.

Jupp, Nancy

22870. *Nairn Golf Club [Handbook].* Derby & Cheltenham, England: New Centurion, 1957, 32p, illustrated, wrappers, 13.5cm.

Karpovich, Peter V.

22890. *A Study of Some Phsysiological Effects of Golf.* Springfield, Massachusetts: Y.M.C.A. College, offprint, 1928, 48p, wrappers, 24cm, offprint from The American Physical Education Review.

Kaser, Arthur Leroy

22910. *Fore! A Farce in One Act Wherein Golf Plays A Leading Part.* Boston: Walter H. Baker, 1st ed. [1931] 18p, illustrated, wrappers, 18.5cm.

Kavanagh, James Edward

22930. *Golf Made Easy: How to Play Without Stress or Strain.* New York: William-Frederick Press, 1st ed. 1953, 62p, illustrated, cloth, 21.5cm, foreword by Tommy Kerrigan.

Kay, Thomas

22950. *The Prestwick St. Nicholas Golf Club [Handbook].* London: Golf Clubs Association [ca1947] 33p, illustrated, wrappers, 18.5cm.

Kebo Valley Club

22970. *The Kebo Valley Club Sixtieth Anniversary Year 1888-1948.* Bar Harbor, Maine: Privately Printed, 1st ed. 1948 [14p] illustrated, illustrated wrappers, 43cm.

Keeler, O.B.

22990. *Golf in North Carolina.* Raleigh, North Carolina: N.C. Department of Conservation and Development, 1st ed. [ca1938] [52p] illustrated, illustrated wrappers, 18cm.

23000. *The Autobiography of An Average Golfer.* New York: Greenberg, 1st ed. 1925, 247p, cloth, 18.5cm.

23010. *The Boy's Life of Bobby Jones.* New York: Harpers', 1st ed. 1931, 308p, illustrated, cloth, 18.5cm. later printing.

Keene, Francis Bowler

23030. *Lyrics of the Links; Poetry, Sentiment and Humor of Golf.* New York: Appleton, 1st ed. 1923, 126p, decorative cloth, 16.5cm, foreword by Grantland Rice.

23040. 1st UK ed. London: Cecil Palmer [1923] 126p, decorative cloth, 16cm.

Kelso Golf Club

23060. *Kelso Golf Club Bazaar Cookery Book.* [Edinburgh] Privately Printed, 1st ed. 1914, 105p, cloth, 21cm.

Kenilworth Golf Club

23080. *Kenilworth Golf Club [Handbook].* Bristol & London: Temple Publicity Services [ca1951] 15p, illustrated, wrappers, 18.5cm.

Kennard, Edward [Mrs]

23100. *The Golf Lunatic and His Cycling Wife.* London: Hutchinson, 1st ed. 1902, 341p, decorative cloth, 18.5cm.

23110. 1st American ed. New York: Brentano's, 1902, 341p, decorative cloth, 18.5cm.

Kennedy, Daniel Edwards

23130. *Golf in Sapphira's Days.* Brookline, Massachusetts: Queen's Shop, 1st ed. 1910, 12p, illustrated wrappers, 20cm.

Kent, John Hoyt

23150. *Rhythm Golf.* NP: Privately Printed, 1st ed. [1958] 78p, illustrated, spiral bound illustrated wrappers, 28cm.

Kerns, Shirley K.

23170. *Fifty Years of Brae Burn, 1897-1947.* West Newton, Massachusetts: Privately Printed, 1st ed. 1947, 79p, illustrated, cloth, 27.5cm.

Kerr, John

23190. *The Golf Song Book.* Edinburgh: J. Kenyon Lees, 1st ed. [1903] 84p, illustrated wrappers, 27cm.

Killarney Golf and Fishing Club

23210. *Killarney Golf and Fishing Club [Handbook].* Cheltenham & London: Ed. J. Burrow [ca1951] 24p, illustrated, illustrated wrappers, 18.5cm.

King, J.B.

23230. *St. Austell Golf Club [Handbook]*. London: Golf Clubs Association, 1924, 20p, illustrated, wrappers, 18.5cm.

Kirkaldy, Andrew [Andra]

23250. *Fifty Years of Golf: My Memories*. London: T. Fisher Unwin, 1st ed. 1921, 224p, illustrated, cloth, 22.5cm, as told to Clyde Foster.

23260. 1st American ed. New York: Dutton, 1921, 224p, illustrated, cloth, 22cm.

23270. *My Fifty Years of Golf: Memories*. London: T. Fisher Unwin, 2d ed. 1921, 224p, illustrated, cloth, 22cm. note: previously titled "Fifty Years of Golf: My Memories," as told to Clyde Foster.

Knaresborough Golf Club

23290. *Knaresborough Golf Club [Handbook]*. Knaresborough, England: Privately Printed, 1929, 48p, illustrated, wrappers, 12cm.

Know the Game-Golf

23310. *Know the Game-Golf*. Wakefield, England: Educational Production, 1st ed. 1952, 32p, illustrated, illustrated wrappers, 13.5cm, later printings.

Knox, Edmund George Valpy [Evoe]

23330. *Mr. Punch on the Links*. edited by. London: Methuen, 1st ed. 1929, 147p, illustrated, decorative cloth, 19cm.

23340. 1st American ed. New York: Rae D. Henkle, 1929, 147p, illustrated, decorative cloth, 23cm.

Knox, Ronald A.

23360. *The Viaduct Murder*. New York: Simon & Schuster, 1st American ed. 1926, 252p, cloth, 19cm. note: first edition not located.

Koehl, Albert E.

23380. *Ardsley Country Club*. Ardsley on Hudson, New York: Privately Printed, 1st ed. 1955, 27p, illustrated, cloth, 26cm.

Kraetz, Ruben

23400. *Golf in Ten Lessons: with the Rules of Golf and 200 Golfing Tips; a complete golf instruction manual covering every phase of the game.* St. Louis, Missouri: Golf Publications, 1st ed. [1938] 48p, illustrated, illustrated wrappers, 28cm.

Lachenmeir, Rudy

23420. *Are You A Gope or A Golfer.* Portland, Oregon: Privately Printed, 2d ed. rev. [1952] 20p, illustrated, illustrated wrappers, 13cm. note: first edition published in 1944 not located.

Ladies Championship Golf 1893-1932 in aid of the Golfers' Cot.

23440. *Ladies Championship Golf 1893-1932 in aid of the Golfers' Cot.* London: Privately Printed, 1st ed. 1932, 76p, illustrated, wrappers, 21cm, introduction by Bernard Darwin.

Lake Placid Club Golf Courses

23460. *Lake Placid Club Golf Courses.* Lake Placid, New York: Lake Placid Club, 1st ed. 1910, 188p, illustrated, wrappers, 20cm.

Lamberhurst Golf Club

23480. *Lamberhurst Golf Club [Handbook].* Bristol & London: Temple Publicity Services [ca1951] 12p, illustrated, illustrated wrappers, 18.5cm.

Lancaster Golf Club

23500. *Lancaster Golf Club [Handbook].* Lancaster, England: John B. Barber, 1933, 35p, illustrated, illustrated wrappers, 22cm.

23510. *Lancaster Golf Club Souvenir Booklet.* Ashton Hall, England: Privately Printed, 1st ed. [ca1933] 38p, illustrated, illustrated wrappers, 22cm.

Lancaster, H. Boswell

23530. *Ridiculous Golf, In Story and In Verse.* London: Arthur H. Stockwell, 1st ed. [ca1938] 88p, cloth, 18.5cm.

23535. pbk. ed. [ca1938] 88p, wrappers, 18.5cm.

Langford, William B.

23550. *Golf Course Architecture in the Chicago District.* Chicago: Privately Printed, 1st ed. 1915, 17p, illustrated, wrappers, 23cm.

Lansdown Golf Club

23570. *Lansdown Golf Club [Handbook].* London & Bath: Mendip Press, 1939, 32p, illustrated, wrappers, 18cm.

Lardner, George E.

23590. *Cut Your Score: The Book of Commonsense Golf.* New York: Viking Press, 1st ed. 1933, 120p, illustrated, decorative cloth, 18.5cm, foreword by Francis Ouimet.

23600. *Golf Technique Simplified.* London: Putnam's, 1st UK ed. 1933, 240p, illustrated, decorative cloth, 18cm, foreword by Francis Ouimet. UK title of "Cut Your Score."

23610. *How to Play Golf.* Girard, Kansas: Haldeman Julius, 1st ed. [1927] 64p, illustrated, wrappers, 12.5cm.

Lardner, Rex

23630. *Out of the Bunker and into the Trees or the Secret of High-Tension Golf.* Indianapolis, Indiana: Bobbs-Merrill, 1st ed. [1960] 187p, illustrated, cloth, 21cm.

Lariar, Lawrence

23650. *Golf and Be Damned.* New York: Prentice-Hall, 1st ed. [1954] 128p, illustrated, decorative cloth, 28cm.

23660. *You've Got Me in A Hole: A collection of the best golfing cartoons by the foremost comic artists.* New York: Dodd, Mead, 1st ed. [1955] [90p] illustrated, decorative cloth, 27.5cm.

23670. 1st UK ed. London: Hammond, Hammond, 1956 [90p] illustrated, cloth, 24.5cm.

Lawless, Peter

23690. *The Golfer's Companion.* edited by. London: J.M. Dent, 1st ed. 1937, 498p, illustrated by Harry Roundtree, cloth, 19.5cm, later printing.

Layer, A.P.

23710. *The Simplicity of the Golf Swing.* London: L. Upcott Gill, 1st ed. 1911, 72p, decorative cloth, 16.5cm, later printings.

23720. 1st American ed. New York: James Pott [ca1911] 72p, decorative cloth, 16.5cm, later printings.

Leach, Henry

23740. *Great Golfer's in the Making: Being autobiographical accounts of the early progress at the most celebrated players.* edited by. London: Methuen, 1st ed. 1907, 299p, illustrated, decorative cloth, 22cm.

23750. 1st American ed. Philadelphia: George W. Jacobs [ca1907] 299p, illustrated, decorative cloth, 22cm.

23760. *Letters of A Modern Golfer to his Grandfather; Being the Correspondence of Richard Allingham, Esq.* London: Mills & Boon, 1st ed. 1910, 309p, cloth, 18.5cm.

23770. *The Happy Golfer: Being some experiences, reflections and a few deductions of a wandering player.* London: Macmillan, 1st ed. 1914, 414p, illustrated, cloth, 19.5cm.

23780. *The Spirit of the Links.* London: Methuen, 1st ed. 1907, 314p, cloth, 19cm.

Leamington Golf Club

23800. *Leamington Golf Club [Handbook].* Cheltenham & London: Ed. J. Burrow [ca1937] 22p, illustrated, illustrated wrappers, 16.5cm.

Leicestershire Golf Club

23820. *Leicestershire Golf Club [Handbook].* Cheltenham & London: Ed. J. Burrow [ca1938] 18p, illustrated, illustrated wrappers, 16.5cm.

Leigh, Dell

23840. *Golf At Its Best on the L.M.S.* London: London Midland & Scottish Railway, 1st ed. 1925, 117p, illustrated, illustrated wrappers, 23.5cm.

23850. *Twelve of the Best on the L.M.S.* London:London Midland & Scottish Railway [ca1930] 60p, illustrated, illustrated wrappers, 24cm. later printings.

Leigh-Bennett, Ernest Pendarves

23870. *An Errant Golfer.* [London] Hurst & Blackett, 1st ed. [1929] 288p, illustrated by H. H. Harris, cloth, 18.5cm.

23880. *Some Friendly Fairways.* [London] Southern Railway, 1st ed. [ca1930] 57p, illustrated, illustrated boards, 21.5cm.

23890. *Southern Golf.* London: Southern Railway, 1st ed. 1935, 167p, illustrated, illustrated boards, 21.5cm.

Leitch, Cecil

23910. *Golf.* London: Thorton Butterworth, 1st ed. 1922, 253p, illustrated, cloth, 22cm.

23920. 1st American ed. Philadelphia: Lippincott, 1922, 276p, illustrated, decorative cloth, 21.5cm.

23930. *Golf for Girls.* London: George Newnes, 1st ed. [ca1911] 91p, illustrated, illustrated wrappers, 18cm.

23940. 1st American ed. New York: American Sports Publishing [1916] 94p, illustrated, pictorial cloth, 19cm, foreword by Marion Hollins.

23945. pbk. ed, [1916] 94p, illustrated, illustrated wrappers, 19cm.

23950. *Golf Simplified.* London: Thorton Butterworth, 1st ed. 1924, 126p, illustrated, cloth, 18.5cm, later printing.

Leman, G. E.

23970. *A Short History of the Origins of Golf At Northam and the Foundation of the Present Royal North Devon Golf Club.* Bideford, England: Privately Printed, 1st ed. [ca1926] 16p, wrappers, 14cm.

Lemmon, George J.

23990. *About Golf.* Dallas, Texas: Crockett-James, 1st ed. 1941, 151p, illustrated by Bud James, leatherette, 21cm.

Leng, John

24010. *Leng's Golfer's Manual.* Dundee & London: John Leng, 1st ed. 1907, 96p, illustrated, illustrated wrappers, 15cm.

Let's Play Golf

24030. *Let's Play Golf.* Chicago: Chicago Daily Fee Golf Association, 1st ed. [1933] 16p, illustrated wrappers, 21.5cm.

Letchworth Golf Club

24050. *Letchworth Golf Club [Handbook]*. Cheltenham & London: Ed. J. Burrow [ca1938] 18p, illustrated, illustrated wrappers, 16.5cm.

Level, Jack

24070. *St. George's Golf and Country Club Thirtieth Anniversary.* Stony Brook, New York: Privately Printed, 1st ed. 1945, 39p, illustrated, illustrated wrappers, 13cm.

Liphook Golf Club

24090. *The Liphook Golf Club [Handbook]*. London: Golf Clubs Association, 1925, 32p, illustrated, wrappers, 18.5cm.

Lippincott, Horace Mather

24110. *A History of the Philadelphia Cricket Club 1854 to 1954.* Chestnut Hill. Pennsylvania: Privately Printed, 1st ed. 1954, 132p, illustrated, decorative cloth, 23.5cm.

Listen To This One

24130. *Listen to This One.* NP: United States Rubber, 1st ed. [ca1933] 20p, illustrated, illustrated wrappers, 15cm.

Littlestone Golf Club

24150. *Littlestone Golf Club [Handbook]*. Bristol & London: Temple Publicity Services [ca1951] 24p, illustrated, wrappers, 18.5cm.

Llandrindod Golf Club

24170. *The Llandrindod Golf Club [Handbook]*. London: Golf Clubs Association [1948] 28p, illustrated, wrappers, 18.5cm.

Locke, Arthur D'Arcy [Bobby]

24190. *Bobby Locke on Golf.* London: Country Life, 1st ed. 1953, 196p, illustrated, cloth, 23.5cm, foreword by Bernard Darwin.

24200. 1st American ed. New York: Simon & Schuster, 1954, 196p, illustrated, cloth, 23cm, foreword by Bernard Darwin.

24210. *Golf Hints.* [England] Lotus, 1st ed. [ca1955] 36p, illustrated, illustrated wrappers, 18cm.

24220. *How to Improve Your Putting*. Buffalo, New York: Dunlop Tire & Rubber, 1st ed. [1949] [10p] illustrated, illustrated wrappers, 16.5cm.

24230. *The Basis of My Game*. London: Slazengers, 1st ed. [ca1950] [14p] illustrated, illustrated wrappers, 20.5cm.

Long Ashton Golf Club

24250. *Long Ashton Golf Club [Handbook]*. London: Alex Matthews [ca1939] 25p, illustrated, wrappers, 18cm.

Longcliffe Golf Club

24270. *Longcliffe Golf Club [Handbook]*. Derby & Cheltenham, England: New Centurion, 1938, 28p, illustrated, wrappers, 13.5cm.

Longhurst, Henry

24290. *Addington Golf Club [Handbook]*. London: Golf Clubs Association [ca1953] 23p, illustrated, wrappers, 18cm.

24300. *Golf*. London: J.M. Dent, 1st ed. 1937, 303p, illustrated, cloth, 19.5cm, later printing.

24310. 1st American ed. Philadelphia: Davis McKay, 1937, 303p, illustrated, cloth, 19.5cm.

24320. *Golf in Ireland*. [Ireland] National Tourist Publicity, 1st ed. [1953] 12p, illustrated, illustrated wrappers, 23cm.

24330. *Golf Mixture*. London: Werner Laurie, 1st ed. [1952] 203p, illustrated by Adam Horne, cloth, 21.5cm, introduction by P.B. Lucas.

24340. *It Was Good While It Lasted*. London: J.M. Dent, 1st ed. 1941, 342p, illustrated, cloth, 21.5cm.

24350. *John O' Gaunt Golf Club [Handbook]*. Sutton Park, England: W.G. Groves, 1950 [28p] illustrated, wrappers, 21.5cm.

24360. *Mere Golf and Country Club [Handbook]*. London: John Langdon, 1947, 32p, illustrated, wrappers, 18.5cm.

24370. *Round in Sixty-Eight*. London: Werner Laurie, 1st ed. [1953] 173p, illustrated, cloth, 21.5cm.

24380. *The Wilderness Country Club [Handbook]*. [England] Privately Printed [ca1937] 15p, illustrated, illustrated wrappers, 17cm.

24390. *Turnberry Hotel and Its Golf Courses*. Turnberry, Scotland: Privately Printed, 1st ed. [ca1958] 16p, illustrated, illustrated wrappers, 20.5cm.

24400. *Turnberry Hotel and the Ailsa Golf Course*. Turnberry, Scotland: Privately Printed, 1st ed. [ca1953] 13p, illustrated, illustrated wrappers, 20.5cm.

24410. *Unwritten Contract*. London: Professional Golfer's Co-Operative Association, 1st ed. 1952 [12p] illustrated by Hunt Roberts, wrappers, 13.5cm.

24420. *West Sussex Golf Club [Handbook]*. Hants & London: Temple Publicity Services [ca1960] 28p, illustrated, illustrated wrappers, 18.5cm.

Looker, Samuel J.

24440. *On the Green: An Anthology for Golfers*. London: Daniel O'Connor, 1st ed. 1922, 232p, illustrated by Claud Lovat Fraser, cloth, 17cm.

Lorenz, LeRoy B.

24460. *The Science of Golf*. San Gabriel, California: Privately Printed, 1st ed. [ca1955] 24p, illustrated, illustrated wrappers, 21.5cm.

Loring, Phillip Quincy

24480. *Rhymes of A Duffer*. Portland, Maine: Privately Printed, 1st ed. [ca1915] [18p] wrappers, 16cm.

Los Angeles Country Club

24500. *History of the Los Angeles Country Club*. Los Angeles: Privately Printed, 1st ed. [ca1936] 14p, illustrated, wrappers, 18.5cm.

Loscalzo, Dic

24520. *On the Links*. Brooklyn, New York: Associated Feature Service, 1st ed. 1926, 45p, illustrated, illustrated wrappers, 25.5cm.

24530. 2d ed rev. 1927, 45p, illustrated, illustrated wrappers, 25cm.

Low, John Laing

24550. *Concerning Golf*. London: Hodder & Stoughton, 1st ed. 1903, 217p, cloth, 18.5cm, chapter on driving by Harold H. Hilton. later printing.

Lowe, W.W.

24570. *Bedrock Principles of Golf*. London: Collins, 1st ed. 1937 191p, illustrated, cloth, 21cm, foreword by Leonard Crawley.

24580. pbk. ed. [ca1937] 191p, illustrated, illustrated wrappers, 18cm.

Lyme Regis Golf Club

24600. *Lyme Regis Golf Club [Handbook]*. Bristol & London: Temple Publicity Services [ca1951] 20p, illustrated, illustrated wrappers, 18.5cm.

Lynham, John M.

24620. *The Chevy Chase Club: A History 1885-1957*. Chevy Chase, Maryland: Privately Printed, 1st ed. [1958] 127p, illustrated, decorative cloth, 26.5cm.

Lyttleton, R.H.

24640. *Out-Door Games: Cricket and Golf*. London: J.M. Dent, limited ed. [150 copies] 1901, 252p, illustrated by Arthur Rackham, 1/2 leather/cloth and vellum, 20cm.

24650. 1st trade ed. 1901, 252p, illustrated by Arthur Rackham, decorative cloth, 20cm.

Macbeth, James Currie

24670. *Golf From A to Z*. London: Putnam, 1st ed. 1935, 150p, illustrated, cloth, 18.5cm.

24680. *Golf: Professional Methods British & American*. Dunfermline, Scotland: Privately Printed, 1st ed. [ca1930] 39p, illustrated, wrappers, 15cm.

24690. *Methods of the Golf Masters*. London: Silvertown Co. 1st ed. [ca1934] 40p, illustrated, wrappers, 15cm.

24700. *Modern [1933] Golfing Methods by British and American Experts*. Dunfermline, Scotland: Privately Printed, 1st ed. 1933, 40p, illustrated, illustrated wrappers, 15cm.

24710. *One Way Golf, The Secret and Simplicity of the Perfect Swing*. Dunfermline, Scotland: Privately Printed, 1st ed. [1935] 48p, illustrated, wrappers, 15.5cm.

Maccauvlei Golf Club

24730. *Maccauvlei Golf Club*. Vereenigina, South Africa: Privately Printed, 1st ed. [ca1948] [12p] illustrated, illustrated wrappers, 20.5cm.

MacDonald, Charles Blair

24750. *National Golf Links of America*. [New York] Privately Printed, limited ed. [100 copies] [ca1912] 24p, illustrated, boards, 24.5cm.

24760. *Scotland's Gift, Golf: Reminiscences 1872-1927*. New York: Scribners, limited ed. [260 copies] signed, slipcased, 1928, 340p, illustrated, 1/2 vellum, illustrated boards, 25.5cm

24770. 1st trade ed. 1928, 340p, illustrated, cloth, 25.5cm.

24780. facsimile ed. Stamford, Connecticut: Classics of Golf, 1985, 340p, illustrated, cloth, 25.5cm, foreword by Herbert Warren Wind, afterword by Alistair Cooke.

MacDonald, John S.

24800. *Deck and Home Golf: The Oval Series*. London: George Routledge, 1st ed. [1905] 116p, illustrated, cloth, 18cm.

MacDonald, Robert G. [Bob]

24820. *Golf*. Chicago: Wallace Press, 1st ed. [1927] 210p, illustrated, decorative cloth, 28cm.

24830. *Golf At A Glance, The Pocket Pro*. Chicago: Bruce-Roberts, 1st ed. 1931 [40p] illustrated by Frederic Tellander, cloth, 14cm, introduction by P.A. Vaile. later printings.

Macey, C. A.

24850. *Golf Through Rhythm.* Crowborough, England: Crowborough Beacon Golf Club, 1st ed. [1957] 86p, illustrated, illustrated wrappers, 16.5cm, forewords by Tom Scott and C.O. Hezlet.

Machrihanish Golf Club

24870. *Machrihanish Golf Club.* Machrihanish, Scotland: Privately Printed, 1st ed. [ca1919] 24p, illustrated, cloth, 13cm.

Mackenzie, Alister J.

24890. *Golf Architecture: Economy in Course Construction and Green Keeping.* London: Simpkin, Marshall, Hamilton, Kent, 1st ed. 1920, 135p, illustrated, cloth, 16cm, introduction by H.S. Colt.

24900. *Dr. Mackenzie's Golf Architecture.* Worcestershire, England: Grant Books, limited ed. [700 copies] 1982, 85p, illustrated, cloth, 24cm, compiled and arranged by H.R. Grant, introduction by Robert Trent Jones, a commentary by Peter Thomson and Michael Wolveridge.

Mackenzie, Alister J. and L.A. & P.J.A. Berckmans

24920. *Description of the Bobby Jones Golf Course with an Historical Sketch of Fruitlands.* Augusta, Georgia: Privately Printed, 1st ed. [ca1934] [16p] wrappers, 23cm.

Maclaren, Muir

24940. *The Australian Golfer's Handbook.* Sydney, Australia: Langside, 1st ed. 1957, 256p, illustrated, cloth, 21.5cm.

24950. 2d ed. 1960, 223p, illustrated, cloth, 21.5cm.

MacLean, G.A.

24970. *Golf Through the Ages, or, The History of the Game, From B.C. to 1975 A.D.* Los Angeles: Western Book, 1st ed. [1923] 67p, illustrated by Lewis Hymers, decorative cloth, 19cm.

Maclennan, R.J.

24990. *Golf At Gleneagles.* Glasgow: McCorquodale, 1st ed. [1921] 144p, illustrated, illustrated boards, 20cm.

MacLeod, John

25010. *The Golfer's Dictionary.* Sydney, Australia: Dunvegan, 1st ed. [ca1935] [74p] illustrated by Mirren, illustrated wrappers, 12.5cm.

MacMillan, Ray

25030. *Masterminding Golf.* [USA] Privately Printed, 1st ed. [1960] 62p, illustrated, cloth, 26.5cm.

Macnamara, T.J.

25050. *The Gentle Golfer.* Bristol, England: J.W. Arrowsmith, 1st ed. 1905, 180p, illustrated by Arthur Morland, illustrated wrappers, 16cm.

MacPherson, Duncan

25070. *Golf Simplified: a graphic presentation of practical golf instruction for the beginning and the advanced player.* Chicago: Duncan MacPherson & William Pool, 1st ed. 1936, 96p, illustrated, illustrated boards, 20.5cm.

Magowan, David

25090. *The Scarsdale Golf Club 1898-1948.* Hartsdale, New York: Privately Printed, limited ed. [800 copies] 1948, 81p, illustrated, cloth, 24cm.

Maiden, Stewart

25110. *Ten Lessons in Golf.* [Atlanta, Georgia] Privately Printed, 1st ed. [ca1930] 32p, illustrated, illustrated wrappers, 23cm, preface by O.B. Keeler.

Manchester Courier

25130. *Manchester Courier Guide to Lancashire, Cheshire, Derbyshire and North Wales Golf.* Manchester, England: Manchester Courier, 1st ed. 1914, 152p, illustrated linen wrappers, 18.5cm.

Manchester Golf Club

25150. *The Manchester Golf Club [Handbook].* London: Ed. J. Burrow [ca1936] 23p, illustrated, wrappers, 16.5cm.

Manchester Guardian

25170. *Golf in 1938.* Manchester, England: Manchester Guardian, 1st ed. 1938, 32p, illustrated wrappers, 13.5cm.

25180. *Golf in 1939.* Manchester, England: Manchester Guardian, 2d ed. 1939, 32p, illustrated wrappers, 13cm.

Mangrum, Lloyd

25200. *Golf: A New Approach.* New York: Whittlesey House, 1st ed. [1949] 127p, illustrated, cloth, 24.5cm, foreword by Bing Crosby. later printings.

25210. 1st UK ed. London: Nicholas Kaye, 1949, 143p, illustrated, cloth, 23.5cm, foreword by Bing Crosby.

25220. *How to Break 90 At Golf.* Greenwich, Connecticut: Fawcett, 1st ed. [1952] 144p, illustrated, illustrated wrappers, 23.5cm, with Otis Dypwick.

25230. *How To Drive A Golf Ball [Flip Book].* NP: NP, 1st ed. [ca1955] [54p] illustrated, wrappers, 6cm.

25240. *How to Play Better Golf.* Greenwich, Connecticut: Fawcett, 1st ed. [1954] 144p, illustrated, illustrated wrappers, 23.5cm, with Otis Dypwick. previously titled "How to Break 90 at Golf."

Manion, James S.

25260. *Culbertson's Contract Golf.* New York: Bridge World, 1st ed. 1932, 64p, illustrated by Mawson Phillips, decorative cloth, 18.5cm, introduction by Grantland Rice, foreword by Ely Culbertson

25270. 1st UK ed. London: George Allen & Unwin, 1933, 64p, illustrated by Mawson Phillips, illustrated boards, 18.5cm.

Manning, Reg

25290. *From Tee to Cup.* Phoenix, Arizona: Reganson, 1st ed. 1954, 111p, illustrated, decorative cloth, 21.5cm.

Mannings Heath Golf Club

25310. *Mannings Heath Golf Club [Handbook].* London: Golf Clubs Association [ca1955] 23p, illustrated, wrappers, 18cm.

Manual for Caddies

25330. *Manual for Caddies*. Chicago: Chicago Park District, 1st ed. 1937, 48p, illustrated, illustrated wrappers, 21.5cm.

Mappin, G.E.

25350. *The Golfing You*. [London] Skeffington, 1st ed. [ca1948] 128p, cloth, 18.5cm.

Marietta

25370. *Six Golf Stories*. Dublin, Ireland: Hodges, Figgis, 1st ed. 1905, 143p, wrappers, 17.5cm.

Marquand, John P.

25390. *Life At Happy Knoll*. Boston: Little, Brown, 1st ed. [1957] 167p, illustrated by John Morris, cloth, 20.5cm. later printing.

Marshall, Keith

25410. *Golf Galore*. London: Nicholas Kaye, 1st ed. 1960, 123p, illustrated by Graham, cloth, 20.5cm.

25420. 1st American ed. New York: A.S. Barnes, 1960, 123p, illustrated by Graham, cloth, 20.5cm.

Marshall, Robert

25440. *The Enchanted Golf Clubs*. New York: Frederick A. Stokes, 1st American ed. [1920] 152p, illustrated by Stuart Hay, illustrated boards, 18.5cm, American title of "The Haunted Major."

25450. 1st Canadian ed. Toronto: S.B. Gundry [ca1920] 152p, illustrated by Stuart Hay, illustrated boards, 18.5cm.

25460. *The Haunted Major*. London: Alexander Moring, 1st ed. 1902, 192p, illustrated by Harry Furniss, decorative cloth, 17cm, later printings.

25470. 2d ed. Edinburgh: Moray Press, 1951, 192p, illustrated by John Mackay, cloth, 16.5cm.

25480. 3d ed. Edinburgh: Scottish Academic Press, 1973, 192p, illustrated by Harry Furniss, cloth, 19.5cm, introduction by Henry Longhurst.

25490. 1st American ed. New York: Ives Washburn, 1960, 192p, illustrated by John Mackay, decorative cloth, 17cm.

Martin, Harry Brownlaw

25510. *Fifty Years of American Golf.* New York: Dodd Mead, limited ed. signed, slipcased [355 copies] 1936, 423p, illustrated, cloth, 23.5cm, foreword by Grantland Rice.

25520. 1st trade ed. 1936, 423p, illustrated, decorative cloth, 23.5cm.

25530. facsimile ed. [New York] Argosy-Antiquarian, slipcased, 1966, 423p, illustrated, decorative cloth, 25cm.

25540. *Golf for Beginners.* New York: Modern Sports, 1st ed. [1930] 98p, illustrated, illustrated wrappers, 24cm, introduction by Walter Hagen.

25550. *Golf Made Easy.* New York: Modern Sports, 1st ed. [1932] 97p, illustrated, illustrated wrappers, 22.5cm, introduction by Walter Hagen. note: previously titled "Golf for Beginners."

25560. *Golf Yarns: The Best Things about the Game of Golf.* New York: Dodd Mead, 1st ed. 1913, 85p, illustrated, illustrated boards, 17cm.

25570. *Great Golfers in the Making.* New York: Dodd Mead, 1st ed. 1932, 268p, illustrated, decorative cloth, 19.5cm.

25580. 1st UK ed. London: John Lane, 1932, 268p, illustrated, decorative cloth, 21.5cm.

25590. *How to Play Golf: An Easy Way to Learn.* New York: Modern Sports, 1st ed. [1936] 98p, illustrated, illustrated wrappers, 24cm, introduction by Walter Hagen. note: previously titled "Golf for Beginners."

25600. *Pictorial Golf.* New York: Dodd, Mead, 1st ed. 1928, 243p, illustrated, decorative cloth, 19.5cm.

25610. *Pictorial Golf: Practical instruction for the beginner and valuable hints for the star.* London: John Lane, 1st UK ed. 1928, 243p, illustrated, cloth, 21.5cm.

25620. *Sketches Made At the Winter Golf League of Advertising Interests, at Pinehurst, North Carolina, January 1915.* New York: Publishers Typesetting, limited ed. [no limitation cited] 1915 [102p] illustrated, illustrated boards, 17cm.

25630. *The Garden City Golf Club [Golden Anniversary] 1899-1949.* Garden City, New York: Privately Printed, limited ed. [600 copies] 1949, 67p, illustrated, cloth, 30.5cm.

25640. *The Making of A Champion.* New York: Harry C. Lee, 1st ed. [ca1928] 32p, illustrated, illustrated wrappers, 17.5cm.

25650. *What's Wrong with Your Golf Game.* New York: Dodd Mead, 1st ed. 1930, 240p, illustrated, decorative cloth, 20cm.

25660. 1st UK ed. London: John Lane, 1930, 240p, illustrated, decorative cloth, 21.5cm

Martin, Harry Brownlaw and A.B. Halliday

25680. *St. Andrews [New York] Golf Club, 1888-1938.* Hastings-on-Hudson, New York: Privately Printed, limited ed. signed [500 copies] 1938, 146p, illustrated, decorative cloth, 23cm.

Massachusetts Golf Association

25700. *Caddie Instruction Manual.* Boston: Massachusetts Golf Association, 1st ed. [1946] 61p, illustrated, wrappers, 15cm.

25710. 2d ed rev. 1955, 61p, illustrated, wrappers, 15cm.

Masse, S. M.

25730. *Caddy Savvy: The Know-How of Expert Caddying.* Cleveland, Ohio: Privately Printed, 1st ed. [1947] 24p, illustrated, illustrated wrappers, 22cm.

Massy, Arnaud

25750. *Golf.* London: Methuen, 1st English language ed. 1914, 160p, illustrated, cloth, 19cm, translated form the French by A.R. Allison.

Maughan, William Charles

25770. *Picturesque Musselburgh and Its Golf Links.* London: Simpkin, Marshall, Hamilton, Kent, 1st ed. 1906, 108p, illustrated by Gemmell Hutchinson, decorative cloth, 18.5cm.

[May, George S.]

25790. *Highlights of George S. May's Tam O' Shanter Golf Tournaments, 1941-1956.* Chicago: George S. May, 1st ed. 1956, 9p, wrappers, 28cm.

Mayer, Dick

25810. *How To Think and Swing Like A Golf Champion.* New York: Crowell, 1st ed. [1958] 211p, illustrated, decorative cloth, 20cm. later printing.

McAlister, Alexander J.

25830. *The Eternal Verities of Golf: A Study in Philosophy and the Ancient Game.* [Greensboro, North Carolina] Privately Printed, Autograph edition, signed [1911] [28p] illustrated, cloth, 19.5cm.

McAndrew, J.

25850. *Golfing Step By Step.* Glasgow: Mitchell, 1st ed. [ca1910] 133p, illustrated, gilt stamped leather, 21.5cm.

McCallister, George

25870. *Golfercises [Flipbook].* Northridge, California: Photo-Aid, 1st ed. [ca1960] [218p] illustrated, illustrated wrappers, 8.5cm.

McConnaughey, James

25890. *Just Swing the Clubhead.* [New York] A. Stein, offprint [ca1946] [16p] illustrated, illustrated wrappers, 18cm, offprint from Collier's Magazine.

McCormick, J.

25910. *Fore: How to Play Good Golf.* Rotorua, New Zealand: Rotorua & Bay of Pleanty Publications, 1st ed. 1932, 66p, illustrated, illustrated wrappers, 19cm.

McFrederick, Roy L.

25930. *The Golfer's Handbook, A Manual on Golf As It Is Played and Taught by the Old Masters.* Manila, Phillipines: Sugar News Press, 1st ed. 1926, 116p, illustrated, wrappers, 20.5cm.

McGregor, George F.

25950. *Open Reflections.* [London] Privately Printed, 1st ed. [1948] 15p, illustrated wrappers, 20.5cm.

25960. *Open Reflections 1949.* [London] Privately Printed, 1st ed. 1949, 28p, illustrated, wrappers, 21.5cm.

25970. *Open Reflections 1950.* [London] Privately Printed, 1st ed. [1951] 42p, illustrated wrappers, 21.5cm.

25980. *Open Reflections 1952*. [London] Privately Printed, 1st ed. 1952, 35p, illustrated wrappers, 21.5cm. note: 1951 reflections chapter contained in this edition.

McKinlay, S.L.

26000. *The Millport Golf Club [Handbook]*. London: Golf Clubs Association [ca1948] 19p, illustrated, wrappers, 18.5cm.

26010. *Western Gailes 1897-1947*. Gailes, Scotland: Privately Printed, 1st ed. 1947, 23p, illustrated, decorative cloth, 18cm.

McKinney, Richmond

26030. *Luck Takes A Hand*. Memphis, Tennessee: S.C. Toof, 1st ed. [1941] 8p, illustrated wrappers, 21cm.

McLaren, R.M.

26050. *The Honourable Company of Edinburgh Golfers 1744-1944*. Gullane, Scotland: Privately Printed, 1st ed. 1944, 23p, wrappers, 21.5cm, with C.B. Clapcott.

McLean, Jack

26070. *One Knuckle Grip*. Glasgow: Scottish Daily Express, 1st ed. [ca1939] [16p] illustrated, illustrated wrappers, 24.5cm.

26080. *Why Not Beat Bogey*. London: Blackie & Son, 1st ed. 1937, 88p, illustrated, cloth, 18cm.

McMahan, Valarie

26100. *Bumps: The Golf Ball Kid and Little Caddies*. East Aurora, New York: Roycrofters, 1st ed. [1929] 88p, illustrated, decorative boards, 27.5cm.

McMaugh, P.

26120. *Golf Green Construction.* New South Wales, Australia: Australian Turf Grass Research Institute, 1st ed. [ca1955] 36p, illustrated, wrappers, 22cm.

McMurtie, John

26140. *The Golfers' Guide and Official Handbook for Scotland 1901-1902.* Glasgow, Scotland: Privately Printed, 1st ed. [ca1902] 416p, illustrated, decorative cloth, 12cm.

McRae, D.G.

26160. *The Principle of Human Automotion As Applied to Golf.* Seattle, Washington: Applied Human Automotion, 1st ed. 1945, 48p, illustrated, illustrated wrappers, 25cm.

McSpadden, Joseph Walker

26180. *How to Play Golf: Compiled from the best English and American authorities.* edited by. New York: Thomas Y. Crowell, 1st ed. [1907] 195p, cloth, 14cm.

Medina, Standish F.

26200. *A History of the Westhampton Country Club 1890-1955.* Westhampton, New York: Privately Printed, 1st ed. [1955] 154p, illustrated, cloth, 28cm.

Merrill, Anthony F.

26220. *The Golf Course Guide.* New York: Thomas Y. Crowell, 1st ed. [1950] 418p, cloth, 18.5cm.

Metcalfe, Leigh and Ted Mertz

26240. *Today's Humor, The Golf Number.* edited by. Oak Park, Illinois: Today's Humor, 1st ed. 1927, 64p, illustrated, illustrated wrappers, 15.5cm.

Metropolitan Golf Association

26260. *Caddie Management Manual.* New York: Metropolitan Golf Association, 1st ed. 1956, 38p, wrappers, 19cm.

26270. *Electric Golf Cart Survey in the Metropolitan New York Area.* New York: Metropolitan Golf Association, 1st ed. 1956, 33p, illustrated, wrappers, 17.5cm.

26280. *Golf Car Usage and Control in the Metropolitan New York Area.* New York: Metropolitan Golf Association, 1st ed. 1960, 36p, wrappers, 20cm. previously titled "Electric Golf Cart Survey."

26290. *Manual of Caddie Management.* New York: Metropolitan Golf Association, 1st ed. 1932, 24p, wrappers, 23cm.

Metz, Dick

26310. *Short Cuts to Improve Your Golf.* Racine, Wisconsin: Rainfair, 1st ed. [1940] 24p, illustrated, illustrated wrappers, 23cm.

26320. *The Secret to Par Golf: Golf made easy for men and women.* New York: Macmillan, 1st ed. [1940] [64p] illustrated, cloth, 33cm.

Metzger, Sol

26340. *Putting Analyzed: A book on perplexing phase of golf covering the game. Dedicated to the dubs, of whom the author is one, who go down to the Links with brave hearts, high hopes-and little more. Done for the purpose of adding a lot more-the clearance of the conflicting theories that make us fozzle on putts.* Garden City, New York: Doubleday, Doran, 1st ed. 1929, 102p, illustrated, decorative cloth, 19cm, later printings.

Meyer, Fred

26360. *The Golf Special, A Musical Foozle, A Musical Comedy in Three Acts [Book and Music].* NP: Privately Printed, 1st ed. 1909, 38p, illustrated, illustrated wrappers, 30.5cm.

Meyrick & Queens Park Golf Club

26380. *The Meyrick & Queens Park Golf Club [Handbook].* London: Golf Clubs Association, 1938, 51p, illustrated, wrappers, 18.5cm.

Mickleover Golf Club

26400. *Mickleover Golf Club [Handbook].* Cheltenham & London: Ed. J. Burrow [ca1938] 16p, illustrated, illustrated wrappers, 16.5cm.

Middlecoff, Cary

26420. *Advanced Golf.* Englewood Cliffs, New Jersey: Prentice-Hall, 1st ed. [1957] 230p, illustrated, cloth, 21.5cm, edited by Tom Michael.

26430. *Cary Middlecoff's Master Guide to Golf.* Englewood Cliffs, New Jersey: Prentice-Hall, deluxe ed. [1960] 266p, illustrated by Edward O. Bailey, decorative cloth, 27.5cm, edited by Tom Michael.

26440. 1st trade ed. [1960] 266p, illustrated by Edward O. Bailey, decorative cloth, 23.5cm, edited by Tom Michael. later printings.

26450. abridged ed. Greenwich, Connecticut: Fawcett [1963] 112p, illustrated, illustrated wrappers, 23.5cm, later printings.

26460. *Golf Doctor.* New York: Whittlesey House, 1st ed. [1950] 103p, illustrated, cloth, 24.5cm, foreword by Bob Hope.

26470. 1st UK ed. London: Nicholas Kaye, 1952, 112p, illustrated, cloth, 21.5cm.

Miles, Alfred H.

26490. *Golfer's Calendar: A Collection of Amusing Poems on the Game.* London: G. Delgado, 1st ed. 1913 [30p] illustrated, illustrated wrappers, 14cm.

Miller, Douglass B.

26510. *So You Want to Play Golf.* Wooster, Ohio: Privately Printed, 1st ed. [1947] 32p, illustrated, illustrated wrappers, 19cm.

Miller, Helen Markley

26530. *Striving to Be Champion: Babe Didrickson Zaharias.* Chicago: Kingston House, 1st ed. [1961] 191p, illustrated by Richard Mlodock, cloth, 21cm.

Miller, T.D.

26550. *Famous Scottish Links and Other Golfing Papers.* Edinburgh: R.&R. Clark, 1st ed. 1911, 150p, illustrated, cloth, 18.5cm.

26560. *The History of the Royal Perth Golfing Society: A Century of Golf in Scotland, with a selection of the Golfing verses [hitherto unpublished] by the late Neil Ferguson Balir, Esq. of Bathayock.* Perth, Scotland: Munro Press, 1st ed. 1935, 80p, illustrated, decorative cloth, 24.5cm.

Miller, Theodore T.

26580. *Essex County Club, Its History, Its Traditions*. Manchester-By-The-Sea, Massachusetts: Privately Printed, 1st ed. 1954, 31p, illustrated, illustrated wrappers, 22.5cm.

Mitchell, Abe

26600. *Down to Scratch*. London: Methuen, 1st ed. 1933, 145p, illustrated, cloth, 19cm, edited by J. Martin. later printings.

26610. *Essentials of Golf*. London: Hodder & Stoughton, 1st ed. [1927] 191p, illustrated, cloth, 22cm, edited by J. Martin. later printings.

26620. 1st American ed. New York: George H. Doran [1927] 195p, 20cm, cloth, edited by J. Martin. later printings.

26630. *Length on the Links: A Book for Players in all Stages Revealing the Secrets of the Long Ball*. London: Methuen, 1st ed. 1935, 138p, illustrated, cloth, 18.5cm, edited by J. Martin. later printings.

Moncado, Hilario Camino

26650. *360° Power Swing*. Los Angeles: Filipine Federation of America, 1st ed. [1951] 66p, illustrated, illustrated wrappers, 26.5cm.

Montague, William Kelley

26670. *The Golf of Our Fathers*. Duluth, Minnesota: Privately Printed, limited ed.[no limitation cited] 1952, 119p, illustrated, decorative cloth, 26.5cm.

26680. 2d ed. rev. 1953, 119p, illustrated, decorative cloth, 26.5cm.

26690. *Rule Changes: A Supplement to the Golf of Our Fathers*. Duluth, Minnesota: Privately Printed, 1st ed. 1961, 15p, illustrated wrappers, 25.5cm.

Moone, Theodore

26710. *Golf From A New Angle: Being letters from a scratch golfer to his son at college*. London: Herbert Jenkins, 1st ed. 1934, 248p, illustrated, cloth, 18.5cm, foreword by J.H. Taylor.

26720. 2d ed. rev. 1934, 248p, illustrated, cloth, 18.5cm, foreword by J.H. Taylor.

Moore, Bertha

26740. *Bunkered: A Duologue for Two Women.* London & New York: Samuel French, 1st ed. [1922] 12p, wrappers, 18.5cm.

Moore, Charles W.

26760. *The Mental Side of Golf.* New York: Horace Liveright, 1st ed. 1929, 167p, 1/4 cloth, illustrated boards, 19cm, foreword by Gene Sarazen. later printing.

Moran, Frank

26780. *Book of Scottish Golf Courses.* Edinburgh: S.M.T. Magazine & Scottish Country Life, 1st ed. 1939, 127p, illustrated, illustrated wrappers, 22.5cm, introduction by James Braid.

26790. 2d ed. 1945, 111p, illustrated, wrappers, 22cm, introduction by George Duncan.

26800. 3d ed. 1947, 128p, illustrated, illustrated wrappers, 21cm, introduction by Dai Rees.

26810. 4th ed. 1949, 108p, illustrated, illustrated wrappers, 21.5cm, introduction by John Paton.

26820. *Golfers' Gallery.* Edinburgh: Oliver & Boyd, 1st ed. 1946, 196p, illustrated, cloth, 18.5cm.

26830. *Gullane Golf Club [Handbook].* Derby & Cheltenham, England: New Centurion [1955] 28p, illustrated, wrappers, 18cm.

26840. *Westlinks Golf Course New Club, North Berwick [Handbook].* Derby & Cheltenham, England: New Centurion [ca1954] 64p, illustrated, wrappers, 18.5cm.

Morey, Albert A.

26860. *Tee-Time, Enjoy It and Live!* Chicago: Franklin House, 1st ed. [1952] 44p, illustrated by Cliff Ulrich, illustrated wrappers, 20cm.

Morris, Warren Emerson

26880. *The Toltec Twist, or, My Dad's Notebook on Golf.* Mexico City, Mexico: Privately Printed, 1st ed. 1955, 79p, illustrated, decorative cloth, 22.5cm.

Morrison, Alex J.

26900. *A New Way to Better Golf.* New York: Simon & Schuster, 1st ed. 1932, 186p, illustrated, cloth, 20cm, foreword by Rex Beach. later printings.

26910. 1st UK ed. London: William Heinemann, 1932, 179p, illustrated, cloth, 21cm, introduction by Bernard Darwin. later printings.

26920. 1st Canadian ed. Toronto: Musson [1932] 178p, illustrated, cloth, 20.5cm, foreword by Rex Beach. later printings.

26930. *Better Golf Without Practice.* New York: Simon & Schuster, 1st ed. [1940] 158p, illustrated, decorative cloth, 27cm, introduction by Clarance Buddington Kelland. later printings.

26940. *Pocket Guide to Better Golf.* New York: Simon & Schuster, 1st ed. 1934, 103p, illustrated, cloth, 16.5cm.

Morrison, Erwin G. [Morie]

26960. *Here's How in Golf.* Garden City, New York: Doubleday, 1st ed. 1949, 128p, illustrated, cloth, 25cm.

26970. 1st UK ed. London: Thorson's, 1950, 128p, illustrated, cloth, 21.5cm.

26980. *Here's How to Play Money Golf.* Garden City, New York: Doubleday, 1st ed. 1953, 64p, illustrated, illustrated boards, 19.5cm.

26990. *Life with Par.* Garden City, New York: Doubleday, 1st ed. 1958, 96p, illustrated, illustrated boards, 20.5cm.

Morrison, John Stanton Fleming

27010. *Around Golf.* London: Arthur Barker, 1st ed. 1939, 246p, illustrated, decorative cloth, 24cm, foreword by John Beck.

Morrison, Stuart

27030. *Golf Faults: How to Improve Your Game Fifty Percent.* London: George Newnes, 1st ed. 1912, 23p, illustrated, illustrated wrappers, 24.5cm.

Mortimer, Charles G. and Fred Pignon

27050. *The Story of The Open Championship [1860-1950].* London: Jarrolds, 1st ed. 1952, 248p, illustrated, cloth, 21cm.

Moseley Golf Club

27070. *Moseley Golf Club [Handbook]*. Derby & Cheltenham, England: New Centurion, 1939, 40p, illustrated, wrappers, 13cm.

Moses, R.J.H.

27090. *Fore!* London: Eyre & Spottiswoode, 1st ed. 1937, 145p, illustrated by Mel, cloth, 18cm.

Mountain View Country Club

27110. *Early Days of the Mountain View Country Club 1898-1927*. Greensboro, Vermont: Privately Printed, 1st ed. 1927 [9p] illustrated, wrappers, 19cm.

Mowbray Golf Club

27130. *Mowbray Golf Club [Handbook]*. Cape Town, South Africa: Privately Printed, 1st ed. 1932, 28p, illustrated, illustrated wrappers, 11cm.

Murray, Henry Arthur

27150. *More Golf Secrets*. Kingswood, England: Elliot's, 1st ed. 1954, 140p, illustrated, cloth, 18.5cm, preface by Algy Easterbrook.

27160. 1st American ed. New York: Emerson, 1955, 160p, illustrated, cloth, 18.5cm, preface by Algy Easterbrook.

27170. *The Golf Secret*. Kingswood, England: Elliot's, 1st ed. [1953] 142p, illustrated, cloth, 18.5cm, preface by Algy Easterbrook. later printings.

27180. 1st American ed. New York: Emerson, 1954, 142p, illustrated, cloth, 18.5cm, preface by Algy Easterbrook.

27190. 2d American ed. rev. 1954, 160p, illustrated, cloth, 18.5cm, preface by Algy Easterbrook.

Murray, J.P.

27210. *Golfing in Ireland*. Dublin: Harpers, 1st ed. 1952, 255p, illustrated, decorative cloth, 21cm. note: see also Martin E. Coffey " Golfing in Ireland."

Murray, Robinson

27230. *Are Golfer's Human?* New York: Prentice-Hall, 1st ed. [1951] 133p, illustrated by The Roth Foursome, cloth, 23cm.

Myers, Edward L.

27250. *Experiences of A Caddy.* Philadelphia: Dorrance, 1st ed. [1927] 96p, illustrated by James E. Mathews, Jr., pictorial cloth, 19cm.

Mylrea, D.T.

27270. *Sale Golf Club, Twenty-First Anniversary 1913-1934.* Manchester, England: Privately Printed, 1st ed. 1934, 16p, illustrated, illustrated wrappers, 23.5cm.

Naismith, Ted

27290. *Golf.* Melbourne, Australia: Privately Printed, 1st ed. [ca1948] 114p, illustrated, illustrated wrappers, 21.5cm, introduction by J.M. Dillon.

Nash, George C.

27310. *General Forcursue and Co.; More Letters to the Secretary of A Golf Club.* London: Chatto & Windus, 1st ed. 1936, 212p, illustrated by Christopher Millett, cloth, 19cm.

27320. *Golfing in North Ireland.* Belfast: Tourist Information Centre Association [ca1955] 100p, illustrated, illustrated wrappers, 18.5cm.

27330. *Golfing in Ulster.* Belfast: Ulster Tourist Development Association, 1949, 96p, illustrated, illustrated wrappers, 18cm. later printings.

27340. *Letters to the Secretary of A Golf Club.* London: Chatto & Windus, 1st ed. 1935, 195p, illustrated by Christopher Millett, cloth, 19cm.

27350. *Whelks Postbag: Still More Letters to the Secretary of A Golf Club.* London: Chatto & Windus, 1st ed. 1937, 187p, illustrated by Christopher Millett, cloth, 19cm.

National Golf Foundation

27370. *Beginning Golf, The Game.* Chicago: National Golf Foundation, 1st ed. [1948] 70p, illustrated, illustrated wrappers, 10cm.

27380. *Golf Fundamentals*. Chicago: National Golf Foundation, 1st ed. [ca1949] [12p] illustrated, illustrated wrappers, 13.5cm, note: see also "Golf Lessons."

27390. *Golf in Physical Education*. Chicago: National Golf Foundation, 1st ed. 1941, 48p, illustrated, illustrated wrappers, 23cm.

27400. *Golf Lessons: The Fundamentals As Taught by Foremost Professional Instructors*. Chicago: National Golf Foundation [1950] [28p] illustrated, illustrated wrappers, 21.5cm, introduction by Herb Graffis. later printings. previously titled "Golf Fundamentals."

27410. *Golf Operators Handbook: Miniature Putting Courses; Golf Driving Ranges; Par-3 Golf Courses*. Chicago: National Golf Foundation, 1st ed. 1956, 104p, illustrated, illustrated wrappers, 28cm, edited by Ben Chlevin.

27420. *Golf Range Operator's Handbook*. Chicago: National Golf Foundation, 1st ed. 1947, 34p, illustrated, illustrated wrappers, 28cm, later printings.

27430. *How to Improve Your Golf*. Chicago: National Golf Foundation, 1st ed. [ca1952] 71p, illustrated, illustrated wrappers, 21cm, later printings.

27440. *Miniature Golf Courses*. Chicago: National Golf Foundation, 1st ed. 1949, 24p, illustrated, illustrated wrappers, 28cm.

27450. *Planning and Building the Golf Course*. Chicago: National Golf Foundation, 1st ed. [ca1958] 28p, illustrated, illustrated wrappers, 28cm, later printings.

27460. *Planning and Building the Par-3 or Executive Golf Course Manual*. Chicago: National Golf Foundation, 1st ed. [ca1960] 30p, illustrated, illustrated wrappers, 28cm.

27470. *Public Opinion Survey. General Public and Golf Players*. Dunedin, Florida/Los Angeles: National Golf Foundation/John B. Knight, 1st ed. 1955, 13p, wrappers, 28cm.

27480. *Suggestions for Conducting Intramural Golf Tournaments.* Chicago: National Golf Foundation, 1st ed. [ca1950] [8p] illustrated wrappers, 28cm.

Neath Golf Club

27500. *Neath Golf Club [Handbook].* Bristol & London: Temple Publicity Services [ca1951] [10p] illustrated, wrappers, 18.5cm.

Neff, Sylva Kreider

27520. *Know Your Golf!* St. Paul, Minnesota: Brown & Bigelow, 1st ed. [ca1940] 28p, illustrated, illustrated wrappers, 14cm.

Neill, A.S.

27540. *The Booming of Bunkie.* London: Herbert Jenkins, 1st ed. [ca1925] 318p, cloth, 18.5cm.

Nelson, Byron

27560. *How To Score Better Than You Swing.* Evanston, Illinois: Golf Digest, 1st ed. [ca1955] [32p] illustrated, illustrated wrappers, 14cm.

27570. *Winning Golf.* New York: A.S. Barnes, 1st ed. [1946] 190p, illustrated, cloth, 25.5cm, foreword by Grantland Rice.

Newbould, T. Palmer

27590. *The Dieppe Golf Club.* Dieppe, France: Privately Printed, 1st ed. 1912, 56p, illustrated, decorative cloth, 15cm.

Newman, Josiah

27610. *Newman's Guide to London Golf: Being a Concise Guide to the Recognized Golf Clubs within 25 miles of Charing Cross.* London: Players Company, 1st ed. 1913, 288p, illustrated, leather, 18cm.

27620. limited special presentation ed. [9 copies] 1913, 288p, illustrated, leather, aeg, 18cm.

27630. *The Official Golf Guide to the United Kingdom 1903-04.* London: The Official Golf Guide Publishing Co. 1st ed. 1903, 448p, illustrated, cloth, 27.5cm.

Newmark, M. H.

27650. *Something About Golf, with a few Ramblings by Marco R. Newmark.* Los Angeles: Privately Printed, 1st ed. 1922, 15p, illustrated, illustrated wrappers, 16cm.

Newton Abbot Golf Club

27670. *Newton Abbot Golf Club [Handbook].* Bristol & London: Temple Publicity Services [ca1954] 16p, illustrated, illustrated wrappers, 18.5cm.

Niblick [Charles Stedman Hanks]

27690. *Hints to Golfers.* Salem, Massachusetts: Salem Press, 1st ed. 1902, 147p, illustrated, decorative cloth, 22cm, later printings.

Niblick [R.L. Kitching]

27710. *Introduction to Golf.* London: Lincoln Williams, 1st ed. [ca1932] 32p, wrappers, 18.5cm.

Niblick [Reginald Sigel]

27730. *Par Golf: Principles of the Natural Swing and Guides to Practice.* New York: Par Golf, 1st ed. [1926] 153p, illustrated, leatherette, 19cm.

Niblick Club

27750. *The Niblick Club 1922-1947.* Philadelphia: Privately Printed, 1st ed. 1947, 111p, illustrated, cloth, 23cm.

Nisbet's Golf Year Book

27770. *Nisbet's Golf Year Book 1905.* London: James Nisbet, 1st ed. 1905, 498p, cloth, 18.5cm, edited by John L. Low. note: first year title "Golfers' Year Book."

27780. 2d ed. 1906, 492p, cloth, 18.5cm, edited by John L. Low.

27790. 3d ed. 1907, 536p, cloth, 18.5cm, edited by John L. Low.

27800. 4th ed. 1908, 562p, cloth, 18.5cm, edited by John L. Low.

27810. 5th ed. 1909, 596p, cloth, 18.5cm, edited by John L. Low.

27820. 6th ed. 1910, 598p, cloth, 18.5cm, edited by John L. Low.

27830. 7th ed. 1911, 654p, cloth, 18.5cm, edited by John L. Low.

27840. 8th ed. 1912, 612p, cloth, 18.5cm, edited by John L. Low.

27850. 9th ed. 1913, 644p, cloth, 18.5cm, edited by Vyvyan G. Harmsworth.

27860. 10th ed. 1914, 554p, cloth, 18.5cm, edited by Vyvyan G. Harmsworth.

Nolan, William H.

27880. *Caddie Routine.* North Bennington, Vermont: Privately Printed, 1st ed. [1951] [22p] illustrated, illustrated wrappers, 12.5cm.

North Foreland Golf Club

27900. *The North Foreland Golf Club [Handbook].* Bristol & London: Temple Publicity Services [ca1951] 28p, illustrated, illustrated wrappers, 18.5cm.

North Manchester Golf Club

27920. *North Manchester Golf Club [Handbook].* London: Ed. J. Burrow [ca1938] 24p, illustrated, wrappers, 16.5cm.

Northbourne Golf Club

27940. *Northbourne Golf Club [Handbook].* Bristol & London: Temple Publicity Services [ca1951] 20p, illustrated, illustrated wrappers, 18.5cm.

Norval, Ronald

27960. *King of the Links: The Story of Bobby Locke.* Cape Town, South Africa: Maskew Miller, 1st ed. [ca1951] 108p, illustrated, cloth, 21.5cm.

Norwood, Joe

27980. *Help Yourself to Joe Norwood's Swing.* Los Angeles: Privately Printed, 1st ed. [1941] [10p] illustrated, illustrated wrappers, 28cm.

Novak, Joe

28000. *How to Put Power and Direction in Your Golf.* New York: Prentice-Hall, 1st ed. 1954, 187p, illustrated, cloth, 25.5cm, 3-D viewer enclosed in envelope attached to front cover.

28010. *Par Golf in 8 Steps.* New York: Prentice-Hall, 1st ed. 1950, 131p, illustrated, cloth, 20.5cm, later printings.

28020. 1st UK ed. London: Herbert Jenkins, 1951, 128p, illustrated, cloth, 20.5cm, later printings.

Nuneville

28040. *Illustrated Lessons in Golf.* Philadelphia: Innes, 1st ed. [ca1924] 128p, illustrated, cloth, 18cm.

Oahu Country Club

28060. *Oahu Country Club, The First Fifty Years 1906-1956.* Honolulu, Hawaii: Privately Printed, 1st ed. 1956 [16p] illustrated, illustrated wrappers, 25.5cm.

Oak Bluff Country Club

28080. *Oak Bluff Country Club.* Martha's Vineyard, Massachusetts: Privately Printed, 1st ed. [ca1914] [26p] illustrated, illustrated wrappers, 18.5cm.

Oak Park Country Club

28100. *Oak Park Country Club, Fifth Anniversary 1914-1919.* Oak Park, Illinois: Privately Printed, 1st ed. 1919, 35p, illustrated, wrappers, 27cm.

Oakley Country Club

28120. *Oakley Country Club 1898-1948: Notes On A Happy Half-Century.* Watertown, Massachusetts: Privately Printed, 1st ed. 1948, 49p, illustrated, decorative cloth, 18.5cm.

Oakwood Club

28140. *Oakwood Club 1905-1955, Fiftieth Anniversary.* Cleveland, Ohio: Privately Printed, 1st ed. 1955, 32p, illustrated, illustrated boards, 23cm.

Oban Golf Club

28160. *Oban Golf Club [Handbook].* London: Golf Clubs Association, 1915, 20p, illustrated, illustrated wrappers, 18.5cm.

Official Golf Guide

28180. *Official Golf Guide 1947.* New York: A.S. Barnes, 1st ed. 1947, 256p, illustrated, illustrated wrappers, 17cm, edited by William D. Richardson.

28190. *Official Golf Guide 1948.* New York: A.S. Barnes, 2d ed. 1948, 256p, illustrated, illustrated wrappers, 17cm, edited by Fred Corcoran.

28200. *Official Golf Guide 1949*. New York: A.S. Barnes, 3d ed. 1949, 256p, illustrated, illustrated boards, 18.5cm, edited by Fred Corcoran.

Ogg, Willie

28220. *Golf As I Know It*. New York: Vantage Press, 1st ed. [1961] 86p, cloth, 20cm, foreword by Robert L. Russell.

Old Link Golf Club

28240. *The Old Link Golf Club [Handbook]*. Cheltenham: Ed. J. Burrow [ca1938] 28p, illustrated, illustrated wrappers, 16.5cm.

Old Player [W.E. Riorden]

28260. *Golf and How to Play It*. London: Horace Cox, 1st ed. 1905, 164p, illustrated, decorative cloth, 18cm.

Oldest Member

28280. *The Etiquette and Traditions of Golf*. London: Silvertone [ca1920] 24p, illustrated, illustrated wrappers, 15.5cm.

Olgiati, Jake

28300. *Pocket Golf Book Illustrated*. Brioni, Italy: Privately Printed, 1st ed. 1924, 55p, illustrated, cloth, 16cm.

Olympia Fields Country Club

28320. *Olympia Fields Country Club*. Chicago: Privately Printed, 1st ed. [ca1923] [24p] illustrated, wrappers, folio, 37cm.

O'Malley, Bill

28340. *Golf Fore Fun*. San Mateo, California: The Golfer Magazine, 1st ed. [1953] [70p] illustrated, illustrated wrappers, 21.5cm, later printing.

28350. *Golf Fore Fun! A Book of Golf Cartoons*. New York: Prentice-Hall, reprint ed. [1953] [80p] illustrated, illustrated boards, 22.5cm, introduction by Bing Crosby.

O'Reilly, Nan

28370. *Bobby Jones Had To Defeat Himself*. New York: McClure's Magazine, offprint [1927] 31p, illustrated, illustrated wrappers, 14cm, offprint from McClure's Magazine.

Ormskirk Golf Club

28390. *Ormskirk Golf Club Golden Jubilee 1899-1949.* Ormskirk, England: Privately Printed, 1st ed. 1949 [16p] illustrated, wrappers, 15.5cm.

O'Rourke, Randall M.

28410. *The Truth About Golf.* Detroit, Michigan: Privately Printed, 1st ed. [1955] 33p, illustrated, wrappers, 15.5cm.

28420. *To Golf Here's How To Teach It.* Detroit, Michigan: Privately Printed, 1st ed. 1960, 10p, wrappers, 21.5cm.

Osborn, Robert

28440. *How to Play Golf.* New York: Coward McCann, 1st ed. [1949] [30p] illustrated, illustrated boards, 12cm.

Ouimet, Francis

28460. *A Game of Golf: A Book of Reminiscences.* Boston: Houghton Mifflin, limited ed. signed, slipcased [550 copies] 1932, 273p, illustrated, cloth, 21.5cm, introduction by Bernard Darwin.

28470. 1st trade ed. 1932, 273p, illustrated, decorative cloth, 20.5cm, introduction by Bernard Darwin.

28480. facsimile ed. Boston: Francis Ouimet Caddie Scholarship Fund, 1963, 273p, illustrated, decorative cloth, 20cm, introduction by Bernard Darwin.

28490. facsimile ed. limited [250 copies] Cincinnati, Ohio: Old Golf Shop, 1978, 273p, illustrated, gilt stamped leather, 21cm, issued for The Memorial Tournament 1978.

28500. *Golf Facts For Young People.* New York: Century, 1st ed. 1921, 207p, illustrated, decorative cloth, 18.5cm.

28510. *The Rules of Golf [Revised] Illustrated and Explained.* Garden City, New York: Garden City, 1st ed. [1948] 90p, illustrated by Art Krenz, cloth, 21.5cm.

Oyler, T.H.

28530. *The Golfer's Glossary or Lexicon of the Links.* Maidstone, England: W.P. Dickinson, 1st ed. [ca1920] [52p] illustrated by C.P. Hawlles, illustrated wrappers, 18cm.

Ozone Club

28570. *Down the Fairway and in the Rough with the Ozone Club 1901-1927*. Philadelphia: Privately Printed, 1st ed. 1927, 148p, illustrated, cloth, 23cm.

Pa Golf

28590. *Fore!* Sydney, Australia: Privately Printed, 1st ed. [ca1934] 82p, illustrated, illustrated wrappers, 18.5cm.

Pach, Al

28610. *Artists and Writers Golf Association*. [New York] Artists and Writers Golf Association, 1st ed. 1948 [120p] illustrated, spiral bound vinyl, 30.5cm, captions by Rube Goldberg.

Padgham, Alfred Harry

28630. *The Par Golf Swing*. London: George Routledge, 1st ed. 1936, 134p, illustrated, cloth, 18.5cm, preface by Evan M. MacColl.

Panton, John

28650. *My Way of Golf*. Glasgow: Scottish Field, 1st ed. [1951] 24p, illustrated, illustrated wrappers, 21.5cm.

Park, Jr., William

28670. *The Art of Putting*. Edinburgh: J&J Gray, 1st ed. 1920, 47p, illustrated, cloth, 22.5cm.

28680. 1st American ed. [United States] Donald Mathieson [1921] 47p, illustrated, cloth, 22.5cm.

Parris, C. L.

28700. *The Truth About Putting*. Savannah, Tennessee: Parris Manufacturing, 1st ed. [1953] 20p, illustrated, illustrated wrappers, 22cm.

Parrish, Samuel L.

28720. *Some facts, Reflections and Personal Reminiscences, connected with the Introduction of the Game of Golf into the United States, more especially as associated with the Formation of the Shinnecock Hills Golf Club [incorporated September 22, 1891]*. Southampton, New York: Privately Printed, 1st ed. [1923] 20p, illustrated, wrappers, 25cm.

Pazzetti, Jr., V.J.

28740. *Saucon Valley Country Club: Green Committee Summary Report and Statistical Review-1951 Amateur Championship of the USGA, September 10/15/51.* Saucon Valley, Pennsylvania: Privately Printed, 1st ed. [1951] 117p, illustrated, cloth, 28cm, assisted by William F. Gordon.

Peet, William F.

28760. *The Beginnings of Golf in Saint Paul and the Early History of the Town and Country Club.* St. Paul, Minnesota: Privately Printed, 1st ed. 1930 [13p] wrappers, 19cm.

28770. *The Story of Town and Country Club 1888-1948, Sixtieth Anniversary.* St. Paul, Minnesota: Privately Printed, 1st ed. 1948, 31p, illustrated, illustrated wrappers, 27.5cm.

Peille, Pentland

28790. *Clanbrae: A Golfing Idyll.* Edinburgh & London: William Blackwood, 1st ed. 1908, 324p, decorative cloth, 18cm.

Pendleton, Alexander

28810. *Better Golf with Brains.* Mount Morris, Illinois: Kable Brothers, 1st ed. [1941] 62p, illustrated by Jack Walther, illustrated wrappers, 21.5cm.

Pennard Golf Club

28830. *Pennard Golf Club [Handbook].* Cheltenham, England: Ed. J. Burrow, 1941, 24p, illustrated, wrappers, 16.5cm.

Pennink, Frank

28850. *Homes of Sport: Golf.* London: Peter Garnett, 1st ed. 1952, 209p, illustrated, cloth, 18.5cm.

Penzance Golf Club

28870. *Penzance Golf Club [Handbook].* London: Golf Club Publicity Association, 1914, 20p, illustrated, illustrated wrappers, 18cm.

Perkins, Helen B and Roy F.

28890. *Wannamoisett Country Club 1898-1948, Fiftieth Anniversary Year.* Rumford, Rhode Island: Privately Printed, 1st ed. 1948, 47p, illustrated, 1/4 cloth, decorative boards, 23cm.

Peterhead and the Peterhead Golf Club

28910. *Peterhead and the Peterhead Golf Club [Handbook].* London: Golf Clubs Association, 1939, 25p, illustrated, wrappers, 18.5cm.

Pettitt, Roy A.

28930. *The Straight-Line Golf Swing.* NP: Privately Printed, 1st ed. [1946] 23p, wrappers, 18.5cm.

Phillips, Michael J.

28950. *How to Play Miniature Golf: A Complete and Correct Description of the Art of the Newest Sport.* Los Angeles: Keystone, 1st ed. [1930] 82p, illustrated, illustrated wrappers, 20.5cm.

Philmont Country Club

28970. *Since The Spring of 1906... Philmont Country Club 1906-1946.* Philadelphia: Privately Printed, 1st ed. 1946 [16p] illustrated, tied wrappers, 22cm.

Philpot, George A.

28990. *The Birstall Golf Club [Handbook].* London: Golf Clubs Association, 1938, 28p, illustrated, wrappers, 18.5cm.

29000. *The Bournemouth Golf Club [Handbook].* Nottingham, England: Golf Club Publishing Service [ca1936] 27p, illustrated, wrappers, 18.5cm.

29010. *The Bridport & West Dorset Golf Club [Handbook].* London: Golf Clubs Association [ca1946] 39p, illustrated, wrappers, 18cm.

29020. *The Chigwell Golf Club [Handbook].* London: Golf Clubs Association, 1939, 23p, illustrated, wrappers, 18.5cm.

29030. *The Cleethorpes Golf Club [Handbook].* Nottingham, England: Golf Club Publishing Service, 1937, 34p, illustrated, wrappers, 18.5cm.

29040. *The Grimsley Golf Club [Handbook].* Nottingham, England: Golf Club Publishing Service [ca1938] 36p, illustrated, wrappers, 18.5cm.

29050. *The North Wales Golf Club [Handbook].* London: Golf Clubs Association [ca1947] 27p, illustrated, wrappers, 18.5cm.

29060. *The Reading Golf Club [Handbook].* London: Golf Clubs Association [ca1947] 29p, illustrated, wrappers, 18.5cm.

Photographic Study of Pebble Beach Golf Links

29080. *A Photographic Study of Pebble Beach Golf Links, Stroke by Stroke.* Carmel, California: Carmel Work Center, 1st ed. [1952] [48p] illustrated, illustrated wrappers, 28cm.

Pickworth, H.O. [Ossie]

29100. *Golf the Pickworth Way.* Sydney, Australia: John Reeve SportsBooks, 1st ed. [ca1949] 48p, illustrated, illustrated wrappers, 28cm, as told to John Reeve, foreword by Nick Stafford.

Pignon, Fred J.C.

29120. *Spalding Golfer's Year Book 1960.* London: Stanley Paul, 1st ed. 1960, 127p, illustrated, illustrated wrappers, 18cm.

Platte, Jules

29140. *Better Golf Through Better Practice.* Englewood Cliffs, New Jersey: Prentice-Hall, 1st ed. [1958] 169p, illustrated, cloth, 21cm, with Herb Graffis.

Play It Pro

29160. *Play It Pro: Golf from Beginner to Winner.* New York: Masthead, 1st ed. [1960] 66p, illustrated, illustrated wrappers, 18cm.

Pocket Pro

29380. *Pocket Pro.* New York: Norsil, 1st ed. [1948] 22p, illustrated, spiral bound flip cards, 11cm.

Pollock, William H.

29400. *You, the Golfer.* Milwaukee, Wisconsin: Privately Printed, 1st ed. [1937] 182p, leatherette, 16.5cm.

Pond, Harold M.

29420. *Guide to 1,870 North American Golf Courses.* Chicago: Popular Mechanics Press, 1st ed. [1954] 286p, illustrated by Art Huhta, illustrated wrappers, 19cm.

Pontypridd Golf Club

29440. *Pontypridd Golf Club [Handbook]*. Cheltenham, England: Ed. J. Burrow [ca1924] 28p, illustrated, illustrated wrappers, 16.5cm.

Popa, Nicholas

29460. *Caddy Tip$*. Worthington, Ohio: Privately Printed, 1st ed. 1953, 15p, illustrated, illustrated wrappers, 16cm.

Portmarnock Golf Club

29480. *Portmarnock Golf Club [Handbook]*. Cheltenham & London: Ed. J. Burrow [ca1939] 16p, illustrated, wrappers, 16.5cm.

Potters Bar Golf Club

29500. *The Potters Bar Golf Club [Handbook]*. London: Golf Clubs Association, 1926, 32p, illustrated, wrappers, 18.5cm.

Prain, Eric M.

29520. *Live Hands: A Key to Better Golf*. London: Adam & Charles Black, 1st ed. 1946, 55p, illustrated, cloth, 17.5cm, introduction by Bernard Darwin.

29530. 2d ed. rev. 1947, 63p, illustrated, cloth, 17.5cm, introduction by Bernard Darwin.

29540. *The Oxford and Cambridge Golfing Society 1898-1948*. edited by. contributors: Bernard Darwin, Harold Beveridge, Seton Gordon, Oliver Lyttelton, G.L. Mellin, R.C. Robertson-Glasgow, R.B. Vincent,, E.F. Storey, Guy Campbell, Dudley Scholey. London: Eyre & Spottiswoode, 1st ed. 1949, 245p, illustrated, cloth and leather, 21cm.

Preedy, Arthur

29560. *Home Park Golf Club, From Birth To Jubilee*. Kingston-upon-Thames, England: Privately Printed, 1st ed. 1950, 55p, wrappers, 25cm.

Prestatyn Golf Club

29580. *Prestatyn Golf Club [Handbook]*. Bristol & London: Temple Publicity Services [ca1951] 20p, illustrated, illustrated wrappers, 18.5cm.

Prestbury & Upton Golf Club

29600. *The Prestbury & Upton Golf Club [Handbook].* Cheltenham & London: Ed. J. Burrow [ca1950] 32p, illustrated, illustrated wrappers, 18.5cm.

Price, Charles

29620. *Golf Magazine's Pro Pointers and Stroke Savers.* New York: Harpers, 1st ed. [1960] 253p, illustrated by Lealand Gustavson & John Gallagher, cloth, 23.5cm, instruction editors: Jimmy Demaret, Gene Sarazen and Louise Suggs.

Prince's Golf Club

29640. *Prince's Golf Club [Handbook].* London: Golf Clubs Association, 1932, 31p, illustrated, wrappers, 18.5cm.

Professional Golfers' Association [UK]

29660. *Teaching Manual.* London: Professional Golfers' Association, 1st ed. [ca1950] 36p, illustrated, wrappers, 22cm.

Professional Golfers' Association [U.S.]

29700. *Education and Teaching Clinics and Seminars.* Dunedin, Florida: Professional Golfers' Association, 1st ed. 1956 [28p] illustrated, illustrated wrappers, 28cm.

29710. *Golf's Professional Man.* [Chicago] Professional Golfer's Association, 1st ed. [ca1943] [26p] wrappers, 18cm.

29720. *Greener Pastures At Dunedin Isles.* Chicago: Professional Golfers' Association, 1st ed. [ca1946] [20p] illustrated, illustrated wrappers, 30.5cm.

29730. *P.G.A. Teachers Guide.* Chicago: Professional Golfer's Association, 1st ed. [ca1951] 81p, illustrated, wrappers, 27.5cm, foreword by Robert T. [Bobby] Jones, Jr.

29740. *The Book of Golf: On the Occasion of the Ninth Biennial Ryder Cup Matches, Pinehurst, N.C. Nov. 2 and 4, 1951.* Chicago: Professional Golfers' Association, 1st ed. 1951, 115p, illustrated, decorative cloth, 28cm.

29745. pbk ed. 1951, 115p, illustrated, illustrated wrappers, 28cm.

29750. *Tournament and Player Record Book for 1934*. Chicago: Professional Golfers' Association of America, 1st ed. [1935] 43p, wrappers, 23cm.

29760. *Tournament and Player Record Book for 1935*. Chicago: Professional Golfers' Association of America, 2d ed. [1936] 109p, wrappers, 23cm. note: title change to "Official Record Book" in 1937.

29770. *Official Record Book 1936-37*. Chicago: Professional Golfers' Association, 3d ed. 1937, 154p, wrappers, 22.5cm. note: previously titled Tournament and Player Record Book.

29780. *Official Record Book 1938-39*. Chicago: Professional Golfers' Association, 4th ed. 1939, 163p, wrappers, 21.5cm.

29790. *Official Tournament Record Book 1940-41*. Chicago: Professional Golfers' Association, 5th ed. 1941, 180p, wrappers, 22.5cm.

29800. *Official Tournament Record Book 1941-49*. Chicago: Professional Golfers' Association, 6th ed. 1949, 273p, wrappers, 23cm.

29810. *Official Tournament Record Book 1950-58*. Dunedin: Florida, Professional Golfers' Association, 7th ed. 1958, 414p, wrappers, 21.5cm. note: supplements were issued in 1950,1952,1953,1954,1955,1956,1957

29820. *Official Tournament Record Book 1959-1964*. Dunedin, Florida: Professional Golfers' Association, 8th ed. 1965, 434p, wrappers, 21cm.

Pryde, Robert D.

31000. *The Early History of Golf in New Haven, Connecticut*. New Haven, Connecticut: Privately Printed, 1st ed. 1952, 15p, illustrated, wrappers, 23cm.

Punch Magazine

31020. *Mr. Punch on the Links*. London: Educational Book, 1st ed. [ca1935] 240p, illustrated, decorative cloth, 19.5cm, edited by J.A. Hammerton. Volume in the "New Punch Library."

31030. *Mr. Punch's Golf Stories Told By His Merry Men*. London: Educational Book, 1st ed. [ca1909] 191p, illustrated, decorative cloth, 17.5cm, edited by J.A. Hammerton.

31040. reprint ed. London: Carmelite House [ca1909] 191p, illustrated, illustrated wrappers, 18.5cm, edited by J.A. Hammerton.

31050. *That Game of Golf and Some Other Sketches.* London: Simpkin, Marshall, Hamilton, Kent, 1st ed. 1902, 99p, illustrated by Tom Browne, decorative cloth, 24.5cm.

31060. *The Funny Side of Golf, From the Pages of Punch.* London: Punch, 1st ed. [ca1909] 116p, illustrated, 1/4 cloth, illustrated boards, 26cm.

Puttenham Golf Club

31080. *Puttenham Golf Club [Handbook].* Bristol & London: Temple Publicity Services [ca1951] 16p, illustrated, illustrated wrappers, 18cm.

Q., A.

31100. *The Swing in Golf and How to Learn It.* London: A.&C. Black, 1st ed. 1919, 82p, cloth, 18cm, later printing.

Radcliffe, Claude

31120. *Holed Out In One: An Original Farcical Play.* London & New York: Samuel French, 1st ed. [1919] 39p, wrappers, 18cm.

Ramsey, Lon W.

31140. *Secrets of Winning Golf Matches: A Guide to Strategy and Tactics for the Competitive Amateur Golfer.* New York: Pilot, 1st ed. [1960] 38p, illustrated, illustrated wrappers, 21.5cm.

Rappaport, Milt

31160. *Oh, No!, A Golf Duffer's Handbook.* New York: Simon & Schuster, 1st ed. 1956, 64p, illustrated wrappers, 20cm, foreword by Byron Nelson.

Ratho Park Golf Club

31180. *Ratho Park Golf Club [Handbook].* London: Golf Clubs Association, 1948, 35p, illustrated, wrappers, 18.5cm.

Rattray, Jeanette Edwards

31200. *Fifty Years of the Maidstone Club 1891-1941*. Bridgehampton, New York: Privately Printed, limited ed. [500 copies] 1941, 194p, illustrated, decorative cloth, 30.5cm.

Ray, Edward

31220. *Driving, Approaching, Putting*. London: Methuen, 1st ed. 1922, 47p, illustrated boards, 17cm, later printings.

31230. 1st American ed. New York: Robert M. McBride, 1922, 47p, illustrated, pictorial boards, 17cm, later printings.

31240. *Golf Clubs and How To Use Them*. London: Methuen, 1st ed. 1922, 55p, illustrated boards, 16.5cm, later printings.

31250. 1st American ed. New York: Robert M. McBride, 1922, 53p, pictorial boards, 17cm, later printings.

31260. *Inland Golf*. London: T. Werner Laurie, 1st ed. [ca1914] 234p, illustrated, cloth, 18.5cm.

Reach, Milton

31280. *Night Golf*. Springfield, Massachusetts: Privately Printed, 1st ed. [ca1955] [8p] illustrated, illustrated wrappers, 28cm.

Read, Opie Percival

31300. *Opie Read on Golf*. Chicago: Golfers Magazine, 1st ed. [1925] [38p] french fold, illustrated, wrappers, 17cm.

Rebar, J.N. and James Jaske and George W. Doran

31320. *Cross-Word Golf: A Game for Two Players*. New York: Dutton, 1st ed. [1933] 95p, illustrated, cloth, 19cm.

31330. 1st UK ed. London: Rich & Cowan, 1933, 95p, illustrated, wrappers, 20cm.

Redditch Golf Club

31350. *Redditch Golf Club [Handbook]*. Cheltenham & London: Ed. J. Burrow [ca1936] 32p, illustrated, illustrated wrappers, 16.5cm.

Redmond, Jack

31370. *Golf Training*. Chicago: Privately Printed, 1st ed. [1930] 32p, illustrated, illustrated wrappers, 23cm.

Rees, Dai [David]

31390. *Dai Rees on Golf.* London: Gerald Duckworth, 1st ed. 1959, 176p, illustrated, cloth, 24.5cm, foreword by Bernard Darwin.

31400. 1st American ed. New York: A.S. Barnes, 1960, 176p, illustrated, cloth, 23.5cm, foreword by Bernard Darwin.

31410. *Golf My Way.* London: Heinemann, 1st ed. 1951, 88p, illustrated, cloth, 21.5cm, introduction by Ernest Bland. later printing.

Rehling, Conrad Henry

31430. *Golf for the Physical Education Teacher and Coach.* Dubuque, Iowa: Wm. C. Brown, 1st ed. [1954] 128p, illustrated, spiral bound illustrated wrappers, 28cm.

Reid, Hastings C.

31450. *The Key to the Rules of Golf and Definitions: A Comprehensive Analysis with Special Cross-Entry Index.* Sydney, Australia: Shepherd Press, 1st ed. 1946, 106p, leather, 20.5cm, foreword by W.E. Bain.

31460. 2d ed. rev. *The Key to the Rules of the Game of Golf and Definitions: A Comprehensive Analysis of the Revised Code with Special Cross-Entry Index.* Sydney, Australia: Shepherd Press, 1950, 145p, illustrated boards, 20.5cm, foreword by C.W. Rundle.

Reid, William

31480. *Golfing Reminiscences: The Growth of the Game, 1887-1925.* Edinburgh: J.&J. Gray, 1st ed. 1925, 140p, illustrated, cloth, 18.5cm.

Renick, Marion

31500. *Champion Caddy.* New York: Scribner's, 1st ed. 1943, 131p, illustrated by John Fulton, decorative cloth, 20cm.

Ressich, John

31520. *Thir Braw Days.* London: Ernest Benn, 1st ed. 1933, 127p, cloth, 18.5cm.

Revell, Alexander H.

31540. *Pro and Con of Golf.* Chicago: Rand McNally, 1st ed. [1915] 276p, illustrated, decorative cloth, 17cm.

Reville, Ralph H.

31560. *Golf in Canada, Along the Line of the Canadian Pacific.* [Canada] Canadian Pacific, 1926, 24p, illustrated, illustrated wrappers, 23.5cm.

Revolta, Johnny

31580. *6 Lessons from Johnny Revolta.* Evanston, Illinois: Golf Digest, 1st ed. [1954] 15p, illustrated, illustrated wrappers, 21cm.

Revolta, Johnny and Charles Cleveland

31600. *Johnny Revolta's Short Cuts to Better Golf.* New York: Thomas Y. Crowell, 1st ed. [1949] 203p, illustrated by Jerry Gibbons, cloth, 21.5cm, introduction by Ellsworth Vines.

31610. 2d ed. rev. [1956] 203p, cloth, 21cm.

Reynolds, Frank

31630. *Hamish McDuff.* London: Methuen, 1st ed. 1937, 48p, illustrated, illustrated boards, 24.5cm, foreword by Bernard Darwin.

31640. *The Frank Reynolds Golf Book: Drawings from Punch.* London: Methuen, 1st ed. 1932, 102p, illustrated, illustrated boards, 28cm, introduction by Bernard Darwin.

31650. 1st American ed. New York: Frederick A. Stokes [ca1932] 102p, illustrated, pictorial cloth, 28cm, introduction by Bernard Darwin.

Rhode Island Country Club

31670. *Rhode Island Country Club 1911-1951.* West Barrington, Rhode Island: Privately Printed, 1st ed. 1952 [76p] illustrated, illustrated wrappers, 24.5cm.

Rhodes, Hal

31690. *Fundamental Principles of Golf.* Harrison Hot Springs, Canada: Privately Printed, 2d ed. 1952, 65p, illustrated, illustrated wrappers, 30.5cm. note: first edition not located.

Ricardo, W.H.

31710. *Golfing Parodies.* [England] Privately Printed, [ca1930] [14p] illustrated wrappers, 20cm, offprint from the South Wales News.

31720. *Out-of-Bounds Poems. No.1-History of the the Hittites.* [England] Privately Printed, 1st ed. [ca1927] [5p] wrappers, 16.5cm.

31730. *Out-of-Bounds Poems. No.2-The Coming of the Moles.* [England] Privately Printed, 1st ed. [ca1927] [9p] wrappers, 16.5cm.

Rice, Grantland

31750. *Fore-With A Glance Aft.* [New York] Conde Nast, 1st ed. [ca1929] 47p, illustrated, pictorial boards, 32cm.

31760. *Sam Snead, Mystery Man of Golf.* New York: Sports Magazine, 1st ed. [1949] [4p] illustrated wrappers, 15cm.

31770. *The Bobby Jones Story: from the writings of O.B. Keeler.* Atlanta, Georgia: Tupper & Love, 1st ed. [1953] 303p, illustrated, decorative cloth, 21cm, preface by Bobby Jones. later printing.

31780. 1st UK ed. London: W. Foulsham [ca1953] 304p, illustrated, decorative cloth, 21cm, special foreword by Bernard Darwin, preface by Bobby Jones.

31790. limited ed. facsimile [300 copies]. Cincinnati, Ohio: Old Golf Shop, 1980, 304p, illustrated, pictorial leather, 21.5cm, special foreword by Bernard Darwin, preface by Bobby Jones.

Rice, Grantland and Clare Briggs

31810. *The Duffer's Handbook of Golf.* New York: Macmillan, limited ed. signed [500 copies] 1926, 163p, illustrated, tartan cloth, 25cm.

31820. 1st trade ed. New York: Macmillan, 1926, 163p, illustrated, decorative cloth, 25cm.

Rich, Endicott G. and Johnson Foley

31840. *You Can Think Ten Strokes Off Your Game, We Did! How two weekend golfers substituted reason for practice.* Nutley, New Jersey: Privately Printed, 1st ed. 1931, 43p, wrappers, 15.5cm.

Richardson, William D. [Bill]

31860. *The Eastern Golfer.* Syracuse, New York: Eastern Golfer, 1st ed. 1939, 72p, illustrated, illustrated wrappers, 30.5cm.

Richardson, William D. [Bill] and Lincoln A. Werden

31880. *Annual Golf Review 1931*. New York: Golfer's Year Book, 1st ed. 1932, 80p, illustrated, illustrated wrappers, 29cm.

31890. *Annual Golf Review 1933*. New York: Golfer's Year Book, 2d ed. 1934, 66p + 42p, illustrated, illustrated wrappers, 28cm.

31900. *Annual Golf Review 1934*. New York: William D. Richardson, 3d ed. 1935, 120p, illustrated, illustrated wrappers, 28cm. note: Annual Golf Review 1932 is contained in the Golfer's Year Book 1932.

31910. *Golfer's Yearbook 1930*. New York: Golfer's Year Book, 1st ed. 1930, 686p, illustrated, leatherette, 19cm.

31920. *Golfer's Yearbook 1931*. New York: Golfer's Year Book, 2d ed. 1931, 806p, illustrated, decorative cloth, 18.5cm.

31930. *Golfer's Yearbook 1932. Containing the supplement of the 1932 Annual Golf Review*. New York: Golfer's Year Book, 3d ed. 1932, 438p, illustrated, decorative cloth, 29cm.

31940. *Golfer's Yearbook 1933. Containing the United States Golf Association Records*. New York: Golfer's Year Book, 4th ed. 1933, 182p, illustrated, decorative cloth, 29cm.

Richmond County Country Club

31960. *Historical Souvenir Book of the Fiftieth Anniversary of the Richmond County Country Club 1888-1938*. Dongan Hills, New York: Privately Printed, 1st ed. 1938 [28p] illustrated, wrappers, 29cm.

Ricornus, C.A.P. [William D. Moffat]

31980. *The Goat Club Golf Book: the Rules of the Game as Played by the Ancient and Honorable Order of Goats*. New York: Knapp, 1st ed. [1911] [24p] illustrated, decorative cloth, 13.5cm.

Ridgewood Country Club

32000. *The Ridgewood Country Club History 1890-1940*. Ridgewood, New Jersey: Privately Printed, 1st ed. 1940, 102p, illustrated, spiral bound illustrated wrappers, 28cm.

Risk, Robert K.

32020. *Songs of the Links*. Edinburgh: George A. Morton, 1st ed. 1904, 48p, wrappers, 19.5cm.

32030. 2d ed. rev. London: Duckworth, 1919, 79p, illustrated by H.M. Bateman, cloth, 25cm.

Robb, James

32050. *Murrayfield Golf Club, The Story of Fifty Years.* Edinburgh: Privately Printed, 1st ed. 1947, 80p, illustrated by Tom Curr, cloth, 21.5cm.

Robbie, J. Cameron

32070. *The Chronicle of the Royal Burgess Golfing Society of Edinburgh, 1735-1935.* Edinburgh: Morrison & Gibb, 1st ed. 1936, 111p, illustrated, cloth, 21.5cm.

32080. *The Chronicle of the Royal Burgess Golfing Society of Edinburgh 1735-1935. Volume I.* Broxburn, Scotland: Alna Press, reprint ed. 1983, 111p, illustrated, decorative cloth, 21.5cm.

Roberts, Arthur E.

32100. *Handbook for Caddies.* Cincinnati, Ohio: H.R. Alcorn, 1st ed. 1914, 40p, illustrated, illustrated wrappers, 14.5cm, foreword by Chick Evans. later printings

Roberts, Henry

32120. *The Green Book of Golf 1923-1924.* San Francisco: Privately Printed, 1st ed. [1923] 534p, illustrated, gilt stamped leather, 26cm.

32130. *The Green Book of Golf 1925-1926.* San Francisco: Privately Printed, 2d ed. 528p, leather, 26cm.

Robertson, A.J.

32150. *The A.B.C. of Golf.* London: Henry J. Drake 1st ed. [ca1904] 110p, illustrated, decorative cloth, 13cm.

Robertson, Frank N.

32170. *Golf Gleanings Old and New and the History of the Maritime Seniors' Golf Association.* Saint John, Canada: Privately Printed, 1st ed. 1953, 100p, illustrated, decorative cloth, 26.5cm.

Robertson, Kolin

32190. *Some Yorkshire Golf Courses.* Leeds, England: Apsley Press, 1st ed. 1935, 132p, illustrated, 22cm.

Robertson, Maud Gordon [Mrs]

32210. *Hints to the Lady Golfers.* London: Walbrook, 1st ed. 1909, 61p, illustrated by Annie Bell, cloth, 18.5cm.

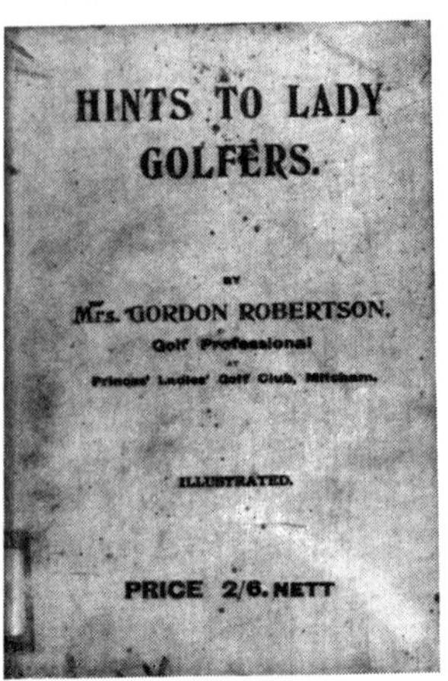

Robinson, Larry

32230. *Golf Secrets of the Pros.* New York: Arco, 1st ed. [1956] 144p, illustrated, decorative cloth, 24cm, introduction by Ray Gill. later printing.

32240. pbk. ed. Greenwich, Connecticut: Fawcett [1956] 144p, illustrated, illustrated wrappers, 23.5cm, later printings.

Robinson, Lawrence

32260. *History of the Blind Brook Club.* Port Chester, New York: Privately Printed, 1st ed. 1947, 19p, illustrated wrappers, 17cm.

Robinson, W. Heath

32280. *Humors of Golf.* London: Methuen, 1st ed. 1923, 50p, illustrated, illustrated boards, 28cm, introduction by Bernard Darwin.

32290. 1st American ed. New York: Dodd, Mead, 1923, 50p, illustrated, illustrated boards, 28cm, introduction by Bernard Darwin.

32300. reprint ed. London: Duckworth, 1975, 50p, illustrated, cloth, 27.5cm, introduction by Bernard Darwin.

Rodgers, Phillip H.

32320. *How to Play St. Andrews Old Links Course [Handbook].* Bristol & London: Temple Publicity Services [ca1951] 28p, illustrated, wrappers, 18.5cm.

Romsey Golf Club

32340. *Romsey Golf Club [Handbook].* Bristol & London: Temple Publicity Services [ca1951] 12p, illustrated, illustrated wrappers, 18.5cm.

Rooney, J.P.

32360. *Play Good Golf.* Tralee, Ireland: Kerryman, 1st ed. [ca1939] 144p, illustrated, illustrated wrappers, 21.5cm.

Rose, William Ganson and Charles Milton Newcomb

32380. *Cut Down That Score: The Psychology of Golf.* Cleveland, Ohio: Privately Printed, 1st ed. 1925, 79p, illustrated, illustrated boards, 17cm, introduction by Chick Evans, Jr.

Ross, Campbell

32400. *More Fun on the Fairway.* Cape Town, South Africa: South African Golf, 1st ed. [1945] 74p, illustrated by L.B. Hilton, illustrated wrappers, 21cm, introduction by Robert Burnett.

32410. *The Fun on the Fairway.* Cape Town, South Africa: South African Golf, 1st ed. [ca1943] 61p, illustrated by George Pilkington, illustrated wrappers, 21.5cm.

Ross, Charles

32430. *The Haunted Seventh.* London: John Murray, 1st ed. 1922, 320p, cloth, 18.5cm.

Ross, Donald J.

32450. *A Partial List of Prominent Golf Courses Designed by Donald J. Ross.* Pinehurst, North Carolina: Privately Printed, 1st ed. 1930 [12p] wrappers, 14cm [revised to 1930].

Rother Golf Club

32470. *The Rother Golf Club [Handbook].* London: Golf Clubs Association, 1924, 36p, illustrated, wrappers, 18.5cm.

Rotherfield, John

32490. *The Official Handbook of Golf in Somerset 1938-1939.* London: Somerset County Golf Union, 1939, 72p, illustrated, illustrated wrappers, 18cm.

Rothwell, J.H. and F. Purchas

32510. *Brighton and Hove Golf Club Jubilee 1887-1937.* Brighton, England: Privately Printed, 1st ed. 1937, 23p, illustrated, 1/4 cloth, boards, 24.5cm.

Rough and the Fairway

32530. *Rough and the Fairway: An Enquiry by the Agenda Club into the Golf Caddie Problem.* London: Heinemann, 1st ed. 1912, 163p, wrappers, 18.5cm.

[Roundtree, Harry]

32550. *The Tale of the S.L.A. [Simple Life Association].* [Glasgow] Privately Printed, limited ed. [16 copies] 1912, 23p, illustrated by Harry Roundtree, leather, raised bands, aeg, 37.5cm.

Rowland, Ralph

32570. *The Humors of Golf.* London & Belfast: McGaw Stevenson & Orr, 1st ed. [ca1903] 48p, illustrated, illustrated boards, 24cm.

Royal and Ancient Game of Goff

32590. *The Royal and Ancient Game of Goff, Exhibit from the White Horse Cellar-A.G. Spalding Collection of Golfing Curios.* New York: Browne-Vintners, 1st ed. [ca1950] 14p, illustrated, illustrated wrappers, 28cm.

Royal and Ancient Golf Club of St. Andrews

32610. *Decisions by the Rules of Golf Committee of the Royal and Ancient Golf Club 1909-1910.* St. Andrews: W.C. Henderson, 1st ed. [1911] 36p, cloth, 21cm.

32620. *Decisions by the Rules of Golf Committee of the Royal and Ancient Golf Club 1909-1913.* St. Andrews: Royal and Ancient Golf Club of St. Andrews, 2d ed. [1914] 139p, decorative cloth, 21.5cm.

32630. *Decisions by the Rules of Golf Committee of the Royal and Ancient Golf Club 1909-1919.* St. Andrews: W.C. Henderson, 3d ed. [1920] 143p, decorative cloth, 21.5cm.

32640. *Decisions by the Rules of Golf Committee of the Royal and Ancient Golf Club 1909-1924.* St. Andrews: W.C. Henderson, 4th ed. [1925] 148p, decorative cloth, 21.5cm.

32650. *Decisions by the Rules of Golf Committee of the Royal and Ancient Golf Club 1909-1928.* St. Andrews: W.C. Henderson, 5th ed. [1929] 151p, decorative cloth, 21.5cm.

32660. *Decisions by the Rules of Golf Committee of the Royal and Ancient Golf Club 1934*. St. Andrews: W.C. Henderson, 6th ed. [1935] 190p, decorative cloth, 21.5cm.

32670. *Royal and Ancient Golf Club of St. Andrews Report for 1948*. St. Andrews: Royal and Ancient Golf Club of St. Andrews, 1st ed. 1949, 30p, illustrated, wrappers, 21.5cm.

Royal Bombay Golf Club

32690. *Centenary Souvenir Handbook of the Royal Bombay Golf Club 1842-1942*. Bombay, India: Privately Printed, 1st ed. 1942, 77p, cloth, 15.5cm.

Royal Eastbourne Golf Club

32710. *Royal Eastbourne Golf Club [Handbook]*. London: Golf Clubs Association, 1938, 35p, illustrated, wrappers, 18.5cm.

Royal Jersey Golf Club

32730. *The Royal Jersey Golf Club [Handbook]*. Bristol & London: Temple Publicity Services [ca1950] 32p, illustrated, illustrated wrappers, 18cm.

Royal Lytham and St. Annes Golf Club

32750. *Royal Lytham and St. Annes Golf Club Diamond Jubilee 1898-1958*. Liverpool, England: Privately Printed, 1st ed. 1958, 8p, illustrated wrappers, 18.5cm.

32760. *Royal Lytham and St. Annes Golf Club [Handbook]*. London: Golf Clubs Association, 1938, 31p, illustrated, wrappers, 18.5cm.

Royal Montreal Golf Club

32780. *The Royal Montreal Golf Club 1873-1923*. Montreal: Privately Printed, 1st ed. 1923, 48p, illustrated, illustrated wrappers, 26cm.

Royal Sydney Golf Club

32800. *Short History of the Royal Sydney Golf Club*. Sydney, Australia: Privately Printed, 1st ed. 1949, 55p, illustrated, cloth, 21.5cm.

Royal Worlington and Newmarket Golf Club

32820. *The Royal Worlington and Newmarket Golf Club [Handbook]*. Bristol & London: Temple Publicity Services [ca1950] 16p, illustrated, wrappers, 18.5cm.

Ruby, Earl

32840. *The Caddy-Cism: A Manual for Caddies.* Louisville, Kentucky: Privately Printed, 1st ed. [1937] 31p, illustrated, illustrated wrappers, 16cm.

Rugby Golf Club

32860. *Rugby Golf Club [Handbook].* Bristol & London: Temple Publicity Services [ca1951] 24p, illustrated, illustrated wrappers, 18.5cm.

Runyan, Paul

32880. *Golf Is A Game.* New York: Calvert Distillers, 1st ed. [1939] 24p, illustrated, illustrated wrappers, 35cm.

Ryan, Joseph Edmond G.

32900. *Golfers' Green Book 1902: containing complete details of the Golf Clubs drawing membership from Chicago. Tabulated results of club contests-Western Golf Association.* Chicago: National Golf Bureau, 1902, 311p, illustrated, decorative cloth, 15cm. note: preface states initial earlier edition. [not located].

S., G.

32920. *Northern Golf Club, Abridged History 1896-1946.* Aberdeen, Scotland: Privately Printed, 1st ed. 1946, 32p, illustrated, illustrated wrappers, 21cm.

Sabin, Edwin L.

32940. *The Magic Mashie and other Golfish Stories.* New York: A. Wessels, 1st ed. 1902, 210p, illustrated, decorative cloth, 19cm.

Salisbury and South Wilts Golf Club

32960. *The Salisbury and South Wilts Golf Club [Handbook].* London: Golf Clubs Association, 1939, 16p, illustrated, wrappers, 18.5cm.

Salmond, J.B.

32980. *The Story of the R.&A.: Being the history of the first two hundred years of the Royal and Ancient Golf Club of St. Andrews.* London: Macmillan, 1st ed. 1956, 256p, illustrated, decorative cloth, 21.5cm, foreword by Bernard Darwin.

Saltburn-by-the-Sea Golf Club

33000. *Saltburn-by-the-Sea Golf Club [Handbook]*. London: Golf Clubs Association [ca1949] 18p, illustrated, wrappers, 18.5cm.

Sampson, Harold A.

33020. *Primer of Golf Instruction*. Burlingame, California: Privately Printed, 1st ed. 1932, 65p, illustrated, decorative cloth, 20cm.

33030. *Golf Instruction Simplified*. Burlingame, California: Privately Printed, 2d ed. [1950] 95p, illustrated, cloth, 21.5cm. note: second edition of "Primer of Golf Instruction."

Sandy Lodge Golf Club

33050. *Sandy Lodge Golf Club 1910-1960, 50 Years Anniversary*. Northwood, England: Privately Printed, 1st ed. 1960, 32p, illustrated, illustrated wrappers, 25cm.

Santa Fe Railroad

33070. *Come and Golf in California*. Chicago: Santa Fe Railroad, 1931, 38p, illustrated, illustrated wrappers, 23cm.

Santee, Ross

33090. *The Bar X Golf Course*. New York: Farrar & Rinehart, 1st ed. [1933] 159p, illustrated, cloth, 19cm. with scorecard.

33100. reprint ed. Flagstaff, Arizona: Northland Press, 1971, 89p, illustrated, decorative cloth, 23.5cm.

Sapper [H. C. McNeile]

33120. *Uncle Jame's Golf Match*. London: Hodder & Stoughton, 1st ed. [ca1932] 61p, decorative cloth, 12cm.

33130. reprint ed. London: St. Hugh's Press [ca1949] 59p, wrappers, 12cm.

Sarazen, Gene

33150. *Gene Sarazen's Commonsense Golf Tips*. Chicago: Wilson-Western Sporting Goods, 1st ed. [1924] 104p, illustrated, decorative cloth, 17cm, introduction by Francis Ouimet.

33160. *Thirty Years of Championship Golf: The Life and Times of Gene Sarazen*. New York: Prentice-Hall, 1st ed. [1950] 276p, illustrated, cloth, 20cm, with Herbert Warren Wind, introduction by Robert T. Jones. Jr. later printings.

33170. *Want To Be A Golf Champion?* Minneapolis, Minnesota: General Mills, 1st ed. [1945] 29p, illustrated, illustrated wrappers, 12.5cm.

Sarazen, Gene and others

33190. *From Tee To Cup.* and Denny Shute, Ralph Guldahl, Johnny Revolta [Chicago] Wilson Sporting Goods, 1st ed. 1937, 64p, illustrated, gilt leather, 18cm.

33200. *The Golf Clinic.* and Sam Snead, Lloyd Mangrum, Jim Ferrier, Ellsworth Vines, Ed Oliver. Chicago: Ziff-Davis, 1st ed. [1949] 157p, illustrated, cloth, 20.5cm, foreword by Mark Cox.

33205. 1st UK ed. London: Kaye, 1951, 165p, illustrated, cloth, 20cm.

Sargent, George

33210. *Golf, The Proper Way.* New York: American Golfer Magazine, 1st ed. 1912, 20p, illustrated, illustrated wrappers, 20cm.

Saxe, John Godfrey

33220. *The Jones' Golf Swing and Other Suggestions.* New York: Privately Printed, 1st ed. [ca1948] 13p, wrappers, 23.5cm.

33230. 2d ed rev. New York: Privately Printed, 1949, 29p, cloth, 21.5cm, foreword by Ernest Jones.

33235. pbk. ed. 1949, 29p, wrappers, 21.5cm.

33240. *The Jones' Golf Swing, with Practical Suggestions by Many Experts.* New York: Privately Printed, 3d rev. ed. 1951, 42p, illustrated, cloth, 21.5cm, foreword by Ernest Jones.

33245. pbk. ed. 1951, 42p, wrappers, 21.5cm.

Scatchard, Charles

33260. *The Pannal Golf Club [Handbook].* London: Golf Clubs Association [ca1960] 19p, illustrated, illustrated wrappers, 18.5cm.

Schleman, Helen Blanche

33280. *Group Golf Instruction.* New York: A.S. Barnes, 1st ed. 1934, 80p, illustrated, wrappers, 23cm, technical adviser Virginia Hayes.

Schon, Leslie

33300. *The Psychology of Golf*. London: Methuen, 1st ed. 1922, 120p, illustrated, cloth, 19cm.

33310. 1st American ed. Boston: Small, Maynard [1923] 121p, decorative cloth, 19cm.

Schrite, J. Ellsworth

33330. *Divots for Dubs*. [Fernwood, Pennsylvania] Privately Printed, 1st ed. [1934] 96p, illustrated by Shane Miller, cloth, 20.5cm.

Scollard, Clinton

33350. *The Epic of Golf*. Boston: Houghton Mifflin, 1st ed. 1923, 98p, illustrated, 1/4 cloth, illustrated boards, 21cm.

Scot [F.A. Bald]

33370. *Consistent Golf, or, How to Become A Champion*. London: Arthur H. Stockwell, 1st ed. [ca1934] 80p, illustrated, boards, 18cm.

Scotland Home of Golf

33390. *Scotland Home of Golf*. Edinburgh: Scottish Tourist Board, 1960, 16p, illustrated, illustrated wrappers, 23cm, foreword by S. L. McKinlay.

33400. *Scotland Home of Golf*. Edinburgh: Scottish Tourist Board, 1978, 47p, illustrated, illustrated wrappers, 29.5cm.

33410. *Scotland Home of Golf*. [Edinburgh] Scottish Tourist Board, 1981, 54p, illustrated, illustrated wrappers, 21cm.

Scott, Lewis

33430. *Par Golf; with 1934 Rule Changes*. Los Angeles: Richfield Oil, 1st ed. [1934] 47p, illustrated, illustrated wrappers, 11.5cm.

Scott, Tom

33450. *A Century of Golf 1860-1960*. edited by. [England] Masius & Fergusson, 1st ed. [1960] 39p, illustrated, illustrated wrappers, 17.5cm.

33460. *Aldeburgh Golf Club [Handbook]*. London: Temple Publicity Services [ca1957] 16p, illustrated, illustrated wrappers, 18.5cm.

33470. *Ashridge Golf Club [Handbook]*. Bristol & London: Temple Publicity Services [ca1955] 24p, illustrated, illustrated wrappers, 18.5cm.

33480. *Barton-On-Sea Golf Club [Handbook]*. London: Temple Publicity Services [ca1958] 28p, illustrated, illustrated wrappers, 18.5cm.

33490. *Burnham & Berrow Golf Club [Handbook]*. London: Temple Publicity Services [ca1957] 28p, illustrated, illustrated wrappers, 18.5cm.

33500. *Camberley Heath Golf Club [Handbook]*. Bristol & London: Temple Publicity Services [ca1950] 40p, illustrated, illustrated wrappers, 18cm.

33510. *Chipstead Golf Club [Handbook]*. London: Temple Publicity Services [ca1960] 12p, illustrated, illustrated wrappers, 18.5cm.

33520. *Dartford Golf Club [Handbook]*. Bristol & London: Temple Publicity Services [ca1955] 16p, illustrated, illustrated wrappers, 18cm.

33530. *Ealing Golf Club [Handbook]*. London: Temple Publicity Services [ca1960] 16p, illustrated, illustrated wrappers, 18.5cm.

33540. *Fifty Miles of Golf Round London*. edited by. London: Herbert Jenkins, 3d ed. 1952, 184p, illustrated wrappers, 18.5cm. note: see also "Fifty Miles of Golf Round London."

33550. *Filey Golf Club [Handbook]*. Bristol & London: Temple Publicity Services [ca1957] 28p, illustrated, illustrated wrappers, 18.5cm.

33560. *Formby Golf Club [Handbook]*. Bristol & London: Temple Publicity Services [ca1958] 28p, illustrated, illustrated wrappers, 18.5cm.

33570. *Golf At Brighton: Hollingsbury Park, Dyke and Waterhall Courses [Handbook]*. Bristol & London: A Temple Production [ca1951] 20p, illustrated, wrappers, 18cm.

33580. *Golf with the Experts*. London: Heinemann, 1st ed. 1959, 180p, illustrated, cloth, 19.5cm.

33590. 1st American ed. New York: A.S. Barnes, 1960, 180p, illustrated, cloth, 23.5cm.

33600. *Golfing Technique in Pictures*. London: Hulton Press, 1st ed. 1957, 128p, illustrated, cloth, 28cm, foreword by Lord Brabazon.

33610. 1st American ed. New York: Pitman, 1957, 128p, illustrated, cloth, 28cm, foreword by Lord Brabazon.

33620. *Hayling Golf Club [Handbook]*. London: Temple Publicity Services [ca1955] 20p, illustrated, illustrated wrappers, 18.5cm.

33630. *Hillside Golf Club [Handbook]*. London: Temple Publicity Services [ca1958] 20p, illustrated, illustrated wrappers, 18.5cm.

33640. *Hornsea Golf Club [Handbook]*. Bristol & London: Temple Publicity Services [ca1960] 16p, illustrated, illustrated wrappers, 18.5cm.

33650. *Hull Golf Club [Handbook]*. London: Temple Publicity Services [ca1960] 20p, illustrated, illustrated wrappers, 18.5cm.

33660. *Hythe & Dibden Golf Club [Handbook]*. Bristol & London: Temple Publicity Services [ca1951] 16p, illustrated, illustrated wrappers, 18.5cm.

33670. *King's Lynn Golf Club [Handbook]*. London: Temple Publicity Services [ca1960] 12p, illustrated, illustrated wrappers, 18.5cm.

33680. *Knole Park Golf Club [Handbook]*. London: Temple Publicity Services [ca1955] 16p, illustrated, illustrated wrappers, 18cm.

33690. *Moor Park Golf Club [Handbook]*. London: Temple Publicity Services [ca1960] 32p, illustrated, illustrated wrappers, 18.5cm.

33700. *Notts Golf Club [Handbook]*. Bristol & London: Temple Publicity Services [ca1955] 20p, illustrated, wrappers, 18.5cm.

33710. *Prince's Sandwich [Handbook]*. Hants & London: Temple Publicity Services [ca1960] 24p, illustrated, illustrated wrappers, 18.5cm.

33720. *Royal Cromer Golf Club [Handbook]*. London: Temple Publicity Services [ca1960] 28p, illustrated, illustrated wrappers, 18cm.

33730. *Royal Porthcawl Golf Club [Handbook]*. London: Temple Publicity Services [ca1960] 24p, illustrated, illustrated wrappers, 18.5cm.

33740. *Saunton Golf Club [Handbook]*. London: Temple Publicity Services [ca1960] 32p, illustrated, illustrated wrappers, 18.5cm.

33750. *Scarborough South Cliff Golf Club [Handbook]*. Bristol & London: Temple Publicity Services [ca1951] 36p, illustrated, illustrated wrappers, 18.5cm.

33760. *Seacroft Golf Club [Handbook]*. London: Temple Publicity Services [ca1960] 12p, illustrated, illustrated wrappers, 18.5cm.

33770. *Sunningdale Ladies Golf Club [Handbook]*. London: Temple Publicity Services [ca1960] 16p, illustrated, illustrated wrappers, 18.5cm.

33780. *Teignmouth Golf Club [Handbook]*. London: Temple Publicity Services [ca1960] 24p, illustrated, wrappers, 18.5cm.

33790. *The Bedford and County Golf Club [Handbook]*. Bristol & London: A Temple Production, 1948, 20p, illustrated, illustrated wrappers, 18cm.

33800. *The Berkshire Golf Club [Handbook]*. London: Temple Publicity Services [ca1955] 28p, illustrated, wrappers, 18.5cm.

33810. *The Bigbury Golf Club [Handbook]*. London: Temple Publicity Services [ca1957] 12p, illustrated, illustrated wrappers, 18cm.

33820. *The Ferndown Golf Club [Handbook]*. London: Temple Publicity Services [ca1957] 36p, illustrated, illustrated wrappers, 18cm.

33830. *The Royal Birkdale Golf Club [Handbook]*. London: Temple Publicity Services [ca1955] 28p, illustrated, wrappers, 18.5cm.

33840. *The Royal Cinque Ports Club [Handbook]*. Bristol & London: Temple Publicity Services [ca1951] 26p, illustrated, illustrated wrappers, 18.5cm

33850. *The Royal Eastbourne Golf Club [Handbook]*. Bristol & London: Temple Publicity Services [ca1951] 32p, illustrated, illustrated wrappers, 18cm.

33860. *The Royal Norwich Golf Club [Handbook]*. London: Temple Publicity Services [ca1960] 12p, illustrated, wrappers, 18.5cm.

33870. *The Seaford Golf Club and Dormy House Club [Handbook]*. London: Temple Publicity Services [ca1960] 28p, illustrated, illustrated wrappers, 18cm.

33880. *The South Herts Golf Club [Handbook]*. London: Temple Publicity Services [ca1955] 36p, illustrated, illustrated wrappers, 18cm.

33890. *The Western-Super-Mare Golf Club [Handbook]*. London: Temple Publicity Services [ca1955] 24p, illustrated, illustrated wrappers, 18cm.

33900. *The Wilderness Golf Club [Handbook]*. London: Temple Publicity Services [ca1960] 16p, illustrated, illustrated wrappers, 18.5cm:

33910. *Thurlestone Golf Club [Handbook]*. Bristol & London: Temple Publicity Services [ca1960] 28p, illustrated, illustrated wrappers, 18.5cm.

33920. *Tyrrells Wood Golf Club [Handbook]*. Bristol & London: Temple Publicity Services [ca1955] 14p, illustrated, illustrated wrappers, 18.5cm.

33930. *Westgate and Birchington Golf Club [Handbook]*. Bristol & London: Temple Publicity Services [ca1951] 24p, illustrated, illustrated wrappers, 18.5cm.

33940. *Wimbledon Park Golf Club [Handbook].* Bristol & London: Temple Publicity Services [ca1951] 16p, illustrated, illustrated wrappers, 18.5cm.

33950. *Woodhall Spa Golf Club [Handbook].* London: Temple Publicity Services [ca1960] 20p, illustrated, wrappers, 18.5cm.

33960. *Yelverton Golf Club [Handbook].* London: Temple Publicity Services [ca1960] 23p, illustrated, illustrated wrappers, 18.5cm.

Scott, Tom and Geoffrey Cousins

33980. *Golf for the Not So Young.* London: Peter Davies, 1st ed. 1960, 208p, illustrated, cloth, 19.5cm, foreword by Gene Sarazen.

33990. *Golf Begins At 45.* New York: A.S. Barnes, 1st American ed. [1960] 208p, illustrated, cloth, 21cm, foreword by Gene Sarazen. American title of "Golf for the Not So Young."

Scott, Tom and Webster Evans

34010. *The Golfers' Year.* London: Nicholas Kaye, 1st ed. 1950, 187p, illustrated, cloth, 22cm.

34020. *The Golfers' Year, Volume II.* London: Nicholas Kaye, 1st ed. 1951, 132p, illustrated, cloth, 21.5cm.

Scottish Golfer [R.K. Ross]

34040. *Swing-Minded.* Cornwall, England: Privately Printed, 1st ed. 1932, 38p, boards and wrappers, 13cm.

Scribner, Romeyn B.

34080. *Senior Golf: Golf Is More Fun After Fifty-Five.* Golf, Illinois: Evans Scholars Foundation, limited ed. [1000 copies] 1960, 175p, illustrated, cloth, 23cm, edited by Frank Matey, forewords by Charles Evans, Jr. and John R. Williams.

Seagrave, Alice D.

34100. *Golf Retold: The Story of Golf in Cleveland.* Cleveland, Ohio: Cleveland Women's Golf Association, 1st ed. [1940] 148p, illustrated, cloth, 21.5cm.

Seattle Golf Club

34120. *Seattle Golf Club 1900-1950, Fiftieth Anniversary.* Seattle, Washington: Privately Printed, 1st ed. 1950 [24p] illustrated, illustrated wrappers, 29cm.

Secrets of Winning Golf Matches

34140. *Secrets of Winning Golf Matches with a Total Concept for Winning Golf and 12 Winning Golf Discoveries.* Golf, Illinois: Golf Capital Publishers, 1st ed. [1959] [98p] illustrated, wrappers, 28cm.

Selangor Golf Club

34160. *Twelve Under Fours: An Informal History of the Selangor Golf Club; Diamond Jubilee, 1953.* Kuala Lumpur, Malaya: Privately Printed, 1st ed. 1953, 169p, illustrated, decorative cloth, 21.5cm.

Selby, Don

34180. *Examiner Golf Foto Lessons.* San Francisco: San Francisco Examiner, 1st ed. [ca1955] 49p, illustrated, illustrated wrappers, 30cm.

Servos, Lancelot Cressy

34200. *Practical Instruction in Golf.* Boston: Privately Printed, 1st ed. [1905] 92p, illustrated, cloth, 23cm.

34210. 2d ed. rev. Emmaus, Pennsylvania: Rodale Press [1938] 175p, illustrated, cloth, 18.5cm.

Seton-Karr, Henry and others

34230. *Golf: Greening's Useful Handbook Series.* and Harold Hilton, Harold Beveridge, Dr. Macnamara, Mary Hezlet, Dr. J.G. McPherson, H.G. Hutchinson, S. Mure Fergusson. London: Greening, 1st ed. 1907, 128p, illustrated linen wrappers, 18cm.

Seymour, Bert

34250. *All-About Golf; How to improve your game.* London and Melbourne: Ward, Locke, 1st ed. 1924, 304p, illustrated, decorative cloth, 18.5cm.

Shanklin & Sandown Golf Club

34270. *The Shanklin & Sandown Golf Club [Handbook].* London: Golf Clubs Association, 1939, 31p, illustrated, wrappers, 18cm.

Sharon Country Club

34290. *The Sharon Country Club Sixtieth Anniversary 1895-1955.* Sharon, Connecticut: Privately Printed, 1st ed. 1955, 30p, illustrated, illustrated wrappers, 18.5cm.

Shaw, James E.

34310. *Prestwick Golf Club, A History and Some Records.* Glasgow: Jackson, 1st ed. 1938, 143p, illustrated, cloth, 25cm, introduction by Bernard Darwin.

Shaw, Joseph T.

34330. *Out of the Rough.* New York: Windward House, 1st ed. [1934] 237p, illustrated by Paul Brown, cloth, 20.5cm.

34340. reprint ed. Garden City, New York: Garden City Publishing, 1937, 237p, cloth, 21cm.

34350. 1st Australian ed. Sydney, Australia: Angus & Robertson, 1934, 219p, illustrated, cloth, 18.5cm.

Shenstone, F.S.

34370. *Golf Rules and Decisions: A Summary of the Rules of Golf, with Decisions, Tables of Penalties and General Index.* London: Methuen, 1st ed. 1924, 132p, cloth, 17cm.

34380. 2d ed. 1924, 132p, cloth, 17cm.

34390. 3d ed. rev. 1927, 132p, cloth, 17cm.

34400. 4th ed. rev. 1935, 128p, cloth, 16.5cm, rev. by J. Bruce Kerr.

Shepherd, Jr., James

34420. *Golf Shots: A Book for Beginners, describing and illustrating the different strokes in the game.* Hyannis, Massachusetts: Privately Printed, 1st ed. 1924, 81p, illustrated, cloth, 19cm.

Sheridan, John Desmond

34440. *It Stance to Reason: The Intelligent Rabbit's Guide to Golf.* Dublin, Ireland: Talbot Press, 1st ed. 1947, 98p, illustrated by Warner, cloth, 18cm.

Sherwood Forest Golf Club

34460. *Sherwood Forest Golf Club [Handbook].* Cheltenham & London: Ed. J. Burrow [ca1938] 16p, illustrated, illustrated wrappers, 16.5cm.

Shinnie, Robert Lester

34480. *The Book of Kingussie: Kingussie Golf Club Bazaar.* Kingussie, Scotland: Badenoch Record, 1st ed. 1911, 85p, illustrated, illustrated wrappers, 25cm.

Shirley Park Golf Club

34500. *The Shirley Park Golf Club [Handbook].* London: Golf Clubs Association [ca1955] 23p, illustrated, wrappers, 18.5cm.

Shooters' Hill Golf Club

34520. *Shooters' Hill Golf Club [Handbook].* Cheltenham & London: Ed. J. Burrow [ca1938] 20p, illustrated, illustrated wrappers, 16.5cm.

Shore, Julian

34540. *Rattle His Bones.* New York: William Morrow, 1st ed. 1941, 315p, cloth, 19cm.

Shotte, Cleeke [John Hogben]

34560. *The Golf Craze: Sketches and Rhymes.* Edinburgh & London: T. N. Foulis, 1st ed. [1905] 123p, cloth, 17.5cm.

34565. pbk. ed. [1905] 123p, illustrated wrappers, 17.5cm.

Shultz, I. Robert M.

34580. *Directory of Municipal and Tax Supported Golf Courses.* Chicago: National Golf Foundation, 1st ed. 1959, 14p, illustrated, wrappers, 28cm.

Sidmouth Golf Club

34600. *The Sidmouth Golf Club [Handbook].* London: Golf Clubs Association, 1931, 24p, illustrated, wrappers, 18.5cm.

Simpson, Harold

34620. *Seven Stages of Golf, and other Golf Stories in Picture and Verse.* London: John Ouseley, 1st ed. 1909, 21p, illustrated by G.E. Shepherd, illustrated boards, 33cm.

Simpson, S. Raleigh

34640. *A Green Crop.* London: Arthur H. Stockwell, 1st ed. [ca1937] 80p, cloth, 18cm.

34650. *The Lyre of the Links.* London: Murray Erenden, 1st ed. [ca1920] 76p, cloth, 18cm.

Sirrah

34670. *Slaves of the Links: A Golf Comedy.* London: Cornish, 1st ed. 1914, 141p, illustrated wrappers, 18.5cm.

Sitwell Park Golf Club

34690. *Sitwell Park Golf Club [Handbook].* Cheltenham & London: Ed. J. Burrow [ca1937] 20p, illustrated, illustrated wrappers, 17cm.

Sixty, Billy

34710. *Golfax.* Milwaukee, Wisconsin: Milwaukee Journal, 2d ed. rev. [1946] [32p] illustrated, illustrated wrappers, 18cm. note: first edition not located.

Sixty, Sr., Billy and Billy Sixty, Jr.

34730. *Have Fun Golfing in the 60's.* Milwaukee, Wisconsin: Milwaukee Journal, 1st ed. [ca1960] 31p, illustrated, illustrated wrappers, 28cm.

Skuse, Dick

34750. *One Hundred Years, The Olympic Club Centennial 1860-1960.* edited by. San Francisco: Privately Printed, 1st ed. 1960, 160p, illustrated, decorative cloth, 29.5cm, with Cedric Tarr & Fran Tuckueiler.

Slack, L. Ert

34770. *Golf Putting.* Indianapolis, Indiana: Privately Printed, 1st ed. [1936] 31p, illustrated, wrappers, 16cm.

Sleepy Hollow Country Club.

34790. *The Sleepy Hollow Country Club: A Brief Description of the Grounds and Buildings.* Scarborough, New York: Privately Printed, 1st ed. 1919, 26p, illustrated, 1/4 cloth, boards, 26cm.

34800. *The Sleepy Hollow of Today: A Brief Description of the enlarged facilities now available to the members.* Scarborough, New York: Privately Printed, 1st ed. 1931, 18p, illustrated, illustrated wrappers, 25.5cm.

Smith, Alex

34820. *Lessons in Golf.* New York: Arthur Potlow, 1st ed. 1907, 183p, illustrated, cloth, 23cm.

Smith, Banjo

34840. *Columbia Country Club 1948-1952*. Columbia, South Carolina: Privately Printed, 1st ed. 1952, 49p, illustrated, illustrated wrappers, 15.5cm.

Smith, Charles

34860. *Aberdeen Golfers: Record and Reminiscences*. London: Privately Printed, limited ed. [150 copies] 1909, 167p, illustrated, decorative cloth, 24.5cm.

Smith, Everett M.

34880. *Synonym Golf, A New Indoor Game*. New York: Mohawk Press, 1st ed. 1931 [90p] illustrated, decorative cloth, 20.5cm.

Smith, Frank Stewart

34900. *How You Can Become A Good Putter*. Los Angeles: Kumback, 2d ed. [1922] 35p, illustrated, illustrated wrappers, 15.5cm. note: first edition not located.

34910. *Putting*. Philadelphia: Fox Manufacturing, 5th ed. 1925, 47p, illustrated, wrappers, 15.5cm. note: first through fourth editions not located.

Smith, Garden C.

34930. *Side Lights of Golf*. London: Sisley's, 1st ed. [ca1907] 153p, illustrated, cloth, 18cm.

Smith, George F.

34950. *Hints to Golfers*. Elgin, Scotland: Privately Printed, 1st ed. [1929] 46p, illustrated, illustrated wrappers, 19.5cm.

Smith, Joseph Stanley Kellet and B.S. Weastell

34970. *The Foundations of Golf*. London: Methuen, 1st ed. 1925, 82p, illustrated, cloth, 18.5cm.

34980. 1st American ed. New York: Robert M. McBride, 1926, 82p, illustrated, cloth, 18.5cm.

Smith, R. Boyd

35000. *The History of the Sylvania Country Club*. Sylvania, Ohio: Privately Printed, 1st ed. [1959] [68p] illustrated, limp leather 3 ring binder, 28cm.

Snaith, J.C.

35020. *Curiouser and Curiouser.* London: Hutchinson, 1st ed. [1935] 288p, cloth, 19cm.

35030. *Lord Cobbleigh Disappears.* New York: Appleton, 1st American ed. 1936, 309p, cloth, 19cm, US title of "Curiouser and Curiouser."

Snead, Sam

35050. *How To Hit A Golf Ball From Any Sort of Lie.* Garden City, New York: Doubleday, 1st ed. [1950] 74p, illustrated, illustrated wrappers, 22.5cm, edited by Mark Cox, preface by Herb Graffis. later printings.

35060. 1st UK ed. Kingswood, England: World's Work [1950] 74p, illustrated, illustrated wrappers, 22.5cm, edited by Mark C. Cox.

35070. *How to Play Golf, and Professional Tips on Improving Your Score.* Garden City, New York: Garden City, 1st ed. [1946] 173p, illustrated, decorative cloth, 25.5cm.

35080. 2d ed. rev. [1952] 160p, illustrated, decorative cloth, 25.5cm, also special section by Bert Katzenmeyer.

35090. *Natural Golf.* New York: A.S. Barnes, 1st ed. [1953] 208p, illustrated, cloth, 23cm, edited by Tom Shehan, introduction by Fred J. Corcoran.

35100. *Sam Snead's Celebrity Golf Tips.* Norwalk, Connecticut: Golf Digest, 1st ed. 1960, 31p, illustrated, illustrated wrappers, 21cm.

35110. *Sam Snead's Quick Way to Better Golf.* [New York] Sun Dial Press, 1st ed. [1938] [76p] illustrated, illustrated wrappers, 35.5cm.

35120. *Sam Snead's Secrets of Golf.* Sydney, Australian: Consolidated Press, 1st ed. [ca1960] 96p, illustrated, illustrated wrappers, 13.5cm.

35130. *Stop-Action Golf Book, 2-4 Iron [flip book].* [Atlanta, Georgia] Coca-Cola, 1st ed. [ca1960] [46p] illustrated, illustrated wrappers, 7cm.

Snead, Sam and Bob Considine

35150. *How To Cut Strokes Off Your Golf Game*. New York: True Magazine, offprint [1945] [5p] illustrated, illustrated wrappers, 18.5cm, offprint from True Magazine.

Sneddon, Richard

35170. *The Golf Stream*. Philadelphia: Dorrance, 1st ed. [1941] 75p, illustrated by Bob Crosby, cloth, 19cm.

Snell, George P.

35190. *Golf At Hotel Del Monte*. Del Monte, California: Privately Printed, 1st ed. [ca1904] 30p, illustrated, illustrated wrappers, 17cm.

Somerset and Its Golf

35210. *Somerset and Its Golf*. Dundee, Scotland: Simmath House, 1st ed. [ca1932] 96p, illustrated, suede wrappers, 17cm.

Souchak, Mike and Cary Middlecoff and Sam Snead

35230. *Improve Your Golf*. New York: Koster-Dana, 1st ed. 1959 [13p] illustrated, illustrated wrappers, 19.5cm.

Soutar, Daniel C.

35250. *The Australian Golfer*. Sydney, Australia: Angus & Robertson, 1st ed. 1906, 259p, illustrated, cloth, 20.5cm.

35260. 2d ed. Melbourne, Australia: E. W. Cole, 1908, 259p, illustrated, cloth, 21cm.

Southern California Golf Association

35280. *History of Golf in Southern California*. Los Angeles: Southern California Golf Association, 1st ed. 1925, 56p, illustrated, leather, 22.5cm.

Southport Municipal Golf Links

35300. *The Southport Municipal Golf Links [Handbook]*. Derby & Cheltenham, England: New Centurion, 1933, 32p, illustrated, wrappers, 18.5cm.

Spalding, Anthony

35320. *Golf for Beginners*. London: Link House, 1st ed. [ca1935] 56p, illustrated, illustrated wrappers, 18.5cm.

Sports Illustrated

35340. *Ten Top Tips.* by the editors of Sports Illustrated. Portland, Oregon: Jantzen, 1st ed. [1958] [21p] illustrated, illustrated wrappers, 15cm, later printings.

35350. *Tips on Top Performance: with golf tips from Sam Snead and Mickey Wright.* by the editors of Sports Illustrated. [Detroit] Ford Motor [ca1955] [10p] illustrated by Anthony Ravielli, illustrated wrappers, 21cm.

St. Andrew's Golf Club

35370. *St. Andrews Golf Club [Handbook].* Dundee, Scotland: Dundee Printers, 1934, 24p, illustrated, illustrated wrappers, 17.5cm.

St. Augustine's Golf Club

35390. *The St. Augustine's Golf Club [Handbook].* Bristol & London: Temple Publicity Services [ca1951] 24p, illustrated, illustrated wrappers, 18.5cm.

St. Cloud Country Club

35410. *The St. Cloud Country Club [Handbook].* Paris: Privately Printed [ca1927] 19p, illustrated, illustrated wrappers, 16cm.

St. Joseph Country Club

35430. *Fore!, St. Joseph Country Club Yearbook.* St. Joseph, Missouri: Privately Printed, 1st ed. [ca1953] [60p] illustrated, decorative cloth, 26.5cm.

Stainton, J.H.

35450. *The Golf Courses of Yorkshire.* Sheffield, England: Sheffield Telegraph, 1912, 171p, illustrated, illustrated wrappers, 17.5cm.

Stancliffe [Stanley Clifford]

35470. *An Astounding Golf Match.* London: Methuen, 1st ed. 1914, 312p, decorative cloth, 19cm.

35480. *Golf Do's and Don'ts: Being a very little about a good deal, together with some new saws for old-wood and knots in the golfer's line which may help a good memory for forgetting.* London: Methuen, 1st ed. 1902, 64p, illustrated, illustrated boards, 17cm. later printings.

35490. 1st American ed. New York: Frederick A. Stokes [ca1930] 64p, illustrated boards, 17cm.

35500. *Quick Cuts to Good Golf*. London: Methuen, 1st ed. 1920, 61p, illustrated boards, 17cm. later printings.

35510. 1st American ed. New York: Frederick A. Stokes [ca1920] 61p, illustrated boards, 17cm.

35520. *The Autobiography of A Caddy-Bag*. London: Methuen, 1st ed. 1924, 86p, illustrated boards, 17cm.

Stanley Golf Club

35540. *Stanley Golf Club House [Dedication Brochure]*. New Britain, Connecticut: Privately Printed, 1st ed. 1933 [16p] illustrated, illustrated wrappers, 19.5cm.

Stanley, Dave [pseud for David Dachs]

35560. *A Treasury of Golf Humor*. New York: Lantern Press, 1st ed. [1949] 383p, illustrated by Cobbledick, decorative cloth, 20cm.

Stanley, Dave [pseud for David Dachs] and George C. Ross

35580. *The Golfer's Own Book*. New York: Lantern Press, 1st ed. [1956] 342p. illustrated, decorative cloth, 21cm.

Stanley, Louis T.

35600. *Fontana Golf Book*. London: Collins, 1st ed. 1957, 127p, illustrated by Charles Green, illustrated wrappers, 18cm.

35610. *Fresh Fairways*. London: Methuen, 1st ed. 1949, 220p, illustrated, cloth, 18.5cm.

35620. *Green Fairways*. London: Methuen, 1st ed. 1947, 204p, illustrated, cloth, 18cm.

35630. *Master Golfers in Action*. London: Macdonald, 1st ed. 1950, 143p, illustrated, cloth, 24.5cm, introduction by Henry Cotton.

35640. *Style Analysis*. London: Naldrett Press, 1st ed. 1951, 103p, illustrated, cloth, 27.5cm, foreword by Sir Guy Campbell.

35650. *Swing to Better Golf*. London: Collins, 1st ed. 1957, 256p, illustrated, cloth, 25cm, foreword by Ronnie White.

35660. 1st American ed. New York: Thomas Y. Crowell, 1957, 256p, illustrated, cloth, 25cm, foreword by Ronnie White.

35670. *The Book of Golf.* London: Max Parrish, 1st ed. [1960] 147p, illustrated, cloth, 26.5cm.

35680. *The Golfer's Bedside Book.* London: Methuen, 1st ed. 1955, 197p, illustrated, cloth, 21.5cm, preface by Richard Burton, introduction by C.K. Cotton.

35690. *The Woman Golfer.* London: Macdonald, 1st ed. 1952, 128p, illustrated, cloth, 21.5cm, introduction by Diana Critchley.

35700. *How to Be A Better Woman Golfer.* New York: Thomas Y. Crowell, 1st American ed. [1952] 127p, illustrated, cloth, 21.5cm, American title of "The Woman Golfer."

35710. *This Is Golf.* London: W.H. Allen, 1st ed. 1954, 192p, illustrated, cloth, 21.5cm, preface by Cyril Tolley.

35720. 1st American ed. New York: A. S. Barnes, 1954, 192p, illustrated, cloth, 21.5cm, preface by Cyril Tolley.

35730. *This Is Putting.* London: W.H. Allen, 1st ed. [ca1957] 191p, illustrated, cloth, 21.5cm, preface by Ken Bousfield.

35740. 1st American ed. New York: Citadel Press [1957] 191p, illustrated, cloth, 21.5cm, preface by Ken Bousfield.

Stark, A.

35760. *Physical Training for Golfers: Improve your game by jerks.* St. Andrews: W.C. Henderson, 1st ed. [ca1937] 62p, illustrated, illustrated wrappers, 18.5cm, forewords by J.H. Taylor and Hector Thompson, preface by Jack McLean.

Steele, Chester K.

35780. *The Golf Course Mystery.* New York: George Sully, 1st ed. [1919] 303p, illustrated, cloth, 19cm.

35790. reprint ed. Cleveland: International Fiction Library [ca1925] 303p, cloth, 18.5cm.

Stein, Jennette A. and Emma F. Waterman

35810. *Golf for Beginning Players*. Columbus, Ohio: Privately Printed, 1st ed. [1934] 31p, illustrated wrappers, 23cm.

35820. 2d ed. rev. 1935, 31p, illustrated wrappers, 23cm.

35830. 3d ed. rev. 1938, 31p, illustrated wrappers, 23cm.

Steinberg, Harris B.

35850. *The Hackers: Twelve Golf Drawings*. New York: Independent Offset Lithographers, limited ed. signed [500 copies] 1956 [28p] illustrated, spiral bound illustrated wrappers, 21.5cm.

Stewart, Hal D.

35870. *The Nineteenth Hole, A Play in One Act*. London: Samuel French, 1st ed. 1933, 20p, wrappers, 18.5cm.

Stibbons, Fred

35890. *Norfolk's Caddie Poet: His Autobiography, Impressions and Some of His Verses*. Norfolk, England: Rounce & Wortley, 1st ed. 1923, 79p, illustrated wrappers, 20cm, introduction by Sir Ernest Wild.

Stillings, Leo

35910. *Golf Fundamentals and Helpful Hints: A Brief direct way to good golf*. McHenry, Illinois: Privately Printed, 1st ed. 1935, 28p, illustrated, wrappers, 16.5cm.

Stobbs, John

35930. *Camberley Heath Golf Club [Handbook]*. London: Golf Clubs Association [ca1955] 26p, illustrated, illustrated wrappers, 18.5cm.

Stoddard, William Leavitt

35950. *The New Golfer's Almanac: Carefully Compiled and Computed on an Ingenious astrological basis for the year 1910 A.D. and containing a Calender and reliable Weather Predictions for every Month, besides an Entertaining Miscellany of Golfing Literature and Information, hitherto [probably] unassembled in a single book*. Boston: Houghton Mifflin, 1st ed. 1909, 89p, illustrated by Arthur Wingate Bartlett, 1/4 cloth, illustrated boards, 19.5cm.

Story of The Open 1860-1960

35970. *The Story of The Open 1860-1960*. Dundee, Scotland: Dundee Evening Telegraph and Post, 1st ed. 1960, 11p, illustrated, illustrated wrappers, 24.5cm.

Strang, Lewis C.

35990. *Golf and Business*. New York: Roland, 1st ed. [1925] 22p, wrappers, 15cm.

Stratford-on-Avon Golf Club

36010. *The Stratford-on-Avon Golf Club [Handbook]*. London: Golf Clubs Association [ca1946] 33p, illustrated, wrappers, 18cm.

Strazza, Frank

36030. *Golf's Inside Secrets*. Westport, Connecticut: Golf Research Institute, 1st ed. [1955] 12p, illustrated, illustrated wrappers, 23.5cm.

Stringer, Mabel A.

36050. *Golfing Reminiscences*. London: Mills & Boon, 1st ed. 1924, 254p, illustrated, cloth, 22cm.

Stroke-O-Matic Golf Stroke Training

36070. *Stroke-O-Matic Golf Stroke Training*. South Bend: Indiana, South Bend Golf Research, 1st ed. [1953] 67p, illustrated, spiral bound illustrated wrappers, 21.5cm.

Strong, Horace D.

36090. *Thru the Years at the Brooklawn Country Club 1895-1945, 50th Anniversary*. Fairfield, Connecticut: Privately Printed, 1st ed. 1945, 20p, illustrated, illustrated wrappers, 28cm.

Sturgess, Don

36110. *Basic Golf*. New York: Coleman Golf Product, 1st ed. [1954] [36p] illustrated by Marc Legis, spiral bound illustrated wrappers, 8.5cm.

Suggs, Louise

36130. *Par Golf for Women*. New York: Prentice-Hall, 1st ed. [1953] 120p, illustrated, decorative cloth, 21cm, foreword by Ben Hogan.

36140. 1st UK ed. London: George G. Harrap, 1954, 128p, illustrated, cloth, 21.5cm, foreword by Ben Hogan.

Suggs, Louise and others

36160. *Golf for Women.* and Marlene Baurer Hagge, Beverly Hanson, Jackie Pung, Barbara Romak, Joyce Ziske, Ruth Jessen. Garden City, New York: Doubleday, 1st ed. [1960] 192p, illustrated, cloth, 23cm, foreword by Tommy Armour.

36170. pbk ed. New York: Cornerstone Library [1960] 192p, illustrated, illustrated wrappers, 20cm.

Sullivan, Des

36190. *Essex Falls Country Club 1896-1950.* Essex Falls, New Jersey: Privately Printed, 1st ed. 1950 [34p] illustrated, wrappers, 22cm.

Susie Takes Up Golf

36210. *Susie Takes Up Golf.* Minneapolis, Minnesota: Board of Park Commissioners, 1st ed. [1940] 32p, illustrated by Betty Dagett, illustrated wrappers, 21.5cm.

Sutphen, William G. Van Tassel

36220. *Harper's Official Golf Guide 1901: A directory of all golf clubs and associations in the United States, together with statistical tables, the rules of golf and other general information.* New York: Harper's, 1901, 332p, illustrated, 1/4 cloth illustrated boards, 24cm.

36230. *The Nineteenth Hole: Being Tales of the Fair Green.* New York: Harper's, 1st ed. 1901, 190p, illustrated, 1/2 cloth. marbled boards, 19.5cm.

36240. *The Official Golf Guide 1902.* New York: Grafton Press, 1902, 372p, illustrated, 1/2 cloth, boards, 23cm.

36250. *The Peripatetic Hazard.* New York: Brooks Brothers, 1st ed. 1921, 35p, illustrated wrappers, 11.5cm.

Sutton, Martin A.F.

36270. *Golf Course Design, Construction and Upkeep.* edited by. London: Simpkin Marshall, 1st ed. 1933, 152p, illustrated, cloth, 24.5cm, introduction by Bernard Darwin, contributors-P. Mackenzie Ross, T. Simpson, Robert Trent Jones, C.H. Alison, C.K. Cotton.

36280. 2d ed. rev. Reading, England: Sutton & Sons, 1950, 192p, illustrated, cloth, 24.5cm.

Sutton, Martin H.F.

36300. *Laying Out and Upkeep of Golf Courses and Putting Greens.* London: Simpkin, Marshall, Hamilton, Kent, 1st ed. [ca1906] 47p, illustrated, illustrated wrappers, 18.5cm.

36310. *The Book of the Links: A Symposium on Golf.* edited by. by Sir George Riddell, Bernard Darwin, H.S. Colt, A.D. Hall. London: W.H. Smith, 1st ed. [1912] 212p, illustrated, cloth, 24.5cm.

Swanson, Henry E.

36330. *Fifty Years of Woodland Golf Club 1902-1952.* Auburndale, Massachusetts: Privately Printed, 1st ed. 1952, 32p, illustrated, illustrated wrappers, 23cm.

Swanston Golf Club

36350. *Swanston Golf Club [Handbook].* London: Golf Clubs Association [ca1948] 18p, illustrated, wrappers, 18.5cm.

Taylor, Arthur V.

36370. *Origines Golfianae; the Birth of Golf and its Early Childhood as revealed in a chance-discovered Manuscript from a Scottish Monastery.* Woodstock, Vermont: Elm Tree Press, limited ed. slipcased [500 copies] 1912, 58p, illustrated, decorative cloth, 21cm.

Taylor, Bert Leston

36390. *A Line o' Gowf or Two.* New York: Knopf, 1st ed. 1923, 185p, illustrated, cloth, 19cm.

Taylor, John Henry

36410. *Golf: My Life's Work.* London: Johnathan Cape, 1st ed. 1943, 236p, cloth, 20cm, introduction by Bernard Darwin. later printing.

36420. *Southampton Public Golf Courses [Handbook].* Southampton, England: Russell, 1935, 40p, illustrated, wrappers, 17.5cm.

36430. *Taylor on Golf: Impressions, Comments and Hints.* London: Hutchinson, 1st ed. 1902, 328p, illustrated, decorative cloth, 20cm, later printings.

36440. 1st American ed. New York: D. Appleton, 1902, 328p, illustrated, decorative cloth, 18.5cm.

Taylor, Joshua

36460. *The Art of Golf.* London: T. Werner Laurie, 1st ed. [ca1913] 161p, illustrated, decorative cloth, 18.5cm, with a chapter on the Evolution of the Bunker by J.H. Taylor.

36470. 1st American ed. New York: Outing [ca1913] 150p, illustrated, cloth, 18cm.

36480. *The Lure of the Links.* London: Heath Cranton, 1st ed. [1920] 89p, boards, 19cm.

Taylor, William Duncan

36500. *Wallasey Golf Club, 1891-1953.* Wallasey, England: Privately Printed, 1953, 68p, illustrated, illustrated wrappers, 21cm.

Tedesco Country Club

36520. *Tedesco Country Club 1903-1953.* Swampscott, Massachusetts: Privately Printed, 1st ed. 1953, 63p, illustrated, cloth, 21.5cm.

Tee Party on the Green

36540. *Tee Party on the Green; Being a St. Paul golf directory and a condensed compendium and a record of Minnesotas ten important events.* St. Paul, Minnesota: W.C. Canby, 1st ed. 1925, 304p, illustrated, suede leather, 19.5cm.

Teeple, David Shea

36560. *How To Cheat At Golf.* Chicago: Privately Printed, 1st ed. [1958] 63p, illustrated by Hugh Brown, spiral bound boards, 19cm.

Tehidy Park Golf Club

36580. *Tehidy Park Golf Club [Handbook].* London: Golf Clubs Association [ca1947] 43p, illustrated, wrappers, 18.5cm.

This Golf From Tee To Green

36620. *This Golf From Tee To Green.* London: Silvertown [1936] [14p] illustrated, illustrated wrappers, 14 cm.

Thom, M.D.

36640. *It's A Golf Rule.* Glasgow: Evening Citizen, 1st ed. [1951] [20p] illustrated, illustrated wrappers, 22cm.

36650. *Tricky Golf Rules.* Glasgow: Evening Citizen, 1st ed. [1952] 48p, illustrated, illustrated wrappers, 21.5cm.

Thomas, David

36670. *Instructions To Young Golfers.* London: Museum Press, 1st ed. 1959, 126p, illustrated by George Houghton, cloth, 21.5cm.

Thomas, Jr., George C.

36690. *Golf Architecture in America: Its Strategy and Construction.* Los Angeles: Times-Mirror Press, 1st ed. 1927, 342p, illustrated, decorative cloth, 22cm.

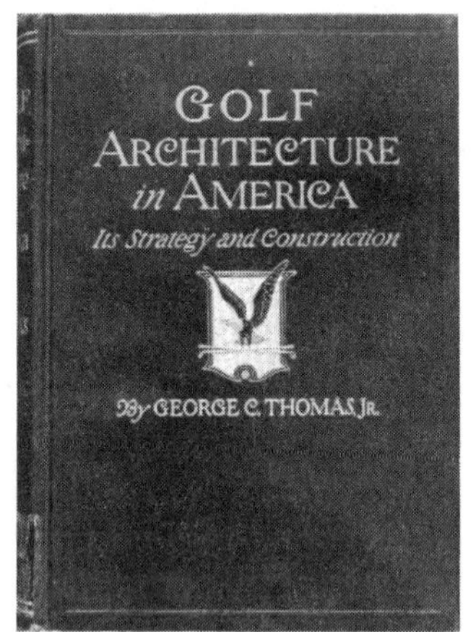

Thompson, Kenneth R.

36710. *The Mental Side of Golf: A study of the game as practiced by champions.* New York: Funk & Wagnalls, 1st ed. 1939, 153p, illustrated, cloth, 18.5cm.

36720. 2d ed. rev. 1947, 198p, illustrated, decorative cloth, 18.5cm.

36730. 1st UK ed. London: Frederick Muller, 1955, 157p, illustrated, cloth, 18.5cm.

Thompson, M.B.

36750. *Miniature Golf: A Treatise on the Subject containing business building ideas.* Denver, Colorado: Central States, 1st ed. [1930] 64p, illustrated, 1/4 cloth, illustrated boards, 23cm.

Thompson, P.B.

36770. *The Experience of A Dub Golfer.* New York: Edgar H. Wells, 1st ed. [ca1925] [8p] illustrated, illustrated wrappers, 15cm.

Thompson, Phillips B.

36790. *Simplifying the Golf Stroke: based on the theory of Ernest Jones.* New York: Laurence Gomme, 1st ed. 1929 [12p] illustrated, boards, 15cm.

Thompson, W.J.

36810. *Commonsense Golf.* Toronto: Thomas Allen, 1st ed. [1923] 147p, illustrated, decorative cloth, 19cm.

Thomson, Bernard [Ben]

36830. *How to Play Golf.* New York: Prentice-Hall, 1st ed. 1939, 65p, illustrated, cloth, 22cm, later printings.

Thomson, Dave

36850. *Practical Golf.* Rosalyn, Virginia: Dave Thomsom Publishing, 1st ed. [1923] 48p, cloth, 15cm.

Thomson, Jimmy

36870. *Hit' em a Mile! How to Drive A Golf Ball.* New York: Sun Dial Press, 1st ed. [1940] [46p] illustrated, illustrated wrappers, 32.5cm, edited by Geoffrey Field, introduction by Herb Graffis.

Thomson, Will J. A.

36890. *Golfing Memories, including a short history of the Titirangi Golf Club and excerpts from golf lies and otherwise.* Auckland, New Zealand: Privately Printed, 1st ed. [1951] 77p, illustrated by J. Turkington & W. Baxter, wrappers, 21cm.

Tillinghast, Arthur W.

36910. *Cobble Valley Golf Yarns and other Sketches.* Philadelphia: Philadelphia Printing & Publishing, 1st ed. [1915] 295p, illustrated, cloth, 19cm.

36920. *Planning A Golf Course.* Philadelphia: Privately Printed, 1st ed. [ca1917] [24p] illustrated, wrappers, 21.5cm.

36930. *The Mutt and other Golf Yarns; A New Cobble Valley Series.* [Philadelphia] Privately Printed, limited ed. signed [250 copies] 105p, illustrated by Ross Morley, leather, 19cm.

36940. 1st trade ed. 1925, 105p, cloth, 18.5cm.

Tolley, Cyril

36960. *Drive and Iron [Flicker Book].* London: Flicker Productions, 1st ed. [ca1930] [100p] wrappers, 7.5cm.

36970. *The Modern Golfer.* London: W. Collins, 1st ed. 1924, 292p, illustrated, cloth, 21.5cm.

36980. 1st American ed. New York: Knopf, 1924, 213p, illustrated, cloth, 21cm.

Torquay Golf Club

37000. *The Torquay Golf Club [Handbook].* London: Golf Clubs Association, 1932, 43p, illustrated, wrappers, 18.5cm.

Toski, Bob

37020. *Beginner's Guide to Golf.* New York: Grosset & Dunlap, 1st ed. [1955] 80p, illustrated, illustrated wrappers, 27cm.

Townshend, Richard Baxter

37040. *Inspired Golf.* London: Methuen, 1st ed. 1921, 64p, illustrated boards, 17cm.

37050. 1st American ed. New York: Henry Holt, 1921, 64p, pictorial boards, 16.5cm.

Trabue, Ann

37070. *History of the Los Angeles Country Club.* Los Angeles: Privately Printed, 1st ed. 1936, 40p, illustrated, suede leather, 23.5cm.

Travers, Jerome Dunstan

37090. *Travers' Golf Book.* New York: Macmillan, 1st ed. 1913, 242p, illustrated, decorative cloth, 19cm. later printing.

Travers, Jerome Dunstan and James J. Crowell

37110. *The Fifth Estate: Thirty Years of Golf.* New York: Knopf, 1st ed. 1926, 259p, illustrated, decorative cloth, 20.5cm. later printing.

Travers, Jerome Dunstan and Grantland Rice

37130. *The Winning Shot.* Garden City, New York: Doubleday, Page, 1st ed. 1915, 258p, illustrated, decorative cloth, 18.5cm.

37140. 1st UK ed. London: T. Werner Laurie [1915] 258p, illustrated, cloth, 18.5cm.

Travis, Walter J.

37160. *Practical Golf.* New York: Harper's, 1st ed. 1901, 225p, illustrated, decorative cloth, 20cm.

37170. 2d ed. rev. 1903, 251p, illustrated, decorative cloth, 20cm.

37180. 3d ed. rev. 1909, 266p, illustrated, decorative cloth, 20.5cm.

Travis, Walter J. and Jack White

37200. *The Art of Putting.* London: Macmillan, 1st ed. 1904, 31p, illustrated, illustrated wrappers, 19.5cm, edited by G.W. Beldam.

Treat, Archibald

37220. *Golf And Lawyers.* San Francisco: E.L. Bosqui, 1st ed. 1932, 13p, illustrated wrappers, 18cm.

Trevor, George

37240. *A Blind Man Breaks 80.* Buffalo, New York: Buffalo Association for the Blind, 1st ed. 1957 [16p] wrappers, 27cm. note: in Braille.

Trezevant, J. T.

37260. *Dallas Country Club.* Dallas, Texas: Privately Printed, 1st ed. [ca1914] [24p] illustrated, illustrated wrappers, 27cm.

Triefus, Paul

37280. *The Most Excellent Historie of MacHamlet, hys handicap, or, as you swipe it, with hys tryalls and tribulations in the game of golfe and contaynyng many and sundrie typps thereon, both prettie and profitable and most delightfully discoursed, as it hath beene divers tymes acted by the Noe-Trumper dramatick players, adorned with many pleasaunt and merrie pictures here for the first tyme displayed by Sidney Rogerson.*

[London] Simpkin, Marshall, Hamilton, Kent, 1st ed. 1922, 35p, illustrated by Sidney Rogerson, 1/4 cloth, illustrated boards, 20.5cm.

Trimingham, Eldon H.

37300. *Golf in Bermuda.* Hamilton, Bermuda: Bermuda Golf Association, 1st ed. 1952 [12p] illustrated, illustrated wrappers, 19cm.

Tripp, William A.

37320. *The Geometry of Golf.* New York: Vantage Press, 1st ed. [1960] 57p, illustrated, cloth, 20.5cm.

Triscott, C. Pette

37340. *Golf in Six Lessons.* London: Athletic Publications, 1st ed. [ca1924] 48p, illustrated, cloth, 18.5cm, later printing.

37350. 1st American ed. Philadelphia: David McKay [1925] 48p, illustrated, cloth, 18.5cm.

[Trump, John Fuller]

37390. *From A Hundred and Two to Eighty Two in A Month or Two.* Springfield, Ohio: Golf Secrets, 1st ed. [1934] 45p, illustrated, illustrated wrappers, 19cm.

37400. 2d ed. rev. 1937, 62p, illustrated, illustrated wrappers, 19cm.

37410. 3d ed. rev. 1939, 80p, illustrated, decorative cloth, 19cm, later printings.

Tucker, Cecil Finn

37430. *Nineteenth Hole Romances and the Devious Methods of Joseph Blotchford.* Melbourne, Australia: Melbourne Publishing, 1st ed. [ca1927] 150p, cloth, 18cm.

Tucker, William H.

37450. *A Golf Course For Your Community.* New York: William H. Tucker, 1st ed. [ca1925] [5p] wrappers, 16cm.

Tuckerman, Walter R.

37470. *A History of the Burning Tree Club.* Bethesda, Maryland: Privately Printed, 1st ed. 1948, 23p, illustrated wrappers, 22cm.

Tufts, Richard S.

37490. *The Principles Behind the Rules of Golf.* Pinehurst, North Carolina: Privately Printed, 1st ed. 1960, 102p, illustrated, cloth, 20.5cm.

37500. 2d ed. rev. 1961, 122p, illustrated, cloth, 19.5cm.

Tulloch, W.W.

37520. *The Life of Tom Morris, with Glimpses of St. Andrews and its Golfing Celebrities.* London: T. Werner Laurie, 1st ed. [ca1908] 334p, illustrated, decorative cloth, 22cm.

37530. facsimile limited ed. [200 copies] slipcased. London: Ellesborough Press, 1982, 334p, illustrated, leather, aeg, raised bands, 22cm.

37540. facsimile ed. London: Ellesborough Press, 1982, 334p, illustrated, decorative cloth, 22cm.

Turner, Rupert

37560. *Novelty Golf Match: George Henriques Playing with Golf Clubs versus Major Hayter Playing with Bow and Arrow.* Edgemoor, England: Privately Printed, 1st ed. 1942 [10p] illustrated, leatherette, 23cm.

Turnesa, Jim

37580. *12 Lessons to Better Golf.* New York: Prentice-Hall, 1st ed. [1953] 180p, illustrated, cloth, 20.5cm.

37590. *Low Score Golf.* London: Herbert Jenkins, 1st ed. 1953, 133p, illustrated, cloth, 23.5cm, UK title of "12 Lessons to Better Golf."

37600. *Jim Turnesa, Driver: A Swing Analysis in Slow Motion [Flip Book].* Dallas, Texas: John E. Campbell, 1st ed. [ca1950] [140p] illustrated, illustrated wrappers, 7cm.

Tuthill, Mex

37620. *Golf Without Gall.* London: Hutchinson, 1st ed. [ca1940] 102p, illustrated by 'Scrum', decorative cloth, 18.5cm.

Two Counties Golf Guide-Lancashire and Cheshire

37640. *Two Counties Golf Guide: Being the Itinerary of the Golf Courses in Lancashire and Cheshire.* Manchester, England: Service Publicity, 1st ed. 1939, 128p, illustrated wrappers, 21.5cm.

Two Hundred Funny Golf Stories As Told at the 19th

37660. *200 Funny Golf Stories As Told At the 19th.* London: W. Foulsham, 1st ed. [ca1932] 92p, cloth, 14.5cm.

Two of His Kind [G.D. Fox]

37680. *The Six Handicap Golfer's Companion.* London: Mills & Boon, 1st ed. 1909, 120p. illustrated by Jack White, cloth, 18 cm, with chapters by Harold H. Hilton and H.S. Colt.

Tyler, Ralph G.

37700. *A Handbook of Golf for Beginners.* Hanover, New Hampshire: Privately Printed, 1st ed. [1914] 41p, wrappers, 15.5cm.

37710. *The Golf Oracle or Golf Made Easy for the Vest Pocket.* NP: Privately Printed, 1st ed. [1913] 23p, wrappers, 13.5cm.

Tyner, Frederick D.

37730. *The Golfer's Dream.* Minneapolis, Minnesota: Colwell Press, 1st ed. [1936] [30p] illustrated by Carl Rawson, 1/4 cloth, illustrated boards, 19cm.

Tyrrells Wood Golf Club

37750. *The Tyrrells Wood Golf Club [Handbook].* London: Golf Clubs Association [ca1951] 16p, illustrated, wrappers, 18cm.

Ulen Country Club

37770. *The Ulen Country Club Silver Anniversary 1924-1949.* Lebanon, Indiana: Privately Printed, 1st ed. 1949, 20p, illustrated, wrappers, 28.5cm.

United Services Golf Club

37790. *United Services Golf Club [Handbook]*. Bristol & London: Temple Publicity Services [ca1951] 16p, illustrated, illustrated wrappers, 18.5cm.

United States Golf Association

37810. *Calkin System of Calculating Handicap*. New York: United States Golf Association, 1st ed. 1927 [6p] wrappers, 21cm.

37820. *Record Book of the U.S.G.A. Championships and International Events*. New York: United States Golf Association, 1st ed. 1947, 84p, wrappers, 21.5cm, supplement 1948.

37830. *Record Book of the USGA Championships 1895-1953*. New York: United States Golf Association, 2d ed. 1953, 305p, wrappers, 22cm, supplements: 1954, 55, 56, 57, 58, 59, 60.

37840. *Record Book of the USGA Championships 1895-1961*. New York: United States Golf Association, 3d ed. 1961, 224p, cloth, 21.5cm, supplements: 1962, 63, 64, 65, 66, 67, 68, 69.

37850. *Record Book of the USGA Championships*. Far Hills, New Jersey: United States Golf Association, 4th ed. 1972, 637p, wrappers, 22.5cm, supplements: 1972, 73, 74, 75, 76, 77, 78, 79.

37860. *Record Book of the USGA Championships 1895-1959 and 1960-1980 [2 Volumes]*. Far Hills, New Jersey: United States Golf Association, 5th ed. 1980, 420p each, wrappers, 23cm, supplements: 1981, 82, 83, 84, 85.

37870. *The Conduct of Women's Golf*. New York: USGA, 1st ed. 1945, 16p, wrappers, 19cm.

37880. 2d ed. 1951, 15p, wrappers, 20cm.

37890. 3d ed. 1954, 42p, wrappers, 18.5cm.

37900. 4th ed. 1956, 42p, wrappers, 19.5cm.

37910. 5th ed. 1957, 52p, wrappers, 19.5cm.

37920. 6th ed. 1958, 63p, wrappers, 20cm.

37930. 7th ed. 1959, 63p, wrappers, 19.5cm.

37940. 8th ed. 1960, 63p, wrappers, 19.5cm.

37950. 9th ed. 1962, 63p, wrappers, 19.5cm.

37960. 10th ed. 1963, 63p, wrappers, 19.5cm.

37970. 11th ed. 1964, 63p, wrappers, 19.5cm.

United States Government Printing Office

37990. *Hickory Golf Shafts: Commercial Standard CS 18-29.* Washington, DC: United States Government Printing Office, 1st ed. 1930, 14p, illustrated, wrappers, 21cm.

United States Senior's Golf Association

38010. *Senior Golf in the United States, Canada and Great Britain.* [New York] United States Senior's Golf Association, 1st ed. [ca1936] [34p] illustrated, wrappers, 24.5cm.

Universal Golf Dictionary

38030. *Universal Golf Dictionary: Summary of Golf and Golf Etiquette.* Springfield, Massachusetts: Universal Golf, 1st ed. [1934] 68p, wrappers, 15.5cm.

[Urry, J.M.]

38050. *To St. Andrews for the Open Championship 1946.* [England] Privately Printed, 1st ed. 1946, 15p, wrappers, 21cm.

Uzzell, Thomas H.

38070. *Golf in the World's Oldest Mountains.* Murray Bay, Canada: Mason Richelieu, 1st ed. [ca1926] [40p] illustrated, pictorial boards, 28cm.

Vachell, H.A.

38090. *The New Forest Golf Club [Handbook].* London: Golf Clubs Association, 28p, 1925, illustrated, wrappers, 18cm.

Vaile, Pembroke A.

38110. *Golf on the Green.* New York: John Wanamaker, 1st ed. 1915, 108p, illustrated, decorative cloth, 17cm.

38120. *How To Approach.* Chicago: Thos E. Wilson, 1st ed. [1919] 53p, illustrated, illustrated wrappers, 19.5cm.

38130. *How To Drive.* Chicago: Thos E. Wilson, 1st ed. [1919] 91p, illustrated, illustrated wrappers, 19.5cm.

38140. *How To Learn Golf: Spalding Primer Series.* New York: American Sports Publishing, 1st ed. [1919] [66p] illustrated, illustrated wrappers, 17cm.

38150. *How To Put and Training for Golf.* Chicago: Thos E. Wilson, 1st ed. [1919] 63p, illustrated, illustrated wrappers, 19.5cm.

38160. *Modern Golf.* London: Adam & Charles Black, 1st ed. 1909, 252p, illustrated, decorative cloth, 19.5cm.
38170. 2d ed. rev. 1914, 256p, illustrated, decorative cloth, 20cm.

38180. *Putting Made Easy: The Mark G. Harris Method.* Chicago: Reilly & Lee, 1st ed. [1935] 95p, illustrated, cloth, 18cm.

38190. *Scientific Putting.* Chicago: Berkley-Ralston, 4th ed. [1927] 48p, illustrated, illustrated wrappers, 16cm. note: earlier editions not located.

38200. *Swerve or the Flight of the Gull.* London: J. Tamblyn, 1st ed. 1905, 83p, illustrated, illustrated wrappers, 18.5cm.

38210. *The Illustrated Rules of Golf.* Chicago: Thos. E. Wilson, 1st ed. [1919] 84p, illustrated by H.B. Martin, illustrated wrappers, 16cm.

38220. *The New Golf.* New York: Dutton, 1st ed. 1916, 289p, illustrated, decorative cloth, 20.5cm.
38230. 2d ed. rev. 1917, 31p, illustrated, decorative cloth, 20.5cm.

38240. *The Short Game.* Chicago: Berkley-Ralston, 1st ed. [1928] 40p, illustrated, illustrated wrappers, 23.5cm, later printings.
38250. 1st UK ed. London: Duckworth, 1936, 136p, illustrated, cloth, 18.5cm, introduction by Henry Longhurst.

38260. *The Soul of Golf.* London: Macmillan, 1st ed. 1912, 355p, illustrated, decorative cloth, 20cm.

Van Loan, Charles E.

38280. *Fore!* New York: George H. Doran, 1st ed. [1918] 328p, decorative cloth, 18cm, foreword by Robert H. Davis. later printing.

38290. 1st Canadian ed. Toronto: Doubleday [1918] 328p, decorative cloth, 18.5cm, foreword by Robert H. Davis.

38300. reprint Memorial ed. New York: George H. Doran, 1919, 328p, 1/4 cloth, boards, 20cm, foreword by Robert H. Davis.

Vander Meulen, John M.

38320. *Getting Out of the Rough.* New York: George H. Doran, 1st ed. [1926] 143p, cloth, 18.5cm.

Vardon, Alfred and E.W.J. Wilson

38340. *Golfing Hints.* Weston-Super Mare, England: Lawrence Bros. 1st ed. [1912] 36p, illustrated, illustrated wrappers, 18.5cm.

Vardon, Harry

38360. *Golf Club Selection.* Newark, Ohio: Burke Golf Company, 1st ed. [1916] 48p, illustrated, embossed leather, 13cm.

38370. *How to Play Golf.* London: Methuen, 1st ed. 1912, 298p, illustrated, cloth, 18.5cm.

38380. 1st American ed. Philadelphia: George W. Jacobs [ca1912] 298p, illustrated, cloth, 19cm.

38390. *My Golfing Life.* London: Hutchinson, 1st ed. 1933, 281p, illustrated, cloth, 21.5cm.

38400. limited facsimile ed. [300 copies] Dublin, Ohio: The Memorial Tournament, 1981, 281p, illustrated, leather, 21.5cm, issued for the 1981 Memorial Tournament

38410. limited facsimile ed. [200 copies] slipcased, London: Ellesborough Press, 1985, 281p, illustrated, gilt stamped leather, aeg, raised bands, 21.5cm.

38420. *Progressive Golf.* London: Hutchinson, 1st ed [1920] 160p, illustrated, cloth, 18.5cm. later printing.

38430. *The Complete Golfer.* London: Methuen, 1st ed. 1905, 283p, illustrated, cloth, 22cm, later printings.

38440. 1st American ed. New York: McClure, Phillips, 1905, 283p, illustrated, 22cm. later printings.

38450. reprint ed. New York: Arno Press/Golf Digest, 1977, 287p, illustrated, decorative cloth, 21.5cm.

38460. *The Gist of Golf.* New York: George H. Doran, 1st American ed. [1922] 153p, illustrated, cloth, 19cm. American title of "Progressive Golf."

Vardon, Harry and others

38490. *Success At Golf: Hints for the Player of Moderate Ability.* and Alexander Herd, George Duncan, Wilfrid Reid, Lawrence Ayton, Jack White, Tom Ball. London: Fry's Magazine, 1st ed. [ca1914] 143p, illustrated, illustrated boards, 16.5cm, introduction by R.E. Howard. later printings.

38500. *Success at Golf.* and Alexander Herd, George Duncan, Wilfrid Reid, Lawrence Ayton, Francis Ouimet. Boston: Little Brown, 1st American ed. 1914, 116p, illustrated, cloth, 18.5cm, introduction by John G. Anderson. later printings.

Venturi, Ken

38520. *Let's Analyze Your Golf Swing.* Portland, Oregon: Jantzen, 1st ed. [ca1960] 20p, illustrated, illustrated wrappers, 15cm.

Verulam Golf Club

38540. *The Verulam Golf Club [Handbook].* London: Golf Clubs Association, 1934, 24p, illustrated, wrappers, 18.5cm.

Veteran

38560. *The Secret of Golf for Occasional Players.* London: Methuen, 1st ed. 1922, 47p, cloth, 17cm, later printings.

38570. *Golf for Occasional Players.* New York: Robert M. McBride, 1922, 47p, pictorial boards, 17cm, American title of "The Secret of Golf for Occasional Players." later printings.

Von Nida, Norman

38590. *Golf Is My Business.* Sydney, Australia: Shakespeare Head Press, 1st ed. 1956, 210p, illustrated, cloth, 19.5cm, with Muir Maclaren, forewords by Henry Cotton, Peter Thomson, Ed Furgol.

38600. 1st UK ed. London: Frederick Muller, 1956, 210p, illustrated, cloth, 19.5cm, later printing.

38610. pbk ed. London: Panther, 1957, 192p, illustrated, illustrated wrappers, 18cm, with Muir Maclaren, foreword by Henry Cotton.

38620. *Golf Isn't Hard.* London: Sampson Low, Marston, 1st ed. 1949, 91p, illustrated, cloth, 19.5cm, foreword by Hector Morrison.

Voorhies, Clifton L.

38640. *The Mental Game of Golf.* La Mesa, California: Privately Printed, 1st ed. [ca1950] 24p, wrappers, 21cm.

Walker, Oscar W.

38660. *Practical Golf Lessons from A New Angle.* Ballycastle, Northern Ireland: J.S. Scarlett, 1st ed. 1949, 54p, illustrated, illustrated wrappers, 18.5cm.

Walker, Robert

38680. *Ham Manor Residential Golf Club [Handbook].* Bristol & London: Temple Publicity Services [ca1951] 24p, illustrated, wrappers, 18.5cm.

38690. *The Newquay Golf Club [Handbook].* Bristol & London: Temple Publicity Services [ca1951] 44p, illustrated, wrappers, 18.5cm.

38700. *The Southerndown Golf Club [Handbook].* Bristol & London: Temple Publicity Services [ca1955] 16p, illustrated, illustrated wrappers, 18.5cm.

38710. *The Verulam Golf Club [Handbook]*. Bristol & London: Temple Publicity Services [ca1957] 28p, illustrated, illustrated wrappers, 18.5cm.

Walmer and Kingsdown Golf Club

38730. *Walmer and Kingsdown Golf Club [Handbook]*. Cheltenham, England: Ed. J. Burrow [ca1937] 16p, illustrated, illustrated wrappers, 16.5cm.

Walsall Golf Club

38750. *Walsall Golf Club [Handbook]*. Cheltenham & London: Ed. J. Burrow [ca1938] 24p, illustrated, illustrated wrappers, 16.5cm.

Walsh, Leigh

38770. *How to Teach Yourself the Expert Golf Swing*. San Francisco: A.M. Regan, 1st ed. [1956] 63p, illustrated, wrappers, 27.5cm.

Walsh, Tom

38790. *The Picture Way to Better Golf*. [Chicago] Privately Printed, 1st ed. [1937] 29p, illustrated, spiral bound illustrated wrappers, 21.5cm.

Ward, Hugh

38810. *Effortless Golf*. New York: Alumni Publications, 1st ed. [1956] 15p, illustrated, illustrated wrappers, 17.5cm, introduction by Mrs. Mortimer Hay.

Waring, G.

38830. *Golf: A Scientific Approach, The Mechanics of the Game*. Newcastle upon Tyne, England: Leyland Motors, offprint, 1958, 11p, illustrated, wrappers, 17.5cm, offprint from The Leyland Journal, July 1947.

Washington Golf and Country Club

38850. *History of the Washington Golf and Country Club*. Arlington, Virginia: Privately Printed, 1st ed. 1947, 36p, illustrated, illustrated wrappers, 23cm.

Wason, E. R.

38870. *Golf Without Tears.* Aberdeen, Scotland: Aberdeen Journals, 1st ed. [ca1951] 40p, illustrated, illustrated wrappers, 18.5cm, with Gordon Durward.

Waters, T.F.R.

38890. *A History of the Royal Hong Kong Golf Club.* Hong Kong: Privately Printed, 1st ed. 1960, 101p, illustrated, decorative cloth, 19cm.

Watson, A. Campbell

38910. *Podson's Golfing Year.* London: W. & R. Chambers, 1st ed. [ca1930] 128p, illustrated by D.M. Sutherland, illustrated wrappers, 18.5cm.

Watson, Gilbert

38930. *A Caddie of St. Andrews.* New York: Henry Holt, 1st ed. 1907, 373p, illustrated, decorative cloth, 18.5cm.

38940. *Skipper.* Edinburgh & London: William Blackwood, 1st ed. 1906, 256p, decorative cloth, 19cm, later printing.

Watson, J.W.

38960. *Little Lessons in Golf.* Kansas City, Missouri: Schmelzer Arms, 1st ed. [ca1921] 48p, illustrated, illustrated wrappers, 18cm.

Weaver, Wyn

38980. *Golf Clubs, An Eccentric Sketch [A Play].* New York: Samuel French, 1st ed. 1925, 13p, wrappers, 18.5cm.

Webb, Warren H.

39000. *Lessons on Golf.* London: World of Golf, 2d ed. 1907, 61p, illustrated, cloth, 15.5cm. note: first edition not located.

39010. 4th American ed. Philadelphia: Privately Printed, 1915, 100p, illustrated, cloth, 17.5cm. note: earlier American editions not located.

Webling, W. Hastings

39030. *An Interrupted Golf Match and Other Stories.* Toronto, Canada: Miln-Bingham, 1st ed. [1910] 31p, illustrated wrappers, 24.5cm.

39040. *Fore: A Few More Golf Shots*. Brantford, Canada: Privately Printed, limited ed. [no limitation cited] [1908] [20p] illustrated, illustrated folding panorama, 19cm.

39050. *Fore: The Call of the Links*. Boston: H.M. Caldwell, 1st ed. [1909] 73p, illustrated, pictorial cloth, 19cm.

39060. *Golf: In Verse and Reverse*. [Brantford, Canada] Privately Printed, 1st ed. 1924 [20p] wrappers, 16cm.

39070. *Locker Room Ballads*. New York: Brentano's, 1st ed. [1925] 95p, illustrated by C.R. Snelgrove, pictorial cloth, 19cm.
39080. 1st UK ed. London: Brentano's [ca1925] 95p, illustrated by C.R. Snelgrove, pictorial cloth, 18cm.

39090. *On and Off the Links*. [Brantford, Canada] Privately Printed, 1st ed. 1921 [16p] wrappers, 18cm.

Weetman, Harry
39110. *Golf [Flicker Book] Drive and 7-Iron Shot*. [England] NP, 1st ed. [ca1960] [96p] illustrated, wrappers, 7.5cm.

39120. *The Way to Golf*. London: Ward, Lock, 1st ed. 1953, 159p, illustrated, cloth, 21.5cm, foreword by Tom Scott.

Weidemnkopf, Ralph
39140. *The Science of Controlled Relaxation in Golf... and How to Apply it to Your Game*. Chagrin Falls, Ohio: Privately Printed, 1st ed. [1936] 20p, wrappers, 23.5cm.

Weiss, Mike
39160. *100 Handy Hints on How to Break 100*. New York: Prentice-Hall, 1st ed. [1951] 118p, illustrated, cloth, 20.5cm, later printings.

Wendehack, Clifford Charles
39180. *Golf and Country Clubs; a survey of the requirements of planning, construction and equipment of the modern club house*. New York: William Helburn, 1st ed. 1929, 51p/156p-plates, illustrated, cloth, 33.5cm.

Wentworth Club
39200. *Wentworth Club [Handbook]*. London: Golf Clubs Association [ca1959] 62p, illustrated, wrappers, 18cm.

Wesson, Douglas Bertram

39220. *I'll Never Be Cured and Don't Much Care: The History of an Acute Attack of Golf and Pertinent Remarks Relating to Various Places of Treatment.* New York: J.H. Sears, 1st ed. [1928] 196p, illustrated by Wyncie King, decorative cloth, 20.5cm.

West Wilts Golf Club

39240. *West Wilts Golf Club [Handbook].* London: Golf Clubs Association, 1938, 24p, illustrated, wrappers, 18.5cm.

West, Henry Litchfield

39260. *Lyrics of the Links.* New York: Macmillan, 1st ed. 1921, 180p, illustrated by George M. Richards, decorative cloth, 19cm.

39270. *The Columbia Country Club As it Was in the Beginning.* Chevy Chase, Maryland: Privately Printed, 1st ed. 1938 [14p] illustrated, illustrated wrappers, 19.5cm.

Western Golf Association

39290. *Caddie Committee Manual.* Chicago: Western Golf Association, 1st ed. [1947] 40p, illustrated, illustrated wrappers, 22cm.

39300. *Caddie Master Manual.* Golf, Illinois: Western Golf Association, 1st ed. [1955] 24p, illustrated, illustrated wrappers, 21.5cm.

39310. *Camera Tour of Caddieville USA.* Golf, Illinois: Western Golf Association, 1st ed. [ca1955] 24p, illustrated, illustrated wrappers, 21.5cm.

39320. *New Caddie Committee Guide and Electric Cart Survey.* Golf, Illinois: Western Golf Association, 1st ed. [1955] 35p, illustrated, illustrated wrappers, 21.5cm.

39330. *Pin Pointers.* Chicago: Western Golf Association, 1st ed. [1948] 20p, illustrated, illustrated wrappers, 21.5cm.

39340. *Recruiting and Retaining Your Caddies.* Chicago: Western Golf Association, 1st ed. [1951] 20p, illustrated, illustrated wrappers, 21.5cm.

Westgate-on-Sea and Birchington Golf Club

39360. *The Westgate-on-Sea and Birchington Golf Club [Handbook].* London: Golf Clubs Association, 1926, 20p, illustrated, wrappers, 18cm.

Weston-Super Mare Golf Club

39380. *The Weston-Super Mare Golf Club [Handbook].* London: Golf Clubs Association [ca1955] 15p, illustrated, wrappers, 18.5cm.

Wethered, H. N.

39400. *The Perfect Golfer.* London: Methuen, 1st ed. 1931, 246p, illustrated, cloth, 19cm.

Wethered, H. N. and T. Simpson

39420. *The Architectural Side of Golf.* London: Longmans, Green, limited ed. large paper [50 copies] 1929, 210p, illustrated, decorative cloth, 25cm, preface by J.C.Squire.

39430. 1st trade ed. 1929, 210p, illustrated, decorative cloth, 24.5cm.

39440. *Design for Golf.* London: Sportsman's Book Club. reprint ed. 1952, 203p, illustrated, cloth, 21cm, preface by J.C. Squire. previously titled "Architectural Side of Golf."

Wethered, Joyce

39460. *Golfing Memories and Methods.* London: Hutchinson, 1st ed. 1933, 255p, illustrated, cloth, 21cm, later printing.

39470. reprint ed. London: Sportsman's Book Club, 1954, 255p, illustrated, cloth, 21.5cm.

Wethered, Joyce and others

39490. *The Game of Golf, The Lonsdale Library.* and Roger Wethered, Bernard Darwin, Horace Hutchinson, T.C. Simpson. London: Seeley, Service, deluxe ed. 1931, 251p, illustrated, 1/4 leather, decorative cloth, 21cm.

39500. 1st trade ed. 1931, 251p, illustrated, cloth, 21cm. later printing.

Wethered, Roger

39520. *The Temple Golf Club [Handbook].* Derby & Cheltenham, England: New Centurion [ca1938] 22p, illustrated, wrappers, 16cm.

Wethered, Roger and Joyce

39540. *Golf From Two Sides*. London: Longmans, Green, 1st ed. 1922, 197p, illustrated, cloth, 21.5cm, prefatory note by H. Newton Wethered.

39550. 2d ed. rev. 1925, 214p, illustrated, cloth, 20cm, preface by H. Newton Wethered.

Weymouth Golf Club

39570. *The Weymouth Golf Club [Handbook]*. Bristol & London: Temple Publicity Services [ca1951] 12p, illustrated, illustrated wrappers, 18cm.

Wheatley, Vera

39590. *Mixed Foursomes: A Saga of Golf*. London: Thorton Butterworth, 1st ed. 1936, 125p, illustrated by Laurie Taylor, cloth, 18.5cm.

Whitcombe, Charles Albert

39610. *Charles Whitcombe on Golf*. London: Alexander-Ouseley, 1st ed. 1931, 66p, illustrated, cloth, 18.5cm.

39620. *Golf*. London: Sir Isaac Pitnam, 1st ed. 1949, 150p, illustrated, decorative cloth, 18.5cm, with a foreword and a chapter on the rules by Robert H. K. Browning

39630. *Golf Shots: The Drive, Fairway Hazard Pocket Pro Series No. 1*. London: Niblick Publishing, 1st ed. [ca1933] 12p, illustrated, illustrated wrappers, 15.5cm.

39640. *Golf Shots: The Iron, Fairway Hazard Pocket Pro Series No. 2*. London: Niblick Publishing, 1st ed. [ca1933] 12p, illustrated, illustrated wrappers, 15.5cm.

39650. *Golf Shots: The Mashie Niblick, Fairway Hazard Pocket Pro Series No. 3*. London: Niblick Publishing, 1st ed. [ca1933] 12p, illustrated, illustrated wrappers, 15.5cm.

39660. *Golf Shots: Niblick and Putter, Fairway & Hazard Pocket Pro Series No 4*. London: Niblick Publishing, 1st ed. [ca1933] 12p, illustrated, illustrated wrappers, 15.5cm.

Whitcombe, Ernest R.

39680. *How To Play Meyrick Park Golf Course [Handbook]*. Bristol & London: Temple Publicity Services [ca1951] 32p, illustrated, wrappers, 18.5cm.

39690. *The Golf I Teach: A book of Instruction in two parts for beginners and others.* Bournemouth, England: Privately Printed, 1st ed. 1947, 134p, illustrated by D.C.W. Sabine, cloth, 18cm, foreword by Humphrey McMaster.

Whitcombe, Reginald Arthur

39710. *Golf's No Mystery: A Book for Golfers and Beginners.* London: J.M. Dent, 1st ed. 1938, 127p, illustrated, illustrated wrappers, 18.5cm, foreword by Peter Lawless.

White, Jack

39730. *Easier Golf.* London: Methuen, 1st ed. 1924, 115p, illustrated, cloth, 19cm. later printing.

39740. 1st American ed. New York: Robert M. McBride, 1924, 115p, illustrated, cloth, 19cm.

39750. *Putting.* London: Country Life, 1st ed. 1921, 48p, illustrated, pictorial cloth, 17.5cm, prefatory notes by J.H. Taylor, James Braid, Alex. Herd, George Duncan and a commentary by Bernard Darwin.

White, Ronald James

39770. *Golf As I Play It.* London: G. Bell, 1st ed. 1953, 160p, illustrated, cloth, 21.5cm, foreword by Leonard Crawley.

White, Stewart-Edward

39790. *The Shepper-Newfounder.* Garden City, New York: Doubleday, Doran, 1st ed. 1931, 107p, illustrated by H.T. Webster, cloth, 18.5cm.

Whiteford, James F.

39810. *Tam At Golf or the Nineteenth Hole.* [London] Privately Printed, 1st ed. 1939, 10p, illustrated wrappers, 18cm.

Whitlatch, Marshall

39830. *Golf for Beginners and Others.* New York: Outing, 1st ed. 1910, 280p, illustrated, cloth, 21cm.

39840. 2d ed. New York: Macmillan, 1921, 280p, illustrated, cloth, 19cm. note: New Publisher.

39850. 2d ed. rev. New York: Macmillan, 1923, 338p, illustrated, cloth, 19cm.

Whitney, Howard F.

39900. *Decisions on the Rules of Golf.* New York: United States Golf Association, 1st ed. 1927 [129p] wrappers, 24cm.

Whitton, Ivo Harrington

39920. *Golf.* Melbourne, Australia: Robertson & Mullens, 1st ed. 1947, 95p, illustrated, illustrated wrappers, 18cm, introduction by Eric S. Quirk.

Who's Who in Golf-Directory of Golf Clubs and Members

39940. *Who's Who in Golf and Directory of Golf Clubs and Members.* London: Stanley, 1st ed. 1909 [1000p] decorative cloth, 21cm.

Wickersham, Price and Frank Lauder

39960. *The K.C.G.A. Caddie Book: A Complete Caddie System with Information for Golfers.* Kansas City, Missouri: Kansas City Golf Assoc. 1st ed. [1921] 114p, illustrated, illustrated wrappers, 17.5cm.

Wickham, Verne

39980. *The Municipal Golf Course: Organizing and Operating Guide.* Chicago: National Golf Foundation, 1st ed. 1955, 120p, illustrated, illustrated wrappers, 28cm.

Wild, Morton

40000. *Inwood Country Club Fiftieth Anniversary 1901-1951.* Inwood, New York: Privately Printed, 1st ed. 1951, 101p, illustrated, decorative cloth, 26.5cm.

Wild, Payson Sibley and Bert Leston Taylor

40040. *The Links of Ancient Rome.* Chicago: Brothers of the Book, 1st ed. 1912 [16p] illustrated by F. Fox, illustrated wrappers, 18.5cm.

Wilderness Country Club

40060. *Wilderness Country Club and Golf Course [Handbook].* London: Golf Club Association, 1930, 31p, illustrated, wrappers, 18.5cm.

Wilkinson, Elizabeth Doddridge

40080. *History of the Toledo Women's District Golf Association.* Toledo, Ohio: Privately Printed, 1st ed. [1931] 79p, illustrated, gilt stamped leather, 23cm.

Williams, Eddie

40100. *How To Improve Your Golf with the Developar.* Louisville, Kentucky: Privately Printed, 1st ed. [ca1958] [8p] illustrated, illustrated wrappers, 23cm.

Williams, Lewis

40120. *Golf Without Tears.* London: Harmony Press, 1st ed. [ca1940] 32p, cloth, 18cm.

Willmott, J.E.

40140. *Sutton Coldfield Golf Club Jubilee 1899-1939.* Sutton Coldfield, England: Privately Printed, 1st ed. 1939, 24p, illustrated, illustrated wrappers, 18.5cm.

Wilson Sporting Goods

40160. *For the Esquire of the Golf Links.* Chicago: Wilson Sporting Goods, 1st ed. [1938] 30p, illustrated, illustrated wrappers, 35.5cm.

40170. *Presenting the 7-Up Golf Tips by the Experts.* Evanston, Illinois: National Sports Almanac, 1st ed. [1957] [32p] illustrated, illustrated wrappers, 10cm.

Wilson, Enid and Robert Allen Lewis

40190. *So That's What I Do!* London: Methuen, 1st ed. 1935, 127p, illustrated, cloth, 21.5cm, forewords by Joyce Wethered and Henry Cotton.

Wilson, Harry Leon

40210. *So This is Golf!* New York: Cosmopolitan, 1st ed. 1923, 46p, illustrated by M.L. Blumenthal, 1/4 cloth, boards, 19cm.

40220. 1st UK ed. London: John Lane, 1923, 52p, illustrated by Fougasse, decorative cloth, 18cm.

Wilson, Kenneth

40240. *It's All in the Swing: Self Help for the Average Golfer.* London: Putnam, 1st ed. 1947, 155p, illustrated, cloth, 18.5cm.

40250. *To Better Golf in Two Strides.* London: Putnam, 1st ed. 1938, 156p, illustrated, cloth, 18.5cm.

Winchester Golf Club

40270. *Rules for Caddies.* Winchester, Massachusetts: Privately Printed, 1st ed. 1926, 9p, wrappers, 15cm.

Wind, Herbert Warren

40290. *Golf Tips From the Top Professionals.* Greenwich, Connecticut: Fawcett, 1st ed. [1958] 144p, illustrated by Anthony Ravielli, illustrated wrappers, 23.5cm, abridged from "Tips From the Top." later printings.

40300. *On the Tour with Harry Sprague.* New York: Simon & Schuster, 1st ed. [1960] 94p, illustrated, decorative cloth, 20.5cm, introduction by Jimmy Demaret.

40310. *The Complete Golfer.* New York: Simon & Schuster, 1st ed. 1954, 315p, illustrated, cloth, 25cm, introduction by Robert T. Jones, Jr. later printings.

40320. 1st UK ed. London: Heinemann, 1954, 398p, illustrated, cloth, 21.5cm, introduction by Robert T. Jones, Jr. later printing.

40330. *The Story of American Golf: Its Champions and Its Championships.* New York: Farrar, Strauss, 1st ed. slipcased, 1948, 502p, illustrated, decorative cloth, 27.5cm.

40340. 2d ed. rev. New York: Simon & Schuster, 1956, 564p, illustrated, 1/4 cloth, illustrated boards, 25cm.

40350. 3d ed. rev. New York: Knopf, 1975, 591p, illustrated, decorative cloth, 27.5cm.

40360. *Thorny Lea Golf Club 1900-1950, 50th Anniversary.* Brockton, Massachusetts: Privately Printed, 1st ed. 1950 [14p] illustrated, illustrated wrappers, 28cm.

40370. *Tips from the Top: 52 golf lessons by the Country's leading pros from Sports Illustrated.* edited by. New York: Prentice-Hall, 1st ed. 1955, 105p, illustrated by Anthony Ravielli, cloth, 22.5cm.

40380. 1st UK ed. London: Country Life, 1956, 105p, illustrated by Anthony Ravielli, cloth, 23cm.

40390. reprint ed. New York: Bramhall House, [1956] 105p, illustrated by Anthony Ravielli, cloth, 22.5cm.

40400. *Tips from the Top: Book 2; More golf lessons by the Country's leading pros from Sports Illustrated.* Englewood Cliffs, New Jersey: Prentice-Hall, 1st ed. 1956, 105p, illustrated by Anthony Ravielli, cloth, 22.5cm.

40410. 1st UK ed. London: Country Life, 1957, 105p, illustrated by Anthony Ravielli, cloth, 23cm.

40420. reprint ed. New York: Bramhall House [1956] 105p, illustrated by Anthony Ravielli, cloth, 22.5cm.

Windermere Golf Club

40440. *The Windermere Golf Club [Handbook].* London: Golf Clubs Association [ca1949] 17p, illustrated, wrappers, 18cm.

Wing, Frank

40460. *Fore! Eighty Two Sketches of the Same Number of Minneapolis Golfers.* [Minnesota] Augsburg Publishing House, 1st ed. 1929 [82p] illustrated, illustrated wrappers, 30.5cm.

Wingate, Roland

40480. *12 Money Shots in Golf.* Boston: Acushnet, 1st ed. [ca1935] [16p] illustrated, illustrated wrappers, 15cm.

40490. *Saving Strokes.* Boston: Privately Printed, 1st ed. 1934, 110p, illustrated, decorative leatherette, 20.5cm, introduction by Wilson E. Mackay.

40495. pbk. ed. 1934, illustrated, illustrated wrappers, 20.5cm.

Winter, Ed

40510. *Simplified Golf Instructions.* Savannah, Georgia: Privately Printed, 1st ed. [ca1950] 32p, illustrated, illustrated wrappers, 15cm.

Woan, Harry

40530. *Swing Secrets Analysed, Explained and Simplified.* Longbridge, England: Austin Motor, 1st ed. 1934, 39p, illustrated, illustrated wrappers, 14.5cm.

Wodehouse, P.G.

40550. *Divots.* New York: George H. Doran, 1st ed. [1927] 316p, decorative cloth, 20cm. American title of "The Heart of A Goof"

40560. reprint ed. New York: A.L. Burt [1927] 316p, cloth, 20cm.

40570. *Golf Without Tears.* New York: George H. Doran [1924] 330p, cloth, 20cm. American title of "The Clicking of Cuthbert."

40580. reprint ed. New York: A.L. Burt, 330p, cloth, 20cm.

40590. *The Clicking of Cuthbert.* London: Herbert Jenkins, 1st ed. 1922, 256p, decorative cloth, 18.5cm. later printings.

40600. *The Heart of A Goof.* London: Herbert Jenkins, 1st ed. 1926, 314p, decorative cloth, 18.5cm. later printing.

40610. *Wodehouse on Golf.* New York: Doubleday, Doran, 1st ed. 1940, 844p, decorative cloth, 20cm. later printing.

Wollaston Golf Club

40630. *Wollaston Golf Club, The Story of the Old Club, Fiftieth Anniversary 1895-1945.* Milton, Massachusetts: Privately Printed, 1st ed. 1945, 59p, illustrated, decorative cloth, 21.5cm.

Woman Golfer [Mabel S. Hoskins]

40650. *Golf for Women.* New York: Moffat, Yard, 1st ed. 1916, 263p, illustrated, decorative cloth, 20cm.

Wood, Craig

40670. *How to Play Golf.* Buffalo, New York: Dunlop, 1st ed. [1935] [16p] illustrated, illustrated wrappers, 10.5cm, introduction by Vincent Richards.

40680. *How to Play Golf.* Victoria, Australia: Dunlop Rubber, 3d Australian ed. [ca1946] 48p, illustrated, illustrated wrappers, 11.5cm. note: earlier editions not located.

Wood, Harry B.

40700. *Golfing Curios and The Like: with an Appendix comprising a Bibliography of Golf.* London: Sherratt & Hughes, limited ed. [150 copies] 1911, 151p, illustrated, 1/4 vellum, cloth, 29cm.

40710. 1st trade ed. London: Sherratt & Hughes, 1910, 149p, illustrated, cloth, 23cm.

40720. reprint ed. Manchester, England: Pride, 1980, 151p, illustrated, cloth, 24cm.

Woodbury, Roy F. and Charlotte Isabel Claflin

40740. *Caddying Erie County.* Buffalo, New York: Juvenile Protective Department, 1st ed. 1935, 44p, illustrated, illustrated wrappers, 23cm.

Woodhall Spa Golf Club

40760. *The Woodhall Spa Golf Club [Handbook].* Bristol & London: Temple Publicity Services [ca1951] 16p, illustrated, wrappers, 18cm.

Woodhead, Arthur L.

40780. *A History of Huddersfield Golf Club from 1891-1949.* Huddersfield, England: Privately Printed, 1st ed. 1949, 34p, illustrated, wrappers, 21.5cm.

Wrexham Golf Club

40800. *The Wrexham Golf Club [Handbook].* London: Golf Clubs Association, 1937, 23p, illustrated, wrappers, 18.5cm.

Wright, Harry

40820. *A Short History of Golf in Mexico and the Mexico City Country Club.* New York: Privately Printed, limited ed. [no limitation cited] signed, 1938, 126p, illustrated, pictorial cloth, 26.5cm.

Wyke Green Golf Club

40840. *Wyke Green Golf Club [Handbook].* Derby & Cheltenham, England: New Centurion [ca1935] 20p, illustrated, wrappers, 18cm.

Wynne, Anthony

40860. *Death of A Golfer.* Philadelphia: Lippincott, 1st ed. [1937] 314p, decorative cloth, 19cm.

40870. 1st UK ed. London: Hutchinson [ca1938] 253p, illustrated wrappers, 18cm.

Yakima Country Club

40890. *Yakima Country Club, Dedication of the New Club House.* Yakima, Washington: Privately Printed, 1st ed. 1949 [16p] illustrated, illustrated wrappers, 23cm.

Yelverton Golf Club

40910. *The Yelverton Golf Club [Handbook].* London: Golf Clubs Association, 1938, 15p, illustrated, wrappers, 18.5cm.

You and Your Golf Course

40930. *You and Your Golf Course.* Kansas City, Missouri: Sports Co. 1st ed. [ca1955] [10p] illustrated by Walt Ditzen, illustrated wrappers, 10.5cm.

You Can Break 80

40950. *You Can Break 80.* [New York] Palmer Products, 1st ed. 1930, 143p, illustrated, illustrated wrappers, 24.5cm.

Young, Charley

40970. *Tips from Western New York Golf Pros.* Buffalo, New York: Buffalo Evening News, 1st ed. [ca1955] 18p, illustrated, illustrated wrappers, 21.5cm.

Young, Jerome Artz

40990. *Documentary Proof That Insanity Is Hereditary.* Springfield, Massachusetts: Privately Printed, 1st ed. 1951 [26p] illustrated, spiral bound wrappers, 21.5cm.

Your Golf Clubs & How To Care For Them

41010. *Your Golf Clubs & How To Care For Them.* White Sulphur Springs, West Virginia: Green Brier Golf Co. 1st ed. [ca1955] [15p] illustrated, illustrated wrappers, 30.5cm.

Zaharias, Mildred Didrickson Babe

41030. *Championship Golf.* New York: A.S. Barnes, 1st ed. [1948] 125p, illustrated, cloth, 23cm, foreword by Walter Hagen.

41040. 1st UK ed. London: Sampson, Low, 1949, 125p, illustrated, cloth, 19.5cm, foreword by Walter Hagen.

41050. *This Life I've Led: My Autobiography.* New York: A.S. Barnes, 1st ed. [1955] 242p, illustrated, cloth, 21cm, as told to Harry Paxton.

41060. 1st UK ed. London: Robert Hale, 1956, 242p, illustrated, cloth, 21cm, as told to Harry Paxton.

Zimmerman, Charles T.

41080. *Sixty Years of Hartford Golf Club 1896-1955.* West Hartford, Connecticut: Privately Printed, 1st ed. 1955, 68p, illustrated, illustrated wrappers, 28cm.

Zodiac Home Golf Ball Booklet

41100. *Zodiac Home Golf Ball Booklet. Golf & How To Play it. [as Told by the Zomites].* Birmingham, England: Martins Birm Golf Ball Maker, 1st ed. [ca1910] [32p] illustrated, illustrated wrappers [shaped] 17.5cm.

Zoghbie, Joseph M.

41120. *Golf Club Directory 1947.* Olean, New York: National Directory, 1st ed. 1947, 134p, illustrated, illustrated wrappers, 30.5cm.

Part IV

The Hard Core Era

1961-1985

THE HARD CORE ERA 1961 TO 1985.

This most recent era of the game has been distinguished, I think, by much more interest on the part of many golfers in establishing the true history of the game, and a goodly numbers of books published in the era reflected this increased interest.

Certainly not the least of these works were those of the late Steven J. H. van Hengel of Amsterdam and, in concert, Ian Henderson and David Stirk. Consistent with our approach in offering little more than identifying the literature of the sport, we choose not to become involved in that scholarly activity. We tend to dismiss the entire question with an airy wave of the hand by saying the game of golf, as we know it today, was probably "invented" in St. Andrews, Scotland, when the Old Course was reduced from 22 holes to 18 holes in 1764.

But to get back to golf literature!

In the previous era, as we divide the history into quarters, we mentioned the great spate of books devoted to learning how to play the game. This era of which we now write doubled that emphasis in spades. Every champion worthy of his title—and some, perhaps, not quite as worthy—-was pursued by publishers and a deluge of books of golf instruction drowned the ever-hopeful hacker who stayed up at night worrying about where to place his right thumb on the club. Such books make up the majority of golf books published since 1960.

I remember offering the opinion in my bibliography of some twenty years ago that it was probably symptomatic of the nature of the two great nations which embraced golf with so much fervor that the British, generally, produced books which spoke of the history of the game while the Americans were more intrigued with how to do it.

Perhaps one feature of this newest era is that the generality has been turned around. In more recent years in Europe, the emergence of such skilled players as Jacklin, Lyle, Ballesteros and Langer (and others) has inspired a succession of books which offer in agonizing detail how to stand to the ball, how to grip the club and how to swing the club with style and grace. At the same time in America, Herbert Warren Wind, Charles Price, Ross Goodner and Tom Boswell—to name just a few of the many fine writers—are producing books which will become a part of the storied literature of the game. To those listed, we would be remiss if we did not add such additional writers as Peter Dobereiner, Pat Ward-Thomas, Dan Jenkins, Michael Hobbs, Lorne Rubenstein and still others, such as Sir Peter Allen and Warner Shelly, who may not have earned their green fees as a "working writer" but have contributed lovely books to the game's literature.

Still, the instruction books spew forth!

Complicating the high-handicapper's search for the elusive answer are such modern innovations as the videocassette which offer us unintelligible verbiage translated into incomprehensible visual images.

Holy smokes! Some of us are old enough to remember when a kid went out to caddie at the local club. Maybe he could read but that wasn't on his mind. He had enough sense to try to emulate the swing of the man who shot par, but he looked for bird nests or lost balls when carrying the bag of the guy who whiffed every third shot. We would hazard the guess that if Sarazen or Snead or Palmer or Wild Bill Mehlhorn ever read a book of instruction, the world would not know today of the wonders they performed.

On the other hand and in the interest of honest reporting, we hear that Larry Nelson never touched a club until he was twenty-one, but by reading Ben Hogan's book he was playing to scratch within a short time. Perhaps, like golfers, some are better "readers" than others. We read Hogan's book and, to date, we haven't won the PGA Championship or the United States Open!

All of which is not intended to denigrate the importance of a book of golf instruction nor to ascribe genius to someone who can shoot par without the ability to read. We are trying to identify golf literature; we are not at all sure that books of golf instruction meet that standard of excellence.

It is appropriate in writing of golf literature after 1960 to mention that the increased interest on the part of many golfers in the history and tradition of the game has spawned a number of books which reflect the greatly increased interest in the collecting of the game's artifacts. While this hobby is almost as old as the game itself, only a handful of books from the past spoke to the interest. Since 1960, more and more books have been written on the subject and are of great interest to the collector. Similarly, the ever-increasing interest in old golf literature—and the relative scarcity of such books—has led to an active "re-print" publishing effort. Some of these are published by small, almost private, publishing houses such as, in England, Grant Books, Ellesborough Press and The Partick Press in Scotland, and in America, by Robert Macdonald's "Classics of Golf" and the private efforts of Charles Dufner and Patrick Kennedy.

Of special interest to collectors, whether they be collectors of golf books or old clubs or old balls or "golf antiques," the following titles should be noted: "The Curious History of the Golf Ball," by John Stuart Martin; "Golf in the Making" by Ian Henderson and David Stirk; Pat Kennedy's exquisite work in "Golf Club Trademarks," Alick Watt's "Collecting Old Golfing Clubs;" "Golf Collector's Price Guide" by John Taylor; "The Sourcebook of Golf" by Don Kennington and "The Encyclopedia of Golf Collectibles" by John and Morton Olman. All of these books have been published in the "Hard Core" era.

Finally, we think it worthy of note that the United States Golf Association embarked on a "Rare Book Program" some years ago in which that august organization offers a reprint of notable literature from the past which is selected for its general interest to the golfer of today. The program is distinguished by the excellence of book production and the limited numbers of each edition. It is of some interest to note that already some of these have become "collector's items."

And thus endeth the fourth and, to date, final era of golf.

Abersoch Golf Club

43000. *Abersoch Golf Club [Handbook].* Bristol & London: Temple Publicity Services [1966] 8p, illustrated, illustrated wrappers, 18.5cm.

Aboyne Golf Club

43020. *Aboyne Golf Club 1883-1983.* Aboyne, Scotland: Privately Printed, 1st ed. 1983, 32p, illustrated, illustrated wrappers, 21cm.

Adams, G.C.

43040. *History of Barwon Heads Golf Club 1907-1973.* Melbourne, Australia: Privately Printed, limited ed. [no limitation cited] 1973, 85p, illustrated, cloth, 22cm.

Adams, John

43060. *Huntercombe Golf Club 1900-1983.* Henley-on-Thames, England: Privately Printed, 1st ed. 1984, 68p, illustrated, illustrated wrappers, 24.5cm.

Adamson, Alistair Beaton

43080. *Allan Robertson, Golfer. His Life and Times.* Worcestershire, England: Grant Books, limited ed. slipcased [1055 copies] 1985, 92p, illustrated, decorative cloth, 23cm. research into the archives of The Royal and Ancient Golf Club of St. Andrews by R.A.L. Burnet. note: 55 copies are publishers presentation copies.

43090. *In The Wind's Eye: North Berwick Golf Club.* [North Berwick, Scotland] Privately Printed, 1st ed. [1980] 92p, illustrated, cloth, 23cm.

Adwick, Ken

43110. *Alphabet of Golf.* London: Pelham, 1st ed. 1973, 201p, illustrated, cloth, 21.5cm, foreword by Gary Player.

43120. *Dictionary of Golf.* New York: Drake, 1st American ed. 1974, 199p, illustrated by George Stokes, cloth, 21.5cm, foreword by Gary Player. American title of "Alphabet Golf."

43130. *Golf.* London: Pelham, 1st ed. 1975, 96p, illustrated, illustrated boards, 25cm, foreword by Tony Jacklin.

43140. *X-Ray Way to Master Golf.* London: Pelham, 1st ed. 1970, 159p, illustrated, cloth, 21.5cm. as told to James Green, foreword by Neil Coles.

43150. 1st American ed. Newfoundland, New Jersey: Walter R. Hessner, 1970, 159p, illustrated cloth, 21.5cm. as told to James Green, foreword by Neil Coles.

Albury, Chuck

43170. *Dunedin Country Club 1925-1970.* Dunedin, Florida: Privately Printed, 1st ed. 1970, 34p, illustrated, illustrated wrappers, 21cm.

Alcott, Amy

43190. *Golf Tips from Amy Alcott.* Norwalk, Connecticut: Golf Digest, 1st ed. [1983] [12p] illustrated, illustrated wrappers, 14cm.

Alenson, John

43210. *Ten Decades 1882-1982: A Story of the Events Which Go to Make the History of 100 Years of the Australian Golf Club.* Sydney, Australia: Privately Printed, 1st ed. 1982, 215p, illustrated, cloth, 24.5cm.

Alfano, Peter

43230. *Grand Slam.* New York: Stadia Sports, 1st ed. 1973, 160p, illustrated, illustrated wrappers, 19.5cm.

Alicoate, John C.

43250. *Reference Year Book of Golf.* Canoga Park, California: International Golfer 1st ed. [1971] 992p, illustrated, illustrated boards, 22.5cm.

43260. *Reference Yearbook of Golf 1972.* 2d ed. [1972] 528p, illustrated, illustrated wrappers, 23cm.

43270. *Reference Yearbook of Golf 1972-73.* 3d ed. [1972] 975p, illustrated, decorative cloth, 22.5cm.

Allen, Frank Kenyon and others

43290. *The Golfer's Bible.* and Tom Lo Presti, Dale Mead, Barbara Romack. New York: Doubleday, 1st ed. 1968, 159p, illustrated, illustrated wrappers, 25.5cm.

Allen, Mark

43310. *Royal Portrush Golf Club Coastal Erosion Appeal Fund.* Portrush, Ireland: Privately Printed, 1st ed. 1983 [16p] illustrated, illustrated wrappers, 15cm.

Allen, Peter

43330. *Famous Fairways: A Look at the World of Championship Courses.* London: Stanley Paul, 1st ed. 1968, 164p, illustrated, cloth, 24.5cm.

43340. *Play the Best Courses: Great Golf in the British Isles.* London: Stanley Paul, 1st ed. 1973, 264p, illustrated by Biro, cloth, 23.5m.

Alles, Jane P.

43360. *The History of the Philadelphia Country Club 1890-1965.* Gladwyne, Pennsylvania: Privately Printed, limited ed. [no limitation cited] 1965, 87p, illustrated, decorative cloth, 25.5cm.

Alliss, Peter

43380. *Alliss Through the Looking Glass.* with Bob Ferrier. London: Cassell, 1st ed. 1963, 300p, illustrated, cloth, 21cm. later printing.

43390. *An Autobiography.* London: Collins, 1st ed. 1981, 192p, illustrated, cloth, 23.5cm.

43400. pbk. ed. Glasgow: Fontana/Collins, 1982, 253p, illustrated, illustrated wrappers, 18cm.

43410. *Lasting the Course.* London: Stanley Paul, 1st ed. 1984, 206p, illustrated, cloth, 26cm.

43420. *More Bedside Golf.* London: Collins, 1st ed. 1982, 88p, illustrated by Colin Whitlock, illustrated boards, 24.5cm.

43430. *Peter Alliss' Bedside Golf.* London: Collins, 1st ed. 1980, 88p, illustrated by Bill Tidy, illustrated boards, 24.5cm.

43440. *Play Golf with Peter Alliss.* with Renton Laidlaw. London: BBC, 1st ed. [ca1977] 128p, illustrated, illustrated wrappers, 23.5cm.
43450. 2d ed. rev. London: Willow Books, 1983, 125p, illustrated, illustrated boards, 23.5cm.

43460. *The Duke.* London: New English Library, 1st ed. 1983, 191p cloth, 21.5cm.

43470. *The Golfer's Logbook.* London: Collins, 1st ed. 1984, 119p, illustrated, illustrated boards, 23.5cm.

43480. *The Open: The British Open Championship Since the War.* with Michael Hobbs. London: Collins, 1st ed. 1984, 256p, illustrated, cloth, 24.5cm.

43490. *The Shell Book of Golf.* London: David & Charles, 1st ed. 1981, 231p, illustrated cloth, 23cm.

43500. *The Who's Who of Golf.* London: Orbis, 1st ed. 1983, 381p, illustrated cloth, 24.5cm, with Michael Hobbs.
43510. 1st American ed. Englewood Cliffs, New Jersey: Prentice-Hall, [1983] 381p, illustrated cloth, 24.5cm. foreword by Arnold Palmer.

Alliss, Peter and Alec
43530. *The Parkstone Golf Club [Handbook].* Hants & London: Temple Publicity Services, 1965, 40p, illustrated, illustrated wrappers, 18.5cm.

Alliss, Peter and Paul Trevillion.
43570. *Easier Golf.* London: Stanley Paul, 1st ed. 1969, 142p, illustrated, cloth, 23cm.
43580. 1st American ed. New York: A.S. Barnes, 1970, 142p, illustrated, cloth, 21cm.

Alpert, Holis and Ira Mothner and Harold Schonberg.

43600. *How to Play Double Bogey Golf.* New York: Quadrangle/ New York Times, 1st ed. [1975] 177p, illustrated by David Harbaugh, cloth, 21cm.

Amazing Golf Ball

43620. *The Amazing Golf Ball.* Forth Worth, Texas: AMF Ben Hogan, 1st ed. [1978] 16p, illustrated, illustrated wrappers, 18cm.

American Society of Golf Course Architects

43640. *Master Planning: The Vital First Steps in Golf Course Construction.* Chicago: American Society of Golf Course Architects, 1st ed. [ca1977] [8p] illustrated, illustrated wrappers, 22.5cm.

43650. *Planning the Municipal Golf Course.* Chicago: American Society of Golf Course Architects, 1st ed. [ca1976] 8p, illustrated, illustrated wrappers, 23cm.

43660. *Planning the Real Estate Development Golf Course.* Chicago: American Society of Golf Course Architects, 1st ed. [ca1977] [6p] illustrated, illustrated wrappers, 23cm.

43670. *Selecting Your Golf Course Architect.* Chicago: American Society of Golf Course Architects, 1st ed. [ca1977] [6p] illustrated, illustrated wrappers, 21.5cm.

Amick, William W.

43690. *The Executive Golf Course.* Daytona Beach, Florida: Privately Printed 1st ed. [ca1975] [16p] illustrated, illustrated wrappers, 20cm.

Anderson, Carlyle E.

43710. *Glen View Club 1897-1982.* Golf, Illinois: Privately Printed, 1st ed. 1982, 12p, illustrated, illustrated wrappers, 28cm.

Anderson, Harold E. and others

43730. *Golf Club Construction: Design, Fitting, Repair. PGA Home Study Program.* and William Hardy, John Henrich, Howard E. Smith. Palm Beach Gardens, Florida: Professional Golfers' Association, 1st ed. [1968] 54p, illustrated wrappers, 28cm.

Anderson, Robert

43750. *A Funny Thing Happened on the Way to the Clubhouse.* London: Arthur Barker, 1st ed. [1971] 127p, illustrated by Doug Smith, illustrated wrappers, 18cm.

43760. *Heard At the Nineteenth: A light-hearted look at the game of golf.* edited by. London: Stanley Paul, 1st ed. 1966, 125p, illustrated by A.S. Graham, cloth, 19.5cm.

Anderson-Davis, Thomas

43780. *The Ryder Cup Heritage.* Norton Grove, Illinois: PGA Golf, 1st ed. [1983] [18p] illustrated, illustrated wrappers, 23cm.

Andrews, Gene

43800. *Scientific Analysis of the Plumb-Bob Method of Reading Greens.* Hacienda Heights, California: Privately Printed, 1st ed. [1968] [12p] illustrated, illustrated wrappers, 16.5cm.

Angas, Major

43820. *The Golf Swings in the Plural: A course for professional instructors, folio 1, A reconciliation of the conflicting teachings of the different pros.* Saxton Rivers, Vermont: Privately Printed, 1st ed. [1962] 61p, illustrated, illustrated wrappers, 28cm.

Annandale Golf Club

43840. *Annandale Golf Club-75th Anniversary 1906-1981.* Pasadena, California: Privately Printed, 1st ed. 1981, 69p, illustrated wrappers, 28cm.

Anthony, Greg

43860. *Building Clubhead Speed, Leverage and Centrifugal Force in the Golf Swing.* Glendale, California: Privately Printed, 1st ed. [ca1985] [352p] illustrated, spiral bound wrappers, 28cm.

Apawamis Club

43880. *The Apawamis Tradition 1890-1965.* Rye, New York: Privately Printed, 1st ed. 1965, 36p, spiral bound wrappers, 28cm.

Apple, Audrey

43900. *History of Richmond Country Club 1924-1978*. Richmond, California: Privately Printed, 1st ed. 1978, 77p, cloth, illustrated, 28cm.

Argea, Angelo

43920. *The Bear and I: The Story of the World's Most Famous Caddie*. New York: Atheneum, 1st ed. 1979, 148p, illustrated, cloth, 20.5cm, with Jolee Edmonston, foreword and commentary by Jack Nicklaus.

Armitage, J.C.

43940. *The 100th Open Championship Held at Royal Birkdale Golf Club from July 7th-10th, 1971*. Altricham, England: Cheshire Printing, limited ed. [no limitation cited] 1971 [14p] illustrated by Ionicis, tied wrappers, 28.5cm.

Armour, Richard

43960. *Golf Is A Four-Letter Word: the intimate confessions of a hooked slicer*. New York: McGraw Hill, 1st ed. [1962] 115p, illustrated by Leo Hershfield, decorative cloth, 20cm.

43970. 1st UK ed. London: Hammond, Hammond, 1962, 123p, illustrated by Leo Hershfield, decorative cloth, 21cm.

Armour, Tommy

43990. *Play Better Golf: The Drive*. New York: The News, 1st ed. [1964] [23p] illustrated, wrappers, 13.5cm.

44000. *Play Better Golf: The Irons*. New York: The News, 1st ed. [1963] [22p] illustrated, wrappers, 13.5cm.

44010. *Tommy Armour's ABC's of Golf*. New York: Simon & Schuster, 1st ed. [1967] 187p, illustrated by Henri Arnold, cloth, 21cm.

Arnold, John

44030. *Riversdale Golf Club: A History 1892-1977*. Ashburton Australia: Privately Printed, 1st ed. 1977, 128p, illustrated, cloth, 21.5cm.

Arran Golf Guide

44050. *Arran Golf Guide*. [Arran, Scotland] Privately Printed, 1985, 20p, illustrated, illustrated wrappers, 20.5cm.

Arthur, Allan

44070. *The Country Club, Its First 75 Years 1889-1964*. Cleveland, Ohio: Privately Printed, 1st ed. 1964, 74p, illustrated cloth, 21.5cm.

Ashford Manor Golf Club

44090. *History of Ashford Manor Golf Club*. Ashford, England: Privately Printed, 1st ed. 1966, 102p, illustrated cloth, 21.5cm.

Augusta National Golf Club

44110. *Arnold Palmer's Scrapbook*. Augusta, Georgia: Augusta National Golf Club, 1st ed. 1964 [40p] illustrated, gilt leather, 43.5cm.

44120. *Portraits: Early Members of the Augusta National Golf Club*. Augusta, Georgia: Augusta National Golf Club, 1st ed. [ca1962] [44p] illustrated wrappers, 23.5cm.

44130. *The Masters: The First Forty One Years*. Augusta, Georgia: Augusta National Golf Club, 1st ed. [1978] 128p, illustrated, decorative cloth, 30cm.

44140. 2d ed. *The Masters 1978*. 80p, illustrated, decorative cloth, 30.5cm.

44150. 3d ed. *The Masters 1979*. 80p, illustrated, decorative cloth, 30.5cm.

44160. 4th ed. *The Masters 1980*. by Loran Smith. 79p, illustrated, decorative cloth 30.5cm.

44170. 5th ed. *The Masters 1981*. by Loran Smith. 80p, illustrated, decorative cloth, 30.5cm.

44180. 6th ed. *The Masters 1982*. by Loran Smith. 79p, illustrated, decorative cloth, 30.5cm.

44190. 7th ed. *The Masters 1983*. edited by George Peper. 80p, illustrated, decorative cloth, 30.5cm.

44200. 8th ed. *The Masters 1984*. edited by George Peper. 80p, illustrated, decorative cloth, 30.5cm.

44210. 9th ed. *The Masters 1985*. edited by George Peper. 80p, illustrated, decorative cloth, 30.5cm.

Aultman, Dick

44600. *101 Ways to Win*. and Editors of Golf Digest. Norwalk, Connecticut: Golf Digest, 1st ed. [1980] 192p, illustrated by Elmer Wexler, illustrated wrappers, 22.5cm.

44610. *Better Golf in Six Swings*. Norwalk, Connecticut: Golf Digest, 1st ed. [1982] 160p, illustrated by Anthony Ravielli, cloth, 23cm.

44620. *Golf Digest's Golf Primer*. and editors of Golf Digest. Norwalk, Connecticut: Golf Digest, 1st ed. [1977] 46p, illustrated by Elmer Wexler, wrappers, 13.5cm.

44630. *Learn to Play Golf*. and editors of Golf Digest. Chicago: Rand McNally, 1st ed. 1969, 72p, illustrated, illustrated boards, 23.5cm.

44640. *The Square-To-Square Golf Swing: Model Method for the Modern Player*. and editors of Golf Digest. Norwalk, Connecticut: Golf Digest, 1st ed. [1970] 127p, illustrated by Anthony Ravielli, cloth, 27.5cm, foreword by Bert Yancey. later printings.

44650. pbk. ed. New York: Bantam, 1971, 122p, illustrated by Anthony Ravielli, illustrated wrappers, 18cm, foreword by Bert Yancey.

Aultman, Dick and Ken Bowden

44670. *The Methods of Golf's Masters*. New York: Coward, McCann & Geoghegan, 1st ed. [1975] 191p, illustrated by Anthony Ravielli, cloth, 28cm, introduction by Herbert Warren Wind.

44680. *Masters of Golf, learning from their methods*. London: Stanley Paul, 1st UK ed. 1976, 191p, illustrated by Anthony Ravielli, cloth, 27.5cm, introduction by Herbert Warren Wind. UK title of "Methods of Golf's Masters."

Automobile Association [UK]

44700. *AA Guide to Golf in Great Britain*. London: Automobile Association, 1977, 328p, illustrated, illustrated wrappers, 22cm, consultant editor Tom Scott, foreword by Gary Player. later printings.

Automobile Club of Southern California

44720. *Golf Courses of California and Nevada*. Los Angeles: Automobile Club of Southern California [1962] 91p, wrappers, 17.5cm.

Bailey, Bill

44730. *Executive Golf: "How To Win Big."* Los Angeles: Entrepreneur Group, [1985] 204p, illustrated, illustrated wrappers, 21cm. introduction by Gene Littler.

Bailey, John W.

44740. *Enthusiastic Amateur Golfer Wanders the World*. Grand Rapids, Michigan: Privately Printed, 1st ed. [1965] 101p, illustrated, cloth, 20.5cm.

Baird, Archie

44760. *Golf on Gullane Hill: A Celebration of 100 Years of Gullane Golf Club*. [Aberlady, Scotland] Privately Printed, limited ed. [no limitation cited] [1982] 67p, illustrated, cloth, 23cm.

44770. 2d ed. rev. limited [no limitation cited] 1985, 67p, illustrated, cloth, 23cm.

Baird, Frederick R.

44790. *Crystal Downs Golf Club*. Frankfurt, Michigan: Privately Printed, 1st ed. 1981, 31p, illustrated wrappers, 23cm.

Baker, Alene and Elaine Lustig

44810. *Golf: To Play this Game You Gotta Have Balls and Clubs and Trees*. Orlando, Florida: Twosome, 1st ed. [1984] [25p] illustrated by Joanne Thorton, spiral bound illustrated wrappers, 16.5cm.

Baker, Stephen

44830. *How to Play Golf in the Low 120's*. Englewood Cliffs, New Jersey: Prentice-Hall, 1st ed. [1962] [92p] illustrated cloth, 21cm.

44840. 1st UK ed. London: Frederick Muller, 1962, 92p, illustrated, cloth, 21cm.

Ball, Brian

44860. *Death of A Low Handicapped Man*. New York: Walker, 1st American ed. 1978, 224p, cloth, 20cm. note: first edition not located.

Ballard, Jimmy

44880. *How to Perfect Your Golf Swing: Using 'Connection' and the Seven Common Denominators*. Norwalk, Connecticut: Golf Digest, 1st ed. [1981] 160p, illustrated by Jim McQueen, cloth, 23cm, with Brennan Quinn, foreword by John Brodie.

Ballater Golf Club

44900. *Ballater Golf Club [Handbook]*. Aberdeen, Scotland: Northern Publications, 1980, 36p, illustrated, illustrated wrappers, 18.5cm.

Ballesteros, Severiano

44920. *Seve Tours: Golf Tours of Spain*. [Spain] Iberia Air Lines, 1st ed. 1981, 64p, illustrated, illustrated wrappers, 27cm.

Ballesteros, Severiano and Dudley Doust

44940. *Seve: The Young Champion*. London: Hodder & Stoughton, 1st ed. 1982, 156p, illustrated, cloth, 24.5cm., foreword by Lee Trevino.

44950. 1st American ed. Norwalk, Connecticut: Golf Digest, 1982, 156p, illustrated by Jim McQueen, cloth, 24.5cm, foreword by Lee Trevino.

Barber, Jerry

44970. *The Art of Putting*. Los Angeles: LaLanne-Barber, 1st ed. [1967] 24p, illustrated, illustrated wrappers, 21.5cm.

Barker, Roland

44990. *The Bass River Golf Club 1900-1974*. South Yarmouth, Massachusetts: Privately Printed, 1st ed. 1974 [36p] illustrated, illustrated wrappers, 21.5cm.

Barkow, Al

45010. *Golf's Golden Grind: The History of the Tour*. New York: Harcourt Brace Jovanovich, 1st ed. [1974] 310p, illustrated cloth, 21cm.

Barnaby, J.W.

45030. *The History of the Royal Melbourne Golf Club, Volume II: 1941 to 1968*. Melbourne, Australia: Privately Printed, 1st ed. 1972, 60p, illustrated, decorative cloth, 21.5cm.

45040. *The History of the Sorrento Golf Club*. Melbourne, Australia: Privately Printed, 1st ed. 1974, 49p, illustrated, decorative cloth, 21.5cm.

Barnett, Ted

45060. *Golf Is Madness*. Norwalk, Connecticut: Golf Digest, 1st ed. [1977] 128p, illustrated by Marcus Hamilton, cloth, 21cm.

Baron, Harry

45080. *Golf Resorts of the U.S.A.* New York: New American Library, 1st ed. [1967] 335p, illustrated by Irwin Schonhorn, cloth, 28cm, foreword by Robert Trent Jones.

45090. pbk. ed. New York: New American Library, 1968, 352p, illustrated, illustrated wrappers, 18cm.

45100. *NBC Sports Guide 1967*. New York: Ridge Press/Grosset & Dunlap, 1st ed. [1967] 159p, illustrated, illustrated wrappers, 18.5cm.

Barratt, Michael

45120. *Golf with Tony Jacklin: Step by step, a great professional shows an enthusiastic amateur how to play every stroke of the game*. London: Arthur Barker, 1st ed. [1978] 136p, illustrated, cloth, 24.5cm.

Barrier, Smith

45140. *GCO: The First Forty-Four Years*. Greensboro, North Carolina: Greensboro Chamber of Commerce, 1st ed. [1982] 127p, illustrated, decorative cloth, 30.5cm.

Barry, Hugh

45160. *Elanora, A History of Elanora Country Club*. Narrabeen, Australia: Privately Printed, 1st ed. 1977, 206p, illustrated cloth, 28cm.

Bartlett, Charles

45180. *Chicago Golf Club Diamond Jubilee 1892-1967.* Chicago: Privately Printed, 1st ed. 1967 [28p] illustrated, illustrated wrappers, 21.5cm.

45190. *The New 1969 Golfer's Almanac.* edited by. New York: Bantam, 1st ed. 1969, 208p, illustrated, illustrated wrappers, 18cm, preface by Herb Graffis.

Bartlett, Michael

45210. *Bartlett's World Golf Encyclopedia.* New York: Bantam, 1st ed. 1973, 486p, illustrated wrappers, 18cm.

45220. *The Golf Book.* edited by. New York: Arbor House, 1st ed. [1980] 282p, illustrated cloth, 25.5cm, foreword by Alistair Cooke.

Bartnett, Edmond P.

45240. *Seventy Years of Wykagyl 1898-1968.* New Rochelle, New York: Privately Printed, 1st ed. 1968, 139p, illustrated, decorative cloth, 26.5cm.

Bassler, Charles T. and Nevin H. Gibson

45260. *You Can Play Par Golf.* New York: A.S. Barnes, 1st ed. [1966] 102p, illustrated, cloth, 21cm.

45270. 2d ed. large print, New York: A.S. Barnes [1966] 102p, illustrated, cloth, 25cm.

Batchelor, Jr., E.A.

45290. *Country Club of Detroit, A History 1897-1979.* Detroit, Michigan: Privately Printed, 1st ed. 1978, 21p, illustrated wrappers, 15cm.

Bateman, Graham

45310. *Selkirk Golf Club 1883-1983, A Century of Golf in Selkirk.* Selkirk, Scotland: Privately Printed, 1st ed. 1983, 28p, illustrated, illustrated wrappers, 21cm.

Bath Golf Club

45330. *Bath Golf Club Centenary Festival 1880-1980.* Bath, England: Privately Printed, 1st ed. 1980, 16p, illustrated, illustrated wrappers, 21.5cm.

Batten, Jack

45350. *Toronto Golf Club 1876-1976.* Toronto: Privately Printed, 1st ed. 1976, 128p, illustrated, cloth, 20.5cm.

Bayless, Dan

45370. *Riviera's Fifty Golden Years.* Pacific Palisades, California: Privately Printed, 1st ed. [1976] 108p, illustrated, decorative cloth, 21.5cm.

Beames, Peter

45390. *Walk Thru to Par.* Los Angeles: Jefferson International, 1st ed. 1984, 137p, illustrated, cloth, 23cm. with Frederic Swan.

45400. 2d ed. rev. 1985, 137p, illustrated, decorative cloth, 23cm.

Beard, Frank

45420. *Pro: Frank Beard on the Golf Tour.* edited by Dick Schaap. New York: World, 1st ed. 1970, 323p, illustrated, cloth, 21.5cm.

45430. *Shaving Strokes.* New York: Grosset & Dunlap, 1st ed. [1970] 126p, illustrated by Murray Olderman, cloth, 21cm.

45440. pbk. ed. [1970] 126p, illustrated, illustrated wrappers, 21cm.

Beard, James B. and Harriet Beard and David P. Martin

45460. *Turfgrass Bibliography from 1672 to 1972.* Ann Arbor, Michigan: Michigan State University Press, 1st ed. 1977, 730p, cloth, 23.5cm.

Beardwood, John B.

45480. *History of the Los Angeles Country Club 1898-1973.* Los Angeles: Privately Printed, 1st ed. 1973, 125p, illustrated, decorative cloth, 25cm.

Beasley, Chauncey Haven

45500. *The Magnificent Golf Foursome: Julius Caesar & Calpurnia vs. Mark Anthony & Cleopatra.* New York: Vantage Press, 1st ed. [1977] 57p, illustrated, cloth, 20cm. in Latin with English translation.

45510. *The Most Difficult Golf Course in America, Golfus Latine.* New York: Vantage Press, 1st ed. [1966] 61p, illustrated, cloth, 20cm.

Beck, Fred

45530. *89 Years in A Sand Trap*. New York: Hill & Wang, 1st ed. 1965, 181p, illustrated by Paul Coker, cloth, 20.5cm.

Bedell, Lew

45550. *Every Golfer Should Have One*. Hollywood, California: Hillary, 1st ed. [ca1965] [49p] illustrated, illustrated wrappers, 21cm.

Bell, Clarance

45570. *Eighty Golfing Years, A History of North Adelaide Golf Club 1905-1985*. Adelaide, Australia: Privately Printed, 1st ed. 1985, 204p, illustrated, decorative cloth, 24cm.

Bell, Peggy Kirk

45590. *A Woman's Way to Better Golf*. New York: Dutton, 1st ed. 1966, 128p, illustrated, cloth, 23cm. with Jerry Claussen, foreword by Patty Berg. later printings.

45600. 1st UK ed. London: Cassell, 1967, 128p, illustrated, cloth, 23cm. later printings.

Bend Golf & Country Club

45620. *Historical Review of the Bend Golf & Country Club*. Bend, Oregon: Privately Printed, 1st ed. 1981 [6p] illustrated, illustrated wrappers, 28cm.

Bender, Josephene

45640. *Kent Country Club, When Kent Was Young, An Early History and Reminiscences*. Grand Rapids, Michigan: Privately Printed, 1st ed. 1980 [16p] illustrated, illustrated wrappers, 21.5cm.

Bendert, Tommy

45660. *Golf Is My Life: Adventures of an amateur in search of happiness*. Union, New York: Privately Printed, 1st ed. 1983, 101p, wrappers, 19cm.

Benedictus, David

45680. *Guru and the Golf Club*. London: Anthony Blond, 1st ed. 1969, 203p, cloth, 21.5cm.

Benham, L.W.

45700. *Golftique: A Price Guide to Old Golf Clubs and Other Golf Memorabilia*. Trumbull, Connecticut: Privately Printed, 1st ed. [1977] 50p, illustrated wrappers, 15cm.

Bennett, Arthur

45720. *Southern California Golf Directory.* edited by. Los Angeles: Southern California Golf Directory, 1st ed. 1963, 52p, illustrated, illustrated wrappers, 28cm.

Bennett, Guy

45740. *Sunningdale Story, A Short History of Sunningdale Golf Club from Its First Beginning*. Sunningdale, England: Privately Printed, 1st ed. 1962, 15p, wrappers, 21cm.

Benson

45760. *Keeping An Eye on Your Balls*. Leyland, England: Media Graphics, 1st ed. [1983] [52p] illustrated, illustrated wrappers, 21cm, introduction by Hiram G. Ball.

Benson, Frederick S.

45780. *The History of Canoe Brook Country Club from 1964 to 1976*. Summit, New Jersey: Privately Printed, 1st ed. 1976, 27p, illustrated wrappers, 28cm.

Berg, Patty

45800. *Inside Golf for Women*. Chicago: Contemporary, 1st ed. [1977] 86p, illustrated, cloth, 27.5cm. foreword by Carol Mann, preface by Kathy Whitworth.

45810. pbk. ed. [1977] 86p, illustrated, illustrated wrappers, 27.5cm.

Berkhamsted Golf Club

45830. *Berkhamsted Golf Club [Handbook]*. Kingston Upon Thames, England: Temple Publicity Services, 1972, 16p, illustrated, illustrated wrappers, 18cm.

Bernardoni, Gus

45850. *Golf God's Way.* Carol Stream, Illinois: Creation House, 1st ed. [1978] 224p, illustrated, cloth, 23cm, foreword by Pat Boone.

Bernier, Bob

45870. *Pro-Golf Teaching Manual.* Tucson, Arizona: Roadrunner Technical Publications, 1st ed. [1964] 63p, illustrated, illustrated wrappers, 21cm.

BGSR Guide

45890. *BGSR Guide to British Golf Courses.* Berkshire, England: British Golf Society Register, 1st ed. [ca1985] 128p, illustrated, illustrated wrappers, 21cm.

Biddulph, Michael

45910. *The Golf Shot.* London: Heinemann, 1st ed. 1980, 116p, illustrated cloth, 23.5cm.

Bidwell, Dale L.

45930. *History of the Texas Association of Left Handed Golfers 1938-1982.* Houston, Texas: National Association of Left Handed Golfers, 1st ed. [1983] 159p, illustrated, spiral bound illustrated wrappers, 28cm.

Birdie

45950. *Golf: The game of A lifetime.* [Jacksonville, Florida] PGA Tour, 1st ed. [1982] [16p] illustrated, illustrated wrappers, 20.5cm.

Bisher, Furman

45970. *Augusta Revisited: An Intimate View.* Birmingham, Alabama: Oxmoor House, 1st ed. [1976] 186p, illustrated, cloth, 28cm.

45980. *The Birth of A Legend: Arnold Palmer's Golden Year 1960.* Englewood Cliffs, New Jersey: Prentice-Hall, 1st ed. [1972] 174p, illustrated, cloth, 21cm, foreword by Murray Olderman.

Bizell, H.A. Buz

46000. *Sunset Ridge Country Club: Our first fifty years 1923-1972.* Northbrook, Illinois: Privately Printed, limited ed. [1500 copies] 1973, 62p, illustrated, decorative cloth, 28cm.

Black, Andrew

46020. *The Golf Courses of Scotland.* London: Macdonald, 1st ed. 1974, 130p, illustrated, illustrated wrappers, 20.5cm.

Black, Kevin

46040. *Six 9 Hole Perthshire Golf Courses [Part I].* Crieff, Scotland: Boolavogue, 1st ed. 1970, 27p, illustrated, illustrated wrappers, 20.5cm.

46050. *Five 9 Hole Perthshire Golf Courses [Part II].* Crieff, Scotland: Boolavogue, 1st ed. 1970, 23p, illustrated, illustrated wrappers, 20.5cm.

Blackburn, Norman

46070. *Lakeside Golf Club of Hollywood, 50th Anniversary Book.* Burbank, California: Cal-Ad, limited ed. [1150 copies] [1974] 344p, illustrated, decorative cloth, 28cm, foreword by Bing Crosby.

Blake, Christopher and Stuart McDowall and Jennifer Devlen

46090. *The 1978 Open Championship At St. Andrews: An economic impact study.* Edinburgh: Scottish Academic Press, 1st ed. [1979] 33p, wrappers, 21cm.

Blake, Mindy

46110. *Golf: The Technique Barrier.* London: Souvenir Press, 1st ed. 1978, 115p, illustrated cloth, 23.5cm. introduction by Harry Weaver.

46120. 1st American ed. New York: Norton, 1979, 115p, illustrated, cloth, 23.5cm.

46130. *The Golf Swing of the Future.* London: Souvenir Press, 1st ed. 1972, 124p, illustrated by Colin Reid, cloth, 23.5cm. introduction by Harry Weaver.

46140. 1st American ed. New York: Norton, 1973, 124p, cloth, 23.5cm.

46150. pbk. ed. New York: Pocket Books, 1974, 159p, illustrated by Dom Lupo, illustrated wrappers, 17.5cm.

Blalock, Jane

46170. *The Guts to Win.* Norwalk, Connecticut: Golf Digest, 1st ed. [1977] 158p, illustrated, cloth, 23cm. with Dwayne Netland, introduction by Billie Jean King.

Blue Mound Golf and Country Club

46190. *The Story of Blue Mound Golf and Country Club.* Wauwatosa, Wisconsin: Privately Printed, 1st ed. slipcased [ca1976] [44p] illustrated, decorative cloth, 21cm.

Bluth, Robert G.

46210. *Golf.* editor. Chicago: Athletic Institute, 1st ed. [ca1979] 44p, illustrated by Dom Lupo, illustrated boards, 21cm.

Bolt, Tommy

46230. *How to Keep Your Temper on the Golf Course.* New York: David McKay, 1st ed. [1969] 145p, illustrated by Fred Conway, cloth, 20cm. with William C. Griffith, foreword by Jimmy Demaret.

46240. *The Hole Truth: Inside Big-Time Big-Money Golf.* Philadelphia: Lippincott, 1st ed. [1971] 187p, illustrated, cloth, 21cm, with Jimmy Mann. later printings.

Bond, Michael

46260. *Paddington Hits Out.* London: Collins, 1st ed. [1977] [48p] illustrated by Barry Wilkinson, illustrated wrappers, 14.5cm.

Bookatz, Barnett

46280. *Oakwood Club, 75th Anniversary.* Cleveland, Ohio: Privately Printed, 1st ed. 1980, 63p, illustrated, decorative cloth, 22.5cm.

Borissow, Michael

46300. *The Naked Fairways.* Cranbrook, England: Cranbrook Golf Club, 1st ed. [1984] 192p, illustrated wrappers, 17.5cm.

Boros, Julius

46320. *How to Play Golf with an Effortless Swing.* Englewood Cliffs, New Jersey: Prentice-Hall, 1st ed. [1964] 160p, illustrated, cloth, 22.5cm.

46330. *How to Win At Weekend Golf.* Greenwich, Connecticut: Fawcett, 1st ed. [1965] 112p, illustrated, illustrated wrappers, 23.5cm. previously titled "How To Play Golf With An Effortless Swing."

46340. reprint ed. Greenwich, Connecticut: Fawcett [1967] 128p, illustrated, illustrated wrappers, 18cm.

46350. *Swing Easy, Hit Hard.* New York: Harper & Row, 1st ed. [1965] 158p, illustrated by Lealand Gustavson, cloth, 23.5cm.

46360. pbk. ed. New York: Cornerstone Library, 1968, 158p, illustrated by Lealand Gustavson, illustrated wrappers, 20.5cm. introduction by George Bayer.

Bortstein, Larry

46380. *Who's Who in Golf.* NP: Bert Randolph Sugar, 1st ed. 1972, 142p, illustrated, illustrated wrappers, 21.5cm.

Boswell, Charles

46400. *Now I See.* New York: Meredith Press, 1st ed. 1969, 208p, cloth, 20.5cm, with Curt Anders. later printing.

Boswell, James W.

46420. *Golf: From Another Angle.* Tallahassee, Florida: Sports Innovations, 1st ed. [1983] 173p, illustrated, cloth, 21.5cm.

Bourke, Kevin

46440. *Cobram-Barooga Golf Club Jubilee History 1928-1978.* Cobram, Australia: Privately Printed, limited ed. [800 copies] 1978, 87p, illustrated, decorative cloth, 20cm.

Bowden, C. Mal

46460. *Golfer's Diary, Where He Keeps Scores I Can't Forget, or, Lies Lies Lies.* Dallas, Texas: Privately Printed, 1st ed. [1962] [24p] illustrated, illustrated wrappers, 19cm.

Bowden, Ken

46480. *The Golf Gazetter.* London: Golf Gazetter, 1st ed. 1968, 224p, wrappers, 21.5cm.

46490. 2d ed. rev. 1973, 248p, illustrated, illustrated wrappers, 21.5cm.

Bowen, Bob and B.J. Clemence

46510. *Golf Everyone.* Winston Salem, North Carolina: Hunter, 2d ed. [1984] 140p, illustrated, illustrated wrappers, 23cm. note: first edition not located.

Bowling, Maurine

46530. *Tested Ways of Teaching Golf Classes.* Dubuque, Iowa: Wm. C. Brown, 1st ed. [1964] 84p, illustrated, spiral bound illustrated wrappers, 28cm.

Box, Sydney

46550. *Alibi in the Rough.* London: Robert Hale, 1st ed. 1977, 176p, cloth, 18.5cm.

Boy, Angelo V.

46570. *Psychological Dimensions of Golf.* Durham, New Hampshire: Evergreen, 1st ed. [1980] 138p, wrappers, 27.5cm.

Bradford, Leland P. and Robert A. Hunt

46590. *The Tin Whistles 1904-1979.* Pinehurst, North Carolina: Privately Printed, 1st ed. 1979 [26p] illustrated, decorative suede wrappers, 22.5cm.

Bradley, Bettie

46610. *The Mississauga Golf and Country Club 1906-1981.* Mississauga, Canada: Privately Printed, 1st ed. 1981, 135p, illustrated cloth, 28cm.

Branson, V.M.

46630. *Kooyonga 1923-1928, The Story of A Golf Club.* Adelaide, Australia: Privately Printed, limited ed. signed [1500 copies] 1983, 133p, illustrated cloth, 26cm.

Brett, Frank

46650. *Cutten Club 1931-1981.* Guelph, Canada: Privately Printed, 1st ed. 1981, 60p, illustrated, illustrated wrappers, 23cm.

Brewer, Gay

46670. *Gay Brewer Shows You How To Score Better Than You Swing.* Norwalk, Connecticut: Golf Digest, 1st ed. [1968] 160p, illustrated, cloth, 23cm.

46680. pbk. ed. New York: Cornerstone Library, 1969, 160p, illustrated, illustrated wrappers, 20.5cm.

46690. *Gay Brewer's Golf Guidebook: Basic Form and Playing Technique for Young People.* New York: McGraw-Hill, 1st ed. 1968, 79p, illustrated by Ric Del Rossi cloth, 13cm, with Roger Ganem.

46700. pbk. ed. New York: McGraw-Hill, 1968, 79p, spiral bound illustrated wrappers, 13cm.

Brickman, E.

46720. *A Brief Introduction to the Club and St Andrews Courses.* St. Andrews, Scotland: Royal and Ancient Golf Club of St. Andrews, 1st ed, 1969, 15p, illustrated, illustrated wrappers, 18cm.

Brickman, E. and R.A.L. Burnet and J. Lawson and W. Loudon

46740. *The Royal and Ancient Golf Club of St. Andrews.* Derby, England: Pilgrim Press, 1st ed. [1984] 24p, illustrated, illustrated wrappers, 23cm.

Brittenden, R.T.

46760. *Golf in New Zealand.* Auckland, New Zealand: South Island Promotion, 1979, 11p, illustrated, illustrated wrappers, 20cm.

Broadstone Golf Club

46780. *The Broadstone Golf Club [Handbook].* Cheltenham, England: New Centurion, 1966, 20p, illustrated, wrappers, 18cm.

Broadus, Jr., Catherine and Loren

46800. *From Loneliness To Intimacy: Help for the Golf Widow and Other Lonely People.* Atlanta, Georgia: John Knox Press, 1st ed. [1976] 94p, cloth, 20cm.

Brod, Howard W.

46820. *By Golf Possessed.* Phoenix, Arizona: Brod Studios, 1st ed. [1972] 106p, illustrated, spiral bound illustrated wrappers, 21.5cm.

Brody, Sidney Steve

46840. *How to Break 90 Before You Reach It!* New York: William-Frederick Press, 1st ed. 1967, 47p, illustrated wrappers, 21.5cm. note: second edition not located.

46850. 3d ed. NP: North River Press, 1980, 90p, illustrated wrappers, 21.5cm. foreword by Wally Phillips.

Bromborough Golf Club

46870. *Bromborough Golf Club 1904-1979*. Bromborough, England: Privately Printed, 1st ed. 1979 [32p] illustrated, illustrated wrappers, 20.5cm.

Brooklawn Country Club

46890. *A Brief History of Golf At Brooklawn Country Club*. Fairfield, Connecticut: Privately Printed, 1st ed. [ca1974] [6p] illustrated, illustrated wrappers, 21.5cm.

Brookmans Park Golf Club

46910. *Brookmans Park Golf Club 1930-1980*. Hatfield, England: Privately Printed, 1st ed. 1980 [16p] illustrated, illustrated wrappers, 20cm.

Brooks, Dick

46930. *The Offensive Golfer: A handbook for compulsive hackers*. Englewood Cliffs, New Jersey: Prentice-Hall, 1st ed. [1963] 128p, illustrated, decorative cloth, 24.5cm.

Brown, Eric Chalmers

46950. *Knave of Clubs*. London: Stanley Paul, 1st ed. 1961, 158p illustrated cloth, 21cm.

46960. *Out of the Bag*. London: Stanley Paul, 1st ed. 1964, 158p, illustrated, cloth, 21cm, with Allan Herron.

Brown, Gene

46980. *The Complete Book of Golf, A New York Times Scrapbook History*. New York: Arno Press, 1st ed. 1980, 206p, illustrated, decorative cloth, 27.5cm, introduction by Frank Litsky.

Brown, John Arthur

47000. *Short History of Pine Valley*. Clementon, New Jersey: Privately Printed, 1st ed. slipcased, 1963, 38p, illustrated, decorative cloth, 28cm. later printing.

Brown, M. Gillette

47020. *Fell's Teen Age Guide to Winning Golf.* New York: Frederick Fell, 1st ed. [1963] 134p, illustrated, cloth, 22.5cm.

Brown, Virginia Pounds

47040. *Grand Old Days of Birmingham Golf.* Birmingham, Alabama: Beech & Boaks, 1st ed. 1984, 60p, illustrated, illustrated wrappers, 28cm.

Browne, Liam

47060. *The Royal Dublin Golf Club 1885-1985.* Dublin, Ireland: Privately Printed, 1st ed. 1985, 96p, illustrated, decorative cloth, 21cm.

Browning, Robert H.K.

47080. *Golf in Devon and Cornwall.* London: Golf Clubs Association [ca1970] 60p, illustrated, illustrated wrappers, 18.5cm.

47090. *Golf in Somerset and Gloucestershire.* London: Golf Clubs Association [ca1975] 36p, illustrated, illustrated wrappers, 18.5cm.

Brownlee, R.C.

47110. *Dunbar Golf Club, A Short History 1794-1980.* Dunbar, Scotland: Privately Printed, 1st ed. 1980, 33p, illustrated, illustrated wrappers, 20.5cm.

Bruce, Ben and Evelyn Davies

47130. *Beginning Golf.* Belmont, California: Wadsworth, 1st ed. [1962] 62p illustrated, illustrated wrappers, 20.5cm.

47140. 2d ed. rev. 1969, 58p, illustrated, illustrated wrappers, 20cm. later printings.

Bruce-Watt, Jeremy

47160. *Gleneagles Hotel Diamond Jubilee Souvenir Book 1924-1984.* London: Gleneagles Hotel, 1st ed. presentation copy [1984] 56p, illustrated, gilt stamped leather, 29.5cm, foreword by George Younger.

47165. *Gleneagles Hotel Diamond Jubilee Souvenir Book 1924-1984*. Perthshire, Scotland: Privately Printed, 1st ed. [1984] 54p, illustrated, decorative cloth, 30cm.

Bruff, Nancy

47180. *The Country Club*. New York: Bartholomew House, 1st ed. 1969, 338p, cloth, 21cm.

Bryden, R.I. and D.T. Hood

47200. *The Kintansett Club A Brief History 1922-1968*. Marion, Massachusetts: Privately Printed, 1st ed. 1968, 180p, illustrated, decorative cloth, 25cm.

Brzoza, Walter C.

47220. *Putting Secrets of the Old Masters*. Schenectady, New York: Parkway Press, 1st ed. [1968] 25p, illustrated, illustrated wrappers, 20cm.

Bulawayo Golf Club

47240. *The Bulawayo Golf Club 1895-1970*. Bulawayo, Zimbabwe: Privately Printed, 1st ed. 1970, 68p, illustrated, illustrated wrappers, 28cm.

Bunker, Linda K. and De De Owens

47260. *Golf: Better Practice for Better Play*. New York: Leisure Press, 1st ed. [1984] 270p, illustrated, illustrated wrappers, 23cm.

Burd, Ron

47280. *Ron Burd's Basic Principles of Golf*. [South Africa] Privately Printed, 1st ed. [ca1966] 28p, illustrated, illustrated wrappers, 18.5cm.

Burden, E.A.R.

47300. *A History of St. Enodoc Golf Club*. St. Enodoc, England: Privately Printed, 1st ed. [1965] 64p, illustrated, illustrated wrappers, 21.5cm.

Burke, Jr., Jack

47320. *The Three Dimensions of Golf*. Toledo, Ohio: Curtin & Pease, 1st ed. [1966] 131p, illustrated in 3-Dimension, illustrated wrappers, 21cm, with 3-D glasses.

Burke, Jr., Jack and others

47340. *How To Solve Your Golf Problems*. and Byron Nelson, Johnny Revolta, Paul Runyan and Horton Smith. South Norwalk, Connecticut: Golf Digest, 1st ed. [1963] 190p, illustrated by James McQueen, cloth, 23.5cm.

47350. pbk. ed. New York: Cornerstone Library, 1964, 190p, illustrated by James McQueen, illustrated wrappers, 20cm.

47360. 1st UK ed. London: Nicholas Kaye, 1964, 190p, illustrated by James McQueen, cloth, 23cm.

Burke, John

47380. *Southwold Golf Club 1884-1984*. Southwold, England: Privately Printed, 1st ed. 1984, 60p, illustrated, illustrated wrappers, 21cm.

Burning Tree Club

47400. *Burning Tree Club, A History 1922-1962*. Bethesda, Maryland: Privately Printed, limited ed. [no limitation cited] slipcased [1962] 232p, illustrated, decorative cloth, 25cm.

47410. *Burning Tree Club, The Fifth Decade 1963-1972*. Bethesda, Maryland: Privately Printed, limited ed. [no limitation cited] slipcased [1972] 144p, illustrated, decorative cloth, 25.5cm.

Cady, Michael

47430. *AA 1986 Guide to Golf Courses in Britain*. edited by. Hamshire, England: Automobile Association [1985] 268p, illustrated, illustrated boards, 21cm.

Cain, Howard

47450. *Briarwood Country Club 1958-1983*. Deerfield, Illinois: Privately Printed, 1st ed. 1983 [8p] illustrated, illustrated wrappers, 28cm.

Cake, Patrick

47470. *The Pro-Am Murders*. Aptos, California: Proteus Press, 1st ed. 1979, 285p, illustrated, cloth, 20cm.

Calafato, Guy T. [Mrs]

47490. *Deal Golf and Country Club 1898-1973, Commemorative History*. Deal, New Jersey: Privately Printed, 1st ed. 1973 [30p] illustrated, wrappers, 19cm.

Calgary Golf & Country Club

47510. *Calgary Golf & Country Club 1897-1972, 75th Anniversary.* Calgary, Canada: Privately Printed, 1st ed. 1972, 29p, illustrated, spiral bound wrappers, 23cm.

Camp, Keith

47530. *Leighton Buzzard Golf Club Diamond Club Jubilee 1925-1985.* Leighton Buzzard, England: Privately Printed, 1st ed. 1985, 27p, illustrated, illustrated wrappers, 21cm.

Campbell, Bailey

47550. *Golf Lessons from Sam Snead.* New York: Duell: Sloan and Pearce, 1st ed. [1964] 126p, illustrated, cloth, 21cm.

47560. pbk. ed. New York: Hawthorn [1964] 126p, illustrated, illustrated wrappers, 21cm.

Campbell, Duncan C.

47580. *The Royal Montreal Golf Club 1873-1973.* Montreal: Privately Printed, 1st ed. 1973, 220p, illustrated, cloth, 22.5cm. foreword by George R.W. Owen.

47590. pbk. ed. 1973, 220p, illustrated, illustrated wrappers, 22.5cm.

Campbell, John

47610. *Greenkeeping.* Harwich, England: A. Quick, 1st ed. 1982, 88p, illustrated, illustrated wrappers, 21.5cm.

Campbell, Patrick

47630. *How to Become A Scratch Golfer.* London: Anthony Blond, 1st ed. 1963, 144p, illustrated, cloth, 17.5cm.

47640. 1st American ed. New York: Norton [1963] 144p, illustrated by Quentin Blake, decorative cloth, 20cm.

47650. *Patrick Campbell's Golfing Book.* London: Blond & Briggs, 1st ed. 1972, 127p, illustrated by Quentin Blake, cloth, 21.5cm.

Canham, Peter

47670. *Introduction to Golf.* Canberra, Australia: Australian Government Publishing Service, 1st ed. 1975, 20p, illustrated, illustrated wrappers, 14.5cm, foreword by Frank Stewart..

Cappers, Elmer Osgood

47690. *Centennial History of The Country Club 1882-1982.* Brookline, Massachusetts: Privately Printed, 1st ed. 1981, 155p, illustrated, cloth, 25.5cm.

Capps, Howard

47710. *Take the Wrists Out, A Life in Golf.* St. Helena, California: Illuminations Press, 1st ed. [1985] 158p, illustrated wrappers, 21.5cm.

Carlisle, Robert D.

47730. *The Montclair Golf Club, A Way of Life 1893-1983.* Montclair, New Jersey: Privately Printed, 1st ed. 1984, 314p, illustrated, pictorial leather, 25.5cm.

Carpenter, Ashley

47750. *In the Rough.* London: Kilcrane, 1st ed. [1984] [32p] illustrated, illustrated wrappers, 29.5cm.

Carpenter, Edward

47770. *Subjective Golf Strategy.* Chicago: Adams Press, 1st ed. [1979] 110p, illustrated, wrappers, 28cm.

Carpenter, Joseph

47790. *Only Golfers Know the Feeling.* Providence, Rhode Island: Mowbray, 1st ed. [1983] [68p] illustrated, cloth, 23cm.

Carr, Dick

47810. *You Too, Can Golf in the Eighties: An effective strategy for reducing strokes.* Hicksville, New York: Exposition Press, 1st ed. [1977] 64p, illustrated, cloth, 20cm.

Casper, Billy

47830. *295 Golf Lessons.* edited by Earl Puckett. Northfield, Illinois: Digest Books, 1st ed. [1973] 80p, illustrated, illustrated wrappers, 27.5cm.

47840. *Billy Casper's My Million Dollar Shots.* New York: Grosset & Dunlap, 1st ed. [1970] 223p, illustrated, cloth, 21cm.

47850. pbk. ed. New York: Bantam, 1971, 223p, illustrated, illustrated wrappers, 18cm.

47860. *Chipping and Putting: Golf around the green.* New York: Ronald Press, 1st ed. [1961] 114p, illustrated, cloth, 25.5cm, with Don Collett, foreword by Arnold Palmer.

47870. *Golf Shotmaking with Billy Casper.* Norwalk, Connecticut: Golf Digest, 1st ed. [1966] 176p, illustrated, cloth, 23cm.
47880. pbk. ed. New York: Cornerstone Library, 1969, 192p, illustrated, illustrated wrappers, 20.5cm.
47890. pbk. ed. New York: Pocket Books, 1970, 192p, illustrated, illustrated wrappers, 18cm.

47900. *Saving Strokes Around the Green.* Norwalk, Connecticut: Golf Digest, 1st ed. [1973] [14p] illustrated, illustrated wrappers, 16.5cm.

47910. *The Good Sense of Golf.* Englewood Cliffs, New Jersey: Prentice-Hall, 1st ed. [1980] 160p, illustrated, cloth, 22.5cm, with Al Barkow.

Chabody, Philip and Florence
47930. *The 86 Proof Pro.* New York: Exposition Press, 1st ed. [1974] 184p, cloth, 20.5cm.

Chamberlain, Faustina E.
47950. *Charley Emery; Pro: Biography of A Maine Golf Pro.* West Baldwin, Maine: Privately Printed, limited ed. [no limitation cited] signed [1982] 166p, illustrated, decorative cloth, 21.5cm.

Chamberlain, Peter
47970. *Good Golf.* London: Queen Anne Press, 1st ed. [1985] 159p, illustrated, cloth, 26cm.
47980. *Winning Golf.* New York: Sterling, 1st American ed. 1985, 159p, illustrated, cloth, 26cm. American title of "Good Golf."
47990. pbk. ed. 1985, 159p, illustrated, illustrated wrappers, 26cm.

Chandler, Leonard R.
48010. *A History of Essex Golf & Country Club 1902-1983.* Windsor, Canada: Privately Printed, 1st ed. 1983, 83p, illustrated, illustrated wrappers, 21.5cm.

Chape, T. and W. Ogilvie

48030. *Newbiggin Golf Club Centenary 1884-1984.* Newbiggin, England: Privately Printed, 1st ed. 1984, 81p, illustrated, decorative cloth, 20cm.

Chapman, H.J.

48050. *The Story of the Dalhousie Golf Club 1868-1968.* Carnoustie, Scotland: Privately Printed, 1st ed. 1968, 47p, illustrated, wrappers, 18.5cm.

Charles, Bob

48070. *Left-Hander from New Zealand: A Book of Golf Instruction.* London: Hodder & Stoughton, 1st ed. [1965] 139p, illustrated, cloth, 21.5cm, with Roger P. Ganem, foreword by Gary Player.

48080. *Left-Handed Golf.* Englewood Cliffs, New Jersey: Prentice-Hall, 1st American ed. [1965] 127p, illustrated, decorative cloth, 23cm. with Roger Ganem, foreword by Mark H. McCormack. American title of "Left-Hander from New Zealand."

48090. *The Bob Charles Left-Handers Golf Book.* Sydney, Australia: Angus & Robertson, 1st ed. 1985, 104p, illustrated, cloth, 24cm, with Jim Wallace.

48100. 1st American ed. Englewood Cliffs, New Jersey: Prentice-Hall, 1985, 104p, illustrated, illustrated wrappers, 24cm, with Jim Wallace, foreword by Jack Nicklaus.

48110. 1st UK ed. London: Angus & Robertson [1985] 104p, illustrated, cloth, 24cm.

Chattanooga Golf and Country Club

48130. *At the End of the Trolley. A History of the Chattanooga Golf and Country Club 1896-1961.* Chattanooga, Tennessee: Privately Printed, 1st ed. 1961, 50p, illustrated, illustrated wrappers, 24cm.

Cheatum, Billye Ann

48150. *Golf.* Philadelphia: W.B. Saunders, 1st ed. [1969] 116p, illustrated by James Bonner, illustrated wrappers, 23cm.

Cherellia, George

48170. *All About Hitting the Sweet Spot.* Champion, Illinois: Stipes Publishing, 1st ed. [1975] 91p, illustrated by David Ardisson, illustrated wrappers, 27.5cm.

48180. *Tempo: The heart of the golf swing.* Hollywood, California: Creative Sports, 1st ed. [1971] 68p, illustrated, illustrated wrappers, 21cm.

Cherry Hills Country Club

48200. *Cherry Hills Country Club [Handbook].* Durham, North Carolina: Golf Course Profiles 1st ed. [1978] [27p] illustrated, illustrated wrappers, 18cm.

Cheves, Ike

48220. *Play Better Golf.* NP: Knight Publications, 1st ed. [1966] 80p, illustrated, cloth, 22cm.

Chevin Golf Club

48240. *Chevin Golf Club [Handbook].* London: Golf Clubs Association [ca1965] 24p, illustrated, illustrated wrappers, 18cm.

Chieger, Bob and Pat Sullivan

48260. *Inside Golf: Quotations on the Royal and Ancient Game.* New York: Atheneum, 1st ed. 1985, 271p, illustrated wrappers, 21cm.

Chinnock, Frank

48280. *How to Break 90 Consistently.* Philadelphia: Lippincott, 1st ed. [1976] 144p, illustrated by Ed Vebell, cloth, 23cm.

Chlevin, Ben

48300. *Golf for Industry: A Planning Guide.* Chicago: National Golf Foundation, 1st ed. 1962, 50p, illustrated, illustrated wrappers, 28cm.

Chodosh, Maureen and Maggie Weiss

48320. *The Golfer's Cookbook: Recipes Collected At Pebble Beach.* Edmonton, Canada: Hurtig, 1st ed. [1984] 296p, illustrated, cloth, 21.5cm.

Chui, Edward

48340. *Golf.* Pacific Palisades, California: Goodyear, 1st ed. [1969] 88p, illustrated, illustrated wrappers, 21.5cm.

Cincinnati Country Club

48360. *Cincinnati Country Club 1903-1975.* Cincinnati, Ohio: Privately Printed, 1st ed. 1975, 84p, cloth, 17.5cm.

Clarke, R.N.

48380. *A Sudbrook Chronicle, Being A History of Richmond Golf Club 1891-1932.* Richmond, England: Privately Printed, limited ed. [100 copies] 1976, 44p, illustrated, spiral bound illustrated wrappers, 29.5cm.

Clarke, Richard W.

48400. *The Bedford Golf & Tennis Club 1890-1965.* Katonah, New York: Privately Printed, 1st ed. 1965, 26p, illustrated, wrappers, 23.5cm.

Clement, Joe

48420. *Classic Golf Clubs: A Pictorial Guide.* Jackson, Mississippi: Classic Golf Clubs, 1st ed. [1980] 198p, illustrated, illustrated wrappers, 27.5cm.

Clements, William R.

48440. *Historical Highlights Miami Valley Golf Club.* Dayton, Ohio: Privately Printed, 1st ed. 1963, 14p, illustrated wrappers, 21cm.

Clovelly Country Club

48460. *Clovelly Country Club 1932-1982, 50th Anniversary.* Cape Town, South Africa: Privately Printed, 1st ed. 1982, 16p, illustrated, illustrated wrappers, 25cm.

Cobe, Albert

48480. *Great Spirit.* Chicago: Childrens Press, 1st ed. [1970] 64p, illustrated, illustrated boards, 17cm. with George Elrick and R.E. Simon Jr.

Cochran, Alastair and John Stobbs

48500. *The Search for the Perfect Swing.* London: Heinemann, 1st ed. [1968] 242p, illustrated, cloth, 26.5cm.

48510. 1st American ed. Philadelphia: Lippincott [1968] 242p, illustrated, cloth, 26.5cm. later printings.

Cockfield, A.S. and Herb McNally

48530. *Mount Bruno Country Club, Some Historical Notes 1918-1978.* Montreal: Privately Printed, 1st ed. 1978, 28p, illustrated, illustrated wrappers, 21.5cm.

Colburn, Neil

48550. *The Pro Golf Teacher.* La Mesa, California: Commercial Printing, 1st ed. [1980] 113p, illustrated, illustrated wrappers, 21cm.

Coldstream Country Club

48570. *Coldstream Country Club 25th Anniversary 1959-1984.* Cincinnati, Ohio: Privately Printed, 1st ed. 1984, 67p, illustrated, wrappers, 28cm.

Colebank, Albert

48590. *A History of Red Hill Country Club.* Cucamonga, California: Privately Printed, 1st ed. 1972, 77p, illustrated, wrappers, 27.5cm.

Coles, Neil

48610. *Neil Coles on Golf.* London: Stanley Paul, 1st ed. 1965, 125p, illustrated, cloth, 23cm, preface by Geoffrey Cousins.

Coll, Ben

48630. *The Country Club.* New York: Carlton Press, 1st ed. [1961] 97p, illustrated, cloth, 20cm.

Collier, Sargent F.

48650. *Green Grows Bar Harbor, Reflections from Kebo Valley.* Bar Harbor, Maine: Privately Printed, 1st ed. [1964] 107p, illustrated, pictorial cloth, 23cm, introduction by Cleveland Amory.

Collins, David R.

48670. *Super Champ! The Story of Babe Didrickson Zaharias.* Austin, Texas: Eakin Press, 1st ed. [1982] 77p, illustrated, illustrated boards, 21.5cm.

Colmer, Albert W.K. and Ivor D. Ray

48690. *History of the Ardglas Castle and Ardglas Golf Club.* Ardglas, Northern Ireland: Privately Printed, 1st ed. 1982, 42p, illustrated, illustrated wrappers, 22cm.

Colomb, Reggie

48710. *Rutland Country Club, A Continuing Tradition.* Rutland, Vermont: Privately Printed, 1st ed. [1985] [152p] illustrated, illustrated wrappers, 28cm.

Colver, J. Arthur

48730. *A History of Lindrick Golf Club 1891-1979.* Sheffield, England: J.W. Northend, 1st ed. 1980, 168p, illustrated, cloth, 21.5cm.

Colville, George M.

48750. *Five Open Champions and The Musselburgh Golf Story.* Musselburgh, Scotland: Colville Books, limited ed. [no limitation cited] signed, 1980, 115p, illustrated, 1/2 leather, gilt cloth, raised bands, 23.5cm, foreword by Peter Alliss.

48760. 1st trade ed. 1980, 115p, illustrated, cloth, 24cm.

Comer, John L.

48780. *Putting: A New Approach.* Oklahoma City: Privately Printed, 2d ed. rev. 1962, 25p, illustrated, wrappers, 21.5cm. note: first edition not located.

Comrie, Leslie and William Dakers and Allen Wright

48800. *Liberton Golf Club 1920-1980.* Edinburgh, Scotland: Privately Printed, 1st ed. 1980, 54p, illustrated, gilt stamped leather, 25cm.

Conley, Harvey

48820. *Golf Made Easy the H.A.R.D. Way.* Rockaway, New York: Privately Printed, 1st ed. [ca1965] 22p, illustrated, illustrated wrappers, 21.5cm.

Connolly, Robert

48840. *Carnaby Threep's Golf Class.* [Johannesburgh, South Africa] Sunday Times, 1st ed. [1970] 52p, illustrated, illustrated wrappers, 18cm.

Conron, Brandon

48860. *The London Hunt and Country Club.* London, Canada: Privately Printed, 1st ed. 1985, 108p, illustrated, decorative cloth, 20.5cm.

Cooke, Bernard

48880. *Newnes All Color Golf Guide.* Feltham, England: Newnes, 1st ed. [1984] 92p, illustrated, illustrated boards, 29.5cm.

Cooper, Jim

48900. *A.G. Spalding & Bros. Pre-1930 Clubs, Trademarks, Sub-Marks and etc. and other Spalding collectables; featuring the collection of Jim The Spalding Man Cooper.* Kannapolis, North Carolina: Privately Printed, 1st ed. [1985] 78p, illustrated, illustrated wrappers, 28cm.

Coopman, Edwin J.

48920. *History of the San Francisco Golf Club.* San Francisco, California: Privately Printed, limited ed. [1000 copies] 1978, 95p, illustrated, decorative cloth, 20cm.

Copt Heath Golf Club

48940. *Copt Heath Golf Club 1907-1977.* Solihull, England: Privately Printed, 1st ed. 1977 [8p] illustrated, illustrated wrappers, 21cm.

48950. *Copt Heath Golf Club 1910-1985.* Solihull, England: Privately Printed, 1st ed. 1985, 16p, illustrated, illustrated wrappers, 21cm.

Corcoran, Fred

48970. *Unplayable Lies.* New York: Duell, Sloan and Pearce, 1st ed. 1965, 274p, illustrated, cloth, 23.5cm, with Bud Harvey, foreword by Bing Crosby. later printing.

Cornish, Geoffrey S. and William G. Robinson

48990. *Golf Course Design. An Introduction.* Amherst, Massachusetts: Privately Printed, 1st ed. [ca1972] [12p] illustrated, illustrated wrappers, 21.5cm.

49000. 2d ed. rev. 1979, 20p, illustrated wrappers, 21.5cm.

Cornish, Geoffrey S. and Ronald W. Whitten

49020. *The Golf Course*. New York: Rutledge Press, 1st ed. 1981, 320p, illustrated, cloth, 27.5cm. foreword by Robert Trent Jones. later printings.

49030. limited ed. facsimile, slipcased [200 copies] London: Ellesborough Press, 1984, 320p, illustrated, leather, aeg, raised bands, 27.5cm.

Cossey, Rosalynde

49050. *Golfing Ladies: Five Centuries of Golf in Great Britain and Ireland*. London: Orbis, 1st ed. 1984, 256p, illustrated, cloth, 24.5cm, foreword by Vivien Saunders.

Costelloe, A.J.

49070. *Faversham Golf Club 1902-1983*. Bristol, England: Summit Publications, 1st ed. 1983, 32p, illustrated, illustrated wrappers, 21cm.

Cotton, C.K.

49090. *Porters Park Golf Club [Handbook]*. Kingston Upon Thames, England: Temple Publicity Services, 1971, 16p, illustrated, illustrated wrappers, 18.5cm.

Cotton, Henry

49110. *Golf: A Pictorial History*. Glasgow: Collins, 1st ed. [1975] 240p, illustrated, cloth, 25cm, foreword by Sam Snead.

49120. *A History of Golf Illustrated*. Philadelphia: Lippincott, 1st American ed. [1975] 240p, illustrated, cloth, 25cm, foreword by Sam Snead. American title of "Golf, A Pictorial History."

49130. *Henry Cotton Says...* London: Country Life, 1st ed. 1962, 80p, illustrated by Roy Ullyett, cloth, 19cm.

49140. *Play Better Golf.* Newton Abbot, England: David & Charles, 2d ed. 1973, 80p, illustrated by Roy Ullyett, cloth, 20cm. note: reissue of "Henry Cotton Says."

49150. *Henry Cotton's Guide to Golf in the British Isles.* Manchester, England: Cliveden Press, 1st ed. 1969, 124p, illustrated, cloth, 29cm.

49160. *Study the Golf Game with Henry Cotton.* London: Country Life, 1st ed. 1964, 236p, illustrated, cloth, 25cm.

49170. *Thank's for the Game: The best of golf with Henry Cotton.* London: Sidgwick & Jackson, 1st ed. 1980, 176p, illustrated, cloth, 24.5cm.

49180. pbk. ed. 1980, 176p, illustrated, illustrated wrappers, 24.5cm.

49190. *The Picture Story of the Golf Game.* London: World Distributors, 1st ed. [ca1965] 157p, illustrated, illustrated boards, 27.5cm.

Country Club of Fairfield

49210. *The Country Club of Fairfield 1914-1966.* Fairfield, Connecticut: Privately Printed, 1st ed. 1966 [30p] illustrated, illustrated wrappers, 23cm.

Cousins, Geoffrey

49230. *Golf in Britain: A Social History from the beginnings to the present day.* London: Routledge & Kegan Paul, 1st ed. 1975, 176p, illustrated, cloth, 23.5cm.

49240. *Lords of the Links: The story of professional golf.* London: Hutchinson Benham, 1st ed. 1977, 176p, illustrated, cloth, 21.5cm.

49250. *Manor House Hotel Golf Course [Handbook].* Devon, England: Privately Printed [ca1965} 12p, illustrated, illustrated wrappers, 20.5cm.

49260. *The Handbook of Golf: A guide to the game and its techniques.* London: Sir Isaac Pitman, 1st ed. 1969, 147p, illustrated, cloth, 21.5cm.

Cousins, Geoffrey and Bill Cox

49280. *The State Express: The book of golf.* [London] Privately Printed, 1st ed. 1962, 64p, illustrated, illustrated wrappers, 20.5cm.

Cousins, Geoffrey and Don Pottinger

49300. *An Atlas of Golf.* London: Thomas Nelson, 1st ed. [1974] 96p, illustrated, cloth, 27.5cm.

Cousins, Geoffrey and Tom Scott

49320. *A Century of Opens.* London: Frederick Muller, 1st ed. 1971, 232p, illustrated, cloth, 21.5cm.

Cowell, A.T.

49340. *Kidderminster Golf Club [Handbook].* Kingston Upon Thames, England: Temple Publicity Services, 1971, 28p, illustrated, illustrated wrappers, 18.5cm.

Cox, A. Bertran

49360. *Fairways Of the Mount 1927-1977, Mount Osmond Club.* Adelaide, Australia: Privately Printed, 1st ed. 1977, 107p, illustrated, decorative cloth, 24.5cm.

49370. *Out of the Rough, A History of the Mount Lofty Golf Club 1925-1975.* Adelaide, Australia: Privately Printed, 1st ed. 1975, 103p, illustrated, decorative cloth, 24.5cm.

Cox, Paul and Jim Koger

49390. *The City That Broke Par.* [Columbus, Georgia] Privately Printed, 1st ed. 1971, 192p, illustrated, cloth, 22.5cm, introduction by Lee Trevino, foreword by Fred Corcoran.

Cox, Wiffy

49410. *The Wiffy Cox Story.* [London] Privately Printed, limited ed. [no limitation cited] [ca1970] 96p, illustrated, cloth, 23cm.

Cox, William J. [Bill]

49430. *Improve Your Game.* Hammondsport, England: Penguin Books, 1st ed. 1963, 140p, illustrated, illustrated wrappers, 18cm, foreword by John Arlott.

49440. 1st American ed. Baltimore, Maryland: Penguin Books, 1963, 140p, illustrated, illustrated wrappers, 18cm, foreword by John Arlott.

Cox, William J. [Bill] and Nicholas Tremayne

49460. *Bill Cox's Golf Companion.* London: J.M. Dent, 1st ed. 1969, 215p, illustrated, decorative cloth, 21.5cm, foreword by John Arlott.

49470. pbk. ed. 1969, 215p, illustrated, illustrated wrappers, 21.5cm.

Coyne, John

49490. *Better Golf.* edited by. Chicago: Follett, 1st ed. [1972] 224p, illustrated, illustrated boards, 25cm.

49500. *The New Golf for Women.* edited by. New York: Doubleday, 1st ed. [1973] 223p, illustrated, cloth, 25.5cm, foreword by Bob Toski, introduction by Kathy Whitworth.

49510. *Golf For Women.* London: Angus & Robertson, 1st UK ed. 1975, 223p, illustrated, cloth, 25cm. UK title of "New Golf For Women."

Craft, Linda and Penny Zavichas

49530. *The Craft-Zavichas Golfer's Cookbook.* Jacksboro, Texas: Privately Printed, 1st ed. [1979] 188p, illustrated by Anne Nelson, spiral bound illustrated wrappers, 21.5cm.

49540. *The Craft-Zavichas Golfer's Cookbook II.* Waco, Texas: Privately Printed, 2d ed. rev. [1983] 219p, illustrated, spiral bound illustrated wrappers, 23cm. foreword by Kathy Whitworth.

Crafter, Brian

49560. *Winning Golf.* South Yarra, Australia: Currey O'Neil, 1st ed. 1983, 120p, illustrated, cloth, 27.5cm, with Bill Pritchard.

Crane, Leo

49580. *Putting: The Name of the Game.* Pomona, California: Privately Printed, 1st ed. [1966] 8p, illustrated wrappers, 15.5cm.

Cranford, Peter G.

49600. *The Winning Touch in Golf: A Psychological Approach.* Englewood Cliffs, New Jersey: Prentice-Hall, 1st ed. [1961] 171p, illustrated by Lealand Gustavson, cloth, 21.5cm, introduction by Cary Middlecoff. later printings.

49610. reprint ed. New York: Bramhall House [ca1965] 171p, illustrated by Lealand Gustavson, cloth, 21.5cm.

49620. 1st UK ed. London: Herbert Jenkins, 1962, 171p, cloth, 21.5cm.

Crawford, Iain

49640. *Scottish Brewers Open Guide to the Old Course & St. Andrews.* [Edinburgh] Scottish Brewers 1st ed. [1982] 100p, illustrated, illustrated wrappers, 20cm.

49650. *The Open Guide to Royal St. George's and Sandwich.* [Edinburgh] Bluebird, 1st ed. [1981] 98p, illustrated, illustrated wrappers, 20cm.

49660. *The Open Guide to Royal Troon & Kyle.* [Edinburgh] Bluebird, 1st ed. [1982] 99p, illustrated, illustrated wrappers, 20.5cm.

Creagh, John

49680. *Golden Years of Australian Golf.* edited by. Sydney: K.G. Murray, 1st ed. [ca1977] 193p, illustrated, illustrated wrappers, 27.5cm.

Crehan, William

49700. *Who's Who in Golf.* edited by. New York: Champion Sports, 1st ed. 1971, 130p, illustrated, illustrated wrappers, 21cm.

Crisp, Martha O. and Ruth A. Leffer

49720. *Women's Long Island Golf Association, The First Fifty Years 1930-1980.* [New York] Privately Printed, 1st ed. [1980] [28p] wrappers, 28cm.

Cromie, Robert

49740. *Golf for Boys and Girls.* Chicago: Follett, 1st ed. [1965] 96p, illustrated, illustrated wrappers, 20.5cm, preface by Bill Casper, Jr.

49750. *Par for the Course: A Golfer's Anthology.* edited by. New York: Macmillan, 1st ed. [1964] 303p, cloth, 23.5cm. later printing.

Crosbie, Provan

49770. *Fairways and Foul.* London: Robert Hale, 1st ed. 1964, 192p, cloth, 19.5cm.

Crouch, William H.

49790. *Guide to the Analysis of Golf Courses and Country Clubs.* Chicago: American Institute of Real Estate Appraisers, 1st ed. [1968] 60p, illustrated wrappers, 28cm, with Robert J. Gemeinhardt and Mrs. Herbert L. Blackstone. later printing.

Cruickshank, Charles

49810. *The Tang Murders.* London: Robert Hale, 1st ed. 1976, 182p, cloth, 18.5cm.

Cruickshank, Frederick D.

49830. *The History of the Weston Golf and Country Club.* Toronto, Canada: Privately Printed, limited ed. [1000 copies] 1980, 114p, illustrated, decorative cloth, 21cm. later printing.

Daly, Fred

49850. *Golfing in Northern Ireland.* Belfast, Northern Ireland: Northern Ireland Tourist Board, 1st ed. [ca1971] [6p] illustrated, illustrated wrappers, 21.5cm.

Dante, Joseph [Joe] and Len Elliot

49870. *The Four Magic Moves to Winning Golf.* New York: McGraw-Hill, 1st ed. [1962] 218p, illustrated by William Canfield, cloth, 20cm.

49880. pbk. ed. New York: Cornerstone Library, 1963, 191p, wrappers, 20 cm.

49890. *What's Wrong With Your Golf? Why you hit those bad shots, and how to get rid of them.* New York: Simon & Schuster, 1st ed. [1978] 128p, illustrated by Dom Lupo, cloth, 23.5cm.

Darbyshire, L. Claughton

49910. *Go Golfing in Britain: A hole-by-hole survey of 25 famous seaside courses.* [London] The Sunday Times, 1st ed. [1961] 75p, illustrated, cloth, 19.5cm.

Daro, August

49930. *The Inside Swing: Key to Better Golf.* New York: Thomas Y. Crowell, illustrated. 1st ed. [1972] 124p, illustrated, cloth, 23cm, with Herb Graffis, introduction by Claude Harmon.

Davidson, R.E.

49950. *Golfing At Yokine, Being a brief history of the Western Australian Golf Club Incorporated 1928-1967.* Mt. Yokine, Australia: Privately Printed, 1st ed. 1967, 96p, illustrated, cloth, 24cm.

Davies, John

49970. *Yardley Country Club, A Casual History 1928-1978.* Yardley, Pennsylvania: Privately Printed, 1st ed. 1978, 25p, illustrated, illustrated wrappers, 14cm.

Davies, Peter

49990. *Davies' Dictionary of Golfing Terms.* New York: Simon & Schuster, 1st ed. [1980] 188p, illustrated by Fran Carson, cloth, 25.5cm.

Davis, William

50010. *The Punch Book of Golf.* edited by. London: Hutchinson, 1st ed. [1973] 112p, illustrated, cloth, 24cm. later printings.

Davis, William H.

50030. *Great Golf Courses of the World.* Norwalk, Connecticut: Golf Digest, 1st ed. [1974] 278p, illustrated, cloth, 27.5cm.

50040. *100 Greatest Golf Courses-and then some!* Norwalk, Connecticut: Golf Digest, 1st ed. [1982] 279p, illustrated, cloth, 27.5cm. later printings.

Davyhulme Park Golf Club

50060. *Davyhulme Park Golf Club, 75th Anniversary.* Davyhulme, England: Privately Printed, 1st ed. 1985 [36p] illustrated, illustrated wrappers, 21.5cm.

Dawkins, George

50080. *Keys to the Golf Swing.* Englewood Cliffs, New Jersey: Prentice-Hall, 1st ed. [1976] [114p] illustrated by Tony Kokinos, cloth, 28cm.

DB Golf Annual

50100. *The DB Golf Annual 1974.* edited by Terry McLean and Jim Wallace. Auckland, New Zealand: MOA, 1st ed. 1974, 125p, illustrated, cloth, 26cm.

50110. 2d ed. 1975, 140p, illustrated, cloth, 26cm. edited by Jim Wallace.

50120. 3d ed. 1976, 141p, illustrated, cloth, 26cm. edited by Jim Wallace.

50130. 4th ed. 1977, 141p, illustrated, cloth, 26cm. edited by Jim Wallace.

50140. 5th ed. 1978, 157p, illustrated, cloth, 26cm. edited by Jim Wallace.

50150. 6th ed. 1979, 157p, illustrated, cloth, 26cm. edited by Jim Wallace.

50160. 7th ed. 1980, 157p, illustrated, cloth, 26cm. edited by Jim Wallace.

Deegan, Paul

50180. *Jack Nicklaus: The Golden Bear.* Mankato, Illinois: Creative Education, 1st ed. [1974] [30p] illustrated, illustrated boards, 24cm.

DeGuerre, Christian and Patrice Failliott

50200. *Europe's Golf Guide.* Puteaux, France: Robert Laffont, 1st ed. 1982, 778p, illustrated, illustrated boards, 23cm, with Petra Giesen.

Delgany Golf Club

50220. *Delgany Golf Club 75th Anniversary 1908-1983*. Delgany, Ireland: Privately Printed, 1st ed. 1983 [24p] illustrated, illustrated wrappers, 29.5cm.

Dellor, Ralph

50240. *British Golf Courses: A Guide to Courses in the British Isles*. edited by. London: Lansdowne, 1st ed. 1974, 439p, illustrated wrappers, 18.5cm.

DeMonte, John

50260. *A Collection and Portfolio of Golf Humor*. Tucson, Arizona: Raycol Products, 1st ed. [1983] [16p] illustrated by O. Cox & C.F. Maraschiello, illustrated wrappers, 23cm.

50270. *The Kings James' Versions of the Game of Golfe*. Tucson, Arizona: Josephson, 1st ed. [1980] 72p, illustrated, illustrated wrappers, 27.5cm.

50280. *The Kings James' Version of the Game of Golfe, Book II*. Tucson, Arizona: Raycol Products, 1st ed. [1982] 52p, illustrated, illustrated wrappers, 27.5cm.

Denis, Frank T.

50300. *The Kanawaki Golf Club 50th Anniversary Book*. Caughnawaga, Canada: Privately Printed, 1st ed. 1964, 36p, illustrated, illustrated wrappers, 23cm.

Dentino, Tom

50320. *The Basic Golf Swing*. [Aboard the Royal Viking Sky] Privately Printed, 1st ed. [1970] [14p] illustrated, illustrated wrappers, 21cm.

Detrick, R. Blaine

50340. *Golf and the Gospel: How To Improve Your Score in the Game of Life*. Lima, Ohio: C.S.S. 1st ed. [1985] 78p, illustrated, illustrated wrappers, 21cm.

Devine, Dominic

50360. *Three Green Bottles*. Garden City, New York: The Crime Club/Doubleday, 1st American ed. 1972, 211p, cloth, 20.5cm. note: first edition not located.

Devlin, Bruce

50380. *Australia's Bruce Devlin Championship Golf [Flip Book].* [Australia] Thumbfix International, 1st ed. 1970 [120p] illustrated, illustrated wrappers, 8.5cm.

50390. *Bruce Devlin Flip Book Instructions, Drive & Wedge.* [Australia] Thumbfix International, 1st ed. 1971 [60p] illustrated, illustrated wrappers, 16.5cm.

50400. *Play Like the Devil.* Sydney, Australia: Angus and Robertson, 1st ed. 1967, 135p, illustrated by Peter Harrigan, cloth, 23.5cm, foreword by Gary Player, with Jack Pollard

50410. 1st American ed. Garden City, New York: Doubleday, 1970, 144p, cloth, 23cm.

50420. pbk. ed. New York: New American Library, 1971, 141p, illustrated wrappers, 18cm, later printings.

Dexter, E.R. Ted

50440. *My Golf.* London: Arthur Barker, 1st ed. [1982] 113p, illustrated, cloth, 21.5cm.

Dexter, E.R. Ted and Clifford Makins

50460. *Deadly Putter.* London: George Allen & Unwin, 1st ed. 1979, 151p, cloth, 21.5cm.

Dexter, E.R. Ted and Michael McDonnell

50480. *The World of Golf.* London: Purnell, 1st ed. [1970] 141p, illustrated, illustrated boards, 25.5cm.

Dey, Jr., Joseph C.

50500. *Golf.* New Brunswick, New Jersey: Boy Scouts of America, 1st ed. 1977, 72p, illustrated by Dom Lupo, illustrated wrappers, 20.5cm.

50510. 2d ed. rev. 1984, 80p, illustrated, illustrated wrappers, 20.5cm.

50520. *Golf Rules in Pictures.* New York: USGA/Grosset & Dunlap, 1st ed. [1964] 88p, illustrated by George Kraynak, illustrated wrappers, 27 cm. introduction by Wm. Ward Foshay. later printings.

Deyo, M.E.

50550. *The Easy Way to Stay in Shape for Golf.* Davenport, Iowa: Information Services, 1st ed. [1971] 94p, illustrated, spiral bound illustrated wrappers, 21.5cm.

Diaz, Carroll

50570. *Golf: A beginner's guide.* Palo Alto, California: Mayfield Publishing, 1st ed. 1974, 87p, illustrated, illustrated wrappers, 20.5 cm.

Dickinson, Patric

50590. *The Good Minute: An Autobiographical Study.* London: Victor Gollancz, 1st ed. 1965, 218p, cloth, 21.5cm.

Dickson, Pat

50610. *Short History of the Clovelly Country Club.* [South Africa] Privately Printed, 1st ed. 1974, 68p, illustrated, illustrated wrappers, 21cm.

Directory of Amateur Golfers

50630. *Directory of Amateur Golfers, Volume 1-Arizona, Nevada, Utah.* Tucson, Arizona: Amateur Golfers Association, 1st ed. 1976, 192p, illustrated, cloth, 28cm.

Dobereiner, Peter

50650. *Down the Nineteenth Fairway: A Golfing Anthology.* London: Andre Deutch, 1st ed. [1982] 205p, illustrated by Tim Havers, cloth, 23.5cm.

50660. 1st American ed. New York: Atheneum, 1983, 205p, illustrated, cloth, 23cm.

50670. *For the Love of Golf: The Best of Dobereiner.* London: Stanley Paul, 1st ed. 1981, 256p, illustrated by John Hassall, cloth, 23cm.

50680. *The World of Golf: The Best of Peter Dobereiner.* New York: Atheneum, 1st American ed. 1981, 287P, cloth, 21cm. American title of "For the Love of Golf: The Best of Dobereiner."

50690. *Stroke, Hole or Match?* London: David & Charles, 1st ed. [1976] 192p, illustrated by Bert Kitchen, illustrated boards, 17cm.

50700. *Golf Explained: How to Take Advantage of the Rules.* New York: Sterling, 1st American ed. 1977, 192p, illustrated by Bert Kitchen, cloth and boards, 22.5cm. American title of "Stroke, Hole or Match."

50710. *The Book of Golf Disasters.* London: Stanley Paul, 1st ed. 1983, 179p, illustrated by John Ireland, cloth, 21.5cm.

50720. 1st American ed. New York: Atheneum, 1984, 179p, cloth, 21.5cm.

50730. *The Game with A Hole in It.* London: Faber & Faber, 1st ed. 1970, 142p, cloth, 20cm.

50740. *The Glorious World of Golf.* New York: McGraw-Hill, 1st ed. [1973] 250p, illustrated, cloth, 27cm.

50750. *The Golfers-The Inside Story.* London: Collins, 1st ed. 1982, 190p, cloth, 21cm, foreword by Henry Cotton.

Doherty, Mike

50770. *Golf Classics Price and Identification Guide.* Studio City, California: Golf Classics, 1st ed. [1978] 74p, illustrated, leather 3 ring binder, 28cm.

Dolan, Anne Reilly

50790. *Congressional Country Club 1924-1984.* Washington, DC: Privately Printed, 1st ed. 1984, 108p, illustrated, decorative cloth, 30cm.

Donohue, Charles and Paul Care

50810. *Guide To Golf in Hampshire.* Southhampton, England: Paul Care Publications, 1977, 68p, illustrated, illustrated wrappers, 18.5cm.

Donovan, Robert [Bob]

50830. *GHO'84-The New Era; Sammy Davis Greater Hartford Open.* Hartford, Connecticut: Greater Hartford Jaycees, 1st ed. [1985] [102p] illustrated, cloth, 22cm.

Douglas, J.H. and E.R. Wastnedge

50850. *A History of Carlisle Golf Club.* Carlisle, England: Privately Printed, 1st ed. 1985, 71p, illustrated, illustrated wrappers, 21cm.

Doyle, Rick

50855. *How To Cheat At Golf.* Las Vegas, Nevada: R&M Publishing, 1st ed, 1985, 64p, illustrated, illustrated wrappers, 13.5cm.

Drought, James

50870. *The Master, A Modern Chronicle.* Macomb, Illinois: Western Illinois Press, 1st ed. 1971, 129p, illustrated wrappers, 23cm.

Drysdale, Alasdair M.

50890. *The Golf House Club, Elie: A Centenary History.* Elie, Scotland: Privately Printed, 1st ed. 1975, 157p, illustrated, cloth, 18.5cm.

Dulack, Thomas

50910. *Pork, or the Day I Lost the Masters.* New York: Dial Press, 1st ed. 1968, 209p, cloth, 21cm.

Dunany Country Club

50930. *The Story of the Dunany Country Club.* Lachute, Canada: Privately Printed, 1st ed. 1967 [8p] illustrated wrappers, 21.5cm.

Dundas Valley Golf and Curling Club

50950. *Dundas Valley Golf and Curling Club 1929-1979, 50th Anniversary.* Dundas, Canada: Privately Printed, 1st ed. 1979 [32p] illustrated, illustrated wrappers, 14cm.

Dunlop, Sandy

50970. *The Golfing Bodymind.* London: Wildwood House, 1st ed. 1980, 153p, illustrated, cloth, 21.5cm.

Dunn, Edward, T.

50990. *The Park Club of Buffalo 1903-1978.* Buffalo, New York: Privately Printed, 1st ed. 1978, 46p, illustrated, illustrated wrappers, 21.5cm.

Dunnett, Dorothy,

51010. *Match For A Murderer.* Boston: Houghton Mifflin, 1st ed. 1971, 306p, cloth, 21cm.

Dunsmore, Colin

51030. *In Celebration of the Golden Anniversary of the New South Wales Golf Club, 1928-1978*. New South Wales, Australia: Privately Printed, 1st ed. 1978 [42p] illustrated, wrappers, 21.5cm.

Durien, Ted

51050. *The First Fifty Years, 1925-1975: Monterey Penisula Country Club*. Monterey, California: Privately Printed, 1st ed. 1975, 127p, illustrated, decorative cloth, 25.5cm.

Dwyer, D.H.

51070. *Killara Golf Club, A History*. Turramurra, Australia: Privately Printed, 1st ed. 1966, 109p, illustrated, cloth, 28cm.

East London Golf Club

51090. *East London Golf Club 1893-1968*. Cape Province, South Africa: Privately Printed, 1st ed. 1968, 82p, illustrated, illustrated wrappers, 28cm.

East Lothian Golf

51110. *East Lothian Golf*. Musselburgh, Scotland: East Lothian District Council, 1st ed. [ca1983] 30p, illustrated, illustrated wrappers, 27.5cm.

Easterbrook, L.F.

51130. *Ipswich Golf Club [Handbook]*. London: Golf Clubs Association [ca1965] 15p, illustrated, wrappers, 18.5cm.

Eastern Airlines

51150. *Eastern's Guide To Great Golf Courses*. NP: Eastern Airlines [1966] 63p, illustrated, illustrated wrappers, 21.5cm.

Eaton, Harry

51170. *Dunmurry Golf Club 75th Anniversary 1905-1980*. Belfast, Northern Ireland: Privately Printed, 1st ed. [ca1981] [28p] illustrated, illustrated wrappers, 25.5cm.

Ebert, Bill

51190. *The Invitation.* Burlingame, California: Bill Eber Associates, 1st ed. [ca1983] 170p, illustrated, decorative cloth, 23cm.

Eddy, Jackie

51210. *The Second Slice: over 250 Delicious, Time Saving Recipes for Golfers and People on the Go.* Toronto: Key Porter Books, 1st ed. [1985] 217p, cloth, 23cm.

Edmondson, Jolee

51230. *The Woman Golfer's Catalogue.* New York: Stein & Day, 1st ed. 1980, 211p, illustrated, cloth, 27.5cm, foreword by Carol Mann.

51240. pbk. ed. 1980, 211p, illustrated, illustrated wrappers, 27.5cm.

Edwards, Leslie

51260. *A Short History of the Royal Liverpool Golf Club and of Championships Played Over the Links [1983 Walker Cup Edition].* Liverpool, England: Privately Printed, 1st ed. 1983, 40p, illustrated, decorative cloth, 21cm.

51270. *The Royal Liverpool Golf Club, 1869-1969; A Short History of the Club and of Championships Played over the Hoylake Links.* Liverpool, England: Privately Printed, 1st ed. 1969, 24p, decorative cloth, 18.5cm.

51280. *The West Lancashire Golf Club Centenary 1873-1973.* Liverpool, England: Privately Printed, 1st ed. 1973, 13p, illustrated, illustrated wrappers, 21cm.

Egan, John

51300. *Castlebar Golf Club 1910-1985.* Castlebar, Ireland: Privately Printed, 1st ed. 1985, 52p, illustrated, illustrated wrappers, 20.5cm.

El Caballero Country Club

51320. *El Cabellero Country Club, Silver Anniversary, 1957-1982.* Tarzana, California: Privately Printed, 1st ed. [1982] 22p, illustrated, decorative cloth, 28.5cm.

Eldred, Patricia

51340. *Kathy Whitworth.* Mankato, Minnesota: Creative Educational Society, 1st ed. [1975] 31p, illustrated, illustrated boards, 24cm.

Eldridge, Ashton G.

51360. *A History of the Huntington Country Club, 1910-1980.* Huntington, New York: Privately Printed, 1st ed. 1981, 170p, illustrated, decorative cloth, 23cm.

Elements of Golf Course Layout and Design

51380. *Elements of Golf Course Layout and Design.* London: Golf Development Council, 1st ed. [ca1968] 18p, illustrated, illustrated wrappers, 18.5cm.

Elliot, Charles

51400. *East Lake Country Club History, Home Course of Bobby Jones.* Atlanta, Georgia: Cherokee Publishing, 1st ed. 1984, 79p, illustrated, cloth, 27.5cm, foreword by Furman Bisher.

Elliot, Len and Barbara Kelly

51420. *Who's Who in Golf.* New Rochelle, New York: Arlington House, 1st ed. [1976] 208p, cloth, 23.5cm.

Ellis, Jr., Wes

51440. *All-Weather Golf.* Princeton, New Jersey: Van Nostrand, 1st ed. [1967] 108p, illustrated, cloth, 23cm. with George Sullivan, foreword by Tommy Bolt.

Ellroy, Jones

51460. *Brown's Requiem.* New York: Avon, 1st ed. [1981] 256p, illustrated wrappers, 17.5 cm.

Emery, David

51480. *The Ryder Cup '85.* London: Pelham, 1st ed. 1985, 160p, illustrated, cloth, 23.5cm, introduction by Tony Jacklin.

51490. *Who's Who In International Golf.* London: Sphere Books, 1st ed. 1983, 128p, illustrated, illustrated wrappers, 19.5cm.

51500. 1st American ed. New York: Facts On File [1983] 128p, illustrated, cloth, 19.5cm.

Emery, Fred

51520. *Colonel Bogey's Coloring Book for Golfers.* Washington, DC: Privately Printed, limited ed. [500 copies] [1981] [46p] illustrated by Tom Morris, illustrated wrappers, 21cm.

Erewash Valley Golf Club

51540. *The Erewash Valley Golf Club 75 Anniversary 1905-1980.* Stanton-by-Dale, England: Privately Printed, 1st ed. 1980, 67p, illustrated, cloth, 21.5cm.

Esquire Magazine

51560. *The Name of the Game Is Golf.* editors of Esquire Magazine. NP: Faultless Golf Balls, 1st ed. [ca1968] [16p] illustrated, illustrated wrappers, 14cm.

Eurogolf 1972

51580. *Eurogolf 1972.* London: Eurogolf, 1st ed. 1972, 251p, illustrated wrappers, 21cm. consultants; Henry Longhurst, Dai Rees, Peter Alliss, Dave Thomas. later printings.

Evans, Webster

51600. *Encyclopedia of Golf.* London: Robert Hale, 1st ed. 1971, 320p, illustrated, cloth, 22.5cm.

51610. 2d ed. rev. London: Robert Hale, 1974, 320p, illustrated, cloth, 22.5cm.

51620. 1st American ed. New York: St. Martin's Press, 1971, 320p, illustrated, cloth, 23cm.

51630. 2d American ed. rev. New York: St. Martins, 1974, 320p, illustrated, cloth, 22.5cm. later printing.

51640. *Rubs of the Green: Golf's Triumphs and Tragedies.* London: Pelham, 1st ed. 1969, 157p, illustrated, cloth, 21.5cm.

Exmoor Country Club

51660. *Exmoor Country Club Seventy-Fifth Anniversary, 1896-1971.* Highland Park, Illinois: Privately Printed, 1st ed. 1972, 60p, illustrated, illustrated wrappers, 28cm.

Fairlie, Jack

51680. *Chicagoland Golf Course Guide.* Park Ridge, Illinois: ASK, 1st ed. [1974] 70p, illustrated, illustrated wrappers, 23cm.

Fairways; a Detailed Graphic Description of all Los Angeles City and County-operated Golf Courses

51700. *Fairways; a Detailed Graphic Description of all Los Angeles City and County-operated Golf Courses.* [Los Angeles] Format Publications, 1st ed. [1967] 164p, illustrated, illustrated wrappers, 13.5cm.

Faldo, Nick

51720. *Enjoying Golf With Nick Faldo, A personal guide to the game.* London: St. Michael, 1st ed. [1985] 128p, illustrated, illustrated wrappers, 21.5cm.

51730. *The Rough with the Smooth: Breaking into Professional Golf.* London: Stanley Paul, 1st ed. 1980, 172p, illustrated, cloth, 21.5cm, with Mitchell Platts, foreword by Peter Oosterhuis.

Faulkner, Max

51750. *Golf-Right From the Start.* London: Newnes, 1st ed. 1965, 119p, illustrated by George Houghton, cloth, 18.5cm, foreword by George Houghton.

51760. *Play Championship Golf All Your Life.* London: Pelham, 1st ed. 1972, 135p, illustrated by Paul Trevillion, cloth, 21.5cm, with Tom Scott. later printing.

Fenton, Ronnie

51780. *The Easy Road to Good Golf.* Sugar Hill, New Hampshire: Harrison, 1st ed. [1962] 51p, illustrated, illustrated wrappers, 20cm.

Fernando, Pam and Sam J. Kadirgamar and Reggie Candappo

51800. *Royal Colombo Golf Club 100 Years 1879-1979.* Colombo, Sri Lanka: Privately Printed, 1st ed. 1979, 175p, illustrated, illustrated wrappers, 28cm.

Finegan, James W.

51820. *The Great Links of Ireland.* Plymouth Meeting, Pennsylvania: Weyerhauser Co. 1st ed. [ca1977] 24p, illustrated, illustrated wrappers, 28cm.

Finger, Joseph S.

51840. *The Business End of Building or Re-Building A Golf Course.* Houston, Texas: Privately Printed, 1st ed. [1972] 47p, illustrated, illustrated wrappers, 27.5cm.

Finsterwald, Dow

51860. *Fundamentals of Golf.* New York: Ronald Press, 1st ed. [1961] 145p, illustrated, cloth, 25cm, with Larry Robinson.

51870. *The Wedges, Pitching and Sand [Flipbook].* New York: Sterling, 1st ed. [1965] 128p, illustrated, illustrated wrappers, 12.5cm.

Fishman, Lew

51890. *Golf Magazine's Short Cuts to Better Golf.* New York: Harper & Row, 1st ed. [1979] 179p, illustrated by Dom Lupo & Lealand Gustavson, cloth, 23.5cm.

Flaherty, Thomas [Tom]

51910. *The Masters: The Story of Golf's Greatest Tournament.* New York: Holt, Rinehart & Winston, 1st ed. [1961] 150p, illustrated, cloth, 22.5cm, introduction by Arnold Palmer.

51920. *The U.S. Open [1985-1965]; The Complete Story of the United States Championship of Golf.* New York: Dutton, 1st ed. 1966, 224p, illustrated, cloth, 21cm.

Flick, Jim

51940. *Square-to-Square Golf in Pictures: An Illustrated Study of the Modern Swing Techniques.* Norwalk, Connecticut: Golf Digest, 1st ed. [1974] 125p, illustrated, cloth, 27.5cm, with Dick Aultman. later printings

Fogarty, Colleen

51960. *The Powelton Club, The First Hundred Years 1882-1982.* Newburgh, New York: Privately Printed, 1st ed. 1982, 92p, illustrated, illustrated wrappers, 23cm.

Foote, Edwin B.

51980. *Oakmont Country Club: The First Seventy-Years.* Oakmont, Pennsylvania: Privately Printed, 1st ed. 1980, 80p, illustrated, illustrated boards, 30cm.

Ford, Doug

52000. *The Wedge Book.* Norwalk, Connecticut: Golf Digest, 1st ed. [1963] 126p, illustrated by James McQueen, decorative cloth, 23cm, preface by Julius Boros. later printings.

52010. 1st UK ed. London: Nicholas Kaye, 1964, 126p, cloth, 22.5cm.

Forest Lake Club

52030. *Forest Lake Club From Its Beginning Through 1964.* Columbia, South Carolina: Privately Printed, 1st ed. 1965, 85p, illustrated, cloth, 21.5cm.

Forfar Golf Club

52050. *Forfar Golf Club 1871-1971.* Forfar, Scotland: Privately Printed, 1st ed. 1971, 36p, illustrated, wrappers, 16.5cm.

Forrester, Fred

52070. *The Guildford Golf Club, A Centenary 1886-1985.* Guildford, England: Privately Printed, 1st ed. 1985, 16p, illustrated, illustrated wrappers, 14.5cm.

Forse, Harry

52090. *The Seventy Second Hole.* Greenfield, Indiana: Mitchell-Fleming, 1st ed. [1976] 190p, cloth, 21.5cm.

Fort Wayne Country Club

52110. *Fort Wayne Country Club Diamond Jubilee 1908-1983.* Fort Wayne, Indiana: Privately Printed, 1st ed. 1983, 64p, illustrated, illustrated wrappers, 25.5cm.

Fossum, Bruce and Mary Dagraedt

52130. *Golf.* Boston: Allyn and Bacon, 1st ed. [1969] 90p, illustrated, illustrated wrappers, 21cm.

Foster, David

52150. *Thinking Golf.* London: Pelham, 1st ed. 1979, 187p, illustrated, cloth, 21.5cm, foreword by Henry Cotton.

Fox, William Price

52170. *Doctor Golf.* Philadelphia: Lippincott, 1st ed. [1963] 176p, illustrated by Charles Rodrigues, decorative cloth, 20.5cm.

52180. pbk. ed. Greenwich, Connecticut: Fawcett, 1964, 176p, illustrated, illustrated wrappers, 18cm.

Foxley, Gladys L.

52200. *A History of Bexley Heath Golf Club 1907-1977*. Bexley Heath, England: Privately Printed, 1st ed. 1977, 71p, illustrated, illustrated wrappers, 21.5cm.

Fraser, George and James Mearns

52220. *Royal Aberdeen Golf Club [Handbook]*. Aberdeen, Scotland: Mearns, [1968] 46p, illustrated, illustrated wrappers, 18cm.

Fraser, George MacDonald

52240. *McAuslan in the Rough*. New York: Knopf, 1st American ed. 1974, 209p, decorative cloth, 21cm. note: first edition not located.

Frazer, Sue R. and Harry B.

52260. *Overbrook Golf Club 1900 to 1975*. Bryn Mawr, Pennsylvania: Privately Printed, limited ed. [no limitation cited] [1977] 53p, illustrated, gilt stamped leather, 20.5cm.

Frazier, Bernard W.

52280. *Records and Statistics, Firestone Country Club*. Akron, Ohio: Firestone, 1st ed. 1975 [14p] wrappers, 21.5cm.

Frederick, Adrian

52300. *The 1984 South African PGA Golf Annual*. Johannesburg, South Africa: A Thomas Publication, 1st ed. 1984, 160p, illustrated, illustrated wrappers, 29.5cm.

Fredericks, Victor

52320. *For Golfers Only*. New York: Frederick Fell, 1st ed. [1964] 192p, illustrated, cloth, 21cm.

French, Adrian

52340. *World Senior Golf International Team Matches and World Senior Championships, A History*. Los Angeles: Privately Printed, 1st ed. 1977 [46p] illustrated, suede leather 3 ring binder, 28cm.

Frick, Ford

52360. *This is St. Andrews 1888-1973*. Hastings on Hudson, New York: Privately Printed, 1st ed. 1973 [16p] illustrated, wrappers, 21.5cm.

Friendly Fairways of Michigan

52380. *Friendly Fairways of Michigan; A directory of public, municipal and semi-private golf courses located within the state of Michigan*. Royal Oak, Michigan: Friendly Fairways of America, 1st ed. [1979] 235p, illustrated wrappers, 21.5cm.

Frothingham, John G.

52400. *The Country Club of New Canaan 1893-1968*. New Canaan, Connecticut: Privately Printed, 1st ed. 1968, 29p, illustrated, wrappers, 27.5cm.

Fukushima, Robert

52420. *Kagero Golf Club Fiftieth Anniversary 1925-1975*. Sacramento, California: Privately Printed, 1st ed. 1975 [16p] illustrated, illustrated wrappers, 28cm.

Fulkerson, Neal and John T. Thatcher

52440. *The Garden City Golf Club, Seventy Fifth-Anniversary, 1899-1974*. Garden City, New York: Privately Printed, limited ed. [1000 copies] 1974, 49p, illustrated, cloth, 30.5cm.

Furness Golf Club

52460. *Furness Golf Club, A Centenary Story 1872-1972*. Barrow-in-Furnace, England: Privately Printed, 1st ed. 1972, 48p, illustrated, decorative cloth, 21cm.

Gair, Jonothan

52480. *The Australian Masters, 1979-1982*. Melbourne, Australia: Australian Masters Golf Tournament, limited ed. [2000 copies] 1983, 64p, illustrated, cloth, 30.5cm.

Galin, Saul

52500. *Golf in Europe: A traveler's guide to 200 of Europe's best golf courses*. New York: Hawthorn, 1st ed. 1967, 281p, illtrated, cloth, 23.5cm.

Gallup, Don

52520. *Golf Courses of Colorado, A Guide to Public and Resort Courses*. Estes Park, Colorado: Colorado Leisure Sports, 1st ed. [1984] 320p, illustrated, illustrated wrappers, 21.5cm.

Gallwey, W. Timothy

52540. *The Inner Game of Golf*. New York: Random House, 1st ed. [1981] 207p, cloth, 23.5cm. later printings.

Galvano, Phil

52560. *Secrets of the Perfect Golf Swing*. Englewood Cliffs, New Jersey: Prentice-Hall, 1st ed. [1961] 176p, illustrated, decorative cloth, 21cm.

Gambatese, Joe

52580. *Golf Guide 1963*. New York: Snibbe, 1st ed. 1963, 91p, illustrated, illustrated wrappers, various, note: covers will vary in size and text as copies were produced for sales promotions thru 1979.

52590. *Pro Am Guide To Golf*. Maplewood, New Jersey: Hammond, 1st ed. [1981] 91p, illustrated, illustrated wrappers, 21cm.

Gammond, Peter

52610. *Bluff Your Way In Golf*. London: Bluffer's Guide, 1st ed. [1985] 64p, illustrated wrappers, 18cm.

Garrity, J.T.

52630. *Golfer's Guide to Florida Courses*. New York: Cornerstone Library, 1st ed. [1973] 191p, illustrated, illustrated wrappers, 20.5cm, foreword by William W. Amick.

Gates, John B.

52650. *Round Hill Club, 1972-1979*. Greenwich, Connecticut: Privately Printed, limited ed. [600 copies] 1979, 108p, illustrated, decorative cloth, 23cm.

52660. *The First Seventy-Five Years of the United States Seniors Golf Association 1905-1980*. editor. [New York] United States Seniors Golf Association, limited ed. [1500 copies] [1980] 144p, illustrated, decorative cloth, 23cm.

Gault, William C.

52680. *The Long Green.* New York: Dutton, 1st ed. [1965] 160p, cloth, 20cm.

Gedye, Michael

52700. *Golf in Portugal.* London: Fairgreen Publications, 1st ed. [ca1975] [13p] illustrated, illustrated wrappers, 18cm.

52710. *Golf in the Sun 1974-75.* London: Fairgreen Publications, 1st ed. [1975] 192p, illustrated, illustrated wrappers, 17.5 cm, with comments by Peter Alliss.

52720. *Holiday Golf in Spain & Portugal.* London: Fairgreen, 1st ed. 1970, 126p, illustrated wrappers, 18cm.

Geiberger, Al

52740. *Tempo: Golf's Master Key.* Norwalk, Connecticut: Golf Digest, 1st ed. [1980] 160p, illustrated, cloth, 25.5cm, with Larry Dennis.

Gerzin, Walt

52760. *Eclectic Golf: Featuring the AWH Takeaway.* Wayzata, Minnesota: Ralph Turtinem, 1st ed. [1976] 72p, illustrated, illustrated wrappers, 21.5cm.

Gibbins, James

52780. *Sudden Death.* London: Collins, 1st ed. 1983, 210p, cloth, 19.5cm.

Gibson, Nevin H.

52800. *A Pictorial History of Golf.* New York: A.S. Barnes, 1st ed. [1968] 237p, illustrated, cloth, 28cm.

52810. 2d ed. rev. 1974, 282p, illustrated, cloth, 27.5cm.

52820. *Great Moments in Golf.* South Brunswick & New York: A.S. Barnes, 1st ed. [1973] 193p, illustrated, cloth, 25cm.

Gibson, Nevin H. and Tom Kouzmenoff

52840. *Golf's Greatest Shots by the World's Greatest Golfers.* Great Neck, New York: Todd & Honeywell, 1st ed. 1981, 176p, illustrated, cloth, 22.5cm.

Gibson, W.H.

52860. *Curragh Golf Club Centenary 1883-1983*. Curragh, Ireland: Privately Printed, 1st ed. 1983, 27p, illustrated, wrappers, 21cm.

Gilchrist, Reg

52880. *The Knott End Story, History of A Golf Club*. Preston, England: Lakeland, 1st ed. [1983] 120p, illustrated, illustrated wrappers, 20.5cm.

Gillen, Donald J.

52900. *The History of Wolferts Roost Country Club*. Albany, New York: Privately Printed, 1st ed. 1985, 36p, illustrated, illustrated wrappers, 21.5cm.

Giller, Norman

52920. *The Book of Golf Lists*. edited by. London: Sidgwick & Jackson, 1st ed. 1985, 187p, illustrated, illustrated wrappers, 21.5cm.

Gleason, Dan

52940. *The Great, The Grand and the Also-Ran: Rabbits and Champions on the Pro Golf Tour*. New York: Random House, 1st ed. [1976] 238p, cloth, 21cm.

Gleason, Jr. John F.

52960. *A Brief History of the Shaker Heights Country Club*. Cleveland, Ohio: Privately Printed, 1st ed. [ca1978] 10p, wrappers, 18cm.

Glenn, Peter

53000. *The Golfer's Guidebook: A Guide to the PGA Winter-Spring Tour*. New York: Peter Glenn, 1st ed. 1965, 93p, illustrated wrappers, 20.5cm.

Goates, Ray

53020. *Los Angeles City Bicentennial Honor of Golf Champions*. Los Angeles: Los Angeles 200 Committee, 1st ed. 1981 [14p] illustrated, illustrated wrappers, 28cm.

Godlington, Doug

53040. *The Un-Golfer*. Ottowa: Ottowa Sports Publishing, 1st ed. [ca1974] [100p] illustrated, illustrated wrappers, 18cm.

Golf

53060. *Golf.* London: Training and Education Associates, 1st ed. 1973, 48p, illustrated, wrappers, 21cm.

53070. 2d ed. 1974, 48p, illustrated, cloth, 21cm.

Golf

53090. *Golf.* St. Peters, Australia: Gregory's, 1st ed. 1983, 85p, illustrated, illustrated wrappers, 25cm, later printings.

Golf & Club Magazine

53110. *Great Golf Cartoons from Golf & Club Magazine.* Santa Monica, California: Werner, 1st ed. [1971] 66p, illustrated, illustrated wrappers, 27.5cm.

Golf Canada

53130. *Golf Canada.* Ottowa: Canadian Government Office of Tourism [ca1984] 84p, wrappers, 23cm, introduction by Gary Gowan.

Golf Course Superintendents Association of America

53150. *History of the Northern Ohio Chapter of the Golf Course Superintendents Association of America 1923-1976.* [Cleveland, Ohio] Privately Printed, 1st ed. 1976, 12p, illustrated, illustrated wrappers, 28cm.

Golf Courses California and Nevada

53170. *Golf Courses California and Nevada.* [Los Angeles] Automobile Club of Southern California [1970] 105p, illustrated, illustrated wrappers, 21.5cm.

Golf Courses in New York State

53190. *Golf Courses in New York State.* Albany, New York: NY State Department of Commerce, 1st ed. [ca1968] [8p] illustrated, illustrated wrappers, 21cm.

Golf Courses of Victoria

53210. *Golf Courses of Victoria, A Listing of over 300 golf courses in the State of Victoria, Australia.* Victoria, Australia: Victorian Government Travel Center [ca1980] 40p, illustrated, illustrated wrappers, 27.5 cm.

Golf Digest Magazine

53230. *15 Point Annual Check-Up*. Norwalk, Connecticut: Golf Digest, 1st ed. [1983] [32p] illustrated, illustrated wrappers, 14cm.

53240. *80 5-Minute Golf Lessons: from the world's greatest teaching professionals*. Norwalk, Connecticut: Golf Digest, 1st ed. [1968] 159p, illustrated, cloth, 24cm, introduction by Richard Aultman.

53250. 1st UK ed. London: Pelham, 1969, 159p, illustrated, cloth, 22cm.

53260. *All About Putting*. New York: Golf Digest/Coward McCann & Geoghegan, 1st ed. [1973] 191p, illustrated by Dick Kohfield, cloth, 22.5cm.

53270. 1st UK ed. London: Kaye & Ward, 1973, 191p, cloth, 22.5cm.

53280. *Arnold Palmer*. New York: Grosset & Dunlap, 1st ed. [1967] 159p, illustrated, illustrated boards, 19cm. editors of Golf Digest.

53290. pbk. ed. 1968, 159p, illustrated, illustrated wrappers, 18cm.

53300. *Better Golf for Boys*. New York: Dodd, Mead, 1st ed. [1965] 62p, illustrated, cloth, 18cm. editors of Golf Digest.

53310. 1st UK ed. London: Kaye, 1966, 93p, illustrated, cloth, 21.5cm. introduction by Brian Huggett.

53320. *Better Golf*. London: Kaye, 2d UK ed. 1974, 93p, illustrated, cloth, 21.5cm. note: previously titled "Better Golf For Boys."

53330. *Gene Littler Presents 38 Checkpoints To Improve Your Swing*. Evanston, Illinois: Golf Digest, 1st ed. [ca1962] [16p] illustrated, illustrated wrappers, 8cm. editors of Golf Digest.

53340. *Golf: A Golden Pocket Guide*. New York: Western Publishing, 1st ed. [1968] 28p, illustrated by James J. Hulley, illustrated boards, 16.5cm, editors of Golf Digest.

53350. *Golf Digest's 20 Ways To Hit It Farther*. Norwalk, Connecticut: Golf Digest, 1st ed. [1982] [44p] illustrated by Anthony Ravielli, illustrated wrappers, 21.5cm. editors of Golf Digest with Dick Aultman.

53360. *Golf Digest's Pocket Golf Tips*. Norwalk, Connecticut: Golf Digest, 1st ed. [1977] 23p, illustrated, wrappers, 14cm. later printings.

53370. *How to Break 90 At Golf*. Greenwich, Connecticut: Fawcett, 1st ed. [196] 112p, illustrated, illustrated wrappers, 23.5cm. editors of Golf Digest.

53380. *Instant Golf Lessons*. Norwalk, Connecticut: Golf Digest, 1st ed. [1978] 255p, illustrated by Elmer Wexler & Stan Drake, illustrated wrappers, 20.5cm. later printings.

53390. *Rand McNally Golf Course Guide*. Chicago: Rand McNally, 1st ed. [1966] 200p, illustrated, illustrated wrappers, 28cm. Golf Digest editors.

53400. *The Art of Putting*. Norwalk, Connecticut: Golf Digest [1976] [28p] illustrated, illustrated wrappers, 14cm.

53410. *The Best of Golf Digest: The First 25 Years*. Norwalk, Connecticut: Golf Digest, 1st ed. [1975] 224p, illustrated, cloth, 28cm, foreword by William H. Davis.

53415. *The Golf Digest Almanac*. edited by John P. May. Norwalk, Connecticut: Golf Digest, 1st ed. [1984] 771p, illustrated, cloth, 21cm.

53420. *The Golf Digest Almanac 1985*. edited by John P. May. Norwalk, Connecticut: Golf Digest, 2d ed. [1985] 893p, illustrated, illustrated wrappers, 21cm.

53450. *Three Pillars of Power*. Norwalk, Connecticut: Golf Digest, 1st ed. [1965] [28p] illustrated, illustrated wrappers, 22cm.

53460. *Tips From the Tour*. Norwalk, Connecticut: Golf Digest, 1st ed. [1985] [28p] illustrated, illustrated wrappers, 14cm.

53470. *Travelers Guide to Golf*. Norwalk, Connecticut: Golf Digest, 1st ed. [1976] 192p, illustrated, illustrated wrappers, 27.5cm, introduction by Jack Nicklaus.

Golf Fitness Instruction Course

53480. *Golf Fitness Instruction Course*. Compton, California: Diversified Products, 1st ed. [1984] 48p, illustrated, illustrated wrappers, 23cm.

Golf Foundation

53500. *Making Room for Golf.* [London] Golf Foundation, 1st ed. [1963] 52p, illustrated, cloth, 28cm.

Golf Guidebook

53520. *Golf Guidebook.* New York: Maco Magazine, 1st ed. [1965] 128p, illustrated, illustrated wrappers, 23.5cm.

Golf in Scandinavia

53540. *Golf in Scandinavia.* NP: Scandinavia Airlines [ca1972] [16p] illustrated, illustrated wrappers, 21.5cm.

Golf in Spain

53560. *Golf in Spain.* [Spain] Ministerio De Informacion Y Turismo, 1971 [48p] illustrated, illustrated wrappers, 22cm. later printing.

Golf in the Sun

53580. *Golf in the Sun.* London: British European Airways/English Digest, 1st ed. 1963, 96p, illustrated illustrated wrappers, 18.5cm, foreword by Pat Ward-Thomas. note: see also Michael Gedye, "Golf in the Sun."

53590. 2d ed. 1965, 112p, illustrated, illustrated wrappers, 18.5cm, foreword by Peter Alliss.

53600. 3d ed. 1971, 122p, illustrated, illustrated wrappers, 18.5cm, foreword by Peter Alliss.

Golf It Up

53620. *Golf It Up! Golf Tips for Juniors.* Palm Beach Gardens, Florida: PGA Junior Golf Foundation [ca1983] 15p, illustrated, illustrated wrappers, 21.5cm.

Golf Magazine

53640. *America's Golf Book.* New York: Scribner's, 1st ed. [1970] 291p, illustrated, decorative cloth, 22.5cm.

53650. *Georgia Guide To Golf.* Atlanta, Georgia: Georgia Department of Industry & Trade [ca1970] [14p] illustrated, illustrated wrappers, 23cm. by editors of Golf Magazine.

53660. *Golf Magazine's Handbook of Putting.* New York: Harper & Row, 1st ed. [1973] 191p, illustrated, cloth, 23.5cm.

53670. 1st UK ed. London: Pelham, 1st UK ed. 1975, 191p, illustrated, cloth, 22cm.

53680. *Golf Magazine's Pro Pointers and Stroke Savers.* New York: Award Books, 1964, 250p, illustrated by Lealand Gustavson & John Gallagher, illustrated wrappers, 18cm, instruction editors; Jimmy Demaret, Gene Sarazen, Louise Suggs.

53690. *Golf Magazine's Tips from the Teaching Pros.* New York: Harper & Row, 1st ed. [1969] 228p, illustrated by Dom Lupo & Lealand Gustavson, cloth, 23.5cm.

53700. *Golf Magazine's Winning Pointers from the Pros.* New York: Harper & Row, 1st ed. [1965] 274p, illustrated by Lealand Gustavson & Dom Lupo, cloth, 23.5cm, instruction editors Gene Sarazen, Peggy Kirk Bell.

53710. pbk. ed. New York: Award Books [1965] 302p, illustrated by Lealand Gustavson & Dom Lupo, illustrated wrappers, 18cm.

53720. *Golf Magazine's: Your Long Game.* New York: Harper & Row, 1st ed. [1964] 188p, illustrated by Lealand Gustavson, cloth, 23.5cm, instruction editors; Jimmy Demaret, Gene Sarazen, Peggy Kirk Bell, introduction by Gene Sarazen.

53730. pbk. ed. New York: Award Books, 1968, 188p, illustrated by Lealand Gustavson, illustrated wrappers, 17.5cm.

53740. *Golf Magazine's: Your Short Game.* New York: Harper & Row, 1st ed. [1962] 203p, illustrated by Lealand Gustavson & Joe Farris, cloth, 23.5cm, instruction editors; Jimmy Demaret, Gene Sarazen, Louise Suggs, foreword by Bobby Jones.

53750. pbk. ed. New York: Award Books, 1968, 203p, illustrated, illustrated wrappers, 17.5cm.

53760. *Kwik Pro.* editors of Golf Magazine. Glen Falls, New York: Glen Falls Insurance, 1st ed. [ca1963] 23p, illustrated, illustrated wrappers, 11cm.

53770. *The Greenbriar's Sam Snead Teaches Golf.* Akron, Ohio: Firestone Tire & Rubber, 1st ed. 1966, 23p, illustrated, illustrated wrappers, 18cm. by editors of Golf Magazine.

Golf Monthly Magazine

53790. *That's Golf: from facts and incidents in the Golfer's Handbook.* Glasgow: Munro-Barr, 1st ed. [ca1979] 40p, illustrated by Peter Davidson, illustrated wrappers, 20cm.

Golf Par Excellence 1980

53810. *Golf Par Excellence 1980.* Edenbridge, England: Cripplegate, 1st ed. 1980, 160p, illustrated, illustrated wrappers, 30cm.

Golf Quotes

53830. *Golf Quotes.* Lombard, Illinois: Greatest Quotations [1984] 75p, illustrated, spiral bound wrappers, 14.5cm.

Golf Slang

53850. *Golf Slang.* [Los Angeles] CC of California, 1978, 23p, wrappers, 21.5cm.

Golf: Where to Play and Where to Stay

53870. *Golf: Where to Play and Where to Stay.* Cheshire, England: McMillan Martin [ca1983] 200p, illustrated, illustrated wrappers, 21cm, foreword by Neil Coles.

Golf World Magazine [UK]

53890. *The Piccadilly World of Golf 1972.* London: Wayland, 1st ed. 1972, 220p, illustrated, cloth, 15.5cm.

53900. *The Piccadilly World of Golf 1973-1974.* London: Wayland, 2d ed. 1973, 224p, illustrated, cloth, 25.5cm.

Golf World Magazine [U.S.]

53920. *The World of Golf 1973.* Southern Pines, North Carolina: Golf World Magazine, 1st ed. 1973, 160p, illustrated, cloth, 27.5cm.

53930. *The World of Golf 1974.* 2d ed. 1974, 160p, illustrated, cloth, 27.5cm.

53940. *The World of Golf 1975.* 3d ed. 1975, 160p, illustrated, cloth, 27.5cm.

53950. *The World of Golf 1976.* 4th ed. 1976, 164p, illustrated, cloth, 27.5cm.

53960. *Turf Mirth Compiled from the Pages of Golf World.* [Southern Pines, North Carolina] Golf World, 1st ed. [ca1962] [60p] illustrated, illustrated wrappers, 23cm.

Golfers Guide To The Counties of Kent, Surrey, Sussex

53980. *Golfers Guide To The Counties of Kent, Surrey, Sussex.* Brighton, England: Golf World [1967] 143p, illustrated, illustrated wrappers, 21cm.

Golfer's Digest

54000. *Golfer's Digest, Volume I.* edited by Lawrence Robinson and James Graham. Chicago: Golfer's Digest Association, 1st ed. [1966] 320p, illustrated, illustrated wrappers, 28cm.

54010. *Golfer's Digest, Volume II.* edited by John May. Chicago: Follett, 2d ed. [1967] 320p, illustrated, illustrated wrappers, 28cm.

54020. *Golfer's Digest, Volume III.* edited by Tom Michael. Chicago: Follett, 3d ed. [1968] 320p, illustrated, illustrated wrappers, 28cm.

54030. *Golfer's Digest, Volume IV.* edited by John May. Northfield, Illinois: Gun Digest, 4th ed. 1970] 320p, illustrated, illustrated wrappers, 28cm.

54040. *Golfer's Digest, Volume V.* edited by Earl Puckett. Chicago: Digest Books, 5th ed. [1972] 320p, illustrated, illustrated wrappers, 28cm.

54050. *Golfer's Digest, Volume VI.* edited by Earl Puckett. Northfield, Illinois: Digest Books, 6th ed. [1974] 320p, illustrated, illustrated wrappers, 28cm.

54060. *Golfer's Digest, Volume VII.* edited by Earl Puckett and Robert Cromie. Chicago: Follett, 7th ed. [1976] 288p, illustrated, illustrated wrappers, 28cm.

Golfer's Trilogy

54080. *The Golfer's Trilogy: The Driver Book; The Putter Book; The Wedge Book.* by Sam Snead, Bob Rosburg, Doug Ford. New York: Cornerstone Library, 1965, 160p; 159p; 160p, illustrated by James McQueen, illustrated wrappers, 20cm, boxed, or individual copies, prefaces by Julius Boros, Billy Casper, Jr., Byron Nelson.

Golfers' Guide To Georgia

54100. *Golfers' Guide To Georgia 1980.* Atlanta, Georgia: 72 Inc, 1980, 45p, illustrated, illustrated wrappers, 27.5cm.

Goodban, J.W.D.

54120. *History of the English Golf Union 1924-1984*. Wokingham, England: Privately Printed, 1st ed. 1984, 55p, illustrated, illustrated wrappers, 21cm.

54130. *Royal North Devon Golf Club, A Centenary Anthology, 1864-1964*. Bideford, England: Privately Printed, 1st ed. 1964, 96p, illustrated, decorative cloth, 26.5cm, foreword by P.A. Ward-Thomas.

Goodman, Edward D.

54150. *Meadowbrook Country Club, A Descriptive History from Its Beginnings in 1957 thru 1984*. Richmond, Virginia: Privately Printed, 1st ed. 1984, 48p, illustrated, illustrated wrappers, 23cm.

Goodner, Ross

54170. *Golf's Greatest: The Legendary World Golf Hall of Famers*. Norwalk, Connecticut: Golf Digest, 1st ed. [1978] 240p, illustrated, cloth, 25cm, foreword by Don Collett.

54180. *The 75 Year History of Shinnecock Hills Golf Club*. Southampton, New York: Privately Printed, limited ed. [500 copies] [1966] 44p, illustrated, decorative cloth, 23cm.

Gordin, Richard D. and Roderick W. Myers

54200. *Golf Fundamentals*. Columbus, Ohio: Charles E. Merrill, 1st ed. [1973] 73p, illustrated, illustrated wrappers, 21cm.

Gordon, Bob

54220. *Basic Golf*. Waltham, Massachusetts: American Publishing, 1st ed. [1972] 96p, illustrated, illustrated wrappers, 22.5cm. later printings.

Gottlieb, Bea

54240. *I Have The Secret of Putting*. New York: Privately Printed, 1st ed. [ca1965] 12p, illustrated wrappers, 20.5cm.

Graff, Stan

54260. *So You Want to Play Golf: The Golf Swing Explained Simply & Logically*. Hilton Head, South Carolina: Privately Printed, 1st ed. [1974] 69p, illustrated, illustrated wrappers, 22.5cm.

Graffis, Herb

54280. *Esquire's World of Golf: What Every Golfer Must Know.* New York: Esquire/Trident Press, 1st ed. [1965] 240p, illustrated by Lealand Gustavson, decorative cloth, 23.5cm, foreword by Tommy Armour and Sam Snead.

54290. 1st UK ed. London: Frederick Muller, 1966, 269p, cloth, 22.5cm.

54300. pbk. ed. New York: Pocket Books, 1967, 240p, illustrated wrappers, 18cm.

54310. *The PGA: The Official History of the Professional Golfers' Association of America.* New York: Crowell, 1st ed. [1975] 559p, illustrated, cloth, 25cm.

54320. *TWA and Your Golf Professional Want You to Have this In-Flight Golf Lesson.* Chicago: TWA, 1st ed. [1971] [8p] illustrated, illustrated wrappers, 21.5cm.

Graham, A.S.

54340. *Graham's Golf Club.* London: Stanley Paul, 1st ed. 1965, 124p, illustrated, cloth, 21cm, foreword by Henry Longhurst

Graham, David

54360. *Your Way to Winning Golf.* Trumbull, Connecticut: Golf Digest, 1st ed. 1985, 190p, illustrated by Bob Giuliani, cloth, 25cm, with Larry Dennis, introduction by Jack Nicklaus.

Graham, Ian R.

54380. *The Merchants of Edinburgh Golf Club 1907-1982.* Edinburgh, Scotland: Privately Printed, limited ed. [10 copies] 1982 [118p] illustrated, leather, 29cm.

Graham, Lou

54400. *Mastering Golf.* Chicago: Contemporary, 1st ed. [1978] 106p, illustrated, cloth, 28cm, with John Bibb.

54410. pbk. ed. [1978] 106p, illustrated, illustrated wrappers, 28cm.

Grant, Donald

54430. *Donald Ross of Pinehurst and Royal Dornoch.* Dornoch, Scotland: Privately Printed, 1st ed. [1973] 40p, illustrated, illustrated wrappers, 21cm, introduction by Frank Moran.

54440. *Personal Memories of Royal Dornoch Golf Club 1900-1925*. Dornoch, Scotland: Privately Printed, 1st ed. [ca1978] 48p, illustrated, illustrated wrappers, 20.5cm, foreword by Herbert Warren Wind, a recollection by Roger Wethered.

54450. 2d ed. rev. 1985, 48p, illustrated, illustrated wrappers, 21cm. foreword by Tom Watson.

Graves, Robert Muir

54470. *A Practice Golf Facility for Athletic Fields*. San Francisco: Privately Printed, 1st ed. 1961 [10p] illustrated, wrappers, 28cm.

Gray, Harry J.

54490. *Last Blast At Wethersfield*. [Hartford, Connecticut] United Technologies, 1st ed. [1983] [92p] illustrated, cloth, 22 cm.

Green, Michael

54510. *The Art of Coarse Golf*. London: Hutchinson, 1st ed. 1967, 126p, illustrated, cloth, 21cm. later printing.

54520. pbk. ed. London: Arrow, 1971, 126p, illustrated wrappers, 18.5cm.

Greenhaw, Wayne

54540. *The Golfer*. Philadelphia: Lippincott, 1st ed. [1967] 219p, cloth, 20cm.

Gregson, Jim

54560. *Golf Rules O.K.* London: Adam & Charles Black, 1st ed. 1984, 63p, illustrated, illustrated wrappers, 21cm.

Gregson, Malcom

54580. *Golf with Gregson*. London: Stanley Paul, 1st ed. 1968, 127p, illustrated, cloth, 21cm.

Gregston, Gene

54600. *Hogan: The Man Who Played for Glory*. Englewood Cliffs, New Jersey: Prentice-Hall, 1st ed. [1978] 192p, illustrated, cloth, 23cm.

Gren

54620. *The Duffer's Guide to Golf; A Second Slice*. London: Columbus Books, 1st ed. 1984, 80p, illustrated, illustrated wrappers, 13.5cm.

Gresswell, Peter

54640. *Weekend Golfer*. London: John Murray, 1st ed. [1977] 192p, illustrated by Gina, cloth, 21.5cm.

Grimsley, Will

54660. *Golf: Its History, People and Events*. Englewood Cliffs, New Jersey: Prentice-Hall, 1st ed. [1966] 331p, illustrated, cloth, 28cm, special section by Robert Trent Jones, foreword by Robert Tyre Jones, Jr. later printing.

Grode, James P.

54680. *The Full Gospel Golfer As Revealed by the Holy Spirit*. Clearwater, Florida: Privately Printed, 1st ed. [ca1983] [42p] illustrated, illustrated wrappers, 21.5cm.

Grout, Jack

54700. *Jack Grout's Golf Clinic*. North Palm Beach, Florida: Athletic Institute, 1st ed. [1985] 194p, illustrated, illustrated wrappers, 25.5cm. introduction by Jack Nicklaus.

54710. *Let Me Teach You Golf As I Taught Jack Nicklaus*. New York: Atheneum, 1st ed. 1975, 164p, illustrated by Jim McQueen, cloth, 26cm, with Dick Aultman, foreword by Jack Nicklaus.

54720. 1st UK ed. London: Cassell, 1977, 164p, cloth, 26cm.

Guaranteed Golf Lesson

54740. *The Guaranteed Golf Lesson*. [New York] Golf Research Institute, 1st ed. [1968] 62p, illustrated, illustrated wrappers, 28cm.

54750. 2d ed. rev. [1974] 63p, illustrated, illustrated wrappers, 28cm.

54760. 3d ed. rev. New York: Allen Advertising [1975] 80p, illustrated, illustrated wrappers, 28cm.

Guide to Golf Courses in the U.K.

54780. *Guide to Golf Courses in the U.K.* [London] IPC Business Press, 1st ed. 1973, 274p, wrappers, 20.5cm.

Guiney, David

54800. *The Dunlop Book of Golf*. Lavenham, England: Eastland Press, 1st ed. 1973, 212p, illustrated by George Houghton, cloth, 21.5cm.

54810. 1st Irish ed. Dublin, Ireland: Irish Dunlop, 1973, 212p, illustrated by George Houghton, illustrated wrappers, 18.5cm.

Gullick, Bill

54830. *The Country Club Caper.* Garden City, New York: Doubleday, 1st ed. 1971, 234p, cloth, 20.5cm.

Gunn, Harry E. [Dr]

54850. *How to Play Golf with Your Wife and Survive.* Matteson, Illinois: Greatlakes Living Press, 1st ed. [1976] 184p, illustrated by Dick Drew, illustrated wrappers, 21.5cm.

Haber, James

54870. *Golf Made Easy: How to Achieve A Consistently Effective Golf Swing.* New York: Scribner's [1974] 154p, illustrated by Carol Slade, illustrated wrappers, 20.5cm.

54880. *Mastering the Art of Winning Golf.* Toronto: Pagurian Press, 1st ed. [1976] 192p, illustrated, cloth, 22.5cm.

54890. pbk. ed. Toronto: Pagurian Press [1976] 192p, illustrated, illustrated wrappers, 22.5cm.

Hackett, Buddy

54910. *The Truth About Golf and Other Lies.* Garden City, New York: Doubleday, 1st ed. [1968] 124p, illustrated by Gahan Wilson, decorative cloth, 19.5cm.

Hackey, Bob

54930. *Golf Annual '74: World Golf Hall of Fame Edition.* edited by. Pinehurst, North Carolina: Diamonhead, 1st ed. [1974] 373p, illustrated, illustrated wrappers, 28cm.

Hahn, James & Lynn

54950. *Nancy Lopez, Golfing Pioneer.* St. Paul, Minnesota: EMC, 1st ed. [1979] 38p, illustrated, illustrated boards, 23cm.

54960. *Patty! The Sports Career of Patricia Berg.* Mankato, Minnesota: Crestwood House, 1st ed. [1981] 47p, illustrated, illustrated boards, 21.5cm. edited by Dr. Howard Schroeder.

Hahn, Paul

54980. *From the Pen and Camera of Paul Hahn.* Southern Pines, North Carolina: Golf World Magazine, 1st ed. [ca1965] [32p] illustrated, illustrated wrappers, 21.5cm.

54990. *Paul Hahn Shows You How to Play Trouble Shots.* New York: David McKay, 1st ed. [1965] 110p, illustrated by Lealand Gustavson, decorative cloth, 23.5cm, introduction by Arnold Palmer.

Hahn, Jr., Paul

55010. *No Trick To It.* Boca Raton, Florida: Privately Printed, 1st ed. [1975] 39p, illustrated, illustrated wrappers, 20cm.

Haliburton, Thomas

55030. *Rabbit into Tiger.* London: Heinemann, 1st ed. 1964, 168p, illustrated, cloth, 21cm.

Halifax Golf and Country Club

55050. *Programme Commemorating the Official Opening of the New Course, Halifax Golf and Country Club.* Kinsac Lake, Canada: Privately Printed, 1st ed. 1970 [14p] illustrated, illustrated wrappers, 21.5cm.

Hall, Joan H.

55070. *The Victoria Club 1903-1978.* Riverside, California: Privately Printed, 1st ed. 1978, 66p, illustrated, illustrated wrappers, 21cm.

Hamilton, David

55090. *Early Aberdeen Golf: Golfing Small-talk in 1636.* Glasgow & Oxford: Partick Press, limited ed. signed [450 copies] 1985, 32p, illustrated by Lady Felicity Fisher, decorative cloth, 21cm. with the assistance of Father Howard Docherty, Samuel Cooper, William S. Watt and Rev J.H. Hamilton. note: a few presentation copies were issued.

55100. *Early Golf in Glasgow 1589-1787.* Oxford: Partick Press, limited ed. signed [250 copies] 1985, 21p, illustrated by Hazell Campbell & Lady Felicity Fisher, decorative cloth, 23.5cm. note: a few presentation copies were issued.

55110. *The Good Golf Guide to Scotland.* Edinburgh: Canongate, 1st ed. 1982, 168p, illustrated by Harry Horse, illustrated wrappers, 19.5cm. foreword by Sean Connery.

Hamilton, Rory

55130. *A Golfer's Guide to Wee Places: Luffness, Gullane, Muirfield.* Hawick, Scotland: Hawick News, 1st ed. 1980, 12p, illustrated, illustrated wrappers, 22cm.

Handy, Ike S.

55150. *How to Hit A Golf Ball Straight.* San Francisco: Cameron, 1st ed. [1967] 144p, illustrated, illustrated boards, 22.5cm. introduction by R.W. Cameron.

Hannan, Chris

55170. *Outlands Golf Club Golden Anniversary 1931-1981.* Dundas, Australia: Privately Printed, 1st ed. 1981 [48p] illustrated, wrappers, 21.5cm.

Hannay, Sebastian [pseud for Mary Louise Wyatt]

55190. *All Square: A Light Hearted Rhyming Guide to the Rules of Golf and Other Verses.* Bognor Regis, England: Privately Printed, 1st ed. [ca1980] [42p] illustrated, illustrated wrappers, 21cm.

Harbottle, George

55210. *The Northumberland Golf Club Story, A Historical Account of the First 80 Years of the Life of the Club.* Newcastle-upon-Tyne, England: Privately Printed, 1st ed. 1978, 108p, illustrated, cloth, 21cm.

Hardcastle, Michael

55230. *Aim for the Flag.* Chicago: Follett, 1st American ed. 1969, 192p, decorative cloth and library binding, 22cm. note: first edition not located.

Hardy, Merrill D. and Eleanor A. Walsh

55250. *Golf.* Santa Monica, California: Goodyear, 1st ed. [1980] 112p, illustrated, illustrated wrappers, 21cm. edited by J. Tillman Hall

Harker, J.R.

55270. *The Finchley Golf Club, A Brief History from It's Foundation in 1929.* Finchley, England: Privately Printed, 1st ed. 1981 [16p] illustrated, illustrated wrappers, 21.5cm.

Harney, Paul

55290. *Golf Is A Simple Game.* [USA] Minute Man Companies, 1st ed. [1972] [12p] illustrated, illustrated wrappers, 16.5cm.

55300. *How to Putt. A Flip Vision Golf Manual.* New York: Sterling, 1st ed. [1965] 128p, illustrated, illustrated wrappers, 12.5cm.

Harriman, Edward

55320. *The Story of Eastward Ho.* Chatham, Massachusetts: Privately Printed, 1st ed. 1978 [8p] illustrated wrappers, 19cm.

Harris, Richard

55340. *Drive For Show Putt for Dough [Part I]. How to Take the Fun out of Golf [Part II].* Chicago: Peacock Press 1st ed. [1972] 80p, illustrated, illustrated wrappers, 27.5cm.

55350. *How to Take the Fun Out of Golf.* LaJolla, California: Harris & Associates, 1st ed. [1970] 64p, illustrated by Wiley Smith, illustrated boards, 18cm. foreword by Bob Lunn.

Hart, Al

55370. *Golfun: A humorous Approach to A Serious Subject.* Arlington, Virginia: H&A Printing, 1st ed. 1966 [90p] illustrated by Joe Holder, illustrated wrappers, 21.5cm.

Hart-Thomast, Ken

55390. *Minehead and West Somerset Golf Club 1882-1982.* Minehead, England: Privately Printed, 1st ed. 1982, 40p, illustrated, illustrated wrappers, 24cm.

Hartley, George

55410. *A History of St. George's Hill Golf Club 1913-1983.* Weybridge, England: Privately Printed, 1st ed. 1983, 90p, illustrated, decorative cloth, 25cm.

Harvey, John C.

55430. *The Golfer's Repair and Maintenance Handbook.* Chicago: Contemporary, 1st ed. [1984] 126p, illustrated, illustrated wrappers, 23cm.

Hasegawa, Sam

55450. *Johnny Miller.* Mankato, Minnesota: Creative Education, 1st ed. [1975] 31p, illustrated by Fred Dingler, illustrated boards, 24cm.

Haslam, Peter

55470. *The World of Scottish Golf.* edited by. London: Golf World [1985] 82p, illustrated, illustrated wrappers, 27.5cm.

Hawkes, Ken

55490. *BBC Book of Golf.* edited by. by Peter Alliss, Harry Carpenter, Henry Longhurst, Mark McCormack, Tom Scott. London: British Broadcasting, 1st ed. 1975, 144p, illustrated, illustrated wrappers, 23.5cm.

Hawkins, Rodney

55510. *Golf At Letchworth.* Letchworth, England: Privately Printed, 1st ed. [1985] 168p, illustrated, cloth, 24cm.

Hawtree, F.W.

55530. *The Golf Course: Planning, Design, Construction & Maintenance.* London: E. & F.N. Spon, 1st ed. 1983, 212p, illustrated, illustrated boards, 15cm. foreword by Henry Cotton.

55540. 1st American ed. New York: E. & F.N. Spon, 1983, 212p, illustrated, illustrated boards, 15cm. foreword by Henry Cotton.

Hay, Alex

55560. *Skills & Tactics of Golf.* New York: Arco, 1st ed. [1980] 151p, illustrated, cloth, 22cm.

55570. *The Golf Manual.* London: Faber & Faber, 1st ed. [1980] 173p, illustrated, cloth, 27.5cm. foreword by Michael Bonallack.

55580. *The Handbook of Golf.* London: Pelham, 1st ed. 1984, 252p, illustrated, cloth, 23.5cm. foreword by Peter Alliss

55590. *The Mechanics of Golf.* London: Robert Hale, 1st ed. 1979, 136p, illustrated, cloth, 23cm.

55600. 1st American ed. New York: St. Martins Press, 1979, 136p, illustrated, cloth, 23cm.

Hay, Alex and Bill Robertson

55620. *Young Golfer.* London: Angus & Robertson, 1st ed. [1980] 96p, illustrated, illustrated boards, 24.5cm.

Hayling Golf Club

55640. *Hayling Golf Club Centenary 1883-1983.* Hayling Island, England: Privately Printed, 1st ed. 1983, 27p, illustrated, illustrated wrappers, 23.5cm.

Haynie, Sandra

55660. *Golf: A Natural Course for Women.* edited by James Lynch and Carole Collins. New York: Atheneum, 1st ed. 1975, 208p, illustrated, cloth, 21.5cm.

Hazell, Ann

55680. *A Slice of History, Blackwood Golf Club 1930-1980.* Hawthorndene, Australia: Investigator Press, 1st ed. 1979, 88p, illustrated, decorative cloth, 21.5cm.

Heager, Ronald

55700. *Kings of Club.* London: Stanley Paul, 1st ed. 1968, 159p, illustrated, cloth, 21cm. foreword by Dave Thomas.

Healey, Kay

55720. *Heritage of Oakland Hills as of 1982.* Birmingham, Michigan: Privately Printed, 1st ed. 1982, 23p, illustrated, illustrated wrappers, 25cm.

Heath, Ian

55740. *The Golden Rules of Golf.* London: Transworld Books, 1st ed. 1984, 47p, illustrated, illustrated wrappers, 15 cm.

Hebron, Michael

55760. *See and Feel the Inside Move the Outside.* [New York] Privately Printed, 1st ed. [1984] 116p, illustrated, illustrated wrappers, 25.5cm.

Heck, Phyllis Fraser

55780. *History of the Dayton Country Club 1896-1976*. Dayton, Ohio: Privately Printed, 1st ed. 1976, 144p, illustrated, illustrated wrappers, 28cm.

Heise, Jack G.

55800. *How You Can Play Better Golf Using Self-Hypnosis*. North Hollywood, California: Wilshire, 1st ed. [1961] 128p, illustrated, illustrated wrappers, 21cm. later printings.

55810. *Super Golf with Self-Hypnosis*. London: Elliots, 1st UK ed. 1962, 109p, illustrated, cloth, 18.5cm. UK title of "How You Can Play Better Golf Using Self-Hypnosis."

Helmes, Charles T. and Kenneth W. Price

55830. *Waccabuc Country Club: Seventy Five Years of History, 1912-1982*. Waccabuc, New York: Privately Printed, 1st ed. 1983, 51p, illustrated, cloth, 27.5cm.

Henderson, Ian T. and David I. Stirk

55850. *Golf in the Making*. Crawley, England: Henderson & Stirk, limited ed. signed [300 copies] 1979, 332p, illustrated, leather, 24cm.

55860. 1st trade ed. 1979, 332p, illustrated, cloth, 24cm.

55870. 2d ed. rev. 1982, 332p + [18p] illustrated, cloth, 24cm.

55880. *Royal Blackheath*. Crawley, England: Henderson & Stirk, 1st ed. 1981, 159p, illustrated, cloth, 23.5cm, foreword by F. Pocock.

55890. *Shortspoon-Major F.P. Hopkins 1830-1913, Golfing Artist and Journalist*. Crawley, England: Henderson & Stirk, limited ed. signed, slipcased [750 copies] 1984, 71p, illustrated, pictorial cloth, 24cm.

55900. *The Compleat Golfer: An Illustrated History of the Royal and Ancient Game*. London: Victor Gollancz, 1st ed. 1982, 96p, illustrated, cloth, 20cm.

55905. *The Heritage of Golf: An Illustrated History*. Crawley, England: Henderson & Stirk, 1985, 1st ed. 112p, illustrated, cloth, 20cm. note: revised and expanded edition of "The Compleat Golfer."

Hendren, J.

55920. *The Knock Golf Club, A History 1895-1982*. Belfast, Northern Ireland: Privately Printed, 1st ed. [1982] 104p, illustrated, cloth, 25cm.

Hendry, W. Garden

55940. *The Dynamic Anatomy of the Golf Swing, A Scientific Approach to Improvement At Golf*. Littleton, Massachusetts: PSG Publishing, 1st ed. [1985] 119p, illustrated, cloth, 23.5cm.

Henning, Harold

55960. *Drive Around Southern Africa with Harold Henning*. Benmore, Transvaal: J.M. Samuel, 1st ed. [1974] 96p, illustrated, illustrated wrappers, 23.5cm.

55970. *Harold Henning's Golfer's Guide of Southern Africa*. Johannesburg, South Africa: Newport Publishers, 1st ed. [ca1984] 168p, illustrated, spiral bound illustrated wrappers, 21cm.

Henry Stambaugh Golf Course

55990. *Henry Stambaugh Golf Course 50th Anniversary 1923-1973*. Youngstown, Ohio: Privately Printed, 1st ed. 1973, 20p, illustrated, illustrated wrappers, 23cm.

Hepburn, Tom and Selwyn Jacobson

56010. *America's Most Difficult Golf Holes*. Los Angeles: Price, Stern, Sloan, 1st ed. 1983 [38p] illustrated, illustrated wrappers, 28.5cm.

56020. *Australia's Most Difficult Golf Holes*. Sydney, Australia: Collins, 1st ed. 1982 [38p] illustrated, illustrated wrappers, 29cm.

56030. *Canada's Most Difficult Golf Holes*. Toronto: Totem Books, 1st ed. 1983 [38p] illustrated, illustrated wrappers, 29cm.

56040. *Even More of Australia's Most Difficult Golf Holes*. Sydney: Collins, 1st ed. 1983 [38p] illustrated, illustrated wrappers, 29cm.

56050. *Great Britain and Ireland's Most Difficult Golf Holes*. London: Willow Books, 1st ed. 1983 [38p] illustrated, illustrated wrappers, 29cm.

56060. *Great Golf Holes of New Zealand*. Auckland, New Zealand: Collins, 1st ed. 1981 [38p] illustrated, illustrated wrappers, 29cm.

56070. *Great Golf Holes of South Africa*. Marshalltown, South Africa: Collins, 1st ed. 1984 [38p] illustrated, illustrated wrappers, 29cm.

56080. *New Zealand's Toughest Golf Courses, Book II*. Sydney: Collins, 1st ed. 1983 [38p] illustrated, illustrated wrappers, 29cm.

56090. *South East Asia's Toughest Golf Holes*. Singapore: Eastern Universities Press, 1st ed. 1984 [38p] illustrated, illustrated wrappers, 29cm.

56100. *The World's 72 Toughest Golf Holes*. Los Angeles: Price/Stern/Sloan, 1st ed. 1984, 158p, illustrated, cloth, 25.5cm.

Hergenroeder, Ernie and Doug Wright and Corb Hillum

56120. *The Conduct Compendium of Golf*. San Jose, California: H&A, 1st ed. [1979] 64p, illustrated, illustrated wrappers, 21.5cm.

Hermanson, Roger F.

56140. *The Rules of Golf in Programmed Form*. Dunedin, Florida: Professionals Golfer's Association of America, 1st ed. 1968, 118p, illustrated boards, 23.5cm. foreword by Joseph C. Dey, Jr.

Herold, Donald [Don]

56160. *Adventures in Golf, or How to Golf Your Troubles Away*. New York: Franklin Watts, 1st ed. [1965] 94p, illustrated, cloth, 23.5cm.

Heuer, Karla L.

56180. *Golf Course, A Guide to Analysis and Valuation*. Chicago: American Institute of Real Estate Appraisers, 1st ed. 1980, 128p, illustrated, cloth, 23.5cm. with Cecil McKay, Jr.

Hewerston, Cyril

56200. *Walton Heath Golf Club, The Story of the First Seventy-five Years, 1904-1979.* Tadworth, England: Privately Printed, 1st ed. 1979, 54p, illustrated, illustrated wrappers, 24.5cm.

Hexter, Paul L.

56220. *You Can Play Golf Forever.* Chicago: Contemporary, 1st ed. [1979] 65p, illustrated, cloth, 27.5cm.

56230. pbk. ed. [1979] 65p, illustrated, illustrated wrappers, 27.5cm.

Hibbard, Angus

56250. *Golf and the Glen View Club.* Golf, Illinois: Privately Printed, offprint [ca1970] [10p] illustrated, wrappers, 23cm. offprint from Association of Choice.

Hick, Keith C.

56270. *The Hesketh Golf Club 1885-1985.* Southport, England: Privately Printed, limited ed. [750 copies] 1985, 264p, illustrated, cloth, 23.5cm.

Hickok, Darrell

56290. *Play Better Golf.* [Arizona] Knight Publications, 1st ed. [1966] 80p, illustrated by Larry Prestwick and George Lee, illustrated wrappers, 21.5cm.

Hill, Dave and Nick Seitz

56310. *Teed Off.* Englewood Cliffs, New Jersey: Prentice-Hall, 1st ed. [1977] 217p, illustrated, cloth, 21cm.

Hilton Park Golf Club

56330. *Hilton Park Golf Club Jubilee Year 1927-1977.* Glasgow, Scotland: Privately Printed, 1st ed. 1977, 32p, illustrated, illustrated wrappers, 21cm.

Hingst, Geneive and Mary Ellen McKee

56350. *The Game of Golf; Programmed Instructions of Playing Procedures.* Dubuque, Iowa: William C. Brown, 1st ed. [1968] 87p, illustrated, spiral bound illustrated wrappers, 28cm.

Hirst, Ruth and Jean Lockwood

56370. *Meltham Golf Club.* Meltham, England: Privately Printed, 1st ed. 1982, 20p, illustrated, illustrated wrappers, 21cm.

Hitch, Thomas Kemper and Mary Ishii Kuranote

56390. *Wailae Country Club, The First Half Century.* Honolulu, Hawaii: Privately Printed, limited ed. [1800 copies] [1981] 220p, illustrated, decorative cloth, 28cm.

Hitchcock, Jimmy

56410. *Master Golfer.* London: Stanley Paul, 1st ed. 1967, 192p, illustrated, cloth, 21cm.

Hobbs, Michael

56430. *50 Masters of Golf.* Ashbourne, England: Moorland, 1st ed. [1983] 192p, illustrated, cloth, 23.5cm.

56440. *Golf for the Connoisseur: A Golfing Anthology.* London: Batsford, 1st ed. 1979, 256p, illustrated, cloth, 23cm. foreword by Henry Longhurst.

56450. *Golf to Remember.* London: Batsford, 1st ed. 1978, 168p, illustrated, cloth, 23.5cm. with Peter Alliss.
56460. 1st American ed. Garden City, New York: Doubleday, 1978, 168p, illustrated, cloth, 23cm. with Peter Alliss.

56470. *Great Opens: Historic British and American Championships 1913-1975.* London: David & Charles, 1st ed. [1976] 156p, illustrated, cloth, 21.5cm. foreword by Henry Cotton.
56480. 1st American ed. South Brunswick & New York: A.S. Barnes, 1977, 156p, illustrated, cloth, 21.5cm. foreword by Henry Cotton.

56490. *In Celebration of Golf.* London: Granada, 1st ed. 1982, 212p, illustrated, cloth, 23.5cm. foreword by Henry Cotton.
56500. 1st American ed. New York: Scribner's, 1983, 212p, illustrated, cloth, 23.5cm. foreword by Henry Cotton.

Hoddinott, Howard H.

56520. *Kingsknowe Golf Club Limited 1908-1983, A History.* Edinburgh: Privately Printed, 1st ed. 1983, 66p, illustrated, decorative cloth, 25cm.

Hoffman, Arthur

56540. *The Golfer's Catalog*. Oconomowoc, Wisconsin: Communigraphics, 1st ed. [1984] 48p, illustrated, illustrated wrappers, 20cm.

Hoffman, Bob

56560. *Functional Isometrics Contraction for Golf*. York, Pennsylvania: Bob Hoffman Foundation, 1st ed. [1963] 18p, illustrated, illustrated wrappers, 28cm.

Hollingsworth, Dean and Andrew Birmingham and Robert Pender

56580. *Golf: Par Fore*. Boston: American Press, 1st ed. [1982] 123p, illustrated, illustrated wrappers, 21.5cm.

Hoot, Brad

56600. *Golf Is An Easy Game: A Formula for Improvement for Weekend Golfers*. Nashville, Tennessee: CBH, 1st ed. [1983] 76p, illustrated by Howard Hoot, illustrated wrappers, 21cm. preface by E.E. 'Bubber' Johnson.

Hope, Bob

56620. *Bob Hope's Confessions of A Hooker: My Lifelong Love Affair with Golf*. Garden City, New York: Doubleday, 1st ed. 1985, 230p, illustrated, cloth, 25.5cm. with Dwayne Netland, foreword by Gerald R. Ford.

56630. *Confessions of A Hooker*.1st UK ed. London: Stanley Paul, 1985, 230p, illustrated, cloth, 25.5cm. with Dwayne Netland, foreword by Gerald R. Ford. UK title of "Bob Hope's Confessions of A Hooker."

Hopkins, Anthony

56650. *Songs for Swinging Golfers*. London: Michael Joseph, 1st ed. 1981, 59p, illustrated by Alex Hay, illustrated boards, 13.5cm. later printings.

Hopkins, John

56670. *Beacon Golfing Handbook*. Northampton, England: Beacon, 1st ed. [1983] 223p, illustrated, illustrated wrappers, 24.5cm.

56680. *Nick Faldo in Perspective*. London: George Allen & Unwin, 1st ed. 1985, 172p, illustrated, cloth, 23.5cm.

Hornabrook, John

56700. *Golden Years of New Zealand Golf.* Christchurch, New Zealand: Whitcombe & Tombs, 1st ed. 1967, 154p, illustrated, cloth, 21cm. foreword by Bryan Silk.

Hornby, D.

56720. *The History of the Seaton Carew Golf Club 1874-1974.* Durham, England: Privately Printed, 1st ed. 1974, 108p, illustrated, decorative cloth, 23cm.

Hornung, Paul

56740. *Story of Muirfield Village Golf Club and The Memorial Tournament.* Dublin, Ohio: Golden Bear Publishing, limited ed. [525 copies] [1985] 189p, illustrated, leather, 21.5cm. introduction by Jack Nicklaus.

56750. 1st trade ed. [1985] 189p, illustrated, decorative cloth, 21.5cm. introduction by Jack Nicklaus.

Horton, Thomas

56770. *Golf: The Long Game.* London: Batsford, 1st ed. 1969, 112p, illustrated, cloth, 18.5cm.

56780. *Golf: The Short Game.* London: Batsford, 1st ed. 1970, 111p, illustrated, cloth, 18.5cm.

Hosmer, Howard C.

56800. *From Little Acorns, The Story of Oak Hill 1901-1976.* Rochester, New York: Privately Printed, 1st ed. 1977, 104p, illustrated, cloth, 25cm.

56810. *The Year of the Diamond: Being an Account of the First Seventy-Five Years of the Country Club of Rochester.* Rochester, New York: Privately Printed, limited ed. [1000 copies] 1971, 100p, illustrated, decorative cloth, 22.5cm.

Houghton, George

56830. *Addict in Bunkerland.* London: Country Life, 1st ed. 1962 [100p] illustrated, cloth, 22cm. introduction by Bob Hope.

56840. *Believe It Or Not-That's Golf: A Miscellany of 1000 Oddities, Facts and Personal Profiles.* London: William Luxombe, 1st ed. 1974, 199p, illustrated, cloth, 21.5cm.

56850. *Full Confessions of A Golf Addict.* London: Pelham, 1st ed. 1966, 147p, illustrated, cloth, 21.5cm.

56860. *Golf Addict Among the Irish.* London: Country Life, 1st ed. 1965, 117p, illustrated, cloth, 21.5cm.

56870. *Golf Addict Among the Scots.* London: Country Life, 1st ed. 1967, 136p, illustrated, cloth, 21.5cm.

56880. *Golf Addict Goes East.* London: Country Life, 1st ed. 1967, 142p, illustrated, cloth, 21.5cm.

56890. *Golf Addict in Gaucho Land.* London: Pelham, 1st ed. 1970, 198p, illustrated, cloth, 21.5cm.

56900. *Golf Addict Invades Wales.* London: Pelham, 1st ed. [1969] 192p, illustrated, cloth, 21.5cm.

56910. *Golf Addict Strike Again.* London: Country Life, 1st ed. 1963, 102p, illustrated, cloth, 21.5cm.

56920. *Golf Addicts Galore.* London: Country Life, 1st ed. 1968 [94p] illustrated, cloth, 21.5cm. foreword by Ronnie Shade.

56930. *Golf Addicts Omnibus: The Best of George Houghton.* London: Country Life, 1st ed. 1966, 304p, illustrated, cloth, 21.5cm.

56940. *Golf Addicts To the Fore!* Scotland: Gordon Wright, 1st ed. [1985] [118p] illustrated, illustrated wrappers, 18.5cm.

56950. *Golf With A Whippy Shaft.* New York: A.S. Barnes, 1st ed. 1971, 287p, illustrated, cloth, 25cm. foreword by Bob Hope.

56960. *Golfers in Orbit.* London: Pelham, 1st ed. 1968, 141p, illustrated, cloth, 21.5cm.

56970. *Golfers Treasury: A Personal Anthology.* London: Newnes, 1st ed. 1964, 208p, illustrated, cloth, 24.5cm.

56980. *How to Be A Golf Addict.* London: Pelham, 1st ed. [1971] 202p, illustrated, cloth, 21.5cm.

56990. *I Am A Golf Widow*. London: Country Life, 1st ed. 1961, 100p, illustrated, decorative cloth, 21.5cm.

57000. *Just A Friendly .. A Book of Golf Addict Cartoons*. London: Leslie Frewin, 1st ed. 1973, 96p, illustrated, illustrated boards, 24.5cm. foreword by Tony Jacklin.

57010. *Secret Diary of A Golf Addict's Caddie*. London: Country Life, 1st ed. 1964, 98p, illustrated, cloth, 21.5cm.

How To Cut Strokes From Your Score

57030. *How To Cut Strokes From Your Score*. [Pittsburgh, Pennsylvania] Bethlehem Steel, 1st ed. [ca1968] 21p, illustrated, illustrated wrappers, 22cm.

Hubbard Trail Country Club

57050. *Hubbard Trail Country Club 50 Years, 1925-1975*. Hoopeston, Illinois: Privately Printed, 1st ed. 1975 [48p] illustrated, wrappers, 27.5cm.

Hudson, D.C.N.

57070. *Your Book of Golf*. London: Faber & Faber, 1st ed. 1967, 54p, illustrated, illustrated boards, 21cm.

Huggett, Brian

57090. *Better Golf*. London: Stanley Paul, 1st ed. 1964, 95p, illustrated, cloth, 18.5cm. with John Whitbourn, foreword by Dai Rees.

Huggins, Percy

57110. *The Golfer's Miscellany*. New York: Harper & Row, 1st American ed. [1971] 176p, illustrated by Bob Bugg, decorative cloth, 17.5cm. foreword by George Plimpton. note: first edition not located.

57120. *Troon Golf Club [Handbook]*. Troon, Scotland: Privately Printed, 1972, 44p, illustrated, illustrated wrappers, 18cm.

Hughes, E.H.

57140. *History of the Spokane Country Club, 75th Anniversary*. Spokane, Washington: Privately Printed, 1st ed. 1973 [20p] illustrated, wrappers, 21.5cm.

Hughes, Margaret

57160. *A Round with Darwin.* edited by. London: Souvenir Press, 1st ed. 1984, 223p, cloth, 21.5cm.

Hugman, Robert H.H.

57180. *Putting Know-How.* [San Antonio, Texas] Privately Printed, 1st ed. [1963] 54p, illustrated, illustrated wrappers, 17cm.

Hulme, Gerald

57200. *Cheadle Golf Club 1885-1985*. Cheshire, England: Privately Printed, 1st ed. 1985, 64p, illustrated, illustrated wrappers, 25cm.

Humphreys, Eric

57220. *The Dunlop Golfer's Companion.* Lavenham, England: Eastland Press, 1st ed. 1977, 128p, illustrated, cloth, 22.5cm. foreword by Roy Marsh.

Hunt, Orrin T.

57240. *The Joy of Golf.* Jacksonville, Florida: Privately Printed, 1st ed. [1977] 145p, illustrated by Bill Kirby, illustrated wrappers, 28cm.

Hunter, Mac

57260. *Golf for Beginners.* New York: Grosset & Dunlap, 1st ed. [1973] 94p, illustrated, illustrated wrappers, 27cm. foreword by Gene Littler.

57270. 2d ed. 1978, 94p, illustrated, illustrated wrappers, 27.5cm. foreword by Gene Littler.

Hunter, Robert E.

57290. *Royal & Ancient Game of Golf, A Golf Diary of 72 Years.* NP: Privately Printed, 1st ed. [ca1966] 41p, illustrated, wrappers, 21cm.

Huston, Mervyn J.

57310. *Golf and Murphy's Law.* Edmonton, Canada: Hurtig, 1st ed. [1981] 155p, illustrated by Graham Pilsworth, cloth, 21.5cm.

57320. *Great Golf Humor, A Collection of Stories & Articles.* Edmonton, Canada: Hurtig, 1st ed. [1977] 287p, illustrated, cloth, 23cm.

Iarrobino, Grace and Elayne Slaughter

57340. *The Golfer's Cookbook.* Los Angeles: Price, Stern, Sloan, 1st ed. [1968] 91p, illustrated wrappers, 21.5cm.

Idoux, Clete

57360. *Play Better Golf.* [Illinois] Knight Publications, limited ed. [200 copies] [1966] 80p, illustrated by Larry Prestwich and George Lee, illustrated wrappers, 21.5cm.

Ilfracombe Golf Club

57380. *Ilfracombe Golf Club [Handbook].* London: Temple Publicity Services, 1963, 12p, illustrated, illustrated wrappers, 18cm.

Imhoff, Betty P.

57400. *History of the Country Club of York 1899-1975.* York, Pennsylvania: Privately Printed, limited ed. slipcased [1200 copies] 1975, 152p, illustrated, cloth, 25cm.

Indian Valley Country Club

57420. *Indian Valley Country Club 1952-1977.* Telford, Pennsylvania: Privately Printed, 1st ed. 1977 [20p] illustrated, illustrated wrappers, 28cm.

Ingham, John

57440. *Best Golfing Jokes.* London: Wolfe, 1st ed. [1969] 63p, wrappers, 17cm. later printings.

Innes, Michael

57460. *An Awkward Lie*. New York: Dodd, Mead, 1st American ed. [1971] 192p, cloth, 20cm. note: first edition not located.

Instant Golf

57480. *Instant Golf: How To Do It in Slow Motion*. New York: ASF Enterprises, 1st ed. [1973] 95p, illustrated, spiral bound wrappers, 15cm.

Inverness Club

57500. *Inverness Club [Handbook]*. Durham, North Carolina: Golf Course Profiles, 1st ed. [1979] [27p] illustrated, illustrated wrappers, 18cm.

Inverness Golf Club

57520. *Inverness Golf Club 1883-1983*. Inverness, Scotland: Privately Printed, 1st ed. 1983, 32p, illustrated, illustrated wrappers, 21cm.

Ireland: A Golfer's Paradise

57540. *Ireland: A Golfer's Paradise*. Dublin, Ireland: Irish Tourist Board [ca1968] 11p, illustrated, illustrated wrappers, 20.5cm.

Irish Golf Courses 1983/'84

57560. *Irish Golf Courses 1983/'84*. [Dublin] Irish Tourist Board, 1983, 98p, illustrated, illustrated wrappers, 21cm.

Irwin, Hale

57580. *Play Better Golf*. edited by Keith Mackie. London: Octopus Books, 1st ed. 1980, 152p, illustrated, decorative cloth, 28cm. later printing.

Irwin, N.L.

57600. *St. Georges Golf and Country Club, 50 Years 1929-1979*. Islington, Canada: Privately Printed, 1st ed. 1979 [9p] illustrated, wrappers, 23cm.

Isenogle, Kenneth

57620. *Anatomy of Right Handed Golf*. Auburn, New Jersey: Privately Printed, 1st ed. [1980] 28p, illustrated, illustrated wrappers, 21.5cm.

Isle of Purbeck Golf Club

57640. *Isle of Purbeck Golf Club [Handbook]*. Bristol, England: Summit [ca1984] 20p, illustrated, illustrated wrappers, 21cm.

Ives, Elizabeth Stevenson

57660. *The Belvedere Club, Memoirs of Members 1878-1968*. Charlevoix, Michigan: Privately Printed, 1st ed. 1969, 220p, illustrated, cloth, 23cm.

Jacklin, Tony

57680. *100 Jacklin Golfstrips from the Daily Express*. London: Daily Express, 1st ed. [1970] [80p] illustrated by Yaroslav Horak, illustrated wrappers, 19.5cm. script by Iain Reid.

57690. *Golf with Tony Jacklin*. London: J.M. Dent, 1st ed. 1969, 144p, illustrated, illustrated boards, 13cm. with Jack Wood.

57700. pbk. ed. London: Pan Books, 1970, 144p, illustrated, illustrated wrappers, 11cm.

57710. *Golf Step By Step*. New York: Sterling, 1st American ed. [1969] 144p, illustrated, illustrated boards, 12.5cm. American title of "Golf With Tony Jacklin."

57720. pbk. ed. New York: Bantam, 1970, 144p, illustrated, illustrated wrappers, 10.5cm.

57730. *Jacklin: The Champion's Own Story*. London: Hodder & Stoughton, 1st ed. [1970] 192p, illustrated, cloth, 21cm. introduction by Arnold Palmer.

57740. 1st American ed. New York: Simon & Schuster [1970] 192p, illustrated, cloth, 21cm. foreword by Arnold Palmer.

57750. *Tony Jacklin's Guide to Professional Golf*. London: Purnell, 1st ed. [1970] 31p, illustrated, illustrated wrappers, 30cm.

57760. *Tony Jacklin, The First Forty Years*. London: Queen Anne Press, 1st ed. 1985, 24p, illustrated, cloth, 23.5cm. with Renton Laidlaw

Jacklin, Tony and Peter Dobereiner

57780. *Jacklin's Golf Secrets*. London: Stanley Paul, 1st ed. 1983, 109p, illustrated, cloth, 24cm.

Jackson, Barney

57800. *History of the Canadian Open At Glen Abbey.* edited by. Toronto: Privately Printed, 1st ed. [1984] [62p] illustrated, cloth, 28cm.

Jackson, Robert B.

57820. *Supermex: The Lee Trevino Story.* New York: Henry Z. Walck, 1st ed. [1973] 72p, illustrated, cloth, 20.5cm.

Jacobs, John

57840. *Another Consultation with Doctor Golf, John Jacobs Tells How to Groove Your Swing.* London: Beaverbrook Newspapers, 1st ed. [ca1965] [28p] illustrated, illustrated wrappers, 13cm. introduction by Ron Heager.

57850. *Golf.* London: Stanley Paul, 1st ed. 1963, 160p, illustrated, cloth, 24cm. with John Stobbs, foreword by P.B. Lucas. later printings.

57860. *Golf Doctor: Diagnosis, Explanation and Correction of Golfing Faults.* London: Stanley Paul, 1st ed. 1979, 126p, illustrated, cloth, 27.5cm. with Dick Aultman, foreword by Jack Nicklaus.
57870. 1st Australian ed. Auckland, New Zealand: Stanley Paul/Hutchinson, 1979, 126p, illustrated, cloth, 27.5cm. with Dick Aultman, foreword by Jack Nicklaus
57880. *Quick Cures for Weekend Golfers.* New York: Simon & Schuster, 1st American ed. [1979] 126p, illustrated by Anthony Ravielli, cloth, 27.5cm. with Dick Aultman, foreword by Jack Nicklaus. American title of "Golf Doctor."

57890. *John Jacobs Analyses Golf's Superstars.* London: Stanley Paul, 1st ed. 1974, 79p, illustrated, cloth, 18cm. with Ken Bowden.

57900. *Play Better Golf with John Jacobs.* London: Stanley Paul, 1st ed. 1969, 95p, illustrated, illustrated wrappers, 18.5cm. with Ken Bowden.
57910. *Play Better Golf.* 1st American ed. New York: Arco, 1972, 95p, illustrated, illustrated wrappers and library binding, 17.5cm. with Ken Bowden.

57920. *Practical Golf*. New York: Quadrangle, 1st ed. [1972] 192p, illustrated by Anthony Ravielli, cloth, 27.5cm. with Ken Bowden, foreword by Tony Jacklin.

57930. pbk. ed. [1972] 192p, illustrated by Anthony Ravielli, illustrated wrappers, 27.5cm. with Ken Bowden, foreword by Tony Jacklin.

57940. reprint ed. New York: Atheneum, 1983, 192p, illustrated by Anthony Ravielli, cloth, 27.5cm. with Ken Bowden, foreword by Tony Jacklin.

57950. pbk. ed. reprint. New York: Atheneum, 1983, 192p, illustrated by Anthony Ravielli, 27.5cm. with Ken Bowden, foreword by Tony Jacklin.

Jacobs, Linda

57970. *Ellen The Expert*. St. Paul, Minnesota: EMC, 1st ed. [1974] 38p, illustrated by Paul Synder, illustrated boards and wrappers, 23cm.

57980. *Laura Baugh: Golf's Golden Girl*. St. Paul, Minnesota: EMC, 1st ed. 1975, 38p, illustrated, illustrated boards, 22.5cm.

57990. *Lee Elder, The Daring Dream*. St. Paul, Minnesota: EMC, 1st ed. [1976] 39p, illustrated, illustrated boards, 23cm.

James K. Thomson Golden Anniversary

58010. *James K. Thomson Golden Anniversary*. Schenectady, New York: Mowhawk Golf Club, 1st ed. 1968, 15p, illustrated, illustrated wrappers, 21.5cm.

James River Country Club

58030. *James River Country Club Commemorating the Fiftieth Anniversary*. Newport News, Virginia: Privately Printed, 1st ed. 1982 [20p] illustrated, illustrated wrappers, 27.5cm.

James, Joseph [Joe]

58050. *How to Give Up Golf*. South Brunswick and New York: A.S. Barnes, 1st ed. [1970] 106p, illustrated, cloth, 21cm.

58060. *Quiet on the Tee*. New York: A.S. Barnes, 1st ed. [1963] 78p, illustrated, cloth, 20cm.

58070. *So You're Taking Up Golf?* New York: A.S. Barnes, 1st ed. [1969] 89p, illustrated, cloth, 21cm.

58080. *What It Is, Is Golf.* New York: A.S. Barnes, 1st ed. [1965] 79p, illustrated, cloth, 21cm.

January, Don and Al Carrell

58100. *Golf Is A Funny Game.* South Brunswick & New York: A.S. Barnes, 1st ed. [1967] 128p, illustrated, cloth, 21cm.

Jarrett, T.G.

58120. *A History of the New Club, St. Andrews.* St. Andrews, Scotland: Privately Printed, 1st ed. 1982, 61p, illustrated, illustrated wrappers, 21cm.

Jenkins, Dan

58140. *Dead Solid Perfect.* New York: Atheneum, 1st ed. 1974, 234p, cloth, 21cm.

58150. *Sports Illustrated's: The Best 18 Golf Holes in America.* New York: Delacorte Press, 1st ed. [1966] 160p, illustrated, cloth, 31cm. foreword by Ben Hogan.

58160. *The Dogged Victims of Inexorable Fate.* Boston: Little, Brown, 1st ed. [1970] 298p, cloth, 20cm. foreword by Edwin Shrake.

58170. pbk. ed. New York: Berkley, 1973, 286p, illustrated wrappers, 17.5cm. foreword by Edwin Shrake.

Jenny, Albert

58190. *The Royal Game: Stories Around A Little White Ball.* London: P.R.M. Publishers, 1st English language ed. [1962] 101p, illustrated, cloth, 17.5cm. translated from the German by H. Mitchell.

Johnson, Carol Clark and Ann Casey Johnstone

58210. *Golf: A Positive Approach.* Reading, Massachusetts: Addison-Wesley, 1st ed. [1975] 172p, illustrated, illustrated wrappers, 23cm., forewords by Patty Berg and Gary Wiren.

Johnson, Dewayne J. and Robert A. Oliver and Sharon L. Shields

58230. *Golf.* Boston: American Press, 1st ed. [1979] 61p, illustrated, illustrated wrappers, 21cm.

Johnson, Hank

58250. *End Your Fear of Sand Forever.* Norwalk, Connecticut: Golf Digest, 1st ed. [1981] [13p] illustrated, illustrated wrappers, 14cm.

Johnson, William Oscar and Nancy P. Williamson

58270. *Whatta Gal: The Babe Didrickson Story.* Boston: Little, Brown, 1st ed. [1977] 224p, illustrated, cloth, 20.5cm.

Johnson, Jr., Willis

58290. *Peachtree Golf Club.* edited by. Atlanta, Georgia: Privately Printed, 1st ed. 1978, 40p, illustrated, cloth, 28cm.

Johnston, Alastair J.

58310. *The Clapcott Papers.* Edinburgh: Privately Printed, limited ed. slipcased [400 copies] 1985, 517p, illustrated, decorative cloth, 23cm.

58315. special presentation ed. [20 copies] slipcased, 1985, 517p, illustrated, decorative cloth, 23cm.

Jones, A.C.

58330. *The Royal County Down Golf Club [Handbook].* London: Golf Clubs Association [ca1970] 35p, illustrated, illustrated wrappers, 18.5cm.

Jones, Rees L. and Guy L. Rando

58350. *Golf Course Development.* Washington, DC: Urban Land Institute, 1st ed. [1974] 105p, illustrated, wrappers, 28cm. foreword by Karin A. Pick.

Jones, Robert

58370. *British Golf Odyssey.* Monterey, California: Angel Press, 1st ed. [1977] 152p, decorative cloth, 21cm.

58380. *Gulls on the Golf Course.* Philadelphia: Dorrance, 1st ed. [1975] 64p, cloth, 21cm.

58390. *Sherlock Holmes, the Golfer.* Monterey, California: Angel Press, 1st ed. [1981] 182p, illustrated wrappers, 21cm.

Jones, Robert E.

58410. *A History of the Missoula Country Club.* Missoula, Montana: Privately Printed, 1st ed. 1979 [4p] wrappers, 28cm.

Jones, Robert Trent

58430. *Description of the Golden Horseshoe Golf Course At Williamsburgh Inn.* Williamsburg, Virginia: Privately Printed, 1st ed. [ca1965] 11p, illustrated, illustrated wrappers, 23cm.

58440. *Great Golf Stories.* edited by. Edmonton, Canada: Hurtig, 1st ed. [1982] 294p, cloth, 25.5cm.

Jones, Jr., Robert Tyre

58460. *A Short Love Story: The People of St. Andrews and Robert T. [Bobby] Jones, Jr.* Atlanta, Georgia: Atlanta Athletic Club, 1st ed. [ca1973] [12p] illustrated, wrappers, 25.5cm.

58470. *Bobby Jones on Golf.* Garden City, New York: Doubleday, 1st ed. 1966, 246p, illustrated by Anthony Ravielli, cloth, 23.5cm. foreword by Charles Price.

58480. reprint ed. Norwalk, Connecticut: Arno Press/Golf Digest, 1976, 246p, illustrated, decorative cloth, 23cm. later printings.

58490. *Bobby Jones on the Basic Golf Swing.* Garden City, New York: Doubleday, 1st ed. 1969, 63p, illustrated by Anthony Ravielli, cloth, 26cm.

Jones, Tony

58510. *A Brief History of Abergele and Pensarn Golf Club. 75th. Anniversary Year 1910-1985.* Abergele, Wales: Privately Printed, 1st ed. 1985, 7p, illustrated wrappers, 20.5cm.

Josey, Alex

58530. *Golf in Singapore.* Singapore, Malaysia: Asia Pacific Press, 1st ed. 1969, 168p, illustrated, illustrated wrappers, 18cm.

Judd, H. Stanley

58550. *How to Play Golf the Easy Way.* New York: Harper & Row, 1st ed. [1980] 128p, illustrated, wrappers, 20cm. with Pat Mahoney, preface by Andy North.

Junkermeier, John

58570. *The Glorious Past of Stockdale Country Club.* Bakersfield, California: Privately Printed, 1st ed. 1978, 16p, illustrated, wrappers, 21.5cm.

58580. 2d ed. rev. 1984, 24p, illustrated, wrappers, 21.5cm.

Kahn, Liz

58600. *Tony Jacklin: The Price of Success.* London: Hamlyn, 1st ed. [1979] 160p, illustrated, cloth, 23.5cm.

Kahn, Marilyn M.

58620. *Inwood Country Club Seventy-Fifth Anniversary 1901-1976.* Inwood, New York: Privately Printed, 1st ed. 1976, 106p, illustrated, cloth, 26.5cm.

Kane, John Clarke and John Clarke Kane, Jr. and Alexander MacDonald

58640. *Tedesco Country Club 1903-1978.* Swampscott, Massachusetts: Privately Printed, 1st ed. 1978, 43p, illustrated, illustrated wrappers, 28cm.

Kaplan, Jim

58660. *Hillerich & Bradsby: History-Catalogs.* Glencoe, Illinois: Vintage Golf, 1st ed. [1982] [412p] illustrated, wrappers, 28cm.

58670. *MacGregor Golf: History-Catalogs.* Glencoe, Illinois: Vintage Golf, 1st ed. [1980] [380p] illustrated, wrappers, 28cm. later printings.

58680. *Wilson Golf: History -Catalogs.* Glencoe, Illinois: Vintage Golf, 1st ed. [1981] [282p] illustrated, wrappers, 28cm.

Karen Country Club

58700. *Karen Country Club, Past and Future.* Niarobi, Keyna: Privately Printed, 1st ed. [1978] 88p, illustrated, illustrated wrappers, 22.5cm.

Kaskie, Shirli

58720. *A Woman's Golf Game.* Chicago: Contemporary, 1st ed. [1982] 198p, illustrated, cloth, 22.5cm. foreword by Kathy Whitworth.

58730. pbk. ed. [1982] 198p, illustrated, illustrated wrappers, 22.5cm. foreword by Kathy Whitworth.

Kavanaugh, L.V.

58750. *The History of Golf in Canada.* Toronto: Fitzhenry & Whiteside, 1st ed. [1973] 207p, illustrated, cloth, 28cm.

Keane, Christopher

58770. *The Tour.* New York: Stein & Day, 1st ed. 1974, 239p, illustrated, cloth, 23cm.

Kearney, Tom

58790. *A Funny Thing Happened..* [Llandrindod, Wales] Privately Printed, 1st ed. [ca1985] [30p] illustrated wrappers, 20.5cm.

Keith, Nicholas

58810. *Golf: Sportsviewers Guide.* Newton Abbot, England: David & Charles, 1st ed. [1984] 64p, illustrated, illustrated boards, 21cm. foreword by Peter Alliss.

Kelley, Homer

58830. *The Golfing Machine: The Star System of Golf.* Seattle, Washington: Star System Press, 1st ed. [1969] 149p, illustrated, decorative cloth, 21cm. later printings.

Kelley, James E.

58850. *Minnesota Golf: 75 Years of Tournament History.* Minneapolis, Minnesota: O.H. Dahlen, 1st ed. [1976] 288p, illustrated, illustrated wrappers, 23cm.

Kelly, G.M.

58870. *Golf in New Zealand: A Centennial History.* Wellington, New Zealand: New Zealand Golf Association, 1st ed. 1971, 262p, illustrated, cloth, 23.5cm. foreword by G.P. Roberts.

Kemp, Charles F.

58890. *Smart Golf: A Study of the Mental and Emotional Side of Golf.* Fort Worth, Texas: Branch-Smith, 1st ed. 1974, 146p, illustrated, illustrated wrappers, 21cm. foreword by Byron Nelson. later printings.

58900. *The World of Golf & the Game of Life*. St. Louis, Missouri: Bethany Press, 1st ed. [1978] 176p, illustrated, illustrated wrappers, 23cm. introduction by Jay Randolph.

Kennedy, Des and Harry Georgiades

58920. *A Slice of Fun*. Cape Town, South Africa: Howard Timmins, 1st ed. 1965 [72p] illustrated, cloth, 18cm.

Kennedy, Patrick

58940. *Golf Clubs Trademarks: American 1898-1930*. South Burlington, Vermont: Thistle Books, 1st ed. 1984, 99p, illustrated, illustrated wrappers, 23cm.

Kennington, Don

58960. *The Sourcebook of Golf*. London: Library Associates, 1st ed. 1981, 255p, illustrated, cloth, 22cm.

Kenwood Golf and Country Club

58980. *Kenwood 50 Years 1928-1978*. Bethesda, Maryland: Privately Printed, 1st ed. 1978, 16p, illustrated, illustrated wrappers, 28cm.

Kenyon, Michael

59000. *The Shooting of Dan McGrew*. London: Crime Club, 1st ed. 1972, 191p, cloth, 19.5cm.

Keogh, Barbara K. and Carol E. Smith

59020. *Personal Par: A Psychological System of Golf for Women*. Champaign, Illinois: Human Kinetics, 1st ed. [1985] 91p, illustrated, illustrated wrappers, 23.5cm.

Kessler, Kaye W.

59040. *The Golf Club.* New Albany, Ohio: Privately Printed, 1st ed. 1982, 72p, illustrated, decorative cloth, 30.5cm.

Kiehl, Bob

59060. *Duffer Golf or How to Break 100.* Hamilton, Canada: Potlach, 1st ed. [1979] 64p, illustrated by James Simpkins, illustrated wrappers, 18cm.

Kiernan, Thomas

59080. *Wood-Irons.* Englewood Cliffs, New Jersey: Prentice-Hall, 1st ed. [1981] 165p, illustrated, cloth, 20cm.

Killeen, Albert E.

59100. *The Ten Million Dollar Golf Ball.* Atlanta, Georgia: Greenville Press, 1st ed. [1983] 120p, cloth, 21.5cm.

King, Leslie

59120. *Master Key to Good Golf.* London: Monarch Golf Projects Golf Associates, 1st ed. 1976, 144p, illustrated, spiral bound illustrated wrappers, 26cm. foreword by Michael Bonallack.

59130. 1st American ed. Menlo Park, California: Golf Associates, 1980, 144p, illustrated, illustrated wrappers, 26cm. foreword by Michael Bonallack.

59140. *The Master Key to Success at Golf.* London: Hodder & Stoughton, 1st ed. 1962, 157p, illustrated, cloth, 22cm. later printing.

59150. 1st American ed. New York: Harper & Row [1963] 157p, illustrated, cloth, 21cm.

King, W. R.

59170. *Mohawk Golf Club, Three Quarters of A Century.* Schenectady, New York: Privately Printed, 1st ed. 1973, 68p, illustrated, wrappers, 21cm.

Kinney, H.A.

59190. *Brighton and Hove Golf Club, 1887-1973.* Brighton, England: Privately Printed, 1st ed. 1973, 40p, illustrated, cloth, 24.5cm.

Kirkwood, Joe

59210. *The Links of Life*. Oklahoma City, Oklahoma: Links of Life, 1st ed. [1973] 141p, illustrated, cloth, 21cm. as told to Barbara Fey, introduction by Lowell Thomas.

Kissling, John

59230. *Seventy Years: A History of the Metropolitan Golf Club, Oakleigh, Victoria, which includes the History of the Caulfield Golf Club and a short account of early golf in Victoria*. Melbourne, Australia: Macmillan, 1st ed. 1973, 156p, illustrated, cloth, 21.5cm.

Klappenbach, Ernie

59250. *A Forty-two Year History, 1945-1977, Southern Hills Country Club*. Tulsa, Oklahoma: Privately Printed, limited ed. [1500 copies] 1977, 177p, illustrated, decorative cloth, 25cm.

Klein, Dave

59270. *Golf's Big 3*. New York: Stadia Sports, 1st ed. 1972 [70p] illustrated, illustrated wrappers, 15.5cm.

59280. *Great Moments in Golf*. New York: Cowles, 1st ed. [1971] 128p, illustrated, decorative cloth, 21cm.

Kloppenburg, Jerry

59300. *Cure The Yips*. [Milwaukee, Wisconsin] Privately Printed, 1st ed. [1985] [12p] illustrated by James E. Monroe, illustrated wrappers, 21.5cm.

Klugness, Elizabeth and James

59320. *The Nongolfers Cookbook*. Yuma, Arizona: Tower Enterprises, 1st ed. [1982] 156p, illustrated by Michael Sturgill, illustrated wrappers, 21.5cm.

Klute, Mary Carolyn

59340. *Golfers Always Say*. Richmond, Indiana: Privately Printed, 1st ed. [1984] [120p] illustrated, spiral bound wrappers, 10.5cm.

Kneedler, Bob

59360. *Golfitis: Golf It Is.* Ormond Beach, Florida: Privately Printed, 1st ed. [1965] [26p] illustrated, illustrated wrappers, 21.5cm.

Knight, Reg

59380. *Golf for Beginners.* London: Collins, 1st ed. 1970, 176p, illustrated by John Laing, cloth, 15cm. with Sydney Spicer.

59390. *Learn Golf Backwards.* London: Collins, 1st ed. 1965, 125p, illustrated, cloth, 19.5cm. with Sydney Spicer.

Knollwood Country Club

59410. *Knollwood Country Club 1894-1969, 75 Years of Golf.* Elmsford, New York: Privately Printed, 1st ed. 1969, 16p, illustrated, illustrated wrappers, 14cm.

Kocsis, Lee

59430. *Kinks on the Links: with Spiked Footnotes.* Hot Springs Village, Arkansas: Privately Printed, 1st ed. [1982] 40p, illustrated, illustrated wrappers, 21.5cm.

Koehl, Elaine B.

59450. *Ponte Vedra Club 1927-1982, The First Fifty-five Years.* Ponte Vedra, Florida: Privately Printed, 1st ed. 1982, 99p, illustrated, illustrated wrappers, 23cm.

Koehler, Aileen Poole

59470. *Wawashkame Golf Club.* Mackinac Island, Michigan: Privately Printed, 1st ed. [ca1982] 13p, illustrated, illustrated wrappers, 21cm.

Kostis, Peter

59490. *The Inside Path to Better Golf.* Norwalk, Connecticut: Golf Digest, 1st ed. [1982] 186p, illustrated, cloth, 27.5cm. with Larry Dennis.

Kritzer, John B.

59510. *Butterfield Country Club 1920-1970, 50th Anniversary.* Hinsdale, Illinois: Privately Printed, 1st ed. 1970, 128p, illustrated, decorative cloth, 23cm.

Kullman, Jared Jay

59530. *101 Winning Golf Tips*. North Miami, Florida: Merit, 1st ed. 1980, 223p, illustrated, illustrated wrappers, 15cm.

59540. *How to Play Winning Golf*. North Miami, Florida: Merit Publication, 1st ed. [1980] 224p, illustrated, illustrated wrappers, 15cm.

Kushell, Shela M. & Joel P.

59560. *Golf Resorts USA*. La Mirada, California: Automatic Press, 1st ed. [1983] 466p, illustrated, illustrated wrappers, 21.5cm.

Lake, Ivan

59580. *Falmouth Golf Club [Handbook]*. Bournemouth, England: GM Productions, 1974, 32p, illustrated, illustrated wrappers, 18.5cm.

LaLonde, Roy

59600. *Inverness Golf Club 1926-1974*. Inverness, Illinois: Privately Printed, 1st ed. 1974 [32p] illustrated, illustrated wrappers, 23cm.

Lambeth, Harry J.

59620. *A Directory of the Leading Builders of the Nation's Golf Courses*. Washington, DC: Golf Course Builders of America, 1st ed. 1974 [28p] illustrated, illustrated wrappers, 22.5cm.

Lancaster Golf Club

59640. *Lancaster Golf Club 50th Anniversary*. Ashton Hall, England: Privately Printed, 1st ed. 1983, 31p, illustrated, illustrated wrappers, 22cm.

Langdon, David

59660. *How to Play Golf and Stay Happy*. London: Frederick Muller, 1st ed. 1964, 124p, illustrated, cloth, 24.5cm.

59670. pbk. ed. London: Four Square, 1966, 124p, illustrated, illustrated wrappers, 19cm.

59680. *How to Talk Golf: A to Z Glossary of Golf Terms*. London: Eyre Methuen, 1st ed. 1975, 80p, illustrated, illustrated boards, 21.5cm.

Lapham, Robert

59700. *Twenty Years of Life Begins At Forty: The Story of A Unique Golf Tournament.* Harlingen, Texas: Fairway Publishing, 1st ed. [1972] 158p, illustrated, decorative cloth, 22.5cm.

Lardner, Rex

59720. *Downhill Lies and Other Falsehoods or How to Play Dirty Golf.* New York: Hawthorn, 1st ed. [1973] 152p, illustrated by Roy Schlemme, cloth, 21cm.

59730. pbk. ed. [1973] 152p, illustrated by Roy Schlemme, illustrated wrappers, 21cm.

59740. *The Great Golfers.* New York: Putnam's, 1st ed. [1970] 160p, decorative cloth, 20cm.

Larmore, Mary Liz

59760. *The Resort Book for Swingers, A Golfer's Vacation Guide.* Arcadia, California: Foreword Press, 1st ed. [1981] 39p, illustrated, illustrated wrappers, 23.3cm.

Larsen, Herbert [Mrs]

59780. *Women's Metropolitan Golf Association 1899-1974.* [New York] Privately Printed, 1st ed. 1975, 56p, illustrated, wrappers, 28cm.

Larson, Lucy

59800. *Garden State Women's Golf Association 1953-1978.* editor. [New Jersey] Privately Printed, 1st ed. 1978 [16p] illustrated, illustrated wrappers, 28cm.

Laureti, Mario

59820. *All Putts Should Count 1/2 Stroke.* St. Petersburg, Florida: Outdoors Publishing, 1st ed. [1981] 147p, illustrated, illustrated wrappers, 21.5cm.

Law, Janice

59840. *Death Under Par.* Boston: Houghton Mifflin, 1st ed. 1981, 234p, cloth, 21cm.

Lawson, Stewart

59860. *The Original Rules of Golf.* Gullane, Scotland: Honourable Company of Edinburgh Golfers, limited ed. [1000 copies] [1981] 30p, illustrated, embossed illustrated wrappers, 21cm.

Lazaro, Joe

59880. *The Right Touch.* Weston, Massachusetts: John Mahoney, 1st ed. [1978] 142p, illustrated by Elmer Wexler, cloth, 22.5cm. introduction by Bob Hope.

Leahey, Brendan D.

59900. *One Hundred Years At Vesper Country Club.* Tyngsboro, Massachusetts: Privately Printed, 1st ed. 1979, 162p, illustrated, decorative cloth, 28cm.

Lee, Stan

59920. *Golfers Anonymous.* [New York] Madison, 1st ed. [1961] 63p, illustrated, illustrated wrappers, 21.5cm.

Lee-on-the-Solent Golf Club

59940. *Lee-on-the-Solent Golf Club The First 75 Years, A Brief History.* by N. E. H. Lee-on-the-Solent, England: Privately Printed, 1st ed. 1980 [12p] illustrated wrappers, 20.5cm.

Lema, Tony

59960. *Champagne Tony's Golf Tips.* New York: McGraw-Hill, 1st ed. [1966] 147p, illustrated, cloth, 23.5cm. with Bud Harvey.

59970. pbk. ed. New York: Pocket Books [ca1967] 173p, illustrated, illustrated wrappers, 17.5cm. with Bud Harvey.

59980. *Champagne Golf.* London: Cassell, 1st UK ed. 1966, 106p, illustrated, cloth, 23.5cm. with Bud Harvey. UK title of "Champagne Tony's Golf Tips."

59990. *Golfers' Gold: An Inside View of the Pro Tour.* Boston: Little, Brown, 1st ed. [1964] 248p, illustrated, cloth, 21cm. with Gwilyn S. Brown.

60000. pbk. ed. New York: Pocket Books, 1965, 230p, illustrated, illustrated wrappers, 16cm. with Gwilyn S. Brown.

60010. *Tony Lema's Inside Story of the Professional Golf Tour.* London: W. Foulsham, 1st Uk ed. [1964] 191p, illustrated, cloth, 21.5cm. UK title of "Golfers' Gold."

60020. *How To Break 100/90/80.* NP: NP, 1st ed. [ca1965] [20p] illustrated, illustrated wrappers, 16cm.

Lerner, Mark

60040. *Golf Is for Me.* Minneapolis, Minnesota: Lerner Publications, 1st ed. [1982] 48p, illustrated, illustrated boards, 26cm.

Leslie, Bill and Gene O'Brien

60060. *Aim and Hang Loose.* Springfield, Missouri: Davis Development, 1st ed. [1976] 39p, illustrated wrappers, 19cm.

Levine, Stephen M.

60080. *Woodcrest Country Club-A History.* Cherry Hill, New Jersey: Privately Printed, 1st ed. 1985, 52p, illustrated, decorative cloth, 28cm.

Levison, John G.

60100. *A Short History of the Presidio Golf Club.* San Francisco, California: Privately Printed, 1st ed. 1964, 15p, illustrated wrappers, 18cm.

Lewis, Don

60120. *After Dinner Golf.* London: Mowbrays, 1st ed. 1976, 124p, illustrated by Bill Bowden, cloth, 21.5cm, foreword by Tony Jacklin.

Lewis, Robert

60140. *Win Those Saturday Games.* South Lake Tahoe: California, Zanel, 2d ed. [1979] 48p, illustrated, illustrated wrappers, 21.5cm. introduction by Ethel Lee. note: first edition not located.

Lillie, John Adam

60160. *Ninety Years A Golfer, A Tall Story of Reminiscences and Some Reflections.* Edinburgh: Privately Printed, limited ed. [300 copies] 1981, 17p, wrappers, 18cm.

Lindberg, Lindy

60180. *Lindy Lindberg's Spot System of Chipping*. Glendale, California: Lindberg Publishing, 1st ed. [1977] 64p, illustrated, illustrated wrappers, 18.5cm.

Lindholm, R. C.

60200. *Lindy's Golf Course Guide For the Washington-Baltimore Area*. Alexandria, Virginia: Privately Printed, 1st ed. [1983] 258p, illustrated, illustrated wrappers, 25.5cm.

Lindley, Walter C.

60220. *Oahu Country Club Seventy Five Years*. Honolulu, Hawaii: Privately Printed, 1st ed. 1981 [16p] illustrated, illustrated wrappers, 28cm.

Linkert, Lo

60240. *Around the Courses in 19 Holes*. Port Coquitlam, Canada: Dimples Golf Accessories, 1st ed. 1983 [142p] illustrated, illustrated wrappers, 20.5cm.

60250. *Duffers, Hackers and other Golfers*. Vancouver, Canada/ Oakland, New Jersey: Plainsman/Jolex, 1st ed. 1981 [142p] illustrated, illustrated wrappers, 20cm.

60260. *Golftoons*. Vancouver, Canada: Plainsman, 1st ed. [1977] [155p] illustrated, illustrated wrappers, 20.5cm. later printings.

Liss, Howard

60280. *The Masters Tournament*. New York: Dell, 1st ed. 1974, 219p, illustrated wrappers, 17.5cm.

Lister, David

60300. *I'd Like to Help the World to Swing*. Scottsburgh, South Africa: Dansville Investments, 1st ed. [1977] 150p, illustrated, illustrated boards, 24cm.

60310. *The Ultimate Simplification*. Scottsburgh, South Africa: Dansville Investments, 1st ed. [1981] 39p, illustrated, illustrated wrappers, 21cm.

Little Aston Golf Club

60330. *Little Aston Golf Club 1908-1983.* Sutton Coldfield, England: Privately Printed, 1st ed. [1983] 24p, illustrated, illustrated wrappers, 21cm.

Littler, Gene

60350. *How to Master the Irons: An Illustrated Guide to Better Golf.* New York: Ronald Press, 1st ed. [1962] 118p, illustrated, cloth, 25cm, with Don Collett, foreword by Paul Runyan.

60360. *Iron Tactics, My Secrets to Winning Golf.* [Chicago] Ram Golf Group, 1st ed. [ca1962] 15p, illustrated, illustrated wrappers, 23cm.

60370. *Stroke Minder: The Long Irons: The Driver: Sand Wedge: The Pitch Shot; The Short Irons. 5 Volumes. [Flip Book].* Irvine, California: Stroke Minder, 1st ed. [1978] 112p each, illustrated, illustrated wrappers, 11.5cm.

60380. *The Long and Medium Irons. A Flipvision Golf Manual.* New York: Sterling, 1st ed. [1965] 128p, illustrated, illustrated wrappers, 12.5cm.

60390. *The Real Score.* Waco, Texas: Word Books, 1st ed. [1976] 199p, illustrated, cloth, 21.5cm, with Jack Tobin.later printings.

Littlewood, John

60410. *Oxford & Cambridge Golfing Society. The President's Putter, 50 Putters; 1920-1976, A Statistical Analysis.* [London] Privately Printed, 1st ed. 1976, 32p, wrappers, 22cm.

Lloyd, F.B.

60430. *The Seniors: Being the Story of Senior Golf.* Haslemere, England: Seniors Golfers' Society, 3d ed. 1975, 16p, wrappers, 16.5cm. note: first and second editions not located.

Loch, Tony

60450. *Golf Is My Mistress: Memoirs of A Club Professional.* Greenland, New Hampshire: Evergreen, 1st ed. [1981] 170p, wrappers, 27.5cm. with Angelo Boy, preface by Sheila Loch.

Loeffelbein, Robert L.

60470. *How to Goof-Proof Your Golf Game.* Valley Lee, Maryland: Rob Roy Ventures, 1st ed. [1971] 69p, illustrated, illustrated wrappers, 27.5cm.

Logue, John

60490. *Follow the Leader.* New York: Crown, 1st ed. [1979] 210p, cloth, 23cm.

Lohren, Carl

60510. *One Move to Better Golf.* Norwalk, Connecticut: Golf Digest, 1st ed. [1975] 123p, illustrated by Anthony Ravielli, cloth, 28cm. with Larry Dennis, introduction by Deane Beman.

60520. pbk. ed. New York: New American Library, 1976, 152p, illustrated by Anthony Ravielli, illustrated wrappers, 17.5cm.

Long Ball, Add 50 Yards or More to Your Drive

60540. *The Long Ball, Add 50 Yards or more to your drive.* NP: Bost Enterprises, 1st ed. [1978] 95p, illustrated, illustrated wrappers, 28cm.

Long, Gordon

60560. *The Geelong Golf Club 1892-1967.* Melbourne, Australia: Hawthorn Press, 1st ed. 1967, 178p, illustrated, cloth, 21cm.

Longhurst, Henry

60580. *How to Get Started in Golf.* London: Hodder & Stoughton, 1st ed. 1967, 92p, illustrated by Alex Hay, illustrated wrappers, 18cm.

60590. *My Life and Soft Times.* London: Cassell, 1st ed. [1971] 366p, illustrated, cloth, 24.5cm.

60600. *Never on Weekdays.* London: Cassell, 1st ed. 1968, 182p, cloth, 21cm. introduction by Stephen Potter.

60610. *Only on Sundays.* London: Cassell, 1st ed. 1964, 259p, cloth, 21cm. later printings.

60620. *Southport: Golf Centre of Europe.* Southport, England: County Borough, 1st ed. [ca1969] [32p] illustrated, illustrated wrappers, 21.5cm.

60630. *Talking About Golf.* London: Macdonald, 1st ed. 1966, 150p, cloth, 18.5cm.

Longhurst, Henry and Geoffrey Cousins

60650. *Ryder Cup, 1965.* London: Stanley Paul, 1st ed. 1965, 64p, illustrated, cloth, 22.5cm.

60660. *The Old Course At St. Andrews, Henry Longhurst tells you How To Play It and Geoffrey Cousins offers Some Facts & Figures.* London: A.G. Spalding, 1st ed. 1961, 39p, illustrated, illustrated wrappers, 15cm.

Longo, Peter

60680. *Simplified Golf: There's No Trick to It.* Phoenix, Arizona: Phoenix Books, 1st ed. [1980] 144p, illustrated, illustrated wrappers, 27.5cm. later printing.

Longrigg, Doreen

60700. *Ladies on the Fairway.* Turnbridge Wells, England: Midas, 1st ed. 1981, 91p, illustrated, illustrated wrappers, 21cm.

Longue Vue Club

60720. *Longue Vue Club Fiftieth Anniversary 1920-1970*. Verona, Pennsylvania: Privately Printed, 1st ed. 1970 [20p] illustrated, wrappers, 23cm.

Lopez, Nancy

60740. *The Education of A Woman Golfer*. New York: Simon & Schuster, 1st ed. [1979] 191p, illustrated, cloth, 23.5cm. with Peter Schwed. later printings.

60750. 1st UK ed. London: Pelham, 1980, 188p, illustrated, cloth, 22.5cm, with Peter Schwed.

Los Angeles Country Club

60770. *Golden Anniversary of the Clubhouse 1911-1961, Los Angeles Country Club*. Los Angeles: Privately Printed, 1st ed. 1961, 16p, illustrated, illustrated wrappers, 28cm.

Low, George

60790. *The Master of Putting*. New York: Atheneum, 1st ed. 1983, 84p, illustrated, cloth, 21cm. with Al Barkow. later printings.

Lucas, Laddie

60810. *The Sport of Prince's, Reflections of A Golfer*. London: Stanley Paul, 1st ed. 1980, 192p, illustrated, cloth, 23cm.

Lucock, Ted

60830. *Golf Mad*. Durban, South Africa: E. Lucock, 1st ed. 1981 [78p] illustrated, illustrated wrappers, 20.5cm.

60840. *Golfing with Lu*. Durban, South Africa: E. Lucock, 1st ed. [ca1980] [78p] illustrated, illustrated wrappers, 20cm.

Luffness Golf Club and Kilspinde Golf Club

60860. *A Brief History of Luffness Golf Club and Kilspinde Golf Club*. Edinburgh: Privately Printed, 1st ed. 1967, 15p, illustrated, illustrated wrappers, 25.5cm.

Lunemann, Evelyn

60880. *Fairway Danger*. Westchester, Illinois: Benefic Press, 1st ed. [1969] 72p, illustrated by Max Ranft, illustrated boards, 23cm.

Lupovich, Norman

60900. *Elm Ridge Country Club 1924-1974, Our First Fifty Years.* Montreal: Privately Printed, 1st ed. [1974] 69p, illustrated, decorative cloth, 28cm.

Lush, Lorraine

60920. *Golf Lessons.* Adelaide, Australia: Rigby, 1st ed. 1981, 88p, illustrated, illustrated wrappers, 23.5cm.

Lutz, Douglas

60940. *Metropolitan Golf Guide: New York Edition.* New York: Par Magazine, 1st ed. [1970] 128p, illustrated, illustrated wrappers, 21cm.

Luxton, Theodore

60960. *The Dynamics Golf Correspondence Course.* Stourbridge, England: Privately Printed, 1st ed. [1973] 180p, illustrated, illustrated wrappers, 30cm.

60970. *The Real Truth About the Golf Swing.* London: Kingswood Press, 1st ed. [1985] 104p, illustrated by Phil Green, cloth, 24cm.

Lyle, Sandy

60990. *Dunlop Golf Guide-Carnoustie.* Kingswood, England: World's Work, 1st ed. 1982 [46p] illustrated, illustrated wrappers, 21cm. with Bob Ferrier.

61000. *Dunlop Golf Guide-Muirfield.* Kingswood, England: World's Work, 1st ed. 1982 [46p] illustrated, illustrated wrappers, 21cm. with Bob Ferrier.

61010. *Dunlop Golf Guide-Royal Troon.* Kingswood, England: World's Work, 1st ed. 1982 [46p] illustrated, illustrated wrappers, with Bob Ferrier. 21cm.

61020. *Dunlop Golf Guide-Turnberry.* Kingswood, England: World's Work, 1st ed. 1982 [46p] illustrated, illustrated wrappers, 21cm. with Bob Ferrier.

61030. *The Championship Courses of Scotland.* Kingswood, England: World Work's, 1st ed. 1982, 288p, illustrated, cloth, 29.5cm. with Bob Ferrier.

Lyons, Harry and Dick Johnson

61050. *The Hazards of Golf: A Complete How-Not-To Book.* Honolulu, Hawaii: Lyson Creative Enterprises, 1st ed. [1979] 47p, illustrated, illustrated wrappers, 28cm.

M., P.J. [Pennelope J. Mills]

61070. *Golfing Trifles.* edited by. London: Michael Joseph, 1st ed. 1985, 46p, illustrated, cloth, 15cm.

MacCabe, Eddie

61090. *The Ottawa Hunt Club, 75 Years of History 1908-1983.* Ottawa, Canada: Privately Printed, 1st ed. 1983, 134p, illustrated, decorative cloth, 22cm.

Maccabe, J.C.

61110. *The First Eighty Years, Douglas Park Golf Club.* Bearsden, England: Privately Printed, 1st ed. [1982] 145p, illustrated, cloth, 23.5cm.

MacDonald, John

61130. *Crail Golfing Society, A Short History.* Crail, Scotland: Privately Printed, 1st ed. 1983, 15p, wrappers, 21cm.

MacDonald, Robert G. [Bob] and Leo Bolstad

61150. *Golf.* New York: Sterling, 1st ed. [1961] 128p, illustrated, decorative cloth, 19.5cm.

MacKay, Elizabeth

61170. *Royal Dornoch Golf Club 1877-1977.* Dornoch, Scotland: Privately Printed, 1st ed. 1977 [20p] illustrated, illustrated wrappers, 21.5cm.

Mackay, Thomas

61190. *A History of the Liverpool Golf Club.* Lansvale, Australia: Privately Printed, 1st ed. 1972, 32p, illustrated, illustrated wrappers, 21.5cm.

Mackenzie, David A.

61210. *A History of Melrose Golf Club.* Melrose, Scotland: Privately Printed, 1st ed. [1979] 137p, illustrated, illustrated wrappers, 20.5cm.

Mackey, Richard T.

61230. *Golf.* Oxford, Ohio: Miami University, 1st ed. [ca1962] 44p, illustrated, wrappers, 22.5cm.

61240. *Golf: Learn Thru Auditory and Visual Cues.* Dubuque, Iowa: Kendall/Hunt, 1st ed. [1978] 67p, illustrated, illustrated wrappers, 23cm.

Mackie, Keith and Iain Crawford

61260. *Capital Golf: A colour guide to more than 35 courses in and around Edinburgh.* Edinburgh: City of Edinburgh, limited ed. [320 copies] [1984] 70p, illustrated, leather, 21cm, foreword by Jack Nicklaus.

61270. 1st trade ed. [ca1985] 70p, illustrated, illustrated wrappers, 21cm, foreword by Jack Nicklaus.

Mackintosh, Ian M.

61290. *Troon Golf Club, Its History from 1878.* Troon, Scotland: Privately Printed, 1st ed. 1974, 137p, illustrated, decorative cloth, 24cm.

Mackintosh, Ian M. and W.G. Sweet

61310. *Troon Golf Club 1878-1978, Commemorative Brochure.* Troon, Scotland: Privately Printed, 1st ed. 1978, 23p, illustrated, illustrated wrappers, 24cm.

Maclaren, Muir

61330. *The Golfer's Bedside Book.* Sydney, Australia: A.H. & A.W. Reed, 1st ed. 1976, 332p, illustrated by Peter Harrigan, cloth, 18.5cm.

MacVicar, Angus

61350. *Golf in My Gallowses: Confessions of A Fairway Fanatic.* London: Hutchinson, 1st ed. 1983, 178p, illustrated, cloth, 21.5cm, with Jock MacVicar.

61360. *Murder At the Open.* London: John Long, 1st ed. 1965, 184p, cloth, 18cm.

MacWeeney, Paul

61380. *Woodbrook Golf Club, 50th Anniversary Year 1926-1976.* Wicklow, Ireland: Privately Printed, 1st ed. 1976 [36p] illustrated, illustrated wrappers, 15cm.

Mahon, James J.

61400. *Baltusrol, 90 Years in the Mainstream of American Golf.* Plainfield, New Jersey: Privately Printed, 1st ed. [1985] 160p, illustrated, cloth, 28cm.

Mahoney, Jack

61420. *The Golf History of New England.* Wellesley, Massachusetts: New England Golf, 1st ed. [1973] 175p, illustrated, illustrated wrappers, 23cm.

Mahopac Golf Club

61440. *Mahopac Golf Club 1898-1980.* Lake Mahopac, New York: Privately Printed, limited ed. [500 copies] 1980 [20p] illustrated, decorative cloth, 24cm.

Mair, Lewine

61460. *The Dunlop Lady Golfer's Champion.* Lavenham, England: Eastland Press, 1st ed. 1980, 106p, illustrated, cloth, 22.5cm, foreword by Henry Cotton.

Maltby, Ralph

61480. *Golf Club Assembly Manual.* Newark, Ohio: Ralph Maltby Enterprises, 1st ed. 1981, 36p, illustrated, illustrated wrappers, 28cm.

61490. *Golf Club Design, Fitting, Alteration and Repair: The principles and procedures.* Newark, Ohio: Faultless Sports, 1st ed. [1974] 331p, illustrated, decorative cloth, 27.5cm.

61500. 2d ed. rev. Newark, Ohio: Ralph Maltby Enterprises, 1982, 720p, illustrated, decorative cloth, 27.5cm.

61510. *Golf Club Repair in Pictures.* Newark, Ohio: PGA & Ralph Maltby Enterprises, 1st ed. [1978] 104p, illustrated, illustrated wrappers, 28cm, foreword by Joseph O'Brien.

61515. 2d ed. rev. Newark, Ohio: Ralph Maltby Enterprises, 1980, 152p, illustrated, illustrated wrappers, 28cm.

61520. 3d ed. rev. 1982, 185p, illustrated, spiral bound illustrated wrappers, 27.5cm.

Manchester Country Club

61540. *Manchester Country Club 1923-1973.* Manchester, New Hampshire: Privately Printed, 1st ed. 1973, 76p, illustrated, wrappers, 22cm.

Manito Golf & Country Club

61560. *Manito Golf & Country Club, 50 Years 1922-1972.* Spokane, Washington: Privately Printed, 1st ed. 1972, 20p, illustrated, wrappers, 20cm.

Mann, Frederick George

61580. *Lord Rutherford on the Golf Course.* Cambridge, England: Privately Printed, 1st ed. 1976, 33p, illustrated, wrappers, 23.5cm.

Marks, Sara W.

61600. *Fore!... Women Only; An Anatomy of A Woman's Golf Club.* La Brea, California: Sarma, 1st ed. 1966, 77p, illustrated, illustrated wrappers, 21.5cm, introduction by Shirley Spork.

Marr, David

61620. *Woods from the Tee and Fairway. A Flip Vision Golf Manual.* New York: Sterling, 1st ed. [1965] 128p, illustrated, illustrated wrappers, 12.5cm.

Marshall, Harry

61640. *Sixty Years and More, A History of Low Laithes Golf Club.* Wakefield, England: Privately Printed, 1st ed. 1985 [52p] illustrated, illustrated wrappers, 21cm.

Martin, John Stuart

61660. *The Curious History of the Golf Ball: Mankind's Most Fascinating Sphere.* New York: Horizon Press, limited ed. signed, slipcased [500 copies] [1968] 192p, illustrated, decorative cloth, 23.5cm, foreword by Chick Evans.

61670. 1st trade ed. [1968] 192p, illustrated, decorative cloth, 23cm, foreword by Chick Evans.

Maryland Interclub Seniors Golf Association

61690. *A History of MISGA 1976-1985.* [Maryland] Maryland Interclub Seniors Golf Association, 1st ed. 1985, 56p, illustrated, illustrated wrappers, 21.5cm.

Mason, Gard

61710. *Durand Eastman Golf Club Member Information Package: Being a compilation of historical facts information, rules, policies and guide for members and officers a like; and designed to help maintain the continuity and traditions of the Durand Eastman Golf Club.* Rochester, New York: Privately Printed, 1st ed. 1978, 26p, illustrated, wrappers, 28cm.

Mason, J.T.

61730. *Build Yourself A Golf Swing by the Seven Steps of the Mason Methods.* Hamphshire, England: Privately Printed, 1st ed. 1974, 32p, illustrated, illustrated wrappers, 22cm, foreword by F.H. Holmes.

Massereene Golf Club

61750. *Massereene Golf Club 1895-1974.* Antrim, Northern Ireland: Privately Printed, 1st ed. 1975, 15p, illustrated, illustrated wrappers, 25.5cm.

Master Golf

61770. *Master Golf: Learn Golf with the Stars, the Neil Coles Way.* London: Futura, 1st ed. 1977, 63p, illustrated, illustrated wrappers, 30cm, introduction by Alan Mouncer.

Matson, Geoffrey J.

61790. *Off the Tee: Favourite Golfing Stories and Anecdotes of the Famous.* London: W. Foulsham, 1st ed. [1963] 127p, illustrated by Trevor Parkin, cloth, 18cm.

Matthew, D.B.

61810. *Broughty Golf Club History 1878-1978.* Monifieth, Scotland: Privately Printed, 1st ed. 1978, 26p, illustrated, illustrated wrappers, 21cm.

May, John Allan

61830. *Bedside Duffer.* Boston, Massachusetts: Christian Science Monitor, 1st ed. [1969] [62p] illustrated, illustrated wrappers, 14.5cm.

61840. *Duffer's A.B.C.* Boston, Massachusetts: Christian Science Monitor, 1st ed. [1970] [80p] illustrated, illustrated wrappers, 14.5cm.

61850. *Duffer's Discoveries.* Boston, Massachusetts: Christian Science Monitor, 1st ed. [1972] [58p] illustrated, illustrated wrappers, 14.5cm.

61860. *Duffer's Guide.* Boston, Massachusetts: Christian Science Monitor, 1st ed. [1967] [48p] illustrated, illustrated wrappers, 14.5cm.

61870. *Duffer's Progress.* Boston, Massachusetts: Christian Science Monitor, 1st ed. [1968] [48p] illustrated, illustrated wrappers, 14.5cm.

May, Julian

61890. *Lee Trevino, The Golf Explosion.* Mankato, Minnesota: Crestwood House, 1st ed. [1974] 48p, illustrated, illustrated boards, 23cm.

61900. *The Masters.* Mankato, Minnesota: Creative Education, 1st ed. [1975] 47p, illustrated, illustrated boards, 26.5cm.

61910. *The PGA Championship Tournament.* Mankato, Minnesota: Creative Education, 1st ed. [1976] 44p, illustrated, illustrated boards, 26.5cm.

61920. *The U.S. Open Championship.* Mankato, Minnesota: Creative Education, 1st ed. [1975] 47p, illustrated, illustrated boards, 26.5cm.

Mayhew, John F.

61940. *Par Excellence, Highlights of Sixty Five Years at Barton Hills Country Club [1917-1982].* Ann Arbor, Michigan: Privately Printed, 1st ed. 1983, 90p, illustrated, decorative cloth, 28cm.

McAdam, Cliff

61960. *How to Break 90/80/Par.* New York: Winchester Press, 1st ed. [1973] 158p, illustrated, cloth, 22.5cm.

61970. *Golf Illustrated Presents Arnie.* edited by. Temecula, California: Rich Publishing, 1st ed. [1976] 98p, illustrated, illustrated wrappers, 27.5cm.

McAllister, Evelyn Ditton

61990. *Golf for Beginners: A Golfing Handbook.* Ormond Beach, Florida: Privately Printed, 1st ed. [1969] 95p, illustrated, illustrated wrappers, 23cm.

McAndrew, Bert and T. McClurg

62010. *Basic Principles & Practice of Golf.* St. Andrews: Golf School, 1st ed. [ca1975] 28p, illustrated, wrappers, 21cm.

McCarthy, Colman

62050. *The Pleasures of the Game: The Theory Free Guide to Golf.* New York: Dial Press, 1st ed. 1977, 150p, cloth, 22.5cm.

McCleery, Peter

62070. *More Instant Golf Lessons.* edited by. Norwalk, Connecticut: Golf Digest, 1st ed. [1985] 233p, illustrated, illustrated wrappers, 20.5cm.

McCormack, Mark H.

62090. *Arnie: The Evolution of A Legend.* New York: Simon & Schuster, 1st ed. [1967] 318p, illustrated, cloth, 23.5cm.

62100. *Arnold Palmer, The Man and the Legend.* London: Cassell, 1st UK ed. 1967, 318p, illustrated, cloth, 23.5cm, UK title of "Arnie: The Evolution of A Legend."

62110. *Golf '67: World Professional Golf: the Facts and Figures.* London: Cassell, 1st ed. 1967, 310p, illustrated, cloth, 21cm.

62120. *The World of Professional Golf 1968.* Cleveland, Ohio: World, 1st ed. 1968, 480p, illustrated, decorative cloth, 27cm.

62130. *The World of Professional Golf: Golf Annual 1969.* London: Hodder & Stoughton, 1st ed. 399p, illustrated, cloth, 23.5cm.

62135. *The World of Professional Golf: Golf Annual 1969*. Cleveland, Ohio: International Literary Management, 1st American ed. 1969, 399p, illustrated, cloth, 23.5cm.

62140. *The World of Professional Golf: Golf Annual 1970*. London: Hodder & Stoughton, 1st ed. 1970, 464p, illustrated, cloth, 23.5cm.

62145. *The World of Professional Golf: Golf Annual 1970*. Cleveland, Ohio: IMI, 1970, 1st American ed, 464p, illustrated, cloth, 23.5cm.

62150. *The World of Professional Golf: Mark H. McCormack's Golf Annual 1971*. London: Hodder & Stoughton, 1st ed, 1971, 486p, illustrated, cloth, 23.5cm.

62155. *The World of Professional Golf: Mark H. McCormack's Golf Annual 1971*. Cleveland, Ohio: International Literary Management, 1st American ed. 1971, 486p, illustrated, cloth, 23.5cm.

62160. *The World of Professional Golf Annual 1972*. London: Collins, 1st ed. 1972, 528p, illustrated, cloth, 23cm.

62165. *The World of Professional Golf Annual 1972*. New York: Atheneum, 1st American ed. 1972, 528p, illustrated, cloth, 23cm.

62170. *The World of Professional Golf Mark H. McCormack's Golf Annual 1973*. London: Collins, 1st ed. 1973, 559p, illustrated, cloth, 23.5cm.

62175. *The World of Professional Golf Mark H. McCormack's Golf Annual 1973*. New York: Atheneum, 1st American ed. 1973, 559p, illustrated, cloth, 23.5cm.

62180. *The World of Professional Golf Mark H. McCormack's Golf Annual 1974*. London: Collins, 1st ed. 1974, 580p, illustrated, cloth, 23.5cm.

62185. *The World of Professional Golf Mark H. McCormack's Golf Annual 1974*. New York: Atheneum, 1st American ed. 1974, 580p, illustrated, cloth, 23.5cm.

62190. *The World of Professional Golf Mark H. McCormack's Golf Annual 1975*. London: Collins, 1st ed. 1975, 462p, illustrated, cloth, 23.5cm.

62195. *The World of Professional Golf Mark H. McCormack's Golf Annual 1975*. New York: Atheneum, 1st American ed. 1975, 462p, illustrated, cloth, 23.5cm.

62200. *The World of Professional Golf Mark H. McCormack's Golf*

Annual 1976. London: Collins, 1st ed. 1976, 521p. illustrated, cloth, 23.5cm.

62205. *The World of Professional Golf Mark H. McCormack's Golf Annual 1976*. New York: Atheneum, 1st American ed. 1976, 521p, illustrated, cloth, 23.5cm.

62210. *The World of Professional Golf Mark H. McCormack's Golf Annual 1977*. London: Collins, 1st ed. 1977, 563p, illustrated, cloth, 23cm.

62215. *The World of Professional Golf Mark H. McCormack's Golf Annual 1977*. New York: Atheneum, 1st American ed. 1977, 563p, illustrated, cloth, 23cm.

62220. *The World of Professional Golf Mark H. McCormack's Golf Annual 1978*. Brighton, England: Angus & Robertson, 1st ed. 1978, 392p, illustrated, cloth, 23.5cm.

62223. pbk. ed. 1978, 392p, illustrated, illustrated wrappers, 23cm.

62225. *The World of Professional Golf Mark H. McCormack's Golf Annual 1978*. Garden City, New York: Doubleday, 1st American ed. 1978, 392p, illustrated, cloth, 23.5cm.

62230. *Dunhill Golf Yearbook 1979*. London: Springwood Books, 1st ed, 1979, 446p, illustrated, cloth, 23cm.

62235. pbk. ed. 1979, 446p, illustrated, illustrated wrappers, 23cm.

62240. *Dunhill Golf Yearbook 1979*. Garden City, New York: Doubleday, 1st American ed. 1979, 446p, illustrated, cloth, 23cm.

62245. pbk. ed. 1979, 446p, illustrated, illustrated wrappers, 22.5cm.

62250. *Dunhill Golf Yearbook 1980*. London: Springwood Books, 1st ed, 1980, illustrated, cloth, 23cm.

62255. *Dunhill Golf Yearbook 1980*. Garden City, New York: Doubleday, 1st American ed. 1980, 447p, illustrated, cloth, 23cm.

62260. pbk. ed. 1980, 447p, illustrated, illustrated wrappers, 23cm.

62270. *Dunhill World of Professional Golf 1981*. London: Springwood Books, 1st ed, 482p, illustrated, cloth, 23cm.

62275. *Dunhill World of Professional Golf 1981*. San Diego, California: A.S. Barnes, 1st American ed. 1981, 482p, illustrated, cloth, 23cm.

62280. *Dunhill World of Professional Golf 1982*. London: Springwood Books, 1st ed, 558p, illustrated, cloth, 23cm.

62285. *Dunhill World of Professional Golf 1982*. San Diego,

California: A.S. Barnes, 1st American ed. 1982, 558p, illustrated, cloth, 23cm.

62290. *Dunhill World of Professional Golf 1983*. London: Springwood Books, 1st ed. 1983, 544p, illustrated, cloth, 23cm.

62300. *Dunhill World of Professional Golf 1983*. Washington, DC: Acropolis Books, 1st American ed.1983, 544p, illustrated, cloth, 23cm.

62310. *Ebel World of Professional Golf 1984*. London: Springwood Books, 1st ed. 530p, illustrated, cloth, 23cm.

62320. *Ebel World of Professional Golf 1984*. Washington, DC: Acropolis Books, 1st American ed. 1984, 530p, illustrated, cloth, 23cm.

62325. *Ebel World of Professional Golf 1984*. Surrey Hills, Australia: James Fraser, 1st Australian ed, 1984, 530p, illustrated, cloth, 23cm.

62330. *Ebel World of Professional Golf 1985*. London: Springwood Books, 1st ed, 1985, 515p, illustrated, cloth, 23cm.

62335. *Ebel World of Professional Golf 1985*. Cincinnati, Ohio: Old Golf Shop, 1st American ed. 1985, 515p, illustrated, cloth, 23cm.

62600. *The Wonderful World of Professional Golf*. New York: Atheneum, 1st ed. 1973, 467p, illustrated, cloth, 28cm.

McCormick, Bill

62620. *The Complete Beginner's Guide to Golf*. Garden City, New York: Doubleday, 1st ed. 1974, 130p, illustrated by John Lane, cloth, 23cm.

McCue, Carol

62640. *How to Conduct Golf Club Championships*. Evanston, Illinois: Golf Publishers, 1st ed. [1964] 20p, wrappers, 28cm.

62650. 2d ed. rev. 1965, 20p, spiral bound illustrated wrappers, 28cm.

McDiardmid, D.J.

62670. *100 Years of Golf At Machrihanish 1876-1976*. Machrihanish, Scotland: Privately Printed, 1st ed. 1976, 52p, illustrated, illustrated wrappers, 22.5cm, foreword by S.L. McKinlay.

McDonnell, Michael

62690. *Golf: The Great Ones.* London: Pelham, 1st ed. 1971, 147p, illustrated, cloth, 21.5cm.

62700. 1st American ed. New York: Drake, 1973, 147p, illustrated, cloth, 21.5cm.

62710. *Great Moments in Sport: Golf.* London: Pelham, 1st ed. 1974, 200p, illustrated, cloth, 21.5cm.

62720. 1st Canadian ed. Toronto: Pagurian Press [1974] 200p, illustrated, cloth, 21.5cm.

62730. *The Complete Book of Golf.* London: Kingswood Press, 1st ed. [1985] 247p, illustrated, cloth, 24.5cm.

62740. *The World of Golf 1971-1972.* London: Purnell, 1st ed. 1971, 93p, illustrated, cloth, 26.5cm.

McDonough, Bill

62760. *Common Sense Golf.* Southbury, Connecticut: Privately Printed, 1st ed. [1975] 31p, illustrated wrappers, 18cm.

McDougal, Stan

62780. *101 Great Golf Jokes and Stories.* New York: Citadel Press, 1st ed. [1968] 64p, illustrated by Ben Black, illustrated boards, 18.5cm.

62790. *The World's Greatest Golf Jokes.* Secaucus, New Jersey: Citadel Press, 1st ed. [1980] 179p, illustrated, cloth, 23cm.

McDougall, Donald

62810. *Davie.* New York: St. Martin's Press, 1st American ed. [1977] 254p, cloth, 21cm. note: first edition not located.

McGehee, Charles C.

62830. *History of the Southern Seniors Golf Association, Fifty Years On, 1930-1980*. Pinehurst, North Carolina: Privately Printed, 1st ed. 1980, 63p, illustrated, cloth, 28cm.

McGraw, Donald

62850. *The Full Bag, or, The Golf Duffer's Own Handbook; How to Keep From breaking 100*. New York: Exposition Press, 1st ed. [1962] 42p, cloth, 20.5cm.

McGurn, Robert and S.A. Williams

62870. *Golf Power in Motion*. Norwalk, Connecticut: Golf Digest, 1st ed. [1967] 144p, illustrated, cloth, 23cm.

62880. 1st UK ed. London: Souvenir Press, 1968, 144p, illustrated, cloth, 23cm.

62890. pbk. ed. New York: Cornerstone Library, 1974, 144p, illustrated, illustrated wrappers, 20cm.

McHose, John C.

62910. *The Wilshire Country Club 1919-1979*. Los Angeles: Privately Printed, 1st ed. 1979, 56p, illustrated, illustrated wrappers, 20.5cm.

McInerny, Ralph

62930. *Lying Three: A Father Dowling Mystery*. New York: Vanguard Press, 1st ed. [1979] 250p, cloth, 21cm.

McIntosh, Jan

62950. *Hooked on Golf*. Ipswich, Massachusetts: Ipswich Press, 1st ed. [1982] [92p] illustrated, illustrated wrappers, 20.5cm.

McKay, David

62970. *Leith and the Origins of Golf*. Edinburgh: Leith Rotary Club, 1st ed. 1984 [16p] illustrated, illustrated wrappers, 29.5cm.

McKinlay, S.L.

62990. *Gleneagles Hotel Golf Courses, Scotland*. Gleneagles, Scotland: British Transport Hotels [1969] 20p, illustrated, wrappers, 15cm.

McLachlan, Iaen

63010. *Attack the Flag.* Adelaide, Australia: Rigby, 2d ed. 1977, 182p, illustrated, illustrated wrappers, 21cm, note: previously published as "Billy Dunk's Five Under" in 1972 [have not located].

63020. *One Hundred Golf Tips by Leading Australian and New Zealand Golfers.* Adelaide, Australia: Rigby, 1st ed. 1973, 112p, illustrated, cloth, 28cm.

63030. *Putting Tips from the Top.* Adelaide, Australia: Rigby, 1st ed. 1980, 87p, illustrated, cloth, 27cm.

63040. *Swing to Win: The Story and Techniques of Leading Proette, Judy Perkins.* Adelaide, Australia: Rigby, 1st ed. 1975, 95p, illustrated, cloth, 28cm.

McLean, Terry

63060. *A Simpler Place In Time, Golfing in New Zealand.* Auckland, New Zealand: Air New Zealand, 1st ed. [1980] 112p, illustrated, illustrated wrappers, 18.5cm, foreword by Arnold Palmer.

McLeod, Rod

63080. *St. Andrews Old.* London: Souvenir Press, 1st ed. 1970 [118p] illustrated, cloth, 19.5cm, edited by Ken Thomson, foreword by Sean Connery.

McMahon, Thomas G.

63100. *What Price Uniformity? The Golf Handicap Situation.* Los Angeles: Privately Printed, 1st ed. 1966, 21p, wrappers, 28cm.

McQuillan, Eoin

63120. *The Fred Daly Story.* Belfast, Northern Ireland: Blackstaff Press, 1st ed. [1978] 132p, illustrated, wrappers, 21cm.

McTeigue, Michael

63140. *The Keys to the Effortless Golf Swing.* New York: Atheneum, 1st ed. 1985, 93p, illustrated by Jim McQueen, cloth, 21cm, foreword by Ken Bowden.

McWeeney, Paul

63160. *Milltown Golf Club Golden Jubilee.* Milltown, Ireland: Privately Printed, 1st ed. [ca1981] 24p, illustrated, illustrated wrappers, 21cm.

Mearns, James A.G.

63180. *200 Years of Golf, 1780-1980, Royal Aberdeen Golf Club.* Aberdeen, Scotland: Privately Printed, limited ed. [no limitation cited] 1980, 148p, illustrated, decorative cloth, 22.5cm.

Mehalski, Ross and John Skinner

63200. *The Christchurch Golf Club 1873-1973, A Century of Golf in Christchurch.* Christchurch, New Zealand: Privately Printed, 1st ed. 1973 [48p] illustrated, illustrated wrappers, 30cm.

Mehlhorn, Bill

63220. *Golf Secrets Exposed.* Miami, Florida: M & S, 1st ed. 1984, 210p, illustrated, illustrated wrappers, 21.5cm, with Bobby Shave.

Mele, Joseph G. and Charles R. Wayne, Jr.

63240. *A Golfer's Guide to Public Golf Courses in New Jersey, Vol. 1. North Jersey.* Mount Freedom, New Jersey: Garden State Golf Associates, 1st ed. 1985, 99p, illustrated wrappers, 22.5cm.

Menzies, Gordon

63260. *The World of Golf.* edited by. London: British Broadcast Corp. 1st ed. 1982, 224p, illustrated, cloth, 24.5cm, foreword by Peter Alliss.

Merion Golf Club

63280. *Golf At Merion 1896-1976.* Ardmore, Pennsylvania: Privately Printed, 1st ed. 1977, 96p, illustrated, illustrated wrappers, 21cm.

Merrins, Eddie

63300. *Golf for the Young.* New York: Atheneum, 2d ed. 1983, 100p, illustrated, illustrated wrappers, 28cm, with Michael McTeigue. note: first edition not located.

63310. *Swing the Handle-Not the Clubhead.* Norwalk, Connecticut: Golf Digest, 1st ed. [1973] 128p, illustrated by Ed Vebell, cloth, 28cm.

Merwin, Ben

63330. *Idylwylde, First Fifty Years 1922-1972.* Sudbury, Canada: Privately Printed, 1st ed. 1972, 92p, illustrated, decorative cloth, 27.5cm.

Metz, Richard

63350. *The Graduated Swing Method.* New York: Scribners, 1st ed. [1981] 126p, illustrated, cloth, 27cm.

Meyer, D. Swing

63370. *The Method: A Golf Success Strategy.* Columbia, South Carolina: Acorn Press, 1st ed. [1981] [130p] illustrated, 3-ring cloth binder, 28cm, along with supplemental booklet "How To Get the Most Out of The Method."

Michael, Thomas [Tom]

63390. *Golf's Winning Stroke: Putting.* New York: Coward-McCann, 1st ed. [1967] 189p, illustrated, cloth, 21cm, introduction by Cary Middlecoff.

63400. 1st UK ed. London: Souvenir Press, 1968, 189p, illustrated, cloth, 21cm, introduction by Cary Middlecoff.

Michelmore, Cliff

63420. *The Businessman's Book of Golf.* edited by. London: Weldendeld and Nicholson, 1st ed. [1981] 157p, illustrated, cloth, 23.5cm.

Michener, Edward C.

63440. *The Everglades Club, A Retrospective 1919-1985.* Palm Beach, Florida: Privately Printed, 1st ed. slipcased, 1985, 128p, illustrated, gilt stamped leather, 25.5cm.

Micklem, G.H.

63460. *Help in the Interpretation of the Rules of Golf.* Sunningdale, England: Privately Printed, 1st ed. 1979, 74p, illustrated wrappers, 22cm.

Middlecoff, Cary

63480. *The Golf Swing*. Englewood Cliffs, New Jersey: Prentice-Hall, 1st ed. [1974] 230p, illustrated, cloth, 24.5cm, edited by Tom Michael.

63490. 1st UK ed. London: Robert Hale [1974] 230p, illustrated, cloth, 23cm, edited by Tom Michael.

Middlecoff, Cary and Tom Michael

63510. *14 Classic Tips for the New Year, from the CBS Classic at Firestone C.C.* [Norwalk, Connecticut] Golf Digest, 1st ed. 1967 [16p] illustrated by James McQueen, illustrated wrappers, 21cm.

Middleton, Ralph

63530. *Alwoodley Golf Club 1907-1983*. Leeds, England: Privately Printed, 1st ed. 1985, 97p, wrappers, 21cm.

Mill Creek Park Golf Course

63550. *Mill Creek Park Golf Course 50th Anniversary 1972-1957*. Youngstown, Ohio: Privately Printed, 1st ed. 1977, 20p, illustrated, illustrated wrappers, 28cm.

Miller, Beryl Buck

63570. *Play A Round with Beryl Buck Miller*. [Westport, Connecticut] Arnott, 1st ed. [1979] 101p, illustrated, illustrated wrappers, 23cm, foreword by Dick Siderowf.

Miller, Hack

63590. *The New Billy Casper: More Important Things in Life Than Golf*. Salt Lake City, Utah: Deseret Book Co. 1st ed. 1968, 144p, illustrated, illustrated boards, 23cm, foreword by N. Eldon Tanner.

Miller, Johnny

63610. *Pure Golf*. Garden City, New York: Doubleday, 1st ed. 1976, 191p, illustrated by Jim McQueen, cloth, 25.5cm, with Dale Shankland, foreword by John Geersten.

Miller, Richard [Dick]

63630. *America's Greatest Golfing Resorts*. Indianapolis: Bobbs-Merrill, 1st ed. [1977] 239p, illustrated, cloth, 28cm, foreword by Arnold Palmer.

63640. *Triumphant Journey: The Saga of Bobby Jones and the Grand Slam of Golf.* New York: Holt, Rinehart & Winston, 1st ed. [1980] 258p, illustrated, cloth, 23cm.

63650. 1st UK ed. London: Robert Hale, 1981, 258p, illustrated, cloth, 23cm.

Miller, Robert V.

63670. *Golf, The Ageless Game.* So. Yarmouth, Massachusetts: John Curley & Associates, 1st ed. [1985] 80p, illustrated, illustrated boards, 28cm.

Millus, Donald

63690. *On the Southern Greens.* North Myrtle Beach, South Carolina: Itimmelsbach Communications, 1983, 74p, illustrated, illustrated wrappers, 28cm.

Miner, H. Craig

63710. *A History of the Wichita Country Club 1900-1975.* Wichita, Kansas: Privately Printed, 1st ed. 1975, 79p, illustrated, decorative cloth, 25.5cm.

Miron, Charles

63730. *Murder On the 18th Hole.* New York: Manor Books, 1st ed. [1978] 216p, illustrated wrappers, 17.5cm.

Mitchell, William F.

63750. *Cochrane Castle Golf Club, Its History from 1895.* Johnstone, Scotland: Privately Printed, 1st ed. 1980, 76p, illustrated, illustrated wrappers, 25.5cm.

Mobbs, George

63770. *Northamptonshire County Golf Club, History of the Course.* Northampton, England: Privately Printed, 1st ed. 1969, 29p, illustrated, illustrated wrappers, 18.5cm.

Moffatt, F.C.

63790. *Seventy Five Years of Golf, Morpeth Golf Club 1906-1981.* Morpeth, England: Privately Printed, 1st ed. 1981, 24p, illustrated, illustrated wrappers, 21cm.

Monday, Sil

63810. *Golf in the Ohio Sun.* Cleveland, Ohio: The Golfer, 1st ed. 1970, 160p, illustrated, illustrated wrappers, 18.5cm.

Monte Carlo Country Club

63830. *Monte Carlo Country Club presents the Lighter Side of Golf.* Ft. Pierce, Florida: Monte Carlo Country Club, 1st ed. [ca1982] 16p, illustrated, wrappers, 27.5cm.

Moody, Orville

63850. *Golf How by Orville Who?* New York: Hawthorn, 1st ed. [1972] 199p, illustrated, cloth, 22.5cm, with Jim Hiskey, foreword by Lee Trevino.

Moor Park Golf Club

63870. *Moor Park Golf Club [Handbook].* Kingston Upon Thames, England: Temple Publicity Services, 1968, 40p, illustrated, illustrated wrappers, 18.5cm.

Moran, Sharron

63890. *Golf Is A Woman's Game or How to Be A Swinger on the Fairway.* New York: Hawthorn, 1st ed. [1971] 202p, illustrated, cloth, 22.5cm.

Morgan, Jerome E.

63910. *Golf Analysis Log.* Golden, Colorado: Privately Printed, 1st ed. [1979] 70p, illustrated, spiral bound illustrated wrappers, 28cm.

Morgan, John

63930. *Golf.* East Ardsley, England: EP Publishing, 1st ed. 1976, 112p, illustrated, illustrated boards, 20cm.

Morley, David C.

63950. *The Missing Links: Golf and the Mind.* New York: Atheneum, 1st ed. 1976, 234p, cloth, 21cm, technical editor Ken Bowden.

Morley, Michael E.

63970. *The Art and Science of Putting.* Scottsdale, Arizona: Privately Printed, 1st ed. [1982] 115p, illustrated, cloth, 25.5cm.

Morris, H. Messon

63990. *Church Stretton Golf Club [Handbook].* Bournemouth, England: Temple Publicity Services [ca1967] 12p, illustrated, wrappers, 18cm.

Morris, John and Leonard Cobb

64010. *Great Golf Holes of Hawaii.* Auckland, New Zealand: Morris/ Cobb, 1st ed. [1977] 95p, illustrated, illustrated boards, 21cm.

64020. *Great Golf Holes of New Zealand.* Auckland, New Zealand: Morris/Cobb, 1st ed. 1971, 96p, illustrated, illustrated boards, 22cm, with golf tips by Arnold Palmer.

Morse, Charles and Ann

64040. *Lee Trevino.* Mankato, Minnesota: Amecus Street, 1st ed. [1974] 31p, illustrated by Harold Henrikson, illustrated boards, 24cm.

Morton, Cecil W.

64060. *Golf: The Confessions of A Golf Club Secretary.* London: Hammond, Hammond, 1st ed. [1963] 93p, illustrated by John Cooper, decorative cloth, 26.5cm, foreword by Henry Longhurst.

Mosca, Jerry

64080. *Experiencing Golf in Scotland: A Guide To Scottish Courses.* Mankato, Minnesota: Golfing Scotland, 1st ed. [1984] 96p, illustrated, illustrated wrappers, 21.5cm.

Mountain Ash Golf Club

64100. *Mountain Ash Golf Club 1908-1983.* Cefnpennar, Wales: Privately Printed, 1st ed. 1983, 24p, illustrated, illustrated wrappers, 30cm.

Mucha, Steve

64120. *How to Break 100: Golfing Shortcuts the Pros Don't Teach You.* New York: Walker, 1st ed. 1982, 96p, illustrated by David Wool, cloth, 21cm, with Peter Mucha.

64130. pbk. ed. 1982, 96p, illustrated by David Wool, cloth, 21cm, with Peter Mucha.

Muir, Graham

64150. *Dumfries and Galloway Golf Club 1880-1980.* Dumfries, Scotland: Privately Printed, 1st ed. 1980 [64p] illustrated, illustrated wrappers, 21.5cm.

Muirfield Village Golf Club

64170. *Muirfield Village Golf Club [Handbook].* Chapel Hill, North Carolina: Golf Course Profiles, 1st ed. [1977] [27p] illustrated, illustrated wrappers, 18cm.

Mullins, Richard

64190. *The Phoenix Open-A 50 Year History.* Phoenix, Arizona: The Thunderbirds, limited ed. [1000 copies] [1984] 109p, illustrated, cloth, 30cm, edited by Richard M. Stuart.

Mulvoy, Mark

64210. *Sports Illustrated Golf.* New York: Harper & Row, 1st ed. [1983] 156p, illustrated, illustrated boards, 23cm.

64220. pbk. ed. [1983] 156p, illustrated, illustrated wrappers, 23cm, later printings.

Mulvoy, Mark and Art Spander

64240. *Golf: The Passion and the Challenge.* Englewood Cliffs, New Jersey: Prentice-Hall, 1st ed. 1977, 256p, illustrated, cloth, 27cm.

Mulvoy, Jr., Thomas F.

64260. *Wollaston Golf Club: Old in Tradition Young in Spirit. Commemorating Wollaston's Seventy Fifth Anniversary. 1895-1970.* Wollaston, Massachusetts: Privately Printed, 1st ed. 1970, 73p, illustrated, decorative cloth, 23.5cm.

Murdoch, Joseph S.F.

64280. *The Library of Golf 1743-1966, A Bibliography of Golf Books: Indexed Alphabetically, Chronologically and by Subject Matter.* Detroit, Michigan: Gale Research, 1st ed. slipcased, 1968, 314p, illustrated, decorative cloth, 23cm.

64290. *The Library of Golf 1743-1966 revised: 1967-1977 added.* [Lafayette Hill, Pennsylvania] Privately Printed, limited ed. [150 copies] 1978, 56p, illustrated wrappers, 22.5cm.

Murdoch, Joseph S.F. and Janet Seagle

64310. *Golf: A Guide to Information Sources.* Detroit, Michigan: Gale Research, 1st ed. [1979] 232p, cloth, 21.5cm.

Murphy, Michael

64330. *Golf in the Kingdom.* New York: Viking Press, 1st ed. [1972] 205p, illustrated, cloth, 21cm.

64340. pbk. ed. New York: Dell [1972] 203p, illustrated wrappers, 20cm.

Murphy, Thomas J.

64360. *Woodland Golf Club, A 75 Year History 1902-1977.* Auburndale, Massachusetts: Privately Printed, 1st ed. 1977, 135p, illustrated, gilt stamped leather, 28cm.

Murphy, Tom

64380. *Official Used Club Guide 1965.* Provo, Utah: Pro Guide, 1st ed. [1964] 160p, leatherette, 13cm.

Mutter, Bill

64400. *Golf on Ayrshire Coast.* Glasgow: Impact Publications, 1st ed. 1981, 36p, illustrated, illustrated wrappers, 21.5cm, assisted by Alistair Matheson, foreword by Sam Torrance.

Mutter, Charles

64420. *The Story of the Piltdown Golf 1904-1974.* Uckfield, England: Privately Printed, 1st ed. 1974, 14p, illustrated, wrappers, 21cm.

Myers, Kent

64440. *Golf in Oregon.* Portland, Oregon: Ryder Press, 1st ed. [1977] 153p, illustrated, illustrated wrappers, 23cm.

64450. 2d ed. rev. 1981, 154p, illustrated, illustrated wrappers, 23cm.

Naden, C.J.

64470. *Golf.* New York: Franklin Watts, 1st ed. [1970] 64p, illustrated, illustrated boards, 21.5cm.

Naftal, Charles S.

64490. *Games That Golfer's Play.* New York: Deca Unlimited, 1st ed. [1984] 55p, illustrated, illustrated wrappers, 21.5cm.

Nagle, Kel and others

64510. *The Secrets of Australia's Golfing Success.* and Norman Von Nida, Jim Ferrier, Peter Thomson. Melbourne, Australia: Lansdowne Press, 1st ed. 1961, 126p, illustrated, cloth, 23.5cm, foreword by Ossie Pickworth.

64520. 1st UK ed. London: Nicholas Kaye, 1961, 126p, illustrated, cloth, 23.5cm.

Nance, Virginia L. and Elwood Craig Davis

64540. *Golf.* Dubuque, Iowa: Wm. C. Brown, 1st ed. [1966] 86p, illustrated by Francile Otto & Virginia L. Nance, illustrated wrappers, 23cm.

64550. 3d ed. rev. [1975] 102p, illustrated by Francile Otto & Ralph Rivas, illustrated wrappers, 23cm. note: second edition not located.

National Golf Foundation

64570. *Golf Coach's Guide.* North Palm Beach, Florida: National Golf Foundation, 1st ed. [1975] 98p, illustrated by Dom Lupo, illustrated wrappers, 28cm, edited by Richard D. Gordin.

64580. 2d ed. rev. 1978, 98p, illustrated by Dom Lupo, illustrated wrappers, 28cm, edited by Richard D. Gordin.

64590. *Golf Instructor's Guide.* Chicago: National Golf Foundation, 3d ed. revised [1972] 104p, illustrated wrappers, 28cm.

64600. *Golf Operations Handbook and Golf Facility Development Guide.* North Palm Beach, Florida: National Golf Foundation, 1985, unpaginated, updated periodically, illustrated, vinyl 3 ring folder, 28cm.

64610. *Miniature Putting Course and Golf Driving Range Manual.* Chicago: National Golf Foundation, 1st ed. 1971, 60p, illustrated, illustrated wrappers, 28cm.

64620. *Organizing and Operating Public Golf Courses.* Chicago: National Golf Foundation, 1st ed. [ca1971] [270p] illustrated, spiral bound illustrated wrappers, 28cm.

64630. *Par 3 and Executive Golf Course, Planning & Operating Manual.* Chicago: National Golf Foundation, 1st ed. [1974] 31p, illustrated, wrappers, 28cm.

64640. *Planning and Conducting Competitive Golf Events.* Chicago: National Golf Foundation, 2d ed. rev. [1973] 76p, wrappers, 28cm. note: first edition not located.

64650. *Planning Information for Private and Daily Fee Golf Clubs.* North Palm Beach, Florida: National Golf Foundation, 1st ed. [ca1978] unpaginated, illustrated, spiral bound illustrated wrappers, 28cm.

64660. *Planning Information for Private Golf Clubs.* Chicago: National Golf Foundation, 1st ed. [1965] unpaginated, illustrated, spiral bound wrappers, 28cm.

64670. *Speedy Golf.* Chicago: National Golf Foundation, 1st ed. 1969 [38p] illustrated, illustrated wrappers, 28cm.

Nefyn & District Golf Club

64690. *Nefyn & District Golf Club 1907-1982.* Nefyn, Wales: Privately Printed, 1st ed. 1977, 44p, illustrated, illustrated wrappers, 20cm.

Neil, Mark

64710. *The Awful Golfer's Book.* London: Wolfe, 1st ed. [1967] 56p, illustrated, wrappers, 17cm.

Nelford, Jim

64730. *Seasons in A Golfer's Life.* Toronto, Canada: Methuen, 1st ed. [1984] 151p, illustrated, illustrated wrappers, 23cm, with Lorne Rubenstein.

Nelson, Byron

64750. *Shape Your Swing the Modern Way.* Norwalk, Connecticut: Golf Digest, 1st ed. [1976] 127p, illustrated by Anthony Ravielli, cloth, 25.5cm, with Larry Dennis, introduction by Tom Watson.

64760. pbk. ed. [1976] 127p, illustrated by Anthony Ravielli, illustrated wrappers, 25cm, with Larry Dennis, introduction by Tom Watson.

64770. facsimile ed. New York: Classics of Golf, 1985, 127p, illustrated, cloth, 25.5cm, with Larry Dennis, introduction by Herbert Warren Wind, afterword by Tom Watson.

64780. *The Byron Nelson Story.* Cincinnati, Ohio: Old Golf Shop, limited ed. signed, slipcased [600 copies] [1980] 130p, illustrated, leather, 25.5cm, compiled by Mort Olman.

Netland, Dwayne

64800. *The Crosby: Greatest Show in Golf.* Garden City, New York: Doubleday, 1st ed. 1975, 160p, illustrated, cloth, 26cm, prologue by Bing Crosby.

New Yorker Magazine

64820. *Fore!* New York: New Yorker Magazine, 1st ed. [1967] [29p] illustrated, illustrated shaped wrappers, 21cm.

Newbury and Crookham Golf Club

64840. *Newbury and Crookham Golf Club 1873-1973.* Newbury, England: Privately Printed, 1st ed. 1973, 16p, illustrated, illustrated wrappers, 16cm, foreword by Donald Steel.

Nichols, Bobby

64860. *Never Say Never: The Psychology of Winning Golf.* New York: Fleet, 1st ed. [1965] 113p, illustrated, cloth, 22.5cm, introduction by Deane Eagle.

64870. pbk. ed. New York: Pocket Books [1965] 111p, illustrated, illustrated wrappers, 17.5cm, introduction by Deane Eagle.

Nichols, Lois

64890. *Green Hills Country Club 1930-1980.* Millbrae, California: Privately Printed, 1st ed. 1980, 22p, illustrated, suede leather, 23cm.

Nicklaus, Jack

64910. *18 Holes: The master professional describes his tee to green technique to you.* Columbus, Ohio: Grow Ahead Press, 1st ed. [1970] [32p] illustrated by Ron McKee and Ed Vebell, illustrated wrappers, 18cm.

64920. *All About the Grip.* NP: Privately Printed, 1st ed. [1965] [14p] illustrated, illustrated wrappers, 14.5cm.

64930. *Golf My Way.* New York: Simon & Schuster, 1st ed. [1974] 264p, illustrated by Jim McQueen, cloth, 23.5cm, with Ken Bowden, foreword by Jack Grout.

64940. 1st UK ed. London: Wm. Heinemann, 1974, 264p, illustrated by Jim McQueen, cloth, 23.5cm, foreword by Jack Grout. later printings.

64950. pbk. ed. New York: Simon & Schuster [1974] 265p, illustrated by Jim McQueen, illustrated wrappers, 23.5cm, with Ken Bowden, foreword by Jack Grout.

64960. *Jack Nicklaus Golf Handbook: 25 self-contained lessons by the world's greatest golfer.* New York: Benjamin, 1st ed. [1973] 60p, illustrated by James McQueen, illustrated wrappers, 13.5cm.

64970. *Jack Nicklaus Plays The NCR South.* [Cleveland] Ohio Promotion, 1st ed. [1969] 46p, illustrated, wrappers, 10cm.

64980. *Jack Nicklaus, Profile of A Champion.* Cleveland, Ohio: Ohio Promotion, 1st ed. [1968] 50p, illustrated, illustrated wrappers, 27.5cm.

64990. *Jack Nicklaus' Lesson Tee.* Norwalk, Connecticut: Golf Digest, 1st ed. [1977] 157p, illustrated by Jim McQueen, cloth, 27.5cm, with Ken Bowden.

65000. *Jack Nicklaus' Lesson Tee: Back to Basics.* Norwalk, Connecticut: Golf Digest, abridged ed. [ca1977] [14p] illustrated by Jim McQueen, illustrated wrappers, 14cm, with Ken Bowden.

65010. *Jack Nicklaus' Playing Lessons.* Norwalk, Connecticut: Golf Digest, 1st ed. [1981] 142p, illustrated by Jim McQueen, cloth, 27.5cm, with Ken Bowden.

65020. *My 55 Ways to Lower Your Golf Score.* New York: Simon & Schuster, 1st ed. [1964] 125p, illustrated by Francis Golden, cloth, 23.5cm.

65030. 1st UK ed. London: Hodder & Stoughton, 1965, 125p, illustrated by Francis Golden, cloth, 23.5cm.

65040. *On & Off the Fairway: A Pictorial Autobiography.* New York: Simon & Schuster, 1st ed. [1978] 255p, illustrated, cloth, 27.5cm, with Ken Bowden.

65050. *Play Better Golf, the Swing from A-Z.* New York: Pocket Books, 1st ed. 1980, 200p, illustrated by Jim McQueen, Illustrated wrappers, 17.5cm, with Ken Bowden.

65060. *Play Better Golf, Volume II; The Short Game and Scoring.* New York: Pocket Books, 1st ed. 1981, 207p, illustrated, illustrated wrappers, 18cm, with Ken Bowden.

65070. *Play Better Golf, Volume III; Short Cuts To Lower Scores.* New York: Pocket Books, 1st ed. 1983, 207p, illustrated, illustrated wrappers, 18cm, with Ken Bowden.

65080. *Power Plus.* [Ohio] Ohio Promotions, 1st ed. [1966] [14p] illustrated by Barrett Taylor, illustrated wrappers, 14.5cm.

65090. *Practice Tips.* NP: Privately Printed, 1st ed. [1965] 14p, illustrated, illustrated wrappers, 14.5cm.

65100. *Reading and Controlling Putts.* NP: Privately Printed, 1st ed. [1965] [14p] illustrated, illustrated wrappers, 14.5cm.

65110. *Take A Tip From Me.* New York: Simon & Schuster, 1st ed. [1968] 125p, illustrated by Francis Golden, cloth, 23.5cm.

65120. *The Best Way To Better Golf.* Greenwich, Connecticut: Fawcett, 1st ed. [1966] 128p, illustrated, illustrated wrappers, 18cm, later printing.

65130. *The Best Way To Better Golf, Number 2.* Greenwich, Connecticut: Fawcett, 1st ed. [1968] 127p, illustrated, illustrated wrappers, 18cm, later printing.

65140. *The Best Way To Better Golf, Number 3.* Greenwich, Connecticut: Fawcett, 1st ed. [1969] 128p, illustrated, illustrated wrappers, 17.5cm, later printing.

65150. *The Full Swing.* Norwalk, Connecticut: Golf Digest, 1st ed. [1984] 205p, illustrated, cloth, 27.5cm, with Ken Bowden.

65160. limited ed. presentation [50 copies] Norwalk, Connecticut: Golf Digest [1984] 205p, illustrated, gilt stamped leather, 27.5cm, with Ken Bowden.

65170. *The Greatest Game of All: My Life in Golf.* New York: Simon & Schuster, 1st ed. [1969] 416p, illustrated, cloth, 23cm, with Herbert Warren Wind, foreword by Robert Tyre Jones, Jr. later printings.

65180. *Total Golf Techniques.* London: Heinemann, 1st UK ed. [1977] 157p, illustrated, cloth, 28cm, with Ken Bowden.

65190. *Winning Golf.* Columbus, Ohio: Grow Ahead Press, 1st ed. [1969] [32p] illustrated by Ron McKee & Ed Vebell, illustrated wrappers, 27.5cm.

Nickson, E.A.

65210. *The Lytham Century, A History of Royal Lytham and St. Annes Golf Club 1886-1986.* St. Annes-on-the-Sea, England: Privately Printed, limited ed. [no limitation cited] 1985, 166p, illustrated, gilt stamped leather, 26.5cm.

65220. 1st trade ed. 1985, 166p, illustrated, decorative cloth, 26.5cm.

Nicol, Eric, Golf and Dave More

65240. *Golf, The Agony & The Ecstasy.* Edmonton, Canada: Hurtig, 1st ed. [1982] 159p, illustrated, cloth, 23cm.

Nieporte, Tom and Don Sauers

65260. *Mind Over Golf: What 50 Top Pros Can Teach You About the Mysterious Mental Side of Golf.* Garden City, New York: Doubleday, 1st ed. 1968, 112p, illustrated, cloth, 21cm.

65270. 1st UK ed. London: Cassell, 1969, 112p, cloth, 18.5cm.

Noble, John

65290. *The Official Duffer's Rules of Golf.* Brookline, Massachusetts: Bob Adams, 1st ed. [1981] 96p, illustrated, illustrated wrappers, 13.5cm.

Nolan, James

65310. *Of Golf and Dukes and Princes: Early Golf in France.* Worcestershire, England: Grant Books, limited ed. signed [500 copies] 1982, 36p, illustrated, illustrated wrappers, 21cm.

Norland, Jim

65330. *Fifty Years of Mostly Fun: The History of Cherry Hills Country Club 1922-72.* Denver, Colorado: Privately Printed, limited ed. [1000 copies] [1972] 196p, illustrated, decorative cloth, 23cm.

Norman, Greg

65350. *Greg Norman: My Story.* London: Harrap, 1st ed. 1983, 160p, illustrated, cloth, 24cm, with Don Lawrence, foreword by Peter Alliss.

North Carolina Golf State, USA

65370. *North Carolina Golf State, USA.* Raleigh, North Carolina: Department of Natural & Economic Resources [1974] [16p] illustrated, illustrated wrappers, 18cm.

Norval, Ronald

65390. *Gone to the Golf.* Cape Town, South Africa: Howard Timmins, 1st ed. 1965, 230p, cloth, 21cm, introduction by H.E.P. Watermeyer.

Norwood, Joe

65410. *Joe Norwood's Golf-o-Metrics.* Garden City, New York: Doubleday, 1st ed. 1978, 142p, illustrated by George Janes, cloth, 26cm, with Marilyn Smith and Stanley Blicker

Novak, Joe

65430. *Golf Can Be An Easy Game.* Englewood Cliffs, New Jersey: Prentice-Hall, 1st ed. [1962] 164p, illustrated, cloth, 21.5cm.

65440. *Golf.* London: Hennel Locke, 1st UK ed. 1964, 80p, illustrated, illustrated wrappers, 18.5cm, UK title of "Golf Can Be An Easy Game."

65450. *The Novak System of Mastering Golf.* Garden City, New York: Doubleday, 1st ed. 1969, 54p, illustrated by Si Mezerow, illustrated wrappers, 20.5cm.

Nunn, Eddy

65470. *Mechanics of Golf.* Los Angeles: Privately Printed, 1st ed. [1962] 30p, illustrated, illustrated wrappers, 27.5cm.

Oakley Country Club

65490. *Oakley Country Club 1898-1973: Notes on Seventy-five Happy Years.* Watertown, Massachusetts: Privately Printed, 1st ed. 1973, 63p, illustrated, decorative cloth, 18.5cm.

Obitz, Harry and Dick Farley

65510. *Six Days to Better Golf: The Secrets of Learning the Golf Swing*. New York: Harper & Row, 1st ed. [1977] 180p, illustrated by Dom Lupo, cloth, 23.5cm, with Desmond Tolhurst; foreword by Jackie Gleason, preface by Ken Venturi.

O'Brien, Gene

65530. *Aim and Hang Loose*. Wichita, Kansas: Privately Printed, 1st ed. [1985] 78p, illustrated wrappers, 14cm.

O'Byrne, Robert

65550. *Senior Golf*. New York: Winchester Press, 1st ed. [1977] 174p, illustrated, cloth, 23cm, foreword by Julius Boros, special chapter by Robert Trent Jones, "Courses for Seniors."

O'Connor, Anthony

65570. *Golfing in the Green*. London: Martin Brian & O'Keeffe, 1st ed. 1979, 171p, cloth, 21.5cm.

O'Connor, Christy

65590. *Christy O' Connor, His Autobiography*. Dublin, Ireland: Gill and Macmillan, 1st ed. [1985] 139p, illustrated, cloth, 21.5cm, as told to Jim Redmond.

Odell, C. F.

65610. *History of the Pretoria Country Club 1909-1975*. Pretoria, South Africa: Privately Printed, 1st ed. 1977, 168p, illustrated, cloth, 30cm.

O'Donnell, Paddy

65630. *South Africa's Wonderful World of Golf*. Cape Town, South Africa: Don Nelson, 1st ed. 1973, 189p, illustrated, cloth, 21cm.

Old Warson Country Club

65650. *Old Warson Country Club, 10th Anniversary*. St. Louis: Privately Printed, 1st ed. [1964] [16p] illustrated, wrappers, 28cm.

Olman, John M. and Morton W.

65670. *The Encyclopedia of Golf Collectibles: A Collector's Identification and Value Guide*. Florence, Alabama: Books Americana, 1st ed. [1985] 306p, illustrated, decorative cloth, 28cm, foreword by Ben Crenshaw.

65680. pbk. ed. [1985] 306p, illustrated, illustrated wrappers, 28cm, foreword by Ben Crenshaw.

65690. limited ed. special presentation [15 copies] [1985] 306p, illustrated, decorative cloth, 28cm, foreword by Ben Crenshaw.

Olsen, James T.

65710. *Arnold Palmer: King on the Course*. Mankato, Minnesota: Creative Education, 1st ed. [1974] 31p, illustrated, illustrated boards, 24cm.

Olson, Bill and Lo Linkert

65730. *Beat the Links*. Oakland, New Jersey: Jolex, 1st ed. 1979, 96p, illustrated, illustrated wrappers, 20.5cm.

Olson, George W.

65750. *Bamboozled and Hornswogled*. New York: Carlton Press, 1st ed. 1962, 40p, cloth, 20cm.

O'Malley, Bill

65770. *Fore-and Aft*. South Brunswick, New Jersey: A.S. Barnes, 1st ed. [1969] 76p, illustrated, cloth, 21cm.

Oman, Mark

65790. *Portrait of A Golfaholic*. Chicago: Contemporary, 1st ed. [1984] 96p, illustrated by Gary Patterson, illustrated wrappers, 20.5cm.

65800. *The Sensuous Golfer*. Pacific Grove, California: Oman Enterprises, 1st ed. [1976] 63p, illustrated by Nix, illustrated wrappers, 19cm.

O'Neil, Currey

65820. *The Age Pro Golf Tips*. South Yarra, Australia: Currey O'Neil Ross, 1st ed. 1984, 117p, illustrated by Albert Ricardo, illustrated wrappers, 23.5cm, compiled by Trevor Grant.

Orchard Ridge Country Club

65840. *Orchard Ridge Country Club 1924-1984, 60th Anniversary*. Fort Wayne, Indiana: Privately Printed, 1st ed. 1984, 6p, illustrated, illustrated wrappers, 21.5cm.

Original Golf Facts

65860. *The Original Golf Facts 1971*. Stamford, Connecticut: Pearson Productions, 1st ed. 1971, 48p, illustrated, illustrated wrappers, 19cm.

O'Shaughnessy, Gil

65880. *New Zealand Golf Guide*. Nelson, New Zealand: Nelson Printers [1968] 264p, illustrated, illustrated wrappers, 21cm.

O'Shea, Mary Jo

65900. *Laura Baugh*. Mankato, Minnesota: Creative Education, 1st ed. [1976] 31p, illustrated, illustrated boards, 24cm.

Ostermann, H.T.

65920. *Golf in Europe*. Zurich, Switzerland: Editions Golf in Europe, 1st ed. 1961, 285p, illustrated, illustrated wrappers, 21cm.

65930. 2d ed. 1962, 319p, illustrated, illustrated wrappers, 21cm.

65940. 3d ed. 1963, 351p, illustrated, illustrated wrappers, 21cm.

65950. 4th ed. 1964, 362p, illustrated, illustrated wrappers, 21cm.

65960. 5th ed. 1965, 368p, illustrated, illustrated wrappers, 21cm.

65970. 6th ed. 1966, 385p, illustrated, illustrated wrappers, 21cm.

65980. 7th ed. 1967, 410p, illustrated, illustrated wrappers, 21cm.

65990. 8th ed. 1968, 421p, illustrated, illustrated wrappers, 21cm.

66000. 9th ed. 1969, 428p, illustrated, illustrated wrappers, 21cm.

66010. 10th ed. 1970, 420p, illustrated, illustrated wrappers, 21cm.
66020. 11th ed. 1971, 404p, illustrated, illustrated wrappers, 21cm.
66030. 12th ed. 1972, 429p, illustrated, illustrated wrappers, 21cm.

Oswald, Neville C.

66300. *Thurlestone Golf Club, A Short History 1897-1983.* Thurlestone, England: Privately Printed, 1st ed. 1983, 16p, illustrated, wrappers, 21cm.

Owens, De De

66320. *Teaching Golf To Special Populations.* New York: Leisure Press, 1st ed. [1984] 160p, illustrated, illustrated wrappers, 23cm.

Oxford & Cambridge Golfing Society

66340. *Oxford & Cambridge Golfing Society American Tour 1978.* [London] Privately Printed, 1st ed. 1978 [12p] illustrated, illustrated wrappers, 29.5cm.

Pacini, John

66360. *Its Your Honour: An Account of the First Fifty Years of the Penisula Country Golf Club.* Frankston, Australia: Privately Printed, limited ed. [no limitation cited] [1975] 67p, illustrated, decorative cloth, 24cm.

Palangue, Luis

66380. *Portugal 1984, The Golfer's Paradise.* Lisbon: Pascoal & Palanque, 1st ed. 1984, 72p, illustrated, illustrated wrappers, 15cm.

Palmer, Arnold

66400. *495 Golf Lessons.* Chicago: Follett, 1st ed. [1973] 128p, illustrated, illustrated wrappers, 28cm.

66410. *Arnold Palmer Plays Merion.* NP: Arnold Palmer Enterprises, 1st ed. [1971] [44p] illustrated, illustrated wrappers, 10cm.

66420. *Arnold Palmer The Man and the Golfer.* Cleveland, Ohio: Arnold Palmer Enterprises, 1st ed. [1966] 50p, illustrated, illustrated wrappers, 28cm.

66430. *Arnold Palmer's Best 54 Golf Holes.* Garden City, New York: Doubleday, 1st ed. 1977, 206p, illustrated, cloth, 26cm, with Bob Drum.

66440. *Arnold Palmer's Golf Book: Hit it Hard.* New York: Ronald Press, 1st ed. [1961] 142p, illustrated, cloth, 25cm.

66450. 1st UK ed. London: Hodder & Stoughton, 1961, 142p, illustrated, cloth, 25.5cm.

66460. *Go for Broke: My Philosophy of Winning Golf.* New York: Simon & Schuster, 1st ed. [1973] 252p, illustrated, cloth, 22.5cm, with William Barry Furlong.

66470. *Graph-Check System for Golf.* NP: Graph-Check, 1st ed. [ca1963] 72p, illustrated, illustrated vinyl ring binder, 13cm.

66480. *My Game and Yours.* New York: Simon & Schuster, 1st ed. [1965] 158p, illustrated, cloth, 23cm.

66500. 2d ed. rev. pbk. ed. [1983] 157p, illustrated, illustrated wrappers, 23.5cm.

66510. 1st UK ed. London: Hodder & Stoughton, 1965, 158p, illustrated, cloth, 23cm.

66530. pbk. ed. London: Corgi, 1969, 158p, illustrated, illustrated wrappers, 18cm.

66540. 2d ed. rev. pbk. Horsham, England: Ravette [1985] 157p, illustrated, illustrated wrappers, 23.5.

66550. *Portrait of A Professional Golfer.* South Norwalk, Connecticut: Golf Digest, 1st ed. [1964] 110p, illustrated, illustrated boards, 25cm.

66560. 1st UK ed. London: Pelham, 1966, 110p, illustrated, cloth, 24.5cm.

66570. pbk. ed. New York: Pocket Books, 1966, 63p, illustrated, illustrated wrappers, 23cm.

66580. *Situation Golf.* New York: McCall, 1st ed. [1970] 83p, illustrated by Jesus J. Gutierrez, cloth, 31cm.

66590. *Golf Tactics.* London: Kaye and Ward, 1st UK ed. 1970, 95p, illustrated by Jesus J. Gutierrez, cloth, 29.5cm, UK edition of "Situation Golf."

66600. *The Arnold Palmer Method.* New York: Dell, 1st ed. 1968, 235p, illustrated, illustrated wrappers, 18cm.

66610. *The Rolex Book of Golf.* [England] Muttisquash, 1st ed. [1975] [13p] illustrated, illustrated wrappers, 14.5cm.

Palmer, Norman and William V. Levy

66630. *Five Star Golf.* New York: Duell, Sloan and Pearce, 1st ed. [1964] 160p, illustrated by James T. McQueen, cloth, 23cm, foreword by Dwight D. Eisenhower.

Papp, Charles

66650. *Swing It Like A Pendulum.* Hammond, Indiana: Privately Printed, 1st ed. [1965] 37p, illustrated, spiral bound illustrated wrappers, 20cm.

Par Excellance Magazine

66670. *Par Excellance Guide To Wisconsin.* West Allis, Wisconsin: Par Excellance Magazine, 1st ed. 1984, 96p, illustrated, illustrated wrappers, 28cm.

Parsons, R.

66690. *Golfing Thinking.* Cheam, England: Entryown Patents, 1st ed. 1983, 32p, illustrated wrappers, 10.5cm.

Paskow, H. M.

66710. *Instant Golf.* Miami, Florida: Instant Golf, 1st ed. [1965] 21p, illustrated, illustrated wrappers, 21.5cm.

Patey, Bob

66730. *Welcome to the Club.* Melbourne, Australia: Privately Printed, 1st ed. [ca1981] 16p, illustrated by Geoff Gaylord, illustrated wrappers, 18.5cm, foreword by Peter Thomson.

Patten, G.Z.

66750. *Birth of Greatness: The Story of the Honors Course.* Signal Mountain, Tennessee: Patten Press, limited ed. [no limitation cited] [1984] 67p, illustrated, gilt stamped leather, 23cm.

Patterson, A. Willing

66770. *The Story of the Gulph Mills Golf Club 1916-1976.* King of Prussia, Pennsylvania: Privately Printed, 1st ed. 1976, 90p, illustrated, decorative cloth, 22.5cm.

Patton, Carol S.

66790. *Memories and Golf Stories.* [Hartford, Connecticut] Privately Printed, 1st ed. 1977, 24p, illustrated, illustrated wrappers, 23cm.

Paul, Carl F.

66810. *Golf Clubmaking and Repair.* Austin, Texas: Paul Associates, 1st ed. [1984] 539p, illustrated by Robin Richardson, cloth, 28cm.

66820. *Golf Clubs Design and Repair.* Austin, Texas: Golfsmith, 1st ed. [1978] 33p, illustrated, wrappers, 28cm.

Payes, Rachel Cosgrove

66840. *O Charitable Death.* Garden City, New York: Crime Club, 1st ed. 1968, 191p, cloth, 21cm.

Pazdur, Edward F.

66860. *Golf & Country Club Reciprocity Directory 1976.* Irvine, California: Pazdur Publishing, 1st ed. 1976, 136p, illustrated wrappers, 27.5cm. note: title change 2d ed. annual to "Golf and Country Club Guest Policy Directory."

66870. *Golf and Country Club Guest Policy Directory.* Irvine, California: Pazdur Publications, 2d ed. 1977, 167p, illustrated wrappers, 27.5cm.

66880. 3d ed. 1978, 162p, illustrated wrappers, 27.5cm.

66890. 4th ed. 1979, 186p, illustrated wrappers, 27.5cm.

66900. *Private Country Club Guest Policy Directory.* Irvine, California: Pazdur Publications, 5th ed. 1980, 192p, illustrated wrappers, 27.5cm, note title change.

66910. 6th ed. 1981, 218p, illustrated wrappers, 27.5cm.

66920. 7th ed. 1982, 274p, illustrated wrappers, 27.5cm.

66930. 8th ed. 1983, 232p, illustrated wrappers, 27.5cm.

66940. 9th ed. 1984, 224p. illustrated, illustrated wrappers, 27.5cm.

66950. 10th ed. 1985, 224p, illustrated wrappers, 27.5cm.

Pearl, Leonard

67100. *The Big Secret of Good Golf.* NP: Privately Printed, 1st ed. [1962] 23p, illustrated, illustrated wrappers, 15cm, revised and condensed from "A Duffer Discovers The Big Secret of Good Golf." note: this title not located.

Pearson, T.F. [Major]

67120. *Hohne Station Golf Club [Handbook].* Hohne Station, West Germany: Privately Printed, 1974, 17p, illustrated, illustrated wrappers, 19.5cm.

Peden, J.D.

67140. *Uplands Golf Club 1922-1982, Sixtieth Anniversary.* Victoria, Canada: Privately Printed, 1st ed. 1982 [32p] illustrated, illustrated wrappers, 28cm.

Peers, Michael W.

67160. *A History of the Manchester Golf Club 1882-1982.* Manchester, England: Privately Printed, 1st ed. 1982, 148p, illustrated, cloth, 29.5cm.

Peery, Paul D.

67180. *Billy Casper: Winner.* Englewood Cliffs, New Jersey: Prentice-Hall, 1st ed. [1969] 207p, illustrated, cloth, 22.5cm, foreword by Billy Casper.

Penna, Toney

67200. *My Wonderful World of Golf.* New York: Centaur House, 1st ed. 1965, 239p, illustrated, decorative cloth, 21cm, with Oscar Fraley, foreword by Jimmy Demaret.

Pennink, Frank

67220. *Frank Pennink's Choice of Golf Courses.* London: A&C Black, 1st ed. 1976, 293p, illustrated linen wrappers, 20cm.

67230. *Golfer's Companion.* London: Cassell, 1st ed. 1962, 311p, cloth, 16.5cm.

67240. *Royal Ashdown Forest Golf Club, The Old and New Courses [Handbook].* London: Golf Clubs Association [ca1965] 27p, illustrated, wrappers, 18cm.

Peper, George

67260. *Golf's Supershots: How the Pros Played Them-How You Can Play Them.* New York: Atheneum, 1st ed. 1982, 146p, illustrated by Ron Ramsey, cloth, 26cm.

67270. *Scrambling Golf: How to get out of trouble and into the cup.* Englewood Cliffs, New Jersey: Prentice-Hall, 1st ed. [1977] 175p, illustrated, cloth, 23cm, foreword by Ben Crenshaw.

Perkins, W. F.

67290. *Golfer's Guide To Emotional Management.* Cassopolis, Michigan: Privately Printed, 1st ed. [1981] [15p] illustrated wrappers, 16.5cm.

Perrottet, Louis J.

67310. *A History of Canoe Brook Country Club 1901-1965.* Summit, New Jersey: Privately Printed, 1st ed. 1965, 126p, illustrated, wrappers, 23cm.

Perry, Phyllis

67330. *From Green To Gold: The First Fifty Years of the Australian Ladies Golf Union.* Australia: Australian Ladies Golf Union, 2d ed. rev. 1976, 119p, illustrated, cloth, 21.5cm. note: first edition not located.

Petch, Gordon

67350. *Ashdown Over the Years.* Grinstead, England: Privately Printed, 1st ed. 1973, 51p, wrappers, 21cm.

Petnuch, Andrew

67370. *Turn To Golf.* Ft. Walton Beach, Florida: Vitro Press, 2d ed. rev. [1969] 105p, illustrated, illustrated wrappers, 21.5cm. note: first edition not located.

67380. 3d ed. rev. New York, Carlton Press [1975] 160p, illustrated by Bill Stevens, cloth, 20cm.

Phillips, Betty Lou

67400. *Picture Story of Nancy Lopez.* New York: Julian Messner, 1st ed. [1980] 64p, illustrated, illustrated boards, 21cm.

Pickens, Jr., Arthur E.

67420. *The Golf Bum.* New York: Crown, 1st ed. [1970] 223p, cloth, 21cm.

Platt, Kin

67440. *The Kissing Gourami.* New York: Random House, 1st ed. [1970] 214p, cloth, 20cm.

Player, Gary

67460. *124 Golf Lessons.* Chicago: Golfer's Digest Association, 1st ed. [1968] 50p, illustrated by Paul Trevillion, illustrated wrappers, 28cm, script by Iain Reid.

67470. *395 Golf Lessons.* Chicago: Follett, 1st ed. [1972] 112p, illustrated by Gary Keane & Paul Trevillion, illustrated wrappers, 28cm, script by Iain Reid.

67480. *Gary Player on Fitness and Success.* Tadsworth, England: Worlds Work, 1st ed. [1979] 102p, illustrated, illustrated wrappers, 21.5cm, with Norm Harris

67490. *Gary Player Tells You All About The Shakespeare Fiberglass Wondershaft and what it can do for you.* Kalamazoo, Michigan: Shakespeare, 1st ed. [1964] 18p, illustrated, illustrated wrappers, 23cm.

67500. *Gary Player World Golfer.* Waco, Texas: Word Books, 1st ed. [1974] 193p, illustrated, cloth, 21.5cm, with Floyd Thatcher.

67510. 1st UK ed. London: Pelham, 1975, 157p, illustrated, cloth, 21.5cm, with Floyd Thatcher.

67520. *Gary Player's Golf Book for Young People.* Norwalk, Connecticut: Golf Digest, 1st ed. [1980] 110p, illustrated, cloth, 22.5cm. with George Sullivan.

67530. *Gary Player's Golf Class.* [Johannesburg, South Africa] The Star [1968] 48p, illustrated, illustrated wrappers, 18cm.

67540. *Gary Player's Golf Class [Book I] 100 Lessons.* London: Beaverbrook Newspapers, 1st ed. [1967] 84p, illustrated, illustrated wrappers, 16.5cm. with Iain Reid.

67550. *Gary Player's Golf Class [Book II] 100 Lessons.* London: Beaverbrook Newspapers, 1st ed. [1969] 83p, illustrated, illustrated wrappers, 16.5cm. with Iain Reid.

67560. *Gary Player's Golf Class [Book III] 162 Lessons for the Weekender.* London: Sunday Express, 1st ed. [1975] [100p] illustrated, illustrated wrappers, 16.5cm. with Iain Reid.

67570. *Gary Player's Golf Class [Book IV] 170 Lessons for the Weekender.* London: Express Newspaper, 1st ed. [1980] [100p] illustrated, illustrated wrappers, 16.5cm. with Iain Reid.

67580. *Gary Player's Golf Clinic*. Northfield, Illinois: DBI Books, 1st ed. [1981] 160p, illustrated, illustrated wrappers, 27cm.

67590. *Gary Player's Golf Guide*. [Johannesburg, South Africa] The Star, 1st ed. [ca1974] [24p] illustrated, illustrated wrappers, 11cm.

67600. *Gary Player's Golf Secrets*. Englewood Cliffs, New Jersey: Prentice-Hall, 1st ed. [1962] 146p, illustrated, cloth, 23cm.

67610. 2d ed. rev. Greenwich, Connecticut: Fawcett [1964] 112p, illustrated by J. McQueen, illustrated wrappers, 23.5cm.

67620. *Golfing S. A.* [South Africa] South Africa Tourist Corporation, 1st ed. [ca1980] [6p] illustrated, illustrated wrappers, 30cm.

67630. *Good Test for the 1970 U.S. Open, Hazeltine National Golf Club*. NP: Outmart A.G. 1st ed. [1970] [44p] illustrated, illustrated wrappers, 10cm.

67640. *Grand Slam Golf*. London: Cassell, 1st ed. 1966, 133p, illustrated, cloth, 21cm, later printing.

67650. *Improve Your Golf*. [South Africa] Vacuum Oil Company, 1st ed. [ca1962] 20p, illustrated, illustrated wrappers, 11.5cm.

67660. *More Tips From Gary Player*. [Johannesburg, South Africa] The Star, 1st ed. [1968] 64p, illustrated, illustrated wrappers, 19cm.

67670. *Play Better Golf with Gary Player Edutext*. [U.S.A.] Outmart A.G. 1st ed. [1970] 128p, illustrated, wrappers, 28cm.

67680. *Play Golf with Player*. London: Collins, 1st ed. 1962, 190p, illustrated, cloth, 22cm, foreword by Norman Von Nida.

67690. *Positive Golf: Understanding and Applying the Fundamentals of the Game*. New York: McGraw-Hill, 1st ed. [1967] 119p, illustrated, cloth, 23cm.

67700. pbk. ed. New York: Pocket Books, 1968, 149p, illustrated, illustrated wrappers, 18cm.

67710. 1st UK ed. London: Cassell, 1967, 119p, illustrated, cloth, 22.5cm, later printing.

67720. pbk. ed. London: Corgi, 1970, 141p, illustrated, illustrated wrappers, 18cm.

67730. *The Medium Iron to the Green [8 Iron]*. Benoni, Transvaal: Visual Instruction Booklets, 1st ed. [ca1971] [144p] illustrated, illustrated wrappers, 7.5cm.

67740. *The Tee Shot [A flip book]*. Benoni, Transvaal: Visual Instruction Booklets, 1st ed. [ca1971] [144p] illustrated, illustrated wrappers, 7.5cm.

67750. *Weathering Sand and Storm*. [Canada] Peter Jackson, 1st ed. [1971] [12p] illustrated, illustrated wrappers, 13cm.

Plimpton, George

67770. *The Bogey Man*. New York: Harper & Row, 1st ed. [1968] 306p, illustrated, decorative cloth, 21cm.

67780. 1st UK ed. London: Andre Deutch, 1969, 306p, illustrated, cloth, 20.5cm.

67790. pbk. ed. New York: Avon, 1969, 304p, illustrated, illustrated wrappers, 18cm.

Plumridge, Chris

67810. *How To Play Golf*. Feltham, England: Hamlyn, 1st ed. 1979, 62p, illustrated, illustrated boards, 23.5cm.

67820. 1st American ed. Secaucus, New Jersey: Chartwell [1979] 62p, illustrated, illustrated boards, 23.5cm.

67830. *The Book of Golf Disasters & Bizarre Records*. London: Stanley Paul, 1st ed. 1985, 120p, illustrated, illustrated boards, 24.5cm, introduction by Terry Wogan.

Polakoff, P. Byron

67850. *Arnold Palmer and the Golfin' Dolphin*. Chicago: Turnbill & Willoughby, 1st ed. [1984] [38p] illustrated by Deborah Mackall, decorative cloth, 27.5cm.

Pollard, Frank B.

67870. *Golf on the Peninsula: An Illustrated Guide to the World Famous Courses on the Monterey Penisula*. Manhattan Beach: California, Courses & Links, 1st ed. [1973] 32p, illustrated, illustrated wrappers, 28cm.

Pollard, Jack

67890. *Golf: The Australian Way.* edited by. Melbourne, Australia: Lansdowne Press, 1st ed. 1970, 134p, illustrated, decorative cloth, 28cm.

67900. *Gregory's Australian Guide to Golf.* Sydney, Australia: Gregory's, 2d ed. [1964] 288p, illustrated, cloth, 22cm. note: first edition not located.

Poole, William

67920. *The History of Onwentsia 1895-1945.* Lake Forest, Illinois: Privately Printed, 1st ed. 1984, 129p, illustrated, decorative cloth, 26.5cm.

Poppenberg, Mary Kay and Marlene Parrish

67940. *I'd Rather Play Golf Than Cook: A Cookbook for Duffers.* Pittsburgh: Garlic Press, 1st ed. [1976] 94p, illustrated, spiral bound illustrated wrappers, 21.5cm.

Portsea Golf Club

67960. *Portsea Golf Club History 1925-1975. 50th Anniversary Souvenir.* [Melbourne, Australia] Privately Printed, 1st ed. 1975 [12p] illustrated wrappers, 19.5cm.

Postel, Mitchell P.

67980. *History of the Burlingame Country Club.* Burlingame, California: Privately Printed, limited ed. [1500 copies] [1982] 110p, illustrated, leather, 18cm.

Potter, Stephen

68000. *The Complete Golf Gamesmanship.* London: Heinemann, 1st ed. 1968, 177p, illustrated by Frank Wilson, cloth, 21.5cm.

68010. pbk. ed. Harmondsworth, England: Penguin, 1971, 204p, illustrated, illustrated wrappers, 18cm.

68020. *Golfmanship.* New York: McGraw-Hill, 1st American ed. [1968] 177p, illustrated by Frank Wilson, cloth, 20.5cm, American title of "Complete Golf Gamesmanship." later printing.

Pottinger, George

68040. *Muirfield and the Honourable Company.* Edinburgh: Scottish Academic Press, 1st ed. 1972, 146p, illustrated, cloth, 23.5cm.

Powersland, M.

68060. *Great Yarmouth & Caister Golf Club 1882-1982.* Caister-on-Sea, England: Privately Printed, 1st ed. 1982, 15p, illustrated, illustrated wrappers, 30cm.

Pratt, William and Keith Jennison

68080. *Year-Round Conditioning for Part-Time Golfers: How To Feel and Play Your Best All Your Life.* New York: Atheneum, 1st ed. 1979, 122p, illustrated by Jim McQueen, cloth, 21.5cm.

Preston, Charles

68100. *Fore: Golf Cartoons From the Wall Street Journal.* New York: Dutton, 1st ed. 1962, 92p, illustrated, cloth, 25cm.

Price, Charles

68120. *Black's Picture Sports: Golf.* London: Adam & Charles Black, 1st ed. 1976, 95p, illustrated, illustrated boards, 20.5cm, edited by Peter Ryde.

68130. *Esquire's Golfer's Guide 1972.* edited by. [New York] Esquire, 1st ed. 1972 [28p] illustrated, illustrated wrappers, 18.5cm.

68140. *Golfer-at-Large: New Slants on An Ancient Game.* New York: Atheneum, 1st ed. 1982, 241p, cloth, 21cm, introduction by Ben Hogan.

68150. *Shell's Wonderful World of Golf 1963*. NP: Shell Oil, 1st ed. 1963 [24p] illustrated, illustrated wrappers, 25.5cm.

68160. *Sports Illustrated Book of Golf*. and editors of Sports Illustrated. Philadelphia: Lippincott, 1st ed. [1970] 73p, illustrated by Frank Mullins, cloth, 20cm.

68170. *Sports Illustrated Golf*. Philadelphia: Lippincott, 2d ed. rev. [1972] 93p, illustrated, cloth, 20.5cm. note: this is the 2d ed. edition of "Sports Illustrated Book of Golf."

68175. pbk. ed. 2d ed. rev. 93p, illustrated, illustrated wrappers, 20.5cm.

68180. *The American Golfer*. New York: Random House, 1st ed. [1964] 241p, illustrated, cloth, 28cm.

68190. *The World of Golf: A Panorama of Six Centuries of the Games' History*. New York: Random House, 1st ed. [1962] 307p, illustrated, decorative cloth, 28cm, foreword by Bobby Jones.

Price, Charles and George C. Rogers, Jr.

68210. *The Carolina Lowcountry, Birthplace of American Golf 1786*. Hilton Head Island, South Carolina: Sea Pines, 1st ed. 1980, 76p, illustrated by West Fraser, cloth, 25.5cm. note: Two essays; "This Demi Paradise, The Story of Lowcountry Carolina," by Charles Price: "The History of Golf in South Carolina in the Late 18th Century," by George C. Rogers, Jr.

68220. pbk. ed. 1980, 76p, illustrated, illustrated wrappers, 25cm.

Pro Am Guide To Golf

68240. *Pro Am Guide To Golf*. Maplewood, New Jersey: Hammond, 1st ed. [1982] 91p, illustrated, illustrated wrappers, 21cm.

Pro's Handbook of Golf

68260. *Pro's Handbook of Golf*. New York: Maco, 1st ed. [1967] 128p, illustrated, illustrated wrappers, 24cm.

Professional Golfers' Association [European]

68280. *Official Tournament Guide 1972*. London: Professional Golfers' Association, 1st ed. 1972, 143p, illustrated, wrappers, 23cm.

68290. *Official Tournament Guide 1973*. London: Professional Golfers' Association, 2d ed. 1973, 143p, illustrated, wrappers, 23cm.

68300. *Official Tournament Guide 1974*. London: Professional Golfers' Association, 3d ed. 1974, 159p, illustrated, wrappers, 23cm.

68310. *Official Tournament Guide 1975*. London: Professional Golfers' Association, 4th ed. 1975, 159p, illustrated, wrappers, 23cm.

68320. *Official Tournament Guide 1976*. London: Professional Golfers' Association, 1976, 5th ed. 143p, illustrated, wrappers, 23cm.

68330. *European Tournament Players' Division Tournament Guide 1977*. London: Professional Golfers' Association, 6th ed. 1977, 164p, illustrated, wrappers, 23cm, note: previously titled "Official Tournament Guide."

68340. *European Tournament Players' Division Tournament Guide 1978*. London: Professional Golfers' Association, 7th ed. 1978, 175p, illustrated, wrappers, 23cm.

68350. *European Tournament Players' Division Tournament Guide 1979*. London: Professional Golfers' Association, 8th ed. 1979, 184p, illustrated, wrappers, 23cm.

68360. *European Tournament Players' Division Tournament Guide 1980*. London: Professional Golfers' Association, 9th ed. 1980, 198p, illustrated, wrappers, 23cm.

68370. *European Tournament Players' Division Tournament Guide 1981*. not located.

68380. *European Tournament Players' Division Tournament Guide 1982*. London: Professional Golfers' Association, 11th ed. 1982, illustrated, wrappers, 23cm.

68390. *PGA European Tour Official Guide 1983*. London: Professional Golfers' Association, 12th ed. 1983, 195p, illustrated, wrappers, 23cm.

68400. *PGA European Tour Official Guide 1984*. London: Professional Golfers' Association, 13th ed. 1984, 215p, illustrated, wrappers, 23cm.

68410. *PGA European Tour Official Guide 1985*. London: Professional Golfers' Association, 14th ed. 1985, 319p, illustrated, wrappers, 23cm.

Professional Golfers' Association [U.S.]

68700. *Ideas To Assist Golf Clubs & Courses, Make Money & Reduce Costs*. Palm Beach Gardens, Florida: Professional Golfers' Association, 1st ed. [1981] 36p, illustrated, illustrated wrappers, 28cm.

68710. *PGA Book of Golf 1968*. Palm Beach Gardens, Florida: Professional Golfers' Association, 1st ed. 1968, 96p, illustrated, illustrated wrappers, 27.5cm.

68720. *PGA Book of Golf 1969*. Palm Beach Gardens, Florida: Professional Golfers' Association, 2d ed. 1969, 96p, illustrated, illustrated wrappers, 27.5cm.

68730. *PGA Book of Golf 1970*. Palm Beach Gardens, Florida: Professional Golfers' Association, 1970, 3d ed. 96p, illustrated, illustrated wrappers, 27.5cm.

68740. 4th ed. not located.

68750. 5th ed. not located.

67760. *PGA Book of Golf 1973*. Palm Beach Gardens, Florida: Professional Golfers' Association, 6th ed. 1973, 96p, illustrated, illustrated wrappers, 27.5cm.

68770. *PGA Book of Golf 1974*. Palm Beach Gardens, Florida: Professional Golfers' Association, 7th ed. 1974, 96p, illustrated, illustrated wrappers, 27.5cm.

68780. *PGA Book of Golf 1975*. Palm Beach Gardens, Florida: Professional Golfers' Association, 8th ed. 1975, illustrated, illustrated wrappers, 27.5cm.

68790. *PGA Book of Golf 1976*. Palm Beach Gardens, Florida: Professional Golfers' Association, 9th ed. 1976, illustrated, illustrated wrappers, 27.5cm.

68800. *PGA Book of Golf 1977*. Palm Beach Gardens, Florida: Professional Golfers' Association, 10th ed. 1977, illustrated, illustrated wrappers, 27.5cm.

68810. *PGA Book of Golf 1978*. Palm Beach Gardens, Florida: Professional Golfers' Association, 11th ed. 1978, illustrated, illustrated wrappers, 27.5cm.

68820. *PGA Book of Golf 1979*. Palm Beach Gardens, Florida: Professional Golfers' Association, 12th ed. 1979, 96p, illustrated, illustrated wrappers, 27.5cm.

68825. *PGA Book of Golf 1980*. Palm Beach Gardens, Florida: Professional Golfers' Association, 13th ed. 80p, illustrated, illustrated wrappers, 27.5cm. note: title change in 1980.

68830. *Tour 1980*. New York: Times-Mirror, 14th ed. 1980, illustrated, illustrated wrappers, 27.5cm.

68832. *Tour 1981*. New York: Times-Mirror, 15th ed. 1981, 80p, illustrated, illustrated wrappers, 27.5cm.

68834. *Tour 1982*. New York: Times-Mirror, 16th ed. 1982, 88p, illustrated, illustrated wrappers, 27.5cm.

68836. *Tour 1983*. New York: Times-Mirror, 17th ed. 1983, 79p, illustrated, illustrated wrappers, 27.5cm.

68838. *Tour 1984*. New York: Times-Mirror, 18th ed. 1984, 102p, illustrated, illustrated wrappers, 27.5cm.

68840. *Tour 1985*. New York: Times-Mirror, 19th ed. 1985, 96p, illustrated, illustrated wrappers, 27.5cm.

69000. *PGA Caddie Manual*. Dunedin, Florida: Professional Golfers' Association, 1st ed. [1964] 24p, illustrated, illustrated wrappers, 21cm.

69010. *PGA Golf Professionals Guide*. Dunedin, Florida: Professional Golfers' Association, 1st ed. 1963, 97p, spiral bound wrappers, 27.5cm, introduction by Don Waryman.

69020. *Success Stories in the Golf Business*. [Palm Beach Gardens, Florida] PGA, 1st ed. 1978, 49p, illustrated, wrappers, 28cm.

69030. 2d ed. rev. 1981, 68p, illustrated, wrappers, 28cm.

69040. *The Golf Professional At A Military Course*. Palm Beach Gardens, Florida: Professional Golfers' Association, 1st ed. [1981] [24p] illustrated, illustrated wrappers, 28cm.

69050. *The Golf Professional At A Public Course*. Palm Beach Gardens, Florida: Professional Golfers' Association, 1st ed. [1983] 28p, illustrated, illustrated wrappers, 27.5cm.

Quantz, Nancy

69200. *Tee Party [Fore Ladies Only]*. Philadelphia: Whitmore, 1st ed. [1969] 60p, illustrated by Bo Brown, cloth, 21cm.

Quinzi, Joseph

69220. *Back to the Basics in Golf*. [Los Angeles] Privately Printed, 1st ed. [ca1980] 31p, illustrated, illustrated wrappers, 28cm.

Quinzi, Joseph and Catherine McKenzie Shane

69240. *The Women's World of Golf*. Bloomington, Indiana: T.I.S. Publications, 1st ed. [1980] 100p, illustrated, illustrated wrappers, 22.5cm.

Qvist

69260. *Golfermania*. Horsham, England: Ravette, 1st ed. [1985] 78p, illustrated, illustrated wrappers, 20cm.

Radyr Golf Club

69280. *Radyr Golf Club 1902-1977*. Radyr, Wales: Privately Printed, 1st ed. 1977, 24p, illustrated, illustrated wrappers, 16.5cm.

Rafty, Tony

69300. *Tony Rafty's Golfing Greats*. Adelaide, Australia: Rigby, 1st ed. 1983, 135p, illustrated, cloth, 25cm, with Terry Smith.

Ragaway, Martin A.

69320. *Golfer's Dictionary*. Los Angeles: Price/Stern/Sloan, 1st ed. 1984 [76p] illustrated by Rene Rembrand, illustrated wrappers, 17.5cm.

69330. *Sex Before Golf*. Los Angeles: Price/Stern/Sloan, 1st ed. [1982] [46p] illustrated, illustrated wrappers, 15cm, later printings.

69340. *The World's Worst Golf Jokes*. Los Angeles: Price, Stern, Sloan, 1st ed. [1974] [46p] illustrated, illustrated wrappers, 16.5cm.

Ramsay, Allan

69360. *West Sussex Golf Club Golden Jubilee 1931-1981*. Pulborough, England: Privately Printed, 1st ed. 1981 [12p] illustrated, illustrated wrappers, 21cm.

Ramsay, Neil

69380. *Scotland's Golfing Heritage.* Aberlady, Scotland: Privately Printed, 1st ed. [1984] 32p, illustrated, illustrated wrappers, 30cm.

Ramsey, Tom

69400. *25 Great Australian Golf Courses.* Sydney: Australia, Rigby, 1st ed. 1981, 164p, illustrated, cloth, 29cm, foreword by Peter Thomson.

69410. *Golfer's Gift Book.* Adelaide, Australia: Rigby, 1st ed. 1983, 168p, illustrated, cloth, 25.5cm.

69420. *How to Cheat and Hustle At Golf.* Adelaide, Australia: Rigby, 1st ed. 1983, 62p, illustrated by Tony Rafty, illustrated boards, 21cm.

69430. *Tom Ramsey's World of Golf.* Sydney: Paul Hamlyn, 1st ed. 1977, 395p, illustrated, cloth, 28cm, introduction by Peter Thompson.

Rand McNally

69450. *All About Golf.* [Chicago] Rand McNally, 1st ed. [1975] 194p, illustrated, illustrated wrappers, 28cm.

Randolph, Richard C.

69470. *You Will Win Betting on the Golf Course-I'll Betcha: Everything You Should Know About the Nassau and the Press Bets.* Naples, Florida: Di-el Publishers, 1st ed. [1983] 155p, illustrated, illustrated wrappers, 20.5cm.

Rankin, Judy

69490. *A Natural Way to Golf Power.* New York: Harper & Row, 1st ed. [1976] 126p, illustrated by Dom Lupo, cloth, 22.5cm, with Michael Aronstein, foreword by Bob Toski.

69500. pbk. ed. New York: Cornerstone Library, 1977, 192p, illustrated by Dom Lupo, illustrated wrappers, 20cm, with Michael Aronstein, foreword by Bob Toski.

Rarald, Bertil

69520. *Get Fit for Golf.* New York: Bergh Publishing, 1st ed. 1985, 89p, illustrated, illustrated wrappers, 19.5cm.

Rasmussen, Roy and Betty

69540. *1981 Michigan Golfers Map and Guide*. Detroit, Michigan: RSG, 1st ed. 1981, 171p, illustrated, illustrated wrappers, 21cm.

Rasmussen, Wally [Rev]

69560. *The Preaching Pro*. Marshalltown, Iowa: Privately Printed, 1st ed. [1979] 88p, illustrated, illustrated wrappers, 23cm.

Ravielli, Anthony

69580. *What Is Golf?* New York: Atheneum, 1st ed. 1976 [30p] illustrated, decorative cloth, 19cm.

Ray, Ted

69600. *Golf: My Slice of Life*. London: W.H. Allen, 1st ed. 1972, 127p, illustrated by David Langdon, cloth, 21.5cm, introduction by Dai Rees.

Redford, Ken and Nick Tremayne

69620. *Success in Golf*. London: John Murray, 1st ed. 1977, 86p, illustrated, cloth, 21.5cm, foreword by Tom Scott.

Reece, John

69640. *Golf of Course*. Bristol, England: Redcliffe, 1st ed. 1983, 148p, illustrated by Pete Smith, illustrated wrappers, 21cm.

Reed, Betty Jane

69660. *Golfin with A Dolfin*. Minneapolis, Minnesota: T.S. Denison, 1st ed. [1968] [28p] illustrated by June Talarczyk, illustrated boards, 16.5cm.

Rees, Dai [David]

69680. *Golf Today*. London: Arthur Barker, 1st ed. [1962] 119p, illustrated, cloth, 22cm.

69690. *The Key to Golf*. London: Duckworth, 1st ed. 1961, 128p, illustrated, cloth, 21.5cm.

69700. 1st American ed. New York: A.S. Barnes [1961] 127p, illustrated, cloth, 21cm.

69710. *Thirty Years of Championship Golf*. London: Stanley Paul, 1st ed. 1968, 180p, illustrated, cloth, 22.5cm, with John Ballantine.

Refram, Dean and Arthur Burgoyne

69730. *Golf-O-Genics: How to Play Winning Golf Through Progressive Concentration and the Graduated Length Method.* Tampa, Florida: Information Press Service, 1st ed. [1978] 113p, illustrated, cloth, 21cm.

Reid, William

69750. *Seventy Five Years of Golf At Cathkin Braes 1888-1963.* Rutherglen, Scotland: Privately Printed, 1st ed. 1963, 27p, illustrated, illustrated wrappers, 21.5cm.

Reynolds, Frank

69770. *The Frank Reynolds Golf Collection.* North Berwick, Scotland: Hope Letters, 1st ed. [ca1970] [12p] illustrated, decorative leather, 33.5cm.

Reynolds, Morgan B.

69790. *Seventy Years of Belle Meade Country Club 1901-1971.* Nashville, Tennessee: Privately Printed, limited ed. [1500 copies] 1971 [76p] illustrated, decorative cloth, 25cm.

Rhodes, Louis

69810. *Stop Action Golf: The Driver.* NP: Hammond, 1st ed. [1971] [48p] illustrated, illustrated wrappers, 14.5cm.

Richardson, Bruce

69830. *Richardson's Common Sense Golf.* Monterey, Virginia: Privately Printed, 1st ed. [1984] 30p, illustrated wrappers, 21cm.

Richardson, Donald H.

69850. *World Wide Golf Directory.* Washington, DC: World Wide Sports, 1st ed. [1973] 160p, illustrated, illustrated wrappers, 28cm.

Richardson, Forrest B. "Frosty"

69870. *Broadmoor Golf Club.* Seattle, Washington: Superior Publications, 1st ed. [1983] 120p, illustrated, decorative cloth, 28cm.

Rickard, Bill

69890. *Army Golf Club, 1883-1983.* Aldershot, England: Privately Printed, limited ed. [100 copies] [1983] 124p, illustrated, illustrated wrappers, 29.5cm.

Riddell, Gervase Carre

69910. *Practical Golf Course Design and Construction.* Victoria, Australia: Privately Printed, 1st ed. [ca1973] 45p, illustrated, illustrated wrappers, 12.5cm, edited by George Burgess.

Riley, John

69930. *Royal Salisbury Golf Club Commemorative Brochure.* Salisbury, Zimbabwe: Privately Printed, 1st ed. 1968, 44p, illustrated, illustrated wrappers, 28cm.

Rimmer, Norman H.

69950. *Mere Golf & Country Club Golden Jubilee 1934-1984.* Mere, England: Privately Printed, 1st ed. 1985, 84p, illustrated, illustrated wrappers, 20cm, foreword by Neil Coles.

Ringway Golf Club

69970. *Ringway Golf Club 75th Anniversary 1909-1984.* Altrincham, England: Privately Printed, 1st ed. 1984 [12p] illustrated, illustrated wrappers, 25.5cm.

Roberts, Clifford

69990. *The Story of the Augusta National Golf Club.* Garden City, New York: Doubleday, 1st trade ed. 1976, 255p, illustrated, decorative cloth, 26cm.

70000. limited ed. [no limitation cited] slipcased, 1976, 255p, illustrated, decorative cloth, 26cm.

Roberts, Palmer W.

70020. *Fore: The Golfer's International Cookbook.* San Diego, California: Western Specialities, 1st ed. [1978] 120p, illustrated, illustrated wrappers, 15cm, foreword by John W. Brown.

Robertson, G.S.

70040. *A History of the Stromness Golf Courses, with notes on the Kirkwall and Isles Courses.* Stromness, Scotland: Privately Printed, 1st ed. [ca1974] 19p, illustrated, illustrated wrappers, 22.5cm.

Robertson, James K.

70060. *St. Andrews: Home of Golf.* St. Andrews: Citizen Office, 1st ed. 1967, 173p, illustrated by J. Putter, cloth, 21.5cm.

70070. 2d ed. rev. limited [60 copies] 1974, 179p. illustrated, embossed leather, 21 cm.

Robinson, Robby

70090. *Golf Guide to the Caribbean, including the Bahamas & Bermuda.* Denver, Colorado: Shannon Golf Publications, 1st ed. [1983] 255p, illustrated, illustrated wrappers, 23 cm.

Robison, Nancy

70110. *Nancy Lopez: Wonder Woman of Golf.* Chicago: Childrens Press, 1st ed. [1979] 42p, illustrated, illustrated wrappers, 20cm.

Rock Island Arsenal Golf Club

70130. *Rock Island Arsenal Golf Club.* Rock Island, Illinois: Privately Printed, reprint, 1982 [46p] illustrated, wrappers, 14.5cm, note: original edition [ca1906] not located.

Rodrigo, Robert

70150. *The Birdie Book: A Miscellany of Golf.* London: Macdonald, 1st ed. 1967, 219p, illustrated, cloth, 23.5cm, foreword by The Earl of Derby.

Rodrigues, Chi Chi

70170. *Chi Chi's Secrets of Power Golf.* New York: Viking Press, 1st ed. 1967, 78p, illustrated, cloth, 21.5cm, introduction by Sandy Padwe.

70180. *Everybody's Golf Book.* New York: Viking Press, 1st ed. 1975, 152p, illustrated by Simon Paukow, decorative cloth, 23.5cm, with Chuck Fitt, foreword by Byron Nelson.

Rodrigues, Chi Chi and Harry Stroiman

70200. *Chi Chi's Golf Secret.* Des Moines, Iowa: J & H, 1st ed. [1964] 32p, illustrated by James Stevenson, illustrated wrappers, 23cm.

Rominger, O.B.

70220. *The Desert Valley Country Club.* Hicksville, New York: Exposition Press, 1st ed. [1975] 255p, cloth, 20cm.

Rosburg, Bob

70240. *The Putter Book.* South Norwalk, Connecticut: Golf Digest, 1st ed. [1963] 125p, illustrated by James McQueen, decorative cloth, 22.5cm, preface by Bill Casper, Jr.

Ross, A.C. Gordon

70260. *A Mixed Bag of Golfing Verse*. Glasgow: Brown, Son & Ferguson, 1st ed. 1977, 83p, illustrated wrappers, 18cm.

Ross, John M.

70280. *Golf Businessman's Almanac 1968*. New York: Golf Promotions, 1st ed. 1968, 108p, illustrated, illustrated wrappers, 27.5cm.

70290. *Golf Businessman's Almanac 1969*. New York: Golf Promotions, 2d ed. rev. 1969, 106p, illustrated, illustrated wrappers, 27.5cm.

70300. *The Golfer's Coloring Book*. New York: Arnold E. Abramson, 1st ed. [1962] [22p] illustrated by John Gallagher, illustrated wrappers, 35.5cm.

Rotella, Robert J. and Linda K. Bunker

70320. *Mind Mastery for Winning Golf: Using Your Head to Reach Par and to Enjoy Playing*. Englewood Cliffs, New Jersey: Prentice-Hall [1981] 146p, cloth, 22.5cm, foreword by Bob Hope.

70330. pbk. ed. [1981] 146p, illustrated, illustrated wrappers 22.5cm, foreword by Bob Hope.

Royal and Ancient Golf Club of St. Andrews

70350. *Golf Rules Illustrated*. St. Andrews: Royal and Ancient Golf Club of St. Andrews, 1st ed. 1969, 111p, illustrated, illustrated wrappers, 27cm, later printings.

70360. 2d ed. 1972, 111p, illustrated, illustrated wrappers, 27cm.

70370. 3d ed. 1976, 111p, illustrated by Peter Davidson, illustrated wrappers, 27cm.

70380. 4th ed. 1980, 109p, illustrated by Peter Davidson, cloth, 27cm.

70385. 4th ed. 1980, 109p, illustrated by Peter Davidson, illustrated wrappers, 27cm.

70390. 5th ed. 1985, 95p, illustrated by Peter Davidson, illustrated wrappers, 27cm.

Royal Blackheath Golf Club

70450. *Royal Blackheath Golf Club [Handbook]*. Kingston upon Thames: Temple Publicity Services [1970] 16p, illustrated, illustrated wrappers, 18.5cm.

Royal Burgess Golfing Society

70470. *The Royal Burgess Golfing Society of Edinburgh 1735-1985. 250th Anniversary Celebration.* Edinburgh: Privately Printed, 1st ed. 1985, 48p, illustrated, illustrated wrappers, 30cm.

Royal Canberra Golf Club

70490. *Royal Canberra Golf Club Jubilee History 1926-1976.* Canberra, Australia: Privately Printed, limited ed. [2000 copies] 1976, 80p, illustrated, decorative cloth, 21cm.

Royal Cape Golf Club

70510. *Royal Cape Golf Club Centenary Year 1885-1985.* Cape Town, South Africa: Privately Printed, 1st ed. 1985, 48p, illustrated, illustrated wrappers, 21cm.

Royal Dublin Golf Club

70530. *The Royal Dublin Golf Club 1885-1963.* Dublin, Ireland: Privately Printed, 1st ed. 1963 [12p] illustrated, wrappers, 23cm.

Royal Musselburgh Golf Club

70550. *Royal Musselburgh Golf Club 1774-1974.* Prestonpans, Scotland: Privately Printed, 1st ed. 1974 [30p] leatherette, 12cm.

Royal Portrush Golf Club

70570. *Royal Portrush Golf Club [Handbook].* Portrush, Ireland: Privately Printed [ca1980] [28p] illustrated, illustrated wrappers, 19.5cm.

Royal Salisbury Golf Club

70590. *Royal Salisbury Golf Club, 75th Anniversary 1898-1973.* Salisbury, Zimbabwe: Privately Printed, 1st ed. 1973, 19p, illustrated, illustrated wrappers, 28cm.

Rubenstein, Lorne and J. Briggs

70610. *Brantford Golf and Country Club 1879-1979.* Toronto: Privately Printed, 1st ed. 1979 [36p] illustrated, illustrated wrappers, 24cm, foreword by R. Bruce Forbes.

Rudolph, Mason

70630. *The Short Irons [Flipbook].* New York: Sterling, 1st ed. [1965] 128p, illustrated, illustrated wrappers, 12.5cm.

Rule, Bob

70650. *Champions Golf Club 1957-1976.* Houston, Texas: Graphics Unlimited, 1st ed. 1976, 152p, illustrated, cloth, 25.5cm, foreword by Ben Hogan.

Runyan, Paul

70670. *Paul Runyan's Book for Senior Golfers.* New York: Dodd, Mead, 1st ed. [1962] 149p, illustrated, decorative cloth, 22.5cm, foreword by Robert T. Jones, Jr.

70680. *Short Way to Lower Scoring.* Norwalk, Connecticut: Golf Digest, 1st ed. 1979, 175p, illustrated by Anthony Ravielli, cloth, 25cm, with Dick Aultman, foreword by Gene Littler.

Russell, Edwin F.

70700. *Siwanoy Country Club 1901-1976, 75th Anniversary.* Bronxville, New York: Privately Printed, 1st ed. 1976, 20p, illustrated, illustrated wrappers, 28cm.

Russell, George C.

70720. *The Williamwood Golf Club 1906-1981, "Three Over Fours."* Glasgow: Privately Printed, 1st ed. 1981, 40p, illustrated, illustrated wrappers, 21cm.

Ryan, William

70730. *The History of Innis Arden 1899-1973.* Old Greenwich, Connecticut: Privately Printed, 1st ed. 1973, illustrated, illustrated wrappers, 21.5cm.

70740. *The History of Innis Arden 1905-1980.* Greenwich, Connecticut: Privately Printed, 1st ed. 1980, 20p, illustrated, illustrated wrappers, 28cm.

Ryde, Peter

70760. *Halford Hewitt: A Festival of Foursomes.* Winderton, England: Public Schools Golfing Society, 1st ed. [1984] 192p, illustrated, gilt stamped leather, 25cm, foreword by Gerald Micklem.

70770. *Mostly Golf: A Bernard Darwin Anthology.* edited by. London: Adam & Charles Black, 1st ed. 1976, 198p, cloth, 21.5cm.

70780. *Royal and Ancient Championship Records 1860-1980.* edited by. St. Andrews: Royal and Ancient Golf Club of St. Andrews, 1st ed. [1981] 535p, illustrated, cloth, 26cm, foreword by W.R. Alexander.

70790. pbk. ed. 1984, 40p, illustrated, wrappers, 26cm.

70795. *Royal and Ancient Championship Records 1860-1980 Supplement.* edited by. St. Andrews: Royal and Ancient Golf Club of St. Andrews, 1st ed. 1984, 40p, illustrated, wrappers, 26cm.

70800. *Strokesaver. The Official Course Guide, The Royal St. George's Golf Club.* Glasgow: Stroke Sports & Leisure Products, 1st ed. [1981] [34p] illustrated, illustrated wrappers, 18cm.

Sabayrac, Ernie

70820. *Professionalizing The Golf Pro Shop; Why and How to Have A Sale.* Miami Springs, Florida: Privately Printed, 1st ed. [ca1975] 32p, illustrated, illustrated wrappers, 28cm.

Sadler, Allan

70840. *The Magic Move of Golf.* Rye, England: Privately Printed, 1st ed. [1974] [18p] wrappers, 30cm, with Allen C. Sears.

Sagar, Harold

70860. *A History of Purley Downs Golf Club.* Purley, England: Privately Printed, 1st ed. 1983, 87p, illustrated, illustrated wrappers, 21cm.

Salmon, Ross

70880. *Devon Golf Clubs.* Totnes, England: South Devon Agencies, 1984, 28p, illustrated, illustrated wrappers, 21cm.

70890. *Golf Clubs of Cornwall, Isles of Scilly and Jersey.* Newton Abbot, England: Town & Country, 1985, 128p, illustrated, illustrated wrappers, 21cm.

Sanders, Doug

70910. *Come Swing with Me; My Life On and Off the Tour.* Garden City, New York: Doubleday, 1st ed. 1974, 272p, illustrated, cloth, 21cm, with Larry Sheehan.

70920. *Compact Golf.* New York: Thomas Y. Crowell, 1st ed. [1964] 176p, illustrated, decorative cloth, 23cm, introduction by Jerry Claussen.

70930. pbk. ed. abridged. Greenwich, Connecticut: Fawcett [ca1966] 112p, illustrated, illustrated wrappers, 23.5cm.

Sands, Amelia

70950. *Indian Hill Club 1914-1964.* Winnetka, Illinois: Privately Printed, 1st ed. 1964, 20p, illustrated wrappers, 23cm.

Sandy Lodge Golf Club

70970. *Sandy Lodge Golf Club [Handbook].* London: Golf Clubs Association [ca1965] 31p, illustrated, wrappers, 18.5cm.

Sarazen, Gene

70990. *Better Golf After Fifty.* New York: Harper & Row, 1st ed. [1967] 120p, illustrated, cloth, 21cm, with Roger Ganem, foreword by John M. Ross.

71000. pbk. ed. New York: Award Books, 1969, 120p, illustrated, illustrated wrappers, 17.5cm, with Roger P. Ganem.

71010. *Gene Sarazen's World Golf Directory...with Tennis.* Washington, DC: World Sports, 2d ed. [1977] 208p, illustrated, illustrated wrappers, 28cm, note: first edition not located.

71020. *Golf: New Horizons, Pan Am's Guide to Golf Courses Round the World.* New York: Thomas Y. Crowell, 1st ed. [1966] 276p, illustrated, cloth, 20.5cm, with Peter McLean, introduction by Allan Brown.

71030. 2d ed. rev. [1968] 341p, illustrated, cloth, 20cm, with Peter McLean, introduction by Allan Brown.

Sasse, Howard A.

71050. *Putting Facts and Fallacies.* Buffalo, New York: Wood Wand, 1st ed. 1972, 68p, illustrated, illustrated wrappers, 18cm.

Saunders, Vivien

71070. *Successful Golf.* London: Charles Letts, 1st ed. 1980, 95p, illustrated, illustrated wrappers, 21.5cm.

71080. *The Complete Woman Golfer.* London: Stanley Paul, 1st ed. 1975, 144p, illustrated, cloth, 27.5cm, foreword by Peter Alliss.

71090. *The Golfing Mind.* London: Stanley Paul, 1st ed. 1984, 191p, illustrated by Ken Lewis, cloth, 24cm, foreword by Mary Parkinson.

Saunders, Vivien and Clive Clark

71110. *The Young Golfer.* London: Stanley Paul, 1st ed. 1977, 112p, illustrated, cloth, 18.5cm.

71120. pbk. ed. 1977, 112p, illustrated, wrappers, 18.5cm.

Saunton Golf Club

71140. *Saunton Golf Club [Handbook].* Bristol: E.G. Brown, 1984, 20p, illustrated, illustrated wrappers, 21cm.

Savage, E. J.

71160. *The Story of Felixstowe Ferry Golf Club 1880-1980.* Felixstowe Ferry, England: Privately Printed, 1st ed. 1980 [30p] illustrated, illustrated wrappers, 27cm.

Savannah Golf Club

71180. *Brief History of the Savannah Golf Club.* Savannah, Georgia: Privately Printed, 1st ed. 1975, 8p, illustrated wrappers, 21.5cm.

Scarlett, Arthur C.

71200. *Index and Representative Price Guide to Golf Books, 1743-1970.* Richmond, Virginia: Privately Printed, 1st ed. 1979, 37p, illustrated, illustrated wrappers, 28cm.

Schaap, Dick

71220. *Massacre At Winged Foot: The U.S. Open, Minute by Minute.* New York: Random House, 1st ed. [1974] 222p, illustrated, cloth, 21cm.

71230. *The Masters: The Winning of A Golf Classic.* New York: Random House, 1st ed. [1970] 235p, illustrated, cloth, 21cm, introduction by Frank Beard.

71240. pbk. ed. New York: New American Library, 1971, 223p, illustrated, illustrated wrappers, 18cm.

Scharff, Robert

71260. *Golf Magazine's Encyclopedia of Golf.* New York: Harper & Row, 1st ed. [1970] 424p, illustrated, cloth, 26cm, and the editors of Golf Magazine, assisted by Peter D. Eaton.

71270. 2d ed. rev. [1973] 424p, illustrated, illustrated wrappers, 25cm, and editors of Golf Magazine, assisted by Peter D. Eaton.

71280. *Golf Magazine's Great Golf Courses You Can Play: A Guide to Golf Courses Around the World.* New York: Scribner's, 1st ed. [1973] 440p, illustrated, cloth, 22.5cm, and editors of Golf Magazine.

71290. *Golf Magazine's Handbook of Golf Strategy.* New York: Harper & Row, 1st ed. [1971] 232p, illustrated, cloth, 23.5cm, and the editors of Golf Magazine.

71300. *The Collier Quick and Easy Guide to Golf.* New York: Collier, 1st ed. 1963, 96p, illustrated, illustrated wrappers, 28cm.

71310. *Golf: Collier Quick and Easy Series.* New York: Collier, reprint ed. [ca1966] 96p, illustrated, illustrated wrappers, 28cm, originally published under the title "The Collier Quick and Easy Guide to Golf." later printings.

Schmitt, Chuck

71330. *My Golf Clinic.* Fort Wayne, Indiana: Privately Printed, 1st ed. [1967] 31p, illustrated, illustrated wrappers, 21.5cm.

Scholz, Jackson

71350. *Fairway Challenge.* New York: William Morrow, 1st ed. 1964, 224p, illustrated, cloth, 20.5cm.

Schroeter, Reg

71370. *Rivermead Golf Club 1910-1985, the First 75 Years.* Ottawa, Canada: Privately Printed, 1st ed. 1985, bilingual, 78p English/67p French, illustrated, illustrated wrappers, 23.5cm.

Schultz, Charles M.

71390. *Snoopy's Grand Slam.* New York: Holt, Rinehart and Winston, 1st ed. [1972] [60p] illustrated, decorative boards, 17.5cm.

Schumacher, Craig

71410. *Nancy Lopez.* Mankato, Minnesota: Creative Education, 1st ed. [1979] 32p, illustrated, illustrated boards, 21.5cm.

Scotland for Golf

71430. *Scotland For Golf.* Edinburgh: Scottish Tourist Board, [ca1961] 112p, illustrated, illustrated wrappers, 20.5cm. later printings.

Scott, Garnet

71450. *A Centenary History of the Worcestershire Golf Club.* Malvern, England: Privately Printed, 1st ed. 1979, 138p, illustrated, cloth, 21cm, foreword by Tom Scott.

Scott, Mike

71470. *The Crazy World of Golf.* Watford, England: Exely, 1st ed. [1985] [92p] illustrated, illustrated boards, 14cm.

Scott, Tom

71490. *Axe Cliff Golf Club [Handbook].* London: Temple Publicity Services, 1962, 12p, illustrated, illustrated wrappers, 18.5cm.

71500. *Club Golfer's Handbook.* London: Arthur Barker, 1st ed. [1972] 162p, illustrated, cloth, 19.5cm.

71510. *Golf-Begin the Right Way.* Newton Abbot, England: David & Charles, 1st ed. [1974] 127p, illustrated by Alex Hay, cloth, 21.5cm.

71520. *More Golf with the Experts.* London: Heinemann, 1st ed. 1965, 184p, illustrated, cloth, 20cm.

71530. *Secrets of the Golfing Greats.* South Brunswick, New Jersey: A.S. Barnes, 1st American ed. [1965] 184p, illustrated, cloth, 21cm, American title of "More Golf with the Experts."

71540. *Sixty Miles of Golf Around London.* edited by. London: Barrie & Jenkins, 1st ed. 1975.3, 128p, illustrated, illustrated wrappers, 18.5cm.

71550. *Sonning Golf Club [Handbook].* Hants & London: Temple Publicity Services [ca1965] 16p, illustrated, illustrated wrappers, 18.5cm.

71560. *The Concise Dictionary of Golf.* London: Bison, 1st ed. 1978, 256p, illustrated, cloth, 25.5cm.

71570. *The Observer's Book of Golf.* London: Frederick Warne, 1st ed. 1975, 192p, illustrated, cloth, 14cm.

71580. *The Story of Golf: From its Origins to the Present Day.* London: Arthur Barker, 1st ed. [1972] 166p, illustrated, cloth, 21.5cm.

71590. *The Swanage and Studland Golf Club [Handbook].* Hants & London: Temple Publicity Services, 1964, 24p, illustrated, illustrated wrappers, 18.5cm.

71600. *Worcestershire Golf Club [Handbook].* Bournemouth & London: Temple Publicity Services [ca1967] 12p, illustrated, illustrated wrappers, 18.5cm.

Scott, Tom and Geoffrey Cousins

71620. *Golf Secrets of the Masters.* London: Stanley Paul, 1st ed. 1968, 136p, illustrated, cloth, 21cm.

71630. *The Golf Immortals.* New York: Hart, 1st American ed. 1969, 272p, illustrated, cloth, 23cm, American title of "Golf Secrets of the Masters."

71640. pbk. ed. 1969, 272p, illustrated, illustrated wrappers, 23cm.

71650. *The Ind Coope Book of Golf.* London: Stanley Paul, 1st ed. 1965, 143p, illustrated, cloth, 22.5cm.

71660. *The Wit of Golf.* London: Leslie Frewin, 1st ed. 1972, 93p, illustrated by Paul Trevillion, cloth, 19.5cm, foreword by Ted Ray.

Scrabo Golf Club

71680. *Scrabo Golf Club 1907-1982, 75th Anniversary Souvenir Brochure.* Newtownards, Ireland: Privately Printed, 1st ed. [ca1983] 40p, illustrated, illustrated wrappers, 24cm.

Scudamore, Edward

71700. *Royal Wimbledon Golf Club Centenary 1965.* London: Privately Printed, 1st ed. 1965, 28p, wrappers, 22.5cm.

Seagle, Janet

71720. *The Club Makers.* Far Hills, New Jersey: USGA, 1st ed. 1980 [90p] wrappers, 25.5cm.

71730. 2d ed. rev. 1984, 132p, wrappers, 27cm.

71740. 3d ed. rev. 1984, 117p, wrappers, 27.5cm.

Secrets to the Short Game

71760. *Secrets to the Short Game: Pitching, Chipping, Putting.* NP: Best Enterprises, 1st ed. [1976] 94p, illustrated, illustrated wrappers, 27.5cm.

Seifert, H.A.

71780. *The First 75 Years of the Manawatu Golf Club 1895-1970.* Palmerston, New Zealand: Privately Printed, 1st ed. 1970, 104p, illustrated, cloth, 22cm.

Seitz, Nick

71800. *Quick Tips From the CBS Golf Spot.* Norwalk, Connecticut: Golf Digest, 1st ed. [1982] 182p, illustrated, illustrated wrappers, 23cm.

71810. *Super Stars of Golf.* Norwalk, Connecticut: Golf Digest, 1st ed. [1978] 192p, illustrated, cloth, 25.5cm, swing studies by Bob Toski.

Selleck, Jack and Art Bernard

71830. *Golf Is A Trap*. Garden City, New York: Doubleday, 1st ed. 1968, 63p, illustrated, illustrated boards, 19cm.

Sen, Eric

71850. *The Lodhi-Delhi Golf Club*. New Delhi, India: Privately Printed, 1st ed. [1977] [8p] illustrated, illustrated wrappers, 28.5cm.

Shankland, Craig and others

71870. *The Golfer's Stroke-Saving Handbook*. and Dale Shankland, Dom Lupo, Roy Benjamin. Boston: Little, Brown, 1st ed. [1978] 214p, illustrated, cloth, 23.5cm.

71880. *Stroke-Saving for the Handicap Golfer*. and Dale Shankland, Dom Lupo, Roy Benjamin, edited by Peter Alliss. London: Foulsham, 1st UK ed. 1979, 214p, illustrated, cloth, 23.5cm, UK title of "The Golfer's Stroke Saving Handbook ."

Shapiro, Harold

71900. *Get Golf Straight*. Bristol, England: Abson, 1st ed. 1972 [54p] illustrated, wrappers, 9cm, with John Allan May.

Shay, Arthur

71920. *40 Common Errors in Golf and How to Correct Them*. Chicago: Contemporary, 1st ed. [1978] 108p, illustrated, cloth, 27.5cm.

71930. pbk. ed. [1978] 108p, illustrated, illustrated wrappers, 28cm.

Sheehan, Joseph M.

71970. *How Maureen Orcutt Won 10 Metropolitan Golf Championships*. New York: New York Times, 1st ed. [1969] 14p, illustrated, illustrated wrappers, 30cm.

Sheehan, Larry

71990. *Best Golf Humor from Golf Digest*. Norwalk, Connecticut: Golf Digest, 1st ed. [1972] 160p, illustrated, cloth, 25cm, foreword by William H. Davis.

72000. *Great Golf Humor from Golf Digest*. edited by. Norwalk, Connecticut: Golf Digest, 1st ed. [1979] 192p, illustrated, cloth, 23cm.

72010. *The Whole Golf Catalog: Your guide to all the important sources, resources, and services in the world of golf.* New York: Atheneum, 1st ed. 1979, 292p, illustrated, wrappers, 28cm.

Sheldon, Alan

72030. *Rhode Island Country Club 1911-1961, Fiftieth Anniversary.* West Barrington, Rhode Island: Privately Printed, 1st ed. 1962, 80p, illustrated, illustrated wrappers, 23cm.

Sheldon, Colin

72050. *Reigate Heath and Its Golf Club.* Reigate Heath, England: S. Straker, 1st ed. 1982, 66p, illustrated, illustrated wrappers, 24.5cm.

Shell Oil

72070. *Shell's Wonderful World of Golf 1964.* NP: Shell Oil, 1st ed. 1964 [24p] illustrated, illustrated wrappers, 25.5cm. note: for 1962 and 1963 see Herbert Warren Wind #78630 and Charles Price #68150

72080. *Shell's Wonderful World of Golf 1965.* NP: Shell Oil, 1st ed. 1965 [24p] illustrated, illustrated wrappers, 25.5cm.

72090. *Shell's Wonderful World of Golf 1966.* NP: Shell Oil, 1st ed. 1966 [28p] illustrated, illustrated wrappers, 25.5cm.

72100. *Shell's Wonderful World of Golf 1967.* NP: Shell Oil, 1st ed. 1967 [28p] illustrated, illustrated wrappers, 25.5cm.

72110. *Shell's Wonderful World of Golf 1968.* NP: Shell Oil, 1st ed. 1968 [28p] illustrated, illustrated wrappers, 21.5cm.

72120. *Shell's Wonderful World of Golf 1969.* NP: Shell Oil, 1st ed. 1969, 29p, illustrated, illustrated wrappers, 21.5cm.

72130. *Shell's Wonderful World of Golf 1970.* NP: Shell Oil, 1st ed. 1970, 28p, illustrated, illustrated wrappers, 21.5cm.

Shelly, Warner

72150. *Pine Valley Golf Club, A Chronicle.* Clementon, New Jersey: Privately Printed, 1st ed. slipcased [1982] 106p, illustrated, decorative cloth, 28cm.

Sheridan, James

72170. *Sheridan of Sunningdale: My Fifty-Six Years As A Caddie Master.* London: Country Life, 1st ed. 1967, 144p, illustrated, cloth, 21.5cm, foreword by Gerald Micklem.

Sherman, James W.

72190. *Joey Gets the Golf Bug.* Boston: Little, Brown, 1st ed. [1961] 171p, illustrated by Frank Nicholas, decorative cloth, 18.5cm.

Shone, R.K.

72210. *Bedford Golf Club 1892-1967.* Bedford, South Africa: Privately Printed, 1st ed. 1967, 13p, illustrated, illustrated wrappers, 21cm.

Shore, Josselyn M.

72230. *The Story of the Fresh Meadow Country Club.* Great Neck, New York: Privately Printed, 1st ed. 1985, 127p, illustrated, gilt suede leather, 26cm.

Shwerwood, Peter and Gary Alderdice

72250. *Arnold Snead's World's Best Golf Book Ever.* Hong Kong: Lincoln Green, 1st ed. [1982] 96p, illustrated by Roy Bisson, illustrated boards, 28.5cm, foreword by A. Palmer.

Silver Niblick

72270. *The Silver Niblick: A Fond Remembrance and Good Times.* Oneida, New York: Oneida Silversmiths, 1st ed. [1972] 18p, illustrated, decorative cloth, 23cm.

Silvey, Jim

72290. *Golf As I See It.* [Tucson, Arizona] Privately Printed, 1st ed. [1969] 32p, illustrated, illustrated wrappers, 23cm.

72300. *Golf: How to Learn the Total Game.* Tucson, Arizona: Golf Unlimited, 1st ed. [1982] 86p, illustrated, illustrated wrappers, 23cm.

Simek, Thomas and Richard O'Brien

72320. *Total Golf: A behavioral approach to lowering your score and getting more out of your game.* Garden City, New York: Doubleday, 1st ed. 1981, 225p, illustrated by Phillip Jones, cloth, 25.5cm.

Simmons, Marlin L.

72340. *Golf and the Subconscious Mind.* Belleville, Illinois: Privately Printed, 1st ed. [1984] 61p, illustrated, illustrated wrappers, 17.5cm.

Simms, George

72360. *John Player Golf Yearbook 1973.* London: Queen Anne Press, 1st ed. 1973, 320p, illustrated, illustrated boards, 20.5cm.

72370. *John Player Golf Yearbook 1974.* London: Queen Anne Press, 2d ed. 1974, 319p, illustrated, illustrated boards, 20.5cm, compiled by Ken Schofield.

72380. *John Player Golf Yearbook 1975.* London: Queen Anne Press, 3d ed. 1975, 285p, illustrated, illustrated boards, 20.5cm.

72390. *John Player Golf Yearbook 1976.* London: Queen Anne Press, 4th ed. 1976, 288p, illustrated, illustrated boards, 20.5cm.

72400. *The World of Golf 1977.* London: Queen Anne Press, 1st ed. 1977, 224p, illustrated, cloth, 21.5cm.

72410. 1st American ed. New York: Two Continents, 1977, 224p, illustrated, illustrated wrappers, 21.5cm.

72420. *World of Golf 1978.* London: Macdonald and James, 1st ed. 1978, 224p, illustrated, cloth, 21.5cm.

72430. 1st American ed. New York: Two Continents [1978] 224p, illustrated, illustrated wrappers, 21.5cm.

72440. *World of Golf 1979.* London: Macdonald and James, 1st ed. 1979, 256p, illustrated, cloth, 21.5cm.

72460. *World of Golf 1980.* London: Macdonald and James, 1st ed. 1980, 256p, illustrated, cloth, 21.5cm.

Simons, Leonard

72500. *The Royal & Ancient Beginning of Franklin Hills Country Club.* Franklin, Michigan: Privately Printed, 1st ed. 1985 [8p] illustrated, illustrated wrappers, 22.5cm.

Singleton, James [Mrs] and Elliot Thorpe

72520. *Sara Bay Country Club 1926-1976; The Story of Fifty Years of Golf.* Sarasota, Florida: Privately Printed, 1st ed. 1976, 16p, illustrated, wrappers, 21.5cm.

Skerries Golf Club

72540. *Skerries Golf Club.* Skerries, Ireland: Privately Printed, 1st ed. [1977] 24p, illustrated, illustrated wrappers, 15.5cm.

Slack, Ann

72560. *The Mountain View Country Club 1898-1976.* Greensboro, Vermont: Privately Printed, 1st ed. 1976, 48p, illustrated, illustrated wrappers, 23cm.

Smartt, Patrick

72580. *Golf Grave and Gay.* London: Stanley Paul, 1st ed. 1964, 160p, illustrated, cloth, 19.5cm, foreword by Gerald H. Micklem.

72590. *If You Must Play Golf.* London: Stanley Paul, 1st ed. 1963, 126p, illustrated by John Jensen, cloth, 20cm.

72600. 1st American ed. New York: David McKay, 1964, 126p, illustrated by John Jensen, cloth, 18.5cm.

72610. *Sussex Golf, The 19th Century Club.* Crowborough, England: Privately Printed, limited ed. [no limitation cited] [ca1977] 51p, illustrated, wrappers, 21cm.

Smith, Allan E.

72630. *History of Seattle Golf Club 1960-1972.* Seattle, Washington: Privately Printed, 1st ed. 1972, 19p, illustrated, wrappers, 23cm.

Smith, Don

72650. *The Young Sportman's Guide to Golf.* New York: Thomas Nelson, 1st ed. [1961] 95p, illustrated, decorative cloth, 21cm.

Smith, Douglas Larue

72670. *Winged Foot Story: The Golf, The People, The Friendly Trees.* Mamaroneck, New York: Privately Printed, 1st ed. 1984, 192p, illustrated, decorative cloth, 30.5cm, foreword by Felix E. Larkin.

Smith, Emil

72690. *Golf Laffs: 150 cartoons to suit you to a tee.* Spartansburg, South Carolina: Palmetto Printing Service, 1st ed. [1964] [58p] illustrated, illustrated wrappers, 23cm.

Smith, Frederic W.

72700. *Skytop-An Adventure.* Skytop: Pennsylvania, 1st ed. 1963, 48p, illustrated, cloth, 23.5cm.

Smith, Horton and Marian Benton

72710. *The Velvet Touch.* [Ann Arbor, Michigan] Privately Printed, 1st ed. [1965] 193p, illustrated, cloth, 23cm.

Smith, Horton and Dawson Taylor

72730. *The Secret of Holing Putts.* New York: A.S. Barnes, 1st ed. [1961] 156p, illustrated, cloth, 23.5cm, forewords by Walter Hagen and Robert T. Jones, Jr. later printings.

72740. *The Master's Secrets of Holing Putts.* San Diego: A. S. Barnes, 2d ed. rev. 1982, 155p, illustrated, cloth, 23.5cm, forewords by Walter Hagen and Robert T. Jones, Jr. previously titled "The Secret of Holing Putts."

72750. *The Secret of Perfect Putting.* Hollywood, California: Wilshire, 1963, 156p, illustrated, illustrated wrappers, 21cm, forewords by Walter Hagen and Robert T. Jones, Jr. previously titled "The Secret of Holing Putts."

Smith, Jim

72760. *Acton Golf Club, A History.* London: Privately Printed, 1st ed. 1981, 8p, illustrated, wrappers, 20.5cm.

Smith, Kenneth

72780. *Golf Club Alterations and Repairs: A Professional Shop Manual of Instructions.* Kansas City, Missouri: Privately Printed, 1st ed. [1965] 32p, illustrated, illustrated wrappers, 25.5cm.

Smith, Larry

72800. *Golf Pix: A Pictorial Guide to Golfing, Palm Beach County including Tequesta.* Pompano Beach, Florida: Skypix, 1st ed. 1984, 128p, illustrated, illustrated wrappers, 28cm.

Smith, Mel

72820. *Golf Mel's Way.* Glenwood, Illinois: Mel Smith, 1st ed. [1975] 119p, illustrated, illustrated wrappers, 16.5cm.

Smith, Parker

72840. *Golf Techniques: How to Improve Your Game.* New York: Franklin Watts, 1st ed. 1973, 63p, illustrated by Dom Lupo, cloth, 23.5cm.

Smith, R. Craig

72860. *Enjoy Golf and Win.* San Bernadino, California: Wordsmith, 1st ed. [1981] 60p, wrappers, 27cm.

Smith, Seamus

72880. *Grange Golf Club.* Dublin, Ireland: Privately Printed, 1st ed. [1977] 32p, illustrated, illustrated wrappers, 15cm.

Smith, Shirlee H.

72900. *The Tacoma Country and Golf Club.* Tacoma, Washington: Privately Printed, 1st ed. 1980, 73p, illustrated, cloth, 28cm.

Smith, Terry

72920. *Aussie Golf Trivia.* Sydney: Horwitz Grahame, 1st ed. [1985] 128p, illustrated, illustrated boards, 21cm.

72930. *Australian Golf, The First 100 Years.* Sydney: Lester-Townsend, 1st ed. 1982, 203p, illustrated, cloth, 28cm.

72940. *The Complete Book of Australian Golf.* North Sydney, Australia: Jack Pollard, 1st ed. 1975, 229p, illustrated, cloth, 24.5cm.

72950. 2d ed. rev. Ultimo, Australia: Murray, 1978, 295p, illustrated, cloth, 24cm, foreword by David Graham.

72960. *Tony Rafty's Golfers: A Treasury of Stars in Caricature.* Sydney, Australia: John de Beyer, 1st ed. [1975] 192p, illustrated, illustrated wrappers, 25cm, foreword by Peter Thomson.

Smyth, Brian

72980. *Wetherby Golf Club, A Short History.* Wetherby, England: Privately Printed, 1st ed. 1985 [4p] illustrated, illustrated wrappers, 21cm.

Snarr, Myrene and Patricia Corn

73000. *An Illustrated Guide to Northern California Golf Courses.* Los Altos, California: My and Me, 1st ed. 1978, 187p, illustrated, illustrated wrappers, 15cm.

Snead, Sam

73020. *Golf Begins At Forty.* New York: Dial Press, 1st ed. [1978] 175p, illustrated by James McQueen, cloth, 25cm, with Dick Aultman.

73030. *Sam Snead on Golf.* Englewood Cliffs, New Jersey: Prentice-Hall, 1st ed. [1961] 146p, illustrated, cloth, 23cm, preface by Oscar Fraley.

73040. 1st UK ed. London: Kaye & Ward, 1962, 146p, illustrated, cloth, 22.5cm, preface by Oscar Fraley. later printing.

73050. *Sam Snead's Basic Guide to Good Golf.* New York: Grosset & Dunlap, 1968, 121p, illustrated, illustrated wrappers, 21cm, formerly titled "Sam Snead on Golf."

73060. *Sam Snead Teaches You His Simple Key Approach to Golf.* New York: Atheneum, 1st ed. 1975, 178p, illustrated by Jim McQueen, cloth, 26.5cm, with Larry Sheehan, introduction by Ken Bowden.

73070. *Short Cuts to Long Drives.* Norwalk, Connecticut: Golf Digest, 1st ed. [ca1965] 23p, illustrated, illustrated wrappers, 21.5cm.

73080. *The Driver Book.* South Norwalk, Connecticut: Golf Digest, 1st ed. [1963] 126p, illustrated by James McQueen, decorative cloth, 23cm, preface by Byron Nelson.

73090. pbk. ed. New York: Cornerstone Library, 1965, 160p, illustrated by James McQueen, illustrated wrappers, 20cm, preface by Byron Nelson.

73100. *The Education of A Golfer.* New York: Simon & Schuster, 1st ed. 1962, 248p, illustrated by Burt Silverman, decorative cloth, 23cm, with Al Stump.

73110. pbk. ed. Greenwich, Connecticut: Fawcett, 1964, 214p, illustrated, illustrated wrappers, 18cm, with Al Stump.

73120. 1st UK ed. London: Cassell, 1962, 248p, illustrated by Burt Silverman, cloth, 21.5cm, with Al Stump.

73130. reprint ed. London: Sportsman Book Club, 1964, 248p, illustrated by Burt Silverman, cloth, 21.5cm, with Al Stump.

73140. limited ed. facsimile [410 copies] [Dublin, Ohio] The Memorial Tournament, 1984, 248p, illustrated by Burt Silverman, gilt stamped leather, 23cm, with Al Stump.

Soley, Clyne

73160. *How Well Should You Putt? A Search for A Putting Standard.* [San Jose, California] Privately Printed, 1st ed. [1977] 118p, illustrated, illustrated wrappers, 25.5cm, as related to David A. Crawford.

Sorensen, Gary L.

73180. *The Architecture of Golf.* College Station, Texas: Privately Printed, 1st ed. [1976] 106p, illustrated, illustrated wrappers, 27.5cm.

Southampton Golf Club

73200. *Southampton Golf Club 1925-1975.* Southampton, New York: Privately Printed, 1st ed. 1975 [40p] illustrated, illustrated wrappers, 21.5cm.

Southern Hills Country Club

73220. *Brief History and Guide to the Golf Course of Southern Hills Country Club.* Tulsa, Oklahoma: Privately Printed, 1st ed. 1977 [44p] illustrated, illustrated wrappers, 21.5cm.

Spectator's Guide To Golf

73240. *A Spectator's Guide To Golf.* New York: Rolex Watch, 1st ed. [1969] 24p, illustrated, illustrated wrappers, 15.5cm.

Spence, Johnny

73260. *Golf Pro for God.* New York: Centaur House, 1st ed. [1965] 217p, illustrated, cloth, 21cm, with Oscar Fraley, foreword by Billy Graham.

73270. *How to Loose At Golf.* Wheaton, Illinois: Tyndale House, 2d ed. 1971, 192p, illustrated wrappers, 17.5cm, with Oscar Fraley. note: second edition of "Golf Pro For God."

Spicer, Sydney

73290. *Boomerang Golf.* edited by. [England] Sentinel Press, 1st ed. [1968] 97p, illustrated, cloth, 24.5cm.

Spooner, John

73310. *Golf Facts: Product Knowledge-basic information on the art of selling golf equipment.* Chicago: National Sporting Goods Association [1973] 39p, illustrated, wrappers, 21.5cm.

Sports Illustrated

73330. *Golf Lessons From the Pros.* Englewood Cliffs, New Jersey: Prentice-Hall, 1st ed. [1961] 235p, illustrated by Anthony Ravielli, cloth, 22.5cm, editors of Sports Illustrated.

73340. *Sports Illustrated Golf Tips From the Top Professionals.* Greenwich, Connecticut: Fawcett, 1st ed. [1961] 143p, illustrated, illustrated wrappers, 23.5cm, by the editors Sports Illustrated. later printings.

73350. 2d ed. abridged. Greenwich, Connecticut: Fawcett [1966] 112p, illustrated, illustrated wrappers, 23.5cm, by the editors of Sports Illustrated.

Springman, Jack F.

73370. *The Beauty of Pebble Beach.* [Philadelphia] Privately Printed, 1st ed. [1964] [32p] illustrated, decorative cloth, 28cm.

73380. *The Many Faces of the American Golf Course.* [Camden, New Jersey] RCA, 1st ed. [1963] [24p] illustrated, illustrated cloth, 28cm.

St. Andrew's Golf Club

73400. *St. Andrew's Golf Club 1888-1963.* Hastings-on-Hudson, New York: Privately Printed, 1st ed. 1963, 146p/117p, illustrated, decorative cloth, 22.5cm. note: Part- 1-reprint of H.B. Martin's 1938 History; Part 2-update of history 1938-1963.

St. Charles Country Club

73420. *St. Charles Country Club 1905-1965.* St. Charles, Manitoba: Privately Printed, 1st ed. 1966, 24p, illustrated, spiral bound leather, 23cm.

St. Ledger, Alicia

73440. *Monkstown Golf Club 1908-1983*. Monkstown, Ireland: Privately Printed, 1st ed. 1983, 60p, illustrated, illustrated wrappers, 20.5cm.

Stanley, Louis T.

73460. *Golf With Your Hands*. London: Collins, 1st ed. 1966, 256p, illustrated, cloth, 24.5cm, foreword by Gary Player.

73470. 1st American ed. New York: Thomas Y. Crowell, 1967, 256p, illustrated, cloth, 24.5cm, foreword by Gary Player.

73480. *Pelham Golf Year*. London: Pelham, 1st ed. 1981, 443p, illustrated, cloth, 21.5cm.

73490. 2d ed. 1981, 383p, illustrated, cloth, 21.5cm.

73500. 3d ed. 1982, 336p, illustrated, cloth, 21.5cm.

Stanwich Club

73520. *The Stanwich Club*. Stanwich, Connecticut: Privately Printed, 1st ed. [1972] [30p] illustrated, decorative cloth, 23cm.

Starr, Allan D.

73540. *The Easy Way to Lower Your Golf Score*. Honolulu: Privately Printed, 1st ed. [1975] 90p, wrappers, 18cm.

Steel, Donald

73560. *Guiness Book of Golf Facts and Feats*. Enfield, England: Guiness Superlatives, 1st ed. 1980, 256p, illustrated, cloth, 23cm.

73570. 2d ed. rev. 1982, 256p, illustrated, cloth, 23.5cm.

73580. *The Golfer's Bedside Book*. London: B.T. Batsford, 1st ed. 1971, 240p, illustrated by Iconicus, cloth, 21.5cm.

Steel, Donald and Peter Ryde

73600. *The Shell International Encyclopedia of Golf*. London: Ebury Press and Pelham Books, 1st ed. 1975, 480p, illustrated, illustrated boards, 28cm, advisory editor: Herbert Warren Wind, foreword by Arnold Palmer.

73610. *The Encyclopedia of Golf.* New York: Viking Press, 1st American ed. 1975, 480p, illustrated, cloth, 28cm, American title of "The Shell International Encyclopedia of Golf." American advisory editor: Herbert Warren Wind, foreword by Arnold Palmer.

Stephenson, H.G.

73630. *A History of Todmorden Golf Club.* Todmorden, England: Privately Printed, 1st ed. 1983, 32p, wrappers, 16.5cm.

Stern, Leonard and Ed Powers

73650. *The World's Greatest [and funniest] Golf Awards.* Los Angeles: Price, Stern, Sloan, 1st ed. [1985] 10p, illustrated, illustrated boards, 28cm.

Stewart, Jr., Earl and Dr. Harry E. [Bud] Gunn

73670. *Golf Begins At Forty.* Matteson, Illinois: Great Lakes Living Press, 1st ed. [1977] 163p, illustrated, illustrated wrappers, 21.5cm.

73680. *Left-Hander's Golf Book.* Matteson, Illinois: Great Lakes Living Press, 1st ed. [1976] 166p, illustrated, illustrated wrappers, 21.5cm, foreword by Mickey Wright.

Stine, Charley

73700. *1983 Florida Golf Directory.* Winter Haven, Florida: Florida Golf Week, 1st ed. 1983, 160p, illustrated, illustrated wrappers, 21cm.

Stipe, Frank M.

73720. *The Australian.* New York: Vantage Press, 1st ed. [1980] 69p, cloth, 20.5cm.

Stirling Golf Club

73740. *Stirling Golf Club Centenary, 1869-1969.* Stirling, Scotland: Privately Printed, 1st ed. 1969, 16p, illustrated, illustrated wrappers, 20.5cm.

Stirling, John

73760. *Fit for Golf.* London: B.T. Batsford, 1st ed. 1984, 72p, illustrated, illustrated boards, 20cm.

73770. *Golf: The Skills of the Game.* Marborough, England: Crowood Press, 1st ed. [1985] 120p, illustrated, illustrated boards, 23.5cm.

Stobbs, John

73790. *An A.B.C. of Golf.* London: Stanley Paul, 1st ed. 1964, 251p, illustrated, cloth, 21cm.

73800. *At Random Through the Green: A Collection of Writing About Golf.* London: Pelham, 1st ed. 1966, 220p, illustrated, cloth, 21.5cm.

73810. 1st American ed. New York: Merideth Press, 1966, 220p, illustrated, cloth, 21.5cm.

73820. *Tackle Golf This Way.* London: Stanley Paul, 1st ed. 1961, 128p, illustrated, cloth, 18.5cm.

73830. 2d ed. rev. 1975, 128p, illustrated, cloth, 18.5cm.

73840. pbk. ed. 1975, 128p, illustrated, illustrated wrappers, 18.5cm.

73850. *The Anatomy of Golf: Technique and Tactic.* New York: Emerson Books, 1st American ed. [1962] 158p, illustrated, cloth, 20.5cm, American title of "Tackle Golf This Way."

Stokes, Sydney

73870. *History of Ekwanok, Commemorating Its 75th Year.* Manchester, Vermont: Privately Printed, 1st ed. 1974, 63p, illustrated, decorative cloth, 21.5cm.

Stowers, Carlton

73890. *The Unsinkable Titanic Thompson.* Burnet, Texas: Eakin Press, 1st ed. [1982] 234p, illustrated, cloth, 21.5cm.

Stuart, Ian

73910. *Golf in Hertfordshire.* Hitchin, England: Countryside, 1st ed. [ca1972] 149p, illustrated, cloth, 22cm, foreword by George Houghton.

Stutt, J. Hamilton

73930. *The Reclamation of Derelict Lands for Golf.* Richmond, England: Golf Development Council, 1st ed. 1980, 12p, illustrated, illustrated wrappers, 21cm.

Sullivan, George

73950. *The Champions' Guide to Golf.* New York: Fleet, 1st ed. [1966] 113p, illustrated, cloth, 23cm, introduction by Mike Turnesa.

Sunset Magazine

73970. *Golf Course Directory for California.* Menlo Park, California: Lane Book, 1st ed. 1964, 128p, illustrated, illustrated wrappers, 27.5cm.

Surita, Pearson

73990. *The Royal Calcutta Golf Club, 150th Anniversary 1829-1979.* Calcutta, India: Privately Printed, 1st ed. 1979, 130p, illustrated, illustrated wrappers, 26.5cm.

Sussalla, Eddie

74010. *Tournament Player Magazine.* San Diego, California: Scott-Stuart Sports, 1st ed. 1979, 176p, illustrated, illustrated wrappers, 28cm, note: see also "Tournament Player Golf Annual 1978."

Sutin, Helen G. and Beatrice Quinn

74030. *Chips and Putts.* Albany, New York: Cromwell Publications, 1st ed. [1969] [68p] illustrated, illustrated wrappers, 16cm, later printing.

Swarbrick, Brian

74050. *The Duffer's Guide to Bogey Golf.* Englewood Cliffs, New Jersey: Prentice-Hall, 1st ed. [1973] 167p, illustrated by Bob Bugg & Virginia Stewart, cloth, 23.5cm.

74060. pbk. ed. [1973] 167p, illustrated by Bobb Bugg & Virginia Stewart, illustrated wrappers, 22.5cm.

T., O.F.

74080. *Aldeburgh Golf Club The First 100 Years 1884-1984.* Aldeburgh, England: Privately Printed, 1st ed. 1984, 56p, illustrated, decorative cloth, 21cm.

Takahata, S.

74100. *The Story of Kobe Golf Club.* Japan: Privately Printed, 1st ed. 1966, bilingual, 38p English/183p Japanese, illustrated, cloth, 21cm.

Tarbuck, Jimmy

74120. *Tarbuck on Golf.* London: Willow Books, 1st ed. 1983, 120p, illustrated by Richard Willson, cloth, 24.5cm, foreword by Tony Jacklin.

Tarde, Jerry

74140. *How To Hit Crisp Iron Shots.* Norwalk, Connecticut: Golf Digest, 1st ed. [1980] [32p] illustrated, illustrated wrappers, 14cm.

Tavistock Country Club

74160. *Tavistock Country Club 1921-1971.* Tavistock, New Jersey: Privately Printed, 1st ed. 1971 [12p] illustrated, illustrated wrappers, 21.5cm.

Taylor, Chip

74180. *What You Should Know To Putt for [Dough] Bread.* Scottsdale, Arizona: Privately Printed, 1st ed. [1976] 60p, illustrated, illustrated wrappers, 21.5cm.

Taylor, Dawson

74200. *Inside Golf.* Chicago: Contemporary, 1st ed. [1978] 180p, illustrated, cloth, 28cm.

74210. pbk. ed. [1978] 180p, illustrated, illustrated wrappers, 28cm.

74220. *St. Andrews: Cradle of Golf.* South Brunswick, New York: A.S. Barnes, 1st ed. [1976] 207p, illustrated, cloth, 28cm, foreword by Laurie Auchterlonie.

74230. *The Masters: All About its History, Its Records, Its Players, Its Remarkable Course and Even More Remarkable Tournament.* South Brunswick, New Jersey: A.S. Barnes, 1st ed. deluxe [1973] 159p, illustrated, leather, 28cm, note: special copies with a tipped in presentation slip with Brown & Bigelow stamped on back cover.

74240. 2d ed. rev. [1973] 159p, illustrated, cloth, 27.5cm.

74250. 2d ed. rev. deluxe [1973] 159p, illustrated, leather, 28cm.

74260. *The Masters: An Illustrated History.* San Diego: A.S. Barnes, 3d ed. rev. [1981] 223p, illustrated, cloth, 28cm.

Taylor, Hugh

74280. *Golf Dictionary.* edited by. London: F.C. Avis, 1st ed. 1970, 240p, illustrated, cloth, 14cm.

Taylor, J. Fred and W.D. Kerr

74300. *The Beaconsfield Golf Club 1904-1979, Seventy-Fifth Anniversary.* Pointe Claire, Canada: Privately Printed, 1st ed. 1979, 112p, illustrated, decorative cloth, 24cm.

Taylor, James

74320. *Formby Golf Club 1884-1984.* Liverpool, England: Privately Printed, 1st ed. 1984, 29p, illustrated, decorative cloth, 18.5cm.

Taylor, John L.

74340. *Golf Collectors Price Guide.* Milton Keys, England: St. Giles, 1st ed. [1983] 294p, illustrated, cloth, 21.5cm.

74350. *Golf Collectors Price Guide Supplement.* Milton Keys, England: Privately Printed, 1st ed. 1984 [56p] illustrated, spiral bound wrappers, 21cm.

Taylor, Paula

74390. *Golf's Greatest Winner: Jack Nicklaus.* Mankato, Minnesota: Creative Educational Society, 1st ed. [1977] 30p, illustrated, illustrated boards, 18.5cm.

Tea Time At the Masters

74410. *Tea-Time At the Masters: A Collection of Recipes.* Augusta, Georgia: Junior League of Augusta, 1st ed. 1977, 293p, illustrated, spiral bound illustrated wrappers, 23cm, later printings.

Tee Up

74430. *Tee Up*. Los Angeles, California: Miramar, 1st ed. [1962] [12p] illustrated, illustrated wrappers, 19.5cm, editorial advisors-E.J. Dutch Harrison, Frank Bid Holscher.

Teeman, Lawrence

74450. *Consumer Guide Complete Guide to Golf*. New York: Consumer Guide, 1st ed. [1975] 386p, illustrated, illustrated wrappers, 17.5cm.

Templeton, H.A.

74470. *Vector Putting: The Art and Science of Reading Greens and Computing Break*. Fort Worth, Texas: Vector Golf, 1st ed. [1984] 192p, illustrated, decorative cloth, 28cm.

The Open Championship [British]

74490. *The Open Championship 1984*. London: Springwood, 1st ed. 1984, 104p, illustrated, cloth, 26cm, introduction by Gordon B.B. Jeffrey, foreword by Severiano Ballesteros, edited by Bev Norwood.

74500. *The Open Championship 1985*. Ascot, England: Springwood, 2d ed. 1985, 104p, illustrated, cloth, 26p, introduction by B.B. Jeffrey, foreword by Sandy Lyle, edited by Bev Norwood.

Thomas, David

74800. *Modern Golf*. London: Gerald Duckworth, 1st ed. 1967, 128p, illustrated, cloth, 21.5cm, with Ben Wright.

Thomas, Ivor S.

74820. *Formby Golf Club 1884-1972*. Liverpool, England: Privately Printed, 1st ed. 1972, 186p, illustrated, cloth, 24cm, foreword by The Earl of Derby, preface by N.A. Woodhead.

Thomas, P. Richard

74840. *The Country Club Meadville 1905-1976*. Meadville, Pennsylvania: Privately Printed, 1st ed. 1977 [60p] illustrated, illustrated wrappers, 27cm.

Thomson, George A.

74860. *The Story of the Yarra Yarra Golf Club.* Victoria, Australia: Privately Printed, 1st ed. [ca1972] 94p, illustrated, cloth, 20.5cm.

Thomson, Peter and Desmond Zwar

74880. *This Wonderful World of Golf.* London: Pelham, 1st ed. 1969, 222p, illustrated, cloth, 21.5cm.

Timbrook, Bud

74900. *Golf Mystique Solved.* Los Angeles: Timbrook-Stone, 1st ed. 1982, 69p, illustrated, illustrated wrappers, 28cm, foreword by Dick Meyer. note: a few special presentation copies bound in cloth.

Timpson, W.A.

74920. *Hale Golf Club Seventy-Five Years 1903-1978.* Hale, England: Privately Printed, 1st ed. 1978, 36p, illustrated, wrappers, 21cm.

Toski, Bob

74940. *Bob Toski's Complete Guide to Better Golf.* New York: Atheneum, 1st ed. 1977, 135p, illustrated by Jim McQueen, cloth, 23cm, with Dick Aultman.

74950. pbk. ed. 1977, 135p, illustrated by Jim McQueen, illustrated wrappers, 23cm, with Dick Aultman.

74960. *Bob Toski's Guide to Better Golf.* New York: Grosset & Dunlap, 1st ed. [1975] 48p, illustrated by James McQueen, illustrated boards, 23cm, edited by Dick Aultman.

74970. pbk. ed. [1975] 48p, illustrated by James McQueen, illustrated wrappers, 23cm, edited by Dick Aultman.

74980. *12 Short Cuts to Better Golf.* London: Robert Hale, 1st UK ed. 1975, 45p, illustrated, illustrated wrappers, 23cm, edited by Dick Aultman. UK title of "Bob Toski's Guide to Better Golf."

74990. *Golf for A Lifetime.* Norwalk, Connecticut: Golf Digest, 1st ed. [1981] 125p, illustrated, cloth, 28cm, with Jerry Tarde.

75000. *How to Cure Golf's Six Most Common Faults*. Norwalk, Connecticut: Golf Digest, 1st ed. [1974] 14p, illustrated, illustrated wrappers, 14cm.

75010. *The Touch System for Better Golf*. Norwalk, Connecticut: Golf Digest, 1st ed. [1971] 128p, illustrated by Stan Drake, cloth, 28 cm, with Dick Aultman and the editors of Golf Digest. later printings.
75020. pbk. ed. New York: Bantam, 1974, 122p, illustrated by Stan Drake, illustrated wrappers, 18cm, with Dick Aultman and editors of Golf Digest.

Toski, Bob and Jim Flick
75040. *How to Become A Complete Golfer*. Norwalk, Connecticut: Golf Digest, 1st ed. [1978] 287p, illustrated by Jim McQueen, cloth, 25cm, with Larry Dennis.
75050. 2d ed. rev. 1984, 306p, illustrated by Jim McQueen, cloth, 25cm, with Larry Dennis.

Tournament Player Golf Annual
75070. *The Tournament Player Golf Annual 1978*. San Diego, California: Scott-Stuart, 1st ed. [1977] 184p, illustrated, suede wrappers, 27.5cm.note: see also Eddie Sussalla , "Tournament Player Magazine."

Tournament Players' Championship
75090. *Tournament Players' Championship 1982*. [Pontre Vedra, Florida] PGA Tour, 1st ed. 1982, 48p, illustrated, decorative cloth, 27.5cm, edited by Steve Rankin, foreword by Deane Beman.

Tow, Kristen
75110. *International Golf Directory: Resorts, Clubs, Courses Around the World*. edited by. Glendale, California: International Golf Directory, 1st ed. [1974] 112p, illustrated, illustrated wrappers, 28cm.

Townsend, Peter
75130. *Golf: 100 Ways to Improve Your Game*. [London] Chancerel, 1st ed. [1977] 90p, illustrated by Richard Hughes, illustrated boards, 20cm, script by Iain Reid.

Tremayne, Nicholas

75150. *Golf: How to Become A Champion.* London: William Luscombe, 1st ed. 1975, 126p, illustrated, cloth, 21.5cm.

Tresidder, Phil

75170. *The Golfer Who Laughed.* Richmond, Australia: Hutchinson, 1st ed. 1981, 127p, illustrated, cloth, 19.5cm, later printings.

Trevillion, Paul

75190. *Dead Heat: The '69 Ryder Cup Classic.* London: Stanley Paul, 1st ed. 1969, 128p, illustrated, cloth, 22.5cm, foreword by Eric Brown.

75200. *Save Strokes Like the Stars.* London: Stanley Paul, 1st ed. 1970, 236p, illustrated, cloth, 21cm.

75210. 1st American ed. New York: David McKay, 1972, 236p, illustrated, cloth, 20.5cm.

75220. *The Perfect Putting Method.* London: Pelham, 1st ed. 1971, 128p, illustrated, cloth, 21.5cm.

75230. 1st American ed. New York: Winchester Press [1971] 128p, illustrated, cloth, 21.5cm.

75240. *Tony Jacklin in Play.* London: Arthur Barker, 1st ed. [1970] 121p, illustrated, illustrated wrappers, 17.5cm.

Trevino, Lee

75260. *Groove Your Golf Swing My Way.* New York: Atheneum, 1st ed. 1976, 184p, illustrated by Dom Lupo, cloth, 26.5cm, with Dick Aultman.

75270. *Swing My Way.* London: Angus and Robertson, 1st UK ed. [1976] 184p, illustrated by Dom Lupo, cloth, 26.5cm, with Dick Aultman. UK title of "Groove Your Golf Swing My Way."

75280. *I Can Help Your Game.* Greenwich, Connecticut: Fawcett, 1st ed. [1971] 112p, illustrated, illustrated wrappers, 23.5cm, with Oscar Fraley. later printing.

75290. *Can I Help Your Game.* London: W.H. Allen, 1st UK ed. 1972, 160p, illustrated, cloth, 21.5cm, with Oscar Fraley. UK title of "I Can Help Your Game."

75295. pbk. ed. 1972, 160p, illustrated, illustrated wrappers, 21.5cm, with Oscar Fraley. UK title of "I Can Help Your Game."

75300. *Lee's Secret: The fascinating success story of Lee Trevino.* Akron, Ohio: Confidence, 1st ed. [1969] 21p, illustrated, illustrated wrappers, 14cm, with Joe Lazor.

75310. *They Call Me Super Mex.* New York: Random House, 1st ed. [1982] 202p, illustrated, cloth, 21cm, with Sam Blair.

Trevino, Lee and Sam Blair

75330. *The Snake in the Sandtrap [and other misadventures on the tour].* New York: Holt, Rinehart and Winston, 1st ed. 1985, 166p, illustrated, cloth, 21cm.

Trevose Golf Club

75350. *Trevose Golf Club [Handbook].* Bristol, England: E.C. Brown, 1985, 12p, illustrated, illustrated wrappers, 21.5cm.

Tufts, Richard S.

75370. *The Scottish Invasion: Being a brief review of American Golf in Relation to Pinehurst and the Sixty Second National Amateur.* Pinehurst, North Carolina: Pinehurst Publications, 1st ed. [1962] 121p, illustrated, decorative cloth, 19.5cm, foreword by Joseph C. Dey, Jr.

Turnberry Story

75390. *The Turnberry Story.* Turnberry, Scotland: Privately Printed, 1st ed. 1985, 42p, illustrated, illustrated wrappers, 27.5cm.

Turning Point-The 54th Amateur Championship of the United States Golf Association-1954

75410. *Turning Point-The 54th Amateur Championship of the United States Golf Association-1954 Winner Arnold Palmer.* Chattanooga, Tennessee: Pro Group, limited ed. [no limitation cited] [1983] 48p, illustrated, embossed leather, 19cm.

Turnquist, Gary

75430. *Golf: Solving A Puzzle.* Fairport, New York: Privately Printed, 1st ed. [ca1985] 43p, wrappers, 21.5cm.

Tuttle, Anthony

75450. *Drive for the Green.* Garden City, New York: Doubleday, 1st ed. 1969, 341p, cloth, 23.5cm.

Tyler, Martin

75470. *Sportsman's World of Golf.* edited by. London: Marshall Cavendish, 1st ed. 1976, 152p, illustrated, cloth, 29.5cm.

Uitenhage Golf Club

75490. *Uitenhage Golf Club 75th Anniversary 1891-1966.* Uitenhage, South Africa: Privately Printed, 1st ed. 1966, 48p, illustrated, illustrated wrappers, 28.5cm.

UK & Eire 1983 Golf Guide

75510. *UK & Eire 1983 Golf Guide.* Turnbridge Wells, England: Hodgetts of Turnbridge Wells, 1983, 247p, illustrated, illustrated wrappers, 21cm, foreword by Nick Faldo.

Ungvary, Joe

75530. *How To Be A Good Caddy.* Bedford Hts, Ohio: Caddy Master Books, 1st ed. [1961] 24p, illustrated, illustrated wrappers, 13cm.

U.S. Open Official Annual

75550. *85th U.S. Open Official Annual-Oakland Hills.* Cleveland, Ohio: International Merchandising, 1st ed. 1985, 63p, illustrated, leather, 25.5cm, introduction by Arnold Palmer, edited by Mario Paracenzo

United States Golf Association

75800. *Decisions on the Rules of Golf.* Far Hills, New Jersey: United States Golf Association, 1st ed. 1971, unnumbered, loose leaf binder, 23.5cm, issued with annual supplements.

75810. *Golf Committee Manual and USGA Handicap Systems.* New York: United States Golf Association, 1st ed. 1965, 60p, wrappers, 23cm.

75820. 2d ed. 1967, 53p, wrappers, 23cm.

75830. 3d ed. 1971, 54p, wrappers, 23cm.

75840. 4th ed. Far Hills, New Jersey: United States Golf Association, 1974, 54p, wrappers, 23cm.

75850. 5th ed. 1976, 55p, wrappers, 23cm.

75860. 6th ed. 1978, 57p, wrappers, 23cm.

75870. 7th ed. 1982, 59p, wrappers, 23cm.

75880. *USGA Golf Handicap System with USGA Course Rating System for Men and Women and Golf Committee Manual.* Far Hills, New Jersey: United States Golf Association, 1st ed thus. 1984, 72p, wrappers, 23cm, note: previously titled "Golf Committee Manual and USGA Golf Handicap Systems."

75890. *USGA Course Rating System.* Far Hills, New Jersey: United States Golf Association, 1st ed. [1985] 34p, wrappers, 28cm.

75900. *USGA GHIN: Golf Handicap and Information Operations Manual.* Far Hills, New Jersey: United States Golf Association, 1st ed. [1984] 22p, wrappers, 28cm.

75910. *USGA Women's Golf Course Rating System.* Far Hills, New Jersey: United States Golf Association, 1st ed. [1985] 32p, wrappers, 18cm.

United States Junior Chamber of Commerce

77000. *Jaycee Junior Golf Instructional Handbook.* [USA] United States Junior Chamber of Commerce, 1st ed. [ca1962] 25p, illustrated, illustrated wrappers, 21.5cm.

Valentine, Jessie

77020. *Better Golf... definitely.* London: Pelham, 1st ed. 1967, 102p, illustrated, cloth, 21.5cm, as told to George Houghton.

Valli, Jim

77040. *Golf Guide: Central Otago-Southland.* Invercargill, Scotland: Craig Printing, 1st ed. 1979, 56p, illustrated, illustrated wrappers, 20.5cm.

Van Daalen, Nicholas

77060. *International Golf Guide.* Toronto: Pagurian Press, 1st ed. [1976] 190p, illustrated, illustrated wrappers, 23cm.

Van Evera, Maxine

77080. *Building Your Swing for Better Golf with Amy Alcott.* San Diego: A.S. Barnes, 1st ed. [1981] 255p, illustrated by Jan Nichols & Dom Lupo, cloth, 23.5cm.

77090. 1st UK ed. London: Tantivy Press [1981] 255p, illustrated, cloth, 23.5cm.

van Hengel, Steven J. H.

77110. *Early Golf.* Bentveld, Holland: Privately Printed, limited ed. signed [100 copies] 1982, 76p, illustrated, gilt leather, 25.5cm, foreword by Peter Dobereiner.

77120. 1st trade ed. 1982, 76p, illustrated, cloth, 25.5cm, foreword by Peter Dobereiner.

77130. 2d ed. rev. Vaduz, Liechtenstein: Frank P. Van Eck, 1985, 76p, illustrated, illustrated boards, 26cm, foreword by Peter Dobereiner.

77140. *Early Golf: History and Development.* [Holland] Privately Printed, 1st ed. [1972] 14p, illustrated, illustrated wrappers, 27.5cm.

77150. 2d ed. rev. 1974, 35p, illustrated, spiral bound illustrated wrappers, 28.5cm.

van Riper, Jr., Guernsey

77170. *Golfing Greats: Two Top Pros.* Champaign, Illinois: Garrard, 1st ed. [1975] 95p, illustrated, cloth, 23cm.

Van Straten, Cicely

77190. *Caddie For A Crook.* Pretoria, South Africa: Juventus, 2d ed. 1985, 105p, illustrated, illustrated wrappers, 21cm, note: first edition published in 1981 not located.

Vare, E. C.

77210. *Hip Pocket Golf Coach.* Glenwood Springs, Colorado: Privately Printed, 1st ed. [1983] [32p] illustrated, spiral bound plastic cards, 9cm.

Ventreska, Bill

77230. *Play Better Golf.* NP: Knight, 1st ed. [1966] 80p, illustrated, cloth, 22cm.

Venturi, Ken

77250. *Comeback: The Ken Venturi Story.* New York: Duell, Sloan and Pearce, 1st ed. [1966] 184p, illustrated, cloth, 20.5cm, with Oscar Fraley, foreword by Byron Nelson.

77260. *The Venturi System, with Special Material on Shotmaking for the Advanced Golfer.* New York: Atheneum, 1st ed. 1983, 123p, illustrated by Dom Lupo, cloth, 22.5cm, with Al Barkow, special editorial consultant Desmond Tolhurst.

77270. *Venturi Analysis: Learning Better Golf from Champions.* New York: Atheneum, 1st ed. 1981, 160p, illustrated, cloth, 22.5cm, with Al Barkow, foreword by Byron Nelson.

77280. facsimile ed. New York: Classics of Golf [1985] 160p, illustrated, cloth, 23cm, with Al Barkow, foreword by Herbert Warren Wind, afterword by Ed Sneed.

Victor, Al

77300. *Arnie and His Army: A cartoon cavalcade about the world's outstanding sports personality and his wonderfully wacky army of followers.* NP: NP, 1st ed. [ca1964] [186p] illustrated, spiral bound illustrated wrappers, 22cm.

Vidler, Dennis

77320. *Rye Golf Club, the First 90 Years.* Rye, England: Privately Printed, 1st ed. 1984, 160p, illustrated by Alex Graham, cloth, 23cm.

Vietor, Dean

77340. *Your Golf Game's in Big Trouble When...* Watertown, Massachusetts: Ivory Tower, 1st ed. 1984 [47p] illustrated, illustrated wrappers, 27.5cm.

Viney, Lawrence

77360. *Ashridge Golf Club 1932-1982.* Berkhampsted, England: Privately Printed, 1st ed. 1982, 32p, illustrated, illustrated wrappers, 29.5cm.

Viscellette, V.S.

77380. *Golf Club Reconditioning, A Guide For The Beginner or Professional.* Lunenburg, Massachusetts: Lakeside Golf Center, 1st ed. [1964] 30p, illustrated, wrappers, 28cm.

Vroom, Jerry

77400. *So You Want to Be A Golfer!* San Jose, California: Vroom Enterprises, 1st ed. [1973] 48p, illustrated by Larry Daniello, illustrated wrappers, 21.5cm, introduction by Ken Venturi.

Wagenvoord, James

77420. *Golf Diary.* New York: St. Martins Press, 1st ed. [1981] 160p, illustrated, decorative boards, 20.5cm.

Wagner, Corydon

77440. *Pacific Northwest Golf Comes of Age 1892-1926.* Tacoma, Washington: Privately Printed, 1st ed. [ca1973] 8p, wrappers, 22.5cm.

77450. *Tacoma Country & Golf Club 1894-1969, Seventy-Fifth Anniversary.* Tacoma, Washington: Privately Printed, 1st ed. 1969 [8p] wrappers, 21.5cm.

Wagner, Susan F.

77470. *History of Flossmoor Country Club 1899-1979.* Flossmoor, Illinois: Privately Printed, 1st ed. 1979 [20p] illustrated, illustrated wrappers, 21.5cm.

Wales: A Golfing Guide

77490. *Wales: A Golfing Guide for the Business Traveller.* Cardiff, Wales: Wales Tourist Bureau [ca1980] [4p] illustrated, illustrated wrappers, 29.5cm.

Walker, David G.

77510. *Rick Tees Off.* Palm Beach Gardens: PGA Junior Golf Foundation, [1985] 91p, illustrated by William Van Zandt, illustrated wrappers, 23cm, foreword by Jack Nicklaus.

Walker, Robert

77530. *Fairhaven Golf Club [Handbook].* London: Temple Publicity Services [ca1965] 20p, illustrated, illustrated wrappers, 18.5cm.

Wallcock, Lillian

77550. *With A Song in My Cart.* Palm Springs, California: Lillian Wallcock, 1st ed. [1970] [78p] illustrated, cloth, 27cm.

Wallis, Brian

77570. *A History of Horbury and District Golf Club 1907-1965.* Ossett, England: Privately Printed, limited ed. [350 copies] 1965, 91p, illustrated, illustrated wrappers, 20cm.

Ward, Charles

77590. *How to Play Little Aston Golf Course.* London: Temple Publicity Services [ca1965] 12p, illustrated, illustrated wrappers, 10.5cm.

Ward, Peter

77610. *Came Down to Golf: The Story of the Came Down Golf Club dating from the 1890s to the 1980s.* [London] Ellesborough Press, 1st ed. 1984, 175p, illustrated, cloth, 21.5cm.

Ward-Thomas, P.A.

77630. *Masters of Golf.* London: Heinemann, 1st ed. 1961, 257p, illustrated, cloth, 19.5cm.

77640. *Not Only Golf: An Autobiography.* London: Hodder & Stoughton, 1st ed. 1981, 206p, illustrated, cloth, 23.5cm, foreword by Alistair Cooke.

77650. *Shell Golfer's Atlas of England, Scotland and Wales.* London: George Rainbird, 1st ed. [1968] [76p] illustrated, illustrated wrappers, 21.5cm.

77660. *The Long Green Fairway.* London: Hodder & Stoughton, 1st ed. 1966, 192p, cloth, 20.5cm.

77670. *The Royal and Ancient.* Edinburgh: Royal and Ancient Golf Club of St Andrews, 1st ed. 1980, 124p, illustrated, cloth, 23.5cm, foreword by J. Stewart Lawson.

Ward-Thomas, Pat and others

77690. *The World Atlas of Golf.* and Herbert Warren Wind, Charles Price, Peter Thomson, London: Mitchell Beazley, 1st ed. 1976, 280p, illustrated, cloth, 29cm, foreword by Alistair Cooke. later printings.

77700. 1st American ed. New York: Random House, 1976, 280p, illustrated, cloth, 29cm, foreword by Alistair Cooke.

Watson, Alan S.

77720. *The First 100 Years, A History of the Royal Belfast Golf Club 1881-1981.* Belfast, Northern Ireland: Privately Printed, 1st ed. 1981, 104p, illustrated, decorative cloth, 19.5cm.

Watson, Gilbert

77740. *A Short History of Craigmillar Park Golf Club 1895-1974.* Scotland: Privately Printed, 1st ed. 1974, 28p, illustrated, leather, 21cm.

Watson, Tom

77760. *Getting Up and Down: How to Save Strokes from Forty Yards and In.* New York: Random House, 1st ed. [1983] 192p, illustrated by Anthony Ravielli, cloth, 23cm, with Nick Seitz, introduction by Jack Nicklaus.

77770. *The New Rules of Golf.* New York, Random House/ USGA, 1st. trade ed. [1984] 181p, illustrated, cloth, 23cm, with Frank Hannigan.

77780. pbk. ed. [1984] 181p, illustrated, 23cm, with Frank Hannigan.

77790. limited ed. signed [1000 copies] [1984] 181p, illustrated, decorative cloth, 23cm, with Frank Hannigan.

77800. *The Rules of Golf: Illustrated and Explained.* New York: Random House/USGA, 1st ed. [1980] 200p, illustrated, cloth, 23cm, with Frank Hannigan.

77810. pbk. ed. [1980] 200p, illustrated, illustrated wrappers, 23cm, with Frank Hannigan.

77820. *Tom Watson's Key Swing Thoughts.* Norwalk, Connecticut: Golf Digest, 1st ed. [1978] [16p] illustrated by Anthony Ravielli, illustrated wrappers, 14cm.

Watt, Alick

77840. *Collecting Old Golfing Clubs.* Alton, England: A.A. Watt & Son, 1st ed. 1985, 119p, illustrated, cloth, 21cm.

Webber, Louis and Dennis Kennedy

77860. *Golf Manners.* Universal City, Texas: Golf Manners, 1st ed. [1968] 67p, illustrated, illustrated wrappers, 18.5cm.

Wee Burn Country Club

77880. *Wee Burn Country Club, A History.* Darien, Connecticut: Privately Printed, 1st ed. [1979] 64p, illustrated, gilt stamped leather, 23cm.

Weeks, Edward

77900. *Myopia, A Centennial Chronicle 1875-1975.* Hamilton, Massachusetts: Privately Printed, 1st ed. 1975, 151p, illustrated, decorative cloth, 25cm.

Weetman, Harry

77920. *Add to Your Golf Power.* London: Heinemann, 1st ed. 1963, 158p, illustrated, cloth, 21cm, with John Ballentine, foreword by Arnold Palmer.

Weiskoff, Tom

77940. *Go for the Flag: The Fundamentals of Golf.* New York: Meredith Press, 1st ed. [1969] 88p, illustrated, cloth, 23cm.

77950. pbk. ed. New York: Hawthorn [1969] 88p, illustrated, illustrated wrappers, 21cm.

Welch, Jane Faxon and Wade M. Welch and Richard F. Radford

77970. *1000 Questions: The Golfer's Book of Trivia.* Boston: Quinlan Press, 1st ed. 1985, 176p, illustrated, illustrated wrappers, 21.5cm.

Weld, Stanley

77990. *A History of the Great Chebeague Golf Club.* Chebeague Island, Maine: Privately Printed, limited ed. [250 copies] 1962, 83p, illustrated, cloth, 21.5cm.

Welsh, Charles W.

78010. *Seventy Five Years of Golf At The Royal Eastbourne Golf Club 1887-1962.* Eastbourne, England: Privately Printed, 1st ed. 1962, 26p, illustrated, wrappers, 18.5cm.

Wendt, William Paul

78030. *The Distance Builder.* NP: Privately Printed [1982] 20p, illustrated, illustrated wrappers, 21.5cm.

Werner, D. N.

78050. *Great Golfers of the Twentieth Century.* Santa Monica, California: Werner Book, 1st ed. [1971] 74p, illustrated, illustrated wrappers, 27.5cm, and the editors of Golf & Club Magazine.

78060. *Lower Your Golf Score.* Santa Monica, California: Werner Book, 1st ed. [ca1972] 81p, illustrated, illustrated wrappers, 27cm, and the editors of Golf & Club Magazine.

Weslock, Nick

78080. *Your Golf Bag Pro: Nick Weslock's Little Black Book of Key Golf Secrets.* Edmonton, Canada: Hurtig, 1st ed. [1985] 143p, illustrated by Neil Harris, illustrated wrappers, 17.5cm.

Western Golf Association

78100. *Caddie Operations Manual.* Golf, Illinois: Western Golf Association, 1st ed. 1969, 73p, 3-ring vinyl binder, 28cm.

78110. *Case for Caddies.* Golf, Illinois: Western Golf Association, 1st ed. [ca1965] 9p, illustrated, illustrated wrappers, 23cm.

Westmount Golf and Country Club

78130. *Westmount Golf and Country Club 1931-1981.* Kitchener-Waterloo, Canada: Privately Printed, 1st ed. 1981, 162p, illustrated, cloth, 20.5cm.

Weston, John W.

78150. *A History of Coombe Wood Golf Club 1904-1970.* Coombe Wood, England: Privately Printed, 1st ed. 1985, 29p, spiral bound wrappers, 30cm.

Where To Golf in Kansas City

78170. *Where To Golf in Kansas City.* Kansas City, Kansas: Where To Golf in Kansas City Magazine, 2d ed. 1982, 97p, illustrated, illustrated wrappers, 28cm, editor David M. Starling. note: first edition not located.

White, Fairmount Richmond

78190. *Golf in the Seventies for Those in the Sixties: Psychology of Golf.* Newport News: Virginia, White Co. 1st ed. [1962] 31p, illustrated, illustrated wrappers, 21.5cm.

Whitehead, Eric

78210. *Hathstauwk: The Story of Capilano Golf & Country Club.* Vancouver, British Columbia: Privately Printed, 1st ed. [1981] 144p, illustrated, cloth, 24.5cm.

Whiteleaf Golf Club

78230. *Whiteleaf Golf Club [Handbook].* Kingston upon Thames: Temple Publicity Services, 1967, 12p, illustrated, illustrated wrappers, 18cm.

Whitney, Don E.

78250. *Golf from A to Z.* Jackpot, Nevada: Privately Printed, 1st ed. 1982, 106p, illustrated by Lee Watson, illustrated wrappers, 17.5cm.

Wien, Lawrence A.

78270. *The Golf Club At Aspetuck.* New York: Ridge Press, 1st ed. [1974] [44p] illustrated, cloth, 22.5cm.

Wild, Roland

78290. *The Loneliest Game.* Vancouver, Canada: Mitchell Press, 1st ed. [1969] 129p, illustrated by Lew Saw, cloth, 22.5cm.

Wilde, Larry

78310. *The Official Golfer's Joke Book.* New York: Pinnacle, 1st ed. 1977, 206p, illustrated, illustrated wrappers, 17.5cm.

Will, George

78330. *Golf the Modern Way.* Feltham, England: Country Life, 1st ed. [1968] 176p, illustrated, cloth, 22.5cm.

Williams, Ambrose

78350. *The Principles of the Golf Swing.* Australian Capital Territory: T. Watt, 1st ed. 1965, 82p, illustrated, illustrated boards, 21.5cm.

Williams, Arthur C.

78370. *Brooklawn Country Club 1895-1970, 75th Anniversary.* Fairfield, Connecticut: Privately Printed, 1st ed. 1970, 32p, illustrated, illustrated wrappers, 28cm.

Williams, David

78390. *The Science of the Golf Swing.* London: Pelham, 1st ed. 1969, 130p, illustrated, cloth, 21.5cm.

Williams, David [Dave]

78410. *How to Coach and Play Championship Golf.* Englewood Cliffs, New Jersey: Prentice-Hall, 1st ed. [1962] 253p, illustrated, decorative cloth, 22.5cm, edited by Art Casper.

Williams, Evan "Big Cat"

78430. *You Can Hit the Golf Ball Farther.* Norwalk, Connecticut: Golf Digest, [1979] 127p, illustrated, cloth, 23cm, with Larry Sheehan.

78440. pbk. ed. [1979] 127p, illustrated, cloth, 23cm.

Williams, Gwen

78460. *Unique Golf Resorts of the World.* Corona Del Mar, California: Privately Printed, 1st ed. [1983] 204p, illustrated, gilt stamped leather, 28cm.

Williams, Michael

78480. *Daily Telegragh Pocket Sports Facts: Golf.* London: Telegraph Publications, 1st ed. [1984] 128p, illustrated, wrappers, 19cm.

78490. *History of Golf.* London: Deans International, 1st ed, 1985, 192p, illustrated, illustrated boards, 31.5cm.

78500. 1st American ed. Secaucus, New Jersey: Chartwell, 1985, 192p, illustrated, illustrated boards, 31.5cm.

Wilson, Enid

78520. *A Gallery of Women Golfers*. London: Country Life, 1st ed. 1961, 192p, illustrated, cloth, 25cm, foreword by Bernard Darwin.

78530. *Golf for Women*. London: Arthur Baker, 1st ed. [1964] 84p, illustrated, cloth, 21.5cm.

Wilson, J.H.

78550. *The Golfers of A Past Era*. Ayr, Scotland: B. Marshall, limited ed. signed [1000 copies] 1977, 20p, illustrated, portfolio, 34cm, introduction by G.S. Cunningham.

Wilson, Mark

78570. *The Best of Henry Longhurst*. edited by. Norwalk, Connecticut: Golf Digest, 1st ed. [1978] 206p, cloth, 22.5cm, with Ken Bowden, foreword by Alistair Cooke.

Wind, Herbert Warren

78590. *Following Through*. New York: Ticknor & Fields, 1st ed. 1985, 414p, cloth, 23.5cm.

78600. *Golf Quiz*. Norwalk, Connecticut: Golf Digest, 1st ed. [1980] 248p, illustrated, illustrated wrappers, 20.5cm, foreword by Nick Seitz.

78610. *Herbert Warren Wind's Golf Book*. New York: Simon & Schuster, 1st ed. [1971] 317p, cloth, 21.5cm, foreword by Bing Crosby.

78620. *The Lure of Golf*. London: Heinemann, 1st UK ed. 1971, 316p, cloth, 21.5cm, foreword by Bing Crosby. UK title of "Herbert Warren Wind's Golf Book."

78630. *Shell's Wonderful World of Golf 1962*. NP: Shell Oil, 1st ed. 1962 [24p] illustrated, illustrated wrappers, 26cm.

78640. *The Open's Fourth Visit To Winged Foot*. New York: New Yorker Magazine, offprint [1984] [30p] illustrated wrappers, 21.5cm, offprint form the New Yorker Magazine July 16, 1984.

Wiren, Gary

78660. *Golf*. Englewood Cliffs, New Jersey: Prentice-Hall [1971] 118p, illustrated, cloth, 20cm.

78670. pbk. ed. [1971] 118p, illustrated, cloth, 20.5cm.

78680. *Planning and Conducting Junior Golf Programs.* Chicago: National Golf Foundation, 1st ed. [1973] 36p, illustrated, illustrated wrappers, 28cm, edited by Mrs. Wallace H. Hallmeyer, foreword by Jack Nicklaus.

78690. 2d ed. rev. North Palm Beach, Florida: National Golf Foundation, 1978, 32p, illustrated, illustrated wrappers, 28cm.

78700. *Super Power Golf: Techniques for Increasing Distance.* Chicago: Contemporary, 1st ed. [1984] 158p, illustrated, illustrated wrappers, 22.5cm, with Dawson Taylor, foreword by Gary Player.

Wiren, Gary and Richard Coop

78720. *The New Golf Mind.* Norwalk, Connecticut: Golf Digest, 1st ed. [1978] 160p, cloth, 22.5cm, with Larry Sheehan.

78730. pbk. ed. New York: Cornerstone Library, 1981, 160p, illustrated, illustrated wrappers, 20.5cm, with Larry Sheehan.

Wise, Kris Morgan

78750. *The Answers to Par Golf.* [San Diego, California] Privately Printed, 1st ed. [1978] 143p, illustrated, illustrated wrappers, 17.5cm.

Wise, Sidney L.

78770. *Carolina Golfer Directory 1976.* Columbus, South Carolina: Carolina Golfer, 1976, 107p, illustrated, illustrated wrappers, 28cm.

Wishart, J.R.

78790. *Golf Course Guide to Southern Africa.* Wadeville, South Africa: Press-Mag, 1st ed. [1983] 96p, illustrated, illustrated wrappers, 28cm.

78800. 2d ed. 1984, 184p, illustrated, illustrated wrappers, 28cm.

Wishon, Tom W.

78820. *The Golf Club Identification and Price Guide.* Newark, Ohio: Ralph Maltby Enterprises, 1st ed. 1985 [524p] illustrated, illustrated wrappers, 23.5cm.

Wodehouse, P.G.

78840. *Fore: The Best of Wodehouse on Golf.* New Haven & New York: Ticknor & Fields, 1st ed. 1983, 259p, cloth, 21cm, edited with a preface by D.R. Benson.

78850. *The Golf Omnibus.* London: Barrie & Jenkins, 1st ed. 1973, 467p, cloth, 21.5cm.

Wood, A. G.

78870. *Royal Jersey Golf Club [Handbook].* Hants & London: Temple Publicity Services, 1965, 36p, illustrated, illustrated wrappers, 18.5cm.

Wood, Britten B.

78890. *Piqua Country Club History.* Piqua, Ohio: Privately Printed, 1st ed. 1975 [4p] wrappers, 21.5cm.

Woodison, Alan

78910. *Ayrshire Golf Guide.* Aryshire, Scotland: Scottish & Universal Newspaper [1983] 64p, illustrated, illustrated wrappers, 28cm.

Worthing Golf Club

78930. *Worthing Golf Club 1905-1980, Story of the First Seventy-Five Years.* Worthing, England: Privately Printed, 1st ed. 1980, 40p, illustrated, wrappers, 21cm.

Worthington, Gene

78950. *How to Acquire the Perfect Golf Swing. A Golf Instruction Manual.* [Illinois] Privately Printed, 1st ed. [1973] 31p, illustrated, illustrated wrappers, 21.5cm.

Woy, Bucky

78970. *Sign 'em up, Bucky: The Adventures of A Sport Agent.* New York: Hawthorn, 1st ed. [1975] 229p, illustrated, cloth, 21cm, foreword by Julius Boros.

Wright, Jack W.

78990. *Guide To Vancouver Island Golf Courses.* Saanichton, British Columbia: Hancock House [1977] 94p, illustrated, illustrated wrappers, 19cm.

Wright, Mickey

79010. *Play Golf the Wright Way.* Garden City, New York: Doubleday, 1st ed. [1962] 95p, illustrated, cloth, 25.5cm, edited by Joan Flynn Dreyspool. later printing.

Wrinch-Schulz, Joyce

79030. *The First Sixty Years, A History of the Durban Country Club from 1922-1982.* Durban, South Africa: Privately Printed, 1st ed. 1982, 215p, illustrated, cloth, 24cm.

Wunsch, Josephine

79050. *Girl in the Rough.* New York: Silhonette Books, 1st ed. 1981, 188p, illustrated wrappers, 17cm.

Wygant, Stevan

79070. *What's Your Golf I.Q.? A Mint of Often Misunderstood, Misquoted Facts About Handicaps, Wagers, Tournaments and Terms.* [New York] A.G. Spalding, 1st ed. [ca1962] 40p, illustrated, wrappers, 15cm.

Wyoming Valley Country Club

79090. *Wyoming Valley Country Club 1896-1984, A History.* Wilkes Barre, Pennsylvania: Privately Printed, 1st ed. 1984, 32p, illustrated, illustrated wrappers, 28cm.

X, Mr. [Robert Russell]

79110. *Beginner's Guide to Golf.* London: Pelham, 1st ed. 1973, 117p, illustrated, cloth, 21cm.

79120. *Golf Monthly's Lessons with Mr. X.* London: Pelham, 1st ed. [1968] 96p, illustrated, cloth, 21.5cm.

79130. pbk. ed. London: Sphere Books, 1969, 96p, illustrated, illustrated wrappers, 18cm.

79140. *Golf Lessons with Mr. X.* Norwalk, Connecticut: Golf Digest, 1st American ed. 1969, 96p, illustrated, cloth, 21.5cm, American title of "Golf Monthly's Lessons with Mr. X."

79150. *More Golf Lessons with Mr. X.* London: Pelham, 1st ed. [1971] 103p, illustrated, cloth, 21.5cm.

Yeager, George A.

79170. *The First Seventy-Five Years-Orange County Club 1899-1974*. Middletown, New York: Privately Printed, 1st ed. 1974, 28p, illustrated, illustrated wrappers, 28cm.

Yogi, Count

79190. *Five Simple Steps to Perfect Golf*. Los Angeles: Nash, 1st ed. [1973] 138p, illustrated, cloth, 23cm, foreword by Wolfgang Gerdes-Testa, introduction by Tony Ferra.

79200. pbk. ed. New York: Cornerstone Library, 1979, 142p, illustrated, illustrated wrappers, 20cm, foreword by Wolfgang Gerdes-Testa, introduction by Tony Ferra.

Yorgey, Commodore William

79220. *The Commodore Yorgey Scientific Stance and Swing*. Breinigsville, Pennsylvania: Privately Printed, 1st ed. [1972] 15p, illustrated, wrappers, 18cm.

Young, Tom McFarlane

79240. *The Open Championship in Scotland: Prints and History*. Glasgow, Scotland: Melfa, 1st ed. 1985 [18p] illustrated, folio, 28cm, with 6 loose prints.

Your Guide To The Open, St. Andrew's 1970

79260. *Your Guide To The Open, St. Andrew's 1970*. London: Hamlyn, 1st ed. 1970, 30p, illustrated, illustrated wrappers, 27.5cm.

Zadnik, Bertha D.

79280. *The Connecticut Women's Golf Association History, 1919-1969*. [Connecticut] Privately Printed, 1st ed. 1969, 8p, wrappers, 14.5cm.

Zanger, Jack

79300. *Exercises for Better Golf: The Champions Way to A Stronger Game*. New York: Thomas Nelson, 1st ed. [1965] 160p, illustrated by Sam Dion, cloth, 21cm, foreword by Gene Sarazen.

Zender, Bob and Charles B. Cleveland

79320. *Winning Golf, The Professional Way.* New York: Dodd, Mead, 1st ed. [1985] 212p, cloth, 20cm, introduction by Andy North.

Zwar, Desmond

79340. *Golf, The Dictionary.* Melbourne: Sun Books, 1st ed. 1984, 84p, illustrated by Jeff Hook, illustrated wrappers, 20cm.

AUTHOR INDEX

SHORT TITLE INDEX

CLUB HISTORY INDEX

GOLF CLUB	LOCATION	BIB NO
Abergele and Pensarn GC	Abergele, Wales	58510
Aboyne GC	Aboyne, Scotland	43020
Acton GC	London, England	72760
Aldeburgh GC	Aldeburgh, England	74080
Alwoodley GC	Leeds, England	63530
Annandale GC	Pasadena, California	43840
Apawamis Club	Rye, New York	12940
Apawamis Club	Rye, New York	43880
Arbroath Golf Course	Arbroath, Scotland	17980
Ardglas GC	Ardglas, Northern Ireland	48690
Ardsley CC	Ardsley on Hudson, New York	23380
Army GC	Aldershot, England	69890
Ashford Manor GC	Ashford, England	44090
Ashridge GC	Berkhampsted, England	77360
Augusta National GC	Augusta, Georgia	69990
Augusta National GC	Augusta, Georgia	70000
Australian GC	Sydney, Australia	43210
Baltusrol GC	Plainfield, New Jersey	61400
Barton Hills CC	Ann Arbor, Michigan	61940
Barwon Heads GC	Melbourne, Australia	43040
Bass River GC	South Yarmouth, Mass.	44990
Bath GC	Bath, England	45330
Beaconsfield GC	Pointe Claire, Canada	74300
Bedford Golf & Tennis Club	Katonah, New York	48400
Bedford GC	Bedford, South Africa	72210
Belle Meade CC	Nashville, Tennessee	69790
Belvedere GC	Charlevoix, Michigan	57660
Bend Golf & CC	Bend, Oregon	45620
Bexley Heath GC	Bexley Heath, England	52200
Birkdale GC	Southport, England	6970
Blackwell GC	Worcestershire, England	15240
Blackwood GC	Hawthorndene, Australia	55680
Blind Brook Club	Port Chester, New York	32260
Blue Mound Golf and CC	Wauwatosa, Wisconsin	46190
Brae Burn CC	West Newton, Massachusetts	23170

Clovelly CC	Cape Town, South Africa	48460
Clovelly CC	Cape Town, South Africa	50610
Cobram-Barooga GC	Cobram, Australia	46440
Cochrane Castle GC	Johnstone, Scotland	63750
Coldstream CC	Cincinnati, Ohio	48570
Columbia CC	Columbia, South Carolina	34840
Columbia CC	Chevy Chase, Maryland	39270
Concord GC	Sydney, Australia	19580
Congressional CC	Washington, D.C.	50790
Coombe Wood GC	Coombe Wood, England	78150
Copt Heath GC	Solihull, England	48940
Copt Heath GC	Solihull, England	48950
Country Club Meadville	Meadville, Pennsylvania	74840
Country Club of Detroit	Detroit, Michigan	45290
Country Club of Fairfield	Fairfield, Connecticut	49210
Country Club of New Canaan	New Canaan, Connecticut	52400
Country Club of Rochester	Rochester, New York	21500
Country Club of Rochester	Rochester, New York	56810
Country Club of York	York, Pennsylvania	13140
Country Club of York	York, Pennsylvania	57400
Craigmillar Park GC	Edinburgh, Scotland	77740
Crail Golfing Society	Crail, Scotland	15220
Crail Golfing Society	Crail, Scotland	61130
Crystal Downs GC	Frankfurt, Michigan	44790
Curragh GC	Curragh, Ireland	52860
Cutten Club	Guelph, Canada	46650
Dalbeattie GC	Dalbeattie, Scotland	13690
Dalhousie GC	Carnoustie, Scotland	48050
Dallas CC	Dallas, Texas	37260
Davyhulme Park GC	Davyhulme, England	50060
Dayton CC	Dayton, Ohio	55780
Deal Golf and CC	Deal, New Jersey	47490
Deeside GC	Aberdeen, Scotland	14910
Delgany GC	Delgany, Ireland	50220
Detroit GC	Detroit, Michigan	15010
Dieppe GC	Dieppe, France	27590
Direlton Castle GC	Gullane, Scotland	15120
Douglas Park GC	Bearsden, England	61110
Dumfries and Galloway GC	Dumfries, Scotland	64150
Dunany CC	Lachute, Canada	50930

Furness GC	Barrow-in-Furnace, England	52460
Garden City GC	Garden City, New York	25630
Garden City GC	Garden City, New York	52440
Geelong GC	Melbourne, Australia	60560
Glamorganshire GC	Penarth, Wales	18020
Glasgow GC	Glasgow, Scotland	12820
Glen View Club	Golf, Illinois	43710
Glen View Club	Golf, Illinois	56250
Glens Falls CC	Glens Falls, New York	7640
Golf House Club	Elie, Scotland	12440
Grange GC	Dublin, Ireland	72880
Great Chebeague GC	Chebeague Island, Maine	77990
Great Yarmouth & Caister GC	Caister-on-Sea, England	68060
Green Hills CC	Millbrae, California	64890
Guildford GC	Guildford, England	52070
Gullane GC	Gullane, Scotland	44760
Gullane GC	Gullane, Scotland	44770
Gulph Mills GC	King of Prussia, Pennsylvania	66770
Hale GC	Hale, England	74920
Halifax Golf and CC	Kinsac Lake, Canada	55050
Harpenden GC	Harpenden, England	20290
Hartford GC	West Hartford, Connecticut	41080
Hawick GC	Hawick, Scotland	630
Hayling GC	Hayling Island, England	55640
Henry Stambaugh GC	Youngstown, Ohio	55990
Hesketh GC	Southport, England	56270
Highland CC	Attleboro, Massachusetts	20930
Hilton Park GC	Glasgow, Scotland	56330
Home Park GC	Kingston-upon-Thames, Eng.	29560
Honors Course	Signal Mountain, Tennessee	66750
Honourable Company of Edinburgh Golfers	Gullane, Scotland	17960
Honourable Company of Edinburgh Golfers	Gullane, Scotland	26050
Honourable Company of Edinburgh Golfers	Gullane, Scotland	68040
Horbury and District GC	Ossett, England	77570
Hubbard Trail CC	Hoopeston, Illinois	57050
Huddersfield GC	Huddersfield, England	40780
Huntercombe GC	Henley-on-Thames, England	43060

Little Aston GC	Sutton Coldfield, England	60330
Liverpool GC	Lansvale, Australia	61190
Lodhi Delhi GC	New Delhi, India	71850
London Hunt and CC	London, Canada	48860
Longue Vue Club	Verona, Pennsylvania	60720
Los Angeles CC	Los Angeles, California	24500
Los Angeles CC	Los Angeles, California	37070
Los Angeles CC	Los Angeles, California	45480
Low Laithes GC	Wakefield, England	61640
Lucifer Golfing Society	London, England	14480
Luffness GC & Kilspinde GC	Aberlady/Gullane, Scotland	60860
Maccauvlei Golf Club	Vereenigina, South Africa	24730
Machrihanish GC	Machrihanish, Scotland	62670
Mahopac GC	Lake Mahopac, New York	61440
Maidstone Club	Bridgehampton, New York	31200
Manawatu GC	Palmerston, New Zealand	71780
Manchester CC	Manchester, New Hampshire	61540
Manchester GC	Manchester, England	20470
Manchester GC	Manchester, England	67160
Manito Golf & CC	Spokane, Washington	61560
Manly GC	Sydney, Australia	6910
Maritime Seniors Golf Assoc.	Saint John, Canada	32170
Massereene GC	Antrim, Northern Ireland	61750
Meadowbrook CC	Richmond, Virginia	54150
Melrose GC	Melrose, Scotland	61210
Meltham GC	Meltham, England	56370
Merchants of Edinburgh GC	Edinburgh, Scotland	54380
Mere Golf & CC	Mere, England	69950
Merion GC	Ardmore, Pennsylvania	63280
Metropolitan GC	Melbourne, Australia	14890
Metropolitan GC	Melbourne, Australia	59230
Mexico City CC	Mexico City, Mexico	40820
Miami Valley GC	Dayton, Ohio	48440
Mill Creek Park Golf Course	Youngstown, Ohio	63550
Milltown GC	Milltown, Ireland	63160
Minehead & West Somerset GC	Minehead, England	55390
Mississauga Golf and CC	Mississauga, Canada	46610
Missoula CC	Missoula, Montana	58410
Mohawk GC	Schenectady, New York	59170
Monkstown GC	Monkstown, Ireland	73440

Olympia Fields CC	Chicago, Illinois	28320
Olympic Club	San Francisco, California	34750
Onwentsia Club	Lake Forest, Illinois	67920
Orange County GC	Middletown, New York	79170
Orchard Ridge CC	Fort Wayne, Indiana	65840
Ormskirk GC	Ormskirk, England	28390
Ottawa Hunt Club	Ottawa, Canada	61090
Outlands GC	Dundas, Australia	55170
Overbrook GC	Bryn Mawr, Pennsylvania	52260
Oxford & Cambridge Golfing Society	London, England	60410
Oxford & Cambridge Golfing Society	London, England	29540
Ozone Club	Philadelphia, Pennsylvania	28570
Panmure Golf Club	Dundee, Scotland	20620
Park Club of Buffalo	Buffalo, New York	50990
Peachtree GC	Atlanta, Georgia	58290
Penisula Country GC	Frankston, Australia	66360
Pennant Hills GC	Sydney, Australia	22060
Philadelphia CC	Gladwyne, Pennsylvania	43360
Philadelphia Cricket Club	Chestnut Hill, Pennsylvania	24110
Philmont CC	Philadelphia, Pennsylvania	28970
Piltdown Golf	Uckfield, England	64420
Pine Valley GC	Clementon, New Jersey	47000
Pine Valley GC	Clementon, New Jersey	72150
Piqua CC	Piqua, Ohio	78890
Ponte Vedra Club	Ponte Vedra, Florida	59450
Portsea GC	Melbourne, Australia	67960
Powelton Club	Newburgh, New York	51960
Presidio GC	San Francisco, California	60100
Prestwick GC	Prestwick, Scotland	34310
Prestwick St. Nicholas GC	Prestwick, Scotland	17660
Pretoria CC	Pretoria, South Africa	65610
Prince's and Deal	Sandwich, England	11890
Purley Downs GC	Purley, England	70860
Radyr GC	Radyr, Wales	69280
Red Hill CC	Cucamonga, California	48590
Reigate Heath	Reigate Heath, England	72050
Rhode Island CC	West Barrington, Rhode Island	31670
Rhode Island CC	West Barrington, Rhode Island	72030

Royal Dornoch GC	Dornoch, Scotland	61170
Royal Dublin GC	Dublin, Ireland	47060
Royal Dublin GC	Dublin, Ireland	70530
Royal Eastbourne GC	Eastbourne, England	78010
Royal Hong Kong GC	Hong Kong	38890
Royal Liverpool GC	Birkenhead, England	16320
Royal Liverpool GC	Liverpool, England	51260
Royal Liverpool GC	Liverpool, England	51270
Royal Lytham & St. Annes GC	Liverpool, England	32750
Royal Lytham & St. Annes GC	St. Annes-on-the-Sea, England	65210
Royal Lytham & St. Annes GC	St. Annes-on-the-Sea, England	65220
Royal Melbourne GC	Melbourne, Australia	15930
Royal Melbourne GC	Melbourne, Australia	45030
Royal Montreal GC	Montreal, Canada	32780
Royal Montreal GC	Montreal, Canada	47580
Royal Montreal GC	Montreal, Canada	47590
Royal Musselburgh GC	Prestonpans, Scotland	70550
Royal North Devon GC	Bideford, England	54130
Royal North Devon GC.	Bideford, England	23970
Royal Perth Golfing Society	Perth, Scotland	26560
Royal Salisbury GC	Salisbury, Zimbabwe	69930
Royal Salisbury GC	Salisbury, Zimbabwe	70590
Royal Sydney GC	Sydney, Australia	32800
Royal Troon GC	Troon, Scotland	61290
Royal Troon GC	Troon, Scotland	61310
Royal Wimbledon GC	Wimbledon, England	17090
Royal Wimbledon GC	Wimbledon, England	21450
Royal Wimbledon GC	Wimbledon, England	71700
Rutland CC	Rutland, Vermont	48710
Rye GC	Rye, England	77320
Sale GC	Manchester, England	27270
San Francisco GC	San Francisco, California	48920
Sandy Lodge GC	Northwood, England	33050
Sara Bay CC	Sarasota, Florida	72520
Savannah GC	Savannah, Georgia	71180
Scarsdale GC	Hartsdale, New York	25090
Scrabo GC	Newtownards, Ireland	71680
Seaton Carew GC	Durham, England	56720
Seattle GC	Seattle, Washington	16730
Seattle GC	Seattle, Washington	34120

The Country Club	Brookline, Massachusetts	13660
The Country Club	Brookline, Massachusetts	13670
The Country Club	Brookline, Massachusetts	47690
The Country Club	Cleveland, Ohio	44070
The Golf Club	New Albany, Ohio	59040
Thorny Lea GC	Brockton, Massachusetts	40360
Thurlestone GC	Thurlestone, England	66300
Tin Whistles Club	Pinehurst, North Carolina	46590
Titirangi GC	Auckland, New Zealand	36890
Todmorden GC	Todmorden, England	73630
Toronto GC	Toronto, Canada	45350
Town and CC	St. Paul, Minnesota	28760
Town and CC	St. Paul, Minnesota	28770
Uitenhage GC	Uitenhage, South Africa	75490
Ulen CC	Lebanon, Indiana	37770
Uplands GC	Victoria, Canada	67140
Vesper CC	Tyngsboro, Massachusetts	59900
Victoria Club	Riverside, California	55070
Waccabuc CC	Waccabuc, New York	55830
Wailae CC	Honolulu, Hawaii	56390
Wallasey GC	Wallasey, England	36500
Walton Heath GC	Tadworth, England	56200
Wannamoisett CC	Rumford, Rhode Island	28890
Warrender GC	Edinburgh, Scotland	11690
Wawashkame GC	Mackinac Island, Michigan	59470
Wee Burn CC	Darien, Connecticut	15890
Wee Burn CC	Darien, Connecticut	77880
West Lancashire GC	Liverpool, England	51280
West Sussex GC	Pulborough, England	69360
Western Australian GC	Mt. Yokine, Australia	49950
Western Gailes GC	Gailes, Scotland	26010
Westhampton CC	Westhampton, New York	26200
Westmount Golf and CC	Kitchener-Waterloo, Canada	78130
Weston Golf and CC	Toronto, Canada	49830
Wetherby GC	Wetherby, England	72980
Wichita CC	Wichita, Kansas	63710
Williamwood GC	Glasgow, Scotland	70720
Wilshire CC	Los Angeles, California	62910
Winged Foot	Mamaroneck, New York	72670
Wolferts Roost CC	Albany, New York	52900

AFTERWORD

It may seem somewhat strange to finish up by quoting a fine sportswriter who did not particularly care for golf. The late Red Smith was, in the eyes of many, a great writer. By choice, he confined most of his career to the sports desk, which Herb Graffis once described as "the toy department."

In Smith's mind, however, the English language was not something to be toyed with, and day after day he put words together which became strings of pearls.

He once wrote, in quite another context, "What's to be said that hasn't been said? Nothing, when you come down to it!"

I am not sure that everything has been said about golf literature that should have been said, but when you come down to it, there is nothing more to say.

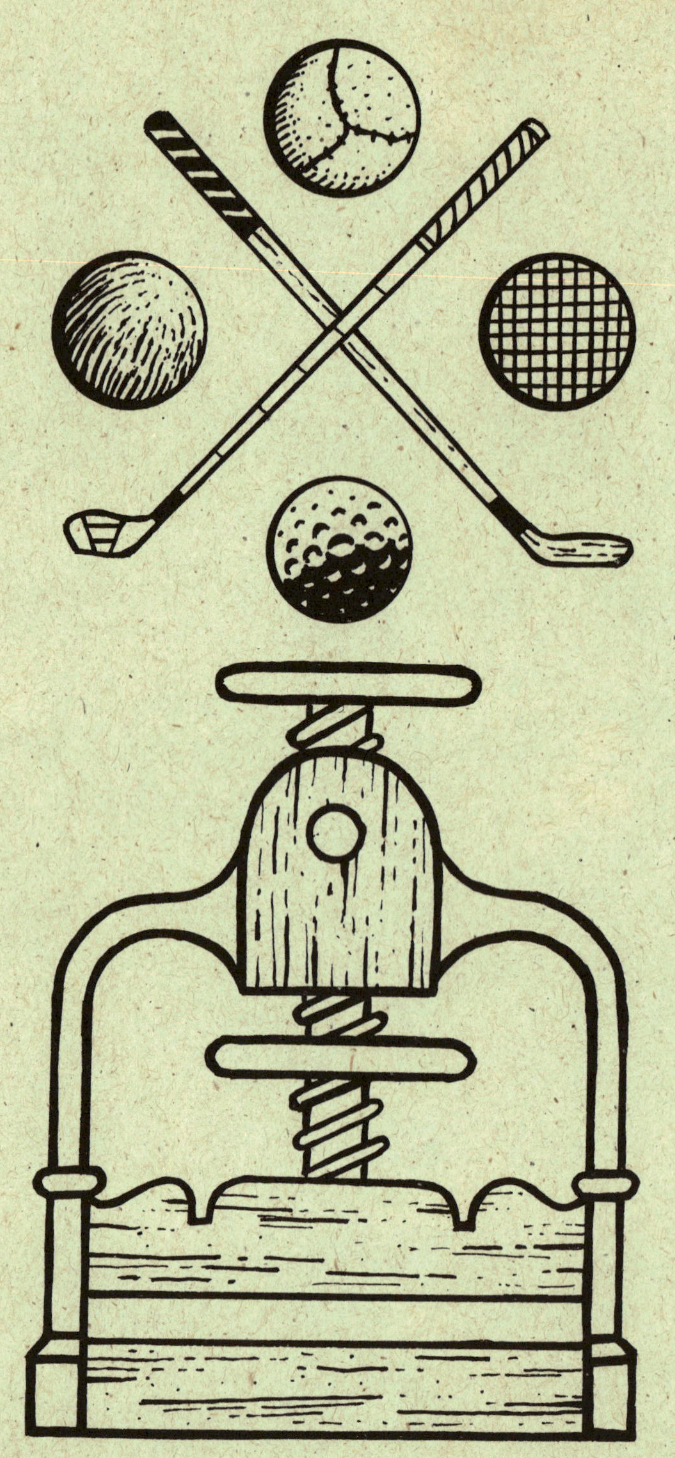